Algebra 2

Response to Intervention

Houghton Mifflin Harcourt

Contents

Introduction

Tier 2: Prerequisite Skills Module Pre-Tests

Tier 2: Prerequisite Skills Post-Tests

Tier 1: Reteach Worksheets

Tier 2: Strategic Intervention Teacher Guides and Worksheets

Response to Intervention

UNIT 1 FUNCTIONS

Student Edition Lessons	Tier 1 Skills	Pre-Tests	Tier 2 Skills Strategic Intervention	Post-Tests	Tier 3 Skills Intensive Intervention
Module 1 Analyzing Functions					
1.1 Domain, Range, and End Behavior	Reteach 1-1	Module 1	4 Algebraic Representations of Transformations	Skill 4	Building Block (Tier 3) worksheets are available online for students who need additional support on prerequisite skills.
1.2 Characteristics of Function Graphs	Reteach 1-2		18 Linear Functions	Skill 18	
			25 Properties of Translations, Reflections, and Rotations	Skill 25	
1.3 Transformations of Function Graphs	Reteach 1-3		27 Rate of Change and Slope	Skill 27	See the teacher page of each Tier 2 Skill lesson for a list of Building Block skills.
1.4 Inverses of Functions	Reteach 1-4				
Module 2 Absolute Value Functions, Equations, and Inequalities					
2.1 Graphing Absolute Value Functions	Reteach 2-1	Module 2	18 Linear Functions	Skill 18	
			19 Linear Inequalities in Two Variables	Skill 19	
2.2 Solving Absolute Value Equations	Reteach 2-2		23 One-Step Equations	Skill 23	
			24 One-Step Inequalities	Skill 24	
2.3 Solving Absolute Value Inequalities	Reteach 2-3		31 Slope and Slope-Intercept Form	Skill 31	

 ADDITIONAL ONLINE INTERVENTION RESOURCES

Tier 1, Tier 2, Tier 3 Skills

Personal Math Trainer will automatically create a standards-based, personalized intervention assignment for your students, targeting each student's individual needs!

Tier 2 Skills

Students scan QR codes with their smart phones to watch Math on the Spot tutorial videos for every Tier 2 skill.

Response to Intervention

UNIT 2 QUADRATIC FUNCTIONS, EQUATIONS, AND RELATIONS					
Student Edition Lessons	**Tier 1 Skills**	**Pre-Tests**	**Tier 2 Skills Strategic Intervention**	**Post-Tests**	**Tier 3 Skills Intensive Intervention**
Module 3 Quadratic Equations					
3.1 Solving Quadratic Equations by Taking Square Roots	Reteach 3-1	Module 3	9 Exponents	Skill 9	Building Block (Tier 3) worksheets are available online for students who need additional support on prerequisite skills.
			24 One-Step Inequalities	Skill 24	
			29 Rational Number Operations	Skill 29	
3.2 Complex Numbers	Reteach 3-2		30 Real Numbers	Skill 30	
3.3 Finding Complex Solutions of Quadratic Equations	Reteach 3-3		32 Solving Quadratic Equations by Completing the Square	Skill 32	See the teacher page of each Tier 2 Skill lesson for a list of Building Block skills.
			33 Solving Quadratic Equations by Factoring	Skill 33	
Module 4 Quadratic Relations and Systems of Equations					
4.1 Circles	Reteach 4-1	Module 4	4 Algebraic Representations of Transformations	Skill 4	
4.2 Parabolas	Reteach 4-2				
4.3 Solving Linear-Quadratic Systems	Reteach 4-3		14 Graphing Linear Nonproportional Relationships	Skill 14	
4.4 Solving Linear Systems in Three Variables	Reteach 4-4		20 Multi-Step Equations	Skill 20	
			32 Solving Quadratic Equations by Completing the Square	Skill 32	
			33 Solving Quadratic Equations by Factoring	Skill 33	
			34 Solving Systems of Linear Inequalities	Skill 34	
			35 Systems of Two Linear Equations	Skill 35	
			36 The Quadratic Formula	Skill 36	
			39 Transforming Quadratic Functions	Skill 39	

Response to Intervention

Student Edition Lessons	Tier 1 Skills	Pre-Tests	Tier 2 Skills Strategic Intervention	Post-Tests	Tier 3 Skills Intensive Intervention
UNIT 3 POLYNOMIAL FUNCTIONS, EXPRESSIONS, AND EQUATIONS					
Module 5 Polynomial Functions					
5.1 Graphing Cubic Functions	Reteach 5-1	Module 5	5 Classifying Polynomials	Skill 5	Building Block (Tier 3) worksheets are available online for students who need additional support on prerequisite skills.
			26 Quadratic Functions	Skill 26	
5.2 Graphing Polynomial Functions	Reteach 5-2		37 Transforming Cubic Functions	Skill 37	
Module 6 Polynomials					See the teacher page of each Tier 2 Skill lesson for a list of Building Block skills.
6.1 Adding and Subtracting Polynomials	Reteach 6-1	Module 6	2 Add and Subtract Polynomials	Skill 2	
6.2 Multiplying Polynomials	Reteach 6-2		3 Algebraic Expressions	Skill 3	
	Reteach 6-3		10 Factoring Polynomials	Skill 10	
6.3 The Binomial Theorem	Reteach 6-4		11 Factoring Special Products	Skill 11	
6.4 Factoring Polynomials	Reteach 6-5				
6.5 Dividing Polynomials			12 Factoring Trinomials	Skill 12	
			22 Multiply Polynomials	Skill 22	
Module 7 Polynomial Equations					
7.1 Finding Rational Solutions of Polynomial Equations	Reteach 7-1	Module 7	1 Add and Subtract Rational Numbers	Skill 1	
			7 Equations Involving Exponents	Skill 7	
7.2 Finding Complex Solutions of Polynomial Equations	Reteach 7-2		30 Real Numbers	Skill 30	

 ADDITIONAL ONLINE INTERVENTION RESOURCES

Tier 1, Tier 2, Tier 3 Skills

Personal Math Trainer will automatically create a standards-based, personalized intervention assignment for your students, targeting each student's individual needs!

Tier 2 Skills

Students scan QR codes with their smart phones to watch Math on the Spot tutorial videos for every Tier 2 skill.

UNIT 4 RATIONAL FUNCTIONS, EXPRESSIONS, AND EQUATIONS

Student Edition Lessons	Tier 1 Skills	Pre-Tests	Tier 2 Skills Strategic Intervention	Post-Tests	Tier 3 Skills Intensive Intervention
Module 8 Rational Functions					
8.1 Graphing Simple Rational Functions 8.2 Graphing More Complicated Rational Functions	Reteach 8-1 Reteach 8-2	Module 8	6 Direct Variation 14 Graphing Linear Nonproportional Relationships 15 Graphing Linear Proportional Relationships 17 Inverse Variation	Skill 6 Skill 14 Skill 15 Skill 17	Building Block (Tier 3) worksheets are available online for students who need additional support on prerequisite skills. See the teacher page of each Tier 2 Skill lesson for a list of Building Block skills.
Module 9 Rational Expressions and Equations					
9.1 Adding and Subtracting Rational Expressions 9.2 Multiplying and Dividing Rational Expressions 9.3 Solving Rational Equations	Reteach 9-1 Reteach 9-2 Reteach 9-3	Module 9	6 Direct Variation 14 Graphing Linear Nonproportional Relationships 15 Graphing Linear Proportional Relationships 17 Inverse Variation	Skill 6 Skill 14 Skill 15 Skill 17	

UNIT 5 RADICAL FUNCTIONS, EXPRESSIONS, AND EQUATIONS

Student Edition Lessons	Tier 1 Skills	Pre-Tests	Tier 2 Skills Strategic Intervention	Post-Tests	Tier 3 Skills Intensive Intervention
Module 10 Radical Functions					
10.1 Inverses of Simple Quadratic and Cubic Functions 10.2 Graphing Square Root Functions 10.3 Graphing Cube Root Functions	Reteach 10-1 Reteach 10-2 Reteach 10-3	Module 10	9 Exponents 16 Inverse Linear Functions	Skill 9 Skill 16	Building Block (Tier 3) worksheets are available online for students who need additional support on prerequisite skills. See the teacher page of each Tier 2 Skill lesson for a list of Building Block skills.
Module 11 Radical Expressions and Equations					
11.1 Radical Expressions and Rational Exponents 11.2 Simplifying Radical Expressions 11.3 Solving Radical Equations	Reteach 11-1 Reteach 11-2 Reteach 11-3	Module 11	9 Exponents 16 Inverse Linear Functions 28 Rational and Radical Exponents	Skill 9 Skill 16 Skill 28	

Response to Intervention

Response to Intervention

UNIT 6 EXPONENTIAL AND LOGARITHMIC FUNCTIONS AND EQUATIONS

Student Edition Lessons	Tier 1 Skills	Pre-Tests	Tier 2 Skills Strategic Intervention	Post-Tests	Tier 3 Skills Intensive Intervention
Module 12 Sequences and Series					
12.1 Arithmetic Sequences	Reteach 12-1	Module 12	3 Algebraic Expressions	Skill 3	Building Block (Tier 3) worksheets are available online for students who need additional support on prerequisite skills.
12.2 Geometric Sequences	Reteach 12-2		13 Geometric Expressions	Skill 13	
12.3 Geometric Series	Reteach 12-3		20 Multi-Step Equations	Skill 20	
Module 13 Exponential Functions					
13.1 Exponential Growth Functions	Reteach 13-1	Module 13	8 Exponential Functions	Skill 8	See the teacher page of each Tier 2 Skill lesson for a list of Building Block skills.
			13 Geometric Sequences	Skill 13	
13.2 Exponential Decay Functions	Reteach 13-2		30 Real Numbers	Skill 30	
13.3 The Base e	Reteach 13-3				
13.4 Compound Interest	Reteach 13-4				
Module 14 Modeling with Exponential and Other Functions					
14.1 Fitting Exponential Functions to Data	Reteach 14-1	Module 14	7 Equations Involving Exponents	Skill 7	
14.2 Choosing Among Linear, Quadratic, and Exponential Models	Reteach 14-2		9 Exponents	Skill 9	
			15 Graphing Linear Proportional Relationships	Skill 15	
			31 Slope and Slope-Intercept Form	Skill 31	
			38 Transforming Linear Functions	Skill 38	
			40 Writing Linear Equations	Skill 40	
Module 15 Logarithmic Functions					
15.1 Defining and Evaluating a Logarithmic Function	Reteach 15-1	Module 15	9 Exponents	Skill 9	
			14 Graphing Linear Nonproportional Relationships	Skill 14	
15.2 Graphing Logarithmic Functions	Reteach 15-2		28 Rational and Radical Exponents	Skill 28	
Module 16 Logarithmic Properties and Exponential Equations					
16.1 Properties of Logarithms	Reteach 16-1	Module 16	7 Equations Involving Exponents	Skill 7	
16.2 Solving Exponential Equations	Reteach 16-2		9 Exponents	Skill 9	
			20 Multi-Step Equations	Skill 20	
			28 Rational and Radical Exponents	Skill 28	

 ADDITIONAL ONLINE INTERVENTION RESOURCES

Tier 1, Tier 2, Tier 3 Skills

Personal Math Trainer will automatically create a standards-based, personalized intervention assignment for your students, targeting each student's individual needs!

Tier 2 Skills

Students scan QR codes with their smart phones to watch Math on the Spot tutorial videos for every Tier 2 skill.

UNIT 7 TRIGONOMETRIC FUNCTIONS

Student Edition Lessons	Tier 1 Skills	Pre-Tests	Tier 2 Skills Strategic Intervention	Post-Tests	Tier 3 Skills Intensive Intervention
Module 17 Unit-Circle Definition of Trigonometric Functions					
17.1 Angles of Rotation and Radian Measure	Reteach 17-1 Reteach 17-2	Module 17	44 Distance and Midpoint Formulas	Skill 44	Building Block (Tier 3) worksheets are available online for students who need additional support on prerequisite skills.
17.2 Defining and Evaluating the Basic Trigonometric Functions			53 Pythagorean Theorem	Skill 53	
			55 Sine and Cosine Ratios	Skill 55	
			56 Special Right Triangles	Skill 56	See the teacher page of each Tier 2 Skill lesson for a list of Building Block skills.
17.3 Using a Pythagorean Identity	Reteach 17-3		58 Tangent Ratio	Skill 58	
Module 18 Graphing Trigonometric Functions					
18.1 Stretching, Compressing, and Reflecting Sine and Cosine Graphs	Reteach 18-1	Module 18	38 Transforming Linear Functions	Skill 38	
			39 Transforming Quadratic Functions	Skill 39	
18.2 Stretching, Compressing, and Reflecting Tangent Graphs	Reteach 18-2		42 Combining Transformations of Quadratic Functions	Skill 42	
18.3 Translating Trigonometric Graphs	Reteach 18-3		57 Stretching, Compressing, and Reflecting Quadratic Functions	Skill 57	
18.4 Fitting Sine Functions to Data	Reteach 18-4				

UNIT 8 PROBABILITY

Student Edition Lessons	Tier 1 Skills	Pre-Tests	Tier 2 Skills Strategic Intervention	Post-Tests	Tier 3 Skills Intensive Intervention
Module 19 Introduction to Probability					
19.1 Probability and Set Theory	Reteach 19-1	Module 19	51 Probability of Compound Events	Skill 51	Building Block (Tier 3) worksheets are available online for students who need additional support on prerequisite skills.
19.2 Permutations and Probability	Reteach 19-2		52 Probability of Simple Events	Skill 52	
19.3 Combinations and Probability	Reteach 19-3				See the teacher page of each Tier 2 Skill lesson for a list of Building Block skills.
19.4 Mutually Exclusive and Overlapping Events	Reteach 19-4				
Module 20 Conditional Probability and Independence of Events					
20.1 Conditional Probability	Reteach 20-1	Module 20	51 Probability of Compound Events	Skill 51	
20.2 Independent Events	Reteach 20-2		52 Probability of Simple Events	Skill 52	
20.3 Dependent Events	Reteach 20-3				
Module 21 Probability and Decision Making					
21.1 Using Probability to Make Fair Decisions	Reteach 21-1	Module 21	48 Making Predictions with Probability	Skill 48	
21.2 Analyzing Decisions	Reteach 21-2		52 Probability of Simple Events	Skill 52	

UNIT 9 STATISTICS					
Student Edition Lessons	**Tier 1 Skills**	**Pre-Tests**	**Tier 2 Skills Strategic Intervention**	**Post-Tests**	**Tier 3 Skills Intensive Intervention**
Module 22 Gathering and Displaying Data					
22.1 Data-Gathering Techniques 22.2 Shape, Center, and Spread	Reteach 22-1 Reteach 22-2	Module 22	41 Box Plots 45 Generating Random Samples 46 Histograms 60 Two-Way Tables	Skill 41 Skill 45 Skill 46 Skill 60	Building Block (Tier 3) worksheets are available online for students who need additional support on prerequisite skills.
Module 23 Data Distributions					See the teacher page of each Tier 2 Skill lesson for a list of Building Block skills.
23.1 Probability Distributions 23.2 Normal Distributions 23.3 Sampling Distributions	Reteach 23-1 Reteach 23-2 Reteach 23-3	Module 23	43 Data Distributions and Outliers 49 Measures of Center and Spread 50 Normal Distributions	Skill 43 Skill 49 Skill 50	
Module 24 Making Inferences from Data					
24.1 Confidence Intervals and Margins of Error 24.2 Surveys, Experiments, and Observational Studies 24.3 Determining the Significance of Experimental Results	Reteach 24-1 Reteach 24-2 Reteach 24-3	Module 24	47 Making Inferences from a Random Sample 54 Scatter Plots and Association 59 Trend Lines and Predictions	Skill 47 Skill 54 Skill 59	

 ADDITIONAL ONLINE INTERVENTION RESOURCES

Tier 1, Tier 2, Tier 3 Skills

Personal Math Trainer will automatically create a standards-based, personalized intervention assignment for your students, targeting each student's individual needs!

Tier 2 Skills

Students scan QR codes with their smart phones to watch Math on the Spot tutorial videos for every Tier 2 skill.

Using HMH Algebra 2 Response to Intervention

 Response to Intervention	Print Resources	Online Resources
TIER 1	**TIER 2 STRATEGIC INTERVENTION**	**TIER 1, TIER 2, AND TIER 3**

Reteach worksheet (one worksheet per lesson) • Use to provide additional support for students who are having difficulty mastering the concepts taught in Algebra 2.	**Skill Intervention worksheets** (one set per skill) • Use for students who require intervention with prerequisite skills taught in Middle School. **Skill Intervention Teacher Guides** (one guide per skill) • Use to provide systematic and explicit instruction, and alternate strategies to help students acquire mastery with prerequisite skills.	 **T1, T2, and T3 skills** • Assign the *Personal Math Trainer,* which will create standards-based practice for all students and customized intervention when necessary. **Progress Monitoring** • Use the *Personal Math Trainer* to assess a student's mastery of skills.
Progress Monitoring • Use *Student Edition Ready to Go On? Quizzes* to assess mastery of skills taught in the Modules. Use for all students. • Use *Assessment Resources Module Quizzes* to assess mastery of skills taught in the Modules. For students who are considerably below level, use Modified Quizzes. For all other students, use Level B.	**Progress Monitoring** • Use *Response to Intervention Module Pre-Tests* or the *Student Edition Are You Ready? Quizzes* to assess whether a student has the necessary prerequisite skills for success in each Module. • Use *Response to Intervention Skill Post-Tests* to assess mastery of prerequisite skills.	**T2 skills** • Use *Math on the Spot* tutorial videos to help students review skills taught in Middle School. **T3 skills** • Use *Building Block Skills* worksheets for struggling students who require additional intervention.

Recommendations for Intervention

Tier 1	For students who require small group instruction to review lesson skills taught in Algebra 2.
Tiers 2–3	For students who require strategic or intensive intervention with prerequisite skills needed for success in Algebra 2.
Tiers 1–3	Intervention materials and the *Personal Math Trainer* are designed to accommodate the diverse skill levels of students at all levels of intervention.

DIAGNOSIS

Tier 2 Module Pre-Tests *(RTI ancillary)*
Tier 2 Are You Ready? Quizzes *(Student Edition)*
Tier 1 Ready to Go On? Quizzes *(Student Edition)*

INTERVENE

Use **Tier 1** Reteach and/or **Tier 2** Skill Worksheets *(RTI ancillary).*
• Uncluttered with minimum words to help all students, regardless of English acquisition
• Vocabulary presented in context to help English learners and struggling readers
• Multiple instructional examples for students to practice thinking-aloud their solutions

Use **Tier 2** Skill Teacher Guides *(RTI ancillary).*
• Explicit instruction and key teaching points
• Alternate strategies to address the different types of learners
• Common misconceptions to develop understanding of skills
• Visual representations to make concept connections
• Checks to fine-tune instruction and opportunities for immediate feedback

MONITOR PROGRESS

Tier 2: Skill Post-Tests *(RTI ancillary)*
Tier 1–2: Assessment Readiness *(Student Edition)*
Tier 1–3: Leveled Module Quizzes *(Assessment Resources online)*

Use **Tiers 1–3** online additional intervention, practice, and review materials.

• Personal Math Trainer
• Math on the Spot videos
• Building Block Skills worksheets with Teacher Guides

• Differentiated Instruction with leveled Practice, Reading Strategies, and Success for English Learners worksheets

MODULE 1

Response to Intervention

Pre-Test: Skills 4, 18, 25, 27

For 1–4, a line has the points (–2, –9), (3, 1), and (6, 7). Find the points for the translation described.

1. 6 units to the left

   _____

2. 3 units down

   _____

3. 5 units to the right

   _____

4. 2 units up

   _____

5. Write an equation for the linear function whose graph is shown.

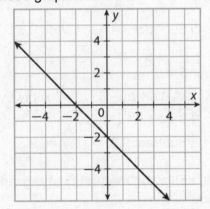

   _____

For 6–7, write an equation representing the linear function described.

6. The *y*-intercept is $\frac{3}{2}$ and the slope is 4.

   _____

7. The slope is 5 and the point $\left(2, -\frac{3}{2}\right)$ is

   on the graph.

   _____

8. The figure shows quadrilateral *CDEF*. Graph the image of the figure after a reflection across the *x*-axis.

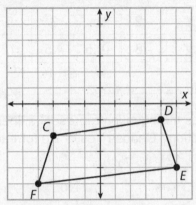

9. A point with coordinates (2, –9) is translated 4 units right and 7 units up. What are the coordinates of its image?

   _____

10. For each table of values, choose whether the rate of change is constant or variable.

A
x	3	5	6	9
y	–5	3	7	19

   ○ Constant   ○ Variable

B
x	–6	–4	–2	0
y	–5	–5	–5	–5

   ○ Constant   ○ Variable

C
x	–8	–7	–9	–6
y	3	6	2	7

   ○ Constant   ○ Variable

D
x	4	9	12	14
y	1	3	7	8

   ○ Constant   ○ Variable

11. What is the slope of the line that passes through the points (–4, 6) and (–8, 3)?

   _____

MODULE 2

Response to Intervention

Pre-Test: Skills 18, 19, 23, 24, 31

1. Write an equation representing the linear function that includes the points given in the table.

x	−2	1	3	6
y	−8	−0.5	4.5	12

_____

2. Does the equation represent a linear function? Choose Yes or No for each.

   A $-12 = 6 + xy$

   ○ Yes   ○ No

   B $\frac{1}{5}x - 6 = 2y$

   ○ Yes   ○ No

   C $4y = \frac{3}{5}x^2 + 1$

   ○ Yes   ○ No

   D $7x + y = 16$

   ○ Yes   ○ No

3. A linear function is graphed on a coordinate plane.

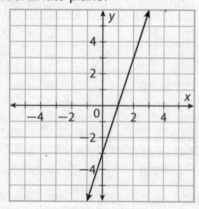

   a. What is the slope of the line?

   _____

   b. What is the y-intercept?

   _____

4. Graph the solution set for the inequality $y > \frac{2}{3}x - 4$.

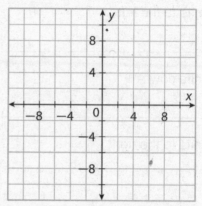

5. For each equation, choose which operation would isolate the variable.

   A $18 = -2.1b$

   ○ Divide by −2.1.   ○ Divide by 2.1.

   B $b - 3.4 = 16.3$

   ○ Subtract 3.4.   ○ Add 3.4.

   C $-\frac{b}{5} = 1.6$

   ○ Multiply by −5.   ○ Multiply by 5.

   D $9.3 + b = -42$

   ○ Subtract 9.3.   ○ Add 9.3.

For 6–8, solve the inequality and graph the solution.

6. $-7 \geq k - 3$

_____

7. $-5 + w < 6$

_____

8. $4 + p < -2$

_____

Name _____ Date _____ Class_____

Response to Intervention
Pre-Test: Skills 9, 24, 29, 30, 32, 33

1. Which inequalities have a solution set appearing as a shaded region above a solid boundary line when graphed? Choose Yes or No for each.

   A $8y + 2x > -14$ ○ Yes   ○ No

   B $18y - x \geq 3$ ○ Yes   ○ No

   C $-x + 3y \leq 9$ ○ Yes   ○ No

   D $6 - 4y \leq 5x$ ○ Yes   ○ No

2. A hot air balloon hovering at an elevation of 240 feet begins to descend. The balloon's descent can be no faster than −16 feet per minute.

   a. Write an inequality that models this situation. Let t represent time in minutes.

   _____

   b. Solve the inequality. Is it possible for the balloon to reach the ground in less than 20 minutes?

   _____

3. Choose Positive or Negative to indicate whether the value of the expression is positive or negative.

   A $-28.15 + 26.34$

   ○ Positive   ○ Negative

   B $-\dfrac{3}{4} - \left(-\dfrac{6}{7}\right)$

   ○ Positive   ○ Negative

   C $40.9 - 38.2$

   ○ Positive   ○ Negative

   D $\dfrac{5}{8} - \dfrac{3}{5}$

   ○ Positive   ○ Negative

4. Write $2\dfrac{3}{8}$ as a decimal.

   _____

5. Write $2.\overline{6}$ as a fraction in simplest form.

   _____

For 6–7, solve each equation by completing the square.

6. $x^2 - 4x = 32$

   _____

7. $x^2 + 16x + 48 = 0$

   _____

8. The width of a rectangle is 14 meters less than the length. The area of the rectangle is 576 square meters. Find the length and the width.

   _____

9. A rectangular prism has a volume of 1080 cm^3. Its dimensions are 5 cm, $(x + 12)$ cm, and $(x + 6)$ cm. What is the value of x?

   _____

10. According to the graph, what are the solutions to the equation $x^2 + x - 2 = 0$?

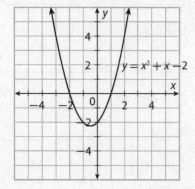

   _____

Response to Intervention
Pre-Test: Skills 4, 14, 20, 32, 33, 34, 35, 36, 39

1. A graph has the points (7, 10), (3, 2), and (−2, 0). Find the points after a vertical compression by a scale factor of $\frac{1}{4}$.

_____

2. Identify the slope and y-intercept of the equation $y = 25 - 6x$.

   slope: _____ y-intercept: _____

3. Solve $-7(9 + 3k) = 12k + 3$.

_____

For 4–6, find the value for c that completes the square.

4. $x^2 + 10x + c$

_____

5. $x^2 + 7x + c$

_____

6. $x^2 - \frac{6}{7}x + c$

_____

For 7–10, solve the quadratic equation.

7. $(x - 8)(x + 7) = 0$

_____

8. $x^2 - 10x = 24$

_____

9. $x^2 + 2x - 48 = 0$

_____

10. $-84 = x^2 - 19x$

_____

11. Solve the system by graphing.
$$\begin{cases} x + y < 1 \\ -x + 2y > 4 \end{cases}$$

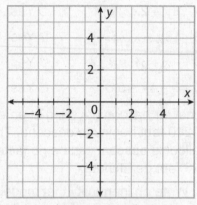

12. Solve the system by substitution.
$$\begin{cases} x + y = 28 \\ x - 3y = 0 \end{cases}$$

_____

13. Does the quadratic equation have the solution

$$x = \frac{-(-3) \pm \sqrt{(-3)^2 - 4(4)(7)}}{2(4)}?$$

Choose Yes or No for each.

A $-3x^2 + 4x - 7 = 0$ ○ Yes ○ No

B $4x^2 = 3x - 7$ ○ Yes ○ No

C $4x^2 - 3x + 7 = 0$ ○ Yes ○ No

D $7x^2 + 4x = 3$ ○ Yes ○ No

14. Is $g(x) = 8x^2$ or $g(x) = 0.45x^2$ wider than the function $f(x) = x^2$?

_____

MODULE 5

Response to Intervention

Pre-Test: Skills 5, 26, 37

1. What are the terms of the following algebraic expression?

   $5x^4 + 6x^3 - 3x^2 + 1$

   _____

2. Choose True or False. Is each term a coefficient in the following expression?

   $5c^4 - 3a^3 + 2c - 4$

   A 5   ○ True ○ False

   B 3   ○ True ○ False

   C 4   ○ True ○ False

   D 2   ○ True ○ False

3. Write the following polynomial in standard form.

   $4a - 5a^2 - 16a^5 + 14 + 13a^3$

   _____

4. Does each equation represent a quadratic function? Choose Yes or No.

   A $y - 3x = -\dfrac{1}{4}x^2$ ○ Yes ○ No

   B $y - 8x = 4x + 5$ ○ Yes ○ No

   C $y - 2x^3 = x^2 - 5$ ○ Yes ○ No

   D $y = \dfrac{1}{5}\left(x - \dfrac{1}{3}\right)^2 + \dfrac{2}{5}$ ○ Yes ○ No

5. State whether the function

   $y = -\dfrac{2}{3}(x + 4)^2 - 6$ has a maximum or

   minimum value. What is the value?

   _____

6. What is the axis of symmetry of the parabola graphed from the equation

   $g(x) = -3(x + 1)^2 + 5$?

   _____

7. Determine the zeros of the quadratic function from its graph.

   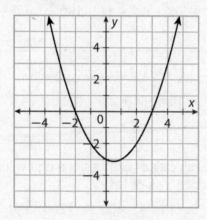

   _____

8. Does each transformation of the parent function $f(x) = x^3$ involve a horizontal translation? Choose Yes or No.

   A $g(x) = \dfrac{1}{3}(x + 1)^3 - 4$ ○ Yes ○ No

   B $h(x) = -1.8x^3 - 0.6$ ○ Yes ○ No

   C $j(x) = \dfrac{3}{2}(x - 12.8)^3$ ○ Yes ○ No

   D $s(x) = (x + 6.7)^3 - 4.2$ ○ Yes ○ No

9. $g(x) = (x - 3)^3 + 2$ is a transformation of the parent cubic function $f(x)^3$. Graph $g(x)$ alongside the parent function shown.

   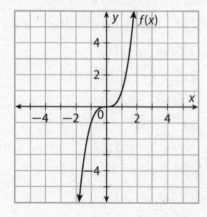

MODULE 6

Response to Intervention

Pre-Test: Skills 2, 3, 10, 11, 12, 22

1. Write the following polynomial in standard form.

   $14c^3 - 7c^2 - 8c^6 + 12 - 18c^2$

   _____

2. Simplify the following expression.

   $(5x^3 + 12x^2 - 4 + 2x) + (-9x^2 + 24x - 6)$

   _____

3. Is each pair of expressions equivalent? Choose Yes or No.

   A $3ab(a+4) - (3a^2b - 12ab)$ and 0

   ○ Yes   ○ No

   B $7n^2 - 5 + 4n^2$ and $3n^2 - 5$

   ○ Yes   ○ No

   C $12(x-7)$ and $12x - 7x$

   ○ Yes   ○ No

   D $\frac{1}{4}p^2(12 - 4p)$ and $-p^3 + 3p^2$

   ○ Yes   ○ No

4. What is the GCF of the terms of the following polynomial?

   $8x^5 - 20x^3$

   _____

5. Can the polynomial be factored by grouping? Choose Yes or No.

   A $4x^5 - 16x^4 + 2x^3 - 8x^2$

   ○ Yes   ○ No

   B $2x^5 + 2x^2 + 4x^3 - 4$

   ○ Yes   ○ No

   C $3x^4 - 15x^3 + 2x - 10$

   ○ Yes   ○ No

   D $5x^4 + 15x^2 + x^3 - 3x$

   ○ Yes   ○ No

6. Choose True or False to indicate whether each term is a perfect square.

   A -36 ○ True   ○ False

   B $16x^2$ ○ True   ○ False

   C x^2y^2 ○ True   ○ False

   D $81p^4$ ○ True   ○ False

7. Factor $81x^4 - y^2$.

   _____

For 8–10, factor each trinomial.

8. $x^2 - x - 56$

   _____

9. $x^2 + 8x - 33$

   _____

10. $x^2 + 5x - 14$

    _____

11. Simplify $5(4x^2 + 9x - 6)$.

    _____

12. Simplify $(9n^2 + 5)^2$.

    _____

13. Explain how to use the FOIL method to multiply two binomials.

    _____

    _____

    _____

14. A rectangle has a length of $6x$ units and a width of $7x^2 + 12x + 9$ units. What is the area of the rectangle?

    _____

Name _____ Date _____ Class_____

For 1–4, draw a dot and arrow above the number line to find the sum or difference.

1. $3\frac{3}{4} - 6 =$ _____

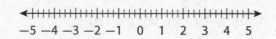

2. $-1.25 - 3.75 =$ _____

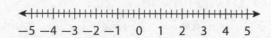

3. $-\frac{1}{4} + 3\frac{1}{2} =$ _____

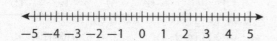

4. $-4.75 - (-2.5) =$ _____

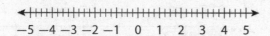

5. Is each number rational? Choose Yes or No.

   A $\frac{13}{115}$ ○ Yes   ○ No

   B $\sqrt{36}$ ○ Yes   ○ No

   C $\sqrt{7}$ ○ Yes   ○ No

   D $3.5\overline{71}$ ○ Yes   ○ No

6. Which of these approximations are true? Choose True or False for each.

   A $2 < \sqrt{7} < 3$ ○ True ○ False

   B $6 < \sqrt{61} < 7$ ○ True ○ False

   C $8 < \sqrt{52} < 9$ ○ True ○ False

   D $9 < \sqrt{93} < 10$ ○ True ○ False

7. The graph represents both sides of an equation involving exponents. Use the graph to determine the solution to the equation.

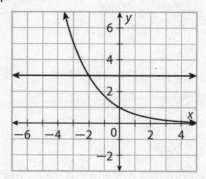

_____

For 8–9, order the numbers from least to greatest.

8. $3.\overline{28}, \frac{143}{37}, \sqrt{5}+2$

_____

9. $\sqrt{45}, 3\pi - 2, 7.\overline{14}$

_____

For 10–11, estimate to three decimal places using a calculator.

10. $\sqrt{19}$

_____

11. $-\sqrt{7}$

_____

12. Write $3.\overline{8}$ as a fraction in simplest form.

_____

Response to Intervention

Pre-Test: Skills 6, 14, 15, 17

1. Which equations represent a direct variation? Choose Yes or No for each.

   A $y = 3x - 5$

   ○ Yes   ○ No

   B $-6x = 2y$

   ○ Yes   ○ No

   C $3.2x - 5y = -7.3$

   ○ Yes   ○ No

   D $5y - 9x = 0$

   ○ Yes   ○ No

2. The constant of variation for a direct variation equation is $\frac{2}{5}$. Choose True or False for each.

   A When $x = -15$, $y = -6$.

   ○ True   ○ False

   B When $x = 20$, $y = 9$.

   ○ True   ○ False

   C When $x = 5$, $y = 2$.

   ○ True   ○ False

   D When $x = -10$, $y = 4$.

   ○ True   ○ False

3. What are the slope and y-intercept of the line?

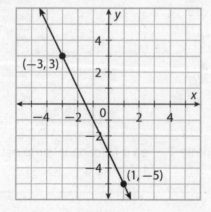

4. The constant of variation for a direct variation equation is $\frac{5}{3}$. Choose True or False for each.

   A When $x = 9$, $y = 15$.

   ○ True   ○ False

   B When $x = -6$, $y = -10$.

   ○ True   ○ False

   C When $x = 2$, $y = 3$.

   ○ True   ○ False

   D When $x = 18$, $y = 20$.

   ○ True   ○ False

5. Choose Direct or Inverse to indicate whether y varies directly or inversely as x.

   A

x	-2	0	3	5
y	-6	0	9	15

   ○ Direct   ○ Inverse

   B

x	1	2	4	6
y	24	12	6	4

   ○ Direct   ○ Inverse

   C

x	2	3	4	6
y	24	16	12	8

   ○ Direct   ○ Inverse

   D

x	-4	-1	3	6
y	-16	-4	12	24

   ○ Direct   ○ Inverse

6. Suppose y varies inversely as x and $y = 3$ when $x = 8$. Write an equation for the inverse variation.

   _____

MODULE
9

Response to Intervention

Pre-Test: Skills 6, 14, 15, 17

1. Which equations represent a direct variation? Choose Yes or No for each.

   A $12x = -3y$

   ○ Yes   ○ No

   B $y - x = 3$

   ○ Yes   ○ No

   C $3x - 12y = -15$

   ○ Yes   ○ No

   D $5y - 14x = 0$

   ○ Yes   ○ No

2. The value of y varies directly with x, and $y = 18$ when $x = 3$. Write a direct variation equation, and then find the value of y when $x = 11$.

   _____

3. Let $y = 3x - 2$.

   a. Complete the table for the equation.

x	−1	0	1	2
y				

   b. Use the table to graph the equation.

   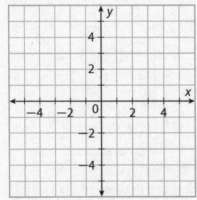

   c. Explain why the relationship is not proportional.

   _____

4. The relationship between x and y is proportional. Write an equation for the relationship.

x	3	6	12	18
y	15	30	60	80

   _____

5. Jasper reads 22 pages per hour. Write an equation that represents the relationship between the total number of pages he reads and the time he spends reading.

   _____

6. Write an equation that describes the proportional relationship.

   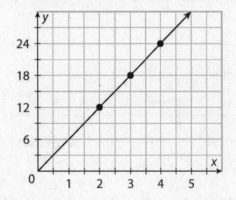

   _____

7. Use the data in the table. Suppose y varies inversely as x. What is the constant of variation?

x	−4	−3	2	8
y	−6	−8	12	3

   _____

8. Suppose y varies inversely as x and $y = 3$ when $x = 13$. Write an equation for the inverse variation.

   _____

MODULE 10

Response to Intervention

Pre-Test: Skills 9, 16

1. Simplify 4^{-4}.

_____

2. Choose True or False. Are each pair of expressions equal?

   A $\left(\dfrac{3}{2}\right)^2$ and $\dfrac{6}{4}$ ○ True ○ False

   B $\left(\dfrac{6}{7}\right)^5$ and $\dfrac{6^5}{7^5}$ ○ True ○ False

   C $\left(\dfrac{1}{3}\right)^{-3}$ and 27   ○ True ○ False

   D $\left(\dfrac{-4}{3}\right)^2$ and $-\dfrac{16}{9}$ ○ True ○ False

3. Simplify $\left(3^{-3}\right)^{-2}$.

_____

4. Simplify $10^4 \cdot 10^{-2} \cdot 10^3$.

_____

5. Choose Yes or No. Is each expression equal to $\dfrac{6^3 \cdot 6^4}{6^2 \cdot 6^3}$?

   A 6^2 ○ Yes ○ No

   C $\dfrac{6^{12}}{6^6}$ ○ Yes ○ No

   B 6^6 ○ Yes ○ No

   D $\dfrac{6^7}{6^5}$ ○ Yes ○ No

6. Simplify $(-2 \cdot 4)^3$.

_____

7. What is the inverse of $f(x) = -\dfrac{1}{6}x + \dfrac{1}{3}$?

_____

8. Choose Yes or No to indicate whether the two functions are inverse functions.

   A $y = 3x - 9;\ y = -\dfrac{1}{3}x + 3$

      ○ Yes   ○ No

   B $y = \dfrac{16}{25}x^2$, where $x \ge 0;\ y = \dfrac{5}{4}\sqrt{x}$

      ○ Yes   ○ No

   C $y = \dfrac{1}{27}x^3;\ y = \dfrac{1}{3}\sqrt[3]{x}$

      ○ Yes   ○ No

   D $y = 32x^5;\ y = \dfrac{1}{2}\sqrt[5]{x}$

      ○ Yes   ○ No

9. Find the inverse of $f(x) = \dfrac{16}{9}x^2$, where $x \ge 0$. Then graph f and f^{-1}.

   $f^{-1}(x) =$ _____

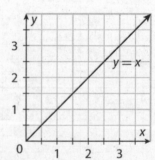

10. What is the inverse of $f(x) = 16x^4$, where $x \ge 0$?

_____

Name _____ Date _____ Class_____

Pre-Test: Skills 9, 16, 28

1. Simplify 6^{-3}.

_____

2. Choose True or False to indicate whether the expressions are equal.

A $\left(\dfrac{2}{3}\right)^2$ and $\dfrac{4}{9}$ ○ True   ○ False

B $\left(\dfrac{6}{5}\right)^4$ and $\dfrac{6^4}{5^4}$ ○ True   ○ False

C $\left(\dfrac{1}{27}\right)^3$ and $\dfrac{1}{3}$ ○ True   ○ False

D $\left(\dfrac{-2}{3}\right)^4$ and $-\dfrac{16}{81}$ ○ True   ○ False

3. Simplify $\left(2^4\right)^{-3}$.

_____

4. Simplify $27^{\frac{1}{3}} + 27^{\frac{2}{3}} + 27^{\frac{3}{3}}$.

_____

5. Write a radical expression that is equal to $63^{\frac{1}{3}}$.

_____

6. Choose True or False to indicate whether the expression is equal to $64^{\frac{1}{3}}$.

A   4   ○ True   ○ False

B $\sqrt[3]{4^3}$ ○ True   ○ False

C $\sqrt[3]{64}$ ○ True   ○ False

D 4^3 ○ True   ○ False

7. What is the simplified form of $10{,}000^{\frac{3}{4}}$?

_____

8. What is the inverse of $f(x) = -\dfrac{1}{8}x + \dfrac{1}{4}$?

_____

9. Choose Yes or No to indicate whether the two functions are inverse functions.

A $y = 4x - 16;$ $y = \dfrac{1}{4}x + 4$

   ○ Yes   ○ No

B $y = \dfrac{9}{4}x^2$, where $x \ge 0;$ $y = \dfrac{3}{2}x$

   ○ Yes   ○ No

C $y = \dfrac{1}{81}x^4$, where $x \ge 0;$ $y = \dfrac{1}{3}\sqrt[4]{x}$

   ○ Yes   ○ No

D $y = 36x^2$, where $x \ge 0;$ $y = \dfrac{1}{6}\sqrt{x}$

   ○ Yes   ○ No

10. Find the inverse of $f(x) = \dfrac{4}{9}x^2$, where $x \ge 0$. Then graph f and f^{-1}.

$f^{-1}(x) = $ _____

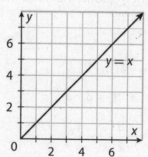

11. What is the inverse of $f(x) = 32x^5$?

_____

MODULE 12

Response to Intervention

Pre-Test: Skills 3, 13, 20

1. Evaluate the expression $\frac{2}{3}p^2 - \frac{1}{6}p + 4$ for $p = -6$.

   _____

2. Choose Yes or No. Is each pair of expressions equivalent?

   A $12(x-4)$ and $12x - 4x$

   ○ Yes   ○ No

   B $5y^3 - 3y^3 + 1$ and $2y^3 + 1$

   ○ Yes   ○ No

   C $\frac{1}{4}a^2(8-4a)$ and $-a^3 + 2a^2$

   ○ Yes   ○ No

   D $3mn(n+3) - (3m^2n + 9mn)$ and 0

   ○ Yes   ○ No

3. Simplify the expression.

   $-\frac{3}{2}x^4y^3 + 2x^3 + \frac{9}{2}x^4y^3 - 3x^3$

   _____

4. Choose Yes or No. Does each equation represent a geometric sequence in explicit form?

   A $a_n = 3^{n-2}$ ○ Yes ○ No

   B $a_n = -4(n-2)$ ○ Yes ○ No

   C $a_1 = 3,\ a_n = 3 \cdot a_{n-1}$ ○ Yes ○ No

   D $a_n = -\frac{3}{2} \cdot \left(-\frac{1}{4}\right)^{n-1}$ ○ Yes ○ No

5. What is the common ratio for the geometric sequence?

   $-2,\ \dfrac{4}{3},\ -\dfrac{8}{9},\ \dfrac{16}{27},\ ...$

   _____

6. A geometric sequence has terms $a_4 = 12$ and $a_6 = 432$.

   a. Write an explicit rule for the sequence. Assume the common ratio is positive.

   _____

   b. What is the value of the 8th term?

   _____

Solve each equation.

7. $c + 6 = -6c + 6$

   _____

8. $-7(6 + 4x) = -3x + 8$

   _____

9. Donna has two monthly payment options for her phone. With Option A, she would pay $40 plus $0.10 for every minute of voice. With Option B, she would pay $30 plus $0.15 per minute of voice. How many minutes of voice per month would she need to use for Option B to cost as much as Option A?

   a. Write an equation that models this situation.

   _____

   b. Solve the equation. How many minutes would she have to use?

   _____

MODULE 13 **Response to Intervention**

Pre-Test: Skills 8, 13, 30

1. Evaluate the exponential function $y = -15(2)^x$ for $x = 3$.

   _____

2. Graph $y = \frac{1}{9}(3)^x$.

   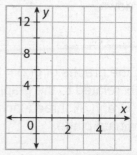

3. Choose True or False to indicate whether the ordered pairs represent a point on the graph of $y = 4(4)^x$.

   A $(-2, 0.25)$ ○ True   ○ False

   B $(0, 1)$ ○ True   ○ False

   C $(1, 8)$ ○ True   ○ False

   D $(2, 64)$ ○ True   ○ False

   _____

4. The population of a town is 25,000 and is expected to decrease 2.5% each year. Find the expected population of the town in 10 years.

   _____

5. What is the common ratio for the geometric sequence?

   $-1, \dfrac{3}{2}, -\dfrac{9}{4}, \dfrac{27}{8}, \ldots$

   _____

6. What is an explicit rule for the geometric sequence?

   $2, -6, 18, -54, \ldots$

   _____

7. Choose Yes or No. Does each equation represent a geometric sequence in explicit form?

   A $a_n = 3^{n+1}$ ○ Yes   ○ No

   B $a_n = -3n + 9$ ○ Yes   ○ No

   C $a_n = -\dfrac{2}{3} \cdot \left(\dfrac{5}{4}\right)^{n-1}$ ○ Yes   ○ No

   D $a_1 = 3, a_n = -3 \cdot a_{n-1}$ ○ Yes   ○ No

8. A geometric sequence has terms $a_5 = 48$ and $a_7 = 12$.

   a. Write an explicit rule for the sequence. Assume the common ratio is positive.

   _____

   b. What is the value of the 8th term?

   _____

9. Which numbers are rational? Choose Yes or No for each.

   A $\sqrt{10} + \sqrt{15}$ ○ Yes   ○ No

   B $0.\overline{123}$ ○ Yes   ○ No

   C $\dfrac{11}{14}$ ○ Yes   ○ No

   D $\pi^2 + 25$ ○ Yes   ○ No

10. What is $\dfrac{23}{11}$ written as a decimal?

    _____

11. What is $0.\overline{5}$ written as a fraction in simplest form?

    _____

12. Order the numbers from least to greatest.

    $\sqrt{72}, 3\pi - 1, 8.\overline{42}$

    _____

MODULE 14 Response to Intervention
Pre-Test: Skills 7, 9, 15, 31, 38, 40

For 1–3, solve each equation.

1. $81^{4x} = 243$

   _____

2. $25^{-x} = \dfrac{1}{125}$

   _____

3. $7^{3x+4} = 343$

   _____

4. Simplify 6^{-2}.

   _____

5. Simplify $10^5 \cdot 10^{-3} \cdot 10^{-2}$.

   _____

6. The relationship between x and y is proportional. Write an equation for the relationship.

x	3	6	9	12
y	12	24	36	48

   _____

7. What are the intercepts of the line described by the equation $x + 5y = 15$?

   _____

8. Which of these equations represents a line with a slope of -3 and a y-intercept of 5? Choose Yes or No for each.

   A $y = -3x + 5$ ○ Yes   ○ No

   B $y = 5x - 3$ ○ Yes   ○ No

   C $3x - y = -5$ ○ Yes   ○ No

   D $3x + y = 5$ ○ Yes   ○ No

9. Write the equation in slope-intercept form of a line with slope 6 and y-intercept -7.

   _____

10. What is the equation of the line whose graph is the graph of $f(x) = x$ shifted 13 units down?

    _____

11. How are the graphs of $g(x) = 3x$ and $h(x) = -3x$ related to the graph of $f(x) = x$? Graph all three functions in the coordinate plane.

    _____

    _____

    _____

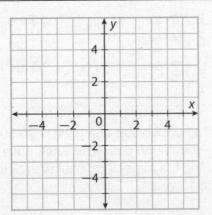

12. What equation models the data in the table?

Number of Hours Worked, x	Amount Earned ($), y
40	850
80	1650
120	2450
160	3250

    _____

MODULE 15

Response to Intervention

Pre-Test: Skills 9, 14, 28

1. Simplify $\left(2^{-3}\right)^2$.

_____

2. Choose True or False to indicate whether the expressions are equal.

   A $\left(\dfrac{3}{2}\right)^2$ and $\dfrac{9}{4}$ ○ True ○ False

   B $\left(\dfrac{3}{4}\right)^{-5}$ and $-\dfrac{3^5}{4^5}$ ○ True ○ False

   C $\left(\dfrac{1}{3}\right)^3$ and $\dfrac{1}{27}$ ○ True ○ False

   D $\left(\dfrac{-4}{3}\right)^{-2}$ and $\dfrac{16}{9}$ ○ True ○ False

3. Simplify $\dfrac{3^5 \cdot 3^{-2}}{3^{-4} \cdot 3^8}$.

_____

4. Simplify $16^{\frac{1}{4}} + 16^{\frac{2}{4}} + 16^{\frac{3}{4}}$.

_____

5. Write a radical expression that is equal to $54^{\frac{1}{4}}$.

_____

6. Choose True or False to indicate whether the expression is equal to $32^{\frac{2}{5}}$.

   A 4   ○ True ○ False

   B $\sqrt{2^5}$ ○ True ○ False

   C $\sqrt[5]{32^2}$ ○ True ○ False

   D 2   ○ True ○ False

7. What is the simplified form of $100,000^{\frac{4}{5}}$?

_____

8. Let $y = \dfrac{1}{2}x - \dfrac{1}{2}$.

   a. Complete the table for the equation.

x	−1	0	1	3
y				

   b. Use the table to graph the equation.

   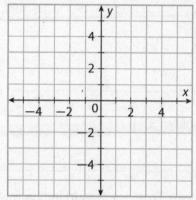

   c. Explain why the relationship is not proportional.

   _____

   _____

9. Consider the equation of the line $y = -\dfrac{3}{2}x - 15$. Which correctly describes the graph of the line? Choose True or False for each.

   A The *y*-intercept is −15
      ○ True   ○ False

   B The *y*-intercept is $-\dfrac{3}{2}$
      ○ True   ○ False

   C The slope is $-\dfrac{3}{2}$.
      ○ True   ○ False

   D The slope is −15.
      ○ True   ○ False

MODULE 16

Response to Intervention

Pre-Test: Skills 7, 9, 20, 28

For 1–3, solve each equation.

1. $81^{3x} = 9$

_____

2. $5^{3x-4} = 25$

_____

3. $\left(\dfrac{1}{16}\right)^{-x} = \dfrac{1}{64}$

_____

4. Simplify $\left(3^{-2}\right)^{3}$.

_____

5. Choose True or False to indicate whether the expressions are equal.

A $\left(\dfrac{5}{4}\right)^{-2}$ and $-\dfrac{25}{16}$ ○ True   ○ False

B $\left(\dfrac{3}{4}\right)^{-5}$ and $\dfrac{4^5}{3^5}$ ○ True   ○ False

C $\left(-\dfrac{5}{3}\right)^{2}$ and $-\dfrac{25}{9}$ ○ True   ○ False

D $\left(\dfrac{1}{3}\right)^{-2}$ and 9   ○ True   ○ False

6. Simplify $\dfrac{5^6 \cdot 5^{-3}}{5^{-2} \cdot 5^8}$.

_____

7. Simplify $27^{\frac{2}{3}} + 27^{\frac{3}{3}} + 27^{\frac{4}{3}}$.

_____

8. Write a radical expression that is equal to $72^{\frac{1}{3}}$.

_____

9. Choose True or False to indicate whether the expression is equal to $81^{\frac{3}{4}}$.

A 27   ○ True   ○ False

B $\sqrt[3]{3^4}$ ○ True   ○ False

C $\sqrt[4]{27}$ ○ True   ○ False

D $\sqrt{9^3}$ ○ True   ○ False

10. What is the simplified form of $1000^{\frac{7}{3}}$?

_____

For 11–13, solve each equation.

11. $c + 6 = -3c + 6$

_____

12. $-4(3 + 2x) = -3x + 8$

_____

13. $3(10m - 9) = -6(2 - 5m)$

_____

14. Dena has two payment options for renting a car. With Option A, she would pay $40 plus $0.40 per mile. With Option B, she would pay $30 plus $0.50 per mile. How many miles would she have to drive using Option B to pay as much as she would if she chose Option A?

a. Write an equation that models this situation.

_____

b. Solve the equation. How many miles would she have to drive?

_____

MODULE 17

Response to Intervention

Pre-Test: Skills 44, 53, 55, 56, 58

1. A segment has coordinates (7, −4) and (−3, 6). What is the midpoint of the segment?

_____

2. What is the distance between a point at (−3, 4) and a point at (2, −5)?

_____

3. Could 9, 40, and 41 be the side lengths of a right triangle? Why or why not?

_____

_____

4. Hannah drives due north and is 53 miles from town after 1 hour. At the same time, Toni drives due east and is 49 miles from town after 1 hour. To the nearest tenth of a mile, what is the straight line distance between the friends after 1 hour?

_____

5. Consider the following triangle. Choose True or False for each statement below.

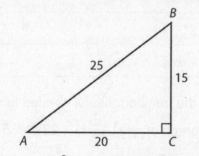

A $\sin A = \dfrac{3}{4}$ ○ True   ○ False

B $\cos A = \dfrac{4}{5}$ ○ True   ○ False

C $\sin B = \cos A$ ○ True   ○ False

D $\cos B = \dfrac{5}{3}$ ○ True   ○ False

6. A 16-foot ladder leans against a wall and forms a 58° angle with the ground. How far away is the base of the ladder from the wall?

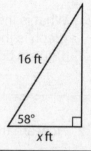

_____

7. In a 45°-45°-90° triangle, if the length of a leg is $5\sqrt{2}$, what is the length of the hypotenuse?

_____

8. Consider the following 30°-60°-90° triangle. Choose True or False for each statement below.

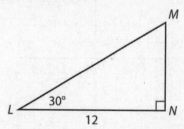

A $m\angle M = 60°$ ○ True   ○ False

B $LM = \sqrt{3} \cdot LN$ ○ True   ○ False

C $LM = 8\sqrt{3}$ ○ True   ○ False

D $MN = 6\sqrt{2}$ ○ True   ○ False

For 9–10, use $\triangle RST$.

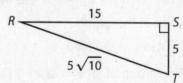

9. What is $\tan T$? Write your answer in simplest form.

_____

10. The tangent of what angle is $\dfrac{1}{3}$?

_____

Response to Intervention

Pre-Test: Skills 38, 39, 42, 57

1. What is the equation of the line whose graph is the graph of $f(x) = x$ shifted 13 units down?

   _____

2. How are the graphs of $g(x) = \dfrac{1}{2}x$ and

   $h(x) = -\dfrac{1}{2}x$ related to the graph of

   $f(x) = x$? Graph all three functions in the coordinate plane.

   _____

   _____

   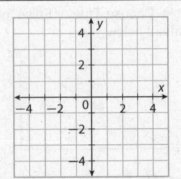

3. Is each statement True or False?

   A The vertex of the graph of
      $g(x) = 3(x-8)^2 - 5$ is (8, 5).

      ○ True   ○ False

   B The vertex of the graph of
      $g(x) = -3(x+2)^2 - 9$ is the highest point of the graph.

      ○ True   ○ False

   C The graph of $g(x) = 3(x-2)^2 + 6$ is wider than the graph of $f(x) = x^2$.

      ○ True   ○ False

   D The graph of $g(x) = -3(x-1)^2 - 5$ is narrower than the graph of $f(x) = x^2$.

      ○ True   ○ False

4. Order the functions from narrowest (most vertically stretched) to widest (most vertically compressed).

   $a(x) = -\dfrac{5}{3}x^2, \quad b(x) = -0.6x^2,$

   $c(x) = \dfrac{2}{3}x^2, \quad d(x) = 1.6x^2$

   _____

5. Choose Yes or No. Does the graph of $f(x) = x^2$ need to be reflected across the x-axis to obtain the graph of each function?

   A $g(x) = -0.3(x-2)^2 + 4$ ○ Yes   ○ No

   B $g(x) = \dfrac{5}{3}(x-3)^2 - \dfrac{2}{3}$ ○ Yes   ○ No

   C $g(x) = 2.5(x+3.5)^2 - 7$ ○ Yes   ○ No

   D $g(x) = -\dfrac{5}{2}(x+3)^2 - 4$ ○ Yes   ○ No

6. List the transformations needed to obtain the graph of $g(x) = -0.25(x+40)^2 - 20$ from the graph of $f(x) = x^2$.

   _____

   _____

   _____

7. List the transformations needed to obtain the graph of $g(x) = \dfrac{5}{3}(x-23)^2 + 35$ from the graph of $f(x) = x^2$.

   _____

   _____

   _____

Name _____ Date _____ Class_____

Response to Intervention
Pre-Test: Skills 51, 52

For 1–4, use the information below. Write each probability as a decimal rounded to three decimal places.

The table below shows the results of a survey of freshmen and sophomore high school students. Each student was asked if he or she prefers to have a study hall for 1st, 2nd, or 3rd period class.

		Year	
		Freshman	**Sophomore**
Preference	1st	18	20
	2nd	5	10
	3rd	25	6

A student is randomly selected from the group.

1. What is the probability that the selected student is a sophomore?

_____

2. What is the probability that the selected student is a freshman or preferred to have a 3rd period study hall?

_____

3. What is the probability that the selected student prefers 1st period study hall and is a sophomore?

_____

4. Are the events "the selected student is a freshman" and "the selected student prefers 2nd period study hall" mutually exclusive? Explain.

_____

5. Two coins are flipped and the side on which they land is noted. List the events in the sample space of this experiment.

_____

For 6–8, use the information below. Write each probability as a simplified fraction.

A number is randomly selected from the set {1, 3, 5, 12, 13, 14, 15, 16, 19, 20}.

6. What is the probability the selected number is even?

_____

7. What is the probability the selected number is greater than 10?

_____

8. What is the probability the selected number is smaller than 5 or greater than 19?

_____

For 9–10, use the information below. Write each probability as a percent.

A review of the budgets of several departments in a company finds that 3 of the 15 budgets have errors.

9. If a department's budget is randomly selected, what is the probability it will have an error?

_____

10. If a department's budget is randomly selected, what is the probability it will NOT have an error?

_____

11. If a 6-sided number cube is rolled, then, in words, what does the event $E = \{1, 2\}$ represent?

_____

Name _____ Date _____ Class_____

Response to Intervention
Pre-Test: Skills 51, 52

For 1–3, use the spinner to find the probability of each event.

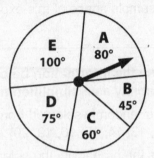

1. the pointer landing on section A

   _____

2. the pointer landing on section C or section D

   _____

3. the pointer not landing on section E

   _____

4. A jar of marbles contains 14 red, 12 green, and 5 blue marbles. If a marble is randomly selected, what is the probability it is green or blue? Write your answer as a decimal rounded to the nearest hundredth.

   _____

For 5–7, use the information below.

A company has two locations and classifies employees as full time or part time. The table below shows the number of employees of each classification at each location.

	Location A	Location B
Full Time	18	10
Part Time	6	14

An employee is randomly selected. Find each probability. Write your answer as a percent. Round to the nearest tenth, if necessary.

5. What is the probability the employee is classified as full time or works at location B?

   _____

6. What is the probability the employee is classified as part time and works at location A?

   _____

7. Are the events "the employee works full time" and "the employee works at location A" mutually exclusive? Explain.

   _____

   _____

8. If E and F are events such that $P(E) = 0.1$, $P(F) = 0.3$, and $P(E$ or $F) = 0.2$, then what is $P(E$ and $F)$?

   _____

MODULE 21

Response to Intervention

Pre-Test: Skills 48, 52

For 1–5, cards are numbered 1–5. A card is selected at random.

1. List the events in the sample space.

   _____

2. What is the probability of choosing an odd number?

   _____

3. What is the probability of choosing a factor of 6?

   _____

4. If cards are randomly selected and replaced 20 times, how many times is an even number expected to be chosen?

   _____

5. If cards are selected and replaced 30 times, how many times is a multiple of 2 expected to be chosen?

   _____

For 6–10, a company surveyed its employees on how they get to work. The results are shown in the table.

Transportation	Number of Responses
Drive alone	65
Drive in a carpool	15
Use public transportation	16
Walk or bike	4

6. How many employees were surveyed?

   _____

7. If an employee is randomly chosen, what is the probability that employee uses public transportation?

   _____

8. If an employee is randomly chosen, what is the probability that employee drives to work alone or in a carpool?

   _____

9. If there are 1500 employees at the company, how many employees would be expected to walk or ride a bike to work?

   _____

For 10–13, a company manufactures light bulbs and finds that some are defective.

10. Batch A has 6 defective bulbs out of 100. What is the percent probability a randomly selected bulb is defective?

    _____

11. Based on Batch A, how many defective bulbs are expected if 2400 bulbs are manufactured?

    _____

12. The company adjusted a machine to try and fix the problem. Batch B has 3 defective bulbs out of 80. What is the probability that a randomly selected bulb is defective?

    _____

13. Did the company's improvements work? Explain.

    _____

    _____

Name _____ Date _____ Class_____

For 1–2, use the given data.

25 10 12 15 19 22 20 8
22 16 12 9 13 19 26 18

1. Make a box plot representing the data.

6 8 10 12 14 16 18 20 22 24 26 28 30

2. Make a histogram representing the data using the intervals shown.

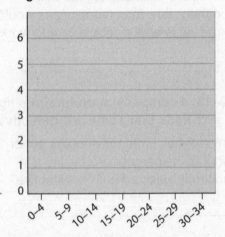

0–4 5–9 10–14 15–19 20–24 25–29 30–34

3. The box plots represent data sets A and B. Is each statement True or False?

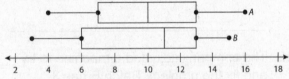

2 4 6 8 10 12 14 16 18

A The minimum for data set B is less than that for data set A.

○ True   ○ False

B The maximum for data set A is less than that for data set B.

○ True   ○ False

C The median for data set B is greater than that for data set A.

○ True   ○ False

D The range for data set A is greater than that for data set B.

○ True   ○ False

4. Choose Yes or No. Can each method be used to get a fair sample of 9 students from 81 students?

A Number the students from 1 to 81. Place each number in a 9-by-9 grid. Draw a number from 1 to 9 out of a hat for the row, replace the number, and draw a number from 1 to 9 for the column. Repeat until 9 students are selected.

○ Yes   ○ No

B Number the students from 1 to 81. Enter **randInt(9, 81)** on a graphing calculator and press enter.

○ Yes   ○ No

C Number the students from 1 to 81. Starting with 1, flip a coin. If the coin comes up heads, the student is selected. Continue until 9 students are selected.

○ Yes   ○ No

D Number the students from 1 to 81. Enter **randInt(1, 81)** on a graphing calculator and press enter until 9 unique numbers have come up.

○ Yes   ○ No

5. A poll asked 250 students if they liked the new school mascot; 120 students were boys. Of the boys, 75% liked the new mascot. Of the girls, 60% liked the new mascot. Use the information to complete the two-way table.

	Like	Do Not Like	TOTAL
Boys			
Girls			
TOTAL			

MODULE 23

Response to Intervention
Pre-Test: Skills 43, 49, 50

For 1–5, use the data set of quiz scores.

26 25 22 23 25 19 28 29
25 26 30 27 26 25 27 22

1. Make a dot plot representing the data.

◄——┼——┼——┼——┼——┼——┼——┼——┼——┼——┼——┼——┼——┼——┼——►

2. Choose True or False for each statement.

   A The first quartile is 23.5.
      ○ True   ○ False

   B The third quartile is 27.
      ○ True   ○ False

   C The interquartile range is 3.
      ○ True   ○ False

   D The median is 26.
      ○ True   ○ False

3. Describe the distribution of the dot plot as skewed to the left, skewed to the right, or symmetric.

   _____

4. What is the range?

   _____

5. What is the mean?

   _____

6. What is the standard deviation rounded to the nearest tenth?

   _____

For 7–13, suppose the heights in inches of the boys at a school are normally distributed with a mean of 67 inches and a standard deviation of 2.5 inches.

7. Make a sketch of the normal curve for the heights showing one, two, and three deviations from the mean. Label the curve with the correct percents.

8. What percent of the boys are no more than 64.5 inches tall?

   _____

9. What is the percent of the boys who are between 67 and 69.5 inches tall?

   _____

10. What is the percent of the boys who are less than 72 inches tall?

   _____

11. What is the probability that a randomly chosen boy is less than 62 inches tall?

   _____

12. What is the probability that a randomly chosen boy is over 67 inches tall?

   _____

13. Between what two heights equidistant from the mean do 95% of the heights fall?

   _____

Name _____ Date _____ Class_____

Response to Intervention
Pre-Test: Skills 47, 54, 59

1. A batch of 12,000 semiconductor chips was produced at a factory. A random sample of 200 of the items revealed that 7 were defective. About how many of the batch are likely to be defective?

_____

A random sample of the ages of pet dogs belonging to a group of students is listed below. Use the data for 2–4.

2 12 8 7 5 8 7 8 9 3 4 1
4 11 5 6 7 8 6 5 4 6 10 6

2. Make a dot plot representing the data.

←++++++++++++++++++++→

3. Make a box plot representing the data.

←++++++++++++++++++++→

4. Choose True or False for each statement.

A About half the dogs are from ages 4 to 8.
  ○ True   ○ False

B A good guess for a likely age of a pet dog is 6.
  ○ True   ○ False

C There are no dogs older than 10.
  ○ True   ○ False

D The range of the ages is 6.
  ○ True   ○ False

The table show the relationship between the hours spent studying for a test and the test scores for 6 students. The maximum possible score on the test is 50. Use the data in the table for 5–10.

Hours	1	2	2	2.5	3.5	4
Score	23	25	29	32	41	45

5. Make a scatter plot of the data.

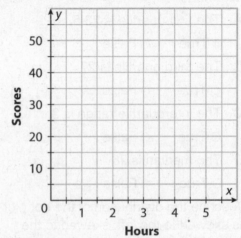

6. What type of correlation does the scatter plot show?

_____

7. Draw a trend line on the scatter plot.

_____

8. What is an equation of the trend line you drew?

_____

9. Use your trend line to predict the score of a student who studies 3 hours.

_____

10. Is your estimation for Question 9 an example of interpolation or extrapolation?

_____

Name _____ Date _____ Class_____

Response to Intervention

Post-Test: Add and Subtract Rational Numbers

Use the number line to find each sum.

1. $\frac{1}{4} + 3\frac{1}{2} =$ _____

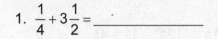

2. $-1.25 + (-3.25) =$ _____

3. $-4\frac{3}{4} + 6\frac{1}{2} =$ _____

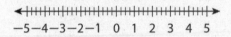

4. Devin used his debit card to buy an item costing \$15.43. Then he made a deposit of \$75.50 to his account. Which of the following correctly represents the overall change in his account?

   A $15.43 + (-75.50)$ ○ Yes   ○ No

   B $-15.43 + 75.50$ ○ Yes   ○ No

   C $75.50 - 15.43$ ○ Yes   ○ No

   D $75.50 + |-15.43|$ ○ Yes   ○ No

5. Find $-1 + 6.2 + (-9.3) + 8.2$.

_____

6. Which describes the result of $2\frac{2}{3} + -\left(5\frac{1}{3}\right)$? Choose True or False for each term.

   A integer   ○ True   ○ False

   B rational number ○ True   ○ False

   C positive number ○ True   ○ False

   D negative number ○ True   ○ False

7. Find $-\frac{1}{2} + 3 + \left(-\frac{7}{2}\right) + 14$.

_____

Use the number line to find each difference.

8. $3\frac{1}{4} - 4 =$ _____

9. $-0.5 - 3.75 =$ _____

10. $-3\frac{3}{4} - \left(-5\frac{3}{4}\right) =$ _____

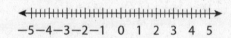

11. Find $2\frac{1}{2} - 8\frac{3}{4} - 7 + 15$.

_____

12. The following terms could describe the number of yards gained or lost in a football game. Choose True or False for each term.

   A rational number ○ True   ○ False

   B whole number   ○ True   ○ False

   C real number   ○ True   ○ False

   D integer   ○ True   ○ False

13. A submarine was submerged at a depth of −24.25 meters. An hour later its depth was −18.07 meters. What was the submarine's overall change in depth?

_____

14. Find $-12.2 - 9 - 7.13 + 4$.

_____

SKILL 2 **Response to Intervention**

Post-Test: Add and Subtract Polynomials

1. List the terms of the following algebraic expression.

   $9k^3 - 18k^2 + 12k - 6$

   _____

2. Tell whether the terms listed below are like terms.

   $7xy^2$ and $7x^2y$

   _____

3. What property is illustrated in the following equation?

   $7x + (13x - 15) = (7x + 13x) - 15$

   _____

4. Which expression is equivalent to the expression $-12 + 15w$?

   A $12 - 15w$

   B $-12 - 15w$

   C $15w + 12$

   D $15w - 12$

5. Simplify $9m^3 + 8 - 5m^3 - 4 + m^2$.

   _____

6. Simplify $-18n^3 + (10 + 11n^3) - 7$.

   _____

7. Choose True or False to indicate whether each polynomial is written in standard form.

   A $8a^3 + 7a^2 + 6 + 5a$ ○ True   ○ False

   B $a + 5a^2 + 8a^3 + 12a^4$ ○ True   ○ False

   C $5a^4 + 12$ ○ True   ○ False

   D $15a^5 + 9a - 6$ ○ True   ○ False

8. Write the following polynomial in standard form.

   $19b^3 - 11b^2 + 19b^5 - 11 + 4b$

   _____

9. Simplify the following expression.

   $(3c^4 + 17c^2 + 17 + 11c) + (13c^2 + 2c + 7)$

   _____

10. A travel agency studied the number of different types of vacation packages it has sold over a 5-year period. The agency modeled the results with the following polynomials.

    Beach: $-8v^2 - 240v + 3600$

    Mountains: $24v^2 - 185v + 1200$

    What polynomial models the total number of vacation packages the agency sold during the 5-year period?

    _____

11. What is the opposite of the polynomial $10f^3 - 4f^2 + 8f - 18$?

    _____

12. Which expression is equivalent to $(3d^2 + 13d) - (17d - 7d^2)$?

    A $-4d^2 - 4d$

    B $-4d^2 + 30d$

    C $10d^2 - 4d$

    D $10d^2 + 30d$

13. Simplify the following expression.

    $(5c^4 + 5c^2 + 5c + 5) - (20c^2 + 9c + 5)$

    _____

SKILL 3

Response to Intervention

Post-Test: Algebraic Expressions

Evaluate each expression for the given value.

1. $5t + 9$ for $t = 4$

_____

2. $y^2 + 6$ for $y = 3$

_____

3. $\frac{1}{2}p^2 - \frac{1}{4}p - 3$ for $p = -8$

_____

4. Which expressions are equivalent? Choose Yes or No for each pair.

A $15(x - 3)$ and $15x - 3x$

   ○ Yes   ○ No

B $2y^2 + 3y^2 - 1$ and $5y^2 - 1$

   ○ Yes   ○ No

C $\frac{1}{3}a^2(9 - 3a)$ and $a^3 - 3a^2$

   ○ Yes   ○ No

D $2ab(a + 3) - (2a^2b + 6ab)$ and 0

   ○ Yes   ○ No

Simplify each expression.

5. $12x - 4x$

_____

6. $-2 + 3p^2 - 4 + 7p^2$

_____

7. $\frac{1}{2}x^3y^2 - 4x^2 + \frac{7}{2}x^3y^2 + x^2$

_____

8. $\frac{2}{3}x(6x + 4) - 10x^2$

_____

9. $a^3b + 3ab(3a^2 - 2) + ab - 2$

_____

10. Which terms describe multiplication? Choose True or False for each term.

    A   product   ○ True   ○ False

    B   quotient   ○ True   ○ False

    C   increased by   ○ True   ○ False

    D   twice   ○ True   ○ False

Write each phrase as an algebraic expression.

11. 5 added to the product of 7 and y

_____

12. the sum of twice m and 3, divided by the difference of 6 and m

_____

13. the product of 7 and t cubed, multiplied by the quantity t minus 12

_____

14. Which expressions are equivalent to the statement, "the product of 5 and x, times the quantity x minus 4?" Choose Yes or No for each expression.

    A $5x(x - 4)$ ○ Yes   ○ No

    B $(5 + x)(x - 4)$ ○ Yes   ○ No

    C $x^2 + x - 20$ ○ Yes   ○ No

    D $5x^2 - 20$ ○ Yes   ○ No

SKILL 4

Response to Intervention

Post-Test: Algebraic Representations of Transformations

A line has the points (–4, 5), (–1, –1), and (3, –9). Find the points for the translation described.

1. 5 units to the right

   _____

2. 2 units down

   _____

3. 3 units to the left

   _____

4. 7 units up

   _____

5. Which transformations describe a vertical translation of a function? Choose Yes or No for each.

   A 17 units down

   ○ Yes   ○ No

   B Reflect across the x-axis.

   ○ Yes   ○ No

   C 3 units up

   ○ Yes ,   ○ No

   D Compress vertically by a factor of 4.

   ○ Yes   ○ No

6. The following terms describe a dilation. Choose True or False for each term.

   A horizontal shift   ○ True   ○ False

   B horizontal stretch   ○ True   ○ False

   C vertical compression ○ True   ○ False

   D vertical reflection   ○ True   ○ False

7. Which transformations include a reflection of a function across the x-axis? Choose Yes or No for each.

   A Multiply each x-coordinate by –1.

   ○ Yes   ○ No

   B Multiply each y-coordinate by $-\frac{1}{2}$.

   ○ Yes   ○ No

   C Subtract 1 from each y-coordinate.

   ○ Yes   ○ No

   D Multiply each y-coordinate by –1.

   ○ Yes   ○ No

For Problems 8–9, a line has the points (–4, –2), (–2, 0), and (3, 5). It is reflected across the y-axis and then translated down by 1 unit.

8. Find the points for the transformation.

   _____

9. Graph the line and the transformation.

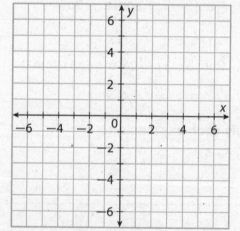

10. A line has the points $(-3, -2)$, $(0, 1)$, and $(2, 3)$. Find the points after a vertical stretch by a scale factor of 3.

   _____

Response to Intervention

Post-Test: Classifying Polynomials

1. List the terms of the following algebraic expression.

   $3a^4 - 7a^3 + 5a^2 - 3$

   _____

2. Tell whether the terms listed below are like terms.

   $7ab^2$ and $6b^2a$

   _____

3. Choose True or False to indicate whether each term is a coefficient in the following expression.

   $14c^3 + 13c^2 - 9c - 11$

   A 14   ○ True   ○ False
   B 13   ○ True   ○ False
   C 9   ○ True   ○ False
   D −11   ○ True   ○ False

4. In the expression $10d^2 + 14d - 13$, what is the constant?

   _____

5. Which polynomial has degree 3?

   A $6f^2 - 9f - 5$ C $2f^4 + 3$

   B $3f$ D $f^3 - 1$

6. What is the degree of the following polynomial?

   $3g^2 + 16 - 5g^3 - 3 + 18g^6$

   _____

7. Choose True or False to indicate whether the polynomial has degree 4.

   A $9h^3 + 12h^2 + 19 + 4h$ ○ True   ○ False
   B $14h + h^2 + 8h^3 + 2h^4$ ○ True   ○ False
   C $12h^4 + 4$ ○ True   ○ False
   D $4h^5 + 9h - 6$ ○ True   ○ False

8. What is the degree of the following monomial?

   $3k$

   _____

9. Write the following polynomial in standard form.

   $9m + 4m^2 - 15m^5 + 16 - 17m^3$

   _____

10. What is the leading coefficient of the following polynomial?

    $5n^2 - 4n + 18 - 5n^3$

    A −5   C 5
    B −4   D 18

11. Classify the following polynomial based on its number of terms.

    $p^3 + 1$

    _____

12. Choose True or False to indicate whether the polynomial is a binomial.

    A $2r^2 + 3r + 1$ ○ True   ○ False
    B $7r + 4r^2$ ○ True   ○ False
    C $4r^4 + 2$ ○ True   ○ False
    D $2r^5 + 7r^3 - 2r - 9$ ○ True   ○ False

13. Which polynomial is a trinomial?

    A $-9s^2$

    B $-8s^2 + 1$

    C $s^2 - 9s + 2$

    D $4s^5 + s^4 + 5s^3 - 6s^2$

14. Which term would you use to classify a polynomial with 6 terms?

    A Monomial   C Trinomial
    B Binomial   D Polynomial

SKILL 6

Response to Intervention
Post-Test: Direct Variation

1. Which equations represent a direct variation? Choose Yes or No for each.

   A $y = 11x - 11$

   ○ Yes   ○ No

   B $-12x = 3y$

   ○ Yes   ○ No

   C $4.5x - 9y = -18$

   ○ Yes   ○ No

   D $6y - 13x = 0$

   ○ Yes   ○ No

Tell whether each equation represents a direct variation. If so, identify the constant of variation.

2. $-18.6x + 6.2y = 0$

   _____

   _____

3. $3x + 4y = -12$

   _____

   _____

Determine whether the values in each table represent a direct variation. If so, identify the constant of variation.

4.

x	-2	0	3
y	-14	0	21

   _____

   _____

5.

x	-5	1	2
y	-9	7	14

   _____

   _____

6. The constant of variation for a direct variation equation is $\frac{2}{3}$. Choose True or False for each.

   A   When $x = -6$, $y = -4$.

   ○ True   ○ False

   B   When $x = 12$, $y = 8$.

   ○ True   ○ False

   C   When $x = 6$, $y = 9$.

   ○ True   ○ False

   D   When $x = -15$, $y = -10$.

   ○ True   ○ False

Write a direct variation equation for each situation. Then solve for the given value of x.

7. The value of y varies directly with x, and $y = 18$ when $x = 3$. Find y when $x = 11$.

   _____

8. The value of y varies directly with x, and $y = 6.5$ when $x = -13$. Find y when $x = -2$.

   _____

9. The distance y from a lightning strike varies directly with the time x it takes to hear thunder. If you hear thunder 15 seconds after seeing lightning that is 3 miles away, how many seconds would it take to hear thunder from lightning that strikes 2 miles away?

   _____

10. The cost y of carnival-ride tickets varies directly with the number of tickets x that are purchased. If it costs $30 for 8 tickets, how much would it cost for 24 tickets?

   _____

SKILL 7

Response to Intervention

Post-Test: Equations Involving Exponents

Choose the best answer.

1. Which equations can be solved using the Equality of Bases Property? Choose Yes or No for each equation.

   A $2^x = 17$ ○ Yes   ○ No

   B $2^x = 64$ ○ Yes   ○ No

   C $\left(\dfrac{1}{3}\right)^x = 27$ ○ Yes   ○ No

   D $64^{2x} = \dfrac{1}{16}$ ○ Yes   ○ No

Solve each equation.

2. $243^{3x} = 27$

   _____

3. $5^{-3x} = 25$

   _____

4. $6^{2x+1} = 36$

   _____

5. $\left(\dfrac{1}{9}\right)^{-x} = \dfrac{1}{243}$

   _____

6. $9^{1-x} = \left(\dfrac{1}{27}\right)^{3x}$

   _____

7. The graph below can be used to solve the equation $3^x = 4$. Choose True or False for each statement.

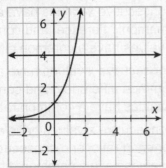

   A The solution is $x \approx 1.26$.

   ○ True   ○ False

   B The input of the intersection point is the solution of the equation.

   ○ True   ○ False

   C The output of the intersection point is the solution of the equation.

   ○ True   ○ False

   D The solution is $x = \dfrac{3}{4}$.

   ○ True   ○ False

Job A offers $700 a month for the first month with a 35% raise every month thereafter. Job B offers $800 a month for the first month with a $25 raise every month thereafter.

8. Write an equation describing when the monthly salaries for both jobs will be equal.

   _____

9. What will be the first month that Job A has a higher salary than Job B?

   _____

SKILL
8

Response to Intervention

Post-Test: Exponential Functions

1. Given a table of x- and y-values, how can you determine if the values satisfy an exponential function?

   A Consecutive x-values have a common difference, and consecutive y-values have a common difference.

   B Consecutive x-values have a common difference, and consecutive y-values have a common ratio.

   C Consecutive x-values have a common ratio, and consecutive y-values have a common difference.

   D Consecutive x-values have a common ratio, and consecutive y-values have a common ratio.

2. Evaluate the exponential function $y = -12(3)^x$ for $x = 2$.

   _____

3. The function $f(x) = 875(1.2)^x$ models a population of fungi in a certain region over time, where x is the time in days. How many fungi will there be in the region in 14 days?

   _____

4. Graph $y = \frac{1}{4}(2)^x$.

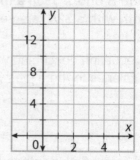

5. Choose True or False to indicate whether the ordered pairs represent a point on the graph of $y = 2(5)^x$.

   A $(-1, 0.4)$ ○ True   ○ False

   B $(0, 2)$ ○ True   ○ False

   C $(1, 10)$ ○ True   ○ False

   D $(2, 100)$ ○ True   ○ False

6. A plot of land sells for $52,000. Its value increases by 5% each year after it is sold. To the nearest dollar, what is the value of the land in 12 years?

   A $54,600   C $655,200

   B $93,385   D $6,746,810

7. Use the following exponential function to decide whether the statements below are True or False.

   $y = 175(1.3)^x$

   A The original amount is 175.

   ○ True   ○ False

   B When $x = 3$, the final amount is about 384.5.

   ○ True   ○ False

   C The growth rate is 3%.

   ○ True   ○ False

   D The function models exponential decay.

   ○ True   ○ False

8. The population of a town is 45,000 and is expected to decrease 3% each year. Find the expected population of the town in 15 years.

   _____

9. A motorcycle sells for $12,000. Its value decreases by 9% each year after it is sold. Find the expected value of the motorcycle in 7 years.

   _____

1. Simplify 7^{-3}.

_____

2. Choose True or False to indicate whether each expression is equal to 1.

   A $\left(\dfrac{3}{7}\right)^0$ ○ True   ○ False

   B 0^1 ○ True   ○ False

   C $(-1)^0$ ○ True   ○ False

   D 0.549^0 ○ True   ○ False

3. Explain how to multiply two powers with the same base.

_____

4. Simplify $10^3 \cdot 10^2 \cdot 10$.

_____

5. Which expression is NOT equal to $\dfrac{5^4 \cdot 5^2}{5 \cdot 5^3}$?

   A $\dfrac{5^6}{5^4}$ C $\dfrac{5^6}{5^3}$

   B 5^2 D 25

6. Simplify $(-3 \cdot 2)^4$.

_____

7. Choose True or False to indicate whether the expressions are equal.

   A $\left(\dfrac{4}{3}\right)^2$ and $\dfrac{8}{6}$ ○ True   ○ False

   B $\left(\dfrac{5}{8}\right)^3$ and $\dfrac{5^3}{8^3}$ ○ True   ○ False

   C $\left(\dfrac{1}{8}\right)^3$ and $\dfrac{1}{2}$ ○ True   ○ False

   D $\left(\dfrac{-2}{3}\right)^5$ and $-\dfrac{32}{243}$ ○ True   ○ False

8. Simplify $\left(4^2\right)^{-3}$.

_____

9. Explain why the following statement is true.

   $\sqrt[5]{1024} = 4$

_____

10. What is the simplified form of $\sqrt[4]{81}$?

    A 3   C 20.25

    B 9   D 324

11. Write a radical expression that is equal to $512^{\frac{1}{3}}$.

_____

12. Choose True or False to indicate whether the expression is equal to $216^{\frac{1}{3}}$.

    A $\sqrt[3]{216}$ ○ True   ○ False

    B $\sqrt[3]{6^3}$ ○ True   ○ False

    C 6   ○ True   ○ False

    D 72   ○ True   ○ False

13. What is the simplified form of $10{,}000^{\frac{3}{4}}$?

    A 1

    B 10

    C 100

    D 1000

14. Simplify $64^{\frac{1}{3}} + 64^{\frac{2}{3}} + 64^{\frac{3}{3}}$.

_____

Response to Intervention
Post-Test: Factoring Polynomials

1. What is the GCF of $8m^3$ and $12m^2$?

   _____

2. Choose True or False to indicate whether the GCF of each pair of monomials is $3x^2$.

   A $3x^2$ and x^2 ○ True   ○ False

   B $6x^3$ and $15x^2$ ○ True   ○ False

   C $3x^5$ and $6x^2$ ○ True   ○ False

   D $3x^3$ and $3x$ ○ True   ○ False

3. List 3 monomials that have a GCF of $5x^3$.

   _____

4. What is the GCF of the terms of the following polynomial?

   $4x^3 - 10x^2$

   _____

5. Factor $7b^6 - 28b^2$.

   _____

6. What is the factored form of $-6m^5 - 9m^3 + 12m$?

   A $-3m(2m^4 + 3m^2 - 4)$

   B $-3m(2m^4 + 3m^2 + 4)$

   C $-3m(-2m^4 - 3m^2 + 4)$

   D $-3(2m^4 + 3m^2 - 4)$

7. Is the polynomial below factored completely? Explain your reasoning.

   $10x^4 - 20x^3 = 5x(2x^3) + 5x(-4x^2)$

   $\qquad\qquad = 5x(2x^3 - 4x^2)$

   _____

8. What is the common binomial factor in the polynomial below?

   $9(2x + 3) - 7x(2x + 3)$

   _____

9. Choose Yes or No to indicate whether the polynomial can be factored by grouping.

   A $10x^3 - 6x^2 + 5x - 3$

      ○ Yes   ○ No

   B $5x^5 + 10x - 6x^3 + 24$

      ○ Yes   ○ No

   C $-4x^3 + 2x^4 - 7x^5 + 21x^6$

      ○ Yes   ○ No

   D $8x^4 - 20x^3 + 6x - 15$

      ○ Yes   ○ No

10. What is the factored form of the following polynomial?

    $9x^4 + 3x^3 + 15x + 5$

    A $(3x^3 + 5)(3x + 1)$

    B $(3x^2 + 5)(3x + 1)$

    C $(3x^3 + 1)(3x + 5)$

    D $(3x^2 + 1)(3x + 5)$

11. What is the GCF of the **first** group of terms in the following polynomial?

    $(40x^6 - 32x^5) + (15x - 12)$

    _____

12. Factor the following polynomial by grouping.

    $18x^5 - 63x^3 + 2x^2 - 7$

    _____

Response to Intervention

Post-Test: Factoring Special Products

1. What term can you use to classify polynomials of the form $a^2 + 2ab + b^2$ or $a^2 - 2ab + b^2$ that describes how they can be factored?

   _____

2. Choose True or False to indicate whether each term is a perfect square.

A	−25	○ True	○ False
B	x^2	○ True	○ False
C	$2y^2$	○ True	○ False
D	$25n^4$	○ True	○ False

3. Factor $h^2 + 16h + 64$.

   _____

4. When factoring a perfect-square trinomial, how do you know whether the factored form of the trinomial should be in the form $(a + b)^2$ or $(a - b)^2$?

   _____

5. Factor $36x^2 - 84x + 49$.

   _____

6. What is the factored form of the following polynomial?

   $9y^2 - 60y + 100$

   A $(3y + 10)(3y - 10)$

   B $(3y + 100)(3y + 100)$

   C $(3y^2 - 10)(3y^2 - 10)$

   D $(3y - 10)(3y - 10)$

7. Is the polynomial below factored correctly? Explain your reasoning.

   $16m^2 - 56m + 49 = (4m + 7)(4m + 7)$

   $\qquad\qquad\qquad = (4m + 7)^2$

   _____

8. The expression $100s^2 + 140s + 49$ represents the area of a square. What is the side length of the square?

   _____

9. How can you tell if a binomial is a difference of two squares?

   _____

10. Choose Yes or No to indicate whether the polynomial is a difference of two squares.

A	$x^2 + 25$	○ Yes	○ No
B	$4y^4 - 9$	○ Yes	○ No
C	$16a^2 - 1$	○ Yes	○ No
D	$8b^2 - 64$	○ Yes	○ No

11. What is the factored form of the following polynomial?

    $9x^2 - 144$

    A $(9x + 144)(9x - 144)$

    B $(3x^2 + 12)(3x^2 - 12)$

    C $(3x + 12)(3x - 12)$

    D $(9x + 12)(9x - 12)$

12. Factor $16y^4 - z^2$.

    _____

13. Explain the error in factoring the difference of two squares. Then find the correct factored form.

    $4d^6 - 81f^4 = (2d + 9f)(2d - 9f)$

    _____

SKILL
12

Response to Intervention
Post-Test: Factoring Trinomials

1. Which is always true about factoring a trinomial of the form $x^2 + bx + c$? Choose True or False for each.

   A You must find the factor pairs of c.

   ○ True   ○ False

   B You must find the factor pairs of b.

   ○ True   ○ False

   C If c is negative, the factors of c will have opposite signs.

   ○ True   ○ False

   D If b is positive, the factors of b will both have the same sign.

   ○ True   ○ False

Factor each trinomial.

2. $x^2 - 13x + 36$

   _____

3. $x^2 - x - 42$

   _____

4. $x^2 + 14x + 33$

   _____

5. $x^2 + 3x - 130$

   _____

6. A carpenter is going to enlarge a rectangular closet that has an area of $x^2 + 5x + 6$ ft^2. The length is $x + 2$ ft. After construction, the area will be $x^2 + 11x + 28$ ft^2 with a length of $x + 7$ ft.

   a. Find the dimensions of the closet before construction.

   _____

   b. Find the dimensions of the closet after construction.

   _____

7. Which trinomials were factored correctly? Choose Yes or No for each.

   A $x^2 + x - 56 = (x - 8)(x + 7)$

   ○ Yes   ○ No

   B $x^2 + 17x + 60 = (x + 5)(x + 12)$

   ○ Yes   ○ No

   C $3x^2 - 16x + 20 = (3x - 10)(x - 2)$

   ○ Yes   ○ No

   D $6x^2 + 7x - 3 = (2x - 3)(3x + 1)$

   ○ Yes   ○ No

Factor each trinomial.

8. $2x^2 - x - 10$

   _____

9. $5x^2 - 22x - 15$

   _____

10. $10x^2 + 21x + 9$

    _____

11. $22x^2 - 23x + 6$

    _____

12. $27x^2 + 48x - 35$

    _____

13. A rectangular garden has an area of $6x^2 + 23x + 7$ square feet. The width of the garden is $2x + 7$ feet. What is the length?

    _____

SKILL 13

Response to Intervention

Post-Test: Geometric Sequences

1. Which equations represent a geometric sequence in explicit form? Choose Yes or No for each.

   A $a_n = 3(n-1)$

   ○ Yes   ○ No

   B $a_n = 4^{n-1}$

   ○ Yes   ○ No

   C $a_1 = 2,\ a_n = 5 \cdot a_{n-1}$

   ○ Yes   ○ No

   D $a_n = -\dfrac{2}{3} \cdot \left(\dfrac{1}{5}\right)^{n-1}$

   ○ Yes   ○ No

Find the common ratio for each geometric sequence.

2. 3, 18, 108, 648, …

   _____

3. 0.5, 2, 8, 32, …

   _____

4. $-4,\ -\dfrac{4}{3},\ -\dfrac{4}{9},\ -\dfrac{4}{27},\ …$

   _____

Write a recursive rule for each geometric sequence.

5. 4, 12, 36, 108, …

   _____

6. 625, 125, 25, 5, …

   _____

7. −2, −12, −72, −432, …

   _____

Write an explicit rule for each geometric sequence.

8. 3, 15, 75, 375, …

   _____

9. −2.5, −5, −10, −20, …

   _____

10. $5,\ \dfrac{5}{4},\ \dfrac{5}{16},\ \dfrac{5}{64},\ …$

   _____

11. Which of these equations represent the geometric sequence 160, 80, 40, 20, …? Choose Yes or No for each.

   A $a_n = 160 \cdot (-2)^{n-1}$

   ○ Yes   ○ No

   B $a_1 = 20,\ a_n = 2 \cdot a_{n-1}$

   ○ Yes   ○ No

   C $a_1 = 160,\ a_n = \dfrac{1}{2} \cdot a_{n-1}$

   ○ Yes   ○ No

   D $a_n = 160 \cdot \left(\dfrac{1}{2}\right)^{n-1}$

   ○ Yes   ○ No

12. A geometric sequence has terms $a_3 = 75$ and $a_5 = 1875$.

   a. Write an explicit rule for the sequence. Assume the common ratio is positive.

   _____

   b. What is the value of the 8th term?

   _____

Name _____ Date _____ Class_____

1. Which equations represent a nonproportional linear relationship between x and y? Choose Yes or No for each.

   A $y = -\dfrac{3}{4}x$

   ○ Yes   ○ No

   B $y = \dfrac{1}{2}x + 9$

   ○ Yes   ○ No

   C $y = -5x - \dfrac{1}{2}$

   ○ Yes   ○ No

   D $y = -\dfrac{2}{3}x + \dfrac{7}{4} - 3$

   ○ Yes   ○ No

2. Let $y = 2x - 3$.

   a. Complete the table for the equation.

x	−1	0	2	3
y				

   b. Use the table to graph the equation.

   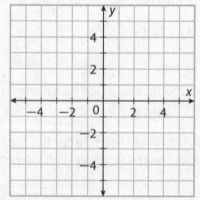

   c. Explain why the relationship is not proportional.

   _____

   _____

3. Consider the equation of the line $y = \dfrac{5}{2}x - 17$. Which correctly describes the graph of the line? Choose True or False for each.

   A The y-intercept is (0, −17).

   ○ True   ○ False

   B The y-intercept is $\left(0, \dfrac{5}{2}\right)$.

   ○ True   ○ False

   C The slope is −17.

   ○ True   ○ False

   D The slope is $\dfrac{5}{2}$.

   ○ True   ○ False

Use the equation to identify the slope and y-intercept of the line. Then graph the line.

4. $y = 1 - \dfrac{1}{2}x$

   slope: _____ y-intercept: _____

   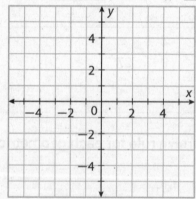

5. The graph of a nonproportional linear relationship between x and y can be represented by the equation $y = mx + b$. What is always true about the value of b?

   _____

   _____

SKILL 15 — Response to Intervention

Post-Test: Graphing Linear Proportional Relationships

1. The relationship between x and y is proportional. Write an equation for the relationship.

x	6	12	18	21
y	18	36	54	63

_____

2. Jasmine bakes 18 muffins per hour at the bakery. Write an equation that represents the relationship between the number of muffins she bakes and the time it takes her to bake them.

_____

3. Choose Yes or No to indicate whether the two quantities have a proportional relationship.

   A The number of hours you work and the amount of money you earn

   ○ Yes   ○ No

   B The side length of a square and the area of the square

   ○ Yes   ○ No

   C The number of water bottles you buy and the amount of money you spend

   ○ Yes   ○ No

   D The amount of money you have and the number of items you can buy

   ○ Yes   ○ No

4. Write an equation that describes the proportional relationship.

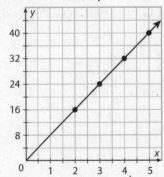

_____

5. Choose True or False for each statement.

   A The graph of a proportional relationship is a line.

   ○ True   ○ False

   B The graph of a proportional relationship passes through the origin (0, 0).

   ○ True   ○ False

   C The graph of a proportional relationship has equation $y = mx + b$, where $b \neq 0$.

   ○ True   ○ False

   D The slope of the graph of a proportional relationship is k, the constant of proportionality.

   ○ True   ○ False

6. What are the slope and y-intercept of the line?

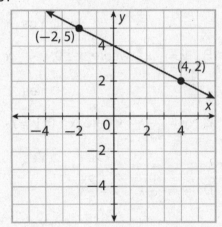

_____

7. An interior designer charges a flat fee for a consultation plus a certain amount per hour of work, as shown in the table. How much does the designer charge for a consultation?

Time (hr)	8	16	24	32
Charge ($)	540	980	1420	1860

   A $55   B $61.25

   C $67.50   D $100

Name _____ Date _____ Class_____

SKILL 16

Response to Intervention

Post-Test: Inverse Functions

1. The table below gives the coordinates $(x, f(x))$ of four points that are on function f. Make a table that shows the coordinates of four points $(x, f^{-1}(x))$ that are on f^{-1}, the inverse of f.

x	0	1	2	3
f(x)	5	6	9	14

   _____

2. What is the inverse of $f(x) = -\frac{1}{4}x - \frac{1}{2}$?

   _____

3. Choose Yes or No to indicate whether the two functions are inverse functions.

   A $y = 3x + 12;\ y = \frac{1}{3}x - 4$

                         ○ Yes   ○ No

   B $y = \frac{4}{9}x^2$, where $x \geq 0;\ y = \frac{2}{3}x$

                         ○ Yes   ○ No

   C $y = \frac{1}{49}x^2$, where $x \geq 0;\ y = 7\sqrt{x}$

                         ○ Yes   ○ No

   D $y = \frac{8}{27}x^3;\ y = \frac{2}{3}\sqrt[3]{x}$

                         ○ Yes   ○ No

4. The function $V(s) = s^3$ gives the volume in cubic units of a cube with side length s units. Find the inverse function $s(V)$. Then use the inverse function to find the side length of a cube with a volume of 64 cubic units.

   _____

   _____

5. Find the inverse of $f(x) = \frac{4}{25}x^2$, where $x \geq 0$. Then graph f and f^{-1}.

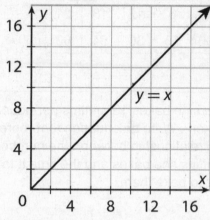

   $f^{-1}(x) =$ _____

6. Choose True or False for each statement.

   A   In inverse functions, the x- and y-values are switched compared to the parent function.

                         ○ True   ○ False

   B   Given a function f, the graph of its inverse f^{-1} is the reflection of f across the line $y = x$.

                         ○ True   ○ False

   C   Inverse functions must pass through the origin (0, 0).

                         ○ True   ○ False

   D   The inverse of a square root function is a cube root function.

                         ○ True   ○ False

7. What is the inverse of $f(x) = 8x^3$?

   A $g(x) = \frac{1}{8}x^3$ B $g(x) = \frac{1}{2}x^3$

   C $g(x) = \frac{1}{8}\sqrt[3]{x}$ D $g(x) = \frac{1}{2}\sqrt[3]{x}$

SKILL 17

Response to Intervention

Post-Test: Inverse Variation

Use the data in the table below to answer Problems 1 and 2.

x	−6	−3	2	9
y	−6	−12	18	4

1. Suppose *y* varies inversely as *x*. What is the constant of variation?

   _____

2. Write an equation for the inverse variation in the table above.

   _____

3. Choose Direct or Inverse to indicate whether *y* varies directly or inversely as *x*.

A
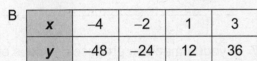

x	−10	−5	1	2
y	−2	−4	20	10

   ○ Direct   ○ Inverse

B

x	−4	−2	1	3
y	−48	−24	12	36

   ○ Direct   ○ Inverse

C

x	−3	−1	2	5
y	27	9	−18	−45

   ○ Direct   ○ Inverse

D

x	−10	−6	5	12
y	−6	−10	12	5

   ○ Direct   ○ Inverse

4. Suppose *y* varies inversely as *x* and *y* = 2 when *x* = 11. Write an equation for the inverse variation.

   _____

5. Choose True or False for each statement.

   A The graph of an inverse variation function has two unconnected sections.

   ○ True   ○ False

   B The graph of an inverse variation passes through the origin (0, 0).

   ○ True   ○ False

   C In an inverse variation, the ratio of the variables *x* and *y* is constant.

   ○ True   ○ False

   D An inverse variation is a relationship that can be represented by a function of the form $xy = k$, where $k \neq 0$.

   ○ True   ○ False

6. Graph $y = \dfrac{-50}{x}$.

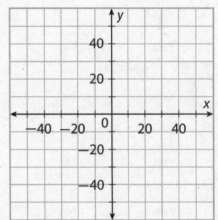

7. The time *t* that it takes a group of workers *w* to build an in-ground swimming pool varies inversely as the number of workers. Suppose 3 workers can build a pool in 15 working days. How many workers would be needed to build a pool in 9 working days?

   A 3   B 15

   C 5   D 45

Response to Intervention
Post-Test: Linear Functions

1. Does the graph represent a linear function? Explain your reasoning.

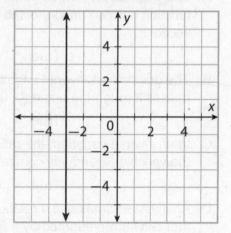

2. Which equations represent a linear function? Choose Yes or No for each.

   A $y = \dfrac{1}{2}x^2 + 4$

   ○ Yes   ○ No

   B $5x - 2y = -21$

   ○ Yes   ○ No

   C $-\dfrac{5}{3}x + 6 = y$

   ○ Yes   ○ No

   D $11 = xy - 2$

   ○ Yes   ○ No

Write an equation representing the linear function described.

3. The y-intercept is $-\dfrac{1}{2}$ and the slope is 5.

4. The slope is $\dfrac{4}{5}$ and the point $\left(0, -\dfrac{2}{3}\right)$ is on the graph.

5. Write an equation representing the linear function that includes the points given in the table.

x	−1	2	5	8
y	7.5	6	4.5	3

6. Write an equation for the linear function whose graph is shown.

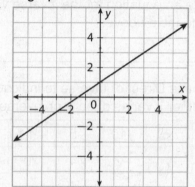

7. A yogurt machine produces $\dfrac{4}{3}$ cups of yogurt every minute. The amount of yogurt the machine produces can be modeled by the equation $y = \dfrac{4}{3}x$.

   a. What do the variables x and y represent in this situation?

   b. What is the rate of change? Interpret the rate of change in terms of the problem situation.

   c. Is the relationship between x and y proportional or nonproportional? Explain in terms of the problem situation.

SKILL 19 Response to Intervention

Post-Test: Linear Inequalities in Two Variables

1. Which inequalities have a solution set appearing as a shaded region above a solid boundary line when graphed? Choose Yes or No for each.

   A $2y - 7x > 14$ ○ Yes   ○ No

   B $6y - 3x \geq 18$ ○ Yes   ○ No

   C $x - 3y \geq 12$ ○ Yes   ○ No

   D $10 - 5y \leq 2x$ ○ Yes   ○ No

Solve each inequality for *y*. Then graph the solution set.

2. $4y - 3x > 24$

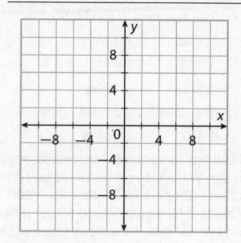

3. $11y - 99 < 10x$

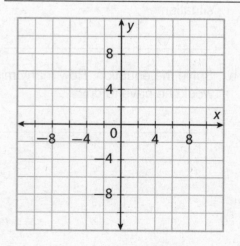

4. $-5x - 2y \geq 12$

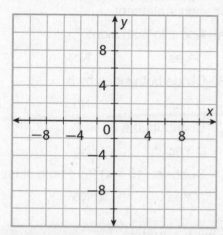

5. Drew has $20 to spend at a closeout sale at the bookstore. Movies cost $3.75 and books cost $2.50.

   a. Write a linear inequality that describes the number of movies, *x*, and books, *y*, that Drew can buy. Then solve for *y*.

   _____

   b. Graph the solution set.

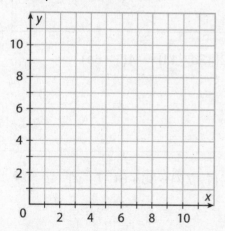

   c. Identify two combinations of movies and books that Drew can afford.

   _____

   _____

SKILL 20 **Response to Intervention**

Post-Test: Multi-Step Equations

1. Consider the equation $6x = 3(15 - x)$. Which could be a useful first step to solving the equation? Choose Yes or No for each statement.

   A Add x to both sides.

   ○ Yes   ○ No

   B Divide both sides by 3.

   ○ Yes   ○ No

   C Distribute the 3.

   ○ Yes   ○ No

   D Subtract $(15 - x)$ from both sides.

   ○ Yes   ○ No

Solve each equation.

2. $n + 5 = -5n + 5$

_____

3. $-8(6 + 5p) = 3p - 5$

_____

4. $2(12a - 11) = -4(1 - 6a)$

_____

5. $-(1 + 7y) = 36 + 6(-7 - y)$

6. $4(3 + 3x) + 2(4 + 8x) = -7 - 4x - 3x - 8$

_____

7. After solving the equation $p + 2(p - 1) = 3p - 2$, Jared came to the solution $3 = 3$. Which is true about the solution Jared found? Choose True or False for each statement.

   A There are no solutions to the equation.

   ○ True   ○ False

   B The equation is an identity.

   ○ True   ○ False

   C There is one solution, $p = 3$.

   ○ True   ○ False

   D The solution is all real numbers.

   ○ True   ○ False

8. Paul has two payment options for renting a car. With Option A he would pay a flat rate of $21 plus $0.25 per mile. With Option B he would pay $0.60 per mile and no flat rate. How many miles would he have to drive using Option B to pay as much as he would if he chose Option A?

   a. Write an equation that models this situation.

   _____

   b. Solve the equation. How many miles would he have to drive?

   _____

SKILL 21

Response to Intervention

Post-Test: Multiply and Divide Rational Numbers

1. Multiply 8(−1.4).

   _____

2. During a cold spell, the temperature drops −10.5 degrees per day. What is the change in the temperature after 4 days?

   _____

3. Choose Positive or Negative to indicate whether each product is positive or negative.

   A 4(−0.75)

   ○ Positive   ○ Negative

   B $-8\left(\dfrac{2}{3}\right)$

   ○ Positive   ○ Negative

   C −9(−1.53)

   ○ Positive   ○ Negative

   D $10\left(\dfrac{1}{3}\right)$

   ○ Positive   ○ Negative

4. Use the number line to simplify the following product.

   3(−1.6)

   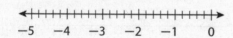

   -5   -4   -3   -2   -1   0

5. Choose True or False for each statement.

   A The product of two negative rational numbers is negative.

   ○ True   ○ False

   B The product of two positive rational numbers is positive.

   ○ True   ○ False

   C The product of a positive rational number and a negative rational number is negative.

   ○ True   ○ False

   D The quotient of two negative rational numbers is negative.

   ○ True   ○ False

6. Multiply $\left(\dfrac{3}{8}\right)\left(-\dfrac{1}{5}\right)\left(-\dfrac{7}{9}\right)$.

   _____

7. A swimming pool loses 820.5 gallons of water in 12.5 hours. The pool loses the same amount of water each hour. What is the change in the amount of water in the swimming pool per hour?

   A −65.64 gal/hr   B −6.564 gal/hr

   C 6.564 gal/hr   D 65.64 gal/hr

8. Simplify $\dfrac{\dfrac{5}{7}}{-\dfrac{8}{11}}$.

   _____

SKILL 22

Response to Intervention

Post-Test: Multiply Polynomials

1. Simplify $4(3x^2 + 8x + 4)$.

_____

2. A rectangle has a length of $(5x)$ units and a width of $(2x^2 + 11x + 5)$ units. What is the area of the rectangle?

_____

3. What is the simplified form of $(4m + 3)(2m - 7)$?

   A $8m^2 + 34m + 21$

   B $8m^2 + 34m - 21$

   C $8m^2 - 22m + 21$

   D $8m^2 - 22m - 21$

4. Explain how to use the FOIL method to multiply two binomials.

_____

5. Choose True or False for each statement.

   A $(3x + 1)(x - 5) = 3x^2 - 14x + 5$

      ○ True   ○ False

   B $(x + 2)(5x^2 - x + 1) = 5x^3 + 9x^2 + x + 2$

      ○ True   ○ False

   C $(6w + 3)^2 = 36w^2 + 36w + 9$

      ○ True   ○ False

   D $(8x + 3)(8x - 3) = 64x^2 - 9$

      ○ True   ○ False

6. Simplify $(7n^2 + 9)^2$.

_____

7. Use the FOIL method to show that $(a - b)^2 = a^2 - 2ab + b^2$. (Hint: Start by writing $(a - b)^2$ as $(a - b)(a - b)$.)

_____

8. Explain the error. Then find the correct solution.

   $$(3x + 11)(3x - 11) = (3x)^2 + 11^2$$
   $$= 9x^2 + 121$$

_____

9. A rectangular prism has length $(x + 5)$ units, height $(x - 1)$ units, and width 3 units. What is the volume of the prism? (Hint: Use the formula $V = lwh$.)

   A $(x^2 + 4x - 5)$ cubic units

   B $(x^2 + 6x - 5)$ cubic units

   C $(3x^2 + 12x - 15)$ cubic units

   D $(3x^2 + 18x - 15)$ cubic units

10. Simplify $(10p - 3)^2$.

_____

Response to Intervention

Post-Test: One-Step Equations

1. What operation would you use to solve the following equation?

$$x + \frac{5}{8} = -\frac{3}{4}$$

_____

2. Solve $b - \frac{4}{5} = \frac{9}{10}$.

_____

3. Which equation can be solved by multiplying by 3.4?

A $3.4 + x = -6.8$

B $10.2 = x - 3.4$

C $3.4x = 13.6$

D $\dfrac{x}{3.4} = 20.4$

4. Do the equations $\dfrac{7}{8}m = 21$ and $7m = 168$ have the same solution? Explain.

_____

5. For each equation, choose which operation would isolate the variable.

A $5.4 + b = -15$

   ○ Subtract 5.4.   ○ Add 5.4.

B $b - 0.89 = 12.11$

   ○ Subtract 0.89.   ○ Add 0.89.

C $24 = -1.5b$

   ○ Divide by -1.5.   ○ Divide by 1.5.

D $-\dfrac{b}{2} = 0.3$

   ○ Multiply by -2.   ○ Multiply by 2.

6. Shari is saving up to buy a new tablet. So far she has saved $73.25. The tablet costs $239. How much more money must Shari save in order to have enough money to buy the tablet?

_____

7. At Nichols High School, 350 students are 10th graders. This is 0.28 of the total student population. What is the student population at Nichols High School?

_____

8. You have already watched 36 minutes of a movie. You are one-fourth of the way through the movie. How long is the movie, in minutes?

_____

9. A football field is in the shape of a rectangle. Its length is 100 yards. Its area is 5333 square yards. Which equation can you solve to find the width of the football field?

A $100 + w = 5333$

B $100w = 5333$

C $w - 100 = 5333$

D $\dfrac{w}{100} = 5333$

10. Tiffany helped raise money for the culinary arts program at her school by selling pies. The total amount she raised can be represented by $12.50p$, where p is the number of pies she sold. Suppose Tiffany raised a total of $150. How many pies did she sell?

_____

SKILL 24

Response to Intervention

Post-Test: One-Step Inequalities

1. For which situations do you need to switch the inequality sign? Choose Yes or No for each.

   A when adding a negative number to both sides

     ○ Yes   ○ No

   B when subtracting any number from both sides

     ○ Yes   ○ No

   C when multiplying both sides by a negative number

     ○ Yes   ○ No

   D when dividing both sides by a negative number

     ○ Yes   ○ No

Solve each inequality and graph the solution.

2. $8 \geq s - 6$

_____

3. $x - 4 \geq -3$

_____

4. $t + 13 < 9$

_____

5. $-7 > -18 + y$

_____

6. $12 \leq -4b$

_____

7. $\dfrac{r}{10} > 5$

_____

8. $-\dfrac{7}{3} \geq -\dfrac{p}{3}$

_____

9. $60 < -10x$

_____

10. $-35 \leq \dfrac{y}{29}$

_____

11. Which inequalities have the solution $x \geq 4$? Choose Yes or No for each.

   A $x - 4 \leq 0$ ○ Yes   ○ No

   B $-\dfrac{x}{2} \leq -2$ ○ Yes   ○ No

   C $\dfrac{x}{6} \geq 24$ ○ Yes   ○ No

   D $-4x \leq -16$ ○ Yes   ○ No

12. A submarine descends from sea level to a shipwreck. The elevation of the shipwreck is –195 feet. The submarine can descend no faster than –13 feet per second. Can the submarine reach the shipwreck in 12 seconds?

   a. Write an inequality that models this situation. Let t represent time in seconds.

_____

   b. Solve the inequality. Is it possible for the submarine to reach the shipwreck in 12 seconds?

_____

SKILL 25

Response to Intervention

Post-Test: Properties of Translations, Reflections, and Rotations

1. Which type of transformation preserves the size, shape and orientation of a figure? Choose Yes or No for each.

   A translation 4 units down

   ○ Yes   ○ No

   B rotation 90° about the origin

   ○ Yes   ○ No

   C translation 3 units left

   ○ Yes   ○ No

   D reflection about the *y*-axis

   ○ Yes   ○ No

Draw the image of the figure after each translation.

2. 2 units right and 4 units down

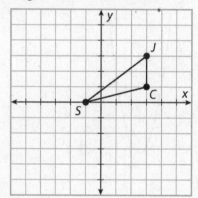

3. 7 units left and 1 unit up

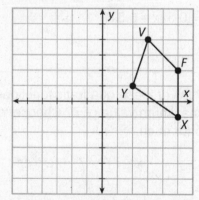

4. A point with coordinates (1, 4) is translated 2 units left and 1 unit down. What are the coordinates of its image?

_____

5. The figure shows quadrilateral *KJXZ*. Graph the image of the figure after a reflection across the *x*-axis.

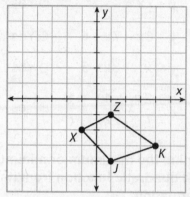

Draw the image of the figure after each rotation.

6. 90° clockwise about the origin

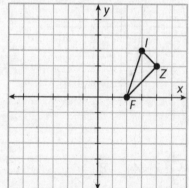

7. 270° counterclockwise about the origin

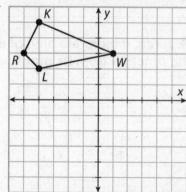

8. A point with the coordinates (0, 2) is rotated 180° about the origin. What are the coordinates of its image?

_____

SKILL 26 **Response to Intervention**

Post-Test: Quadratic Functions

1. Which equations represent a quadratic function? Choose Yes or No for each.

A $y + 2x = -\dfrac{1}{3}x^2$ ○ Yes   ○ No

B $y + 8x = 7x - 4$ ○ Yes   ○ No

C $y - x^3 = 3x + 5$ ○ Yes   ○ No

D $y = \dfrac{2}{7}\left(x + \dfrac{1}{2}\right)^2 + \dfrac{1}{7}$ ○ Yes   ○ No

Determine the maximum or minimum value of each quadratic function from its graph or its equation.

2.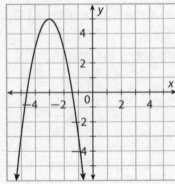

3. $y = \dfrac{4}{3}(x - 4)^2 - 8$

Find the zeros, if there are any, of each quadratic function from its graph.

4.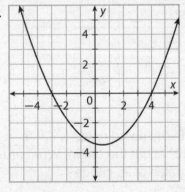

5.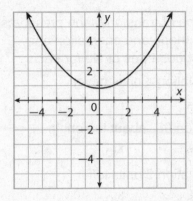

Determine the axis of symmetry of each parabola from its graph or its equation.

6. $y = -2(x - 7)^2 + 12$

7.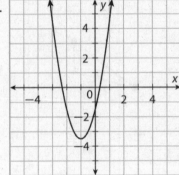

8. $y = 0.5(x + 6.5)^2$

9. Which of these quadratic functions have a maximum value of 7? Choose Yes or No for each.

A $y = \dfrac{1}{2}(x + 7)^2 + 7$ ○ Yes   ○ No

B $y = -\dfrac{1}{2}x^2 + 7$ ○ Yes   ○ No

C $y = 14x^2 + 7$ ○ Yes   ○ No

D $y = -(x - 14)^2 + 7$ ○ Yes   ○ No

SKILL 27

Response to Intervention

Post-Test: Rate of Change and Slope

1. For each table of values, choose whether the rate of change is constant or variable.

A
x	−5	−2	0	3
y	−13	−4	2	11

○ Constant   ○ Variable

B
x	−3	−1	2	4
y	7	−1	2	14

○ Constant   ○ Variable

C
x	−2	−1	2	3
y	−7	0	9	28

○ Constant   ○ Variable

D
x	−5	−2	1	7
y	4	4	4	4

○ Constant   ○ Variable

2. Mr. Sullivan uses the key below to grade his students' tests. Is the rate of change in a student's score with respect to the number of incorrect answers constant? If so, what does the rate of change represent?

Number of Incorrect Answers	0	1	4	7
Score	100	95	80	65

_____

3. What is the rate of change?

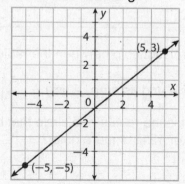

4. What is the average rate of change between (−5, 0) and (0, −3)?

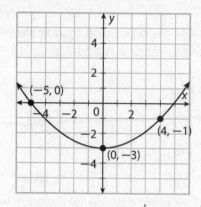

A $-\dfrac{3}{5}$

B $-\dfrac{1}{2}$

C $\dfrac{1}{2}$

D $\dfrac{3}{5}$

5. Choose Yes or No to indicate whether you can use the formula to find the slope of a line.

A $\dfrac{\text{rise}}{\text{run}}$ ○ Yes   ○ No

B $\dfrac{\text{vertical change}}{\text{horizontal change}}$ ○ Yes   ○ No

C $\dfrac{y_2 - y_1}{x_2 - x_1}$ ○ Yes   ○ No

D $\dfrac{\text{change in independent variable}}{\text{change in dependent variable}}$

○ Yes   ○ No

6. What is the slope of the line that passes through the points (−3, −4) and (1, 2)?

_____

SKILL 28 **Response to Intervention**

Post-Test: Rational and Radical Exponents

1. Simplify 8^{-4}.

   _____

2. Choose True or False to indicate whether each expression is equal to 1.

   A $\left(\dfrac{7}{9}\right)^0$ ○ True ○ False

   B 1^0 ○ True ○ False

   C $(-3)^0$ ○ True ○ False

   D 2.85^0 ○ True ○ False

3. Explain how to divide two powers with the same base.

   _____

4. Simplify $11^4 \cdot 11 \cdot 11^2$.

   _____

5. Which expression is NOT equal to $\dfrac{2^3 \cdot 2}{2^2 \cdot 2^5}$?

   A $\dfrac{2^3}{2^7}$ C $\dfrac{2^4}{2^7}$

   B 2^{-3} D $\dfrac{1}{8}$

6. Simplify $(-4 \cdot 5)^3$.

   _____

7. Choose True or False to indicate whether the expressions are equal.

   A $\left(\dfrac{4}{5}\right)^2$ and $\dfrac{8}{10}$ ○ True ○ False

   B $\left(\dfrac{2}{7}\right)^3$ and $\dfrac{2^3}{7^3}$ ○ True ○ False

   C $\left(\dfrac{1}{27}\right)^3$ and $\dfrac{1}{3}$ ○ True ○ False

   D $\left(\dfrac{-3}{4}\right)^3$ and $\dfrac{27}{64}$ ○ True ○ False

8. Simplify $\left(5^3\right)^{-4}$.

   _____

9. Explain why the following statement is true.

   $$\sqrt[4]{1296} = 6$$

   _____

10. What is the simplified form of $\sqrt[3]{343}$?

    A 7   C 21

    B 14   D 49

11. Write a radical expression that is equal to $32^{\frac{1}{5}}$.

    _____

12. Choose True or False to indicate whether the expression is equal to $125^{\frac{1}{3}}$.

    A $\sqrt[3]{125}$ ○ True ○ False

    B $\sqrt[3]{5^3}$ ○ True ○ False

    C 5   ○ True ○ False

    D 5^3 ○ True ○ False

13. What is the simplified form of $100,000^{\frac{2}{5}}$?

    A 10   B 100

    C 1000   D 10,000

14. Simplify $8^{\frac{1}{3}} + 8^{\frac{2}{3}} + 8^{\frac{3}{3}}$.

    _____

15. The relationship between the radius, r, of a circle and its area, A, is $r = \left(\dfrac{A}{\pi}\right)^{\frac{1}{2}}$.

    What is the radius of a circle that has an area of 121π square units?

    _____

Response to Intervention

Post-Test: Rational Number Operations

1. A muffin recipe calls for $1\frac{3}{4}$ cups of milk and $\frac{2}{3}$ cup of oil. How many cups of liquid does the recipe call for?

   _____

2. Annabelle's checking account balance is −$10.37. She makes a deposit of $25. What is her new account balance?

   A −$35.37   C $14.63

   B −$14.63   D $35.37

3. Explain how to subtract a rational number.

   _____

4. Choose Positive or Negative to indicate whether the value of the expression is positive or negative.

   A −14.73 + 15.82

   ○ Positive   ○ Negative

   B $-\frac{5}{8} - \left(-\frac{2}{3}\right)$

   ○ Positive   ○ Negative

   C 36.8 − 45.3

   ○ Positive   ○ Negative

   D $\frac{9}{10} - \frac{6}{7}$

   ○ Positive   ○ Negative

5. The outdoor temperature during the day is 7.8°C. At night, the temperature decreases 10.5°C. What is the night time temperature?

   _____

6. Micah has a large bag of potting soil. For each flower he plants, he scoops $1\frac{1}{4}$ cups of soil out of the bag and dumps it into a hole dug for the flower. He plants a total of 36 flowers. What is the overall change in the amount of soil in the bag?

   _____

7. The price of one share of a certain company declined $2.73 per day for 5 days in a row. What is the overall change in the price of one share of the company?

   _____

8. Choose Positive or Negative to indicate whether the quotient is positive or negative.

   A $\frac{-81}{-9}$

   ○ Positive   ○ Negative

   B 25.5 ÷ −5

   ○ Positive   ○ Negative

   C $-3\frac{2}{3} \div \frac{1}{3}$

   ○ Positive   ○ Negative

   D $\frac{4.9}{-0.7}$

   ○ Positive   ○ Negative

9. Liza wants to divide a $1\frac{4}{5}$-pound bag of granola into small bags. Each bag will hold $\frac{1}{10}$ pound of granola. How many bags of granola can Liza fill?

   _____

Name _____ Date _____ Class _____

Response to Intervention

Post-Test: Real Numbers

1. Which numbers are rational? Choose Yes or No for each.

   A $\sqrt{5}$ ○ Yes   ○ No

   B $1.4\overline{23}$ ○ Yes   ○ No

   C $\dfrac{11}{125}$ ○ Yes   ○ No

   D $\sqrt{16}$ ○ Yes   ○ No

Write each fraction as a decimal.

2. $\dfrac{6}{16}$

   _____

3. $\dfrac{19}{11}$

   _____

4. $22\dfrac{5}{6}$

   _____

Write each decimal as a fraction in simplest form.

5. $0.\overline{8}$

   _____

6. 3.875

   _____

7. Which numbers are irrational? Choose Yes or No for each.

   A $\sqrt{12}$ ○ Yes   ○ No

   B $\dfrac{3\pi}{\pi}$ ○ Yes   ○ No

   C $\pi + 9$ ○ Yes   ○ No

   D $\sqrt{4} + \sqrt{25}$ ○ Yes   ○ No

8. Which of these approximations are true? Choose True or False for each.

   A $2 < \sqrt{3} < 4$ ○ True   ○ False

   B $6 < \sqrt{45} < 7$ ○ True   ○ False

   C $9 < \sqrt{90} < 10$ ○ True   ○ False

   D $100 < \sqrt{121} < 144$ ○ True   ○ False

Estimate to three decimal places using a calculator.

9. $\sqrt{12}$

   _____

10. $-\sqrt{8}$

   _____

Order the numbers from least to greatest.

11. $2.\overline{73}, \dfrac{137}{50}, \sqrt{3} + 2$

   _____

12. $\sqrt{27}, 2\pi - 1, 5.\overline{28}$

   _____

13. Craig is designing two different gardens. One is a square with side length of 7.5 feet. The other is a circle with a diameter of 8 feet.

   a. Find the areas for each garden. Round to 2 decimal places.

   _____

   b. Which garden has the greatest area?

   _____

SKILL 31 **Response to Intervention**

Post-Test: Slope and Slope-Intercept Form

1. Which equations represent a linear function? Choose Yes or No for each.

   A $y = 3x + 6$ ○ Yes   ○ No

   B $x = 12$ ○ Yes   ○ No

   C $x^2 + 4y = -6$ ○ Yes   ○ No

   D $x - y = -2$ ○ Yes   ○ No

Determine the *x*- and *y*-intercept.

2. $x + 5y = 15$

   _____

3.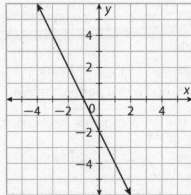

   _____

4. Graph $x - 3y = -3$ using the intercepts.

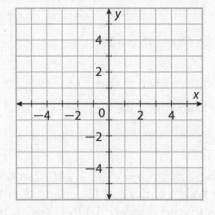

   _____

5. Hannah had 7 peaches after picking for 3 minutes. After picking for 21 minutes, she had 43 peaches. What is the rate of change?

   _____

6. Which of these equations represents the equation of a line with a slope of -2 and a *y*-intercept of 4? Choose Yes or No for each.

   A $y = 4x - 2$ ○ Yes   ○ No

   B $y = -2x + 4$ ○ Yes   ○ No

   C $2x + y = 4$ ○ Yes   ○ No

   D $2x - y = -4$ ○ Yes   ○ No

7. A linear function is graphed on a coordinate plane.

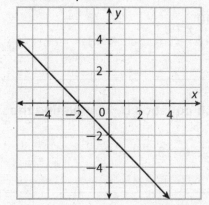

   a. What is the slope of the line?

   _____

   b. What is the *y*-intercept?

   _____

   c. What is the equation of the line in slope-intercept form?

   _____

SKILL 32

Response to Intervention

Post-Test: Solving Quadratic Equations by Completing the Square

1. Which of these is a perfect square trinomial? Choose Yes or No for each.

   A $x^2 + 28x + 196$ ○ Yes   ○ No

   B $4x^2 + 8x - 6$ ○ Yes   ○ No

   C $x^2 - 17x + \dfrac{289}{4}$ ○ Yes   ○ No

   D $9x^2 - 18x - 72$ ○ Yes   ○ No

Find the value for c that completes the square.

2. $x^2 + 4x + c$

   _____

3. $x^2 + 3x + c$

   _____

4. $x^2 - \dfrac{10}{11}x + c$

   _____

Solve each equation by completing the square.

5. $x^2 - 8x = -15$

   _____

6. $x^2 + 10x - 39 = 0$

   _____

7. $x^2 - 50 = 5x$

   _____

8. The width of a rectangle is 11 centimeters less than the length. The area of the rectangle is 242 square centimeters. Find the length and the width.

   _____

9. Choose True or False for each statement about completing the square for an expression of the form $ax^2 + bx + c$.

   A If $a = 1$, then $c = \left(\dfrac{b}{2}\right)^2$ completes the square.

      ○ True   ○ False

   B If $a \neq 1$, and a is a perfect square, then $c = \left(\dfrac{b}{2}\right)^2$ completes the square.

      ○ True   ○ False

   C If $a \neq 1$, then $c = \dfrac{b^2}{4a}$ completes the square.

      ○ True   ○ False

   D If $a \neq 1$, and a is a perfect square, then $c = \dfrac{b^2}{4a}$ completes the square.

      ○ True   ○ False

Solve each equation by completing the square.

10. $4x^2 + 16x = 84$

    _____

11. $9x^2 + 18x - 45 = -5$

    _____

12. $5x^2 - 6x - 15 = 4x$

    _____

13. The equation $h = -16t^2 + 24t + 5$ models the height h of a ball t seconds after it was tossed upward. To the nearest tenth of a second, how long will the ball be in the air?

    _____

SKILL
33

Response to Intervention

Post-Test: Solving Quadratic Equations by Factoring

1. What are the solutions of the quadratic equation $x^2 - 2x - 3 = 0$?

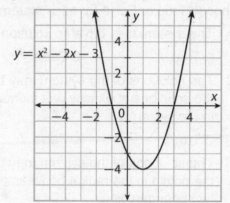

$y = x^2 - 2x - 3$

2. Choose True or False for each statement.

A You can solve a quadratic equation by graphing the related quadratic function and finding its x-intercepts.

○ True　　　　○ False

B The y-intercepts of a quadratic function are the solutions of the related quadratic equation.

○ True　　　　○ False

C If a quadratic function intersects the x-axis at $(-5, 0)$ and $(1, 0)$, the solutions of the related quadratic equation are 5 and -1.

○ True　　　　○ False

D If the solutions of a quadratic equation are -3 and 4, then the related quadratic function has x-intercepts at $(-3, 0)$ and $(4, 0)$.

○ True　　　　○ False

3. What are the solutions of the equation $(x-2)(x+3) = 0$?

A　-2 and -3　　　　C　2 and -3

B　-2 and 3　　　　D　2 and 3

4. What are the solutions of the quadratic equation $x^2 + x = 20$?

_____

5. Explain how to use the Zero Product Property to solve the quadratic equation $x^2 - 5x - 36 = 0$.

_____

6. What are the solutions of the quadratic equation $2x^2 + 3x = 20$?

A　-5 and 4　　　　C　-4 and $\dfrac{5}{2}$

B　-4 and 5　　　　D　$-\dfrac{5}{2}$ and 4

7. A rectangular prism has a volume of 480 cubic inches. Its dimensions are 4 inches, $(x - 3)$ inches, and $(x + 4)$ inches. What is the value of x?

_____

8. What are the solutions of the quadratic equation $3x^2 - 54x + 243 = 0$?

_____

9. What is the solution of the equation $2x^2 + 32x + 128 = 0$?

A　-64　　　　C　-8

B　-16　　　　D　8

10. What are the solutions of the quadratic equation $5x^2 - 605 = 0$?

_____

SKILL 34 **Response to Intervention**

Post-Test: Solving Systems of Linear Inequalities

1. Which point is a solution of the following system of linear inequalities?

$$\begin{cases} x + 2y < 10 \\ 2x - y > -1 \end{cases}$$

   A (1, 3)   C (2, 5)

   B (2, 1)   D (–2, 0)

2. Use the system of inequalities to decide whether each statement is True or False.

$$\begin{cases} 2x - y > 3 \\ 2x + y > 2 \end{cases}$$

   A The boundary line for the inequality $2x - y > 3$ is $2x - y = 3$.

      ○ True   ○ False

   B The boundary line for $2x + y > 2$ is a solid line.

      ○ True   ○ False

   C The system of inequalities has no solution.

      ○ True   ○ False

   D The point where the boundary lines intersect is a solution of the system of inequalities.

      ○ True   ○ False

3. Solve the system by graphing.

$$\begin{cases} x + y \le 5 \\ -3x + y \ge -4 \end{cases}$$

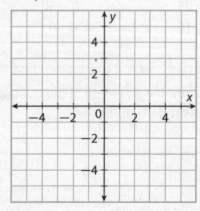

4. Consider a system of linear inequalities in which the boundary lines are parallel. Choose True or False for each statement.

   A The system may have no solution.

      ○ True   ○ False

   B The solutions of the system may be the solutions of exactly one inequality in the system.

      ○ True   ○ False

   C The solutions of the system may be the points in the region between the two boundary lines.

      ○ True   ○ False

   D The solutions of the system may consist only of the points on the two boundary lines.

      ○ True   ○ False

5. Solve the system by graphing.

$$\begin{cases} x - y < -3 \\ x - y \ge 1 \end{cases}$$

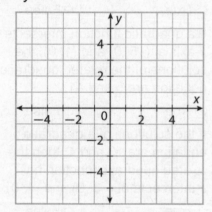

SKILL 35

Response to Intervention

Post-Test: Systems of Two Linear Equations

1. What is the solution of the linear system graphed below?

$$\begin{cases} 3x - y = 0 \\ 3x - y = 4 \end{cases}$$

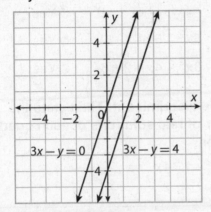

2. Solve the linear system by graphing.

$$\begin{cases} x + y = 5 \\ 2x - y = -2 \end{cases}$$

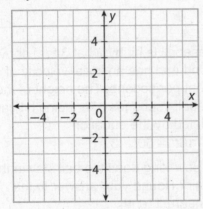

3. Choose True or False for each statement.

A When solving a linear system, if you get an identity, such as $3 = 3$, then the system has infinitely many solutions.

○ True   ○ False

B When solving a linear system, if you get a false statement, such as $5 = 8$, then the system has no solution.

○ True   ○ False

C When graphing a linear system, if the two lines intersect at only one point, then the system has no solution.

○ True   ○ False

D When graphing a linear system, if the two lines are parallel, then the system has infinitely many solutions.

○ True   ○ False

4. Solve the system by substitution.

$$\begin{cases} x + y = 35 \\ x - 4y = 0 \end{cases}$$

5. Solve the system by elimination.

$$\begin{cases} 3x + 4y = -8 \\ x + 2y = -6 \end{cases}$$

6. What is the solution of the linear system?

$$\begin{cases} x - y = -1 \\ 2x + y = 10 \end{cases}$$

A (3, 4)   C (−3, −4)

B (4, 3)   D (−4, −3)

SKILL 36

Response to Intervention

Post-Test: The Quadratic Formula

1. Which quadratic equations have the

   solution $x = \dfrac{-(-7) \pm \sqrt{(-7)^2 - 4(5)(-14)}}{2(5)}$?

   Choose Yes or No for each.

   A $5x^2 - 7x - 14 = 0$ ○ Yes ○ No

   B $5x^2 = 7x + 14$ ○ Yes ○ No

   C $-7x^2 + 5x - 14 = 0$ ○ Yes ○ No

   D $-14x^2 + 5x = 7$ ○ Yes ○ No

Identify *a*, *b*, and *c* for each quadratic equation. Then set up an equation for the solution using the quadratic formula. Do not solve.

2. $3x^2 - 5x - 13 = 0$

   _____

3. $4x^2 + 7x - 25 = 5$

   _____

4. $-x^2 = -7$

   _____

Solve each equation using the quadratic formula.

5. $4x^2 + 4x - 48 = 0$

   _____

6. $-3x^2 + 3 = -2$

   _____

7. $2x^2 - 3x - 8 = -4$

   _____

8. $-4 = 6x - x^2 - 2$

   _____

9. Look at each equation. Does the equation have two real solutions? Select Yes or No for each.

   A $-6x^2 - 3x + 3 = 0$ ○ Yes ○ No

   B $-4x^2 - 4x - 1 = 0$ ○ Yes ○ No

   C $6x^2 + 5x - 1 = 5$ ○ Yes ○ No

   D $3x^2 + 4x + 2 = 6$ ○ Yes ○ No

Find the discriminant. Then state the number of real solutions of each quadratic equation.

10. $4x^2 + 1 = 4x$

    _____

11. $-8x^2 = -6x + 4$

    _____

12. $9x^2 - 7 = -2x$

    _____

13. A baseball is hit by a bat 3 feet above the ground and has an initial velocity of 50 feet per second. The height of the baseball t seconds after being hit can be modeled by the equation $h = -16t^2 + 50t + 3$.

    a. How long does the ball stay in the air? Round your answer to the nearest tenth.

       _____

    b. Calculate the discriminant for a height of 50 feet. Will the baseball ever reach that height? Explain how you know.

       _____

       _____

       _____

SKILL 37

Response to Intervention

Post-Test: Transforming Cubic Functions

1. Which transformation of the parent cubic function $f(x) = x^3$ results in a horizontal translation? Choose Yes or No for each.

   A $g(x) = \dfrac{1}{2}(x - 11)^3 + 14$

   ○ Yes   ○ No

   B $h(x) = -2.25x^3 - 0.75$

   ○ Yes   ○ No

   C $j(x) = \dfrac{2}{5}(x + 108)^3$

   ○ Yes   ○ No

   D $s(x) = (x + 6.07)^3 + 14.12$

   ○ Yes   ○ No

Write an equation for each transformation described of the parent cubic function $f(x) = x^3$.

2. horizontally translated 4 units left

   _____

3. stretched vertically by a factor of 4 and then vertically translated 9 units down

   _____

4. reflected about the x-axis, compressed vertically by a factor of $\dfrac{2}{5}$, and translated horizontally 3 units right

   _____

5. compressed vertically by a factor of 0.25, horizontally translated 4.7 units right, and vertically translated 3.1 units down

   _____

Graph each transformation alongside the parent cubic function $f(x) = x^3$. (The parent function is shown.)

6. $g(x) = x^3 - 2$

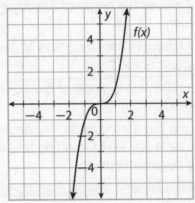

7. $g(x) = (x + 4)^3 + 1$

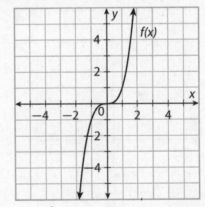

8. The parent cubic function is transformed to create $g(x) = -\dfrac{8}{5}(x + 2)^3 - 7$. Which are included in this transformation? Choose Yes or No for each.

   A a reflection across the x-axis

   ○ Yes   ○ No

   B a horizontal translation to the right

   ○ Yes   ○ No

   C a vertical translation down

   ○ Yes   ○ No

   D a vertical compression

   ○ Yes   ○ No

SKILL 38 Response to Intervention

Post-Test: Transforming Linear Functions

1. When you transform the graph of the linear function $f(x) = mx + b$, how does the value of b affect the graph of $f(x)$?

   A It moves the graph of $f(x)$ left or right.

   B It moves the graph of $f(x)$ up or down.

   C It changes the steepness of the graph of $f(x)$.

   D It reflects the graph of $f(x)$ across the y-axis.

2. How are the graphs of $f(x) = x$ and $f(x) = x + 4$ related? Graph both functions in the coordinate plane.

   _____

   _____

   _____

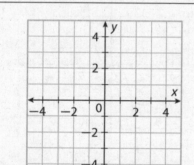

3. What is the equation of the line whose graph is the graph of $f(x) = x$ shifted 10 units up?

   _____

4. Describe how the graph of $f(x) = x - 12$ compares to the graph of $f(x) = x$.

   _____

   _____

   _____

5. Choose True or False for each statement.

   A When you transform the graph of the linear function $f(x) = mx + b$, the value of m affects the steepness of the graph.

   ○ True   ○ False

   B If $0 < m < 1$, then the graph of $f(x) = mx + b$ is steeper than the graph of $f(x) = x$.

   ○ True   ○ False

   C If $m > 1$, then the graph of $f(x) = mx + b$ is less steep than the graph of $f(x) = x$.

   ○ True   ○ False

   D The graph of $f(x) = -mx + b$ is the reflection of $f(x) = mx + b$ across the y-axis.

   ○ True   ○ False

6. How are the graphs of $f(x) = 2x$ and $f(x) = -2x$ related to the graph of $f(x) = x$? Graph all three functions in the coordinate plane.

   _____

   _____

   _____

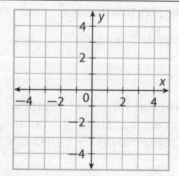

Response to Intervention
Post-Test: Transforming Quadratic Functions

1. Consider the graph of the quadratic function $g(x) = 5x^2$. Which of the following statements is true?

   A It is wider than the graph of $f(x) = x^2$.

   B It is narrower than the graph of $f(x) = x^2$.

   C It is a reflection across the x-axis of $f(x) = x^2$.

   D It is the graph of $f(x) = x^2$ translated 5 units right.

2. How are the graphs of $f(x) = x^2$, $h(x) = 4x^2$, and $g(x) = -4x^2$ related? Graph all three functions in the coordinate plane.

_____

_____

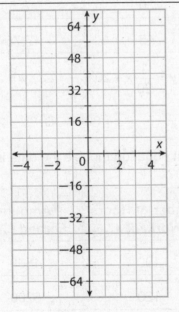

3. Which function's graph is wider than the graph of $f(x) = x^2$?

   A $g(x) = 3x^2$ C $g(x) = 0.6x^2$

   B $g(x) = \dfrac{5}{4}x^2$ D $g(x) = -x^2$

4. In which direction does the graph of $g(x) = -\dfrac{5}{8}x^2$ open?

_____

5. Choose True or False for each statement.

   A The vertex of the graph of $g(x) = 2(x+3)^2 - 7$ is $(3, -7)$.

     ○ True   ○ False

   B The vertex of the graph of $g(x) = -5(x-4)^2 + 9$ is the highest point of the graph.

     ○ True   ○ False

   C The vertex of the graph of $g(x) = -(x-1)^2 + 10$ is $(1, 10)$.

     ○ True   ○ False

   D The graph of $g(x) = 4(x-11)^2 + 15$ is wider than the graph of $f(x) = x^2$.

     ○ True   ○ False

6. Graph $g(x) = -3(x-2)^2 - 4$.

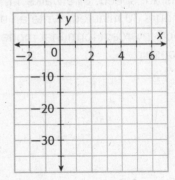

Response to Intervention

Post-Test: Writing Linear Equations

1. An electrician charges a flat fee per job, plus an hourly rate, as shown in the graph.

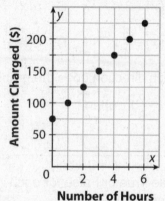

Number of Hours

Choose True or False for each statement.

A The slope of the line that passes through the points is 50.

○ True   ○ False

B The slope represents the electrician's hourly rate.

○ True   ○ False

C The y-intercept of the line that passes through the points is 75.

○ True   ○ False

D The equation $y = 25x + 75$ models the data in the graph.

○ True   ○ False

2. The number of miles a mailwoman walks throughout her day can be modeled with a linear equation. Suppose she walks at a constant speed. She walks 11.25 miles in 4 hours 30 minutes. Write an equation in slope-intercept form that models this relationship.

3. The number of calories Claire consumes at breakfast depends on how much peanut butter she eats with her toast. If she eats 1 tablespoon of peanut butter, she will consume a total of 205 calories. If she eats 2 tablespoons of peanut butter, she will consume a total of 300 calories. Write an equation in slope-intercept form that models this relationship.

4. Which equation models the data in the table?

Number of Miles Driven, x	Amount of Gasoline in Tank (gal), y
0	20
15	19.25
30	18.5
45	17.75

A $y = \dfrac{1}{20}x + 20$ C $y = -20x + 20$

B $y = -\dfrac{1}{20}x + 20$ D $y = 20x + 20$

5. What equation models the data in the table?

Number of Hours Worked, x	Amount Earned ($), y
100	4500
120	5200
140	5900
160	6600

Response to Intervention

Post-Test: Box Plots

The data below shows the prices of several different tablets at an electronics store. Use the data to answer Questions 1–4.

$440 $200 $440 $180 $125 $525 $330

$525 $450 $180 $300 $250 $200 $160

1. Choose True or False for each statement.

   A The minimum value is $125.
      ○ True   ○ False

   B The first quartile is $180.
      ○ True   ○ False

   C The median is $225.
      ○ True   ○ False

   D The third quartile is $445.
      ○ True   ○ False

   E The maximum value is $525.
      ○ True   ○ False

2. Make a box plot to represent the data.

3. What is the range of the tablets' prices?

   _____

4. What is the interquartile range of the prices of the tablets?

   _____

5. Consider a box plot that represents a set of data. Choose True or False for each statement.

   A The left whisker represents about 25% of the data.
      ○ True   ○ False

   B The box represents about 25% of the data.
      ○ True   ○ False

   C The right whisker represents about 25% of the data.
      ○ True   ○ False

The box plots show the average precipitation per month, in inches, for Nashville, Tennessee, and Seattle, Washington. Use the box plots to answer Questions 6–8.

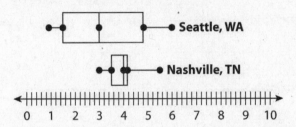

6. Choose True or False for each statement.

   A The minimum average precipitation per month for Seattle is less than that for Nashville.
      ○ True   ○ False

   B The maximum average precipitation per month for Seattle is less than that for Nashville.
      ○ True   ○ False

   C The median average precipitation per month for Nashville is greater than that for Seattle.
      ○ True   ○ False

   D The range of the average precipitation per month for Seattle is about 5 inches.
      ○ True   ○ False

7. Estimate the range of the average precipitation amounts per month for Nashville.

   _____

8. The average precipitation per month for which city has the greater interquartile range? What does this mean in terms of the problem situation?

   _____

SKILL 42 Response to Intervention
Post-Test: Combining Transformations of Quadratic Functions

1. Graph $g(x) = -3(x+2)^2 + 6$.

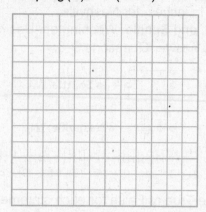

2. Choose Yes or No. Does the graph of $f(x) = x^2$ need to be reflected across the x-axis to obtain the graph of each function?

   A $g(x) = -0.6(x+2)^2 + 5$ ○ Yes ○ No

   B $g(x) = \frac{4}{3}(x-2)^2 - \frac{5}{3}$ ○ Yes ○ No

   C $g(x) = -\frac{2}{5}(x+4)^2 - 3$ ○ Yes ○ No

   D $g(x) = 3.5(x-2.5)^2 - 8$ ○ Yes ○ No

3. List the transformations needed to obtain the graph of $g(x) = -\frac{1}{8}(x-3)^2 + 90$ from the graph of $f(x) = x^2$.

   _____

   _____

   _____

4. A water balloon is dropped from a height of 35 feet above the ground. What is a height function in feet above the ground of the balloon t seconds after the balloon is dropped?

   _____

5. For the graph shown, write a function of the form $g(x) = a(x-h)^2 + k$.

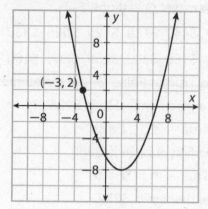

   _____

6. List the transformations needed to obtain the graph of $g(x) = 3.5(x+3)^2 - 5$ from the graph of $f(x) = x^2$.

   _____

   _____

   _____

7. For the graph of $g(x) = -2(x+7)^2 - 5$, is each statement about the transformation from the graph $f(x) = x^2$ True or False?

   A Reflect across the y-axis.

   ○ True   ○ False

   B Translate 3 units to the right.

   ○ True   ○ False

   C Stretch vertically by a factor of 2.

   ○ True   ○ False

   D Translate 5 units down.

   ○ True   ○ False

Name _____ Date _____ Class_____

SKILL 43

Response to Intervention
Post-Test: Data Distributions and Outliers

The published prices, in dollars, of a round-trip plane ticket from Boston to Atlanta on a travel website are listed below. Use the data to answer Questions 1–5.

270, 270, 270, 270, 270, 270, 270, 270, 270, 270, 300, 310, 410, 410, 440, 470

1. Make a dot plot of the data.

←++++++++++++++++++++++++++++++++→

2. Choose True or False for each statement.

   A   The first quartile is 270.

   ○ True   ○ False

   B   The third quartile is 360.

   ○ True   ○ False

   C   The interquartile range is 100.

   ○ True   ○ False

   D   The data value 470 is an outlier.

   ○ True   ○ False

3. Suppose the list of published prices is expanded to include a price of $125. Is $125 an outlier in the new data set? Explain your reasoning.

   _____

4. Describe the distribution of the dot plot in Question 1 as skewed to the left, skewed to the right, or symmetric.

   _____

5. Explain what the distribution means in terms of the problem situation.

   _____

The table lists the times of day that selected students from two different schools wake up each morning. Use the data to answer Questions 6–8.

Time	5:30	6:00	6:30	7:00	7:30
School 1	2	4	6	8	10
School 2	4	5	12	5	4

6. Make a dot plot for School 1.

←++++++++++++++++++++++++++++++++→

7. Make a dot plot for School 2.

←++++++++++++++++++++++++++++++++→

8. Choose True or False for each statement.

   A   The data for School 1 is skewed to the right.

   ○ True   ○ False

   B   For School 1, more than half of the wake-up times are greater than the mean.

   ○ True   ○ False

   C   The data for School 2 is symmetric.

   ○ True   ○ False

   D   For School 2, the wake-up times are evenly distributed about the mean.

   ○ True   ○ False

SKILL 44

Response to Intervention

Post-Test: Distance and Midpoint Formulas

Use the figure for 1–4.

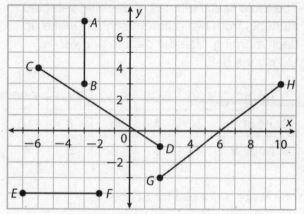

Use the following information for 8–10.

A map is drawn on a coordinate grid. Each unit is equal to 1 mile.

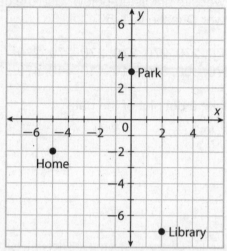

1. What is the midpoint of $\overline{AB}$?

   _____

2. What is the midpoint of $\overline{CD}$?

   _____

3. What is the midpoint of $\overline{EF}$?

   _____

4. What is the midpoint of $\overline{GH}$?

   _____

5. A segment has coordinates (–4, 9) and (0, 7). What is the midpoint of the segment?

   _____

6. A segment has coordinates (8, –5) and (8, 4). What is the midpoint of the segment?

   _____

7. A segment $\overline{ST}$ is graphed on a coordinate plane. The endpoint S is at (–3, 2). The midpoint is at (–3, –2). What are the coordinates of the other endpoint T?

   _____

8. David would like to meet a friend at the halfway point between his home and the library. What is the location of the midpoint between David's home and the library?

   _____

9. What is the distance between the park and the library?

   _____

10. What is the distance between David's home and the park?

    _____

11. A segment measures 10 units. One end of the segment has an endpoint at (3, –6). What is another possible endpoint to this segment?

    _____

SKILL 45
Response to Intervention
Post-Test: Generating Random Samples

1. Choose Yes or No. Can each method be used to get a random sample of 10 students from 100?

   A Number the students from 1 to 100. Place each number in a 10-by-10 grid. Draw a number from 1 to 10 out of a hat for the row, replace the number, and draw a number from 1 to 10 for the column.

   ○ Yes   ○ No

   B Number the students from 1 to 100. Enter **randInt(10, 100)** on a graphing calculator and press enter 10 times.

   ○ Yes   ○ No

   C Number the students from 1 to 100. Starting with 1, flip a coin. If it comes up heads, the student is selected. Continue until 10 students are selected.

   ○ Yes   ○ No

   D Number the students from 1 to 100. Enter **randInt(1, 100)** on a graphing calculator and press enter until 10 unique numbers have come up.

   ○ Yes   ○ No

2. Describe how to use a graphing calculator to select a random sample of 20 from 500 members of a club.

   _____

   _____

3. A store receives a shipment of 500 phones, 10 of which are defective. The manager wants to simulate selecting 40 phones and see how many of that simulation are defective. Describe a method for using a graphing calculator for this simulation.

   _____

   _____

   _____

For 4–6, use the table. The table shows the ages of 36 students in an after-school program for middle school and high school students at a local martial arts studio. A random sample of 10 students is selected, and their ages are bolded in the table.

13	11	18	17	13	16
12	11	16	**12**	**15**	**17**
18	**14**	11	14	16	13
17	16	**11**	14	**13**	12
12	12	**17**	14	13	16
18	16	**12**	14	15	**15**

4. Describe how you could select 10 ages from the table without using technology.

   _____

   _____

5. From the sample shown in the table, what is the average age of the students?

   _____

6. Find the actual average age of the students. How does the average of the sample compare?

   _____

   _____

   _____

SKILL 46

Response to Intervention

Post-Test: Histograms

The data below represent the distances, in miles, that families traveled for vacation. Use the data to answer Questions 1–3.

227 219 687 1005 1048 1020 1466
154 88 343 589 288 155 256

1. Choose True or False for each statement.

   A The minimum distance traveled is 88 miles.

   ○ True   ○ False

   B The maximum distance traveled is 1048 miles.

   ○ True   ○ False

   C If making a frequency table, intervals of 10 miles would be reasonable.

   ○ True   ○ False

   D If making a frequency table, intervals of 250 would be reasonable.

   ○ True   ○ False

2. Use the data to make a frequency table.

Distance Traveled (mi)	Frequency
0–249	
250–499	
500–749	
750–999	
1000–1249	
1250–1499	

3. Use the data to make a histogram.

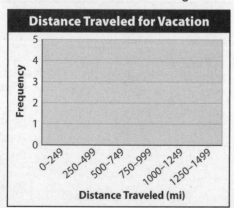

The histogram shows the student enrollment at several school districts in a state. Use the histogram to answer Questions 4–8.

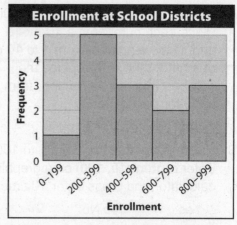

4. How many districts have a student enrollment between 400 and 599?

   _____

5. How many districts have a student enrollment that is less than 400?

   _____

6. How many school districts are included in the histogram?

   _____

7. Estimate the mean enrollment of the school districts included in the histogram.

   _____

8. Estimate the median enrollment of the school districts included in the histogram.

   _____

Response to Intervention

SKILL 47

Post-Test: Making Inferences from a Random Sample

A random sample of people shopping for smartphones were surveyed on the amount they are willing to pay for their phones. The data is listed below. Use the data to answer Questions 1–4.

$50 $100 $400 $150 $250 $300 $150
$200 $100 $150 $200 $250 $200 $400

1. Choose True or False for each statement.

   A   The minimum value is $100.

   ○ True   ○ False

   B   The first quartile is $150.

   ○ True   ○ False

   C   The median is $175.

   ○ True   ○ False

   D   The third quartile is $300.

   ○ True   ○ False

   E   The maximum value is $400.

   ○ True   ○ False

2. Make a dot plot to represent the data.

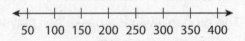

Complete the following statements.

3. Most people are willing to pay between

   $____ , and $_____ for a smartphone.

4. Most people are willing to pay _____

   _____ $250 for a smartphone.

5. Most people are willing to pay _____

   _____ $100 for a smartphone.

6. Make a box plot to represent the data.

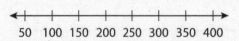

7. Choose True or False for each statement.

   A   About half of people buying smartphones are willing to pay between $150 and $250.

   ○ True   ○ False

   B   No one is willing to pay more than $400 for a smartphone.

   ○ True   ○ False

   C   A good estimate of what people are willing to pay for a smartphone is $200.

   ○ True   ○ False

8. A set of 1200 illustrations is submitted for publication. A random sample of 20 of the items revealed that 2 needed some type of revision. About how many of the set are likely to need revision?

_____

9. There are 3250 students in the Highland School system. A random sample of 100 students revealed that 42 participated in some type of after-school activity. About how many students in the system are involved in some type of after-school activity?

_____

Name _____ Date _____ Class_____

SKILL
48

Response to Intervention

Post-Test: Making Predictions with Probability

Use the information for 1–4. In a board game, the probability of choosing a "Lose a Turn" card is $\frac{2}{15}$.

1. What is a favorable outcome?

   _____

2. What are the possible outcomes?

   _____

   _____

3. During a game, 45 cards have been drawn. Predict how many times a "Lose a Turn" card has been drawn.

   _____

4. If the game contains a total of 300 cards, about how many cards are NOT "Lose a Turn" cards?

   _____

5. A manufacturer conducts a quality review of its cell phones and finds that, on average, 3 out of every 250 phones have a defect. Predict how many phones will have a defect in a batch of 2000 phones.

   _____

6. The results of a survey show that 68 out of 100 people participate in a recycling program in a small community. If there are about 3000 people in the community, predict how many people participate in recycling.

   _____

7. A spinner has 5 equal sections numbered 1–5. How many times would you expect to land on an odd number out of 30 spins?

   _____

Use the following information for 8–10. Organizers for a conference conducted a survey that asked attendees about their main source for news. The results are shown in the table.

News Source	Number of Responses
Newspaper	24
Television Newscast	35
Radio Program	11
Internet	30

8. How many people were surveyed?

   _____

9. If a person was randomly chosen from the conference, what is the probability that person's main source of news is the Internet?

   _____

10. If there are 1200 people at the conference, how many people would you expect get their news from the newspaper?

    _____

11. The probability that a basketball player makes a foul shot is $\frac{4}{5}$. During a game, the player had 11 foul shots. Predict how many foul shots the player missed.

    _____

12. A bag of mints contains pink, green, and yellow mints. You randomly take a handful of mints and count 2 green, 5 pink, and 8 yellow mints. If you fill a bowl with 150 mints, predict how many mints of each color will be in the bowl.

    _____

Response to Intervention

Post-Test: Measures of Center and Spread

1. The number of minutes that Isabella and Connor each spend on chores each day during the school week is shown.

   Isabella: 12, 22, 15, 18, 14

   Connor: 43, 0, 6, 0, 27

   Choose True or False for each statement.

   A The mean number of minutes that Isabella spends on chores each day is about 16.2.

   ○ True   ○ False

   B The median number of minutes that Isabella spends on chores is 15.

   ○ True   ○ False

   C The mean number of minutes that Connor spends on chores each day is about 25.3.

   ○ True   ○ False

   D The median number of minutes that Connor spends on chores is 27.

   ○ True   ○ False

The cost, in dollars, of several watches at a department store are shown. Use the data to answer Questions 2–4.

   11, 16, 98, 30, 85, 69, 100, 75, 90

2. To the nearest cent, what is the mean cost of the watches?

   _____

3. What is the median cost of the watches?

   _____

4. Which measure of central tendency better describes the costs of the watches: the mean or the median? Explain your reasoning.

   _____

Sarah's quiz scores for the semester are shown below. Use the data to answer Questions 5–8.

   85, 87, 98, 82, 77, 88

5. What is Sarah's minimum quiz score? What is her maximum quiz score?

   _____

6. What is the range of Sarah's quiz scores?

   _____

7. What are the first quartile (Q_1) and third quartile (Q_3) of Sarah's quiz scores?

   _____

8. What is the interquartile range (IQR) of Sarah's quiz scores?

   _____

The weight, in pounds, of the defensive tackles on a professional football team are listed below. Use the data to answer Questions 9–11.

   300, 296, 295, 300

9. What is the mean weight?

   _____

10. Complete the table.

Data Value, x	Deviation from Mean, $x - \bar{x}$	Squared Deviation, $\left(x - \bar{x}\right)^2$

11. What is the standard deviation?

   _____

SKILL 50 **Response to Intervention**

Post-Test: Normal Distributions

1. Consider a normal distribution and a normal curve. Choose True or False for each statement.

   A A normal distribution is symmetric about the mean.

   ○ True   ○ False

   B Under a normal curve, 68% of the data fall within 1 standard deviation of the mean.

   ○ True   ○ False

   C Under a normal curve, 96% of the data fall within 2 standard deviations of the mean.

   ○ True   ○ False

   D Under a normal curve, 99.7% of the data fall within 3 standard deviations of the mean.

   ○ True   ○ False

The prices of sneakers at a department store are normally distributed with a mean of $45 and a standard deviation of $8. Use this information to answer Questions 2 and 3.

2. Sketch a normal curve showing the prices of the sneakers at one, two, and three standard deviations from the mean.

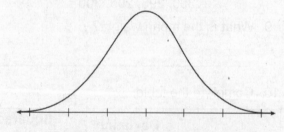

3. What percent of the prices are between $29 and $61? Explain your reasoning.

_____

In a survey, the waist sizes of men are normally distributed with a mean of 34 inches and a standard deviation of 2 inches. Use this information to answer Questions 4 and 5.

4. Sketch a normal curve showing the waist sizes at one, two, and three standard deviations from the mean. Label the curve with the correct percents.

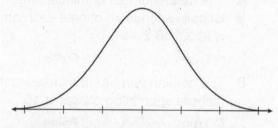

5. What is the probability that a randomly chosen man has a waist size that is between 30 inches and 36 inches? Explain your reasoning.

_____

6. The normal curve below represents the scores of students on a math test. Choose True or False for each statement.

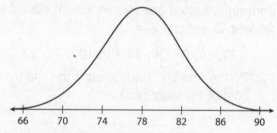

   A The mean test score is 78.

   ○ True   ○ False

   B The standard deviation is 8.

   ○ True   ○ False

   C 47.5% of the test scores are between 78 and 86.

   ○ True   ○ False

SKILL 51

Response to Intervention

Post-Test: Probability of Compound Events

Use this information for 1–3.

A family has 3 children.

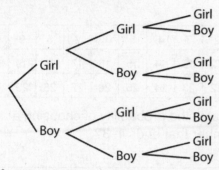

1. What is the probability the family has all girls or all boys?

   _____

2. What is the probability the family has 1 or 2 boys?

   _____

Use this information for 4–5.

A prize machine dispenses prizes one at a time. There are 15 small prizes, 8 medium prizes and 3 large prizes.

3. What is the probability of randomly receiving a large or medium prize?

   _____

4. Are these events mutually exclusive? Explain.

   _____

   _____

5. A student would like to sign up for a class. There are 8 seats open in ceramics, 20 seats in drama, and 9 seats in photography. What is the probability the student randomly receives a seat in drama or photography?

   _____

   _____

Use this information for 6–9.

A city polled 100 residents to see whether they would favor building a park or library. The data is shown below.

	Park	Library	Total
18–30 year olds	28	9	37
31–50 year olds	12	21	33
Over 50	20	10	30
Total	60	40	100

A resident is selected at random. Determine the following probabilities.

6. P(over 50 or favors park)

   _____

7. P(18–30 years old or favors library)

   _____

8. P(31–50 years old or over 50)

   _____

9. Which compound event is mutually exclusive?

   _____

10. State whether the events are mutually exclusive.

    A Getting an odd or prime number on a number cube

    ○ Yes   ○ No

    B Tossing a coin and rolling a number cube

    ○ Yes   ○ No

    C A person having brown hair or blue eyes

    ○ Yes   ○ No

Response to Intervention

Post-Test: Probability of Simple Events

Use this information for 1–3.

Cards are numbered 15–20. A number is selected at random.

1. List the events in the sample space.

   _____

2. What is the probability of choosing an even number?

   _____

3. What is the probability of choosing a number divisible by 3?

   _____

Use this information for 4–5.

A letter is drawn at random from the letters spelling PROBABILITY.

4. What is the probability of selecting a letter at random and selecting a B?

   _____

5. What is the probability of selecting a letter at random and selecting a vowel (A, E, I, O, U)?

   _____

6. In a class, 2 students rode the bus to school, 16 were in a carpool, 8 walked and 4 rode a bike. Determine the probability of each event if a student is chosen at random.

   A P(student rode the bus)

   _____

   B P(student walked)

   _____

   C P(student rides a bike)

   _____

   D P(student in a carpool)

   _____

Use this information for 7–8.

A game consists of choosing numbers at random.

1	2	3	4	5	6	7	8	9	10
11	12	13	14	15	16	17	18	19	20
21	22	23	24	25	26	27	28	29	30

7. What is the probability of choosing a number that ends in 3?

   _____

8. What is the probability of choosing a number that is divisible by 5?

   _____

Use this information for 9–11.

A company manufactures pens and finds that some are leaking.

9. Batch A has 8 leaky pens out of 100. What is the percent probability a randomly selected pen is leaking?

   _____

10. The company adjusted a machine to try and fix the problem. Batch B has 3 leaky pens out of 60. What is the probability a pen in Batch B will leak?

   _____

11. Did the company's improvements work? Explain.

   _____

   _____

12. State whether each experiment has a probability of $\frac{1}{2}$.

   A Rolling an even number on a number cube

   ○ Yes   ○ No

   B Randomly selecting a boy from a class of 10 boys and 20 girls

   ○ Yes   ○ No

SKILL
53

Response to Intervention

Post-Test: The Pythagorean Theorem

For 1–2, find the exact, simplified value of x for the given triangle.

1.

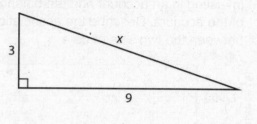

_____

_____

2.

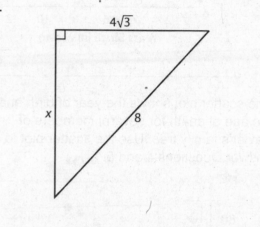

_____

_____

3. Does the Pythagorean Theorem apply to the side lengths of △ABC below? Why or why not?

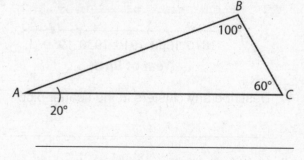

_____

_____

4. Could 16, 30, and 31 be the side lengths of a right triangle? Why or why not?

_____

_____

_____

5. Two friends, Joseph and Darius, each drive out of town at the same time. Joseph drives due south and is 48 miles from town after 1 hour. Darius drives due east and is 54 miles from town after 1 hour. To the nearest tenth of a mile, what is the straight line distance between the friends after 1 hour?

_____

_____

_____

6. A right triangle has one leg with a length of two. Give an example of possible lengths for the other leg and the hypotenuse.

_____

_____

7. Find the altitude, h, in the equilateral triangle below.

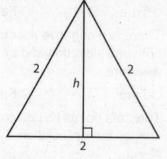

_____

_____

_____

Name _____   Date _____   Class_____

SKILL 54

Response to Intervention
Post-Test: Scatter Plots and Association

The table below shows the elevation above sea level and the atmospheric pressure. Use the table to answer Questions 1 and 2.

Elevation (m)	Atmospheric Pressure (kPa)
0	98
2000	79
4000	63
6000	48
9000	32

1. Make a scatter plot of the data.

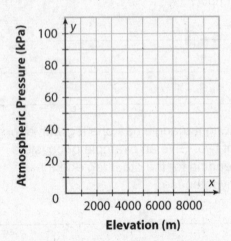

2. Choose True or False for each statement.

A   As the elevation increases, the atmospheric pressure increases.

   ○ True   ○ False

B   There is a negative association between elevation and atmospheric pressure.

   ○ True   ○ False

C   The data points lie basically along a line, so the association is linear.

   ○ True   ○ False

D   The point (0, 98) is an outlier because it is the first data value in the scatter plot.

   ○ True   ○ False

3. The scatter plot shows the relationship between the number of years since investing in an account and the balance of the account. Describe the association between the two sets of data.

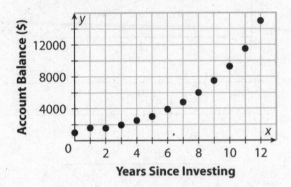

The scatter plot shows the year of birth and the age of death for several members of Xavier's family tree. Use the scatter plot to answer Questions 4 and 5.

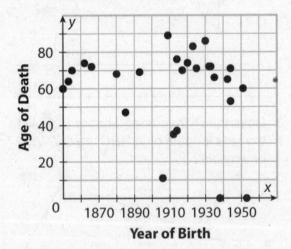

4. Describe any clusters in the scatter plot.

5. Identify two outliers in the scatter plot.

Original content Copyright © by Houghton Mifflin Harcourt. Additions and changes to the original content are the responsibility of the instructor.

SKILL 55

Response to Intervention

Post-Test: Sine and Cosine Ratios

1. Consider the following triangle. Choose True or False for each statement below.

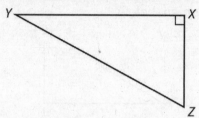

A The leg that is opposite ∠Y is $\overline{XZ}$.

   ○ True   ○ False

B The hypotenuse is $\overline{YZ}$.

   ○ True   ○ False

C $\sin Y = \dfrac{YZ}{XZ}$

   ○ True   ○ False

D $\cos Y = \dfrac{XY}{YZ}$

   ○ True   ○ False

Use △GHJ to answer Questions 2–4.

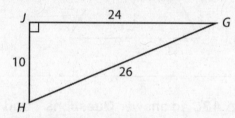

2. What is sin(H)? Write your answer in simplest form.

_____

3. What is cosG? Write your answer in simplest form.

_____

4. What is true about the relationship between sin(H) and cosG?

_____

5. Find the length of $\overline{ST}$. Round your answer to the nearest whole number.

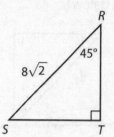

_____

6. A support beam is helping hold up an old utility pole. The base of the support beam is 16 feet from the base of the pole and forms an angle of 63° with the ground. How long is the support beam? Round your answer to the nearest foot.

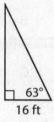

_____

Use △ABC to answer Questions 7 and 8.

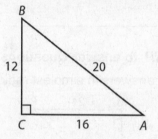

7. The measure of which angle can be found using the expression $\sin^{-1}\left(\dfrac{16}{20}\right)$?

_____

8. To the nearest degree, what is the measure of ∠A?

_____

SKILL 56 Response to Intervention
Post-Test: Special Right Triangles

1. Consider the following $45° - 45° - 90°$ triangle. Choose True or False for each statement below.

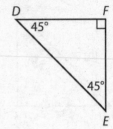

A $\overline{DF} \cong \overline{DE}$

○ True   ○ False

B If $DF = 3$, then $DE = 3\sqrt{3}$.

○ True   ○ False

C If $DE = 8$, then $DF = 4\sqrt{2}$.

○ True   ○ False

D $\triangle DEF$ is an isosceles right triangle.

○ True   ○ False

2. In a $45° - 45° - 90°$ triangle, what is the relationship between the length of the hypotenuse and the length of a leg?

_____

Use $\triangle MNP$ to answer Questions 3 and 4.

Write your answers in simplest radical form.

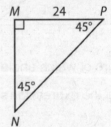

3. What is the length of $\overline{MN}$?

_____

4. What is the length of $\overline{NP}$?

_____

5. Consider the following $30° - 60° - 90°$ triangle. Choose True or False for each statement below.

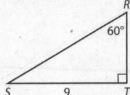

A $RT = 3\sqrt{3}$ ○ True ○ False

B $m\angle S = 30°$ ○ True ○ False

C $RS = 3\sqrt{6}$ ○ True ○ False

D $RS = 2 \cdot RT$ ○ True ○ False

6. The face of a gemstone is in the shape of an equilateral triangle, as shown below. What is the length of each side of the gemstone?

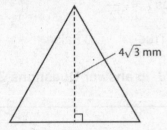

$4\sqrt{3}$ mm

_____

Use $\triangle ABC$ to answer Questions 7 and 8.

Write your answers in simplest radical form.

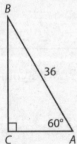

7. What is the length of $\overline{AC}$?

_____

8. What is the length of $\overline{BC}$?

_____

SKILL
57

Response to Intervention

Post-Test: Stretching, Compressing, and Reflecting Quadratic Functions

1. Choose Yes or No. Is the graph of each function wider than the graph of $f(x) = x^2$?

   A $g(x) = \dfrac{2}{3}x^2$ ○ Yes   ○ No

   B $g(x) = -2.1x^2$ ○ Yes   ○ No

   C $g(x) = -\dfrac{3}{2}x^2$ ○ Yes   ○ No

   D $g(x) = 0.9x^2$ ○ Yes   ○ No

2. Graph $g(x) = 5x^2$.

   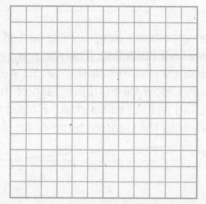

3. How does the graph of $g(x) = 3.5x^2$ compare to the graph of $f(x) = x^2$?

   _____

   _____

4. Order the functions from narrowest (most vertically stretched) to widest (most vertically compressed).

   $a(x) = -\dfrac{3}{5}x^2$, $b(x) = -1.25x^2$,

   $c(x) = \dfrac{4}{3}x^2$, $d(x) = 0.7x^2$

   _____

5. Graph $g(x) = -0.25x^2$.

   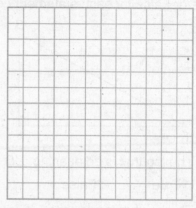

6. How does the graph of $g(x) = -0.75x^2$ compare to the graph of $f(x) = x^2$?

   _____

   _____

7. For the graph of $g(x) = -\dfrac{5}{6}x^2$, is each statement True or False?

   A It is wider than the graph of $f(x) = x^2$.

   ○ True   ○ False

   B It is narrower than the graph of $f(x) = x^2$.

   ○ True   ○ False

   C It is a reflection across the x-axis of $f(x) = \dfrac{5}{6}x^2$.

   ○ True   ○ False

   D It is a vertical stretch away from the x-axis.

   ○ True   ○ False

Response to Intervention
Post-Test: Tangent Ratio

1. Consider the following triangle. Choose True or False for each statement below.

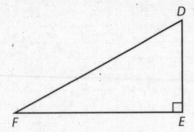

A The leg that is adjacent to $\angle D$ is $\overline{DF}$.

   ○ True   ○ False

B The leg that is opposite $\angle F$ is $\overline{DE}$.

   ○ True   ○ False

C $\tan D = \dfrac{DE}{EF}$

   ○ True   ○ False

D $\tan F = \dfrac{EF}{DE}$

   ○ True   ○ False

Use $\triangle XYZ$ to answer Questions 2–4.

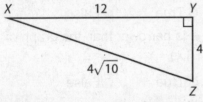

2. What is $\tan Z$? Write your answer in simplest form.

_____

3. The tangent of what angle is $\dfrac{1}{3}$?

_____

4. What is true about the relationship between $\tan X$ and $\tan Z$?

_____

5. Find the length of $\overline{MN}$. Round your answer to the nearest tenth.

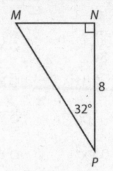

_____

6. The wheelchair ramp will be part of a new school building. The ramp will rise 20 inches and form a 4.8° angle with the ground. How far from the base of the building will the ramp start? Round your answer to the nearest tenth of an inch.

_____

7. To the nearest degree, what is the measure of $\angle Q$?

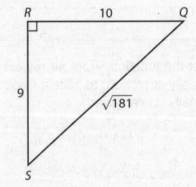

_____

SKILL 59 Response to Intervention
Post-Test: Trend Lines and Predictions

The scatter plot shows the relationship between elevation and atmospheric pressure. Use the scatter plot to answer Questions 1–3.

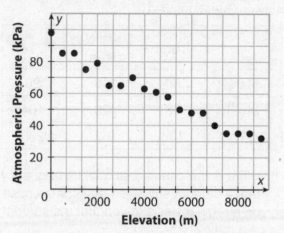

Elevation (m)

The scatter plot and trend line show the relationship between the heights and weights of several patients at a doctor's office. Use the scatter plot to answer Questions 4–8.

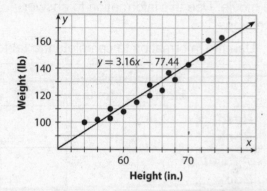

Height (in.)

4. Predict the weight of a person who is 80 inches tall.

_____

1. Choose True or False for each statement.

   A The scatter plot shows a linear association between elevation and atmospheric pressure.

   ○ True   ○ False

5. Is your estimation from Question 4 an example of interpolation or extrapolation? Explain your reasoning.

_____

   B An accurate trend line should have about the same number of points above it as below it.

   ○ True   ○ False

6. Estimate the weight of a person who is 71 inches tall.

_____

   C An appropriate trend line for this scatter plot could pass through (0, 100) and (9000, 40).

   ○ True   ○ False

7. Is your estimation from Question 6 an example of interpolation or extrapolation? Explain your reasoning.

_____

   D An appropriate trend line for this scatter plot could pass through (0, 90) and (8000, 35).

   ○ True   ○ False

2. Draw a trend line on the scatter plot above.

3. What is an equation of the trend line you drew in Question 3?

_____

8. Janelle uses the equation of the trend line to predict the weight of a person who is 100 inches tall. Will Janelle's prediction be reasonable? Explain.

_____

Response to Intervention

Post-Test: Two-Way Tables

A poll of 100 students found that 35% have read a certain book. Of those who have read the book, 60% have seen the movie. Of those who have not read the book, 80% have seen the movie. Use this information to answer Questions 1–5.

1. Use the information to complete the table.

	Seen Movie	Not Seen Movie	TOTAL
Read Book			
Not Read Book			
TOTAL			

2. Choose True or False for each statement.

   A   A total of 35 students have read the book.   ○ True   ○ False

   B   Of those students who have read the book, 60 have seen the movie.
   ○ True   ○ False

   C   Of those students who have not read the book, 80 have seen the movie.
   ○ True   ○ False

   D   A total of 73 students have seen the movie.   ○ True   ○ False

3. What is the relative frequency of having seen the movie?

   _____

4. What is the relative frequency of having seen the movie among those who have read the book?

   _____

5. Is there an association between having read the book and having seen the movie? Explain.

   _____

A group of students were asked if they run for exercise on a regular basis. The results are shown in the two-way table. Use the table to answer Questions 6–10.

	Runs	Does Not Run	TOTAL
Male	60	36	96
Female	78	26	104
TOTAL	138	62	200

6. What is the conditional relative frequency that a student surveyed runs for exercise on a regular basis, given that the student is a male?

   _____

7. What is the conditional relative frequency that a student surveyed is a female, given that she does not run for exercise on a regular basis?

   _____

8. Use the two-way table to create a two-way relative frequency table.

	Runs	Does Not Run	TOTAL
Male			
Female			
TOTAL			

9. What is the joint relative frequency of students surveyed who are female and run for exercise on a regular basis?

   _____

10. What is the marginal relative frequency of students surveyed who do not run for exercise on a regular basis?

   _____

LESSON 1-1

Domain, Range, and End Behavior

Reteach

To represent part of a number line using interval notation use a square bracket if the endpoint is included, use a parenthesis if the endpoint is not included. Use $-\infty$ or $+\infty$ if the interval continues to the left or right.

Example

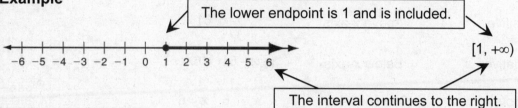

The lower endpoint is 1 and is included.

$[1, +\infty)$

The interval continues to the right.

Use interval notation to represent each number line graph.

1.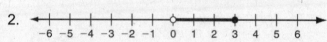

1. _____

2.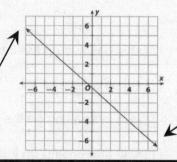

2. _____

To find end behavior for a function, trace the graph to its left ($x \to -\infty$) and right ($x \to +\infty$) ends. If it continues up, $f(x)$ goes to $+\infty$. If it continues down, $f(x)$ goes to $-\infty$.

Example

Left end continues up
As $x \to -\infty$, $f(x) \to +\infty$

Right end continues down
As $x \to +\infty$, $f(x) \to -\infty$

Fill in the end behavior for each function.

3.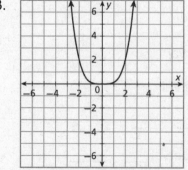

4.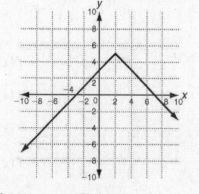

As $x \to -\infty$, $f(x) \to$ _____

As $x \to +\infty$, $f(x) \to$ _____

As $x \to -\infty$, $f(x) \to$ _____

As $x \to +\infty$, $f(x) \to$ _____

LESSON 1-2

Characteristics of Function Graphs

Reteach

Example

Attribute of Function	Graph Characteristic	Interval
Positive	Above x-axis	$(-6, 6)$
Negative	Below x-axis	$(-\infty, -6) \cup (6, +\infty)$
Zero(s)	Crosses x-axis	$x = -6,\ x = 6$
Increasing	Uphill (from left–right)	$(-\infty, 0)$
Decreasing	Downhill (from left–right)	$(0, +\infty)$
Local Maximum	Top of "peak"	$f(x) = 6$ at $x = 0$
Local Minimum	Bottom of "valley"	None

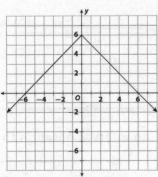

Fill in the blanks for the attributes of the functions shown in the graphs below.

1.

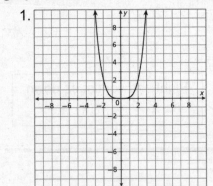

$f(x)$ is positive on the interval _____

$f(x)$ has a zero at $x =$ _____

$f(x)$ is increasing on the interval _____

$f(x)$ is decreasing on the interval _____

$f(x)$ has a local minimum of _____ at $x =$ _____

2.

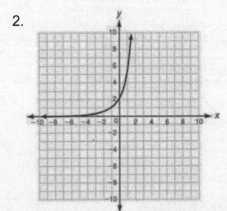

$f(x)$ is positive on the interval _____

$f(x)$ is negative on the interval _____

$f(x)$ has a zero at $x =$ _____

$f(x)$ is increasing on the interval _____

$f(x)$ is decreasing on the interval _____

LESSON 1-3
Transformations of Function Graphs
Reteach

Horizontal Translation	**Vertical Translation**
$f(x) \rightarrow f(x - h)$	$f(x) \rightarrow f(x) + k$
Shifts x and $f(x)$ right h units for $h > 0$	Shifts $f(x)$ up k units for $k > 0$
Shifts x and $f(x)$ left $|h|$ units for $h < 0$	Shifts $f(x)$ down $|k|$ units for $k < 0$

Example

$f(x) = |x + 3|$ <u>Graph shifts left 3 units.</u>

Example

$f(x) = |x| + 3$ <u>Graph shifts up 3 units.</u>

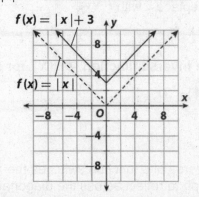

Describe the translation of $f(x) = x^2$ and sketch the graph of the translated function.

1. $f(x) = (x + 1)^2$ _____

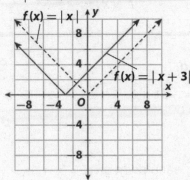

2. $f(x) = x^2 - 2$ _____

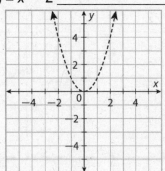

Describe the translation of $f(x) = 2^x$ and sketch the graph of the translated function.

3. $f(x) = 2^x - 4$ _____

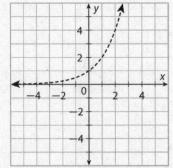

4. $f(x) = 2^{x-1}$ _____

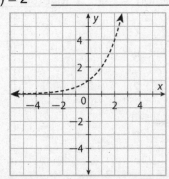

Name _____ Date _____ Class_____

LESSON 1-4

Inverses of Functions
Reteach

To find the inverse of a function:

1. Substitute y for $f(x)$.

2. Solve for x in terms of y.

3. Switch x and y.

4. Replace y with $f^{-1}(x)$.

Example: $f(x) = 6x - 1$

$$y = 6x - 1$$
$$y + 1 = 6x$$
$$\frac{y + 1}{6} = x$$
$$y = \frac{x + 1}{6}$$
$$f^{-1}(x) = \frac{x + 1}{6}$$

Find the inverse function, $f^{-1}(x)$, for the function given.

1. $f(x) = 2x + 5$

2. $f(x) = -3x + 8$

The inverse of a function switches the xs and ys, causing each point on the graph to reflect across the diagonal line $y = x$.

Example

Function			Inverse Function	
x	y		x	y
-2	1		1	-2
0	5		5	0
1	7		7	1

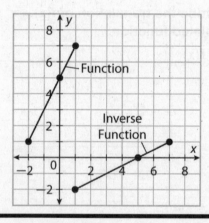

Find the ordered pairs of the inverse function. Graph the function and its inverse.

3.

Function		Inverse Function	
x	y	x	y
1	5		
2	2		
3	-1		

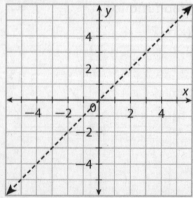

<table>
<tr><td>LESSON
2-1</td><td></td></tr>
</table>

Graphing Absolute Value Functions
Reteach

The graph of the absolute-value parent function is shaped like a V.
To **translate** $f(x) = |x|$ to a new **vertex** (h, k), use $g(x) = |x - h| + k$.

Example

Translate $f(x) = |x|$ so that the vertex is at $(2, -3)$.

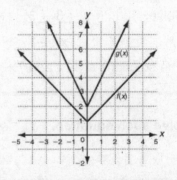

$g(x) = |x - h| + k$	Write the transformation.
$g(x) = |x - 2| + (-3)$	Substitute $h = 2$, $k = -3$.
$g(x) = |x - 2| - 3$	Simplify. Domain: all x; Range: $y \geq -3$

The vertex is $(2, -3)$. The entire graph of the parent function moves when the vertex moves.

To **vertically** stretch or shrink $f(x)$ by a factor of a, use $f(x) \rightarrow a \cdot f(x)$.

To **horizontally** stretch or shrink $f(x)$ by a factor of b, use $f(x) \rightarrow f\left(\dfrac{1}{b}x\right)$.

Example

Stretch the graph of $f(x) = |x| + 1$ vertically by a factor of 2.

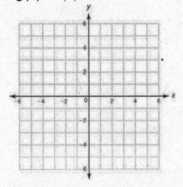

$g(x) \rightarrow a \cdot f(x)$	Write the transformation.
$g(x) = 2(|x| + 1)$	Substitute the factor of 2 for a.
$g(x) = 2|x| + 2$	Distribute. Vertex is at $(0, 2)$.
	Domain: all x; Range: $y \geq 2$

Graph each function. Identify the vertex, domain, and range.

1. $g(x) = |x - 1| + 2$

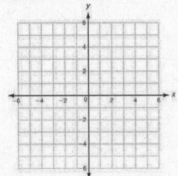

Vertex:_____

Domain:_____

Range:_____

2. $g(x) = |x + 3| - 1$

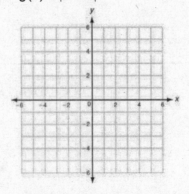

Vertex: _____

Domain: _____

Range: _____

3. $g(x) = 3|x| + 1$

Vertex:_____

Domain:_____

Range:_____

| LESSON 2-2 | **Solving Absolute Value Equations** |

Reteach

There are three steps in solving an absolute-value equation.

Solve $|x - 3| + 4 = 8$.

Step 1: Isolate the absolute-value expression.

$$|x - 3| + 4 = 8$$

$$\underline{\ -4\ -4}$$ *Subtract 4 from both sides.*

$$|x - 3| = 4$$

Step 2: Rewrite the equation as two cases.

$$|x - 3| = 4$$

            Case 1   **Case 2**

Step 3: $x - 3 = -4$ $x - 3 = 4$

Solve. $\underline{+3\ +3}$ $\underline{+3\ +3}$ *Add 3 to both sides.*

           $x = -1$ $x = 7$

The solutions are −1 and 7.

Solve each equation.

1. $|x - 2| - 3 = 5$ 2. $|x + 7| + 2 = 10$

_____   _____

3. $4|x - 5| = 20$ 4. $|2x| + 1 = 7$

_____   _____

LESSON 2-3

Solving Absolute Value Inequalities
Reteach

To solve an absolute-value inequality, first use inverse operations to isolate the absolute-value expression. Then write and solve a compound inequality.

Example

Solve $|x - 2| + 8 < 10$.

    Step 1: Isolate the absolute-value expression.

      $|x - 2| + 8 < 10$

      $\underline{\quad -8 \quad -8 \quad}$ *Subtract 8 from both sides.*

      $|x - 2| \quad < \quad 2$

    Step 2: Solve a compound inequality.

      $|x - 2| < 2$ means $x - 2 > -2$ AND $x - 2 < 2$.

          $\underline{\quad +2 \quad +2 \quad}$ $\underline{\quad +2 \quad +2 \quad}$ *Solve each inequality.*

          $x \quad > \quad 0$ AND $x \quad < 4$

Graph the solution as shown.

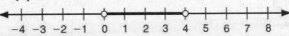

Solve each inequality and graph the solution.

1. $|x| + 12 < 16$ _____

2. $|x - 1| + 5 \le 9$ _____

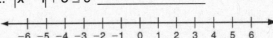

Use a similar method to solve absolute-value inequalities that have a greater-than symbol (>).

Example

Solve $|x - 5| - 4 > -1$.

    Step 1: Isolate the absolute-value expression.

      $|x - 5| - 4 > -1$

      $\underline{\quad +4 \quad +4 \quad}$ *Add 4 to both sides.*

      $|x - 5| \quad > \quad 3$

    Step 2: Solve a compound inequality.

      $|x - 5| > 3$ means $x - 5 < -3$ OR $x - 5 > 3$.

          $\underline{\quad +5 \quad +5 \quad}$ $\underline{\quad +5 \quad +5 \quad}$ *Solve each inequality.*

          $x \quad < \quad 2$ OR $x \quad > 8$

Graph the solution as shown.

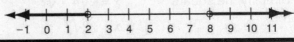

Solve each inequality and graph the solution.

3. $4 + |x| \ge 5$ _____

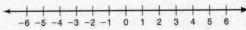

4. $2|x + 2| > 6$ _____

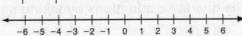

LESSON 3-1 Solving Quadratic Equations by Taking Square Roots
Reteach

Imaginary numbers are the square roots of negative numbers. You can use the following information to simplify the square root of a negative number.

Product Property of Square Roots	Quotient Property of Square Roots	Definition of i
$\sqrt{ab} = \sqrt{a}\sqrt{b}$	$\sqrt{\dfrac{a}{b}} = \dfrac{\sqrt{a}}{\sqrt{b}}$	$i = \sqrt{-1}$

Example Simplify $\sqrt{-32}$.

Rewrite using the Product Rule of Square Roots; then simplify.

$$\sqrt{-32}$$
$$\sqrt{16} \cdot \sqrt{-1} \cdot \sqrt{2}$$
$$4i\sqrt{2}$$

Example Simplify $\sqrt{-\dfrac{3}{4}}$.

Rewrite using the Quotient Rule of Square Roots; then simplify.

$$\sqrt{-\dfrac{3}{4}}$$
$$\sqrt{-1} \cdot \dfrac{\sqrt{3}}{\sqrt{4}}$$
$$i \cdot \dfrac{\sqrt{3}}{2}$$
$$\dfrac{i}{2}\sqrt{3}$$

Simplify the square roots.

1. $\sqrt{-44}$ _____

2. $\sqrt{-\dfrac{5}{9}}$ _____

To solve simple quadratic equations of the form $x^2 = a$, use the method of taking square roots.

Example Solve $x^2 - 28 = 0$.

Add 28 to both sides. $x^2 = 28$

Take the square root. $x = \pm\sqrt{28}$

Simplify the square root. $x = \pm\sqrt{4} \cdot \sqrt{7}$

$$x = \pm 2\sqrt{7}$$

Example Solve $x^2 + 45 = 0$.

Subtract 45 from both sides. $x^2 = -45$

$$x = \pm\sqrt{-45}$$

Take the square root. $x = \pm\sqrt{9} \cdot \sqrt{-1} \cdot \sqrt{5}$

$$x = \pm 3i\sqrt{5}$$

Simplify the square root.

Solve the quadratic equations by taking square roots.

3. $x^2 - 20 = 0$

4. $x^2 + 48 = 0$

_____   _____

Name _____ Date _____ Class_____

Complex Numbers
Reteach

A complex number can be written as follows.

Real Part   Imaginary Part

$$a + bi$$

To add or subtract complex numbers, group and combine the real parts and imaginary parts.

Example Add. $(8-2i)+(-3+5i)$

Group like terms. $(8+(-3))+((-2i)+5i)$

Combine like terms. $5+3i$

Example Subtract. $(-1+23i)-(-6+19i)$

Group like terms. $(-1-(-6))+(23i-19i)$

Combine like terms. $5+4i$

Add or subtract the complex numbers.

1. $(2+11i)+(-10-4i)$ 2. $(6-29i)-(17+8i)$ 3. $(16-5i)+(9i)$

_____   _____   _____

To multiply complex numbers, use the Distributive Property and the fact that $i^2=-1$.

Example Multiply. $(3+2i)(-4-5i)$

Use the Distributive Property. $-12-15i-8i-10i^2$

Substitute -1 for i^2. $-12-15i-8i-10(-1)$

Combine like terms. $-2-23i$

Multiply the complex numbers.

4. $(-8+12i)(10-i)$ 5. $(7-5i)(1+9i)$ 6. $(-1+i)(5+2i)$

_____   _____   _____

LESSON	Finding Complex Solutions of Quadratic Equations
3-3	*Reteach*

One way to solve quadratic equations of the form $ax^2 + bx + c = 0$ is to use the

Quadratic Formula $\qquad x = \dfrac{-b \pm \sqrt{b^2 - 4ac}}{2a}$

Example Solve. $\qquad\qquad\qquad\qquad 2x^2 + 5x + 5 = -1$

Step 1 Write in the form $ax^2 + bx + c = 0$. $\quad 2x^2 + 5x + 6 = 0$

Step 2 Write the Quadratic Formula. $\qquad x = \dfrac{-b \pm \sqrt{b^2 - 4ac}}{2a}$

Step 3 Substitute values. $\qquad\qquad\quad = \dfrac{-5 \pm \sqrt{5^2 - 4(2)(6)}}{2(2)}$

$\qquad\qquad\qquad\qquad\qquad\qquad\quad = \dfrac{-5 \pm \sqrt{25 - 48}}{2(2)}$

Step 4 Simplify. $\qquad\qquad\qquad\quad = \dfrac{-5 \pm \sqrt{-23}}{4}$

$\qquad\qquad\qquad\qquad\qquad\qquad\quad = \dfrac{-5 \pm i\sqrt{23}}{4}$

So, the two solutions are $\dfrac{-5 + i\sqrt{23}}{4}$ and $\dfrac{-5 - i\sqrt{23}}{4}$.

Solve the equations using the Quadratic Formula.

1. $-x^2 - 3x + 9 = 0$

2. $3x^2 - 7x + 10 = 0$

_____

3. $-2x^2 + 5x + 3 = -1$

4. $5x^2 + 4x - 7 = -8$

_____

LESSON 4-1

Circles
Reteach

The standard form of the equation of a circle with center (h, k) and radius r is $(x - h)^2 + (y - k)^2 = r^2$.

Example

To write the equation of the circle with center $(-1, 3)$ and containing the point $(2, 7)$, use the Distance Formula to find the length of the radius.

Step 1 Substitute $d = r$ in the Distance Formula.

$$d = \sqrt{(x_2 - x_1)^2 + (y_2 - y_1)^2}$$

$$r = \sqrt{(x_2 - x_1)^2 + (y_2 - y_1)^2}$$

> By definition, the radius is the distance from the center to any point on the circle.

Step 2 Use $(2, 7)$ and $(-1, 3)$ in the formula for (x_2, y_2) and (x_1, y_1).

$$r = \sqrt{(x_2 - x_1)^2 + (y_2 - y_1)^2}$$

$$r = \sqrt{(2 - (-1))^2 + (7 - 3)^2}$$

$$r = \sqrt{3^2 + 4^2} = \sqrt{9 + 16} = \sqrt{25} = 5$$

Step 3 Substitute center $(-1, 3)$ and radius $r = 5$ into the standard form of the equation of a circle with center (h, k) and radius r.

$$(x - h)^2 + (y - k)^2 = r^2$$

$$(x - (-1))^2 + (y - 3)^2 = 5^2$$

$$(x + 1)^2 + (y - 3)^2 = 25$$

Find the equation of each circle with the given center and point on the circle.

1. Center $(3, -7)$ and containing the point $(8, 5)$

$$r = \sqrt{(8 - 3)^2 + (5 - (-7))^2}$$

_____

_____

$$(x - h)^2 + (y - k)^2 = r^2$$

_____

2. Center $(4, 5)$ and containing the point $(10, 13)$

_____

_____

$$(x - h)^2 + (y - k)^2 = r^2$$

_____

LESSON 4-2
Parabolas
Reteach

	Vertical Parabola	Horizontal Parabola
Vertex	(h,k)	(h,k)
Standard Form	$(x-h)^2 = 4p(y-k)$	$(y-k)^2 = 4p(x-h)$
$p > 0$	Opens up	Opens right
$p < 0$	Opens down	Opens left
Focus	$(h, k+p)$	$(h+p, k)$
Directrix	$y = k - p$	$x = h - p$
Axis of Symmetry	$x = h$	$y = k$

Example Use the information from the table to graph the parabola $(y+1)^2 = 8(x-3)$.

Determine if parabola is vertical or horizontal.	The equation is of the form $(y-k)^2 = 4p(x-h)$, so it is a horizontal parabola.	
Identify the vertex (h,k).	$(3,-1)$	
Find p.	$4p = 8 \rightarrow p = 2$	
Determine direction of opening.	$p > 0$, so the parabola opens right	
Find the focus.	$(h+p,k) \rightarrow (3+2,-1) \rightarrow (5,-1)$	
Find the directrix.	$x = h - p \rightarrow x = 3 - 2 \rightarrow x = 1$	
Find the axis of symmetry.	$y = k \rightarrow y = -1$	

Use the information from the table to graph the parabola along with its focus, directrix, and axis of symmetry.

1. $(x-2)^2 = -4(y-3)$

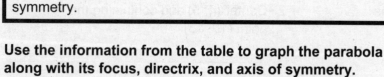
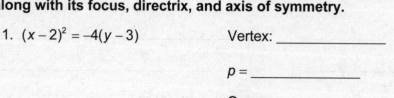

Vertex: _____

$p = $ _____

Opens _____

Focus: _____

Directrix: _____

Axis of symmetry: _____

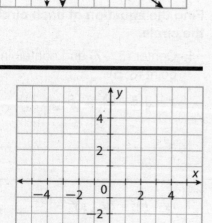

Solving Linear-Quadratic Systems

LESSON 4-3

Reteach

Linear-quadratic systems could have the following types of solutions:

$$y = (x-1)^2 - 3$$
$$y = x - 2$$

$$y = (x-1)^2 - 3$$
$$y = -3$$

$$y = (x-1)^2 - 3$$
$$y = -x - 3$$

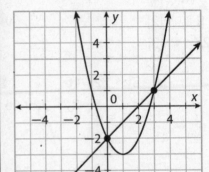

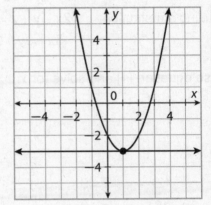

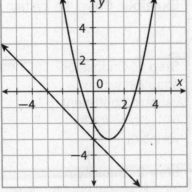

Two Solutions: $(0, -2)$ and $(3, 1)$ One Solution: $(1, -3)$ No Solution

Example Solve the linear-quadratic system algebraically.

$$y - 4 = -(x+2)^2$$
$$2y = -4x$$

Step 1 Solve the linear equation for y.

$$y - 4 = -(x+2)^2$$
$$y = -2x$$

Step 2 Substitute for y in the quadratic equation.

$$-2x - 4 = -(x+2)^2$$

Step 3 Solve for x.

$$-2x - 4 = -(x+2)^2$$
$$-2x - 4 = -(x^2 + 4x + 4)$$
$$-2x - 4 = -x^2 - 4x - 4$$
$$x^2 + 2x = 0$$
$$x(x+2) = 0$$
$$x = 0$$

or

$$x + 2 = 0$$
$$x = -2$$

Step 4 Find y coordinates for solution points.

$$y = -2(0) = 0$$
$$(0,0)$$

$$y = -2(-2) = -4$$
$$(-2,-4)$$

Two Solutions:
$(0,0)$ and $(-2,-4)$

Solve the linear-quadratic systems algebraically.

1. $y + 2 = (x-3)^2$
   $y + 3 = x$

2. $y = -2(x+1)^2$
   $y - 6 = 4x$

3. $y - 2 = -4x^2$
   $y = 2(x+2)$

_____ _____ _____

LESSON 4-4 Solving Linear Systems in Three Variables
Reteach

One way to solve a system of three linear equations is by <u>substitution</u>. Substitution is a good method when there is an equation that has a variable whose coefficient is one.

Example Solve the system using substitution.
$$\begin{cases} x - 2y + 3z = 16 & [1] \\ 2x - y + z = 9 & [2] \\ -5x - 3y + 2z = 1 & [3] \end{cases}$$

Step 1 Choose an equation with a variable coefficient of 1. Solve for that variable.

Choose equation [1] and solve for x.

$$x - 2y + 3z = 16$$
$$x = 2y - 3z + 16$$

Step 2 Substitute for x in equations [2] and [3], and simplify.

$$2x - y + z = 9$$
$$2(2y - 3z + 16) - y + z = 9$$
$$4y - 6z + 32 - y + z = 9$$
$$3y - 5z = -23$$

$$-5x - 3y + 2z = 1$$
$$-5(2y - 3z + 16) - 3y + 2z = 1$$
$$-10y + 15z - 80 - 3y + 2z = 1$$
$$-13y + 17z = 81$$

Step 3 Solve the resulting system for y and z using substitution or elimination.

$$\begin{cases} 3y - 5z = -23 \\ -13y + 17z = 81 \end{cases}$$

$$-13(3y - 5z = -23)$$
$$-3(-13y + 17z = 81)$$
$$-39y + 65z = 299$$
$$39y - 51z = -243$$
$$14z = 56$$
$$z = 4$$

$$3y - 5(4) = -23$$
$$y = -1$$

Step 4 Substitute y and z into the equation for x.

$$x = 2y - 3z + 16$$
$$x = 2(-1) - 3(4) + 16$$
$$x = 2$$

Step 5 Write the solution as an ordered triple.

$$(2, -1, 4)$$

Solve the systems using substitution.

1. $\begin{cases} x + y - z = 8 \\ 2x - 2y - z = 11 \\ x - 5y + 3z = -12 \end{cases}$

2. $\begin{cases} -3x + y - 4z = -12 \\ 5x - 5y + z = 12 \\ 7x + 9y + z = 0 \end{cases}$

_____ _____

LESSON 5-1

Graphing Cubic Functions
Reteach

The graph of the parent function $f(x) = x^3$ can be transformed into $g(x) = a\left(\frac{1}{b}(x-h)\right)^3 + k$.

Each parameter (*a*, *b*, *h*, and *k*) affects the transformation of the function:

a	$\lvert a \rvert < 1$ Vertical Compression	$\lvert a \rvert > 1$ Vertical Stretch	$a < 0$ Reflection over *x*-axis
b	$\lvert b \rvert < 1$ Horizontal Compression	$\lvert b \rvert > 1$ Horizontal Stretch	$b < 0$ Reflection over *y*-axis
h	$h < 0$ Translate Left *h*		$h > 0$ Translate Right *h*
k	$k < 0$ Translate Down *k*		$k > 0$ Translate Up *k*

By using reference points, a graph of the transformed function can be created.

$f(x) = x^3$		$g(x) = a\left(\frac{1}{b}(x-h)\right)^3 + k$	
x	*y*	*x*	*y*
−1	−1	$-b + h$	$-a + k$
0	0	*h*	*k*
1	1	$b + h$	$a + k$

Example Identify the transformations that produce the graph of $g(x) = 2(x+1)^3 - 2$. Then, graph $g(x)$ by applying the transformations to the reference points $(-1, -1)$, $(0, 0)$, and $(1, 1)$.

Transformations	Reference Points			Graph
$a = 2$ Vertical Stretch by 2	Original Points	*x*	*y*	
$b = 1$ No Horizontal Stretch or Compression	$(-1, -1)$	$-1 + (-1) = -2$	$-2 + (-2) = -4$	
$h = -1$ Translate Left 1	$(0, 0)$	-1	-2	
$k = -2$ Translate Down 2	$(1, 1)$	$1 + (-1) = 0$	$2 + (-2) = 0$	

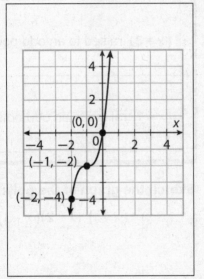

Identify the transformations that produce the graph of the given function. Then, graph the function by applying the transformations to the reference points $(-1, -1)$, $(0, 0)$, and $(1, 1)$.

1. $g(x) = -3(x-4)^3 + 1$

2. $g(x) = \frac{1}{2}(x-2)^3 - 4$

3. $g(x) = -(x+3)^3 + 2$

LESSON 5-2 Graphing Polynomial Functions
Reteach

To sketch $f(x) = a(x - x_1)(x - x_2)...(x - x_n)$:

n = degree a = constant factor	End Behavior	Graph Description	x-intercepts
n odd $a > 0$	as $x \to -\infty$, $f(x) \to -\infty$ as $x \to +\infty$, $f(x) \to +\infty$	Uphill	$(x - x_1)^{odd}$ Crosses x-axis at x_1
n odd $a < 0$	as $x \to -\infty$, $f(x) \to +\infty$ as $x \to +\infty$, $f(x) \to -\infty$	Downhill	
n even $a > 0$	as $x \to -\infty$, $f(x) \to +\infty$ as $x \to +\infty$, $f(x) \to +\infty$	Opens up	$(x - x_2)^{even}$ Tangent to x-axis at x_2
n even $a < 0$	as $x \to -\infty$, $f(x) \to -\infty$ as $x \to +\infty$, $f(x) \to -\infty$	Opens down	

Example Sketch the graph of the polynomial function $f(x) = \left(-\dfrac{1}{5}\right)(x + 3)(x - 1)^3$.

$n = 4$ (even), $a = -\dfrac{1}{5}$ ($a < 0$) $\to$ Opens down	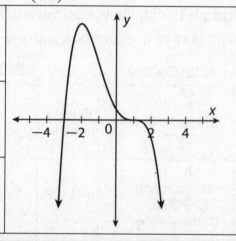
$(x + 3)$ raised to an odd power $\to$ crosses at $x = -3$	
$(x - 1)$ raised to an odd power $\to$ crosses at $x = 1$	

Sketch the graph of the polynomial function.

1. $f(x) = (x + 1)^2 (x - 2)(x - 3)$

2. $f(x) = -2(x + 3)^3 (x - 2)^2$

3. $f(x) = (x - 1)^3 (x + 4)^2$

4. $f(x) = x(x + 3)(x + 1)(x - 1)(x - 3)$

LESSON 6-1

Adding and Subtracting Polynomials

Reteach

Example $\left(-3x^4 + 2x - x^3 - 12\right) + \left(4 + 2x^4 - x^2 + 9x\right)$

1. Write in standard form.	$-3x^4$	$-x^3$		$+2x$	-12
2. Align like terms.	$+\ 2x^4$		$-x^2$	$+9x$	$+4$
3. Add.	$-x^4$	$-x^3$	$-x^2$	$+11x$	-8

$$\left(-3x^4 + 2x - x^3 - 12\right) + \left(4 + 2x^4 - x^2 + 9x\right) = -x^4 - x^3 - x^2 + 11x - 8$$

Add the polynomials.

1. $\left(2x^2 - 7x + 5x^4 + 4x^3 - 11\right) + \left(6x^3 + x^4 - 3x^2 + 10x\right)$ 2. $\left(6x^2 - 9 + x^3\right) + \left(3x^3 - 4 - x\right)$

3. $\left(4a^4 - 9a^2 + 3a^3 - a\right) + \left(-5a^3 + 14 - a\right)$ 4. $\left(y^2 - 5y + 18\right) + \left(2y - y^2 - 11\right)$

Example $\left(-x + 5x^3 + 2x^4 - 10x\right) - \left(4x^2 - 2x - x^4 + 1\right)$

1. Write in standard form.	$2x^4$	$+5x^3$	$-x^2$	$-10x$	
2. Align like terms and add the opposite.	$+\ \ x^4$		$-4x^2$	$+2x$	-1
3. Add.	$3x^4$	$+5x^3$	$-5x^2$	$-8x$	-1

$$\left(-x + 5x^3 + 2x^4 - 10x\right) - \left(4x^2 - 2x - x^4 + 1\right) = 3x^4 + 5x^3 - 5x^2 - 8x - 1$$

Subtract the polynomials.

5. $\left(-4x^3 + 3x^2 - x^4 + 8x\right) - \left(9 + 5x^4 - 3x^2 + 10x\right)$ 6. $\left(x^3 - 7x + 3x^4 - 5\right) - \left(3 + 2x^3 - 4x^2 - 2x\right)$

7. $\left(c^4 + 7c - c^3 - 12\right) - \left(-c^4 + 4c^3 - c^2 + 5\right)$ 8. $\left(3r^3 + r - 8\right) - \left(-2r^2 - 8\right)$

LESSON 6-2	**Multiplying Polynomials**
	Reteach

You can multiply polynomials horizontally or vertically.

Example Find the product by multiplying horizontally. $(x-5)(3x+x^2-7)$

Multiply each term of the first polynomial by each term of the second polynomial, then simplify.

1. Write polynomials in standard form.

$$(x-5)(x^2+3x-7)$$

2. Distribute x and -5.

$$x(x^2)+x(3x)+x(-7)+(-5)(x^2)+(-5)(3x)+(-5)(-7)$$

3. Simplify.

$$x^3+3x^2-7x-5x^2-15x+35$$

4. Combine like terms.

$$x^3-2x^2-22x+35$$

Find the product by multiplying horizontally.

1. $(x+8)(6-2x^2+x)$

2. $(2x-3)(x^2+4-5x)$

_____   _____

Example Find the product by multiplying vertically. $(x-5)(3x+x^2-7)$

1. Write each polynomial in standard form.

2. Multiply -5 and $(3x+x^2-7)$.

3. Multiply x and $(3x+x^2-7)$.

4. Combine like terms.

$$\begin{array}{rrrr} & x^2 & +3x & -7 \\ & & x & -5 \\ \hline & -5x^2 & -15x & +35 \\ x^3 & +3x^2 & -7x & \\ \hline x^3 & -2x^2 & -22x & +35 \end{array}$$

Find the product by multiplying vertically.

3. $(x-3)(5x-8+2x^2)$

4. $(5-3x)(4x^2-1+7x)$

_____   _____

LESSON 6-3

The Binomial Theorem

Reteach

The coefficients of the expansion of $(x + y)^n$ are the numbers in Pascal's triangle. The binomial coefficients are also combinations.

Pascal's Triangle	Combinations	Binomial Expansion
1	$_0C_0$	$(x + y)^0 = 1$
1 1	$_1C_0$ $_1C_1$	$(x + y)^1 = x + y$
1 2 1	$_2C_0$ $_2C_1$ $_2C_2$	$(x + y)^2 = x^2 + 2xy + y^2$
1 3 3 1	$_3C_0$ $_3C_1$ $_3C_2$ $_3C_3$	$(x + y)^3 = x^3 + 3x^2y + 3xy^2 + y^2$

The **Binomial Theorem** summarizes the relationship.

$$(x + y)^n = {}_nC_0x^ny^0 + {}_nC_1x^{n-1}y^1 + {}_nC_2x^{n-2}y^2 + \ldots + {}_nC_{n-1}x^1y^{n-1} + {}_nC_nx^0y^n$$

You can use the Binomial Theorem to expand any binomial.

Expand $(x + y)^5$.

> The sum of the exponents for each term is n.

Step 1 Use the Binomial Theorem with $n = 5$.

$$(x + y)^5 = {}_5C_0x^5y^0 + {}_5C_1x^4y^1 + {}_5C_2x^3y^2 + {}_5C_3x^2y^3 + {}_5C_4x^1y^4 + {}_5C_5x^0y^5$$

Step 2 Use the fifth row of Pascal's triangle to find the coefficients. Continue the pattern and add pairs of terms from the fourth row to find the numbers in the fifth row.

> The sum of the exponents for each term is 5. The exponents of x decrease as the exponents of y increase.

1	3	3	1	$\leftarrow n = 3$
1	4	6	4	1	$\leftarrow n = 4$
1	5	10	10	5	1	$\leftarrow n = 5$

Step 3 Write the coefficients.

$$(x + y)^5 = 1x^5y^0 + 5x^4y^1 + 10x^3y^2 + 10x^2y^3 + 5x^1y^4 + 1x^0y^5$$

Step 4 Simplify.

$$(x + y)^5 = x^5 + 5x^4y + 10x^3y^2 + 10x^2y^3 + 5xy^4 + y^5$$

Use the Binomial Theorem to expand each binomial.

1. $(2x + y)^3 = {}_3C_0(2x)^3y^0 + {}_3C_1(2x)^2y^1 + {}_3C_2(2x)^1y^2 + {}_3C_3(2x)^0y^3$

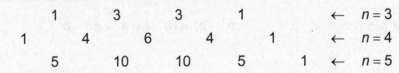

$= {}_3C_0 \cdot 8x^3 + {}_3C_1 \cdot 4x^2y^1 + {}_3C_2 \cdot 2xy^2 + {}_3C_3 \cdot y^3$

$= \underline{\hspace{8cm}}$

$= \underline{\hspace{8cm}}$

2. $(x + 3y)^4 = \underline{\hspace{8cm}}$

$= \underline{\hspace{8cm}}$

$= \underline{\hspace{8cm}}$

Factoring Polynomials
Reteach

Factoring a sum of two cubes:　　　　$a^3 + b^3 = (a+b)(a^2 - ab + b^2)$

Example Factor $125a^3 + 8$.

$$125x^3 + 8$$

Recognize the sum of two cubes.　　　　$(5x)^3 + (2)^3$

Factor using factoring pattern.　　　　$(5x + 2)\left((5x)^2 - (5x)(2) + (2)^2\right)$

Simplify.　　　　$(5x + 2)(25x^2 - 10x + 4)$

Factor.

1. $27x^3 + 1$

2. $m^3 + \dfrac{1}{8}$

3. $p^3 + 216$

_____   _____   _____

Factoring a difference of two cubes:　　　　$a^3 - b^3 = (a-b)(a^2 + ab + b^2)$

Example Factor $27a^3 - 64$.

$$27a^3 - 64$$

Recognize the difference of two cubes.　　　　$(3a)^3 - (4)^3$

Factor using factoring pattern.　　　　$(3a - 4)\left((3a)^2 + (3a)(4) + (4)^2\right)$

Simplify.　　　　$(3a - 4)(9a^2 + 12a + 16)$

Factor.

4. $8x^3 - 1$

5. $b^3 - 1000$

6. $125t^3 - 343$

_____   _____   _____

LESSON 6-5 Dividing Polynomials
Reteach

Example Divide $(x^3 - 2x^2 - 22x + 45)$ by $(x - 5)$ using synthetic division.

$\underline{5}|$					$\underline{5}|$	1	-2	-22	45		$\underline{5}|$	1	-2	-22	45	
			$\llcorner$		$\rightarrow$					$\llcorner$	$\rightarrow$	1			$\llcorner$	$\rightarrow$

	$\underline{5}|$	1	-2	-22	45			$\underline{5}|$	1	-2	-22	45			$\underline{5}|$	1	-2	-22	45	
$\rightarrow$			5				$\rightarrow$			5				$\rightarrow$			5	15		$\rightarrow$
		1			$\llcorner$				1	3		$\llcorner$				1	3		$\llcorner$	

	$\underline{5}|$	1	-2	-22	45			$\underline{5}|$	1	-2	-22	45			$\underline{5}|$	1	-2	-22	45
$\rightarrow$			5	15			$\rightarrow$			5	15	-35	$\rightarrow$			5	15	-35
		1	3	-7	$\llcorner$				1	3	-7	$\llcorner$			1	3	-7	$\underline{|10}$

Quotient: $x^2 + 3x - 7$
Remainder: 10

Divide using synthetic division. Give the quotient and the remainder.

1. $(3x^3 - 4x^2 + x - 16) \div (x - 2)$

2. $(-2x^3 + 3x^2 + 5x + 12) \div (2x - 1)$

Quotient: _____

Remainder: _____

Quotient: _____

Remainder: _____

3. $(5x^3 + 6x^2 - 7x + 8) \div (x + 4)$

4. $(-2x^4 + x^2 + 12x + 1) \div (x - 1)$

Quotient: _____

Remainder: _____

Quotient: _____

Remainder: _____

Finding Rational Solutions of Polynomial Equations
Reteach

Rational Root Theorem:	Possible rational roots are of the form $\dfrac{m}{n}$ where m = factor of the constant term n = factor of the leading coefficient

Example Find the rational zeros of $x^3 - 11x^2 + 23x + 35$, then write the function in factored form.

Step 1: List possible rational roots.

$x^3 - 11x^2 + 23x + 35$	Constant term: 35 Factors: $\pm 1, \pm 5, \pm 7, \pm 35$	Leading Coefficient: 1 Factors: ± 1

Possible Rational Roots: $\dfrac{m}{n} = \dfrac{\pm 1, \pm 5, \pm 7, \pm 35}{\pm 1} = \pm 1, \pm 5, \pm 7, \pm 35$

Step 2: Use synthetic division to test for a zero remainder.

$\underline{1|}$	1	−11	23	35
		1	−10	13
	1	−10	13	$\underline{|48}$

Remainder is not 0, so 1 is not a root.

$\underline{5|}$	1	−11	23	35
		5	−30	−35
	1	−6	−7	$\underline{|0}$

Remainder is 0, so 5 is a root.

Step 3: Factor the remaining quadratic to find the zeros and write the polynomial in factored form.

$x^3 - 11x^2 + 23x + 35 = (x-5)(x^2 - 6x - 7)$ $= (x-5)(x-7)(x+1)$	Rational zeros are 5, 7, and −1, and $f(x) = (x-5)(x-7)(x+1)$.

Find the rational zeros of each polynomial function, then write each function in factored form.

1. $f(x) = 2x^3 + x^2 - 25x + 12$

2. $f(x) = x^3 - 11x^2 + 8x + 20$

_____

3. $f(x) = x^4 - x^3 - 26x^2 - 24x$

4. $f(x) = x^3 + 2x^2 - 13x + 10$

_____

Finding Complex Solutions of Polynomial Equations

LESSON 7-2

Reteach

$a + bi$ and $a - bi$ are <u>complex conjugates</u>.

Example Give the complex conjugate of each number.

$-2 - i$	$4 + 3i$	$5i$
Complex Conjugate: $-2 + i$	Complex Conjugate: $4 - 3i$	Complex Conjugate: $-5i$

Give the complex conjugate of each number.

1. $1 - i$

2. $-1 + 3i$

3. $-2i$

Complex Conjugate Root Theorem:	If $a + bi$ is an imaginary root of a polynomial equation with real-number coefficients, then $a - bi$ is also a root.

Example Write the polynomial function with the least degree and a leading coefficient of 1 that has zeros $1 - 2i$, 5, and –1.

Complex roots come in conjugate pairs → zeros are $1 - 2i$, $1 + 2i$, 5, and –1.

Write the function in factored form. $p(x) = \left(x - (1 - 2i)\right)\left(x - (1 + 2i)\right)(x - 5)(x + 1)$

Multiply the complex conjugate
factors using FOIL, then simplify.

$$= \left[x^2 - (1 + 2i)x - (1 - 2i)x + (1 - 2i)(1 + 2i)\right](x - 5)(x + 1)$$

$$= \left[x^2 + (-1 - 2i - 1 + 2i)x + (1 - 4i^2)\right](x - 5)(x + 1)$$

$$= \left(x^2 - 2x + 5\right)(x - 5)(x + 1)$$

Multiply the binomials.

$$= \left(x^2 - 2x + 5\right)\left(x^2 - 4x - 5\right)$$

Use the distributive property.

$$= x^2\left(x^2 - 4x - 5\right) - 2x\left(x^2 - 4x - 5\right) + 5\left(x^2 - 4x - 5\right)$$

$$= x^4 - 4x^3 - 5x^2 - 2x^3 + 8x^2 + 10x + 5x^2 - 20x - 25$$

Combine like terms.

$$= x^4 - 6x^3 + 8x^2 - 10x - 25$$

Write the polynomial function with the least degree and a leading coefficient of 1 that has the given zeros.

4. 1, –2, and $3 + i$

5. –3, 5, and $2i$

LESSON 8-1
Graphing Simple Rational Functions
Reteach

Graph of $y = \dfrac{1}{x}$

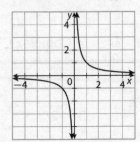

Vertical Asymptote: $x = 0$

Horizontal Asymptote: $y = 0$

Graph of $y = \dfrac{1}{x-1} + 2$

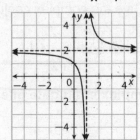

Vertical Asymptote: $x = 1$

Horizontal Asymptote: $y = 2$

Identify the horizontal and vertical asymptotes of the function.

1. $y = \dfrac{2}{x-5} - 3$ 2. $y = \dfrac{5}{x+3} - 1$ 3. $y = \dfrac{-2}{x-4} + 6$ 4. $y = \dfrac{-1}{x} + 7$

_____   _____   _____   _____

Example Write the function in the form $f(x) = \dfrac{a}{x-h} + k$ by using its graph.

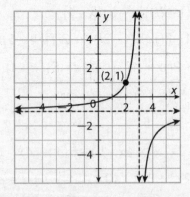

1. Find asymptotes from the graph.

   $x = 3$
   $y = -1$

2. Plug in h and k.

   $f(x) = \dfrac{a}{x-3} - 1$

3. Plug in the given point for x and y.

   $1 = \dfrac{a}{2-3} - 1$

   $2 = \dfrac{a}{-1}$

4. Solve for a.

   $-2 = a$

5. Write the function.

   $f(x) = \dfrac{-2}{x-3} - 1$

Write the functions in the form $f(x) = \dfrac{a}{x-h} + k$ by using the graph.

5.

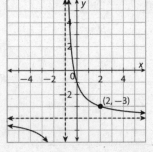

_____

6.

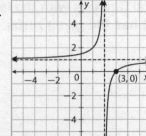

_____

LESSON 8-2
Graphing More Complicated Rational Functions
Reteach

Characteristics of Rational Functions

Vertical asymptotes	Zeros of denominator
Holes	Shared zeros of numerator and denominator
x-intercepts	Zeros of numerator
y-intercept	Value of function at $x = 0$, $f(0)$

Example

Find the vertical asymptote(s), hole(s), x-intercept(s), and y-intercept of: $f(x) = \dfrac{x^2 + 2x - 15}{x^2 - x - 6}$

Step 1 Write function in factored form.

$$f(x) = \frac{x^2 + 2x - 15}{x^2 - x - 6}$$
$$= \frac{(x + 5)(x - 3)}{(x - 3)(x + 2)}$$

Step 2 Find zeros of numerator and denominator.

Zeros of numerator: $x = -5$; $x = 3$
Zeros of denominator: $x = 3$; $x = -2$

Step 3 Find $f(0)$.

$$f(0) = \frac{0^2 + 2(0) - 15}{0^2 - 0 - 6} = \frac{5}{3}$$

Vertical Asymptote	Hole	x-intercept	y-intercept
$x = -2$	$x = 3$	$(-5, 0)$	$\left(0, \dfrac{5}{3}\right)$

Find the vertical asymptote(s), holes, x-intercept(s), and y-intercept of the functions.

1. $f(x) = \dfrac{x + 6}{x^2 - 4x - 12}$

    Vertical Asymptote(s): _____

    Hole(s): _____

    x-intercept(s): _____

    y-intercept: _____

2. $f(x) = \dfrac{x^2 + 7x + 12}{x^2 + 2x - 8}$

    Vertical Asymptote(s): _____

    Hole(s): _____

    x-intercept(s): _____

    y-intercept: _____

3. $f(x) = \dfrac{x^2 - 1}{x - 4}$

    Vertical Asymptote(s): _____

    Hole(s): _____

    x-intercept(s): _____

    y-intercept: _____

4. $f(x) = \dfrac{x + 2}{x^2 + 2}$

    Vertical Asymptote(s): _____

    Hole(s): _____

    x-intercept(s): _____

    y-intercept: _____

LESSON 9-1 Adding and Subtracting Rational Expressions
Reteach

To add or subtract rational expressions, they must have <u>common denominators</u>.

Example Add $\dfrac{x+2}{x-3} + \dfrac{x-1}{x+1}$.

Step 1 Multiply each rational expression by a common factor to get equivalent fractions with a common denominator.

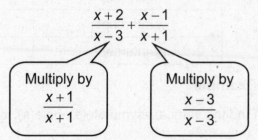

$$\dfrac{x+2}{x-3} \cdot \dfrac{x+1}{x+1} = \dfrac{(x+2)(x+1)}{(x-3)(x+1)} = \dfrac{x^2+3x+2}{(x-3)(x+1)} \qquad \dfrac{x-1}{x+1} \cdot \dfrac{x-3}{x-3} = \dfrac{(x-1)(x-3)}{(x+1)(x-3)} = \dfrac{x^2-4x+3}{(x-3)(x+1)}$$

Common Denominators

Step 2 Add the fractions.

$$\dfrac{x^2+3x+2}{(x-3)(x+1)} + \dfrac{x^2-4x+3}{(x+1)(x-3)} = \dfrac{2x^2-x+5}{(x+1)(x-3)}$$

Step 3 Give excluded values that make the denominator 0.

$$x \neq -1, \ x \neq 3$$

Add or subtract.

1. $\dfrac{3}{x+2} + \dfrac{x+1}{x-5}$

2. $\dfrac{4x}{x(x-2)} + \dfrac{x+7}{x}$

_____

_____

3. $\dfrac{x+8}{x-3} - \dfrac{x-2}{x-1}$

4. $\dfrac{3x}{x+6} - \dfrac{4}{(x-5)(x+6)}$

_____

_____

5. $\dfrac{x-5}{x+3} + \dfrac{x-10}{x^2-9}$

6. $\dfrac{x+4}{x^2-x-2} - \dfrac{x-1}{x^2+x-6}$

_____

_____

Multiplying and Dividing Rational Expressions
Reteach

Example Find the product and any excluded values. $\dfrac{x^2-2x-8}{x^2-1} \cdot \dfrac{x-1}{x^2-x-6}$

Step 1 Factor and multiply.

$$= \dfrac{(x-4)(x+2)(x-1)}{(x+1)(x-1)(x-3)(x+2)}$$

Step 2 Cancel common factors.

$$= \dfrac{(x-4)\cancel{(x+2)}\cancel{(x-1)}}{(x+1)\cancel{(x-1)}(x-3)\cancel{(x+2)}}$$

Step 3 Write simplified product.

$$= \dfrac{x-4}{(x+1)(x-3)}$$

Step 4 Note excluded values.

$$x \neq -2, x \neq -1, x \neq 1, x \neq 3$$

Find the product and any excluded values.

1. $\dfrac{x^2-5x-14}{x^2-16} \cdot \dfrac{x^2-x-20}{x+2}$

2. $\dfrac{x^2+6x-16}{x^2-3x} \cdot \dfrac{x}{x^2-3x+2}$

3. $\dfrac{x^2-14x+45}{6x^2-3x} \cdot \dfrac{3x}{2x^2-50}$

_____   _____   _____

Example Find the quotient and any excluded values. $\dfrac{x^2-x-12}{x+5} \div \dfrac{x^2+9x+18}{2x+10}$

Step 1 Rewrite as multiplication by reciprocal of divisor.

$$= \dfrac{x^2-x-12}{x+5} \cdot \dfrac{2x+10}{x^2+9x+18}$$

Step 2 Factor

$$= \dfrac{(x-4)(x+3)}{x+5} \cdot \dfrac{2(x+5)}{(x+6)(x+3)}$$

Step 3 Multiply

$$= \dfrac{2(x-4)(x+3)(x+5)}{(x+5)(x+6)(x+3)}$$

Step 4 Cancel common factors.

$$= \dfrac{2(x-4)\cancel{(x+3)}\cancel{(x+5)}}{\cancel{(x+5)}(x+6)\cancel{(x+3)}}$$

Step 5 Write simplified product.

$$= \dfrac{2(x-4)}{(x+6)}$$

Step 6 Note excluded values.

$$x \neq -6, x \neq -5, x \neq -3$$

Find the quotient and any excluded values.

4. $\dfrac{x^2-7x-18}{2x^2-32} \div \dfrac{x^2+x-2}{2x-8}$

5. $\dfrac{3x^2+6x+3}{x+5} \div \dfrac{3x+3}{x^2-25}$

6. $\dfrac{2x^2-3x+1}{5x^2} \div \dfrac{12x-6}{10x^3+5x^2}$

_____   _____   _____

Solving Rational Equations
Reteach

Rational equations can be solved algebraically by multiplying through by the LCD.

Example Solve the rational equation algebraically. $\dfrac{x}{x-2}+\dfrac{1}{x-4}=\dfrac{2}{x^2-6x+8}$

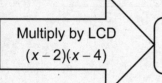

Multiply by LCD
$(x-2)(x-4)$

$\dfrac{x}{x-2}+\dfrac{1}{x-4}=\dfrac{2}{(x-2)(x-4)}$

Factor the denominator
$\dfrac{2}{(x-2)(x-4)}$

Step 1 Multiply each term by the LCD.

$$\dfrac{x}{x-2}(x-2)(x-4)+\dfrac{1}{x-4}(x-2)(x-4)=\dfrac{2}{(x-2)(x-4)}(x-2)(x-4)$$

Step 2 Cancel common factors.

$$\dfrac{x}{\cancel{x-2}}\cancel{(x-2)}(x-4)+\dfrac{1}{\cancel{x-4}}(x-2)\cancel{(x-4)}=\dfrac{2}{\cancel{(x-2)}\cancel{(x-4)}}\cancel{(x-2)}\cancel{(x-4)}$$

$$x(x-4)+(x-2)=2$$

Step 3 Simplify and solve the remaining equation.

$$x^2-4x+x-2=2$$
$$x^2-3x-4=0$$
$$(x-4)(x+1)=0$$
$$x=4 \text{ or } x=-1$$

Step 4 Check for extraneous solutions that are excluded values.

$x=4$ is an excluded value.
$x=-1$ is the solution.

Solve the rational equations algebraically.

1. $\dfrac{x}{x+1}=\dfrac{5x-10}{x^2-x-2}$

2. $\dfrac{x}{x+2}=\dfrac{6-x}{2x-1}$

_____

3. $\dfrac{x}{3}+\dfrac{x+1}{x+2}=x$

4. $\dfrac{2x}{x-5}=\dfrac{3x^2-15x}{x^2-9x+20}$

_____

LESSON 10-1

Inverses of Simple Quadratic and Cubic Functions
Reteach

If $f(x) = x^2$ then $f^{-1}(x) = \sqrt{x}$.

Restrict the domain of a quadratic function when finding its inverse to prevent negative numbers under the radical sign.

Example Restrict the domain of the quadratic function $f(x) = \dfrac{x^2}{6}$ and

find its inverse. Confirm the inverse relationship using composition. Graph the function and its inverse.

Step 1: Restrict the domain to $\{x \mid x \geq 0\}$.

Step 2: Replace $f(x)$ with y.
$$y = \frac{x^2}{6}$$

Step 3: Solve for x.
$$y = \frac{x^2}{6}$$
$$6y = x^2$$
$$\sqrt{6y} = x$$

Step 4: Switch x and y.
$$\sqrt{6x} = y$$

Step 5: Replace y with $f^{-1}(x)$.
$$f^{-1}(x) = \sqrt{6x}$$

Step 6: To confirm the inverse relationship, use the composition $f^{-1}(f(x))$.

$$f^{-1}(f(x)) = \sqrt{6\left(\frac{x^2}{6}\right)}$$
$$= \sqrt{\cancel{6}\left(\frac{x^2}{\cancel{6}}\right)}$$
$$= \sqrt{x^2}$$
$$= x$$

Step 7: Graph by reflecting $f(x)$ over the line $y = x$.

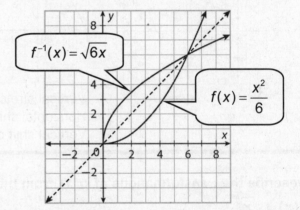

$f^{-1}(x) = \sqrt{6x}$

$f(x) = \dfrac{x^2}{6}$

Restrict the domain of the quadratic function and find its inverse. Confirm the inverse relationship using composition. Graph the function and its inverse.

1. $f(x) = 10x^2$

2. $f(x) = \dfrac{x^2}{7}$

3. $f(x) = x^2 - 6$

4. $y = x^2 + 2$

Graphing Square Root Functions
Reteach

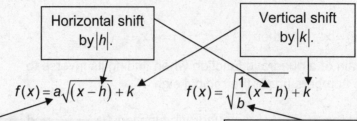

Horizontal shift by $|h|$.

Vertical shift by $|k|$.

$$f(x) = a\sqrt{(x-h)} + k \qquad f(x) = \sqrt{\frac{1}{b}(x-h)} + k$$

Vertical stretch or compression by $|a|$.
Reflect over *x*-axis if $a < 0$.

Horizontal stretch or compression by $|b|$.
Reflect over *y*-axis if $b < 0$.

$f(x) = \sqrt{x}$	$g(x) = 2.5\sqrt{x+2} - 1$	$g(x) = \sqrt{-(x-1)} - 2$

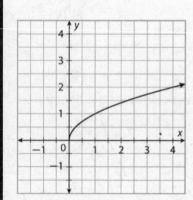 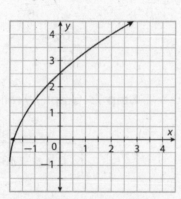 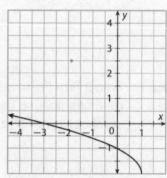

	Vertical stretch by 2.5 Horizontal shift left 2 units Vertical shift down 1 unit	Reflect across y-axis Horizontal shift right 1 unit Vertical shift down 2 units

Describe the transformations of $g(x)$ from the parent function

$f(x) = \sqrt{x}$.

1. $g(x) = -\sqrt{x-5} + 3$

2. $g(x) = \sqrt{2(x+4)} + 1$

_____

3. $g(x) = \sqrt{-\frac{1}{3}x - 6}$

4. $g(x) = 0.4\sqrt{x+8} - 10$

_____

LESSON 10-3

Graphing Cube Root Functions
Reteach

Parent Function: $f(x) = \sqrt[3]{x}$

Transformed Functions:

$f(x) = a\sqrt[3]{x - h} + k$

Vertical Stretch/Compression

Horizontal Shift

Vertical Shift

Reference Point (1, 1)

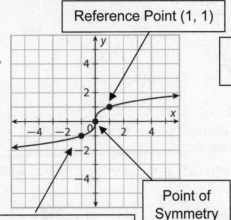

Reference Point (−1, −1)

Point of Symmetry (0, 0)

$f(x) = \sqrt[3]{\dfrac{1}{b}(x - h)} + k$

Horizontal Stretch/Compression

$f(x) = \sqrt[3]{x}$ $f(x) = a\sqrt[3]{x - h} + k$ OR $f(x) = \sqrt[3]{\dfrac{1}{b}(x - h)} + k$

$(0, 0) \longrightarrow (h, k)$ (h, k)

$(1, 1) \longrightarrow (h + 1, a + k)$ $(b + h, 1 + k)$

Example Write the function in the form $f(x) = a\sqrt[3]{x - h} + k$.

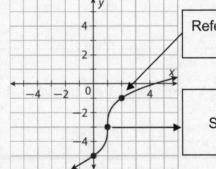

Reference Point (2, −1)

Point of Symmetry: (1, −3)

Step 1: Find h, k, and a.

$(h, k) = (1, -3)$

$(h + 1, a + k) = (1 + 1, a - 3) = (2, -1)$

$a - 3 = -1$

$a = 2$

Step 2: Give the function.

$f(x) = 2\sqrt[3]{x - 1} - 3$

Write the functions in the form given.

1. $f(x) = a\sqrt[3]{x - h} + k$

2. $f(x) = \sqrt[3]{\dfrac{1}{b}(x - h)} + k$

3. $f(x) = a\sqrt[3]{x - h} + k$

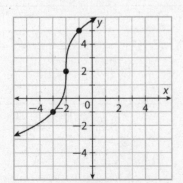
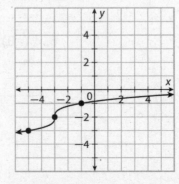
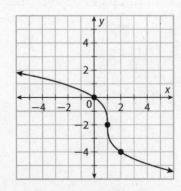

LESSON 11-1 Radical Expressions and Rational Exponents
Reteach

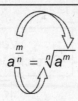

Numerator → Power

$$a^{\frac{m}{n}} = \sqrt[n]{a^m}$$

Denominator → Index

Translate the expressions with rational exponents into radical expressions, then simplify.

Example $625^{\frac{3}{4}} = \left(\sqrt[4]{625}\right)^3 = 5^3 = 125$ **Example** $(-243)^{\frac{2}{5}} = \left(\sqrt[5]{-243}\right)^2 = (-3)^2 = 9$

Simplify the expressions.

1. $25^{\frac{3}{2}}$

2. $(-27)^{\frac{2}{3}}$

3. $(-216)^{\frac{5}{3}}$

4. $(128)^{\frac{4}{5}}$

Translate the radical expressions into expressions with rational exponents, then simplify.

Example $\sqrt[4]{4^2} = 4^{\frac{2}{4}} = 4^{\frac{1}{2}} = 2$ **Example** $\sqrt[3]{6^9} = 6^{\frac{9}{3}} = 6^3 = 216$

Simplify the expressions.

5. $\sqrt[4]{9^2}$

6. $\sqrt[4]{7^8}$

7. $\sqrt[4]{\left(\frac{1}{16}\right)^3}$

8. $\sqrt[3]{(-8)^5}$

LESSON 11-2
Simplifying Radical Expressions
Reteach

Rational exponents are subject to the same properties as integer exponents.

Product of Powers	Quotient of Powers	Power of a Power	Power of a Product	Power of a Quotient	Negative Exponent
$a^m \cdot a^n = a^{m+n}$	$\dfrac{a^m}{a^n} = a^{m-n}$	$\left(a^m\right)^n = a^{m \cdot n}$	$(ab)^m = a^m b^m$	$\left(\dfrac{a}{b}\right)^m = \dfrac{a^m}{b^m}$	$a^{-m} = \dfrac{1}{a^m}$

Example Simplify the expressions. Assume all variables are positive.

$$\left(4x^{\frac{1}{3}}\right)^{\frac{3}{2}} \qquad\qquad\qquad\qquad \left(\frac{5y^{\frac{3}{4}}}{y^{\frac{1}{4}}}\right)^2$$

Power of a Product

$$\left(4x^{\frac{1}{3}}\right)^{\frac{3}{2}} = 4^{\frac{3}{2}}\left(x^{\frac{1}{3}}\right)^{\frac{3}{2}}$$

Quotient of Powers

$$\left(\frac{5y^{\frac{3}{4}}}{y^{\frac{1}{4}}}\right)^2 = \left(5 \cdot y^{\left(\frac{3}{4}-\frac{1}{4}\right)}\right)^2 = \left(5 \cdot y^{\frac{2}{4}}\right)^2 = \left(5y^{\frac{1}{2}}\right)^2$$

Power of a Power

$$= 8\left(x^{\frac{1}{3} \cdot \frac{3}{2}}\right)$$

Power of a Product

$$= 5^2\left(y^{\frac{1}{2}}\right)^2$$

Simplify.

$$= 8x^{\frac{1}{2}}$$

Simplify.

$$= 25y^{\frac{1}{2} \cdot 2} = 25y$$

Simplify the expressions. Assume all variables are positive.

1. $\left(9a^{\frac{2}{3}}\right)^{\frac{5}{2}}$

2. $\left(\dfrac{2b^{\frac{3}{5}}}{b^{\frac{1}{5}}}\right)^2$

3. $\left(27x^{\frac{3}{4}}\right)^{\frac{2}{3}}$

4. $\left(\dfrac{x^{\frac{1}{2}}}{x^{\frac{5}{2}}}\right)^3$

5. $\left(\dfrac{625y^{-3}}{y}\right)^{\frac{1}{4}}$

6. $\left(\dfrac{z^{\frac{5}{6}} \cdot z^{\frac{2}{3}}}{z^{\frac{1}{2}}}\right)^{\frac{1}{5}}$

LESSON 11-3

Solving Radical Equations

Reteach

To solve square root equations, you will need to raise both sides to the 2nd power.

Example Solve $\sqrt{x+7} - 3 = 9$.

Isolate the square root on one side.	Square both sides.	Solve for x.	Check for extraneous solutions.
$\sqrt{x+7} - 3 = 9$ $\sqrt{x+7} = 12$	$\left(\sqrt{x+7}\right)^2 = \left(12\right)^2$ $x + 7 = 144$	$x = 144 - 7$ $x = 137$	$\sqrt{137+7} - 3 \overset{?}{=} 9$ $\sqrt{144} - 3 \overset{?}{=} 9$ $12 - 3 \overset{?}{=} 9$ $9 = 9$ $x = 137$ is a solution.

Example Solve $(3x-5)^{\frac{1}{2}} = x - 5$.

Square both sides.	Simplify and solve by factoring.	Check for extraneous solutions.	Check for extraneous solutions.
$\left((3x-5)^{\frac{1}{2}}\right)^2 = (x-5)^2$ $3x - 5 = x^2 - 10x + 25$	$0 = x^2 - 13x + 30$ $0 = (x-10)(x-3)$ $x = 10$ $\;or\;$ $x = 3$	$(3(10)-5)^{\frac{1}{2}} \overset{?}{=} 10 - 5$ $(30-5)^{\frac{1}{2}} \overset{?}{=} 5$ $25^{\frac{1}{2}} \overset{?}{=} 5$ $5 = 5$ $x = 10$ is a solution.	$(3(3)-5)^{\frac{1}{2}} \overset{?}{=} 3 - 5$ $(9-5)^{\frac{1}{2}} \overset{?}{=} -2$ $4^{\frac{1}{2}} \overset{?}{=} -2$ $2 \neq -2$ $x = 3$ is not a solution.

Simplify each equation. Make sure to check for extraneous solutions.

1. $\sqrt{x-10} + 4 = 7$

2. $x = \sqrt{2x-1}$

3. $\sqrt{2x+10} = x + 1$

_____ _____ _____

4. $3 = (x+6)^{\frac{1}{2}} - 1$

5. $(x+8)^{\frac{1}{2}} = x + 2$

6. $(5x)^{\frac{1}{2}} = 3$

_____ _____ _____

LESSON 12-1 Arithmetic Sequences
Reteach

An **arithmetic sequence** is a list of numbers (or **terms**) with a **common difference** between each number.

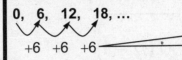

0, 6, 12, 18, ...

+6 +6 +6

Find how much you add or subtract to move from term to term.

The difference between terms is constant.

In this example, $f(1) = 0$, $f(2) = 6$, $f(3) = 12$, $f(4) = 18$, ...
The common difference is 6.

Use the common difference d to write rules for an arithmetic sequence.

A **recursive** rule has this general form: $f(1) = a$ and $f(n) = f(n - 1) + d$ for $n \geq 2$

Substitute $a = 0$ and $d = 6$: $f(1) = 0$ and $f(n) = f(n - 1) + 6$ for $n \geq 2$

An **explicit** rule has this general form: $f(n) = a + d(n - 1)$

Substitute $a = 0$ and $d = 6$ from the example: $f(n) = 0 + 6(n - 1) = -6 + 6n$

Indicate whether each sequence is arithmetic. If so, find the common difference, and write an explicit rule for the sequence.

1. –1, 2, –3, 4, ...

2. 14, 12, 10, 8, ...

3. 3, 6, 9, 27, ...

_____   _____   _____

_____   _____   _____

Write a recursive rule and an explicit rule for each sequence.

4. –5, 0, 5, 10, ...

5. 7, 4, 1, –2, ...

6. 4, 7, 10, 13, ...

_____   _____   _____

_____   _____   _____

Use the explicit rule given to write the first three terms for each sequence.

7. $f(n) = 6 + 3(n - 1)$

8. $f(n) = 16 + \left(-\dfrac{1}{2}\right)(n - 1)$

9. $f(n) = 20 + (-10)(n - 1)$

_____   _____   _____

Geometric Sequences

LESSON 12-2

Reteach

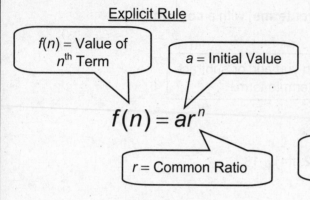

Explicit Rule

$f(n)$ = Value of nth Term

a = Initial Value

$$f(n) = ar^n$$

r = Common Ratio

Recursive Rule

r = Common Ratio

$$f(n) = r \cdot f(n-1)$$

$f(n)$ = Value of nth Term

$f(n-1)$ = Value of Previous Term

Example Write the explicit and recursive rules for a geometric sequence given the table of values.

n	0	1	2	3	4	...
f(n)	7	14	28	56	112	...

Step 1: Find the common ratio, r, by dividing two successive terms.

$$r = \frac{f(2)}{f(1)} = \frac{28}{14} = 2$$

Step 2: Find the initial value, a, from the table.

$$a = f(0) = 7$$

Step 3: Write the explicit rule by plugging in a and r.

$$f(n) = 7 \cdot (2)^n$$

Step 4: Write the recursive rule. ($n \geq 1$ because the initial value, 7, is for $n = 0$.)

$$f(n) = 2 \cdot f(n-1)$$
$$n \geq 1$$
$$f(0) = 7$$

Write the explicit and recursive rules for a geometric sequence given a table of values.

1.

n	0	1	2	3	4	...
f(n)	0.5	1.5	4.5	13.5	40.5	...

2.

n	0	1	2	3	4	...
f(n)	6	3	1.5	0.75	0.375	...

3.

n	0	1	2	3	4	...
f(n)	$\frac{1}{4}$	1	4	16	64	...

4.

n	0	1	2	3	4	...
f(n)	162	18	2	$\frac{2}{9}$	$\frac{2}{81}$	...

LESSON
12-3

Geometric Series

Reteach

To find the sum of a **finite geometric series**, you can use the **summation formula**,

$S(n) = a\left(\dfrac{1-r^n}{1-r}\right)$, where a is the initial term of the series, r is the common ratio between the

terms, and n is the number of terms in the series. To find the sum, you must identify the values of a, r, and n using the information given in the problem. Sometimes a, r, and n are given. Other times you must perform calculations to determine their values.

Examples

Find the sum of the geometric series $-3 - 12 - 48 - 192 - 768$.

- Identify a. The first term is $a = -3$.

- Identify n. There are $n = 5$ terms in the series.

- Determine r. The common ratio is $r = -12 \div (-3) = 4$.

- Use the summation formula:

$$S(n) = a\left(\frac{1-r^n}{1-r}\right) = -3\left(\frac{1-4^5}{1-4}\right) = -3\left(\frac{-1023}{-3}\right) = -3(341) = -1023$$

Find the sum of the geometric series $4 - 12 + 36 - \ldots + 2916$.

- Identify a. The first term is $a = 4$.

- Determine r. The common ratio is $r = -12 \div (4) = -3$.

- Determine n. Set the last term in the series equal to the explicit formula for the associated geometric series:

$$a \cdot r^{n-1} = 2916$$
$$4 \cdot (-3)^{n-1} = 2916$$
$$(-3)^{n-1} = 729$$
$$(-3)^{n-1} = (-3)^6$$
$$n - 1 = 6$$
$$n = 7$$

- Use the summation formula.

$$S(n) = a\left(\frac{1-r^n}{1-r}\right) = 4\left(\frac{1-(-3)^7}{1-(-3)}\right) = 4\left(\frac{2188}{4}\right) = 4(547) = 2188$$

Find the sum of each geometric series.

1. $2 - 8 + 32 - 128 + 512$

2. $4 + 8 + 16 + \ldots + 2048$

_____

LESSON 13-1

Exponential Growth Functions
Reteach

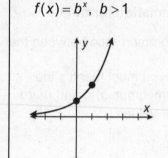

$f(x) = b^x, \ b > 1$

Horizontal Asymptote

$y = 0 \longrightarrow y = k$

Reference Point

$(0, 1) \longrightarrow (h, a + k)$

Reference Point

$(1, b) \longrightarrow (1 + h, ab + k)$

$g(x) = ab^{x-h} + k$

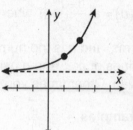

Example State the domain and range of the given function. Then identify the new values of the reference points and the asymptote. Use these values to graph the function.

$g(x) = 4(2^{x-3}) - 1$

Step 1: Identify the parameters a, b, h, and k.

$a = 4, \ b = 2, \ h = 3, \ k = -1$

Step 2: Identify the horizontal asymptote.

$y = -1$

Step 3: Identify the reference points.

$(h, a + k) = (3, 4 + (-1)) = (3, 3)$

$(1 + h, ab + k) = (1 + 3, (4)(2) + (-1)) = (4, 7)$

Step 4: Graph the function.

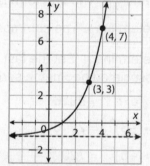

Step 5: Give the domain and range.

Domain $\{x | -\infty < x < \infty\}$,

Range $\{y | y > -1\}$

State the domain and range of the given function. Then identify the new values of the reference points and the asymptote. Use these values to graph the function.

1. $g(x) = 3(4^{x-1}) + 1$

2. $g(x) = \dfrac{1}{2}(2^{x-3}) - 4$

3. $g(x) = 10^{x+5} - 5$

4. $g(x) = 5(3^{x-1}) - 2$

LESSON 13-2

Exponential Decay Functions

Reteach

$f(x) = b^x,\ 0 < b < 1$

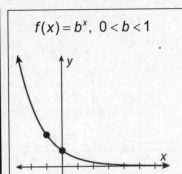

$g(x) = ab^{x-h} + k$

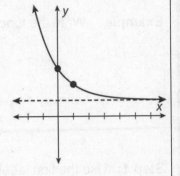

Horizontal Asymptote

$y = 0 \longrightarrow y = k$

Reference Point

$(0, 1) \longrightarrow (h,\ a + k)$

Reference Point

$\left(-1,\ \dfrac{1}{b}\right) \longrightarrow \left(h-1,\ \dfrac{a}{b} + k\right)$

Example State the parent function, decay factor, asymptote, and reference points for the given function.

$$g(x) = 3\left(\dfrac{1}{5}\right)^{x-2} + 4$$

Parent function	Decay factor	Asymptote	Reference points
$f(x) = \left(\dfrac{1}{5}\right)^x$	$b = \dfrac{1}{5}$	$y = 4$	$(h,\ a+k) = (2,\ 3+4) = (2,\ 7)$ $\left(h-1,\ \dfrac{a}{b}+k\right) = \left(2-1,\ \dfrac{3}{\frac{1}{5}}+4\right) = (1,\ 19)$

State the parent function, decay factor, asymptote, and reference points for the given function.

1. $g(x) = 4\left(\dfrac{1}{2}\right)^{x-3} - 2$

2. $g(x) = 7\left(\dfrac{1}{10}\right)^{x+2} + 1$

3. $g(x) = 6(0.3)^{x+3} - 3$

4. $g(x) = -\left(\dfrac{1}{4}\right)^{x-6} - 5$

5. $g(x) = \left(\dfrac{2}{3}\right)^x + 9$

6. $g(x) = -2\left(\dfrac{3}{10}\right)^{x-4} + 7$

The Base e
Reteach

Using reference points, you can find the function for a graph of the form $g(x) = a \cdot e^{x-h} + k$.

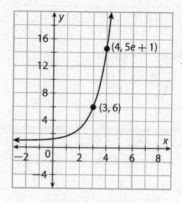

Example   Write the function whose graph is shown.

Step 1: Use the first labeled reference point to find h.

$$(h, a + k) = (3, 6)$$
$$h = 3$$

Step 2: Use the second labeled reference point to find a and k.

$$(1 + h, ae + k) = (4, 5e + 1)$$
$$ae + k = 5e + 1$$
$$a = 5$$
$$k = 1$$

Step 3: Write the equation using a, h, and, k.

$$g(x) = 5e^{x-3} + 1$$

Write the function whose graph is shown.

1.

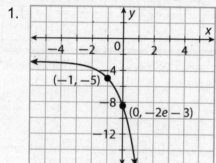

2.

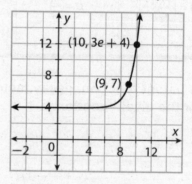

3.

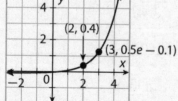

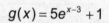

4.

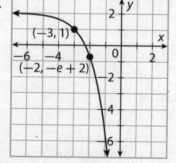

LESSON 13-4 Compound Interest
Reteach

There are three formulas used to model investments that earn **compounding interest**. In each formula, V represents the value of the account at time t, r is the annual interest rate, and P is the principal, or the initial amount invested.

 I. When interest is compounded once per year: $V(t) = P(1+r)^t$

 II. When interest compounded n times per year: $V(t) = P\left(1+\dfrac{r}{n}\right)^{nt}$

  If the account is compounded: *monthly* then $n = 12$, *quarterly* then $n = 4$, *semiannually* then $n = 2$, *daily* then $n = 365$.

 III. When interest is compounded continuously: $V(t) = Pe^{rt}$

When solving compound interest problems where V, P, and r (and sometimes n) are given, you must solve for t. To do this, first determine which formula to use. Then write a model that represents the problem. Solve for t using a graphing calculator. Graph each side of the equation. The x-value of the point of intersection is the solution.

Example

Peter opens an account with $6000 that earns 4.25% interest, compounded semiannually. How long will it take for the account value to be $8000?

Step 1	Step 2	Step 3
Since the account is compounded semiannually, $n = 2$. Use $V(t) = P\left(1+\dfrac{r}{n}\right)^{nt}$.	Substitute using the values given for V, P, r, and n, and simplify. $V(t) = P\left(1+\dfrac{r}{n}\right)^{nt}$ $8000 = 6000\left(1+\dfrac{0.0425}{2}\right)^{2t}$ $8000 = 6000(1.02125)^{2t}$	Graph each side of the equation and use the intersection feature to solve for t. Intersection X=6.8406584 Y=8000

It will take about 6.8 years for the account value to be $8000.

Solve.

1. Fatima opens an account with $1300 that earns 3.5% interest, compounded monthly. How long will it take the account value to be $2500?

2. Eli opens an account with $10,000 that earns 6% interest, compounded continuously. How long will it take the account value to be $20,000?

_____

_____

LESSON
14-1

Fitting Exponential Functions to Data

Reteach

To find an exponential model for a data set, identify the <u>initial value</u> and the <u>growth or decay factor</u>.

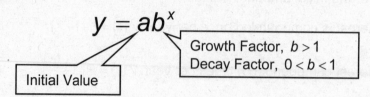

$$y = ab^x$$

Growth Factor, $b > 1$
Decay Factor, $0 < b < 1$

Initial Value

Example Create an approximate exponential model for the data set.

x	y
1.8	4.2
3.2	8.7
4.5	9.1
5.7	11.3
7.1	18.5

Step 1: Find the initial value of the data set from the table.

$a = 4.2$

Step 2: Approximate the growth factor by dividing successive y-values.

$b = \dfrac{11.3}{9.1} = 1.2$

Step 3: Write the function.

$y = 4.2 \cdot 1.2^x$

Step 4: Check the fit by graphing.

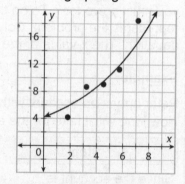

Create an approximate exponential model for the data set.

1.

x	y
0	1.2
1	1.6
2	2.0
3	2.6
4	3.4

_____

2.

x	y
0	56
1	50.4
2	45.4
3	40.8
4	36.7

_____

3.

x	y
0	−20
1	−22
2	−24
3	−27
4	−29

_____

4.

x	y
0	3.0
1	6.3
2	13.2
3	27.8
4	58.3

_____

5.

x	y
0	100
1	80
2	64
3	51
4	41

_____

6.

x	y
0	−5
1	−2.5
2	−1.3
3	−0.6
4	−0.3

_____

LESSON 14-2
Choosing Among Linear, Quadratic, and Exponential Models
Reteach

Using your graphing calculator, you can perform linear, quadratic, or exponential regression on a data set to find the best-fit model. Also, you can plot the regression function with a scatter plot of the data to visually test its fit.

Example

x	y
3	21
12	25
45	49
67	75
90	119

Enter the data into L1 and L2.

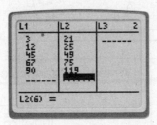

Create a scatter plot of the data using ZOOMSTAT.

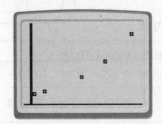

Linear Regression	Quadratic Regression	Exponential Regression
	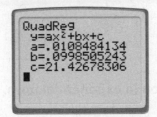	

Plot $y = 1.077x + 11.064$ Plot $y = .0108x^2 + .0999x + 21.427$ Plot $y = 19.771 \cdot 1.02^x$

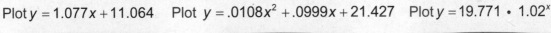
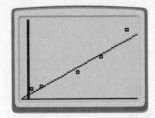
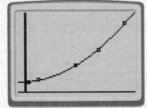

Using a graphing calculator, perform the given regression on the data set and give the best-fit model.

1.	x	y
	1.2	1.7
	2.8	7.0
	3.4	11.8
	5.9	105.1
	7.5	426.3

Exponential

_____

2.	x	y
	23	63
	34	87
	59	141
	71	167
	94	216

Linear

_____

3.	x	y
	3.4	63.4
	8.1	45.5
	12.9	73.8
	15.2	87.4
	17.3	99.8

Quadratic

_____

4.	x	y
	5	157
	10	122
	15	94
	20	73
	25	56

Exponential

_____

LESSON
15-1
Defining and Evaluating a Logarithmic Function
Reteach

Exponential Form   Logarithmic Form

$$b^x = a \qquad \log_b a = x$$

Example

Write the exponential equation in logarithmic form. $3^4 = 81$	Write the logarithmic equation in exponential form. $\log_5 125 = 3$
$3^4 = 81 \rightarrow \log_3 81 = 4$	$\log_5 125 = 3 \rightarrow 5^3 = 125$

Write the given exponential equation in logarithmic form.

1. $2^6 = 64$

2. $4^{-2} = \dfrac{1}{16}$

3. $\dfrac{1}{3}^3 = \dfrac{1}{27}$

_____   _____   _____

Write the given logarithmic equation in exponential form.

4. $\log_7 49 = 2$

5. $\log_2 \dfrac{1}{16} = -4$

6. $\log_8 48 = x$

_____   _____   _____

You can evaluate logarithms using your knowledge of exponents.

Example

$\log_4 64$	What power of 4 is 64?	$4^? = 64$ $4^3 = 64$ $\log_4 64 = 3$
$\log_2 \dfrac{1}{8}$	What power of 2 is $\dfrac{1}{8}$?	$2^? = \dfrac{1}{8}$ $2^{-3} = \dfrac{1}{8}$ $\log_2 \dfrac{1}{8} = -3$

Evaluate each logarithm.

7. $\log_5 625$

8. $\log_8 2$

9. $\log_3 \dfrac{1}{9}$

_____   _____   _____

Graphing Logarithmic Functions

LESSON 15-2

Reteach

	$f(x) = \log_b x$	$g(x) = a\log_b(x - h) + k$
Graph	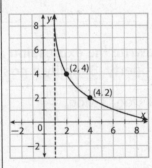(graph with (1, 0) and (b, 1))	a — $\lvert a \rvert > 1 \rightarrow$ vertical stretch by $\lvert a \rvert$ $\lvert a \rvert < 1 \rightarrow$ vertical compression by $\lvert a \rvert$ $a < 0 \rightarrow$ reflection over x-axis
		h — $h > 0 \rightarrow$ shift right h units $h < 0 \rightarrow$ shift left h units
		k — $k > 0 \rightarrow$ shift up k units $k < 0 \rightarrow$ shift down k units
Vertical Asymptote	$x = 0 \longrightarrow$	$x = h$
Reference Point	$(1, 0) \longrightarrow$	$(1 + h, k)$
Reference Point	$(b, 1) \longrightarrow$	$(b + h, a + k)$

Example Graph $g(x) = -2\log_3(x - 1) + 4$ by applying the transformations of $f(x) = \log_3 x$ to the asymptote $x = 0$ and to the reference points $(1, 0)$ and $(b, 1)$.

$g(x) = -2\log_3(x - 1) + 4$		
$a = 2$ $\lvert a \rvert = 2 \rightarrow$ vertical stretch by 2 $a < 0 \rightarrow$ reflection over x-axis $h = 1$ $1 > 0 \rightarrow$ shift right 1 unit $k = 4$ $4 > 0 \rightarrow$ shift up 4 units	Vertical Asymptote $x = 1$ Reference Point $(1 + h, k) = (1 + 1, 4) = (2, 4)$ Reference Point $(b + h, a + k) = (3 + 1, -2 + 4) = (4, 2)$	(graph with points (2, 4) and (4, 2))

Graph $g(x)$. State the vertical asymptote and reference points.

1. $g(x) = 5\log_2(x + 2) - 1$

2. $g(x) = -\log(x + 5) + 2$

3. $g(x) = 3\log_6(x - 4) - 2$

4. $g(x) = -2\log_8(x + 9) + 3$

LESSON 16-1 Properties of Logarithms
Reteach

Product Property	Quotient Property	Power Property
$\log_b (mn) = \log_b m + \log_b n$	$\log_b \left(\dfrac{m}{n}\right) = \log_b m - \log_b n$	$\log_b m^n = n \log_b m$

Use properties to rewrite the expressions as a single logarithm.

Example $\log_4 256 + \log_4 \dfrac{1}{4}$	Example $\log_3 81 - \log_3 3$	Example $\log_{\frac{1}{3}} \left(\dfrac{1}{3}\right)^4$
$\log_4 256 + \log_4 \dfrac{1}{4} = \log_4 \left(256 \cdot \dfrac{1}{4}\right)$ $= \log_4 64$ $= 3$	$\log_3 81 - \log_3 3 = \log_3 \left(\dfrac{81}{3}\right)$ $= \log_3 27$ $= 3$	$\log_{\frac{1}{3}} \left(\dfrac{1}{3}\right)^4 = 4\log_{\frac{1}{3}} \left(\dfrac{1}{3}\right)$ $= 4 \cdot 1$ $= 4$

Rewrite the expression as a single logarithm using the product property. Simplify if possible.

1. $\log_2 \dfrac{1}{8} + \log_2 128$

2. $\log x + \log y$

3. $\log_{\frac{1}{5}} 20 + \log_{\frac{1}{5}} \dfrac{1}{100}$

_____   _____   _____

Rewrite the expression as a single logarithm using the quotient property. Simplify if possible.

4. $\log_8 3 - \log_8 \dfrac{1}{192}$

5. $\log_7 (ab) - \log_7 b$

6. $\log 2000 - \log 200$

_____   _____   _____

Rewrite the expression using the power property. Simplify if possible.

7. $\log_6 6^x$

8. $\log_a a^5$

9. $\log x^2$

_____   _____   _____

Solving Exponential Equations

LESSON 16-2

Reteach

An **exponential equation** contains an expression that has a variable as an exponent.

$5^x = 25$ is an exponential equation.

$x = 2$, since $5^2 = 25$.

Remember: You can take the logarithm of both sides of an exponential equation. Then use other properties of logarithms to solve.

> If $x = y$, then
> $\log x = \log y$
> ($x > 0$ and $y > 0$).

Solve $6^{x+2} = 500$.

Step 1: Since the variable is in the exponent, take the log of both sides.

$$6^{x+2} = 500$$
$$\log 6^{x+2} = \log 500$$

Step 2: Use the Power Property of Logarithms: $\log a^p = p \log a$.

$$\log 6^{x+2} = \log 500$$
$$(x + 2) \log 6 = \log 500$$

> "Bring down" the exponent to multiply.

Step 3: Isolate the variable. Divide both sides by log 6.

$$(x + 2) \log 6 = \log 500$$
$$x + 2 = \frac{\log 500}{\log 6}$$

Step 4: Solve for x. Subtract 2 from both sides.

$$x = \frac{\log 500}{\log 6} - 2$$

Step 5: Use a calculator to approximate x.

$$x \approx 1.468$$

Step 6: Use a calculator to check.

$$6^{1.468+2} \approx 499.607$$

Solve and check. The first two are started for you.

1. $4^{-x} = 32$

     $\log 4^{-x} = \log 32$

     $-x \log 4 = \log 32$

     _____

     _____

2. $3^{4x} = 90$

     $\log 3^{4x} = \log 90$

     $4x \log 3 = \log 90$

     _____

     _____

3. $5^{x-3} = 600$

     _____

     _____

     _____

     _____

Angles of Rotation and Radian Measure

LESSON 17-1

Reteach

To convert angle measures from radians to degrees or from degrees to radians, use the following rule:

Radians → Degrees

Multiply by $\dfrac{180}{\pi}$.

Degrees → Radians

Multiply by $\dfrac{\pi}{180}$.

Example

	Step 1	Step 2
Convert 140° to radians.	Choose the conversion factor. Multiply by $\dfrac{\pi}{180}$.	Multiply, leave in terms of π. $140 \cdot \dfrac{\pi}{180} = \dfrac{7\pi}{9}$
	Step 1	**Step 2**
Convert $\dfrac{4\pi}{7}$ radians to degrees.	Choose the conversion factor. Multiply by $\dfrac{180}{\pi}$.	Multiply, round to nearest degree. $\dfrac{4\pi}{7} \cdot \dfrac{180}{\pi} = \dfrac{720}{7} \approx 103°$

Convert each measure from degrees to radians or from radians to degrees.

1. 160° = _____ radians

2. $\dfrac{4\pi}{5}$ radians = _____ degrees

To find the length of the intercepted arc s for a given angle θ and radius r use the following formula:

$$s = r\theta$$

Example Find the length of the intercepted arc for an angle of 260° with radius 3 inches.

Step 1	Step 2
Convert angle to radians. $260 \cdot \dfrac{\pi}{180} = \dfrac{13\pi}{9}$	Substitute into the formula $s = r\theta$ and calculate. $s = r\theta = (3)\left(\dfrac{13\pi}{9}\right) = \dfrac{13\pi}{3} \approx 13.61$

The intercepted arc length is about 13.6 inches.

Find the length of the intercepted arc for the given angle and radius.

3. $\theta = 18°$, radius = 12 cm

4. $\theta = 105°$, radius = 6 inches

_____

_____

5. $\theta = 256°$, radius = 1.4 m

6. $\theta = 310°$, radius = 45 mm

_____

_____

LESSON 17-2

Defining and Evaluating the Basic Trigonometric Functions

Reteach

To evaluate trigonometric functions for reference angles, you can use a special right triangle made with the *x*-axis in the appropriate quadrant.

Here are the side lengths of special right triangles in the unit circle and the signs of the trigonometric functions in each quadrant.

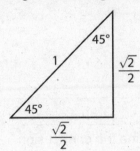 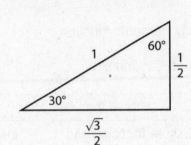 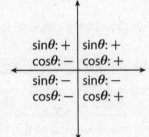

Example

Evaluate the trigonometric function without using a calculator: sin(−225°).

Step 1	Step 2	Step 3
Identify the coterminal angle between 0 and 360°.	Use a special right triangle in the appropriate quadrant.	Choose the correct side length for sine or cosine and use the correct sign.
−225° + 360° = 135°		$\sin(-225°) = \dfrac{\sqrt{2}}{2}$

Evaluate the trigonometric functions without using a calculator.

1. sin 420°

2. cos(−120°)

_____

_____

3. sin(−60°)

4. cos 495°

_____

_____

LESSON 17-3

Using a Pythagorean Identity

Reteach

The Pythagorean Identity, $\sin^2 \theta + \cos^2 \theta = 1$, can be rearranged to solve for $\sin \theta$ and $\cos \theta$.

$$\sin \theta = \pm\sqrt{1 - \cos^2 \theta} \qquad\qquad \cos \theta = \pm\sqrt{1 - \sin^2 \theta}$$

Example

Find the approximate value of the trigonometric function.

Given that $\cos \theta = -0.285$ where $\dfrac{\pi}{2} < \theta < \pi$, find $\sin \theta$.

Step 1	Step 2	Step 3
Use the correct version of the Pythagorean Identity.	Substitute for $\cos \theta$ and evaluate using a calculator. Round to the nearest thousandth.	Determine the correct sign.
Since the cosine is given and sine is desired, use $\sin \theta = \pm\sqrt{1 - \cos^2 \theta}$.	$\sin \theta = \pm\sqrt{1 - (-0.285)^2}$ $\approx \pm 0.959$	$\dfrac{\pi}{2} < \theta < \pi$ refers to Quadrant II where $\sin \theta > 0$. So, $\sin \theta \approx 0.959$.

Find the approximate value of each trigonometric function.

1. Given that $\cos \theta = 0.929$ where $0 < \theta < \dfrac{\pi}{2}$, find $\sin \theta$.

   _____

2. Given that $\sin \theta = 0.548$ where $\dfrac{\pi}{2} < \theta < \pi$, find $\cos \theta$.

   _____

3. Given that $\cos \theta = -0.403$ where $\pi < \theta < \dfrac{3\pi}{2}$, find $\sin \theta$.

   _____

4. Given that $\sin \theta = -0.172$ where $\dfrac{3\pi}{2} < \theta < 2\pi$, find $\cos \theta$.

   _____

LESSON 18-1

Stretching, Compressing, and Reflecting Sine and Cosine Graphs
Reteach

For a sine function, $y = a \sin\left(\dfrac{1}{b}x\right)$.

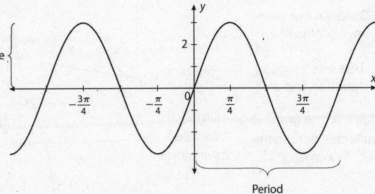

Amplitude = $|a|$

Period = $2\pi \cdot b$

If $a < 0$, the graph is reflected across the x-axis.

Example Write the function shown in the graph above.

Step 1	Step 2	Step 3
Determine the amplitude and reflection to find a.	Determine the period and calculate $\dfrac{1}{b}$.	Write the function in the form $y = a \sin\left(\dfrac{1}{b}x\right)$.
The graph is not reflected, so $a > 0$. The distance from the midline to the maximum is 3. So, $a = 3$.	The period is π radians. $2\pi \cdot b = \pi$ $b = \dfrac{\pi}{2\pi} = \dfrac{1}{2}$. So, $\dfrac{1}{b} = 2$.	$y = 3 \sin 2x$

Write the function shown in the graph in the form $y = a \sin\left(\dfrac{1}{b}x\right)$.

1.

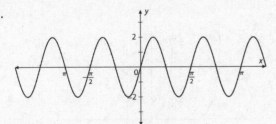

2.

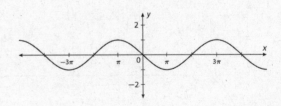

_____

_____

Stretching, Compressing, and Reflecting Tangent Graphs
Reteach

For a tangent function, $f(x) = a\tan\left(\dfrac{1}{b}x\right)$:

Distance between
asymptotes $= \pi b$

Use a reference
point to find a.

Reference
point

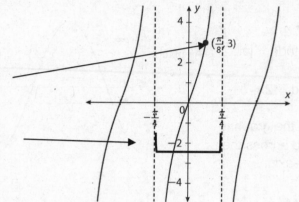

$(\frac{\pi}{8}, 3)$

If $a < 0$, the graph is
reflected across the
x-axis.

Distance
between
asymptotes

Distance between
asymptotes

Example Write the function shown in the graph above.

Step 1	Step 2	Step 3
Determine the distance between asymptotes and calculate b.	Plug the reference point and b into $y = a\tan\left(\dfrac{1}{b}x\right)$ to calculate a.	Write the function in the form $f(x) = a\tan\left(\dfrac{1}{b}x\right)$.
$\dfrac{\pi}{4} - \left(-\dfrac{\pi}{4}\right) = \pi b$ $\dfrac{\pi}{2} = \pi b \qquad$ So, $\dfrac{1}{b} = 2$ $\dfrac{1}{2} = b$	$3 = a\tan\left(2 \cdot \dfrac{\pi}{8}\right)$ $3 = a\tan\left(\dfrac{\pi}{4}\right) \qquad$ So, $a = 3$ $3 = a \cdot 1$	$f(x) = 3\tan 2x$

Write the function shown in the graph.

1.

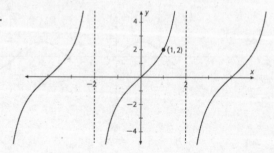

$(1, 2)$

2.

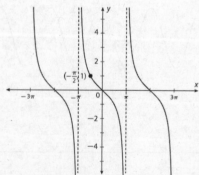

$\left(-\dfrac{\pi}{2}, 1\right)$

_____   _____

LESSON 18-3	**Translating Trigonometric Graphs**
	Reteach

To find the sine function, $f(x) = a \sin\left[\dfrac{1}{b}(x-h)\right] + k$, shown in a given

graph, identify the parameters *a, b, h,* and *k* using the midline, amplitude, period, and a starting point.

Example   Write a sine function for the graph.

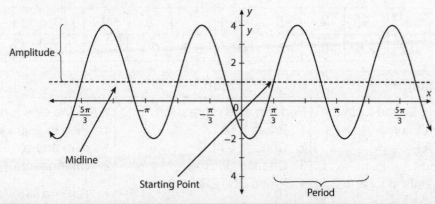

Step 1	Step 2	Step 3	Step 4
Find the midline.	Find the amplitude.	Find a starting point.	Find the period.
$x = 1$ is the midline, so the graph has been translated up 1.	The distance from the midline to the maximum is 3, so the amplitude is 3.	A starting point for one cycle is $\left(\dfrac{\pi}{3}, 1\right)$, so the graph was translated right $\dfrac{\pi}{3}$.	The length of one cycle is $\dfrac{4\pi}{3} - \dfrac{\pi}{3} = \pi$. $2\pi \cdot b = \pi$ $b = \dfrac{1}{2}$
$k = 1$	$a = 3$	$h = \dfrac{\pi}{3}$	$\dfrac{1}{b} = 2$

$$f(x) = 3\sin 2\left(x - \dfrac{\pi}{3}\right) + 1$$

Write a sine function for each graph.

1.

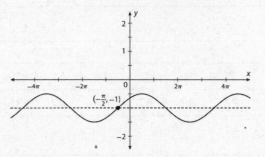

2.

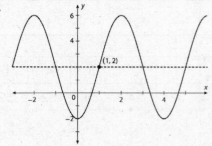

_____   _____

LESSON 18-4

Fitting Sine Functions to Data
Reteach

To fit a sine function, $f(x) = a\sin\left[\dfrac{1}{b}(x-h)\right] + k$, to a given set of data,

use the SinReg function on a graphing calculator.

Example Write an equation for the data in the form $f(x) = a\sin\left[\dfrac{1}{b}(x-h)\right] + k$.

x	1	2	3	4	5	6	7	8	9	10	11	12
y	−3.5	0.2	2.5	−0.8	−3.8	0.3	3.2	0.1	−4.2	0.7	2.9	−0.2

Step 1	Step 2	Step 3
Enter data into L_1 and L_2 in the graphing calculator. 1. Press STAT 2. Choose Edit 3. Enter the data in L_1 and L_2	Perform sine regression. 1. Press STAT 2. Choose CALC 3. Choose SinReg 4. Press ENTER	Write the sine function. 1. Plug in given values for *a*, *b*, *c*, and *d*. 2. Change into $f(x) = a\sin\dfrac{1}{b}(x-h) + k$ by factoring.
		$y = a*\sin(bx+c)+d$ $f(x) = 3.4\sin(1.6x - 3.0) - 0.2$ $f(x) = 3.4\sin 1.6(x - 1.9) - 0.2$

Write an equation for the data in the form $f(x) = a\sin\left[\dfrac{1}{b}(x-h)\right] + k$.

Round to the nearest tenth.

1.

x	−3.1	−2.3	−1.6	−0.8	−0.1	0.7	1.5	2.3	3.0	3.8	4.5	5.3
y	1.9	2.4	2.8	2.3	1.7	2.2	2.6	2.1	1.5	2.0	1.6	2.2

_____

2.

x	1	2	3	4	5	6	7	8	9	10	11	12
y	32	24	39	52	59	68	77	83	67	56	42	35

_____

LESSON 19-1
Probability and Set Theory
Reteach

Basic Set Vocabulary:

- **element** an object in a set (often a number or event)
- **empty set** a set with no elements; symbol is $\varnothing$
- **set** a collection of distinct objects called elements
- **subset** a smaller set of elements within a universal set
- **universal set** a complete collection of elements

The **theoretical probability** of an event is the likelihood that an event will happen, where all possible outcomes are equally likely.

Theoretical Probability of A: $P(A) = \dfrac{\text{number of outcomes for event } A}{\text{total possible outcomes in universal set}} = \dfrac{n(A)}{n(U)}$

---

1. Consider the universal set of all odd numbers between 1 and 15: $U = \{1, 3, 5, 7, 9, 11, 15\}$.

   Complete the chart for each subset of the universal set.

Description of Subset	Set Notation	Number of Elements in Subset	Number of Elements in Universal Set
Multiples of 3	$A = \{$ _____ $\}$	$n(A) =$ _____	$n(U) = 7$
Multiples of 5	$B = \{$ _____ $\}$	$n(B) =$ _____	$n(U) = 7$

Suppose each element in *U* is written on a card. Calculate the theoretical probability of randomly choosing a number of each type from the set of cards.

2. $P(A) = \dfrac{n(A)}{n(U)} =$ _____

3. $P(B) = \dfrac{n(B)}{n(U)} =$ _____

The **intersection** of sets A and B, $A \cap B$, is the set of all elements in **both A and B**.

The **union** of sets A and B, $A \cup B$, is the set of all elements in A **and/or** in B.

The **complement** of set A is the set of all elements in the universal set that are **not** in A.

---

4. Use the Venn diagram at right to organize the elements in $U = \{0, 4, 6, 9, 12, 16, 20\}$, when $C = \{0, 6, 12\}$ and $D = \{0, 4, 16\}$.

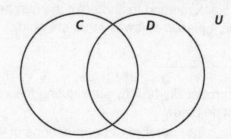

LESSON 19-2 Permutations and Probability
Reteach

To find the number of permutations of 3 objects chosen out of 10 total objects, use the "blank method."

A Draw the number of blanks in which the objects will be placed: ☐ ☐ ☐ .

B Record the number of options you have for the first blank: ☐10☐ ☐ ☐ .

C Record the number of options you have for the second blank, after the first object has been placed: ☐10☐ ☐9☐ ☐ .

D Record the number of options you have for the third blank, after the first two objects have been placed: ☐10☐ ☐9☐ ☐8☐

E Continue until all blanks are filled with a number. Multiply the numbers in the blanks to find the total permutations of 3 objects chosen out of 7 objects: $10 \cdot 9 \cdot 8 = 720$.

You can use this method to find the total number of permutations in the sample space $n(S)$ as well as the total number of permutations of a specific type $n(A)$. Calculate the probability of A as $\dfrac{n(A)}{n(S)}$.

1. A jewelry store clerk will choose 4 pieces of jewelry to display on a shelf. The clerk will choose the 4 pieces randomly from a group of 8 pieces. Solve for $n(S)$, the total number of different possible ways to choose the jewelry to display on the shelf.

   a. Use the space above to draw the appropriate number of blanks.

   b. How many options are there for the first blank, given that the clerk is choosing from 8 pieces? Record that number in the first blank.

   c. After the first piece is placed, how many options are there for the second blank? Record that number in the second blank.

   d. Fill in each remaining blank with the number of options that are left for each one.

   e. Write and solve a multiplication sentence to find how many possible ways there are to choose the jewelry to display on the shelf.

      $n(S) =$ _____

2. Suppose that 5 of the pieces of jewelry the clerk can select from are made of gold. Let event A be "All 4 pieces on display are gold." What is the probability of A?

   a. Use the blank method to find $n(A)$, the number of different possible ways there are to choose 4 pieces of jewelry that are gold.

      $n(A) =$ _____

   b. Find the probability of A by substituting the values you found into the equation below.

   $P(\text{all gold}) = P(A) = \dfrac{\text{number of permutations of 4 gold pieces}}{\text{total possible permutations of 4 pieces}} = \dfrac{n(A)}{n(S)} =$ _____

Combinations and Probability
Reteach

Permutations vs. Combinations

• Remember to use a **permutation** when **order matters** and a **combination** when **order does not matter**.

• There are fewer combinations of a group of objects than there are permutations. You must divide the number of permutations by the number of permutations of the "blanks" in order to find the smaller number of combinations.

To find the number of combinations of 4 objects chosen out of 9 total objects, use the following steps.

A Draw the number of blanks in which the objects will be placed: ☐ · ☐ · ☐ · ☐ .

B Use the "blank method" to find the number of permutations: $\boxed{9} \cdot \boxed{8} \cdot \boxed{7} \cdot \boxed{6} = 3024$.

C Find the factorial of the number of blanks: $4! = 4 \cdot 3 \cdot 2 \cdot 1 = 24$

D Divide the number from **B** by the number from **C**: $\dfrac{3024}{24} = 126$

You can use this method to find the total number of combinations in the sample space $n(S)$ as well as the total number of combinations of a specific type $n(A)$. Calculate the probability of A as $\dfrac{n(A)}{n(S)}$.

For 1–2, determine whether each is an example of a combination or a permutation.

1. Picking a group of 3 winners to come in first place, second place, and third place. _____

2. Picking a group of 3 winners from a group of 8 finalists. _____

3. Mike is choosing 3 books to borrow from a friend. He selects the books from the shelf at random. The shelf contains 11 books.

   a. Use the blank method to find how many permutations there are of 3 books chosen from the 11 on the shelf.

   _____

   b. Find the factorial of the number of blanks.

   _____

   c. Write and solve a division sentence to find the total number of combinations $n(S)$ of 3 books.

   $n(S) =$ _____

4. Suppose that the shelf contains 5 fiction books. Let event A be "All books that Mike chooses are fiction." What is the probability of A?

   a. Write and solve a division sentence to find the total number of combinations $n(A)$ of 3 fiction books.

   $n(A) =$ _____

   b. Find the probability of A by substituting the values you found into the equation below.

   $P(\text{all fiction}) = P(A) = \dfrac{\text{number of combinations of 3 fiction books}}{\text{total possible combinations of 3 books}} = \dfrac{n(A)}{n(S)} =$ _____

LESSON 19-4 **Mutually Exclusive and Overlapping Events**
Reteach

If two events are **mutually exclusive**, then they cannot occur at the same time.
If two events are **overlapping**, then they can occur at the same time.

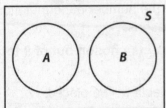
A and *B* are
mutually exclusive

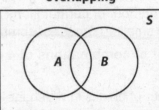
A and *B* are
overlapping

The **Addition Rule** tells you how to find the probability that *A* **or** *B* occurs.

- Addition Rule for mutually exclusive *A* and *B*: $P(A \text{ or } B) = P(A) + P(B)$

- Addition Rule for overlapping *A* and *B*: $P(A \text{ or } B) = P(A) + P(B) - P(A \text{ and } B)$

Examples of the Addition Rule:

- Find the probability that a multiple of 5 or an even number is rolled on a number cube.
  The events are mutually exclusive because they cannot both occur at once:

$$P(A \text{ or } B) = P(A) + P(B) = \frac{1}{6} + \frac{1}{6} = \frac{2}{6} = \frac{1}{3}$$

- Find the probability that a multiple of 3 or an even number is rolled on a number cube.
  The events are overlapping because both occur when 6 is rolled:

$$P(A \text{ or } B) = P(A) + P(B) - P(A \text{ and } B) = \frac{2}{6} + \frac{3}{6} - \frac{1}{6} = \frac{4}{6} = \frac{2}{3}$$

For 1–4, determine whether the two events are mutually exclusive or overlapping.

1. rolling an even number on a die; rolling a 6 on a die _____

2. rolling an odd number on a die; rolling a 2 on a die _____

3. drawing a face card from a deck of cards; drawing a 5 from a deck of cards _____

4. drawing a spade from a deck of cards; drawing a 7 from a deck of cards _____

Use the appropriate version of the Addition Rule to find each probability.

5. *P*(rolling an even number on a die or rolling a 6 on a die) = _____

6. *P*(rolling an odd number on a die or rolling a 2 on a die) = _____

7. *P*(drawing a spade from a deck of cards or drawing a 7 from a deck of cards) = _____

Conditional Probability

LESSON 20-1

Reteach

The **two-way frequency table** shows the genders and grade levels of students who attended a school district meeting.

	Boys	Girls	TOTAL
Middle School	20	25	45
High School	35	20	55
TOTAL	55	45	100

Let A be that a student is a boy and let B be that a student is a middle-schooler. To find the **conditional probability** that a student who is a boy is also a middle-schooler,

use $P(A|B) = \dfrac{P(\textbf{both } \text{middle-schooler } \textbf{and} \text{ boy})}{P(\text{boy})} = \dfrac{n(A \cap B)}{n(B)}$.

- Look at the column that shows event B: This is the **Boys** column. Now look at the cell in this column that shows **both A and B**: the number of middle school boys is 20.

- $n(B)$ is the total in the column: $n(B) = 55$.

- $n(A \cap B)$ is the number in the cell: $n(A \cap B) = 20$.

So, $P(A|B) = \dfrac{n(A \cap B)}{n(B)} = \dfrac{20}{55} \approx 36\%$. The probability that a student is a

middle-schooler, given that he is a boy, is about 36%.

Use the table above to identify the totals, and then calculate the conditional probabilities.

1. Let A be that a student is a high-schooler. Let B be that a student is a boy. Find $P(A|B)$, the probability that a student who is a boy is also a high-schooler.

   a. What is the total in the B column? $n(B) =$ _____

   b. What is the total in the cell for A and B? $n(A \cap B) =$ _____

   c. $P(A|B) = \dfrac{n(A \cap B)}{n(B)} =$ _____

2. Let A be that a student is a girl. Let B be that a student is a middle-schooler. Find $P(A|B)$, the probability that a student who is a middle-schooler is also a girl.

   a. What is the total in the B row? $n(B) =$ _____

   b. What is the total in the cell for A and B? $n(A \cap B) =$ _____

   c. $P(A|B) = \dfrac{n(A \cap B)}{n(B)} =$ _____

LESSON 20-2 — Independent Events

Reteach

If $P(A) = P(A|B)$ and $P(A \text{ and } B) = P(A) \cdot P(B)$, then A and B are independent.

	Prefers Rock	Prefers Classical	TOTAL
Male	12	3	15
Female	24	6	30
TOTAL	36	9	45

The table shows the genders and music preference in a group of people.
Let A be that a person prefers rock and let B be that a person is male.
Are A and B independent?

Method 1: Test whether $P(A) = P(A|B)$.

- $P(A) = \dfrac{36}{45} = \dfrac{4}{5}$ and $P(A|B) = \dfrac{12}{15} = \dfrac{4}{5}$. Therefore, $P(A) = P(A|B) = \dfrac{4}{5}$

  and whether a person likes rock is independent of whether the person is male.

Method 2: Test whether $P(A \text{ and } B) = P(A) \cdot P(B)$.

- $P(A) = \dfrac{36}{45} = \dfrac{4}{5}$, $P(B) = \dfrac{15}{45} = \dfrac{1}{3}$, and $P(A \text{ and } B) = \dfrac{4}{15}$. Therefore,

  $P(A \text{ and } B) = P(A) \cdot P(B) = \dfrac{4}{5} \cdot \dfrac{1}{3} = \dfrac{4}{15}$ and whether a person likes

  rock is independent of whether the person is male.

If events A and B are independent, then $P(A \text{ and } B) = P(A) \cdot P(B)$.

Let C be that a person is female. Let D be that a person prefers rock.
Use the table above to answer the questions.

1. Use **Method 1** to determine whether C is independent of D.

   a. $P(C) = $ _____   b. $P(C|D) = $ _____

   c. Is C independent of D? _____

2. Use **Method 2** to determine whether C is independent of D.

   a. $P(C) = $ _____   b. $P(D) = $ _____   c. $P(C \text{ and } D) = $ _____

   d. Is C independent of D? _____

3. Events E and F are independent. $P(E) = \dfrac{1}{2}$ and $P(F) = \dfrac{2}{5}$. What is

   the probability that both E and F will occur?

   $P(E \text{ and } F) = $ _____

LESSON 20-3

Dependent Events

Reteach

If *A* and *B* are **independent events**, then whether *A* happens or not has no effect on whether *B* happens. In cases of **selection with replacement**, the events are independent.

If *A* and *B* are **dependent events**, then the outcome of *A* has an effect on whether *B* happens. In cases of **selection without replacement**, the events are dependent.

Suppose a card is randomly selected from a deck, the deck is shuffled, and then a second card is drawn from the deck. Let *A* be selecting a spade on the first draw. Let *B* be selecting a spade on the second draw.

- If the first card is replaced, you start with the same set of cards for each draw. In this case, *A* and *B* are **independent** events.

- If the first card is **not** replaced before the second draw, the deck on the second draw is not exactly the same as the deck on the first draw. In this case, *A* and *B* are **dependent** events.

For each pair of events, determine whether *A* and *B* are independent or dependent.

1. Event *A* is rolling a 3 on the first roll of a number cube.
   Event *B* is rolling a 2 on the second roll of the number cube. _____

2. Event *A* is pulling a blue marble from a bag of colored marbles.
   Event *B* is pulling a blue marble on the second draw, given that
   the first marble pulled is **not** put back in the bag. _____

If events A and B are dependent, then $P(A \text{ and } B) = P(A) \cdot P(B|A)$.

A card is randomly selected from a deck and not replaced, the deck is shuffled, and then a second card is selected from the deck. Let *A* be selecting a spade on the first draw. Let *B* be selecting a spade on the second draw. What is the probability of getting a spade on both draws?

- There are 13 spades in a complete deck of 52 cards: $P(A) = \dfrac{13}{52}$

- If a spade is drawn first, there are 12 spades and 51 cards at the start of the second draw: $P(B|A) = \dfrac{12}{51}$

- $P(A \text{ and } B) = P(A) \cdot P(B|A) = \dfrac{13}{52} \cdot \dfrac{12}{51} = \dfrac{1}{17}$

3. A card is randomly selected from a deck and not replaced. The deck is shuffled, and then a second card is drawn. Let *A* be selecting a 2 on the first draw. Let *B* be selecting a 2 on the second draw. What is the probability that a 2 will be drawn both times?

   a. $P(A) = $ _____   b. $P(B|A) = $ _____   c. $P(A \text{ and } B) = $ _____

LESSON
21-1

Using Probability to Make Fair Decisions
Reteach

To make a fair choice between outcomes with equal probability, you can use a random number generator on a graphing calculator.

Example On a class field trip, one student out of a class of 24 is needed to assist the zookeeper in feeding the elephant. Explain how to use a random number generator to choose the student assistant fairly.

Step 1	Step 2
Assign a number to each student, possibly by placing them in alphabetical order.	Use the calculator to choose a number randomly between 1 and 24. 1. Press MATH 2. Choose CALC 3. Choose PRB 4. Choose randInt(5. Type in (1, 24) and press Enter

1.	Agatha
2.	Caroline
3.	Harry
4.	Jack
5.	Jenny
6.	Matilda
7.	Max
and so on…	

```
randInt(1,24)
                    2
■
```

The student whose number is 2 will get to feed the elephant. That is Caroline on the alphabetical list.

Explain how to use a random number generator to make a fair decision in each situation.

1. A group of five friends is trying to decide which movie to watch. Each friend wants to watch a different movie. Explain how to use a random number generator to choose the movie fairly.

_____

2. A soccer team will award one raffle prize to team members who sell candy as a fundraiser. The team members who sell more candy will have a greater probability of winning the prize. Explain how to use a random number generator to award the prize fairly.

_____

3. Students in a classroom earn points for good behavior and participation throughout the week. Explain how the teacher could use a random number generator to fairly award a prize for good behavior and participation at the end of the week.

_____

Analyzing Decisions
Reteach

Bayes' Theorem helps to determine the probability of a conditional event such as the likelihood of an accurate outcome from a medical test.

$$P(B\,|\,A) = \frac{P(A\,|\,B)P(B)}{P(A)} \text{ where}$$

$P(B\,|\,A)$ = the probability of event B occurring given that event A has occurred.

$P(A\,|\,B)$ = the probability of event A occurring given that event B has occurred.

$P(A)$ = the probability of event A occurring.

$P(B)$ = the probability of event B occurring.

Example   Joe has a sore throat and is tested for a strep throat infection by his doctor. The test gives correct positive results 98% of the time. About 25% of all sore throats are caused by strep bacteria. Overall, when doctors use the strep test it gives positive results about 60% of the time. Given that Joe's strep throat test comes back positive, what is the probability that he actually does have strep throat?

Step 1	Step 2	Step 3
Define event A and event B.	To find $P(B\,|\,A)$, first find $P(A\,|\,B)$, $P(B)$, and $P(A)$.	Find $P(B\,|\,A)$, the probability that Joe actually does have strep throat given a positive test result.
Event A = the strep test gives a positive result Event B = Joe has strep throat	$P(A) = 60\%$ $P(B) = 25\%$ $P(A\,|\,B) = 98\%$	$P(B\,|\,A) = \dfrac{P(A\,|\,B)P(B)}{P(A)}$ $= \dfrac{(0.98)(0.25)}{(0.60)}$ $= 0.41$

The probability that Joe actually has strep throat is about 41%.

Use Bayes' Theorem to find the probabilities in the given situation.

1. Some students in a school are suffering from a contagious virus. 95% of the time, a symptom of the virus is an itchy rash. Only 5% of people actually contract the virus, but 9% of the students at the school have a rash. What is the probability that a student who has a rash actually does have the virus?

_____

2. About 1% of the population has disease X. A blood test for disease X gives correct positive results 85% of the time. Overall, about 30% of the time, the blood test gives positive results. If your blood test results are positive, what is the probability that you actually have disease X?

_____

Data-Gathering Techniques
Reteach

Data gathered as a sample can be used to make predictions about the entire population.

Example

A local high school drama department is gathering data about the audience members at its annual spring musical. A total of 624 people attended the show over three nights, and a random sample of 20 audience members per night was surveyed about their connections to the show and the number of tickets they purchased.

Type of Audience Member	Number of Audience Members	Number of Tickets Purchased
Family of Cast	22	96
School Faculty	8	24
Student	19	21
Other Community Member	11	45

Calculate the mean number of tickets purchased by a single audience member.

Step 1	Step 2	Step 3
Sum the total tickets purchased by members of this 60-person sample. $96 + 24 + 21 + 45 = 186$	Divide the number of tickets by the number of people. $\dfrac{186}{60} = 3.1$	Interpret the result. Each audience member purchased ≈ 3.1 tickets.

Predict the total number of tickets purchased by non-students.

Step 1	Step 2	Step 3
Calculate the proportion of tickets purchased by non-students. $\dfrac{96 + 24 + 45}{96 + 24 + 21 + 45} = \dfrac{165}{186}$ $\approx 0.89 = 89\%$	Multiply this percentage by the total population to make your prediction. $(624)(0.89) \approx 555$	Interpret the result. ≈ 555 tickets were purchased by non-students.

Use the data table from the example above to answer the following questions.

1. Predict the total number of tickets purchased by faculty and students. _____

2. Calculate the average number of tickets purchased by family of cast members. _____

3. The drama department would like for 15% of its audience to be other community members not connected to the school. Did the drama department reach its goal with this musical? Explain.

_____

Name _____ Date _____ Class_____

LESSON 22-2

Shape, Center, and Spread
Reteach

Given a data sample, you can use your graphing calculator to determine the distribution's center and spread.

Type of Distribution	Normal	Skewed
Best Measure of Center	Mean	Median
Spread	Standard Deviation	Interquartile Range

Example
Find the mean, median, standard deviation, and interquartile range of the distribution using a graphing calculator.

24	27	19	46	51	33	39	13	30	45	14	28	32	36	41

Step 1	Step 2	Step 3
Enter the data into a list on your graphing calculator.	Calculate the desired information.	Use the down cursor to view the rest of the information.
1. Press STAT. 2. Choose EDIT. 3. Enter the data into L1.	1. Press STAT. 2. Choose CALC. 3. Choose 1-Var Stats. 4. Press Enter.	

1-Var Stats
$\bar{x}=31.86666667$
$\Sigma x=478$
$\Sigma x^2=17068$
$Sx=11.45093051$
$\sigma x=11.06264987$
$\downarrow n=15$

1-Var Stats
$\uparrow n=15$
$minX=13$
$Q_1=24$
$Med=32$
$Q_3=41$
$maxX=51$

$\bar{x} \approx 31.9$ $s \approx 11.1$ Median = 32 $IQR = Q_3 - Q_1 = 41 - 24 = 17$

Find the mean, median, standard deviation, and interquartile range of each distribution using a graphing calculator.

1.
84.2	82.1	85.4	80.9	84.1	87.6	88.3	82.4	90.1	85.2	83.9

2.
0.65	0.45	0.50	0.55	0.50	0.40	0.65	0.60	0.70	0.55	0.45

LESSON 23-1 Probability Distributions
Reteach

A probability distribution shown by a histogram can be used to predict the probability of a particular outcome.

Example The histogram shown below represents the probabilities for possible outcomes of a particular experiment. What is the probability of an outcome greater than 3?

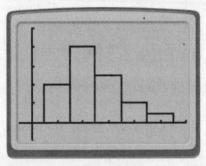

(Note: The x-scale is 1, and the y-scale is 0.1.)

Step 1	Step 2	Step 3
Identify the desired outcome.	Find the probability of each desired outcome from the histogram.	Add the results to find the total probability of the desired outcome.
An outcome greater than 3 means an outcome of 4 or 5.	$P(4) = 0.1$ $P(5) = 0.05$	$P(>3) = P(4) + P(5)$ $= 0.1 + 0.05$ $= 0.15$

The probability of an outcome greater than 3 is 15%.

Use the histogram to answer the following questions.

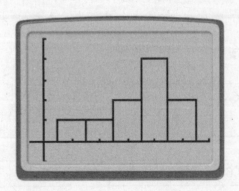

1. What is the probability of an outcome greater than 2?

   _____

2. What is the probability of an odd outcome?

   _____

3. What is the probability of an outcome less than 6?

   _____

LESSON 23-2

Normal Distributions

Reteach

Data that are normally distributed have the following percentages of the data in each part of the distribution.

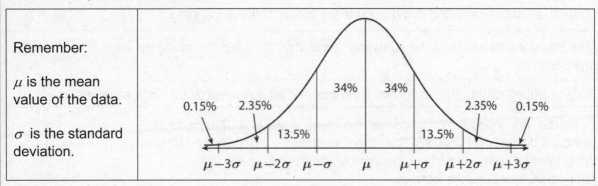

Remember:

μ is the mean value of the data.

σ is the standard deviation.

Example

A factory that makes paper towels measures the diameter of several rolls and determines the data are normally distributed with a mean of 12.1 cm and a standard deviation of 0.02 cm. What percent of the sampled rolls have a diameter between 12.06 cm and 12.14 cm?

Step 1	Step 2	Step 3
Determine how many standard deviations away from the mean for the lower limit of desired values.	Determine how many standard deviations away from the mean for the upper limit of desired values.	Find the percent of data that is between the lower and upper ends of the range.
$12.1 - 12.06 = 0.04 = 2\sigma$ So, $12.06 = \mu - 2\sigma$.	$12.14 - 12.1 = 0.04 = 2\sigma$ So, $12.14 = \mu + 2\sigma$.	The percentage of data between $\mu - 2\sigma$ and $\mu + 2\sigma$ is $13.5 + 34 + 34 + 13.5 = 95\%$.

Use the normal distribution diagram above to determine the percentage of data in the given range with the given mean and standard deviation.

1. The mean height of a group of women is 65 inches. The standard deviation is 2 inches. How many women are between 63 and 67 inches in height?

2. The mean annual income for a population is $25,934 with a standard deviation of $2940. How many people make more than $20,054?

3. The mean volume of milk in a jug is 3780 mL. The standard deviation is 7 mL. What percentage of the jugs have between 3766 and 3794 mL?

4. The mean distance measured in a physics experiment is 16.4 m. The standard deviation is 0.6 m. How many measurements fall between 14.6 m and 18.2 m?

Sampling Distributions

LESSON 23-3

Reteach

For a collection of samples of size *n* from a population:

The mean of the sampling distribution is the mean of the population.	$\mu_{\bar{x}} = \mu$
The standard deviation of the sampling distribution is called the standard error of the mean.	$\sigma_{\bar{x}} = \dfrac{\sigma}{\sqrt{n}}$
The sampling distribution is normal if the population is normal or for large sample size *n*.	

Example For a population of geese, the mean mass is 9.07 kg with a standard deviation of 0.46 kg. Random samples of 20 geese are chosen. What interval captures 68% of the sample means? Assume the population distribution is normal.

Step 1	Step 2	Step 3
Find the mean of the sampling distribution.	Find the standard error of the mean.	In a normal distribution, 68% of the data fall within 1 standard deviation of the mean.
$\mu_{\bar{x}} = \mu = 9.07$	$\sigma_{\bar{x}} = \dfrac{\sigma}{\sqrt{n}} = \dfrac{9.07}{\sqrt{20}} \approx 2.03$	$\mu_{\bar{x}} + \sigma_{\bar{x}} = 9.07 + 2.03 = 11.1$ $\mu_{\bar{x}} - \sigma_{\bar{x}} = 9.07 - 2.03 = 7.04$

So, 68% of the sample means fall between 7.04 kg and 11.1 kg.

A population of second graders has a mean height of 122 cm with a standard deviation of 4 cm. Random samples of 7 second graders are chosen. Assume the population distribution is normal.

1. What interval captures 95% of the sample means?

_____

2. What is the probability that a particular sample has a mean above 123.5 cm?

_____

Bottles of shampoo have a mean volume of 120 mL with a standard deviation of 3 mL. Random samples of 25 bottles of shampoo are chosen. Assume the population distribution is normal.

3. What interval captures 99.7% of the sample means?

_____

4. What is the probability that a particular sample has a mean below 118.2 mL?

_____

Name _____ Date _____ Class_____

Confidence Intervals and Margins of Error
Reteach

To find a confidence interval for a population proportion, use the formula:

$\hat{p} - z_c\sqrt{\dfrac{\hat{p}(1-\hat{p})}{n}} \le p \le \hat{p} + z_c\sqrt{\dfrac{\hat{p}(1-\hat{p})}{n}}$	$\hat{p}$ is the sample proportion.			
	n is the sample size.			
	z_c depends on the degree of confidence.			
	Degree of Confidence	90%	95%	99%
	z_c	1.645	1.96	2.576

Example

In a random sample of 225 voters in the city of Johnsonville, 134 were women. Find a 95% confidence interval for the proportion of all voters in the city who were women.

Step 1	Step 2
Find the sample size n, the proportion $\hat{p}$, and the value of z_c for 95% confidence.	Substitute into the formula to find the lower endpoint of the confidence interval.$$\hat{p} - z_c\sqrt{\dfrac{\hat{p}(1-\hat{p})}{n}} = 0.6 - 1.96\sqrt{\dfrac{0.6(1-0.6)}{225}} \approx 0.54$$
	Step 3
$n = 225$ $\hat{p} = \dfrac{135}{225} = 0.6$ $z_c = 1.96$	Substitute into the formula to find the upper endpoint of the confidence interval.$$\hat{p} + z_c\sqrt{\dfrac{\hat{p}(1-\hat{p})}{n}} = 0.6 + 1.96\sqrt{\dfrac{0.6(1-0.6)}{225}} \approx 0.66$$

It can be stated with 95% confidence that the proportion of women voters in Johnsonville is between 0.54 and 0.66.

Find the confidence interval for the proportion in each situation.

1. In a random survey of 100 households in Arkansas, 36 had a dog for a pet. Find a 90% confidence interval for the proportion of households in Arkansas who have a dog. _____

2. 450 people participated in a random taste test for a new energy drink. 346 participants said they liked the taste of the new drink. Find a 95% confidence interval for the proportion of people who will like the taste of the new drink. _____

3. In a random sample of 2000 bags of potato chips from a particular machine, 22 bags were improperly sealed. Find a 99% confidence interval for the proportion of improperly sealed bags from that machine. _____

LESSON 24-2	**Surveys, Experiments, and Observational Studies**
	Reteach

When you hear reports about the outcome of a particular study, you can decide if the study is a survey, observational study, or experiment.

Survey	Observational Study	Experiment
Measures characteristics of interest about a population using a sample.	Determines whether a factor in a population is related to a characteristic of interest.	Imposes a treatment, then determines if the treatment affected a characteristic of interest.

Example Determine whether each study is a survey, observational study, or experiment.

1. After a test, Mrs. Jackson compares which of her students completed the review assignment with their test scores.	Observational Study	The factor is completing the review. The characteristic of interest is the test score.
2. In a sample of 15 of Mrs. Jackson's students, 9 students completed the review assignment prior to the test.	Survey	The population is Mrs. Jackson's students. The characteristic of interest is completing the review assignment.
3. Mrs. Jackson offers extra credit to some of her students for completing the review assignment and then compares those who were offered extra credit to the students' test scores.	Experiment	The treatment is the offer of extra credit. The characteristic of interest is the test score.

Determine whether each study is a survey, observational study, or experiment.

1. In a random sample of 100 households, 62 have at least two cars. _____

2. In a group of 120 patients with cancerous tumors, 60 are given a new treatment drug and 60 are given the traditional treatment drug. After 6 months, the tumors are re-measured. _____

3. A study reports that college students who have taken a physics course in high school are more likely to pass college science courses. _____

4. In a sample of 250 former college athletes, 56 became coaches in their sport. _____

5. A study reports that girls who play with blocks when they are younger are more likely to be good at math and science. _____

Determining the Significance of Experimental Results
Reteach

Example Determine whether the result is significant and state a conclusion.

A pharmaceutical manufacturer wants to determine if an experimental medicine lowers bad cholesterol in patients with high cholesterol. A treatment group is given the experimental medicine while a control group is not. After 6 weeks, the cholesterol levels are re-measured. The mean cholesterol level of the treatment group is 187 mg/dL while the mean of the control group is 195 mg/dL. The resampling distribution for the difference between $\bar{x}_T$ and $\bar{x}_C$ is normal with a mean of 0 and a standard deviation of 3 mg/dL.

Step 1	State the null hypothesis.	The difference in mean cholesterol levels between those who received the experimental medicine and those who did not is about 0.
Step 2	Find the difference in the means between the treatment group and the control group.	$\bar{x}_T - \bar{x}_C = 187 - 195 = -8$
Step 3	Find the probability (P-value) of the difference of means occurring randomly.	−8 is 3 standard deviations below the mean in the normal resampling distribution and, therefore, has a probability of 0.025. So, $P = 0.025$.
Step 4	If $P \leq 0.05$, then the result is significant.	Since $0.025 \leq 0.05$, the result is significant.
Step 5	Reject or accept the null hypothesis.	The null hypothesis can be rejected; therefore, it can be assumed that the experimental medicine does have an effect on cholesterol level.

Determine whether the result is significant and state a conclusion.

A farmer wants to determine if a new fertilizer will increase his crop yield. The mean yield of the treatment group with the new fertilizer applied is 152 bushels/acre. The mean of the control group with the old fertilizer applied is 148 bushels/acre. The resampling distribution for the difference between $\bar{x}_T$ and $\bar{x}_C$ is normal with a mean of 0 and a standard deviation of 2 bushels/acre.

1. State the null hypothesis.

   _____

2. Find the difference in the means between the treatment group and the control group.

   _____

3. Find the P-value of the difference in means.

   _____

4. Determine if the result is significant and whether or not the null hypothesis is rejected. What conclusion can be drawn?

   _____

Add and Subtract Rational Numbers

KEY TEACHING POINTS

Example 1

Remind students that rational numbers are numbers that can be written as a fraction of two integers. Decimals, fractions, and integers are all rational numbers.

Say: Adding rational numbers using a number line is done in the same way as adding integers using a number line. These number lines are divided into units of 0.25, or $\frac{1}{4}$.

Part A

Say: Locate the first addend on the number line.

Say: The arrow shows the direction and distance to add 2.5 to 0.25.

Say: To add a positive rational number, move right on the number line. Move the whole number part first, then move the decimal fraction part.

Ask: How many tick marks do you move for 0.75? **[Three.]**

Part B

Ask: Should you start on the left or right of zero on the number line? **[left]** Why? **[The first addend is a negative number, and negative numbers are left of zero on the number line.]**

Say: To add a negative rational number, move left on the number line. Move the whole number part, 2 first, then move the fraction part.

Check

Say: Adding positive rational numbers is the same as adding rational numbers without positive or negative signs.

ALTERNATE STRATEGY

Strategy: Use absolute values.

1. Absolute value is the distance a number is from 0 on a number line. Absolute values are always positive. You can add rational numbers with the same sign by adding their absolute values.

2. The absolute value of a positive rational number is the same as the rational number. So, adding two positive rational numbers is the same as adding rational numbers with no signs.

3. Add 0.25 and 2.5 by lining up the decimal points and adding.

    ```
      0.25
    + 2.5
      2.75
    ```

4. Remind students that the absolute value of a negative number is the opposite, or positive, number that is the same distance from 0 on the number line.

5. Add $-\dfrac{1}{2}+\left(-2\dfrac{1}{4}\right)$ by adding the absolute value of each fraction.

$$\left|-\dfrac{1}{2}\right|=\dfrac{1}{2} \text{ and } \left|-2\dfrac{1}{4}\right|=2\dfrac{1}{4}$$

$$\dfrac{1}{2}+2\dfrac{1}{4}=\dfrac{2}{4}+2\dfrac{1}{4}=2\dfrac{3}{4}, \text{ so } -\dfrac{1}{2}+\left(-2\dfrac{1}{4}\right)=-2\dfrac{3}{4}$$

6. The sign of the sum is the same as the sign of the addends. When the addends are positive, the sum is positive. When the addends are negative, the sum is negative.

KEY TEACHING POINTS

Example 2

Make sure students understand the meaning of "absolute value," which is essential in the addition of rational numbers with different signs when not using a number line.

Ask: You can use a number line to add rational numbers. When the second addend is positive, which direction should you move on the number line? **[Right.]** When the second addend is negative, which direction should you move on the number line? **[Left.]**

Say: The sum of rational numbers can also be found using the difference of their absolute values.

Demonstrate how to use absolute values to find the sum.
- First identify the absolute value of each addend.
- Subtract the lesser absolute value from the greater absolute value.
- The sum takes the sign of the rational number with the greater absolute value.

Check

Ask: When you start at 4.75 on the number line and move 7.25 units left, will the result be to the left or right of 0? **[Left.]** Does this make the answer positive or negative? **[Negative.]**

Say: Remember, the sum of the sign is the same as the sum of the rational number with the greater absolute value.

Ask: Should Sylvia pouring lemonade be represented by a positive or negative value? **[Negative.]** What about if she adds more to the pitcher? **[Positive.]**

Check that students correctly choose the starting point and direction of movement on number lines. Have them talk through their reasoning with you.

KEY TEACHING POINTS

Example 3
Remind students of the Commutative and Associative Properties of Addition.
- The Commutative Property of Addition allows addends to be moved around. This means that $3+(-2)+7$ has the same value as $(-2)+3+7$ and $3+7+(-2)$.
- The Associative Property of Addition allows addends to be grouped in any order. This means that $(-2+3)+7$ has the same value as $-2+(3+7)$.

Ask: How is the Commutative Property used in Step 3? **[The numbers are moved around so that the positive numbers are together and the negative numbers are together.]** How is the Associative Property used? **[To add the numbers with the same signs first.]**

Say: After the numbers with the same signs are added, you need to find the sum of the numbers that are left.

Ask: How do you find the sum of rational numbers with different signs? **[By finding the difference of the absolute values.]** Why might you not want to use a number line for this problem? **[The numbers are large and far apart on a number line.]**

Check
Ask: When adding three or more numbers, numbers with the same sign can be grouped for convenience. How might it be convenient to group opposite numbers together? **[The sum of a number and its opposite is zero.]**

Ask: Does the word "ascended" indicate a positive or negative value? **[Positive.]** Explain. **[It means the diver was moving up in the water.]**

Example 4
Review the terms minuend (first number in a subtraction problem) and subtrahend (second number in a subtraction problem).

Ask: How can you subtract 8 – 5 on a number line? **[Start at 8 and move 5 units left.]** So, when you subtract with a positive subtrahend, what direction should you move on the number line? **[Left.]**

Say: When using the number line to subtract a positive subtrahend, always move left. The sign of the minuend does not make any difference.

Say: When both numbers are positive, and the subtrahend is greater than the minuend, the result is a negative number.

Say: Start at 3.5, and then move left 6.7 units. Because the move left is greater than 3.5, the result is to the left of 0, which is a negative value.

Check

Ask: After locating the minuend on the number line, which direction should you move for each of these problems? **[Left.]**

Say: When the subtrahend is a positive number, move left to subtract. This subtrahend is a negative number, so move in the opposite direction, right.

Ask: Is $7\frac{1}{4} - 5$ the same as $5 - 7\frac{1}{4}$? **[No.]**

Say: The Commutative Property does not apply to subtraction, so the numbers in a subtraction problem cannot be moved around.

Say: Remember, the sign of the sum is the same as the sign of the rational number with the greater absolute value.

Ask: Does $5 - 7\frac{1}{4}$ have a positive or negative value? **[Negative.]**

COMMON MISCONCEPTION

Ask: What is a possible error in this student's work?
Use the number line to find the difference.
$-1.25 - 2.5 = -3.25$

Reason incorrect: The student started at –0.75 instead of –1.25.
Solution:

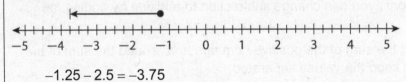

$-1.25 - 2.5 = -3.75$

Say: Remember, on a number line, –1.25 is further left than –1.

KEY TEACHING POINTS

Example 5

Ask: How can you rewrite the expression $-4 - \left(-7\frac{3}{4}\right)$ using addition?

$\left[-4 + \left(+7\frac{3}{4}\right) \text{ or } -4 + 7\frac{3}{4}\right]$ In this addition problem, which addend has the greater absolute value? $\left[7\frac{3}{4}\right]$ Will the answer be positive, or negative? **[Positive.]**

Check

Ask: When subtracting a negative number from a negative number, how do you know if the difference is positive or negative? **[If the absolute value of the subtrahend is greater than the absolute value of the minuend, the difference is positive. If the absolute value of the minuend is greater, the difference is negative.]**

Ask: How can you rewrite the expression $\frac{1}{4} - \left(-3\frac{1}{2}\right)$ using addition?

$\left[\frac{1}{4} + \left(+3\frac{1}{2}\right) \text{ or } \frac{1}{4} + 3\frac{1}{2}\right]$ Will the answer be positive or negative?

Say: Sometimes the context of a problem can help you determine if the difference is positive or negative. To find the overall change in water level, you can subtract the current level from the previous level, $-10.16 - (-25.4)$. By reading the problem, you can tell that the water level has risen, which indicates a positive overall change.

Example 6

Say: Before performing operations, you can change subtraction to addition by adding the opposite.

Say: Using parentheses around the sum of the positive numbers and around the sum of the negative numbers can help you keep the values separated.

Ask: When might you want to group a positive and negative number together? **[Possible answer: When the numbers are opposites, or when the numbers have a sum that is an integer.]**

Ask: After you find the sum of the positive numbers and the sum of the negative numbers, how can you tell if the answer is positive or negative? **[If the sum of the positive and negative sums has the sign of the number with the greater absolute value.]**

Check

Ask: What is the first step in solving each of these problems? **[Change subtraction to addition.]**

COMMON MISCONCEPTION

Ask: What is the error in
$-2.69 + 16.05 - 13.21 - 0.8 = (2.69 + 16.05) + (-13.21 + (-0.8)) = 4.73$?

Reason incorrect:

$$-2.69 + 16.05 - 13.21 - 0.8$$
$$= (2.69 + 16.05) + (-13.21 + (-0.8))$$
$$= 4.73$$

> In this step −2.69 was grouped with the positive numbers instead of negative numbers when adding the opposite.

Solution:

$$-2.69 + 16.05 - 13.21 - 0.8$$
$$= (-2.69) + 16.05 + (-13.21) + (-0.8)$$
$$= (16.05) + \left[(-2.69) + (-13.21) + (-0.8) \right]$$
$$= 16.05 + (-16.7)$$
$$= 0.65$$

Ask: How could this error have been avoided? **[Possible answer: The student could have used parentheses around each negative number first, then used the Commutative Property to move the numbers with the same sign together.]**

ADDITIONAL ONLINE INTERVENTION RESOURCES

Use the following for students who have not mastered the concepts in Skill 1.

- Math on the Spot videos
- Personal Math Trainer with customized intervention
- Building Block worksheets (Skill 2: Add and Subtract Decimals; Skill 3: Add and Subtract Fractions; Skill 4: Add and Subtract Integers)

Name _____ Date _____ Class _____

SKILL 1 **Add and Subtract Rational Numbers**

Example 1

To add rational numbers with the same sign, apply the rules for adding integers. The sum will have the same sign as the rational numbers.

A. Find $0.25 + 2.5$.

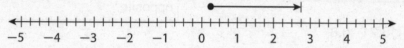

Start at 0.25. Move 2.5 units to the *right* because the second addend is *positive*.

The result is 2.75.

B. Find $-\frac{1}{2} + \left(-2\frac{1}{4}\right)$.

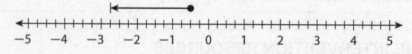

Start at $-\frac{1}{2}$. Move $2\frac{1}{4}$ units to the *left* because the second addend is *negative*.

The result is $-2\frac{3}{4}$.

Vocabulary
Rational numbers
Integers
Addend
Absolute value
Commutative Property of Addition
Associative Property of Addition
Adding the opposite

Check
Use the number line to find each sum.

1. $1\frac{1}{4} + 3\frac{1}{2} = $ _____

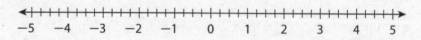

2. $-1.5 + (-2.25) = $ _____

3. $-\frac{9}{4} + (-2) = $ _____

Example 2

To add rational numbers with different signs, find the difference of their absolute values. Then use the sign of the rational number with the greater absolute value.

A. Find $\frac{1}{2} + \left(-3\frac{1}{4}\right)$.

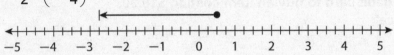

Start at $\frac{1}{2}$. Move $\left|-3\frac{1}{4}\right| = 3\frac{1}{4}$ units to the *left* because the second addend is *negative*.

The result is $-2\frac{3}{4}$.

B. Find $-2.75 + 6.25$.

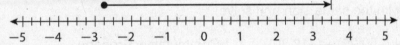

Start at -2.75. Move $|6.25| = 6.25$ units to the *right* because the second addend is *positive*.

The result is 3.5.

Check

Use the number line to find each sum.

4. $-3\frac{3}{4} + 5\frac{1}{2} =$ _____

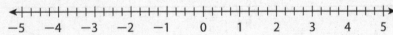

5. $4.75 + (-7.25) =$ _____

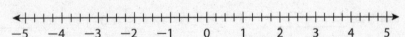

Solve.

6. Sylvia poured out $2\frac{1}{2}$ cups of lemonade from a pitcher. Then she added another $3\frac{1}{4}$ cups. What was the overall change in the amount of lemonade in the pitcher?

Example 3

To add three or more rational numbers, you can apply the Commutative and Associative Properties of Addition to group terms with the same sign before adding.

On Monday, Patrick had a balance of $150.65 in his bank account. On Tuesday, he wrote a check for $50.25 and deposited $75.80. On Wednesday, he used his debit card to buy an item costing $18.30. What is his ending balance?

Step 1 Use *positive* numbers to represent the credits to Patrick's account. Use *negative* numbers to represent the amount he spent.

Step 2 Find $150.65 + (-50.25) + 75.80 + (-18.30)$.

Step 3 Group numbers with the same sign and solve.

$150.65 + 75.80 + (-50.25) + (-18.30)$ Commutative Property

$= (150.65 + 75.80) + (-50.25 + (-18.30))$ Associative Property

$= 226.45 + (-68.55)$ Add the numbers inside the parentheses.

$= 157.90$ Find the difference of the absolute values: $226.45 - 68.55$, and use the sign of the number with the greatest absolute value. The sum is positive.

Patrick's ending balance is $157.90.

Check

Find each sum.

7. $4.5 + (-12) + (-4.5) = $ _____

8. $-2 + 1\frac{1}{4} + 3\frac{1}{2} = $ _____

9. $-2\frac{1}{3} + 1\frac{1}{6} + \left(-3\frac{1}{2}\right) + 4 = $ _____

10. $-7.5 + (-9.2) + 6.8 + (-11.5) = $ _____

11. A deep-sea diver was submerged at a depth of $-50\frac{3}{4}$ feet. She dove an additional 9 feet down and then ascended $24\frac{1}{2}$ feet. What is the new depth of the diver?

_____

Example 4

To subtract rational numbers, apply the same rules you use to subtract integers.

One afternoon, an outdoor thermometer showed a temperature of 3.5°C. That evening the temperature dropped 6.75°. What was the temperature that evening?

Subtract to find the temperature that evening.

Find $3.5 - 6.75$.

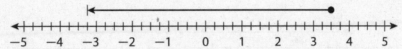

Start at 3.5. Move $|-6.75| = 6.75$ units to the *left* because you are subtracting a *positive* number.

The result is –3.25.

The temperature that night was –3.25°C.

Check

Use the number line to find each difference.

12. $2\frac{1}{2} - 4 =$ _____

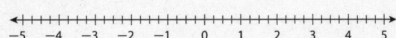

13. $-1.25 - 0.75 =$ _____

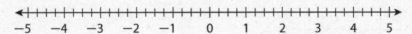

14. $5 - 7\frac{1}{4} =$ _____

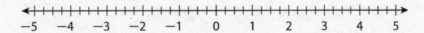

15. What's the Error? Explain the error. Find the correct solution.

$-1.25 - 2.5 = -3.25$

Example 5

To subtract negative rational numbers, move in the opposite direction on the number line.

A geologist was taking rock samples from a cave. His first set of samples was taken from an elevation of –7.75 meters. His second set of samples was taken from an elevation of –4 meters. What is the geologist's change in elevation between samples?

Subtract to find the difference in elevation.

Find $-4-(-7.75)$.

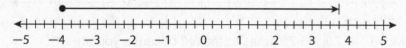

Start at –4. Move $|-7.75| = 7.75$ units to the *right* because you are subtracting a *negative* number.

The result is 3.75.

The geologist's change in elevation between samples is 3.75 m.

Check

Use the number line to find each difference.

16. $-3.25-(-2.5)$ _____

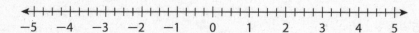

17. $\frac{1}{4}-\left(-3\frac{1}{2}\right)=$ _____

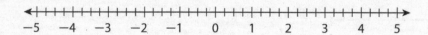

Solve.

18. After a week of record heat, the water level for a river was 25.4 cm below normal. The following week, the water level was 10.16 cm below normal. What is the overall change in water level?

_____

Example 6

To subtract rational numbers, you can add the opposite to change the subtraction problem into an addition problem. Then use the Commutative and Associative Properties of Addition to group terms with the same sign before adding.

Find $11.25 - 14.3 - 5 + 16.22 - 9.4$.

$11.25 + (-14.3) + (-5) + 16.22 + (-9.4)$	Change from subtraction to addition by adding the opposite.
$= 11.25 + 16.22 + (-14.3) + (-5) + (-9.4)$	Commutative Property
$= (11.25 + 16.22) + (-14.3 + (-5) + (-9.4))$	Associative Property
$= 27.47 + (-28.7)$	Add the numbers inside the parentheses.
$= -1.23$	Find the difference of the absolute values: $27.47 - 28.7$, and use the sign of the number with the greatest absolute value. The sum is negative.

The result is -1.23

Check

Solve.

19. $3.2 - 12.1 - 5 + 2.8 =$ _____

20. $2 + 1\frac{1}{4} - 3\frac{1}{2} + 4 =$ _____

21. $-2 - \frac{7}{2} + \frac{1}{4} - 5 =$ _____

22. $-3.9 + 10.15 - 13 + 1.4 =$ _____

23. Explain the Error. Find the correct solution.
$-2.69 + 16.05 - 13.21 - 0.8 = (2.69 + 16.05) + (-13.21 + (-0.8)) = 4.73$

SKILL 1 ADD AND SUBTRACT RATIONAL NUMBERS

Add and Subtract Polynomials

KEY TEACHING POINTS

Example 1

Use contrasting examples to show the difference between like terms and terms that are not like terms.

Say: 4 and –7 are like terms that have no variables.

Say: $3y$ and $8y$ are like terms that have variables.

Say: $-4xy^3$ and $6xy^3$ are like terms that have more than one variable, and include variables with integer exponents.

Say: The following sets of terms are *not* like terms.

$4x$ and -7 $\qquad$ $5x$ and $-2x^2$ $\quad$ $-4x^3y$ and $6xy^3$

Ask: Why are $-4xy^3$ and $6xy^3$ like terms but $-4x^3y$ and $6xy^3$ are not like terms? **[The *x* and *y* have different exponents.]**

Check

Ask: How are st^4 and s^4t alike? **[They both use the variables *s* and *t*, and they both have an exponent of 4.]** How are st^4 and s^4t different? **[The exponent is on different variables.]**

Say: The terms st^4 and s^4t are not like terms because the variables must be raised to the same power. The only difference between like terms is the coefficient.

Example 2

Say: To remember which property is which, you can think of the word "commutative" as related to the word "commute," which is what you do when you go from one place to another.

Ask: How are the terms on each side of the equation $6x + 9 = 9 + 6x$ different? **[The terms have changed positions.]**

Say: The word "associative" is related to the word "associate," which means linked together.

Ask: How are the terms on each side of the equation $(8 + 10x) + 3x = 8 + (10x + 3x)$ different? **[The terms are all in the same order, but they have been grouped differently.]**

Check

Say: Determine which property is used by asking "Do the terms change position or are the terms grouped differently?"

Ask: Can you tell which property is used by looking for parentheses? **[No.]** Which question uses parentheses but illustrates the Commutative Property? **[Question 6]** Why are parentheses used in Question 6? **[To separate the plus sign and the negative sign.]**

KEY TEACHING POINTS

Example 3

Ask: How is the Commutative Property used in $7x + (4 + 3x) + 5 = 7x + (3x + 4) + 5$?
[The terms inside the parentheses change position.]

Say: The Commutative Property is used first to move like terms next to each other.

Emphasize that like terms should be grouped together before adding or subtracting to combine them. Each term and its 'front' sign (+ or −) should be together when rearranging the terms.

Ask: If you remove the parentheses from $(12y^2 - 2) + 4y^2$, what is your next step in simplifying the expression? **[Use the Commutative Property to switch the places of the last two terms, −2 and $+4y^2$.]**

ALTERNATE STRATEGY

Strategy: Use algebra tiles.

1. The algebraic expression $7x + (4 + 3x) + 5$ can be simplified using algebra tiles.

2. Model the expression using algebra tiles. Make four sets of tiles, one to model each term.

x	x	x	x
x	x	x

1	1
1	1

x	x
x

1	1	1
1	1

3. Move tiles into sets of like tiles.

x	x	x	x	x
x	x	x	x	x

1	1	1	1	1
1	1	1	1

4. Write an expression that models the tile sets.

$10x + 9$

For students who are unfamiliar with algebra tiles, explain the difference between positive tiles and negative tiles, and point out that variables have their own tiles.

KEY TEACHING POINTS

Example 4

A monomial contains only one term. "Mono" means one. A polynomial contains more than one term. "Poly" means many.

Ask: How many terms are in the expression $-3z^2$? **[One.]** Is $-3z^2$ a monomial or not? **[Monomial.]**

Ask: How many terms are in the expression $3a + 2$? **[Two.]** Is $3a + 2$ a monomial or not? **[Polynomial.]**

Say: Polynomials and terms are also classified by their degree. The degree of a term is the sum of the exponents in that term. The degree of a polynomial is the greatest sum of the exponents on the variables in each term.

Show this example:

$$\frac{1}{4}c^3d$$

Say: This monomial has degree 4 because the variable c has the exponent 3 and the variable d has an exponent 1. $3 + 1 = 4$.

$$-9x^4 + 12x^2 + 2x + 7$$

Say: This polynomial has degree 4 because the term with the greatest degree is degree 4.

Check

Ask: In the expression $6 + 15a^3 + 12a^5$, what degree is the term $+ 6$? **[0]** Why? **[There are no exponents.]**

Ask: Are there any like terms in $9y^3 + 2 + 7y^3 - y^2$? **[Yes, $9y^3$ and $7y^3$.]**

Say: The standard form of a polynomial is simplified, so combine like terms, then write the terms in decreasing order of degree.

Example 5

Say: Adding polynomials is similar to addition of numbers in expanded form. Just as you can only add hundreds to hundreds, tens to tens, and ones to ones, you can only add terms that are like terms.

Say: When the terms are written vertically, add only the coefficients and keep the variables as they are.

Say: It may help to mark terms in the original problem as you rewrite them.

Check

Ask: There is no term that has the variable and exponent n^3 in the second polynomial. What gets added to $20n^3$? **[Nothing.]**

Say: When there is no matching term in the two polynomial expressions, add nothing, or zero. To write polynomial addition vertically when there are no matching terms, leave a blank space in the vertical column, or put a zero in the space as a placeholder.

Example 6

Say: Subtracting polynomials can be done in the same way as subtracting integers, by adding the opposite.

Ask: When subtracting horizontally, why is it important to write the problem first using the opposite of the terms in the second polynomial? **[Possible answer: It is easy to get the signs mixed up if you don't rewrite it first.]**

Check

Say: In the problem $(7z^4 + 19z^2 + 7z^3 + 20z) - (7z^2 + 19z^3 + 20z)$, there are four terms in the first polynomial and only three terms in the second. Just as with adding polynomials, you can think of this as subtracting zero in that space.

COMMON MISCONCEPTION

Ask: What is the Error?

$$(7m^2 + 5) - (11m^2 - 4) = 7m^2 + 5 - 11m^2 - 4$$
$$= (7m^2 - 11m^2) + (5 - 4)$$
$$= -4m^2 + 1$$

Reason incorrect: To subtract polynomials, you add the opposite of each term. The term -4 in the polynomial should have been changed to $+4$.

Solution:

$$(7m^2 + 5) - (11m^2 - 4) = 7m^2 + 5 - 11m^2 + 4$$
$$= (7m^2 - 11m^2) + (5 + 4)$$
$$= -4m^2 + 9$$

Ask: How could this error have been avoided? **[Possible answer: The student could have used parentheses around each negative number first, then used the Commutative Property to move the numbers with the same sign together.]**

ADDITIONAL ONLINE INTERVENTION RESOURCES

 Use the following for students who have not mastered the concepts in Skill 2.

• Math on the Spot videos

• Personal Math Trainer with customized intervention

• Building Block worksheets (Skill 24: Distributive Property; Skill 84: Simplify Polynomial Expressions)

SKILL 2 Add and Subtract Polynomials

Example 1

In an algebraic expression, a term is a number, a variable, or the product of a number and one or more variables. The coefficient of a term is the term's numerical factor. A constant is a term with no variable.

In the algebraic expression $5x^2 + 3x - 8$, there are 3 terms: $5x^2$, $3x$, and -8. The coefficients of the terms are 5 and 3. The constant is -8.

Like terms have the same variable factors.

Like Terms: 4 and -7; $3y$ and $8y$; $5x^2$ and $-2x^2$; $-4xy^3$ and $6xy^3$
Not Like Terms: $4x$ and -7; $3x$ and $8y$; $5x$ and $-2x^2$; $-4x^3y$ and $6xy^3$

Vocabulary
Term
Coefficient
Constant
Like terms
Commutative Property of Addition
Associative Property of Addition
Combine like terms
Monomial
Polynomial
Standard form of a polynomial

Check
Tell whether the terms are like terms.

1. $-4m$ and $-4m^2$ _____

2. $9n^3$ and $-n^3$ _____

3. $-2pq^2$ and $5pq^2$ _____

4. st^4 and s^4t _____

Example 2

The Commutative Property of Addition states that changing the order of the terms of an expression does not affect the sum. For example,

$$6x + 9 = 9 + 6x \qquad \text{and} \qquad -4 + 7x = 7x + (-4).$$

The Associative Property of Addition states that changing the grouping of the terms of an expression does not affect the sum. For example,

$$(8 + 10x) + 3x = 8 + (10x + 3x) \qquad \text{and} \qquad 5x + (9x + 2) = (5x + 9x) + 2.$$

Check
Name the property that each statement illustrates.

5. $11 + (7 + 5x) = (11 + 7) + 5x$ _____

6. $-1 + 6x = 6x + (-1)$ _____

7. $12 + (4 + 7x) = (4 + 7x) + 12$ _____

8. $3 + (3 + 3x) = (3 + 3) + 3x$ _____

Example 3

To simplify an algebraic expression, use properties and operations to combine the terms that are alike. This is called combining like terms.

A. Simplify $7x + (4 + 3x) + 5$.

$7x + (4 + 3x) + 5$	$=$	$7x + (3x + 4) + 5$	Commutative Property of Addition
	$=$	$(7x + 3x) + (4 + 5)$	Associative Property of Addition
	$=$	$10x + 9$	Combine like terms.

B. Simplify $(8xy^2 + 3xy) + 5xy^2$.

$(8xy^2 + 3xy) + 5xy^2$	$=$	$(3xy + 8xy^2) + 5xy^2$	Commutative Property of Addition
	$=$	$3xy + (8xy^2 + 5xy^2)$	Associative Property of Addition
	$=$	$3xy + 13xy^2$	Combine like terms.

Check

Simplify each algebraic expression by combining like terms.

9. $2x + (9 + x) - 6$ _____

10. $(12y^2 - 2) + 4y^2$ _____

11. $(15wz^2 + 3wz^3) - 5wz^3$ _____

12. $-9a^2 + (5 + 9a^2) - 5$ _____

Example 4

A monomial is a real number, a variable, or the product of a real number and one or more variables with whole-number exponents. A polynomial is a monomial or a sum of monomials.

Monomials: $2y \qquad -3z^2 \qquad \frac{1}{4}c^3d \qquad 15 \qquad 0$

Polynomials: $3a \qquad -4b + 15 \qquad 9c^3 - 12c^2 + 3c + 1 \qquad 4d^4 + 8d^2 + 1$

A polynomial is in standard form if its monomial terms are written in decreasing order according to degree.

Write the polynomial $12x^2 + 7 - 9x^4 + 2x$ in standard form.

$12x^2 + 7 - 9x^4 + 2x$

$= -9x^4 + 12x^2 + 2x + 7$ Write terms in order according to degree.

Check

Write each polynomial in standard form.

13. $6 + 15a^3 + 12a^5$ _____

14. $-12x + 2x^2 - 32$ _____

15. $-10 - 10b - 10b^4$ _____

16. $9y^3 + 2 + 7y^3 - y^2$ _____

Example 5

You can add polynomials vertically or horizontally by adding like terms.

A. Simplify $(3g^4 - 9g^2 + 12) + (2g^4 - 15g^2 + 10)$.
    To add the polynomials vertically, align like terms. Then add coefficients.

$$\begin{array}{r} 3g^4 - 9g^2 + 12 \\ + 2g^4 - 15g^2 + 10 \\ \hline 5g^4 - 24g^2 + 22 \end{array}$$

The sum is $5g^4 - 24g^2 + 22$.

B. Simplify $(10h^2 + 9h + 2) + (3h^2 + 16h + 21)$.
    To add the polynomials horizontally, group like terms. Then add coefficients.

$$\begin{aligned} (10h^2 + 9h + 2) + (3h^2 + 16h + 21) &= (10h^2 + 3h^2) + (9h + 16h) + (2 + 21) \\ &= 13h^2 + 25h^2 + 23 \end{aligned}$$

The sum is $13h^2 + 25h^2 + 23$.

Check
Simplify.

17. $\begin{array}{l} 4j^3 + 7j + 4 \\ + 6j^3 + 12j + 5 \\ \hline \end{array}$

18. $\begin{array}{l} 1k^5 + 7k^2 - 14 \\ + 18k^5 - 1k^2 - 6 \\ \hline \end{array}$

19. $(18m + 13) + (-8 - 9m)$ _____

20. $(20n^3 + 6n^2 + 17 + 2n) + (10n^2 + 10n + 9)$ _____

21. The population of Springfield and the population of Franklin over a
    20-year period can be modeled by the following polynomials, where
    $n = 0$ corresponds to the first year in the 20-year period.

    Springfield: $-12n^2 + 85n + 1300$
    Franklin: $-6n^2 + 73n + 975$

    Write a polynomial that represents the total population of the two towns
    over the 20-year period.

    _____

Example 6

You can subtract polynomials vertically or horizontally. Subtracting a polynomial is the same as adding its opposite. To find the opposite of a polynomial, change each term to its opposite. Then add the coefficients.

A. Simplify $(13p^3 + 19p + 9) - (9p^3 + 17p - 18)$.

To subtract the polynomials vertically, align like terms.

Add the opposite of each term of the polynomial being subtracted.

$$
\begin{array}{r}
13p^3 + 19p + 9 \\
- \quad (9p^3 + 17p - 18)
\end{array}
\longrightarrow
\begin{array}{r}
13p^3 + 19p + 9 \\
+ \; -9p^3 - 17p + 18 \\
\hline
4p^3 + 2p + 27
\end{array}
$$

The difference is $4p^3 + 2p + 27$.

B. Simplify $(7q^2 + 15q) - (q^2 + 11q)$.

$(7q^2 + 15q) - (q^2 + 11q)$

$= 7q^2 + 15q - q^2 - 11q$

To subtract horizontally, find the opposite of each term of the polynomial being subtracted.

$= (7q^2 - q^2) + (15q - 11q)$ Group like terms.

$= \quad 6q^2 \quad + \quad 4q$ Add the coefficients.

The difference is $6q^2 + 4q$.

Check

Simplify.

22.
$$
\begin{array}{r}
18x^5 + x^2 + 14x \\
- \quad (9x^5 + 6x^2 + 9x)
\end{array}
$$

_____

23.
$$
\begin{array}{r}
15y^2 + 5y - 13 \\
- \quad (4y^2 - 4y - 2)
\end{array}
$$

_____

24. $(6w^3 + 3w) - (-2w - 19w^3)$ _____

25. $(7z^4 + 19z^2 + 7z^3 + 20z) - (7z^2 + 19z^3 + 20z)$ _____

26. Explain the Error. Find the correct solution.

$(7m^2 + 5) - (11m^2 - 4) = 7m^2 + 5 - 11m^2 - 4$

$= (7m^2 - 11m^2) + (5 - 4)$

$= -4m^2 + 1$

SKILL 2 ADD AND SUBTRACT POLYNOMIALS

Algebraic Expressions

KEY TEACHING POINTS

Example 1

Remind students that an algebraic expression is one that uses letters to stand for unknown values.

Say: Evaluate means to find the value, so when you evaluate an expression, you find its value. In each expression, replace the variable with the value you are given, then perform any operations.

Review the order of operations.
- Operations inside grouping symbols
- Exponents
- Multiplication and division, from left to right.
- Addition and subtraction, from left to right.

Part A

Say: When there is a coefficient in front of a variable, it indicates multiplication. When you replace the variable with a value, insert parentheses around the variable.

Part B

Ask: What are the rules for multiplying integers? **[Multiply the absolute values. When the signs are the same, the product is positive. When the signs are different, the product is negative.]**

Check

Ask: After evaluating the expression, should you see any variables? **[No.]** Why? **[When you evaluate the expression, you replace the variables with numbers.]**

Say: When you replace a variable with an exponent, the exponent acts on the entire value of the variable.

Point out that when the variable p is replaced by the value -1 in the expression $3p^2 - 2p + 8$, p^2 evaluates as $(-1)^2 = 1$.

The negative sign is included as part of the base, so $(-1)^2$ means $(-1)(-1)$, not $-(1)(1)$.

KEY TEACHING POINTS

Example 2
Part A
Ask: How many terms are in this polynomial? **[4]** How many of the terms use the same variable? **[4]** How many of the terms use the same exponents? **[two have an exponent of 2, two have an exponent of 4]**

Demonstrate how to group the like terms first.
- $2x^2y^5 - 8x^5y^4 + 8x^2y^5 + 6x^5y^4$
- $= (6x^3 - 8x^3) + (-4x^2 + 10x^2)$ Group like terms.
- $= -2x^3 + 6x^2$ Mentally combine the coefficients.

Check
Ask: What are the like terms in $x^2 + 2x - 3x^2 - 4$? **[x^2 and $-3x^2$]**

Say: Signed coefficients follow the same rules for operations as signed numbers. Because the coefficient -3 has a greater absolute value than the coefficient 1, the sum of x^2 and $-3x^2$ is negative, $-2x^2$.

Say: There are four terms in the polynomial $x^2 + 2x - 3x^2 - 4$. The constant 4 is a term, and if there are other constants in the polynomial, the constants may be combined.

ALTERNATE STRATEGY

Strategy: Use visual cues to combine like terms.

1. Remind students that only the coefficient in like terms can be different. Write $-12.5r^5s^2 + 8r^3s^2 - r^5s^2 - 1.2r^3s^2$ on the board. Have students write the expression on paper as an example.

2. Circle the terms with r^5s^2 in blue and circle the terms with r^3s^2 in red. If colored chalk or markers are not available, different shapes may be used.

3. **Say:** Only terms that have the same color (or shape) may be combined.

4. **Ask:** What is the simplified term for the monomials in blue circles? **[$-13.5r^5s^2$]** Simplify the terms with the rectangles. **[$6.8r^3s^2$]**

5. **Say:** The simplified polynomial is written as $-13.5r^5s^2 + 6.8r^3s^2$ because the terms are written in descending order of exponents.

Remind students to include the negative signs inside the circles.

KEY TEACHING POINTS

Example 3

Say: To simplify some algebraic expressions, you must use the Distributive Property first.

Ask: Why is this not a monomial term? $2x(x+2)$ **[It contains a plus sign.]**

Say: When an expression contains parentheses, use the Distributive Property to remove them before you combine like terms. To use the Distributive Property, multiply each term inside the parentheses by the factor outside the parentheses, $2x$.

Multiply $2x(x)$ and $2x(2)$.

Ask: What is $2x(x)$? **[$2x^2$]**

Say: When you multiply the same variable, use an exponent to show how many times the variable is a factor.

Check

Say: Expressions with rational coefficients are treated in the same way as rational numbers.

Review the steps of the solution together:

$\dfrac{1}{3}x(1+9x)-2(3x+4)+\dfrac{2}{3}x^2$

$\dfrac{1}{3}x+3x^2-6x-8+\dfrac{2}{3}x^2$ Remove parentheses using the Distributive Property.

$3x^2+\dfrac{2}{3}x^2+\dfrac{1}{3}x-6x-8$ Rearrange in descending order of exponents.

$\left(3x^2+\dfrac{2}{3}x^2\right)+\left(\dfrac{1}{3}x-6x\right)-8$ Identify like terms. Be careful here, the like terms are not the terms that have like fractions.

$3\dfrac{2}{3}x^2-5\dfrac{2}{3}x-8$ Combine like terms.

Ask: How many times should you use the Distributive Property in $3xy(x^2y-2)-2x^2(xy^2+1)+6xy$? **[2]**

Say: There are two sets of parentheses, so use the Distributive Property twice. In the second set, you multiply $2x^2(xy^2)$ first. You can think of this as each factor individually, $2(x)(x)(x)(y)(y)$. The coefficient is 2 and there are three x variables and two y variables, so the product is $2x^3y^2$.

KEY TEACHING POINTS

Example 4

Say: To write an algebraic expression, variables are used in place of unknown numbers. The sum of x and 3 is written as $x + 3$.

Ask: To write the algebraic expression for 11 minus twice x and 10, how do you decide what the two terms are? **[The main operation is "minus" so that will separate the two terms. The left term is 11, the right term is the product of twice x and 10.]**

Check

Ask: How many operations are given in the phrase "the quotient when 5 more than y squared is divided by 7"? **[2]** What are the operations? **[division and addition]**

Ask: In the phrase, "the sum of t and 8, times the difference of s cubed and $2y$," what does the comma tell you? **[The entire sum is multiplied by the difference of s cubed and $2y$.]** If the comma was left out, how could the algebraic expression be different? **[$t + 8(s^3 - 2y)$, so that the difference is only multiplied by 8.]** What other words could be used to show the entire sum is multiplied by the difference? **[the quantity t plus 8 multiplied by the difference of s cubed and $2y$.]**

COMMON MISCONCEPTION

Ask: What is the error in this problem?

$$2a^5b^3 + 3a^2b - a^5b^3 - 2a^2b = 2a^{14}b^8$$

Reason incorrect: The exponents have been combined instead of just the coefficients.

Solution:
$$2a^5b^3 + 3a^2b - a^5b^3 - 2a^2b$$
$$= 2a^5b^3 - a^5b^3 + 3a^2b - 2a^2b$$
$$= (2 - 1)a^5b^3 + (3 - 2)a^2b$$
$$= a^5b^3 + a^2b$$

Say: Combining like terms only combines the coefficients. Like terms must have exactly the same variables with exactly the same exponents.

ADDITIONAL ONLINE INTERVENTION RESOURCES

 Use the following for students who have not mastered the concepts in Skill 3.

- Math on the Spot videos
- Personal Math Trainer with customized intervention
- Building Block worksheets (Skill 27: Evaluate Expressions)

**SKILL
3**

Algebraic Expressions

Example 1

To evaluate an algebraic expression, substitute the given value for the variable, and then use the order of operations to simplify.

A. Evaluate $10p + 6$ for $p = 5$.

$10p + 6 = 10(5) + 6$ Replace p with 5 since 5 is the given value.

$= 50 + 6$ Order of operations says to multiply first.

$= 56$ Add.

B. Evaluate $-7y - 12$ for $y = -3$.

$-7y - 12 = -7(-3) - 12$ Replace y with -3 since -3 is the given value.

$= 21 - 12$ Order of operations says to multiply first.

$= 9$ Subtract.

C. Evaluate $2x^2 - 4x + 3$ for $x = 2$.

$2x^2 - 4x + 3 = 2(2)^2 - 4(2) + 3$ Replace x with 2 since 2 is the given value.

$= 2(4) - 4(2) + 3$ Order of operations says to evaluate exponents first.

$= 8 - 8 + 3$ Multiply.

$= 3$ Simplify.

Vocabulary

Algebraic expression

Variable

Order of operations

Distributive Property

Like terms

Check

Evaluate each expression for the given value.

1. $3s + 8$ for $s = 7$.

2. $-4t - 16$ for $t = 3$.

3. $25 - 6x$ for $x = -10$.

4. $y^2 - 12$ for $y = 4$.

5. $-t^2 + 2t$ for $x = 2$.

6. $3p^2 - 2p + 8$ for $p = -1$.

Example 2

To simplify an algebraic expression, use the Distributive Property to combine like terms.

A. Simplify $6x^3 - 4x^2 + 10x^2 - 8x^3$.

$6x^3 - 8x^3 - 4x^2 + 10x^2$ Rearrange in descending order of exponents.

$= \left(6x^3 - 8x^3\right) + \left(-4x^2 + 10x^2\right)$ Identify like terms.

$= x^3\left(6 - 8\right) + x^2\left(-4 + 10\right)$ Combine using the Distributive Property.

$= -2x^3 + 6x^2$ Simplify.

B. Simplify $2x^2y^5 - 8x^5y^4 + 8x^2y^5 + 6x^5y^4$.

$-8x^5y^4 + 6x^5y^4 + 2x^2y^5 + 8x^2y^5$ Rearrange in descending order of exponents.

$= \left(-8x^5y^4 + 6x^5y^4\right) + \left(2x^2y^5 + 8x^2y^5\right)$ Identify like terms.

$= x^5y^4\left(-8 + 6\right) + x^2y^5\left(2 + 8\right)$ Combine using the Distributive Property.

$= -2x^5y^4 + 10x^2y^5$ Simplify.

Check

Simplify each expression.

7. $4x - 15x$

8. $\dfrac{1}{3}s + \dfrac{7}{2}s$

9. $x^2 + 2x - 3x^2 - 4$

10. $5 + 12.2p^2 - 3.2 - 8.7p^2$

11. $\dfrac{1}{2}m^2n - 4n^2 - 2m^2n + \dfrac{1}{3}n^2$

12. $-12.5r^5s^2 + 8r^3s^2 - r^5s^2 - 1.2r^3s^2$

Example 3

To simplify an algebraic expression that includes a product of expressions, use the Distributive Property first to remove all parentheses. Then combine like terms.

A. Simplify $2x(x+2)+x^2-5x$.

$2x(x+2)+x^2-5x$

$=2x(x)+2x(2)+x^2-5x$ Multiply expressions using the Distributive Property.

$=2x^2+4x+x^2-5x$ Multiply.

$=2x^2+x^2+4x-5x$ Rearrange in descending order of exponents.

$=(2x^2+x^2)+(4x-5x)$ Identify like terms.

$=x^2(2+1)+x(4-5)$ Combine using the Distributive Property.

$=3x^2-x$ Simplify.

Check

Simplify each expression.

13. $6(3r-7)-2$

14. $\frac{1}{2}x(2x+6)-11$

15. $s^2+3s(3-8s)+s-2$

16. $\frac{1}{3}x(1+9x)-2(3x+4)+\frac{2}{3}x^2$

17. $3a^2b(2a+1)+2a^3b-4a^2b$

18. $3xy(x^2y-2)-2x^2(xy^2+1)+6xy$

Example 4

To write an algebraic expression from a description, you can use word associations:

Operation	Associated Words and Phrases
Add	sum, plus, more than, increased by, added to
Subtract	minus, difference, less than, decreased by, subtracted from
Multiply	product, times, of, twice, multiplied by
Divide	quotient, divided by

Quantities are enclosed in parentheses: ( )

Write each phrase as an algebraic expression.

A. the sum of x and 3: $x + 3$

B. 5 less than y: $y - 5$

C. the product of 7 and b, increased by 2: $7b + 2$

D. the quotient of 11 minus twice x and 10: $\dfrac{11 - 2x}{10}$

E. the quantity r plus s times the quantity r minus s: $(r + s)(r - s)$

Check

Write each phrase as an algebraic expression.

19. x increased by 8

20. the difference of 12 and y

21. the product of 3 and the quantity t minus 4

22. the difference of m and n, divided by the sum of m and n

23. the quotient when 5 more than y squared is divided by 7

24. the sum of t and 8, times the difference of s cubed and 2

25. Explain the Error. Find the correct solution.

$2a^5b^3 + 3a^2b - a^5b^3 - 2a^2b = 2a^{14}b^8$

SKILL 3 ALGEBRAIC EXPRESSIONS

Algebraic Representations of Transformations

KEY TEACHING POINTS

Example 1

Say: When a point is translated right, the *x*-coordinate increases.

Ask: Which coordinate changes and how does it change when a point is translated left? **[The x-coordinate decreases.]** Is it translated up? **[The y-coordinate increases.]** Is it translated down? **[The y-coordinate decreases.]**

Say: When a line is translated, every point on that line moves in the same translation. This means that every point on the original line, or preimage, moves the same distance to reach the new line, or image.

Ask: How are the preimage and image of a translated line related? **[They are parallel.]**

Say: The notation $(x, y) \rightarrow (x + a, y + b)$ is used to represent transformations. The original points are represented by (x, y), the arrow represents a transformation, and the second set of coordinates $(x + a, y + b)$ that include operations, in this case addition, shows how the line is transformed. This notation is called *mapping notation* because it shows the rule for how the preimage is mapped to the image.

Say: When the *x*-value moves 3 units right, the new *x*-value is $x + 3$. When the *y*-value moves one unit down, the new *y*-value is $y - 1$. In mapping notation this is written as $(x, y) \rightarrow (x + 3, y - 1)$.

Check

Review item 2 together.

Say: The translation is moving each point 4 units to the left and 3 units up.

Ask: How is each *x*-value changing? **[They are decreasing by 4.]** How is each *y*-value changing? **[They are increasing by 3.]**

Ask: How is this translation shown using mapping notation? **[$(x, y) \rightarrow (x - 4, y + 3)$]**

Have students assist in completing a table on the board to show the translation.

Point on line	Rule: $(x - 4, y + 3)$	Point on Transformation
$(-1, -4)$	$(-1 - 4, -4 + 3)$	$(-5, -1)$
$(1, -2)$	$(1 - 4, -2 + 3)$	$(-3, 1)$
$(5, 2)$	$(5 - 4, 2 + 3)$	$(1, 5)$

Graph the preimage and image together by locating each point of the preimage and connecting the points to form a line.

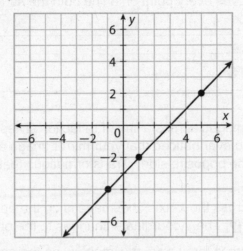

For each point, show a translation of 4 units left and 3 units up. Point out to students that translations can move the preimage in any direction.

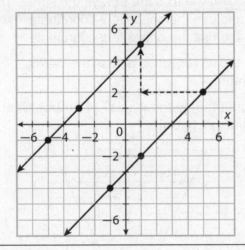

ALTERNATE STRATEGY

Strategy: Use a manipulative.

1. Using an overhead coordinate graph or a large coordinate grid, mark the points (0, –5), (1, –3), and (4, 3) and draw a line through the points.

2. Place the edge of a piece of cardstock, or other rigid straightedge along the line and mark the points on the cardstock.

3. Following the upper point, pull the cardstock up three units. Be sure the cardstock does not twist, but retains the exact slope of the original line.

4. Once again, following one point, move the cardstock left 5 units. Mark the image of the point you followed on the graph and draw a new line down the edge of the cardstock.

5. Pull the cardstock from the grid and check the remaining points.

6. **Ask:** Does the image of each point fall on the new line? **[Yes.]**

7. **Say:** A translation moves every point on a line both the same direction and the same distance.

KEY TEACHING POINTS

Example 2

Say: Reflections are mirror images across a line of reflection. These reflections are across the *x*-axis or *y*-axis. Have you ever noticed that your mirror image appears to be doing the same thing you are, but on the opposite side? Transformations that are reflections produce opposites.

Ask: If a point is reflected across the *x*-axis, the image is on the opposite side of the *x*-axis. Which coordinate changes? **[y]** The *y*-coordinate changes to the opposite value.

Ask: If a point is reflected across the *y*-axis, the image is on the opposite side of the *y*-axis. Which coordinate changes? **[x]** The *x*-coordinate changes to the opposite value.

Say: The rules for reflections over the axis are always the same. To reflect over the *x*-axis, keep the same *x*-coordinate and use the opposite *y*-coordinate. To reflect over the *y*-axis, keep the same *y*-coordinate and use the opposite *x*-coordinate.

Say: Look at the point (4, 5) and its reflection across the *y*-axis.
Point out the points on the graph.

Ask: What is the distance from (4, 5) to the *y*-axis? **[4 units.]** What is the distance from the reflected point (−4, 5) to the *y*-axis? **[4 units.]**

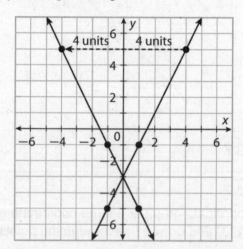

Say: In a reflection, a point and its image are always the same distance from the line of reflection, in this case, from the *y*-axis.

Check

Ask: When the point (−2, 0) is reflected across the *x*-axis, what is the image point? **[(−2, 0)]**

Say: When a point is reflected across the *x*-axis, the *y*-value is multiplied by −1 to find its opposite. For point (−2, 0), the *y*-value is 0. Any number multiplied by 0 is still 0.

Ask: Is the point (−2, 0) and its reflection the same distance from the *x*-axis? **[Yes.]**

COMMON MISCONCEPTION

Ask: What is the error in this problem?
A line has the points (−3, −4),
(−1, −2), and (3, 2). Find the points
after a reflection across the x-axis
and a translation of 1 unit up.

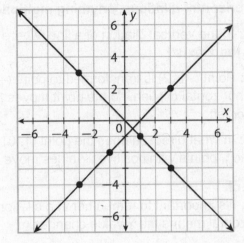

Points on transformation:
(3, −3), (1, −1), and (−3, 3)

Reason incorrect:

The wrong coordinate was multiplied by −1,
so the line reflected across the y-axis, then
translated 1 unit up.

Solution: Multiply each y-value by −1 to reflect
across the x-axis, and then translate the point
1 unit up.

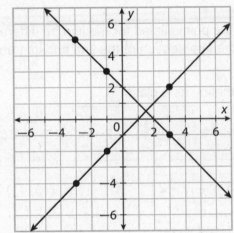

Say: Check your answer by looking at the points you reflected. Move the same distance across the x-axis, and then move one unit up.

KEY TEACHING POINTS

Example 3
Say: A dilation that is a stretch increases one or both of the coordinates by a given factor. When the scale factor has an absolute value greater than 1, the resulting coordinate has a greater absolute value than the original.

Ask: If the scale factor for a dilation is $\frac{1}{c}$, where c is a positive number greater than 1, how will the coordinate change? **[It will become smaller.]** This is called a *compression*.

Say: You can use the words stretch and compress to understand a dilation. Think drawing the line on a rubber surface. If you stretch the rubber horizontally, the line is going to stretch horizontally. If you compress, or push together, the rubber vertically, the line is going to compress vertically.

Ask: In a horizontal dilation, why do points on the *y*-axis not change? **[When points are on the *y*-axis, the *x*-coordinate is 0. Since the *x*-coordinate is what is multiplied by a factor in horizontal dilations, anything multiplied by 0 is still 0.]**

Ask: In the vertical dilation of a line, where will the line and its transformation intersect? **[On the *x*-axis.]**

Say: Point $(-1, 2)$ is transformed to point $(-4, 2)$. Look at the graph of the transformation. This is a horizontal dilation, so the point moves horizontally. Points with negative *x*-values move further left.

Ask: In what direction does the point $(1, 0)$ transform? **[It moves right.]** In a horizontal dilation, points with positive *x*-values move further right.

Check

Say: It's important to remember in a dilation, vertical means the *y*-value changes and horizontal means the *x*-value changes.

Ask: When a point is dilated by a vertical stretch with a scale factor of 5, what coordinate changes and how? **[The *y*-value is multiplied by 5.]** What will the image of the point $(-4, 4)$ be? **(−4, 20)**

Ask: In problem 10, will all of the points listed for the line be different than their transformed points? **[Yes.]** Where should the intersection of the line and its transformation be? **[On the *x*-axis.]**

Create a table for the transformation as a class.

Point on line	Rule: $\left(x, \dfrac{1}{2} \cdot y \right)$	Point on Transformation
$(-3, -2)$	$\left(-3, \left(\dfrac{1}{2} \right) \cdot -2 \right)$	$(-3, -1)$
$(0, 1)$	$\left(0, \left(\dfrac{1}{2} \right) \cdot 1 \right)$	$\left(0, \dfrac{1}{2} \right)$
$(3, 4)$	$\left(3, \left(\dfrac{1}{2} \right) \cdot 4 \right)$	$(3, 2)$

Graph the original line and the transformation as a class.

Point out that the lines intersect on the *x*-axis.

Ask: When a point is dilated by a horizontal compression with a scale factor of $\dfrac{1}{3}$, what coordinate changes and how? **[The *x*-value is multiplied by $\dfrac{1}{3}$.]** What will the image of the point $(3, 4)$ be? **(1, 4)**

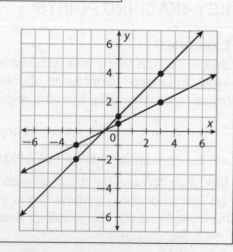

COMMON MISCONCEPTION

Ask: What is the error in this problem?

A line has the points $(-4, -3)$, $(0, -1)$, and $(4, 1)$. Find the points after a vertical stretch by a scale factor of two and a translation two units to the right.

Points on transformation: $(-2, 6)$, $(2, 2)$, $(6, -2)$

Reason incorrect: The incorrect points include a reflection about the x-axis, so the opposite y-value from the correct solution.

Solution: The problem asks for a vertical stretch by a scale factor of 2, so first multiply the y-value by 2. Then, the point should also be translated 2 units up, so add 2 to the x value.

Ask: How can you represent a vertical stretch of 2 and a translation of 2 units up using mapping notation? **$[(x, y) \rightarrow (x + 2, 2y)]$**

Demonstrate how to create a table to model the transformation.

Point on line	Rule: $(x + 2, 2y)$	Point on Transformation
$(-4, -3)$	$(-4 + 2, 2(-3))$	$(-2, -6)$
$(0, -1)$	$(0 + 2, 2(-1))$	$(2, -2)$
$(4, 1)$	$(4 + 2, 2(1))$	$(6, 2)$

ADDITIONAL ONLINE INTERVENTION RESOURCES

Use the following for students who have not mastered the concepts in Skill 4.

- Math on the Spot videos

- Personal Math Trainer with customized intervention

- Building Block worksheets (Skill 103: Transformations)

SKILL 4

Algebraic Representations of Transformations

Example 1

A translation is a type of transformation that shifts the graph of a function *up*, *down*, *right*, or *left*. If *a* and *b* are numbers greater than 0, then do the following:

Translation	Effect on coordinates
Right *a* units	Add *a* to the *x*-coordinate: $(x, y) \rightarrow (x + a, y)$
Left *a* units	Subtract *a* from the *x*-coordinate: $(x, y) \rightarrow (x - a, y)$
Up *b* units	Add *b* to the *y*-coordinate: $(x, y) \rightarrow (x, y + b)$
Down *b* units	Subtract *b* from the *y*-coordinate: $(x, y) \rightarrow (x, y - b)$

A line has the points (–3, –2), (0, 1), and (2, 3). Find the points after a translation of 3 units to the right and 1 unit down. Then graph the line and its transformation.

Point on line	Rule: $(x + 3, y - 1)$	Point on Transformation
$(-3, -2)$	$(-3 + 3, \ -2 - 1)$	$(0, -3)$
$(0, 1)$	$(0 + 3, \ 1 - 1)$	$(3, 0)$
$(2, 3)$	$(2 + 3, \ 3 - 1)$	$(5, 2)$

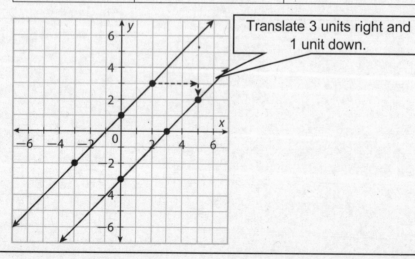

Translate 3 units right and 1 unit down.

Vocabulary

Transformation
Translation
Reflection
Dilation
Scale factor

Check

Find the points for the translation described. Then graph the line and its transformation.

1. A line has the points (–2, 3), (0, 1), and (4, –3). Find the points after a translation of 2 units to the left and 1 unit down.

2. A line has the points (–1, –4), (1, –2), and (5, 2). Find the points after a translation of 4 units to the left and 3 units up.

_____

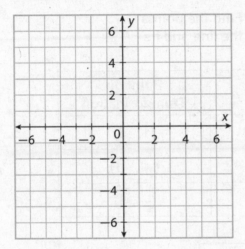

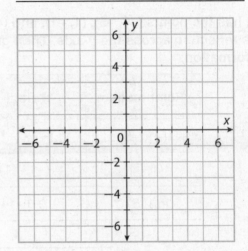

3. A line has the points (–4, 0), (0, –2), and (2, –3). Find the points after a translation of 1 unit up and 2 units to the right.

4. A line has the points (0, –5), (1, –3), and (4, 3). Find the points after a translation of 3 units up and 5 units to the left.

_____

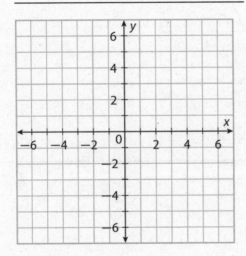

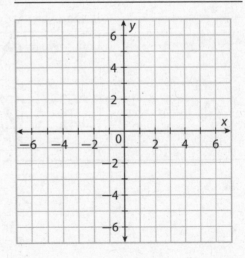

Example 2

A reflection is a type of transformation that reflects the graph of a function across the *x*-axis or *y*-axis.

Reflection	Effect on coordinates
Across the *x*-axis	Multiply each *y*-coordinate by –1: $(x, y) \rightarrow (x, -y)$
Across the *y*-axis	Multiply each *x*-coordinate by –1: $(x, y) \rightarrow (-x, y)$

A line has the points (–1, –5), (1, –1), and (4, 5). Find the points after a reflection across the *y*-axis. Then graph the line and its transformation.

Point on line	Rule: (–x, y)	Point on Transformation
(–1, –5)	$(-1 \cdot (-1), -5)$	(1, –5)
(1, –1)	$(-1 \cdot (1), -1)$	(–1, –1)
(4, 5)	$(-1 \cdot (4), 5)$	(–4, 5)

Reflect across the *y*-axis.

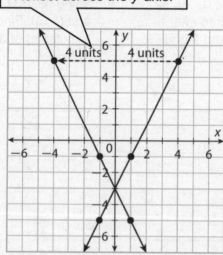

Check

Find the points for the reflection described. Then graph the line and its transformation.

5. A line has the points (−5, −3), (−2, 0), and (3, 5). Find the points after a reflection across the *x*-axis.

_____

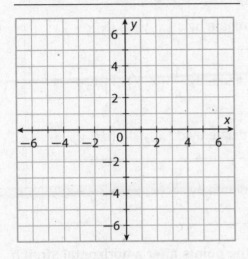

6. A line has the points (−1, −4), (1, 2), and (2, 5). Find the points after a reflection across the *y*-axis.

_____

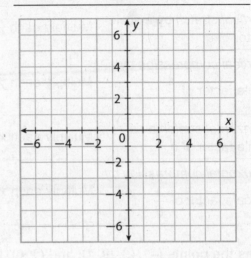

7. Explain the Error. Find the correct solution.

A line has the points (−3, −4), (−1, −2), and (3, 2). Find the points after a reflection across the *x*-axis and a translation of 1 unit up.

Points on transformation: (3, −3), (1, −1), and (−3, 3)

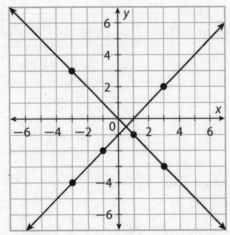

Error:

_____

_____

_____

Correct points on transformation:

_____

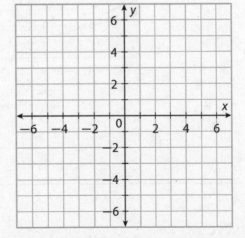

Example 3

A dilation is a type of transformation that stretches or compresses the graph of a function by a scale factor. You can stretch or compress a graph *vertically* in the *y*-direction or *horizontally* in the *x*-direction. If *c* and *d* are numbers greater than 1, then do the following:

Dilation	Effect on coordinates
Vertical stretch by a scale factor of *c*	Multiply each *y*-coordinate by c: $(x, y) \rightarrow (x, c \cdot y)$
Vertical compression by a scale factor of $\dfrac{1}{c}$	Multiply each *y*-coordinate by $\dfrac{1}{c}$: $(x, y) \rightarrow \left(x, \dfrac{1}{c} \cdot y\right)$
Horizontal stretch by a scale factor of *d*	Multiply each *x*-coordinate by d: $(x, y) \rightarrow (dx, y)$
Horizontal compression by a scale factor of $\dfrac{1}{d}$	Multiply each *x*-coordinate by $\dfrac{1}{d}$: $(x, y) \rightarrow \left(\dfrac{1}{d} \cdot x, y\right)$

A line has the points (–1, 2), (0, 1), and (1, 0). Find the points after a horizontal stretch by a scale factor of 4. Then graph the line and its transformation.

Point on line	Rule: $(4 \cdot x, y)$	Point on Transformation
(–1, 2)	$(4 \cdot (-1), 2)$	(–4, 2)
(0, 1)	$(4 \cdot (0), 1)$	(0, 1)
(1, 0)	$(4 \cdot (1), 0)$	(4, 0)

Stretch horizontally by a scale factor of 4.

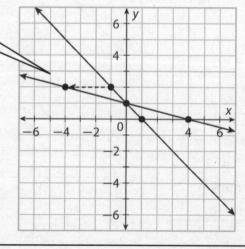

Check

A line has the points (–4, 4), (–1, –2), and (1, –6). Find the points for the dilation described.

8. vertical stretch by a scale factor of 5

9. horizontal stretch by a scale factor of 2

_____   _____

A line has the points (–3, –2), (0, 1), and (3, 4). Find the points for the dilation described. Then graph the line and its transformation.

10. vertical compression by a scale
    factor of $\frac{1}{2}$

11. horizontal compression by a scale
    factor of $\frac{1}{3}$

_____   _____

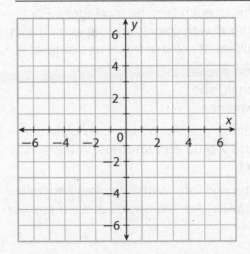   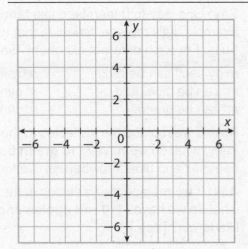

12. Explain the Error. Find the correct solution.

    A line has the points (–4, –3), (0, –1), and (4, 1). Find the points after a vertical stretch by a scale factor of 2 and a translation 2 units to the right.

    Points on transformation: (–2, 6), (2, 2), (6, –2).

    _____

    _____

SKILL 4 ALGEBRAIC REPRESENTATIONS OF TRANSFORMATIONS

Classifying Polynomials

KEY TEACHING POINTS

Example 1

Say: Like terms must have exactly the same variables with exactly the same exponents.

Ask: Why are the terms $-4c$ and $7c^4$ not like terms? **[The variables are the same, but they have different exponents.]**

ALTERNATE STRATEGY

Strategy: Replace variables with categories.

1. **Say:** One way to understand like terms is to think of each term as a category. For example, let's replace variables that use the letter m with colors, and the letter n with fruits. For each different exponent, we'll use a different color or fruit. For example:

   m by itself can be red, n by itself can be apples,
   m^2 can be blue, and n^2 can be bananas, and
   m^3 can be green. n^3 can be strawberries.

2. **Ask:** If we replace the variables in the terms $10m^3n^2$ and $7m^2n^3$ with our colors and fruits, what do we have? **[10 green bananas and 7 blue strawberries]** Are green bananas and blue strawberries like terms? **[No.]**

3. **Ask:** If we replace the variables in the terms $3mn$ and $7mn$ with our colors and fruits, what do we have? **[10 red apples and 7 red apples]** Are red apples and red apples like terms? **[Yes.]**

KEY TEACHING POINTS

Example 2

Say: A monomial is an expression with one term. Terms do not contain any addition or subtraction, so monomials do not include any addition or subtraction.

Ask: In the monomial $-4b^6$, what does the sign "–" mean? **[The 4 is negative.]**

Say: Monomials may contain negative signs. A negative sign is the same as multiplying by -1. This is not the same as using subtraction.

Say: The degree of a monomial is found by adding all of the exponents.

Ask: What degree is the monomial $\frac{2}{3}c^3d^3$? **[6]** Why? **[Add the exponents. 3 + 3 = 6]**

KEY TEACHING POINTS

Example 3

Ask: How do you determine the degree of a monomial? **[Add the exponents of the variables.]**

Say: To write a polynomial, in standard form, you write the monomial with the highest degree first.

Ask: What values do you look at to write a polynomial in standard form? **[The exponents.]**

Check

Ask: In the polynomial, what degree is the term "$- x$"? **[1 or first]** What degree is the term "-5"? **[0]**

Say: If one of the terms in a polynomial is a constant, the constant is the final term when the polynomial is written in standard form.

Example 4

Ask: A binomial is a polynomial with two terms. What other words use the prefix 'bi' to identify two of something? **[Possible answers: Bicycle means two wheels, bifocals have two different lenses, biweekly means every two weeks.]**

Check

Ask: How can you name the polynomial $2y^5 + 7y^3 - 6y - 1$ using both the degree and number of terms? **[$2y^5 + 7y^3 - 6y - 1$ is a 5th degree polynomial or a polynomial with degree 5.]**

COMMON MISCONCEPTION

Ask: What is the error in this problem?

Name the polynomial based on its number of monomial terms.

The polynomial $x^2 + 9x + 14$ is a binomial because its degree is 2.

Reason incorrect: The degree of a polynomial does not determine the name.

Solution: The polynomial $x^2 + 9x + 14$ is a trinomial because there are three terms.

The polynomial is degree 2, so you could say $x^2 + 9x + 14$ is a 2nd degree trinomial.

ADDITIONAL ONLINE INTERVENTION RESOURCES

 Use the following for students who have not mastered the concepts in Skill 5.

- Math on the Spot videos
- Personal Math Trainer with customized intervention
- Building Block worksheets (Skill 29: Evaluate Powers; Skill 43: Graph Functions)

SKILL 5 Classifying Polynomials

Example 1

In an algebraic expression, a term is a number, a variable, or the product of a number and one or more variables. The coefficient of a term is the term's numerical factor. A constant is a term with no variable.

In the algebraic expression $8x^2 - 12x + 4$, there are three terms: $8x^2$, $-12x$, and 4. The coefficients are 8 and -12. The constant is 4.

Like terms have the same variable factors.

Like Terms: 2 and -5 $9a$ and $8a$ $-4c^4$ and $7c^4$ $3fg^2$ and $-5fg^2$

Not Like Terms: $2x$ and -5 $9a$ and $8b$ $-4c$ and $7c^4$ $3f^2g$ and $-5fg^2$

Vocabulary
Term
Coefficient
Constant
Like terms
Monomial
Degree of a
  monomial
Polynomial
Degree of a
  polynomial
Standard form
Leading
  coefficient
Binomial
Trinomial

Check
Tell whether the terms are like terms.

1. $15h$ and $15h^2$_____

2. $-k^3$ and k^3_____

3. $10m^3n^2$ and $7m^2n^3$_____

4. $5pq^4$ and $5q^4p$_____

Example 2

A monomial is a real number, a variable, or the product of a real number and one or more variables with whole-number exponents. The degree of a monomial is the sum of the exponents of its variables. The degree of a nonzero constant is 0. Zero has no degree.

Monomial: $3a$ $-4b^6$ $\frac{2}{3}c^3d^3$ 8   0

Degree: 1   6   6   0   No degree

A polynomial is a monomial or a sum or difference of monomials. The degree of a polynomial is the degree of the monomial term with the greatest degree.

Polynomial: $13m$ $-20n + 20$ $11p - 14p^2 + 14p^3 + 19$ $8q^2 + 19q^4 - 2$
Degree: 1   1   3   4

Check
Find the degree of each monomial or polynomial.

5. $11f^8$_____

6. $6g - 8g^2 + 10g^3$_____

7. $2h^4 - 9h^5 + 5h^9 - 8$_____

8. 2_____

Example 3

A polynomial is in standard form if its monomial terms are written in decreasing order according to degree. When a polynomial is written in standard form, the coefficient of its first term is called its leading coefficient.

Write the polynomial $7x + 16 - 13x^4 + 16x^3$ in standard form. Identify its leading coefficient.

$$7x + 16 - 13x^4 + 16x^3$$
$$= -13x^4 + 16x^3 + 7x + 16 \quad \text{Write terms in order according to degree.}$$

The standard form is $-13x^4 + 16x^3 + 7x + 16$. The leading coefficient is -13.

Check

Write each polynomial in standard form. Then give its leading coefficient.

9. $2x^5 + 20x^3 + x^4$ _____

10. $16 + 17x^2 - 17x$ _____

11. $-5 - x - 2x^4$ _____

12. $2y^4 + 3 + 7y^3 - 4y^2$ _____

Example 4

You can name a polynomial based on its number of monomial terms.

Polynomial	Number of Terms	Name
$3x$	1	Monomial
$3x - 5$	2	Binomial
$2x^2 + 3x - 5$	3	Trinomial
$-8x^3 + 2x^2 + 3x - 5$	4 (or more)	Polynomial

Check

Name each polynomial based on its number of terms.

13. $2x^2 + 11x + 12$ _____

14. $16x^2$ _____

15. $-x + 8$ _____

16. $2y^5 + 7y^3 - 6y - 1$ _____

17. Write a trinomial with degree 4. _____

18. Explain the Error. Find the correct solution.

The polynomial $x^2 + 9x + 14$ is a binomial because its degree is 2.

_____

SKILL 5 CLASSIFYING POLYNOMIALS

Direct Variation

KEY TEACHING POINTS

Example 1
Say: A linear relationship that shows direct variation can always be written in the form: $y = kx$.

Ask: Using the equation $y = kx$, what can you say about y when the value of x is 0? **[The value of y is also 0.]** Does it make any difference what k, the constant of variation, is? **[No, any value multiplied by 0 is still 0.]**

Part A
Say: To determine if an equation represents direct variation, rewrite the equation so that the value for y is on the left side by itself.

Part C
Say: The graph of the equation $y = -3x + 5$ is a line. The graphs of equations that show direct variation are also lines. The difference between equations that show direct variation and other linear equations is that in a direct variation equation, when x is 0, y is also 0.

Ask: In the equation $3x + y = 5$, what is the value of y when x is 0? **[5]** Does the equation represent a direct variation? **[No.]** What term in the equation $3x + y = 5$ shows you that the equation does not represent a direct variation? **[The constant 5]**

Point out that when a linear equation is written in standard form, $Ax + By = C$, if the value of C is anything other than zero, the equation does not represent direct variation.

Check
Ask: What steps must you take to write $5x = -15y$ in the form $y = kx$? **[You need to get y on one side of the equation by itself.]** What must you divide both sides of the equation by in order for y to be alone? **[-15]** You are left with the equation $-\frac{1}{3}x = y$.

Say: You are left with the equation $-\frac{1}{3}x = y$. You can reverse the sides of the equation without changing the meaning. $y = -\frac{1}{3}x$.

Ask: What is the constant of variation? $\left[-\frac{1}{3} \right]$

KEY TEACHING POINTS

Example 2
Part A:
Say: Look at the values in the table closely. Remove the lines from the table, and write a fraction bar between each x and y term.

$$\frac{2}{1} \qquad \frac{4}{2} \qquad \frac{8}{4}$$

Ask: How are the fractions that are formed related? **[They are equivalent.]** In lowest terms, what is the fraction? $\left[\dfrac{2}{1}\right]$

Say: The constant of variation in the equation is $\dfrac{1}{2}$.

Ask: If the fraction $\dfrac{2}{1}$ represents the ratio of the x-value to the y-value, or $\dfrac{x}{y}$, what can you say about the constant of variation? $\left[\textbf{It is the ration of the } \boldsymbol{y}\textbf{-value to the } \boldsymbol{x}\textbf{-value, or } \dfrac{\boldsymbol{y}}{\boldsymbol{x}}.\right]$

Say: Solving the equation $y = kx$ for the constant of variation shows that this is true.

$$y = kx$$
$$\frac{y}{x} = \frac{kx}{x}$$
$$\frac{y}{x} = k$$

Say: When an equation is written in this form, you can say, "Each y-value is k times the corresponding x-value."

Part B
Ask: If you write the ratio of y- and x-values with fraction bars, are the fractions equivalent? **[No.]** Does the table represent a direct variation? **[No.]**

Ask: When a table or equation represents a direct variation, what is the ratio of y to x when the x-value is 0? **[0]**

Check
Ask: In the table for problem 5, what is the value of k? **[3]**

Say: This means that each y-value is 3 times the corresponding x-value.

ALTERNATE STRATEGY

Strategy: Sketch a graph.

1. Remind students that an equation that is a direct variation will form a line that passes through the point (0, 0).

2. **Say:** Graphing the points given in a table will show if the relationship in the table is a direction variation.

3. Graph the table for Problem 5 as a class.

x	0	1	2
y	0	3	6

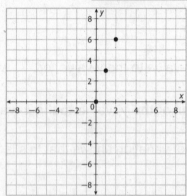 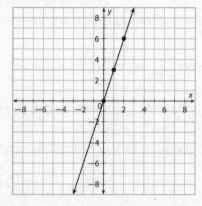

4. **Ask:** When the points are connected and extended, is a line formed? **[Yes.]** Does the line pass through the point (0, 0)? **[Yes.]** Then the relationship in the table is a direct variation.

Have students graph the points from the tables in Problems 6 and 7 to determine if the relationships are direct variations. Check student work for accuracy.

KEY TEACHING POINTS

Example 3
Say: When you are given that a relationship is a direct variation, and you are given corresponding *x*- and *y*-values, you can use the relationship $k = \dfrac{y}{x}$ to write the equation.

Ask: How can you find the constant of variation when you know an *x*- and *y*-value? **[Use the equation $y = kx$ or $k = \dfrac{y}{x}$.]**

Ask: When you know an equation, and you know an *x*-value, how can you find the corresponding *y*-value? **[Substitute the value for *x* into the equation and solve for *y*.]**

Check
Say: Direct variation can be used to solve word problems. Be careful to connect the correct values with the variables *x* and *y*.

Ask: The age of a dog, *x*, varies directly with its equivalent age in human years, *y*. What does the variable *x* represent? **[The age of the dog.]** What does the variable *y* represent? **[The dogs equivalent age in human years.]** In the sentence 'A 4-year-old dog is considered to be 28 in human years,' what is the *x*-value? **[4]** What is the *y*-value? **[28]** In the direct variation equation that represents this relationship, what is the constant of variation?

$$\left[k = \frac{y}{x} = \frac{28}{4} = 7 \right]$$

Say: This means that the corresponding human age (*y*-value) is 7 times the actual age of a dog (*x*-value).

COMMON MISCONCEPTION

Ask: What is the error in this problem?

The value of *y* varies directly with *x*, and $y = 6$ when $x = 15$. Find *y* when $x = 35$.

The equation is $y = 2.5x$. When $x = 35$, $y = 87.5$.

Reason incorrect: The constant of variation was found using $\dfrac{x}{y}$ instead of $\dfrac{y}{x}$.

Solution:

$$k = \frac{y}{x}$$

$$
\begin{array}{ll}
y = kx & \\
6 = k(15) \quad \text{or} & k = \frac{6}{15} \\
k = 0.4 & k = 0.4
\end{array}
$$

So, the equation is $y = 0.4x$.

By substituting the value 35 into the equation for *x*, you find that when $x = 35$, $y = 0.4(35) = 14$.

ADDITIONAL ONLINE INTERVENTION RESOURCES

Use the following for students who have not mastered the concepts in Skill 6.

- Math on the Spot videos
- Personal Math Trainer with customized intervention
- Building Block worksheets (Skill 96: Solve Proportions Using Cross Products)

SKILL 6 | Direct Variation

Vocabulary
Direct
  variation
Constant of
  variation

Example 1

If an equation can be written in the form $y = kx$, then it represents a direct variation, and the constant of variation is k.

Tell whether each equation represents a direct variation. If so, identify the constant of variation.

A. $y = 7x$.
  This equation represents a direct variation because it is in the form $y = kx$. The constant of variation is 7.

B. $-4x + 9y = 0$
  Solve the equation for y.
  $-4x + 9y = 0$

  $\qquad 9y = 4x \qquad$ Add $4x$ to both sides.

  $\qquad y = \dfrac{4}{9}x \qquad$ Divide both sides by 9.

  This equation represents a direct variation because it can be written in the form $y = kx$. The constant of variation is $\dfrac{4}{9}$.

C. $3x + y = 5$
  Solve the equation for y.
  $3x + y = 5$

  $\qquad y = -3x + 5 \qquad$ Subtract $3x$ from both sides.

  This equation does not represent a direct variation because it cannot be written in the form $y = kx$.

Check

Tell whether each equation represents a direct variation. If so, identify the constant of variation.

1. $5x = -15y$

2. $2y = 6x + 3$

3. $4y - 3x = 0$

4. $8x - 2y = 16$

Example 2

Given a table of ordered pairs, you can write an equation to determine whether the values represent a direct variation.

Determine whether the values in each table represent a direct variation. If so, identify the constant of variation.

A.

x	2	4	8
y	1	2	4

Write an equation.

$y = \dfrac{1}{2}x$ *Each y-value is $\dfrac{1}{2}$ times the corresponding x-value.*

This is a direct variation because it can be written as $y = kx$, where $k = \dfrac{1}{2}$.

B.

x	1	3	5
y	−4	−2	0

Write an equation.

$y = x - 5$ *Each y-value is 5 less than the corresponding x-value.*

This is not a direct variation because it cannot be written as $y = kx$.

Check

Determine whether the values in each table represent a direct variation. If so, identify the constant of variation.

5.

x	0	1	2
y	0	3	6

_____

_____

6.

x	−1	0	1
y	3	4	5

_____

_____

7.

x	−1	2	5
y	−5	10	25

_____

_____

8.

x	−6	0	6
y	−2	0	2

_____

_____

9.

x	−6	0	6
y	0	2	4

_____

_____

10.

x	1	3	5
y	1.5	4.5	7.5

_____

_____

Example 3

Given one ordered pair that satisfies a direct variation, you can write the equation. Then you can find other ordered pairs that satisfy the equation.

Write a direct variation equation for each situation. Then solve for the given value of x.

A. The value of y varies directly with x, and $y = 2$ when $x = 8$. Find y when $x = 24$.

Step 1: Find the value of k and write the equation.

$y = kx$ Write the equation for direct variation.

$2 = k(8)$ Substitute 2 for y and 8 for x.

$k = \dfrac{1}{4}$ Solve for k. Divide both sides by 8, and simplify.

The equation is $y = \dfrac{1}{4}x$.

Step 2: Use the equation to find y for the given value of x.

When $x = 24$, $y = \dfrac{1}{4}(24) = 6$.

B. The cost of gasoline, y, varies directly with the number of gallons, x. If it costs \$19.50 for 5 gallons of gas, how much would it cost to fill a 13-gallon tank?

Step 1: Find the value of k and write the equation.

$y = kx$ Write the equation for direct variation.

$19.5 = k(5)$ Substitute 19.5 for y and 5 for x.

$k = 3.9$ Solve for k. Divide both sides by 5, and simplify.

The equation is $y = 3.9x$.

Step 2: Use the equation to find y for the given value of x.

When $x = 13$, $y = 3.9(13) = 50.7$.

It would cost \$50.70 to fill a 13-gallon tank.

Check

Write a direct variation equation for each situation. Then solve for the given value of x.

11. The value of y varies directly with x, and $y = 6$ when $x = 3$. Find y when $x = 10$.

12. The value of y varies directly with x, and $y = 16$ when $x = -2$. Find y when $x = 5$.

_____   _____

_____   _____

13. The value of *y* varies directly with *x*, and *y* = 2 when *x* = −12. Find *y* when *x* = 24.

_____

_____

14. The value of *y* varies directly with *x*, and *y* = −27 when *x* = −45. Find *y* when *x* = −5.

_____

_____

15. The cost of concert tickets, *y*, varies directly with the number of tickets purchased, *x*. Riley spent $64.50 to buy 3 tickets. How much would it cost for him to buy 8 tickets?

_____

16. The amount of packages, *y*, that a delivery service can deliver varies directly with time, *x*, in hours. If the service can deliver 7 packages every 2 hours, how many packages can be delivered in 10 hours?

_____

17. The age of a dog, *x*, varies directly with its equivalent age in human years, *y*. If a 4-year-old dog is considered to be 28 in human years, how old, in human years, is a 7-year-old dog?

_____

18. Explain the Error. Find the correct solution.

The value of *y* varies directly with *x*, and *y* = 6 when *x* = 15. Find *y* when *x* = 35.

The equation is *y* = 2.5*x*. When *x* = 35, *y* = 87.5.

_____

_____

_____

SKILL 6 DIRECT VARIATION

Equations Involving Exponents

KEY TEACHING POINTS

Example 1
Say: The Equality of Bases Property says that if two exponential expressions are equal and have the same base, then the exponents are equal to each other.

Part A
Say: To solve for a variable that is part of an exponent, first isolate the base and exponent on one side of the equation.

Say: Once the base and exponent are isolated, write the value on the other side of the equation as an exponential expression that has the same base.

Ask: How can you find how many times a number is a factor of another number?
[Use division.] How many times is 2 a factor of 16? **[4]**

Say: The number 16 can be written as 2^4. The bases are now the same, so the exponents, x and 2 are equal.

Part B
Say: The variable and its exponent are already isolated in this equation,

$$\left(\frac{1}{25}\right)^{1-3x} = \frac{1}{625}.$$

Ask: How can you determine how many times $\frac{1}{25}$ is a factor of $\frac{1}{625}$? $\left[\textbf{Divide } \frac{1}{625} \textbf{ by } \frac{1}{25}.\right]$

Remind students that dividing by a fraction is the same as multiplying by its reciprocal, so

$$\frac{1}{625} \div \frac{1}{25} = \frac{1}{625} \times \frac{25}{1} = \frac{25}{625} = \frac{1}{25}, \text{ so } \frac{1}{625} = \left(\frac{1}{25}\right)^2.$$

Say: $\left(\frac{1}{25}\right)^{1-3x} = \left(\frac{1}{25}\right)^2$ The bases are now the same, so the exponents, $1 - 3x$ and 2 are equal.

Check
Say: Look at the equation $3\left(\frac{7}{5}\right)^x = \frac{147}{25}$.

Ask: What is the first step in getting the exponential expression by itself? **[Divide both sides by 3.]**

Say: When you divide both sides of the equation by 3, you are left with $\frac{7^x}{5} = \frac{49}{25}$.

Say: Because $\frac{7}{5} \times \frac{7}{5} = \frac{49}{25}$, $\frac{49}{5} = \left(\frac{7}{5}\right)^2$, and $\frac{7^x}{5} = \left(\frac{7}{5}\right)^2$.

Ask: What does the Equality of Bases Property tell you is the value of x? **[$x = 2$]**

COMMON MISCONCEPTION

Ask: What is the error in this problem?

$$15^{-x} = 225^{2x+1}$$

$$15^{-x} = \left(15^2\right)^{2x+1}$$

Solve $15^{-x} = 225^{2x+1}$ for x.

$$-x = 2x + 1$$

$$-3x = 1$$

$$x = -\frac{1}{3}$$

Reason incorrect: The Power Rule was not used after the second step.

Solution:

$$15^{-x} = 225^{2x+1}$$

$$15^{-x} = \left(15^2\right)^{2x+1}$$

$$15^{-x} = 15^{2(2x+1)}$$

$$-x = 2(2x+1)$$

$$-x = 4x + 2$$

$$-5x = 2$$

$$x = -\frac{2}{5}$$

The Power Rule must be used before the Equality of Bases Property.

The Power Rule tells you that when an expression with a power is taken to a power, the expression is evaluated by multiplying the exponents.

The Equality of Bases Property tells you that when two exponential expressions are equal and have the same base, the exponents are equal to each other.

KEY TEACHING POINTS

Example 2

Say: You can use graphing to find the solution to exponential equations. When you graph each side of the equation as a function, the point of intersection of the functions is the solution to the equation.

Ask: What function should be graphed for the left side of the equation? [$y = 6^x$] What function should be graphed for the right side of the equation? [$y = 10$]

Say: When you use a graphing calculator, you need to enter the functions as Y_1 and Y_2. In some cases, you will need to change the viewing window and scale by zooming in or out or going to window settings. Try to locate the point of intersection near the center of your screen.

Say: The intersect feature can be used on the CALC menu to find the point where the two graphs intersect. It is important that you know your graphing calculator.

Ask: To the nearest hundredth, at what point do the two graphed functions intersect? [1.29, 10]

Say: The solution to the equation is the *x*-coordinate at the intersection. Test the value in the original equation to make sure the solution is correct. Remember, you have rounded the solution, so checking the solution will be slightly different than the exact equation.

Show the following work:

$$6^x = 10$$
$$6^{(1.29)} = 10$$
$$10.09 \approx 10$$

Say: The evaluated expression is slightly greater than 10. When you rounded, you rounded up, so this solution makes sense.

Check

Ask: What two functions should be graphed to find the solution for $3^{x-1} = 7$? **[$Y_1 = 3^{x-1}$ and $Y_2 = 7$]**

Ask: What is the graph of the function $Y_2 = 7$? **[A horizontal line.]**

Say: The solution of the equation is the point on the graph of $y = 3^{x-1}$ where $y = 7$.

Ask: When you calculate the intersection, what value is *x*? **[Around 2.77]** The value for *y* should always be the same as a function that is just a constant.

ALTERNATE STRATEGY

Strategy: Sketch a graph.

1. You can sketch the graphs for the two sides of the equation using a table of values to approximate a solution when you don't have a graphing calculator.

2. For the equation $2^x = 5$, the solution will be where the function $2^x = 5$ intersects with the horizontal line at $y = 5$.

3. Demonstrate how to make a table of values for $y = 2^x$. Use values for *x* from 0 to 3.

x	y
0	$2^0 = 1$
1	$2^1 = 2$
2	$2^2 = 4$
3	$2^3 = 8$

4. Explain that you don't need to go any further because you can tell from the table that *x* will lie somewhere between 2 and 3.

5. Sketch a graph of the function $y = 2^x$ using the table of values. Sketch the line $y = 5$.

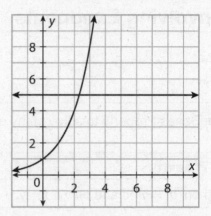

6. **Ask:** What is the approximate solution? **[Possible answers: between 2.3 and 2.5]**

Explain that using a hand drawn graph will give you an approximate value. A graphing calculator can give you a much closer solution.

KEY TEACHING POINTS

Example 3

Say: Systems of equations can be solved by graphing the two functions and finding the point of intersection. This is the same concept as graphing the two sides of an equation. You are trying to find the point where the x and y values are equal for both equations.

Ask: If Sylvia gets the same increase in pay each month, what kind of function models her pay over time? **[linear]** If Sylvia gets a percentage increase each month, what kind of function models her pay over time? **[exponential]**

Say: Over time, an exponential function increases more rapidly than a linear function. For Sylvia, the two jobs will allow her to earn about the same amount after 50 months.

Check

Ask: What function can be used to model the change in Middleburg's population? **[$y = 1500 - 80x$]** In Northtown's population? **[$y = 1000(1 - 0.03)^x$]**

ADDITIONAL ONLINE INTERVENTION RESOURCES

 Use the following for students who have not mastered the concepts in Skill 7.

- Math on the Spot videos

- Personal Math Trainer with customized intervention

- Building Block worksheets (Skill 29: Evaluate Powers; Skill 75: Properties of Exponents; Skill 76: Reading and Writing Exponents)

SKILL 7

Equations Involving Exponents

Example 1

Vocabulary
Equality of
  Bases
  Property
Exponential

You can use the Equality of Bases Property to solve many equations involving exponents.

Equality of Bases Property
If $b > 0$ and $b \neq 1$, then $b^x = b^y$ if and only if $x = y$.

Solve each equation.

A. $\dfrac{7}{2}(2)^x = 56$

$\dfrac{2}{7} \cdot \dfrac{7}{2}(2)^x = \dfrac{2}{7} \cdot 56$ Multiply by the reciprocal to isolate 2^x.

$(2)^x = 16$ Simplify.

$(2)^x = 2^4$ Write 16 as a power of 2.

$x = 4$ Apply the Equality of Bases Property.

B. $\left(\dfrac{1}{25}\right)^{1-3x} = \dfrac{1}{625}$

$\left(\dfrac{1}{25}\right)^{1-3x} = \left(\dfrac{1}{25}\right)^2$ Write $\dfrac{1}{625}$ as a power of $\dfrac{1}{25}$.

$1 - 3x = 2$ Apply the Equality of Bases Property.

$-3x = 1$ Subtract 1 from both sides.

$x = -\dfrac{1}{3}$ Solve for x.

Check

Solve each equation.

1. $4^{-x} = \dfrac{1}{64}$

2. $3\left(\dfrac{7}{5}\right)^x = \dfrac{147}{25}$

3. $243^{3-3x} = 81$

4. $\left(\dfrac{1}{16}\right)^{2-x} = 64^{x-2}$

5. Explain the Error. Find the correct solution.

Solve $15^{-x} = 225^{2x+1}$ for x.   _____

$$15^{-x} = 225^{2x+1}$$ _____

$$15^{-x} = \left(15^2\right)^{2x+1}$$ _____

$$-x = 2x + 1$$ _____

$$-3x = 1$$

$$x = -\frac{1}{3}$$

Example 2

When an equation involving exponents cannot be rewritten so that both sides have the same base, you can solve by graphing both sides of the equation. The solution is the input value for the point of intersection.

Solve $6^x = 10$ by graphing. Round to the nearest hundredth, if necessary.

Step 1: Use a graphing calculator to graph both sides of the equation by letting $Y_1 = 6^x$ and $Y_2 = 10$. Use a viewing window of –2 to 12 with a scale of 1 for both the x- and y-axes.

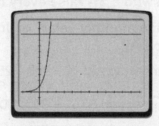

Step 2: Use the intersect feature on the CALC menu to find the input value where the graphs intersect.

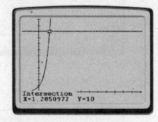

Intersection
X=1.2850972   Y=10

Check

Solve by graphing. Round to the nearest hundredth, if necessary.

6. $2^x = 5$

7. $3^{x-1} = 7$

_____   _____

Example 3

You can also use a graphing calculator to analyze equations that are exponential on one side and linear on the other.

Sylvia was offered two jobs described below.

- **Job A: $900 for the first month with a $25 raise every month thereafter**
- **Job B: $800 for the first month with a 2% raise every month thereafter**

How many months will it take for the monthly salary of Job B to exceed the monthly salary of Job A?

Step 1: Write equations to represent the monthly salaries. Let t represent months.

Job A: $Y_1 = 900 + 25t$ *linear equation*

Job B: $Y_2 = 800(1.02)^t$ *exponential equation*

Step 2: Graph the equations on a calculator.

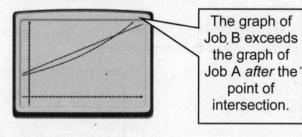

The graph of Job B exceeds the graph of Job A *after* the point of intersection.

Step 3: Solve the equation $900 + 25t = 800(1.02)^t$ using the intersect feature.

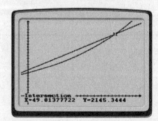

The monthly salary of Job B will exceed Job A's after 50 months.

Check
Solve by graphing. Round to the nearest hundredth, if necessary.

8. $2 + 3x = 2(1.2)^x$ for $x > 0$

9. $17 + 4x = 14(1.12)^x$ for $x > 0$

_____   _____

10. Companies A and B each have 40 employees. Company A increases its workforce by two employees each month, and Company B increases its workforce by an average of 3% each month. To the nearest month, when will Company B have more employees than Company A?

_____

11. Middleburg has 1500 residents and Northtown has 1000 residents. Middleburg's population decreases by 80 people per year, and Northtown's population decreases by 3% per year. After what whole-number year will Northtown have a greater population than Middleburg?

_____

12. Job A offers $1600 a month for the first month with a 2% raise every month thereafter. Job B offers $1600 a month for the first month with a $50 raise every month thereafter. Which job will have a higher monthly salary at 3 years? At 4 years?

_____

SKILL 7 EQUATIONS INVOLVING EXPONENTS

Exponential Functions

KEY TEACHING POINTS

Example 1

Remind students that exponential functions are different than linear functions. The equations of linear functions do not include variables as exponents.

Say: The y-values in a linear function have a common difference as x increases by one unit. The y-values in an exponential function increase by the same ratio as x increases by one unit.

Say: Exponential equations have a variable in the exponent. The equations of linear functions do not include variables as exponents.

Point out the variable in each function.

$$f(x) = 1(4)^x \qquad y = 9\left(\frac{1}{3}\right)^x \qquad f(x) = -6(2)^x$$

Say: In the function $f(x) = 40(1.1)^x$, evaluate the function at x by replacing x with the value 8.

Ask: What value does the exponent 8 act on? **[1.1]** The variable only acts on 1.1. Make sure you use the order of operations to evaluate exponents before you do the multiplication.

Check

Ask: For the function $f(x) = -5(10)^x$ for x = 4, will the answer be negative or positive? **[negative]** Why? **[After evaluating the exponent, the result is multiplied by –5.]** Will the result ever be positive? **[No.]** Why not? **[The result of evaluating the exponent will always be positive because 10 is positive, and a positive multiplied by a negative is always negative.]**

Say: When you replace a variable with an exponent, the exponent acts on the entire value of the variable.

Example 2

Remind students that when the exponent is a negative number, they should use the reciprocal of the base to the opposite exponent.

Ask: What x-values might you always want to include in your table of values? **[Possible answers: 0 and 1]**

Say: Remember, when the exponent is 0, the value of the expression is always 1. When the exponent is 1, the value of the expression is the same as the value of the base. This makes 0 and 1 nice values to include when you make a table of value.

Ask: In this table, each x-value increases by the same difference, 1. How do the y-values change? **[As the x-value increases by 1 unit, the y-value increases by a ratio of 2.]** When the common ratio is 2, the y-value doubles with each successive x-value.

Check

Say: Let's make a table of values for the exponential function $y = 6\left(\frac{1}{3}\right)^x$.

Create the table of values and list the x-values –2 to 2.

Say: To evaluate the function at $x = -2$, use the reciprocal of the base. The reciprocal of $\frac{1}{3}$ is 3.

$$y = 6\left(\frac{1}{3}\right)^{-2}$$

Show the following work:
$$= 6(3)^2$$
$$= 6(9)$$
$$= 72$$

Say: Exponential functions increase or decrease rapidly. When graphing an exponential function, it is common to use a unit other than 1 for the y-axis.

ALTERNATE STRATEGY

Strategy: Use a graphing calculator.

1. Remind students that although a graphing calculator will give them the graph of an exponential function, they must still understand what the function means and how it relates to real situations. They must also know their calculator and how it functions.

2. **Say:** Let $y_1 = -4(0.25)^x$. Be sure to enter the function correctly, and include the variable in the exponent position.

3. **Ask:** For this function, what scale might you choose for each axis? **[The scale used for graphing by hand is 1 for the x-axis and 4 for the y-axis. This is a good choice.]** Note that other choices would work, but the area between the x-values –2 and 2 must be included in the viewing window.

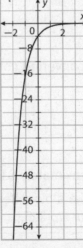

4. **Ask:** Can you use the graph to find the value of y when $x = 10$? **[No]** The calculator will allow you to find the value of y when x equals 10, but not on this graph. You can use a scientific calculator to find the value of y when $x = 10$.

KEY TEACHING POINTS

Example 3

Say: Exponential growth occurs when quality grows at the same rate over time. This does NOT mean the rate of change remains the same.

Ask: What kind of function shows a constant rate of change? **[Linear functions because a straight line has a rate of change that is constant.]**

Say: The equation of a linear function is in the form $y = mx + b$. The variable m tells the slope of the equation. When m is a positive number, the line slants up from left to right. An exponential function that increases in y value as the x value increases shows exponential growth. In the exponential equation $y = ab^x$, when b is greater than one, it is a growth function, and the base, b, is the growth factor.

Ask: In the example problem, what is the initial value of the coin? **[1200]** The initial value is the value when the coin was sold, $1200. What is the growth rate in decimal form? **[0.07]** The coin is increasing in value each year by 7%, which in decimal form is 0.07.

Say: The equation for exponential growth, $y = ab^x$, is one that is used often in real world situations.

Check

Ask: In problem 10, what is the initial value of the home? **[220,000]** What is the growth rate as a decimal? **[0.02]** What function models this situation? **[$y = 220,000(1 + 0.02)^t$]**

COMMON MISCONCEPTION

Ask: What is the Error in this problem?
The tuition at a university is $8500 per year. Tuition increases 4% each year. Write an exponential growth function to model this situation. Then find the cost of tuition at the university in 8 years.

$$y = 8500(1.4)^t$$
$$= 8500(1.4)^8$$
$$\$125,442.07$$

Reason incorrect: The percent was not converted correctly to a decimal.

Solution:
$$y = 8500(1.04)^t$$
$$= 8500(1.04)^8$$
$$\approx \$11,632.84$$

The cost of tuition in 8 years will be approximately $11,632.84.

Say: Simple computation errors can make a big difference in the result. Compute carefully and double check your work.

KEY TEACHING POINTS

Example 4

Say: The function that models exponential decay is very similar to the one that models exponential growth.

Ask: How are the two functions different? **[Instead of adding the growth rate to 1, you subtract the decay rate from 1.]**

Say: In the parent exponential function, $y = ab^x$, the variable b is $1 - r$, the decay rate in a decay function. In this form, b is greater than 0, but less than one. In an exponential function, when the base, b, is greater than 0 but less than one, the value for y decreases as the x value increases.

Ask: In the enrollment example, what is the initial value? **[1050]** What is the decay rate as a decimal? **[0.02]** What is the decay factor? **[0.98]**

Check

Ask: If a tournament begins with 128 teams, and the number of teams decreases by 50% at the end of each round, what is the decay factor? **[0.5]** The decay factor is the same as the decay rate in this case, because it is 50%. What is the decay function? **[$y = 128(0.5)^x$]**

ADDITIONAL ONLINE INTERVENTION RESOURCES

Use the following for students who have not mastered the concepts in Skill 8.

- Math on the Spot videos
- Personal Math Trainer with customized intervention
- Building Block worksheets (Skill 29: Evaluate Powers; Skill 75: Properties of Exponents; Skill 76: Reading and Writing Exponents)

SKILL 8 — Exponential Functions

Example 1

An exponential function models the growth or decay of an initial amount.

The x- and y-values in the table below satisfy a certain exponential function. Notice that consecutive x-values have a common *difference*, whereas consecutive y-values have a common *ratio*.

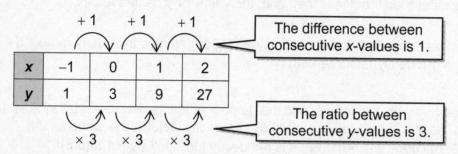

<table>
<tr><td>x</td><td>−1</td><td>0</td><td>1</td><td>2</td></tr>
<tr><td>y</td><td>1</td><td>3</td><td>9</td><td>27</td></tr>
</table>

The difference between consecutive x-values is 1.

The ratio between consecutive y-values is 3.

An exponential function has the form $f(x) = ab^x$, where $a \neq 0$, $b \neq 1$, and $b > 0$. In an exponential function, the independent variable appears as an exponent, and the common ratio is the base b.

Exponential Functions: $f(x) = 1(4)^x$ $y = 9\left(\dfrac{1}{3}\right)^x$ $f(x) = -6(2)^x$

To evaluate an exponential function, evaluate the function at a given x-value. Then simplify the power.

The function $f(x) = 40(1.1)^x$ models the height of a bamboo stalk, in centimeters, after x days. What will its height be after 8 days?

$f(x) = 40(1.1)^x$	Write the function.
$f(8) = 40(1.1)^8$	Substitute 8 for x.
$\approx 40(2.14)$	Use a calculator to simplify 1.1^8.
≈ 85.6	Multiply.

The height of the bamboo plant after 8 days will be about 85.6 cm.

Vocabulary

Exponential function
Exponent
Base
Exponential growth
Final amount
Original amount
Growth rate
Growth factor
Exponential decay
Decay rate
Decay factor

Check

Evaluate each function for the given value.

1. $f(x) = 2(3)^x$ for $x = 3$ _____

2. $y = 4(2)^x$ for $x = 5$ _____

3. $f(x) = -5(10)^x$ for $x = 4$ _____

4. $y = 25(1.5)^x$ for $x = 7$ _____

5. The function $f(x) = 1200(0.9)^x$ models the deer population in a certain region over time, where x is the time in years. Use this model to estimate the expected deer population in the region in 6 years. _____

Example 2

To graph an exponential function, make a table of values. Choose several values of x and find the corresponding values of y. Then graph the points and connect them with a smooth curve.

Graph $y = 3(2)^x$.

Make a table of x- and y-values.

x	y
-1	$3(2)^{-1} = 3\left(\dfrac{1}{2}\right) = \dfrac{3}{2} = 1.5$
0	$3(2)^0 = 3(1) = 3$
1	$3(2)^1 = 3(2) = 6$
2	$3(2)^2 = 3(4) = 12$
3	$3(2)^3 = 3(8) = 24$

Graph the points. Connect them with a smooth curve.

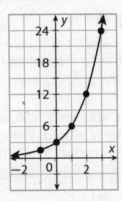

Check

Graph each exponential function.

6. $y = 3(3)^x$

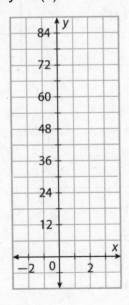

7. $y = \dfrac{1}{2}(4)^x$

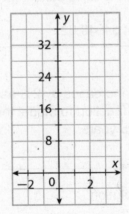

8. $y = 6\left(\dfrac{1}{3}\right)^x$

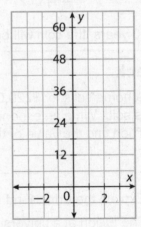

Example 3

Exponential growth occurs when a quantity grows, or increases, at the same rate over time. The function $y = a(1 + r)^t$ models exponential growth.

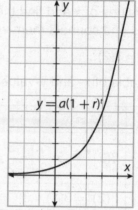

> y represents the final amount.
>
> a represents the original amount.
>
> r represents the growth rate in decimal form.
>
> t represents time.

The function $y = a(1 + r)^t$ is equivalent to the function $y = ab^x$, with $b = 1 + r$, $b > 1$, and $x = t$. In this form, the base b is the growth factor.

A rare coin is sold for $1200, and its value increases by 7% each year after it is sold. Write an exponential growth function to model the situation. Then find the value of the coin in 20 years.

Step 1   Write the exponential growth function for this situation.

$$\begin{aligned} y &= a(1 + r)^t && \text{Use the exponential growth function.} \\ &= 1200(1 + 0.07)^t && \text{Substitute 1200 for } a \text{ and 0.07 for } r. \\ &= 1200(1.07)^t && \text{Simplify.} \end{aligned}$$

Step 2   Find the value of the coin in 20 years.

$$\begin{aligned} y &= 1200(1.07)^t && \text{Use the function from Step 1.} \\ &= 1200(1.07)^{20} && \text{Substitute 20 for } t. \\ &\approx 4643.62 && \text{Use a calculator. Round to the nearest cent.} \end{aligned}$$

In 20 years, the coin will be worth about $4643.62.

Check

9. A home sells for $220,000. Its value increases by 2% each year after it is sold. Write an exponential growth function to model this situation. Then find the value of the home in 15 years.

_____

10. Explain the Error. Find the correct solution.

The tuition at a university is $8500 per year. Tuition increases 4% each year. Write an exponential growth function to model this situation. Then find the cost of tuition at the university in 8 years.

$$\begin{aligned} Y &= 8500(1.4)^t \\ &= 8500(1.4)^8 \\ &\approx \$125,442.07 \end{aligned}$$

_____

Example 4

Exponential decay occurs when a quantity decays, or decreases, at the same rate over time. The function $y = a(1 - r)^t$ models exponential decay.

  y represents the final amount.

  a represents the original amount.

  r represents the decay rate in decimal form.

  t represents time.

The function $y = a(1 - r)^t$ is equivalent to the function $y = ab^x$, with $b = 1 - r$, $0 < b < 1$, and $x = t$. In this form, the base b is the decay factor.

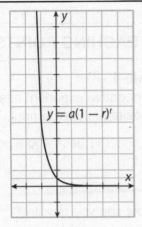

The enrollment at a high school is 1050 and is expected to decrease 2% each year. Write an exponential decay function to model this situation. Then find the expected enrollment at the school in 5 years.

Step 1 Write the exponential decay function for this situation.

$y = a(1 - r)^t$	Use the exponential decay function.
$= 1050(1 - 0.02)^t$	Substitute 1050 for a and 0.02 for r.
$= 1050(0.98)^t$	Simplify.

Step 2 Find the expected enrollment in 5 years.

$y = 1050(0.98)^t$	Use the function from Step 1.
$= 1050(0.98)^5$	Substitute 5 for t.
≈ 950	Use a calculator to simplify.

The expected enrollment at the high school in 5 years is about 950.

Check

11. A certain sports tournament begins with 128 teams. The number of teams decreases by 50% at the end of each round. Write an exponential decay function to model this situation. Then find the number of teams that remain in the tournament at the end of 7 rounds.

_____

12. A car sells for $18,000. Its value decreases by 8% each year after it is sold. Write an exponential decay function to model this situation. Then find the value of the car in 10 years.

_____

SKILL 8 EXPONENTIAL FUNCTIONS

Exponents

KEY TEACHING POINTS

Example 1

Say: A negative exponent has the same effect as taking the reciprocal of the base, and using the opposite of the exponent. This means a negative exponent can be rewritten as a unit fraction with the base and a positive exponent in the denominator, so $9^{-3} = \dfrac{1}{9^3}$.

Check

Ask: How can you rewrite 6^{-4} using a positive exponent? $\left[\dfrac{1}{6^4}\right]$

Ask: How can you rewrite $(-8)^{-3}$ using a positive exponent? $\left[\dfrac{1}{(-8)^3}\right]$ Is the value of the expression positive, or negative? Explain. **[Negative. The exponent is negative, which puts the expression in the denominator with a positive exponent. The base is a negative number. Since the exponent is 3, the base is multiplied an odd number of times, giving the expression a negative value.]**

ALTERNATE STRATEGY

Strategy: Look for a pattern.

1. Remind students that an exponent tells how many times the base is used as a factor.

2. **Say:** As an exponent increases by 1, the base becomes a factor one more time, so you can multiply by the base to find the next higher value.

   Demonstrate this using a table of values.

Expression	$(-10)^1$	$(-10)^2$	$(-10)^3$
Value	-10	$(-10)(-10) = 100$	$(-10)(-10)(-10) = -1000$

$\times (-10) \qquad\qquad \times (-10)$

3. **Say:** If the table starts with a higher exponent and decreases the exponents by 1 for each row, the values change by dividing each row by -10.

   Demonstrate this using a table of values, completing the rows together as they are addressed in Steps 4 and 5.

Expression	$(-10)^2$	$(-10)^1$	$(-10)^0$	$(-10)^{-1}$	$(-10)^{-2}$
Value	100	-10	1	$-\dfrac{1}{10}$	$\dfrac{1}{100}$

$\div (-10) \quad \div (-10) \quad \div (-10) \quad \div (-10)$

4. **Say:** An exponential expression with a power of 1 has the same value as the base. To find the value at a base 0, divide by the base again. What is the base, −10, divided by the base, −10? **[1]** Any value divided by itself is 1, and any base to the power of 0 has a value of 1.

5. **Say:** If you continue this pattern, (decreasing the exponent by 1 is the same as dividing the previous value by the base) you can find the value of negative exponents. The value of $(-10)^{-1}$ is $-\dfrac{1}{10}$ and the value of $(-10)^{-2}$ is $\dfrac{1}{100}$.

6. **Ask:** What pattern do you see when you compare the value for expression that used opposite integers, such as 1 and −1 or 2 and −2? **[The values are reciprocals of each other.]**

KEY TEACHING POINTS

Example 2

Say: If you do not remember the Product of Powers rule, think about the meaning of an exponent. The exponent tells you how many times the base is a factor, so

$$2^2 \cdot 2^3 = (2 \cdot 2)(2 \cdot 2 \cdot 2) = 2 \cdot 2 \cdot 2 \cdot 2 \cdot 2 = 2^5 = 32.$$

Ask: How can you use the meaning of exponents to remember the Quotient of Powers rule? **[Write the factors of the numerator over the factors of the denominator. Cancel out all of the like factors.]** This has the same result as subtracting the number of factors in the denominator from the number of factors in the numerator.

Check

Say: Sometimes to evaluate an algebraic expression, more than one property can be used.

Ask: How can you eliminate the negative exponent in $\dfrac{10^6}{10^{-2}}$ using the Quotient of Powers?

[Subtract the exponents. 6 − (−2) = 8, so $\dfrac{10^6}{10^{-2}} = 10^8$.]

Say: When a negative exponent is in the numerator, it moves the base and exponent to the denominator and takes the opposite exponent.

Ask: What happens when the negative exponent is in the denominator? **[The base and exponent move to the numerator, and the expression takes the opposite exponent.]**

Say: This can be applied to the same problem, $\dfrac{10^6}{10^{-2}}$. The negative exponent can be moved to the numerator as a positive exponent. Apply the Product of Powers, and $\left(10^6\right)\left(10^2\right) = 10^8$.

KEY TEACHING POINTS

Example 3

Say: Writing an exponential expression using all of the factors can often make properties of exponents understandable. The expression $\left(\dfrac{12}{7}\right)^2$ means the fraction is a factor 2 times, or $\left(\dfrac{12}{7}\right)\left(\dfrac{12}{7}\right)$. Multiply fractions by multiplying the numerators and multiplying the denominators, $\left(\dfrac{12 \cdot 12}{7 \cdot 7}\right)$, which can be written as $\dfrac{12^2}{7^2}$.

Say: To find the power of a power, think of the expression inside the parentheses as a variable and apply it as a factor the same number of times as the outer power.

$$\left(4^2\right)^3 = \left(4^2\right)\left(4^2\right)\left(4^2\right)$$

Ask: All of the exponential expressions have the same base. How do you multiply expressions with the same base? **[Add the exponents.]**

COMMON MISCONCEPTION

Ask: What is the Error? $\left(7^4\right)^5 = 7^{4+5} = 7^9$

Reason incorrect: The exponents were added instead of multiplied.

Solution: $\left(7^4\right)^5 = 7^{(4)(5)} = 7^{20}$

Say: Multiply the exponents to find the power of a power. Add the exponents to find the product of powers with the same base.

KEY TEACHING POINTS

Example 4

Say: A radical, or root, is the opposite of an exponent. A radical is used to express the number which when raised to the given power, called the index, results in the value of the radicand, or number under the radical symbol.

Ask: In the radical $\sqrt[3]{27}$ the index is 3 and the radicand is 27. So, what number, when it has an exponent of 3, is equal to 27?

Say: When no index is visible in the radical, it is assumed to be 2. This is read as square root. When the index is 3, the radical is read as cube root.

Check

Ask: What number, when raised to the 4th power, has a value of 10,000? **[10]** How can you check this? **[Multiply 10 as a factor 4 times. $10 \times 10 \times 10 \times 10 = 10,000$]**

KEY TEACHING POINTS

Example 5

Say: Exponents and radicals are inverse operations, in the same way that multiplication and division are inverse operations, and they undo each other. Just as you can write division as multiplication by using the reciprocal, you can write roots and exponents in their opposite form.

Ask: How can the exponential expression $49^{\frac{1}{2}}$ be written as a radical expression? **[$\sqrt{49}$]**

Say: The denominator of the rational exponent is the index of the radical.

Check

Ask: How can $64^{\frac{1}{3}}$ be written as a radical? **[$\sqrt[3]{64}$]** How can $16^{\frac{1}{2}}$ be written as a radical?

[$\sqrt{16}$] What are the values of $\sqrt[3]{64}$ and $16^{\frac{1}{2}}$? **[Both equal 4.]**

Example 6

Say: The properties of exponents, such as the Power of Powers, Product of Powers, and Quotient of Powers, all apply to rational exponent expressions. In some cases, different properties can be used to evaluate the same expression.

Ask: One method uses the Power of a Power Property, the other uses Product of Powers Property. How are these similar? **[Sample answer: A property of a power is really the same factor being applied a number of times. This means you can multiply either by adding the same exponent a number of times, or by multiplying the exponent by the number of times it is a factor.]**

Ask: Why do you write each radicand as a cube? **[The denominator of 3 in the rational exponent indicates an index of 3 in the radical.]**

Check

Ask: The exponential expression $32^{\frac{4}{5}}$ can be rewritten as a power of a power, $\left(32^{\frac{1}{5}}\right)^{4}$.

What is the indicated index when the fractional exponential expression is written as a radical?

[5] What is the radical expression for $32^{\frac{4}{5}}$? $\left[\left(\sqrt[5]{32}\right)^{4}\right]$

ADDITIONAL ONLINE INTERVENTION RESOURCES

 Use the following for students who have not mastered the concepts in Skill 9.

- Math on the Spot videos

- Personal Math Trainer with customized intervention

- Building Block worksheets (Skill 76: Reading and Writing Exponents; Skill 100: Squares and Square Roots)

Exponents

SKILL 9	**Exponents**

Example 1

Recall that a power has two parts: a base and an exponent. The exponent tells how many times the base should be used as a factor. In the expression 2^4, 2^4 is the power, 2 is the base, and 4 is the exponent.

You can simplify powers that have an exponent of 0 or a negative exponent.

Exponent of 0: For every nonzero number a, $a^0 = 1$.

$$8^0 = 1 \qquad \left(\frac{2}{5}\right)^0 = 1 \qquad (-15)^0 = 1$$

Negative Exponent: For every nonzero number a and integer m,

$$a^{-m} = \frac{1}{a^m}.$$

$$12^{-1} = \frac{1}{12^1} = \frac{1}{12} \qquad 9^{-3} = \frac{1}{9^3} = \frac{1}{729} \qquad (-10)^{-2} = \frac{1}{(-10)^2} = \frac{1}{100}$$

Vocabulary

Power
Base
Exponent
Radical symbol
Square root
Cube root
Radicand
Radical expression
Rational exponents

Check

Simplify each expression.

1. 35^0 _____

2. 8.723^0 _____

3. $\left(\frac{7}{9}\right)^0$ _____

4. 3^{-5} _____

5. 6^{-4} _____

6. $(-8)^{-3}$ _____

Example 2

Product of Powers: To multiply two or more powers with the same base, add the exponents.

$$a^m \cdot a^n = a^{m+n} \qquad 2^2 \cdot 2^3 = 2^{2+3} = 2^5 = 32$$

Quotient of Powers: To divide powers with the same base, subtract the exponents.

$$\frac{a^m}{a^n} = a^{m-n}, \ a \neq 0 \qquad \frac{8^9}{8^7} = 8^{9-7} = 8^2 = 64$$

Check

Simplify each expression.

7. $4^3 \cdot 4^5$ _____

8. $5^6 \cdot 5^{-2} \cdot 5^3$ _____

9. $(-3)^7 \cdot (-3)^{-2}$ _____

10. $\frac{12^{10}}{12^6}$ _____

11. $\frac{10^6}{10^{-2}}$ _____

12. $\frac{6^2 \cdot 6^4}{6 \cdot 6^3}$ _____

Example 3

Power of a Product: To raise a product to a power, raise each factor to the power. Then multiply.

$(ab)^m = a^m b^m$ $\qquad\qquad$ $(3 \cdot 5)^2 = 3^2 \cdot 5^2 = 9 \cdot 25 = 225$

Power of a Quotient: To raise a quotient to a power, raise the numerator and the denominator to the power. Then divide.

$\left(\dfrac{a}{b}\right)^m = \dfrac{a^m}{b^m},\ b \neq 0$ $\qquad\qquad$ $\left(\dfrac{12}{7}\right)^2 = \dfrac{12^2}{7^2} = \dfrac{144}{49}$

Power of a Power: To raise a power to a power, multiply the exponents.

$\left(a^m\right)^n = a^{mn}$ $\qquad\qquad$ $\left(4^2\right)^3 = 4^{2(3)} = 4^6 = 4096$

Check

Simplify each expression.

13. $(8 \cdot 5)^3$ _____

14. $(-4 \cdot 10)^2$ _____

15. $(-2 \cdot 7)^{-3}$ _____

16. $\left(\dfrac{9}{5}\right)^2$ _____

17. $\left(\dfrac{4}{11}\right)^3$ _____

18. $\left(\dfrac{-3}{10}\right)^4$ _____

19. $\left(11^2\right)^4$ _____

20. $\left(3^{-3}\right)^{-5}$ _____

21. $\left(12^2\right)^{-1}$ _____

22. Explain the Error. Find the correct solution.

$$\left(7^4\right)^5 = 7^{4+5} = 7^9$$

_____

23. Use the Power of a Power Property to write 5^{12} in three different ways.

_____

Example 4

The radical symbol $\sqrt{\ }$ indicates a nonnegative square root. The symbol $\sqrt[3]{\ }$ indicates a cube root. In general, the symbol $\sqrt[n]{\ }$ indicates an *n*th root.

$$\sqrt{36} = 6 \text{ because } 6 \cdot 6 = 36. \qquad \sqrt[3]{27} = 3 \text{ because } 3 \cdot 3 \cdot 3 = 27.$$

The expression under the radical symbol is the radicand. An expression that contains radicals is a radical expression.

Check

Simplify each expression.

24. $\sqrt{81}$ _____

25. $\sqrt{169}$ _____

26. $\sqrt[3]{8}$ _____

27. $\sqrt[3]{-1}$ _____

28. $\sqrt[4]{10,000}$ _____

29. $\sqrt[4]{256}$ _____

Example 5

An exponent can be expressed as a fraction. Fractional exponents are called rational exponents.

The equations $7 \cdot 7 = 49$ and $49^{\frac{1}{2}} = 7$ are equivalent. The equation $49^{\frac{1}{2}} = 7$ indicates that 7 is the positive number that, when used as a factor twice, equals 49.

In general, a number raised to the power of $\dfrac{1}{n}$ is equal to the *n*th root of that number:

$a^{\frac{1}{n}} = \sqrt[n]{a}$, where $a \geq 0$ and *n* is an integer greater than 1.

You can simplify powers that have a rational exponent.

Simplify $125^{\frac{1}{3}}$.

$$125^{\frac{1}{3}} = \sqrt[3]{125} \qquad \text{Use the definition of } a^{\frac{1}{n}}.$$
$$= \sqrt[3]{5^3} \qquad \text{Rewrite the radicand as a cube.}$$
$$= 5 \qquad \text{Simplify.}$$

Check

Simplify each expression.

30. $8^{\frac{1}{3}}$ _____

31. $121^{\frac{1}{2}}$ _____

32. $81^{\frac{1}{4}}$ _____.

33. $0^{\frac{1}{6}}$ _____

34. $4^{\frac{1}{2}} + 32^{\frac{1}{5}}$ _____

35. $64^{\frac{1}{3}} - 16^{\frac{1}{2}}$ _____

Example 6

You can use the properties of exponents to simplify expressions that contain rational exponents.

Simplify $64^{\frac{2}{3}}$.

Method 1

$$64^{\frac{2}{3}} = 64^{\frac{1}{3} \cdot 2} \qquad \text{Write the exponent as a product.}$$

$$= \left(64^{\frac{1}{3}}\right)^2 \qquad \text{Power of a Power Property}$$

$$= \left(\sqrt[3]{64}\right)^2 \qquad \text{Definition of } a^{\frac{1}{n}}$$

$$= \left(\sqrt[3]{4^3}\right)^2 \qquad \text{Rewrite the radicand as a cube.}$$

$$= (4)^2 \qquad \text{Simplify.}$$

$$= 16 \qquad \text{Simplify.}$$

Method 2

$$64^{\frac{2}{3}} = 64^{\frac{1}{3}} \cdot 64^{\frac{1}{3}} \qquad \text{Rewrite the expression.}$$

$$= \sqrt[3]{64} \cdot \sqrt[3]{64} \qquad \text{Definition of } a^{\frac{1}{n}}$$

$$= \sqrt[3]{4^3} \cdot \sqrt[3]{4^3} \qquad \text{Rewrite each radicand as a cube.}$$

$$= 4 \cdot 4 \qquad \text{Simplify.}$$

$$= 16 \qquad \text{Simplify.}$$

Check

Simplify each expression.

36. $16^{\frac{3}{4}}$ _____

37. $27^{\frac{2}{3}}$ _____

38. $32^{\frac{4}{5}}$ _____

39. $81^{\frac{3}{4}}$ _____

40. $125^{\frac{2}{3}} + 1^{\frac{3}{4}}$ _____

41. $1000^{\frac{2}{3}} - 243^{\frac{4}{5}}$ _____

SKILL 9 EXPONENTS

Factoring Polynomials

KEY TEACHING POINTS

Example 1

Say: Factoring out the greatest common factor of monomial terms can be done by writing the prime factorization for each term. To factor $3a^5 - 18a^4$, find the greatest common factors of the monomials $3a^5$ and $18a^4$.

Show the following work:

$3a^5 = 3 \cdot a \cdot a \cdot a \cdot a \cdot a$

$18a^4 = 3 \cdot 2 \cdot 3 \cdot a \cdot a \cdot a \cdot a$

The greatest common factor of $3a^5$ and $18a^4$ is $3 \cdot a \cdot a \cdot a \cdot a$, or $3a^4$.

Say: The Distributive Property is used to factor the greatest common factor out of polynomials.

Ask: When you factor $3a^4$ out of $3a^5$, what is left? **[a]** When you factor $3a^4$ out of $18a^4$, what is left? **[6]** Notice, the operation, subtraction, remains subtraction.

Say: The factored form of $3a^5 - 18a^4$ is $3a^4(a - 6)$. Use the Distributive Property to check your computations.

Show the following work:
$3a^4(a - 6) = 3a^4(a) - 3a^4(6)$
$= 3a^5 - 18a^4$

Check

Ask: How can you rewrite 6^{-4} using a positive exponent? $\left[\dfrac{1}{6^4} \right]$

ALTERNATE STRATEGY

Strategy: Factor by parts.

1. **Say:** Factoring out the greatest common factor uses the least number of steps to factor a polynomial, but sometimes you may not recognize the factor the first time.

2. **Say:** In the polynomial $-11z^6 - 22z^3 + 121z^2$, the constant factor, or number, -11, is common to each of the three terms. You can factor the constant out first.
   $-11(z^6 + 2z^3 - 11z^2)$

3. **Ask:** Look at the variable part of each term inside the parentheses. The term with the lowest exponent has an exponent of 2. You can also factor z^2 out of each term.
   $-11(z^2)(z^4 + 2z - 11) = -11z^2(z^4 + 2z - 11)$

KEY TEACHING POINTS

Example 2

Say: First, identify the common factors. In the polynomial $8(x-5)-3x(x-5)$ there are two expressions that have a common factor. You can factor out the common factor $(x-5)$ using the Distributive Property.

Say: When factoring polynomials with four terms, the goal is to form two binomials by grouping terms that can be factored into polynomials that have a common binomial factor.

Ask: When $2x^6 + 14x^5 - 3x - 21$ is grouped into $(2x^6 + 14x^5) + (-3x - 21)$, and the GCF is factored from each group, what binomial does each group have in common? **[x + 7]** Why is it necessary to factor –3 from the second group instead of 3? **[So that each group has a common binomial factor.]**

Check

Ask: In the polynomial $3x^5 + 15x^3 + 2x^2 + 10$, how can you group the terms? **[Into $3x^5 + 15x^3$ and $2x^2 + 10$.]** When the GCFs $3x^3$ and are $2x^2 + 10$ factored out, what is the common binomial factor in each group? **[x^2 + 5]**

COMMON MISCONCEPTION

Ask: What is the Error? $4w(w-3)+(-5)(w-3)=(w-3)(4w+5)$

Reason incorrect: When the GCF was factored out of the polynomial, the other factor was written incorrectly.

Solution: $4w(w-3)+(-5)(w-3)=(w-3)(4w-5)$

Say: Watch the signs of the factors carefully. When a negative value is factored out, it can be written as adding a negative, or subtracting a positive.

ADDITIONAL ONLINE INTERVENTION RESOURCES

Use the following for students who have not mastered the concepts in Skill 10.

- Math on the Spot videos

- Personal Math Trainer with customized intervention

- Building Block worksheets (Skill 25: Divide Monomials; Skill 33: Factor GCF from Polynomials; Skill 34: Factor Trinomials; Skill 62: Multiply Binomials)

SKILL 10 — Factoring Polynomials

Example 1

Remember that a monomial is a number, a variable, or the product of a number and one or more variables. A polynomial is a sum of monomials.

Monomials: -4, x, $5xy$ **Polynomials:** $x + 2$, $3x^2 - 5x + 8$

Common factors are factors that are shared by two or more terms. The greatest of the common factors is called the greatest common factor, or GCF.

Factors of 12: 1, 2, **3**, 4, 6, 12   The common factors are 1 and 3.
Factors of 9: 1, **3**, 9   The GCF is 3.

To find the GCF of two or more monomials, write the prime factorization of each monomial. Then find the product of the common factors.

A. Find the GCF of $7x^5$ and $21x^3$.

  Write the prime factorization of each monomial.

  $7x^5 = \mathbf{7 \cdot x \cdot x \cdot x} \cdot x \cdot x$ Find the common factors.
  $21x^3 = 3 \cdot \mathbf{7 \cdot x \cdot x \cdot x}$

  The GCF of $7x^5$ and $21x^3$ is $7 \cdot x \cdot x \cdot x$, or $7x^3$.

You can use the GCF to factor a polynomial. First factor out the GCF from each term of the polynomial. Then factor out the GCF from the polynomial.

B. Factor $3a^5 - 18a^4$.

  $3a^5 - 18a^4 = 3a^4(a) + 3a^4(-6)$ Factor the GCF, $3a^4$, out of each term.

  $= 3a^4(a + (-6))$ Factor the GCF out of the polynomial.

  $= 3a^4(a - 6)$ Rewrite as subtraction.

  The factored form of $3a^5 - 18a^4$ is $3a^4(a - 6)$.

Vocabulary

Monomial
Polynomial
Common factors
Factors
Greatest common factor (GCF)
Prime factorization
Product
Factor out
Binomial
Common binomial factor
Common monomial factor
Factor by grouping

Check

Find the GCF of each pair of monomials.

1. $12y^7$ and $60y^5$ _____

2. m^4 and $9m^3$ _____

3. $-4b^2$ and $-24b^2$ _____

4. $7c^3$ and $18d^3$ _____

Factor each polynomial.

5. $4x^5 + 24x^2$ _____

6. $6x^3 - 42x$ _____

7. $9y^5 + 27y^3 - 18y^2$ _____

8. $-11z^6 - 22z^3 + 121z^2$ _____

Example 2

The GCF of the terms in a polynomial can also be a binomial. This is called a common binomial factor. You factor out a common binomial factor the same way you factor out a common monomial factor.

A. Factor $8(x-5)-3x(x-5)$.

$8(x-5)-3x(x-5)$ $(x-5)$ is the common binomial factor.

$=(x-5)(8-3x)$ Factor out $(x-5)$.

The factored form of $8(x-5)-3x(x-5)$ is $(x-5)(8-3x)$.

You can factor some polynomials that have four terms by grouping. To factor by grouping, make two groups and factor out the GCF of each group.

B. Factor $6x^3+3x+10x^2+5$.

$6x^3+3x+10x^2+5=\left(6x^3+3x\right)+\left(10x^2+5\right)$ Group terms that have common factors.

$=3x(2x^2+1)+5(2x^2+1)$ Factor out the GCF of each group.

$=\left(2x^2+1\right)(3x+5)$ Factor out the GCF of the polynomial.

C. Factor $2x^6+14x^5-3x-21$.

$2x^6+14x^5-3x-21=\left(2x^6+14x^5\right)+\left(-3x-21\right)$ Group terms.

$=2x^5\left(x+7\right)+\left(-3\right)\left(x+7\right)$ Factor out the GCF of each group.

$=\left(x+7\right)\left(2x^5+\left(-3\right)\right)$ Factor out the GCF of the polynomial.

$=\left(x+7\right)\left(2x^5-3\right)$ Rewrite as subtraction.

Check

Factor each expression, if possible.

9. $7(x+6)-9x(x+6)$ _____

10. $-m(m^3+2)+1(m^3+2)$ _____

11. $3y(y+1)-5(y+1)$ _____

12. $-2x^2(x-3)+5(x+3)$ _____

13. Explain the Error. Find the correct solution.

$4w(w-3)+(-5)(w-3)=(w-3)(4w+5)$

_____

Factor each polynomial by grouping.

14. $3x^5+15x^3+2x^2+10$ _____

15. $2x^3+14x^2+x+7$ _____

16. $8x^7+4x^5-6x^2-3$ _____

17. $-5x^6+15x^2+2x^4-6$ _____

18. Can you factor $6x^4+12x^3+4x^2-10x$ by grouping? _____

SKILL 10 FACTORING POLYNOMIALS

Factoring Special Products

KEY TEACHING POINTS

Example 1

Say: Perfect square trinomials are the product of the square of a binomial. You can recognize perfect square trinomials by the perfect square in the first and last term.

Ask: In the trinomial $x^2 + 14x + 49$, what is the first term? **[x^2]** Is x^2 a perfect square? **[Yes.]** What is the last term? **[49]** Is 49 a perfect square? **[Yes.]**

Say: The center term in a perfect square trinomial is twice the product of the square roots of the first and last term. The sign of the center term tells you if the binomial uses addition or subtraction. In the trinomial $x^2 + 14x + 49$, the center term is positive, so the binomial is $x + 7$, and the factored form of $x^2 + 14x + 49$ is $(x + 7)^2$.

Check

Ask: In the trinomial $25g^2 - 20g + 4$, are the first and last terms perfect squares? **[Yes.]** What is the square root of $25g^2$? **[5g]** What is the square root of 4? **[2]** Is the center term double the product of 5g and 2? **[Yes.]** What is the factored form? **[$(5g - 2)^2$]**

Say: Check your answer by squaring the binomial:
$(5g - 2)^2 = (5g - 2)(5g - 2) = 25g^2 - 10g - 10g + 4 = 25g^2 - 20g + 4$

ALTERNATE STRATEGY

Strategy: Use algebra tiles.

1. **Say:** Algebra tiles may be used to factor perfect square trinomials by arranging the tiles into a perfect square.

2. Model the trinomial $x^2 + 10x + 25$ using algebra tiles.

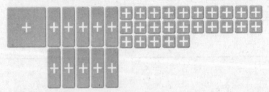

3. Arrange the unit tiles to form a square on their own. Arrange the tiles so that the x^2 tile is in the upper left and the unit tiles are in the bottom right corner of a square. Fill in the missing area with x tiles.

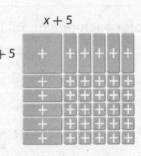

4. The area of a square is the square of the side length. The side length of the square is the binomial factor.

5. The square has a side length of 5. Square the binomial to be sure it is the correct factor for the trinomial $x^2 + 10x + 25$.

Show the work: $(x + 5)^2 = (x + 5)(x + 5) = x^2 + 5x + 5x + 25 = x^2 + 10x + 25$

KEY TEACHING POINTS

Example 2

Say: Binomials that are the difference of two perfect squares can be factored into two binomials. The terms in the factored binomial are the same, but one uses addition and one uses subtraction.

Say: Factor the difference of two squares by finding the square root of each term.

Ask: What is the square root of $9a^4$? **[$3a^2$]** What is the square root of $4b^2$? **[$2b$]**

Write the factored form as two binomials with a first term $3a^2$ and a second term, $2b$. One of the binomial factors uses addition, $\left(3a^2 + 2b\right)$ and the other uses subtraction, $\left(3a^2 - 2b\right)$.

Check

Ask: In the binomial $9m^6 - 81n^2$, the terms are perfect squares. Can you factor out the GCF 9 before using the difference of squares? **[Yes.]** Why? **[Because the terms that are left, m^6 and $9n^2$ are still perfect squares.]** When you factor out 9 first, what is the factored form of $9m^6 - 81n^2$? **[$9(m^3 + 3n)(m^3 + 3n)$]**

COMMON MISCONCEPTION

Ask: What is the Error? $4c^2 - 36 = \left(4c + 6\right)\left(4c - 6\right)$

Reason incorrect: In $4c^2 - 36$, $a = 2c$, not $4c$. So $4c^2 - 36 = (2c + 6)(2c - 6)$.

Solution: $4c^2 - 36 = \left(2c + 6\right)\left(2c - 6\right)$

Say: Be careful when the first term has a coefficient other than 1. Use the square root of the coefficient, not the actual coefficient.

ADDITIONAL ONLINE INTERVENTION RESOURCES

 Use the following for students who have not mastered the concepts in Skill 11.

- Math on the Spot videos

- Personal Math Trainer with customized intervention

- Building Block worksheets (Skill 34: Factor Trinomials)

SKILL 11

Factoring Special Products

Example 1

Remember that the square of an integer is called a perfect square. The first three perfect squares are 1^2, or 1; 2^2, or 4; and 3^2, or 9.

A trinomial of the form $a^2 + 2ab + b^2$ or $a^2 - 2ab + b^2$ is a perfect-square trinomial. A trinomial is a perfect-square trinomial if the following are true:

- The first term is a perfect square.
- The last term is a perfect square.
- The middle term is 2 times one factor of the first term times one factor of the last term.

You can use the rules below to help you factor a perfect-square trinomial.

Factoring Perfect-Square Trinomials	
Perfect-Square Trinomial	**Example**
$a^2 + 2ab + b^2 = (a + b)(a + b)$ $= (a + b)^2$	$x^2 + 2x + 1 = (x + 1)(x + 1)$ $= (x + 1)^2$
$a^2 - 2ab + b^2 = (a - b)(a - b)$ $= (a - b)^2$	$x^2 - 6x + 9 = (x - 3)(x - 3)$ $= (x - 3)^2$

A. Factor $x^2 + 14x + 49$.

$\quad x^2 + 14x + 49 = x^2 + 2(x)(7) + 7^2$ Write in the form $a^2 + 2ab + b^2$.

$\quad\quad\quad\quad\quad\quad = (x + 7)(x + 7)$ Write in the form $(a + b)(a + b)$.

The factored form of $x^2 + 14x + 49$ is $(x + 7)(x + 7)$, or $(x + 7)^2$.

B. Factor $9y^2 - 6y + 1$.

$\quad 9y^2 - 6y + 1 = (3y)^2 - 2(y)(3) + 1^2$ Write in the form $a^2 - 2ab + b^2$.

$\quad\quad\quad\quad\quad = (3y - 1)(3y - 1)$ Write in the form $(a - b)(a - b)$.

The factored form of $9y^2 - 6y + 1$ is $(3y - 1)(3y - 1)$, or $(3y - 1)^2$.

Vocabulary
Perfect square
Trinomial
Perfect-square trinomial
Factor
Binomial

Check
Factor each perfect-square trinomial.

1. $d^2 + 10d + 25$ _____

2. $f^2 - 18f + 81$ _____

3. $16x^2 + 24x + 9$ _____

4. $25g^2 - 20g + 4$ _____

Example 2

Remember that a binomial is a polynomial that has two terms.

Binomials: $4a^4 + 9$ $-6b^3 + 5b^2$ $g^4 + 12g^2$

A binomial of the form $a^2 - b^2$ is a difference of two squares. A binomial is a difference of two squares if the following are true:

- Both terms are perfect squares.

- One term is subtracted from the other term.

You can use the rule below to help you factor a difference of two squares.

Factoring a Difference of Two Squares	
Difference of Two Squares	**Example**
$a^2 - b^2 = (a+b)(a-b)$	$x^2 - 9 = (x+3)(x-3)$

A. Factor $x^2 - 100$.

$$x^2 - 100 = x^2 - 10^2 \qquad \text{Write in the form } a^2 - b^2.$$
$$= (x+10)(x-10) \qquad \text{Write in the form } (a+b)(a-b).$$

The factored form of $x^2 - 100$ is $(x+10)(x-10)$.

B. Factor $9a^4 - 4b^2$.

$$9a^4 - 4b^2 = (3a^2)^2 - (2b)^2 \qquad \text{Write in the form } a^2 - b^2.$$
$$= (3a^2 + 2b)(3a^2 - 2b) \qquad \text{Write in the form } (a+b)(a-b).$$

The factored form of $9a^4 - 4b^2$ is $(3a^2 + 2b)(3a^2 - 2b)$.

Check

Factor each difference of squares.

5. $m^2 - 144$ _____

6. $4y^2 - 121$ _____

7. $9m^6 - 81n^2$ _____

8. $25x^2 - 64y^2$ _____

9. Explain the Error. Find the correct solution.

$$4c^2 - 36 = (4c+6)(4c-6)$$

SKILL 11 FACTORING SPECIAL PRODUCTS

Factoring Trinomials

KEY TEACHING POINTS

Example 1

Say: When the sign of *c* is negative, the *b* term is the sum of a positive and a negative constant, or the difference between the absolute value of the constants in the factored binomials.

Say: In the trinomial $x^2 + 2x - 8$, the *c* term is negative, and *c* is 8. The *b* term is 2.

Ask: What two factors of 8 have a difference of 2? **[4 and 2]**

Say: Because 2 is positive, the factor with the greatest absolute value, 4, must be positive and the factor with the lesser absolute value must be negative 2.

Check

Ask: What is the first step to factor $x^2 + 2x - 8$? **[Write the parentheses to show a product of two binomials.]**

Say: The factors of the first term are both *x*. Write an *x* in each binomial as the first term.

Ask: Is *c* positive or negative? **[Negative.]** What does this mean? **[The factors will have the different signs.]**

Ask: What are the possible factors of 8? **[1 and 8, 2 and 4.]**

ALTERNATE STRATEGY

Strategy: Use algebra tiles.

1. **Say:** Algebra tiles may be used to factor simple trinomials by arranging the tiles into a rectangle.

2. Model the trinomial $x^2 + 5x + 4$ using algebra tiles.

3. Arrange the tiles so that the x^2 tile is in the upper left and the unit tiles are in the bottom right corner of a rectangle. Fill in the missing area with *x* tiles. The tiles must form a perfect rectangle with no gaps and no extra tile.

   x + 4

   x + 1

4. The area of a rectangle is the product of the length and width. The rectangle forms an area model for the two binomials that equal the trinomial when they are multiplied. The length dimensions of the rectangle are the binomial factors.

5. The length of the rectangle is $x + 4$ and the width is $x + 1$. Multiply the two binomials to be sure they are the factors of $x^2 + 5x + 4$.

   Show the work: $(x + 4)(x + 1) = x^2 + 4x + x + 4 = x^2 + 5x + 4$

KEY TEACHING POINTS

Example 2

Say: Trinomials that have a value for *a* that is not 1 follow the same rule for *c*. When *c* is positive, the constant factors have the same sign. When *c* is negative, the constant factors have different signs.

Ask: Could the factors of *a* both be negative? **[Yes.]** How would this change the binomial factors? **[All of the signs would be opposite.]** Why is this not the correct answer? **[You can factor –1 out of each binomial, and the two –1 factors are multiplied to just be 1.]**

Check

Ask: In the polynomial $6x^2 - 17x + 5$, what are the factors of 6? **[1, 2, 3, 6]** What factors for 5 can be used? **[–1, –5]** How can these factors be combined to have a sum of –17? **[(3)(–5) + (2)(–1) = –17]**

Say: The factors of 15 are 1 and 15 or 3 and 5. The factors of 7 are 1 and 7.

Ask: How can the factors be combined to have a sum of –32? **[(5)(–7) + (3)(1) = –32]** What are the binomial factors for $15x^2 - 32x - 7$? **[(5x + 1) (3x – 7)]**

COMMON MISCONCEPTION

Ask: What is the Error? $7x^2 + 40x - 12 = (7x + 2)(x - 6)$

Reason incorrect: The signs in the binomials are reversed.

Solution: $7x^2 + 40x - 12 = (7x - 2)(x + 6)$

Say: Watch the signs of the factors carefully. The value for *b* is positive, so the greater of the outer products or inner products must be positive. Because (7)(6) is greater than (2)(1), the constant 6 must be negative. This error can be avoided by checking your answer using FOIL.

ADDITIONAL ONLINE INTERVENTION RESOURCES

 Use the following for students who have not mastered the concepts in Skill 12.

- Math on the Spot videos

- Personal Math Trainer with customized intervention

- Building Block worksheets (Skill 25: Divide Monomials; Skill 33: Factor GCF from Polynomials)

SKILL 12 Factoring Trinomials

Example 1

	Vocabulary
	Trinomial
	Binomial

When factoring a trinomial with the form $x^2 + bx + c$, pay attention to the sign of c. If c is positive, the factors of c will both have the same sign. If c is negative, one factor will be negative, and one will be positive.

Factor each trinomial.

A. $x^2 + 2x - 8$

Step 1: $(\quad)(\quad)$ Use ( ) to set up a product of two binomials.

Step 2: $(x\quad)(x\quad)$ Write the factors of the first term, x^2.

Step 3: $(x-\quad)(x+\quad)$ Since c is negative, the factors will have opposite signs.

Step 4: $(x-2)(x+4)$ The factors of –8 are $\pm 1 \cdot \pm 8$ or $\pm 2 \cdot \pm 4$. The pair that has a sum of 2 is –2 and 4.

The factored trinomial is $x^2 + 2x - 8 = (x-2)(x+4)$.

B. $x^2 - 8x + 15$

Step 1: $(\quad)(\quad)$ Use ( ) to set up a product of two binomials.

Step 2: $(x\quad)(x\quad)$ Write the factors of the first term, x^2.

Step 3: $(x\pm\quad)(x\pm\quad)$ Since c is positive, the factors will have the same sign.

Step 4: $(x-3)(x-5)$ The factors of 15 are $\pm 1 \cdot \pm 15$ or $\pm 3 \cdot \pm 5$. The pair that has a sum of –8 is –3 and –5.

The factored trinomial is $x^2 - 8x + 15 = (x-3)(x-5)$.

Check

Factor each trinomial.

1. $x^2 + 5x + 4$ 2. $x^2 + 3x - 18$ 3. $x^2 - 5x - 14$ 4. $x^2 - 16x + 55$

_____   _____   _____   _____

Solve.

5. The area of a soccer field is $x^2 + 23x + 132$ m^2. The width of the field is $(x + 11)$ m. What is the length?

_____

Example 2

When factoring trinomials with the form $ax^2 + bx + c$, the result will be in the form $(\square x + \square)(\square x + \square)$. You must choose factors of both a and c so that the sum of the products of the inner and outer terms will be bx.

Factor $2x^2 + 3x - 14$.

Make a table of factor pairs for a and c. Since c is negative, one factor will be positive and one factor will be negative. Find the combination whose sum is equal to $b = 3$.

Factors of a $a = 2$	Factors of c $c = -14$	Outer product + Inner Product
1 and 2	1 and -14	$(1)(-14) + (2)(1) = -12$
1 and 2	2 and -7	$(1)(-7) + (2)(2) = -3$
1 and 2	7 and -2	$(1)(-2) + (2)(7) = 12$
1 and 2	14 and -1	$(1)(-1) + (2)(14) = 27$
1 and 2	-1 and 14	$(1)(14) + (2)(-1) = 12$
1 and 2	-2 and 7	$(1)(7) + (2)(-2) = 3$
1 and 2	-7 and 2	$(1)(2) + (2)(-7) = -12$
1 and 2	-14 and 1	$(1)(1) + (2)(-14) = -27$

> Three is the sum that you're looking for.

Use the correct combination of factored pairs to write the factored trinomial.

The factored trinomial is $2x^2 + 3x - 14 = (2x + 7)(x - 2)$.

Check

Factor each trinomial.

6. $2x^2 + 7x + 3$ 7. $3x^2 + 10x - 8$ 8. $6x^2 - 17x + 5$ 9. $15x^2 - 32x - 7$

_____   _____   _____   _____

10. Explain the Error. Find the correct solution.

$7x^2 + 40x - 12 = (7x + 2)(x - 6)$

SKILL 12 FACTORING TRINOMIALS

Geometric Sequences

KEY TEACHING POINTS

Example 1

Say: Arithmetic sequences move from one term to the next using addition, and geometric sequences move from one term to the next using multiplication.

Ask: If each term is found by multiplying the previous term by a common ratio, how can you find the common ratio? **[Divide any term by the previous term.]**

Say: It does not matter what two consecutive terms are chosen, the ratio is always the same.

Check

Ask: What is $4 \div 2$? **[2]** What is $8 \div 4$? **[2]** What is $16 \div 8$? **[2]** What is the common ratio? **[2]**

Say: You can check that you have the correct common ratio by multiplying each term by the common ratio you found. The product should be the next consecutive term.

Ask: What is $18 \div 54$? $\left[\dfrac{1}{3}\right]$ What is $18 \times \dfrac{1}{3}$? **[6]** What is $6 \times \dfrac{1}{3}$? **[2]**

Example 2

Ask: In both the recursive and explicit rules, the first term a_1 and the common ratio r must be known. How do you determine the common ratio in the sequence 3, 6, 12, 24, …? **[Divide a term by the previous term. $6 \div 3 = 2$]**

Say: In the recursive rule $a_1 = 3$, $a_n = 2 \cdot a_{n-1}$, the first term a_1 is 3, and each term a_n can be found by multiplying 2 times the previous term a_{n-1}.

Say: The explicit formula, $a_n = 3 \cdot 2^{n-1}$, says that you can find any term by multiplying 3 times 2 to the $n - 1$ power where n is the term number.

Check

Ask: What is a_1 in the sequence 5, $\dfrac{10}{3}$, $\dfrac{20}{9}$, $\dfrac{40}{27}$, …? **[5]** What is the common ratio? $\left[\dfrac{2}{3}\right]$

Say: So, the first term is 5, and each term can be found by multiplying $\dfrac{2}{3}$ by the previous term. How can this be written as a recursive rule? $\left[a_1 = 5, \ a_n = \dfrac{2}{3} \cdot a_{n-1}\right]$ You can find any term by multiplying the first term by $\dfrac{2}{3}$ to the $n - 1$ power where n is the term number. How can this be written as an explicit rule? $\left[a_n = 5\left(\dfrac{2}{3}\right)^{n-1}\right]$

Ask: In Problem 9, what is the first term? **[48]** What is the common ratio? $\left[\dfrac{1}{2}\right]$

Say: The value of the terms is decreasing, so the common ratio is greater than 0 and less than 1.

ALTERNATE STRATEGY

Strategy: Use a table.

1. **Say:** A table can help keep terms and their values organized. Set up a table for the geometric sequence −1, −3, −9, −27.

   Represent the sequence in a table. Explain that the first row of the table is the term number and the second row is the value of the term. (Do not include the third row until Step 3.)

n	1	2	3	4
a_n	−1	−3	−9	−27
	$-1(3)^0$	$-1(3)^1$	$-1(3)^2$	$-1(3)^3$

2. Find the common ratio by dividing any term by the previous term. $r = \dfrac{-9}{-3} = 3$

3. Add a third row to the table. In this row, write each term as the product of the first term, −1, and a power of the common ratio, 3. Note that for each term, the power is one less than the term number. This can be used to write the explicit rule,

   $a_n = -1 \cdot 3^{n-1}$.

COMMON MISCONCEPTION

Ask: What is the Error in this problem?

   Write a recursive rule and an explicit rule for the geometric sequence 108, 36, 12, 4, ...

   Recursive rule: $a_1 = 108$, $a_n = 3 \cdot a_{n-1}$

   Explicit rule: $a_n = 108 \cdot 3^{n-1}$

Reason incorrect: The common ratio was found by dividing a term by the following term instead of dividing a term by the previous term.

Solution: The common ratio, using the first two terms, is $36 \div 108 = \dfrac{36}{108} = \dfrac{1}{3}$. The initial term is 108.

So, the correct rules are:

Recursive: $a_1 = 108$, $a_n = \dfrac{1}{3} \cdot a_{n-1}$; **Explicit:** $a_n = 108 \cdot \left(\dfrac{1}{3}\right)^{n-1}$

Say: The terms in the geometric sequence are decreasing. When terms are decreasing, the common ratio is $0 < r < 1$.

KEY TEACHING POINTS

Example 3

Ask: What operation do you use to find the common ratio when you know two consecutive terms? **[Division]**

Say: In some cases you are not given consecutive terms. You can use the general recursive rule to find consecutive terms, then use division to find the common ratio.

Ask: Why do you use the general recursive rule to find consecutive terms instead of the general explicit rule? **[The recursive rule is written using the previous term, the explicit rule is written using the general term.]**

Say: The problem gives you the 3rd term and the 5th term. To find the common ratio, you set the 3rd term equal to the product of the 5th term and the square of the common ratio.

Ask: How would this be different if you knew the 2nd and 5th terms? **[Since the known terms are three places from each other, you need to use the cube of the common ratio, r^3.]**

Say: Once you know the common ratio and any term, you can use the explicit formula to find the first term. You must know the term and the value of the term. In this problem, you know the third term is 4th and the 5th term is $\frac{4}{9}$.

Ask: Why might you prefer to use a lower term to find the first term? **[Possible answers: The exponent will be smaller with a lower term, so it might be easier to calculate.]**

Say: Once you have the formula, it's a good idea to check your answer. You can find the geometric sequence named by the rule, $a_n = 36 \cdot \left(\frac{1}{3}\right)^{n-1}$ by substituting each term number into the rule.

Show the following work:

$$a_1 = 36 \cdot \left(\frac{1}{3}\right)^{1-1} = 36 \cdot \left(\frac{1}{3}\right)^0 = 36 \cdot 1 = 36$$

$$a_2 = 36 \cdot \left(\frac{1}{3}\right)^{2-1} = 36 \cdot \left(\frac{1}{3}\right)^1 = 36 \cdot \frac{1}{3} = 12$$

$$a_3 = 36 \cdot \left(\frac{1}{3}\right)^{3-1} = 36 \cdot \left(\frac{1}{3}\right)^2 = 36 \cdot \frac{1}{9} = 4$$

$$a_4 = 36 \cdot \left(\frac{1}{3}\right)^{4-1} = 36 \cdot \left(\frac{1}{3}\right)^3 = 36 \cdot \frac{1}{27} = \frac{4}{3}$$

$$a_5 = 36 \cdot \left(\frac{1}{3}\right)^{5-1} = 36 \cdot \left(\frac{1}{3}\right)^4 = 36 \cdot \frac{1}{81} = \frac{4}{9}$$

So, the sequence is: $36, 12, 4, \frac{4}{3} \cdot \frac{4}{9} \dots$, The 3rd term is 4 and the 5th term is $\frac{4}{9}$.

Check

Ask: If Rafael needs 500 points for Level 2 and 200,000 points for Level 4, what is the common ratio between levels? **[20]**

Say: Check the common ratio by multiplying Level 2, 500, by 20 to find Level 4. $(500)(20) = 10,000$. Then multiply Level 3, 10,000, by 20 to find Level 5.

Ask: How can you find the score that was needed for Level 1? **[Divide the score for Level 2 by 20.]** What score was needed? **[25]**

Say: One way you can find the score needed to reach Level 6 is to substitute 6 into the explicit rule.

Ask: What other way could you find the score needed for Level 6? **[You could use the recursive rule to keep multiplying each consecutive term by 20.]**

Ask: If you only have the rule, and no terms, which rule, recursive or explicit, would make it easier to find the 20th term in a sequence? **[The explicit rule.]**

ADDITIONAL ONLINE INTERVENTION RESOURCES

 Use the following for students who have not mastered the concepts in Skill 13.

- Math on the Spot videos

- Personal Math Trainer with customized intervention

- Building Block worksheets (Skill 29: Evaluate Powers; Skill 75: Properties of Exponents; Skill 76: Reading and Writing Exponents; Skill 109: Write a Mixed Number as an Improper Fraction)

SKILL 13 — Geometric Sequences

Example 1

In a geometric sequence, the ratio of any term to the previous term is constant. This ratio is called the common ratio, often written as r.

Find the common ratio r of the geometric sequence 1, 4, 16, 64, …

Find the ratio of each term to the previous term:

$$\frac{4}{1} = 4 \qquad \frac{16}{4} = 4 \qquad \frac{64}{16} = 4$$

The common ratio is $r = 4$.

Vocabulary
Geometric sequence
Common ratio
Recursive rule
Explicit rule

Check

Find the common ratio of each geometric sequence.

1. 2, 4, 8, 16, …

2. 16, 8, 4, 2, …

3. 4, 12, 36, 108, …

4. 54, 18, 6, 2, …

_____   _____   _____   _____

Example 2

You can describe a geometric sequence with a recursive rule or an explicit rule. A recursive rule gives the first term and defines the nth term by relating it to the previous term:

> **Recursive Rule**
>
> $a_1 = c$, $a_n = r \cdot a_{n-1}$, where c is a known constant, and r is the common ratio.

An explicit rule defines the nth term as a function of n:

> **Explicit Rule**
>
> $a_n = a_1 \cdot r^{n-1}$, where r is the common ratio.

Write a recursive rule and an explicit rule for the sequence 3, 6, 12, 24, …

The first term is 3, so $a_1 = c = 3$. The common ratio is 2, so $r = 2$.

Write the recursive rule.

$a_1 = c$, $a_n = r \cdot a_{n-1}$ Write the general form for a recursive rule.

$a_1 = 3$, $a_n = 2 \cdot a_{n-1}$ Substitute 3 for c and 2 for r.

The recursive rule is $a_1 = 3$, $a_n = 2 \cdot a_{n-1}$.

Write the explicit rule.

$a_n = a_1 \cdot r^{n-1}$ Write the general form for an explicit rule.

$a_n = 3 \cdot 2^{n-1}$ Substitute 3 for a_1 and 2 for r.

The explicit rule is $a_n = 3 \cdot 2^{n-1}$.

Check

Write a recursive rule and an explicit rule for each geometric sequence.

5. 4, 16, 64, 256, ...

    Recursive rule: _____

    Explicit rule: _____

6. −1, −3, −9, −27, ...

    Recursive rule: _____

    Explicit rule: _____

7. 0.25, 1, 4, 16, ...

    Recursive rule: _____

    Explicit rule: _____

8. 5, $\dfrac{10}{3}$, $\dfrac{20}{9}$, $\dfrac{40}{27}$, ...

    Recursive rule: _____

    Explicit rule: _____

Solve.

9. When you drop a ball, the height to which the ball rises, (bounce height), decreases by a common ratio on each successive bounce. The table shows the heights of a basketball's bounces, in inches, after falling from the hoop.

Bounce	1	2	3	4
Height After Bounce (in.)	48	24	12	6

    a. What is the common ratio of the bounce heights?

       _____

    b. Write a recursive rule describing the bounce heights.

       _____

    c. Write an explicit rule describing the bounce heights.

       _____

10. Explain the Error. Find the correct solution. Write a recursive rule and an explicit rule for the geometric sequence 108, 36, 12, 4, ...

    Recursive rule: $a_1 = 108$, $a_n = 3 \cdot a_{n-1}$

    Explicit rule: $a_n = 108 \cdot 3^{n-1}$

Example 3

Given two terms in a geometric sequence, you can use algebra to find the common ratio and the first term. Then you can write an explicit rule for the sequence.

A geometric sequence has the terms $a_3 = 4$ and $a_5 = \dfrac{4}{9}$. Write an explicit rule for the sequence.

Step 1: Use both known terms to find the common ratio.

$a_5 = a_4 \cdot r$	Write the recursive rule for a_5.
$a_4 = a_3 \cdot r$	Write the recursive rule for a_4.
$a_5 = a_3 \cdot r \cdot r$	Substitute the expression for a_4 into the rule for a_5.
$\dfrac{4}{9} = 4 \cdot r^2$	Substitute $\dfrac{4}{9}$ for a_5 and 4 for a_3.
$\dfrac{1}{9} = r^2$	Divide both sides by 4.
$\dfrac{1}{3} = r$	Take the positive square root to solve for r.

Step 2: Use either of the known terms to find the first term of the sequence.

$a_n = a_1 \cdot r^{n-1}$	Write the general explicit rule.
$4 = a_1 \cdot \left(\dfrac{1}{3}\right)^{3-1}$	Substitute 4 for a_3, $\dfrac{1}{3}$ for r, and 3 for n.
$4 = a_1 \cdot \dfrac{1}{9}$	Simplify.
$36 = a_1$	Multiply both sides by 9 to solve for a_1.

Step 3: Use the values of r and a_1 to write the explicit formula.

The explicit formula is $a_n = 36 \cdot \left(\dfrac{1}{3}\right)^{n-1}$.

Check

Write an explicit rule for each geometric sequence using the given terms from the sequence. Assume that the common ratio r is positive.

11. $a_2 = 6$ and $a_3 = 12$

_____

12. $a_3 = -12$ and $a_4 = -24$

_____

13. $a_3 = 5$ and $a_5 = \dfrac{1}{5}$

_____

14. $a_5 = -2500$ and $a_8 = -312,500$

_____

Solve.

15. Rafael is playing in a video game competition. The number of points he must accumulate to reach the next level forms a geometric sequence. He needs 500 points to complete Level 2 and 200,000 points to complete Level 4.

a. Write an explicit rule for the sequence.

_____

b. How many points must Rafael accumulate to reach Level 6?

_____

c. The record high score for the competition is 31,201,019,453. What level must Rafael reach to beat the high score? How many points would Rafael have if he made it to this level?

_____

SKILL 13 GEOMETRIC SEQUENCES

KEY TEACHING POINTS

Example 1

Say: Linear equations have a set of solutions that form a line on the coordinate plane. In linear equations, the value of one variable depends on the value of another variable. For each one unit of change in the x-value, there is a corresponding change in the y-value.

Say: In a proportional relationship, each set of x and y values have a constant ratio. The graph of a proportional relationship always passes through the origin.

Ask: Does the equation $y = -2x$ model a proportional relationship? **[Yes.]** Why? **[For every increase of 1 x-value, the y-value changes by –2 and when x is 0, y is also 0.]**

Say: When a linear equation is written in the form $y = mx + b$, the relationship is proportional if $b = 0$. When $b \neq 0$, the relationship is not proportional.

Ask: For the equation $y = -2x + 1$, why might the values from –2 to 3 be used in the table? **[Possible answers: They are small integers and will result in integers that are also small, so they should be easy to graph.]**

Say: In order for the line to pass through the origin, when you plug in the x-value 0, the value for y will also be 0. The origin is the point (0, 0).

Check

Say: Look at the equation $y = 15x + 50$ in problem 3.

Ask: Why are no negative values included in the table? **[Possible answer: The situation does not include negative values, because Alex will not work for negative time.]**

Say: For each additional hour Alex works, he earns $15 more, so as x increases by 1, y increases by 15.

Ask: If x and y are always changing at the same rate, does this make the relationship proportional? **[No.]** What are the characteristics of proportional relationships? **[The y to x ratios are always the same, and the line of the graph passes through the origin.]**

Ask: The graph for this problem has time on the x axis and earnings on the y axis. What are the unit intervals used on each axis? **[1 hour on the x-axis and $10 on the y-axis.]**

Graph the points from the table as a class.

Find each point, then connect the points with a line.

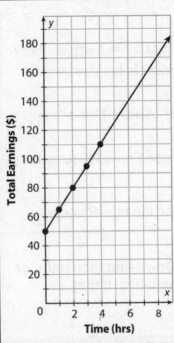

Ask: The graph shows that if Alex works 0 hours, he still earns $50. Is this a proportional relationship? **[No.]** In order for this to be proportional, how much would Alex earn for working 0 hours? **[0 dollars]**

ALTERNATE STRATEGY

Strategy: Determine the ratios from a table.

1. **Say:** You can use a table of values to decide if a relationship is proportional or not.

2. For the equation $y = \frac{1}{2}x - 2$, create a table of values using even numbers from –4 to 4.

    Explain that the even numbers in the table were chosen because the coefficient is also even. This will lead to integer values for both x and y.

Demonstrate how to make a table of values using the equation. Substitute each x-value from the table into the equation to find the corresponding y-value.

x	–4	–2	0	2	4
y	–4	–3	–2	–1	0

3. **Say:** Look at the values in the table. Find the ratio of y to x for each column.

x	–4	–2	0	2	4
y	–4	–3	–2	–1	0
$\frac{y}{x}$	$\frac{-4}{-4} = 1$	$\frac{-3}{-2} = \frac{3}{2}$	$\frac{-2}{0} =$ undefined	$\frac{-1}{2} = -\frac{1}{2}$	$\frac{0}{-4} = 0$

4. Point out that each ratio is different. This tells you the relationship is not proportional.

5. Point out that where x is 0, y is –2. In a proportional relationship, where x is 0, y is also 0.

KEY TEACHING POINTS

Example 2

Say: The linear equation $y = mx + b$ is called the slope-intercept form of a line because it tells the slope m and the y-intercept b directly in the equation. The y-intercept is the point where $x = 0$ and $y = b$.

Ask: When the y-intercept is positive, is it above or below the x-axis? **[Above.]** When the y-intercept is negative, is it above or below the x-axis? **[Below.]**

Ask: Once the y-intercept is located, how do you decide what the second point is? **[Use the slope.]**

Say: The slope is $\frac{2}{3}$. To find a second point, move up 2 units because the numerator is positive, and move right 3 units because the denominator is positive.

Ask: How do you move from the intercept if the slope is negative? **[Down and then right, or up and then left.]** Why? **[Only the numerator or denominator is negative. If they are both negative, then the slope is positive.]**

Check

Ask: In the equation $y = 19 - 52x$, what should you do first? **[Rearrange the equation to $y = mx + b$ form.]** What is the rearranged equation? **[$y = -52x + 19$]**

Say: Notice the negative sign moves with the term. Be careful when using the Commutative Property. It only applies to addition, so you need to think of subtraction as adding a negative. The slope is –52, not 52.

Ask: The slope –52 is not written as a fraction. How should you move from the intercept to find a second point? **[Even though –52 is not written as a fraction, it is still a rational number, and has the same value as $-\frac{52}{1}$. So, you could move up 52 units and left 1 unit to find the second point.]**

Check

Ask: In the equation $y = \frac{1}{3}x - 2$, what point is the y-intercept? **[(0, –2)]** What is the slope? $\left[\frac{1}{3}\right]$

Ask: Explain how you can use the slope and the y-intercept to find a second point on the line. What point can you use as a second point to graph the equation? **[Possible answer: (3, –1)]** **[Possible answer: Start at the y-intercept (0, –2). Use the slope, $\frac{1}{3}$, to move up 1 unit and right 3 units.]**

COMMON MISCONCEPTION

Ask: What is the Error in this problem?

Identify the slope and y-intercept of the

equation $y = -2 - \dfrac{3}{4}x$. Then graph the line.

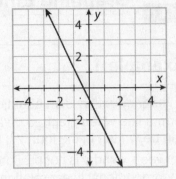

Slope: -2 ***y*-intercept:** $\left(0, -\dfrac{3}{4}\right)$

Reason incorrect: The slope and y-intercept are reversed.

Solution:

Slope: $-\dfrac{3}{4}$ ***y*-intercept:** $(0, -2)$

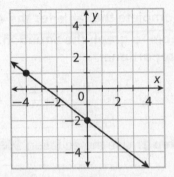

The correct graph is found by plotting a point
at $(0, -2)$ and using the slope to locate a second
point. By moving up 3 units and left 4 units,
a second point can be located at $(1, -4)$.

ADDITIONAL ONLINE INTERVENTION RESOURCES

Use the following for students who have not mastered the concepts in Skill 14.

- Math on the Spot videos
- Personal Math Trainer with customized intervention
- Building Block worksheets (Skill 43: Graph Functions; Skill 44: Graph Linear Functions; Skill 46: Graph Ordered Pairs (First Quadrant); Skill 94: Solve One-Step Inequalities)

Name _____ Date _____ Class_____

Example 1

Vocabulary
Linear equation
Nonproportional
Slope-intercept form
Slope
y-intercept

A linear equation is an equation whose solutions are ordered pairs that form a line when graphed on a coordinate plane. All linear equations can be written in the form $y = mx + b$. When $b \neq 0$, the relationship between x and y is nonproportional. Thus, the graph of a nonproportional linear relationship will *not* go through the origin.

Complete the table for the equation $y = -2x + 1$. Then use the table to graph the equation. Explain why the relationship is not proportional.

x	−2	−1	0	2	3
y					

Step 1: Use the equation $y = -2x + 1$ to find y for each value of x.

x	−2	−1	0	2	3
y	5	3	1	−3	−5

Substitute −2 for x:
$-2(-2) + 1 = 5$

Step 2: Plot ordered pairs from the information in the table. Then draw a line connecting the points to represent all the possible solutions.

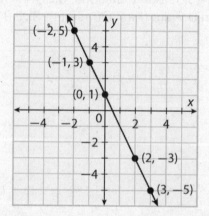

Step 3: The relationship is linear but not proportional because the graph of the line does not go through the origin.

Check

Complete the table for the equation. Then use the table to graph the equation. Explain why the relationship is or is not proportional.

1. $y = \dfrac{1}{2}x - 2$

x	−4	−2	0	2	4
y					

_____

_____

_____

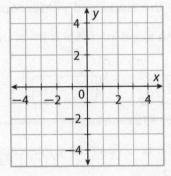

2. $y = -x + 1.5$

x	−3	−1	2	3	5
y					

_____

_____

_____

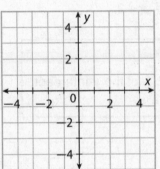

3. Alex works as a carpenter's apprentice. For each job, he earns a flat fee of $50 plus $15 per hour. The equation $y = 15x + 50$ represents his earnings, where x represents the number of hours he works.

   a. Make a table of values representing the amount Alex earns.

Time (hrs)	0	1	2	3	4
Total Earnings ($)					

   b. Draw a graph to represent the situation.

   c. Explain why the relationship is not proportional.

   _____

   _____

   _____

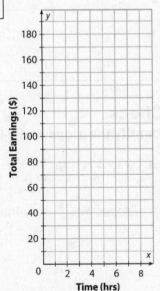

Example 2

The slope-intercept form of the equation of a line is $y = mx + b$, where m is the slope and b is the y-intercept. To quickly graph a line in this form, plot the y-intercept $(0, b)$ and use the slope to find the second point.

A.   Identify the slope and y-intercept of the equation $y = 12x - 31$.

Using the slope intercept form of the equation of a line:

$$y = mx + b$$

$m = 12$ $b = -31$

$$y = 12x - 31$$

The slope is 12, and the y-intercept is $(0, -31)$.

B.   Graph $\dfrac{2}{3}x + 2$.

Step 1:
Since $b = 2$, plot the y-intercept: $(0, b) = (0, 2)$.

Step 2:
The slope is $m = \dfrac{2}{3}$.

Use the slope to find a second point. From $(0, 2)$, count *up* 2 and *right* 3. The new point is $(3, 4)$.

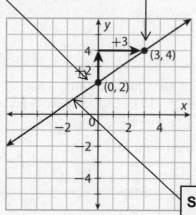

Step 3:
Draw a line through the points.

Check

Identify the slope and y-intercept of each equation.

4. $y = -\dfrac{1}{4}x + 9$

5. $y = 19 - 52x$

Slope: _____ y-intercept: _____

Slope: _____ y-intercept: _____

Graph each equation using the slope and *y*-intercept.

6. $y = \dfrac{1}{3}x - 2$

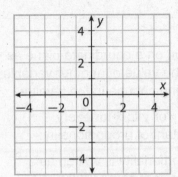

7. $y = -3x + 1$

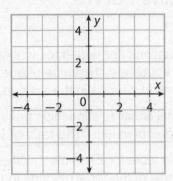

8. Explain the Error. Find the correct solution.
Identify the slope and *y*-intercept of the equation
$y = -2 - \dfrac{3}{4}x$. Then graph the line.

Slope: –2   *y*-intercept: $\left(0, -\dfrac{3}{4}\right)$

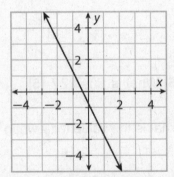

SKILL 14 GRAPHING LINEAR NONPROPORTIONAL RELATIONSHIPS

Graphing Linear Proportional Relationships

KEY TEACHING POINTS

Example 1

Say: Linear equations are equations whose solution can be shown on a coordinate plane as a line. In linear equations, the value of one variable depends on the value of another variable. For each one unit of change in the x-value, there is a corresponding change in the y-value.

Say: Proportional linear relationships have the same ratio of x to y or y to x for every corresponding pair of values. The ratio of y to x is called the constant of proportionality.

Ask: Look at the table for Example 1. When the constant of proportionality is written as a fraction, which row of the table belongs in the numerator? **[The bottom row.]** Which row belongs in the denominator? **[The top row.]**

Say: Tables of values for x and y typically list the values for x first. Be careful not to confuse the two rows.

Ask: What do you look for in each column of the table to decide if the relationship is proportional? **[That the ratios are the same.]**

Say: If the bottom number divided by the top number in the table is the same for each column, the relationship is proportional.

Check

Say: Look at the table in Problem 1.

Ask: What is $20 \div 4$? **[5]** What is $40 \div 8$? **[5]** What is $50 \div 10$? **[5]** What is $60 \div 12$? **[5]** What is k, the constant of proportionality? **[5]**

Ask: In a proportional relationship, this constant is always true. What is the value for y when x is 0? **[0]**

Say: In every proportional relationship, the value for y is 0 when $x = 0$.

COMMON MISCONCEPTION

Ask: What is the Error?

Jonah says that the relationship between x and y is a proportional relationship because as x increases by 1, y increases by 2.

x	2	3	4	5
y	5	7	9	11

Reason incorrect: The ratio of y to x is not constant.

Solution: The relationship is not proportional. The relationship is linear, because as x increases by 1, y increases by 2.

In a proportional relationship, when $x = 0$, y is also 0.

KEY TEACHING POINTS

Example 2

Say: In a proportional relationship, when $x = 0$, y is also 0. This means that the graph of a proportional relationship will always pass through the origin, point (0, 0).

Ask: How can you tell from the graph that this is a proportional relationship? **[It is a straight line that passes through the origin.]**

Ask: What is the slope of a line? **[The ratio of the change in y to the change in x.]**

Say: In a linear proportional relationship, the constant of variation k is the same as the slope.

Ask: As the amount of time Sasha walks increases, how does the distance she travels change? **[It increases.]** As the amount of time Sasha walks decreases, how does the distance she travels change? **[It decreases.]**

Say: The constant of proportionality can be directly related to the context of a problem. You can say that for every 12 minutes Sasha walks, she travels one mile.

Ask: If Sasha walks 0 minutes, how far has she traveled? **[0 miles]**

Ask: Does it matter what points you use for your table? **[No, as long as they are on the line.]**

Check

Ask: In Problem 4, what does the x-value represent? **[Time.]** The y-value? **[Earnings.]**

Ask: How can you tell by looking at the graphs that they represent proportional relationships? **[They are graphs of straight lines that pass through the origin.]**

Say: Once you know the graph represents a proportional relationship, how many points do you need to determine the constant of variation? **[1]**

Ask: What is the constant of variation for Problem 4? **[9]** For Problem 5? **[4]**

Example 3

Say: The graphs in Example 3 do not represent proportional relationships.

Ask: How are these graphs the same as graphs of proportional relationships? **[They are lines.]** How are the different? **[They do not pass through the origin.]**

Say: In a linear relationship that is not proportional, the slope is the rate of change.

Ask: How are the rate of change in a nonproportional relationship and the constant of variation in a proportional relationship related? **[They both show the slope of the graph of the line.]**

Say: In both proportional and nonproportional relationships, the slope is the rate of change. In a proportional relationship, the rate of change is also the constant of variation.

Ask: In a nonproportional linear relationship, you can find the slope using two points on the line. Is this also true of a proportional relationship? **[Yes.]**

Check

Say: Slope can be either positive, as in Problem 6, where the line moves up from left to right, or negative, as in Problem 7, where the line moves down from left to right.

Ask: What values do you use to find the slope of the line in Problem 7? **[The points that are marked (–2, 3) and (1, –3)]** Does it matter which order you use them? **[No, as long as the values correspond for x and y.]**

Example 4

Say: The linear equation $y = mx + b$ is called the slope-intercept form of a line because it tells the slope m and the y-intercept b directly in the equation. The y-intercept is the point where $x = 0$ and $y = b$.

Ask: Using the slope-intercept form of a line, where does the constant of proportionality belong? **[It is the same as the slope, so it replaces m.]**

Ask: What is the difference between rate of change and constant of proportionality? **[The rate of change is the ratio of the change in y to the change in x. The constant of proportionality is the ratio of y to x that is the same for each coordinate in a proportional relationship.]**

Say: The rate of change is constant in both proportional and nonproportional relationships. The ratio of y to x is only constant in proportional relationships.

Ask: In Step 1 you find the rate of change. What does the rate of change tell you on the graph of this relationship? **[A constant rate of change tells you that the graph is linear, and the rate of change tells you the slope of the line.]**

Ask: The initial value is \$35. In the graph of the relationship, what does the initial value tell you? **[The y-intercept.]**

Ask: You know the rate of change, or slope, and the initial value, or y-intercept. How can you write the equation of the line in slope-intercept form? **[Substitute the values you know into the equation $y = mx + b$, so $y = 6x + 35$.]**

Check

Say: In Problem 8, the rate of change is positive because as the values for x increase, the values for y also increase.

Ask: Is the slope positive in Problem 9? Explain. **[No. As the values for x increase, the values for y decrease.]**

ALTERNATE STRATEGY

Strategy: Make and read a graph.

1. You can use a graph to determine if a relationship is linear, find the initial value, and find the rate of change.

2. Graph the points from the table of values shown in Problem 9.

x	1	3	5	6
y	60	36	12	0

3. Connect the points from the table. The points all lie on the same line, so the relationship is linear.

4. The initial value can be read from the graph. It is the point where the line crosses the x- axis. The initial value is 72.

5. The rate of change is the slope. The line moves down 12 units for every 1 unit right. The rate of change is –12.

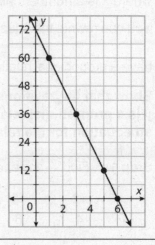

ADDITIONAL ONLINE INTERVENTION RESOURCES

Use the following for students who have not mastered the concepts in Skill 15.
- Math on the Spot videos
- Personal Math Trainer with customized intervention
- Building Block worksheets (Skill 41: Generate Ordered Pairs; Skill 46: Graph Ordered Pairs (First Quadrant); Skill 96: Solve Proportions Using Cross Products)

Name _____ Date _____ Class_____

SKILL
15

Graphing Linear Proportional Relationships

Example 1

A proportional relationship is a relationship between two quantities in which the ratio of one quantity to the other quantity is constant. You can describe a proportional relationship with an equation of the form $y = kx$, where k is a number called the constant of proportionality.

You can rewrite the equation $y = kx$ as $\frac{y}{x} = k$. When two quantities x and y have a proportional relationship, $\frac{y}{x}$ is the constant of proportionality.

Show that the relationship between x and y is a proportional relationship. Then write an equation for the relationship.

x	4	6	8	10
y	12	18	24	30

Step 1   Find $\frac{y}{x}$ for each ordered pair.

$\frac{12}{4} = 3 \qquad \frac{18}{6} = 3 \qquad \frac{24}{8} = 3 \qquad \frac{30}{10} = 3$

Since the ratio $\frac{y}{x} = 3$ for each ordered pair, the relationship between x and y is proportional.

Step 2   Write an equation.

Use the ratio $\frac{y}{x}$, or 3, as the constant of proportionality in the equation $y = kx$.

The equation is $y = 3x$.

Check

Show that the relationship between x and y is a proportional relationship. Then write an equation for the relationship.

1.

x	4	8	10	12
y	20	40	50	60

2.

x	3	6	9	12
y	4.5	9	13.5	18

_____

_____

3. Explain the Error. Then find the correct solution.

Jonah says that the relationship between x and y is a proportional relationship because as x increases by 1, y increases by 2.

x	2	3	4	5
y	5	7	9	11

_____

Example 2

The graph of a proportional relationship is a line that passes through the origin (0, 0). The equation of the line is $y = kx$. The slope of the line is k.

The graph shows the relationship between the amount of time Sasha walks and the total distance she travels. Write an equation for this relationship.

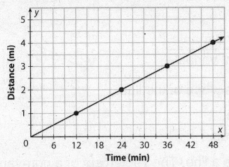

Step 1 Use the points on the graph to make a table.

Time (min)	12	24	36	48
Distance (mi)	1	2	3	4

Step 2 Find the constant of proportionality.

$$\frac{\text{Distance (mi)}}{\text{Time (min)}}: \quad \frac{1}{12} = \frac{1}{12} \quad \frac{2}{24} = \frac{1}{12} \quad \frac{3}{36} = \frac{1}{12} \quad \frac{4}{48} = \frac{1}{12}$$

The constant of proportionality is $\frac{1}{12}$.

Step 3 Write an equation.

$y = kx$ Use $y = kx$. Let x represent time and y represent distance.

$y = \frac{1}{12}x$ Substitute $\frac{1}{12}$ for k.

Check

Write an equation that describes each proportional relationship.

4.

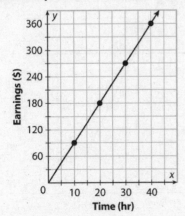

5.

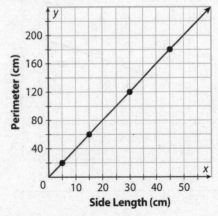

Example 3

The graph at the right is a line, but it is not a proportional relationship because it does not pass through the origin.

For these types of lines, you can describe the relationship between the two quantities using rate of change.

$$\text{rate of change} = \frac{\text{change in dependent variable}}{\text{change in independent variable}}$$

The rate of change of a line is called the slope of the line.

$$\text{Slope} = \frac{y_2 - y_1}{x_2 - x_1} = \frac{\text{vertical change}}{\text{horizontal change}} = \frac{\text{rise}}{\text{run}}$$

You can also use y-intercept to describe a line. The y-intercept of a non-vertical line is the y-coordinate of the point where the line crosses the y-axis.

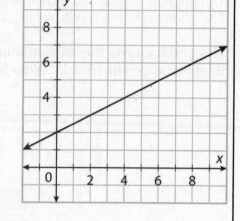

What are the slope and y-intercept of the line?

Step 1 Find the slope.

$$\text{slope} = \frac{y_2 - y_1}{x_2 - x_1} = \frac{7 - 4}{8 - 2} = \frac{3}{6} = \frac{1}{2}$$

Step 2 Find the y-intercept.

The line crosses the y-axis at (0, 3).
So the y-intercept is 3.

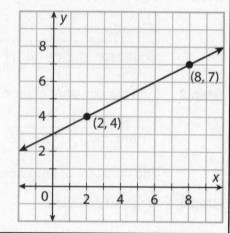

Check

Find the slope and y-intercept of each line.

6.

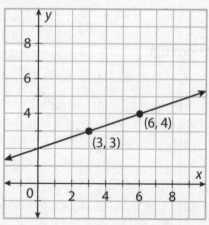

7.

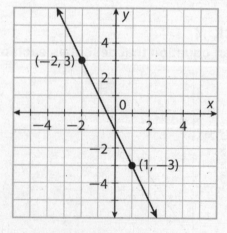

_____   _____

Example 4

The equation $y = mx + b$ is the slope-intercept form of a linear equation. Its graph is a line with slope m and y-intercept b. You can use slope-intercept form to model real-life situations where you are given an initial value (y-intercept, or b) and a rate of change (slope, or m).

You pay a flat fee each month for your television package, plus an additional fee for each streaming movie that you rent, as shown in the table. Confirm that the relationship is linear. Give the rate of change and the initial value.

Number of Movies Rented	2	4	6	7
Monthly Charge ($)	47	59	71	77

Step 1 Confirm that the rate of change is constant.

$$\frac{59-47}{4-2} = \frac{12}{2} = 6 \qquad \frac{71-59}{6-4} = \frac{12}{2} = 6 \qquad \frac{77-71}{7-6} = \frac{6}{1} = 6$$

The relationship is linear because the rate of change is constant, 6. The rate of change represents the cost of renting a movie, $6.

Step 2 Find the initial value.

The initial value is the monthly cost of the package when you rent 0 movies. Use the table. Work backward to find the monthly charge.

$$-2 \qquad -2$$

Number of Movies Rented	0	2	4	6	7
Monthly Charge ($)	35	47	59	71	77

$$-12 \qquad -12$$

The initial value is $35. This is the monthly cost of the TV package when you rent 0 movies.

Check

Confirm that the relationship is linear. Give the rate of change and the initial value.

8.

x	3	6	9	12
y	49	76	103	130

9.

x	1	3	5	6
y	60	36	12	0

SKILL 15 GRAPHING LINEAR PROPORTIONAL RELATIONSHIPS

Inverse Functions

KEY TEACHING POINTS

Example 1

Say: A function that reverses another function is called an inverse function. Recall that multiplication and division are inverse operations because they reverse each other.

Say: Inverse functions are denoted using a negative 1 to the upper right of the function notation, f^{-1}.

Say: For the function $f(x) = 4x + 6$ you can use this chart:

Show the following:

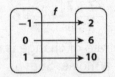 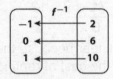

Say: In the function f, the input -1 produces an output of 2.

Ask: The inverse function makes the output the new input. In the inverse function, what is the output when the input is 2? **[−1]**

Say: When you are given a function, you can find the inverse by reversing the x and y. When a function is written in function notation, replace $f(x)$ with y. Use algebra to isolate y, then write the inverse function in function notation.

Check

Say: Look at the function $f(x) = -\dfrac{1}{3}x - 4$.

Ask: What is the first step in finding the inverse function? **[Reverse the x and y,**
$x = -\dfrac{1}{3}y - 4$**]**

Say: Next, solve for y.

Show the following work.

$$x = -\frac{1}{3}y - 4$$
$$x + 4 = -\frac{1}{3}y$$
$$-3x - 12 = y$$
$$y = -3x - 12$$
$$f^{-1}(x) = -3x - 12$$

Ask: What are the slope and *y*-intercept of the original function? **[The slope is $-\frac{1}{3}$ and *y*-intercept is –4.]**

Ask: What are the slope and *y*-intercept of the inverse function? **[The slope is –3 and *y*-intercept is –12.]**

Ask: How are the slopes of the function and its inverse related? **[They are reciprocals.]**

Use the slope and *y*-intercepts to graph the function and its inverse.

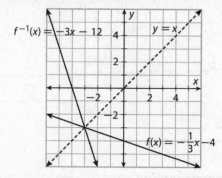

ALTERNATE STRATEGY

Strategy: Use inverse operations.

1. **Say:** The inverse of a function undoes operations in the function. Using inverse operations, you can find the inverse of functions.

2. Look at the function $f(x) = -3x + 2$. Use the function to create a table of values.

x	–2	1	0	1	2
y	8	5	2	–1	–4

3. Using a given value of *x*, you must multiply by –3, then add 2 to find the value of *y*.

4. The inverse of multiplying by –3 is dividing by –3. The inverse of adding 2 is subtracting 2.

5. You can write the inverse function, f^{-1}, using the inverse operations in reverse order. First, subtract 2, then divide by –3.

$f^{-1} = \dfrac{(x-2)}{-3}$, or in slope-intercept form $f^{-1} = -\dfrac{1}{3}x + \dfrac{2}{3}$

6. Make a table of values to check your inverse function. Use the values for *y* in your original functions table as the *x* values in the inverse functions table.

x	8	5	2	–1	–4
y	–2	1	0	1	2

7. You can use the slope and *y*-intercept to graph the function and its inverse, or the tables of values you already have. Since these are linear functions, you only need to graph two points and draw the line that runs through both.

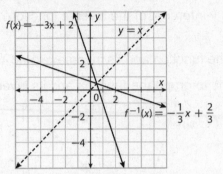

KEY TEACHING POINTS

Example 2

Say: Quadratic functions include a squared variable. Recall that inverse functions are the reverse function, or a function that does the opposite.

Ask: What is the opposite of squaring a number? **[Taking the square root of a number.]**

Say: So, if $y = x^2$, you can take the square root of each side to find the value for *x*. When $y = x^2$, then you know $x = \pm\sqrt{y}$.

Ask: Why does $x = \pm\sqrt{y}$ and not just $x = \sqrt{y}$? **[Possible response: If $x = -3$, there is no radical that can produce a negative value for *x*.]**

Say: The $\pm$ in this equation shows that for some values of *y*, there are two possible values of *x*. For example, in $x = \sqrt{y}$, where $y = 9$, the values for *x* are both +3 and –3.

Ask: The inverse of the function $f(x) = \dfrac{1}{4}x^2$ without the limited domain is $y = \pm 2\sqrt{x}$. Is $y = \pm 2\sqrt{x}$ a function? **[No.]** Why not? **[There can be more than one *y*-value for a given *x*-value. It won't pass the vertical line test.]**

Say: We can limit the domain of the square root equation to $x \geq 0$, the equation becomes $y = 2\sqrt{x}$, which is a square root function.

Say: Notice in the graph of the function and its inverse, the two graphs are reflections over the line $y = x$. This is true of all inverse functions.

Check

Say: What is the first step in finding the inverse function for $f(x) = x^2 - 2$ when $x \geq 0$? **[Reverse the *x* and *y*.]**

Show the following work, explaining each step:
$$y = x^2 - 2$$
$$x = y^2 - 2$$
$$x + 2 = y^2$$
$$\sqrt{x + 2} = y$$
$$f^{-1}(x) = \sqrt{x + 2}$$

Ask: Why do you not need to include the $\pm$ sign in the answer? **[The domain is limited.]**
If the domain were not limited, would the inverse of a function be a function? **[No.]**

Ask: How can you graph the function and its inverse? **[Use a table of values for each.]**

Demonstrate the table of values for each. Reiterate that you can use the same table of values and switch the *x*- and *y*-values.

x	0	1	2	3	4
$f(x)$	-2	-1	2	7	14

x	-2	-1	2	7	14
$f^{-4}(x)$	0	1	2	3	4

Make sure when you switch the values in the table that your inverse function matches the values in the table.

Graph the function and its inverse as a class.

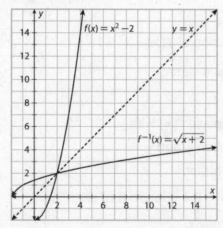

Say: The function in item 11 gives the area of a square in terms of side length.
Ask: What does the inverse function give? **[The side length of a square in terms of area.]**
What function gives you the side length of a square in terms of area? **[$s(A) = \sqrt{A}$]** Why are negative values not included in the solution? **[Length is always positive, so there are no negative lengths.]**

Example 3

Say: Cubic functions include a variable with the exponent 3.

Ask: The original function in Part A does not have the constraint $x \geq 0$. Why is this constraint not necessary? **[When you cube a value, it keeps its sign. If the value is negative, the cube is also negative. This means there will only be one x-value for each y-value in the inverse function.]**

Say: Remember, the steps to finding the inverse of a function are always the same. Switch x and y, solve for y.

Say: You can switch the x- and y-values in the table of values for the function to make a table of values for the inverse function. Check the table to make sure your inverse equation is correct.

Check a few of the values from the table as a class. Show the following work.

$f^{-1}(x) = 2\sqrt[3]{x}$ when $x = -8$ $f^{-1}(x) = 2\sqrt[3]{x}$ when $x = 1$

$$f^{-1}(-8) = 2\sqrt[3]{-8}$$ $$f^{-1}(1) = 2\sqrt[3]{1}$$
$$= 2(-2)$$ $$= 2(1)$$
$$= -4$$ $$= 2$$

Check

Say: Let's find the inverse function of $f(x) = x^3 + 1$.

Complete the following work as a class:

$f(x) = x^3 + 1$	
$y = x^3 + 1$	Replace $f(x)$ with y.
$x = y^3 + 1$	Switch x and y.
$x - 1 = y^3$	Subtract.
$\sqrt[3]{x-1} = \sqrt[3]{y^3}$	Take the cube root of each side.
$\sqrt[3]{x-1} = y$	Simplify.
$f^{-1}(x) = \sqrt[3]{x-1}$	Use f^{-1} to represent the inverse of f.

The inverse of $f(x) = x^3 + 1$ is $f^{-1}(x) = \sqrt[3]{x-1}$.

Ask: If you are given the graph of $f(x) = x^3 - 2$, how could you sketch the graph of the inverse without finding the inverse function first? **[The function and its inverse are reflections over the line $y = x$. Find points on the function, and plot the inverse by reversing the x- and y-values.]**

COMMON MISCONCEPTION

Ask: What is the Error in this problem?

$$y = \frac{1}{64}x^3$$

$$x = \frac{1}{64}y^3$$

$$64x = y^3$$

$$\sqrt[3]{64x} = \sqrt[3]{y^3}$$

$$8\sqrt[3]{x} = y$$

$$f^{-1}(x) = 8\sqrt[3]{x}$$

Reason incorrect: The square root of 64 is given, instead of the cube root of 64.

Solution:

$$y = \frac{1}{64}x^3$$

$$x = \frac{1}{64}y^3$$

$$64x = y^3$$

$$\sqrt[3]{64x} = \sqrt[3]{y^3}$$

$$4\sqrt[3]{x} = y$$

$$f^{-1}(x) = 4\sqrt[3]{x}$$

Ask: How could this error be avoided? **[Check values to make sure the inverse function undoes the original function.]**

ADDITIONAL ONLINE INTERVENTION RESOURCES

Use the following for students who have not mastered the concepts in Skill 16.

- Math on the Spot videos
- Personal Math Trainer with customized intervention
- Building Block worksheets (Skill 85: Simplify Radical Expressions; Skill 100: Squares and Square Roots)

SKILL 16 Inverse Functions

Example 1

Vocabulary

Inverse functions

Quadratic function

Square root function

Cubic function

Cube root function

Remember that in inverse functions, the x- and y-values are switched. This means that, given the graph of a function, f, the graph of its inverse is the reflection of f across the line $y = x$. You use f^{-1} to denote the inverse of the function f.

Given a function, you can use algebra to find its inverse.

Find the inverse of the function $f(x) = 4x + 6$.

Then graph f and f^{-1} in the same coordinate plane.

Step 1 Replace $f(x)$ with y. Then replace x with y and y with x.

$$f(x) = 4x + 6$$
$$y = 4x + 6 \qquad \text{Replace } f(x) \text{ with } y.$$
$$x = 4y + 6 \qquad \text{Switch } x \text{ and } y.$$

Step 2 Solve for y.

$$x = 4y + 6$$
$$x - 6 = 4y \qquad \text{Subtract 6 from each side.}$$
$$\frac{x-6}{4} = y \qquad \text{Divide each side by 4.}$$
$$\frac{1}{4}x - \frac{3}{2} = y \qquad \text{Simplify.}$$

Step 3 Write in function notation. Use f^{-1} to represent the inverse of f.

$$f^{-1} = \frac{1}{4}x - \frac{3}{2}$$

Step 4 Graph f and f^{-1} in the same coordinate plane.

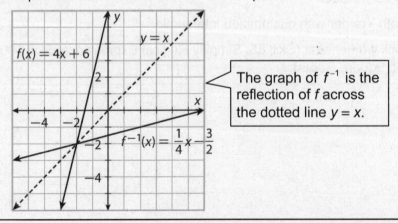

The graph of f^{-1} is the reflection of f across the dotted line $y = x$.

Check

Find the inverse of each linear function. Then graph both *f* and *f*⁻¹ in the same coordinate plane.

1. $f(x) = 2x + 1$

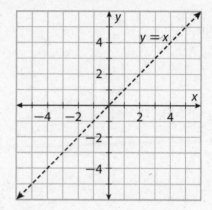

$f^{-1}(x) = $ _____

2. $f(x) = -3x + 2$

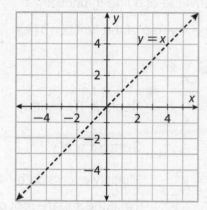

$f^{-1}(x) = $ _____

3. $f(x) = -\dfrac{1}{3}x - 4$

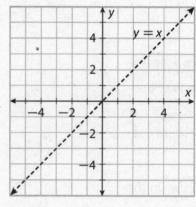

$f^{-1}(x) = $ _____

4. $f(x) = \dfrac{2}{5}x - 5$

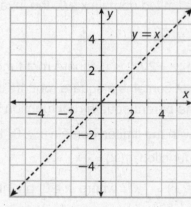

$f^{-1}(x) = $ _____

5. $f(x) = -2x$

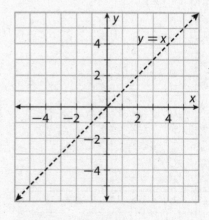

$f^{-1}(x) = $ _____

6. $f(x) = -x$

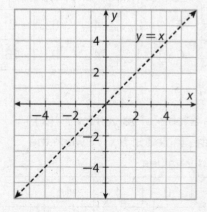

$f^{-1}(x) = $ _____

Example 2

Remember that a quadratic function is a function of the form $f(x) = ax^2$. You can find the inverse of a quadratic function in the same way you found the inverse of a linear function.

A. Find the inverse of the function $f(x) = \dfrac{1}{4}x^2$ for the domain $x \geq 0$.

$$f(x) = \dfrac{1}{4}x^2$$

$$y = \dfrac{1}{4}x^2 \qquad \text{Replace } f(x) \text{ with } y.$$

$$x = \dfrac{1}{4}y^2 \qquad \text{Switch } x \text{ and } y.$$

$$4x = y^2 \qquad \text{Multiply each side by 4.}$$

$$\sqrt{4x} = \sqrt{y^2} \qquad \text{Take the square root of each side.}$$

$$2\sqrt{x} = y \qquad \text{Simplify.}$$

$$f^{-1}(x) = 2\sqrt{x} \qquad \text{Use } f^{-1} \text{ to represent the inverse of } f.$$

With the limited domain $x \geq 0$, the inverse of $f(x) = \dfrac{1}{4}x^2$ is

$$f^{-1}(x) = 2\sqrt{x}.$$

The function $y = 2\sqrt{x}$ is a square root function. A square root function is a function that contains a square root. Its independent variable is in the radicand. The parent square root function is $y = \sqrt{x}$.

In general, with the limited domain $x \geq 0$, the inverse of $f(x) = x^2$ is the square root function $g(x) = \sqrt{x}$.

B. Graph $f(x) = \dfrac{1}{4}x^2$, where $x \geq 0$, and its inverse, $f^{-1}(x) = 2\sqrt{x}$, in the same coordinate plane.

Step 1

Make a table of values for $f(x)$.

x	0	2	4	6	8
f(x)	0	1	4	9	16

Step 2

Make a table of values for $f^{-1}(x)$. Use the table for $f(x)$. Switch the x- and y-values.

x	0	1	4	9	16
f⁻¹(x)	0	2	4	6	8

Step 3

Graph $f(x)$ and $f^{-1}(x)$.

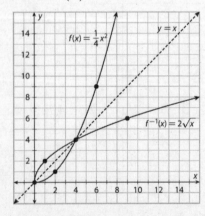

Check

Find the inverse of each quadratic function with the limited domain.
Then graph both f and f^{-1} in the same coordinate plane.

7. $f(x) = \dfrac{1}{9}x^2$ when $x \geq 0$

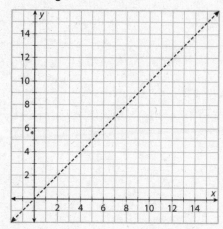

$f^{-1}(x) = $ _____

8. $f(x) = 4x^2$ when $x \geq 0$

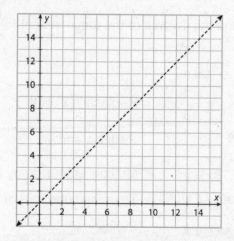

$f^{-1}(x) = $ _____

9. $f(x) = x^2 + 1$ when $x \geq 0$

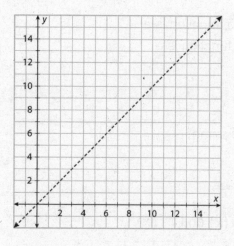

$f^{-1}(x) = $ _____

10. $f(x) = x^2 - 2$ when $x \geq 0$

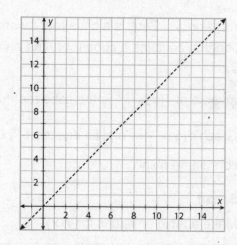

$f^{-1}(x) = $ _____

11. The function $A(s) = s^2$ gives the area A in square units of a square with a side length of s units. Find the inverse function, $s(A)$. Then use the inverse function to find the side length of a square with an area of 121 square units.

$s(A) = $ _____ ; _____

Example 3

A cubic function is a function of the form $f(x) = ax^3$. You can find the inverse of a cubic function in the same way you found the inverses of linear and quadratic functions.

A. Find the inverse of the function $f(x) = \dfrac{1}{8}x^3$.

$$f(x) = \frac{1}{8}x^3$$

$y = \dfrac{1}{8}x^3$ Replace $f(x)$ with y.

$x = \dfrac{1}{8}y^3$ Switch x and y.

$8x = y^3$ Multiply each side by 8.

$\sqrt[3]{8x} = \sqrt[3]{y^3}$ Take the cube root of each side.

$2\sqrt[3]{x} = y$ Simplify.

$f^{-1}(x) = 2\sqrt[3]{x}$ Use f^{-1} to represent the inverse of f.

The inverse of $f(x) = \dfrac{1}{8}x^3$ is $f^{-1}(x) = 2\sqrt[3]{x}$.

The function $y = 2\sqrt[3]{x}$ is a cube root function. A cube root function is a function that contains a cube root. The parent cube root function is $y = \sqrt[3]{x}$.

The inverse of $f(x) = x^3$ is the cube root function $g(x) = \sqrt[3]{x}$.

B. Graph $f(x) = \dfrac{1}{8}x^3$ and its inverse $f^{-1}(x) = 2\sqrt[3]{x}$ in the same coordinate plane.

Step 1

Make a table of values for $f(x)$.

x	−4	−2	0	2	4
f(x)	−8	−1	0	1	8

Step 2

Make a table of values for $f^{-1}(x)$. Use the table for $f(x)$. Switch the x- and y-values.

x	−8	−1	0	1	8
f⁻¹(x)	−4	−2	0	2	4

Step 3

Graph $f(x)$ and $f^{-1}(x)$.

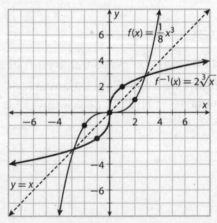

Name _____ Date _____ Class_____

Check

Find the inverse of each cubic function. Then graph both f and f^{-1} in the same coordinate plane.

12. $f(x) = x^3 + 1$

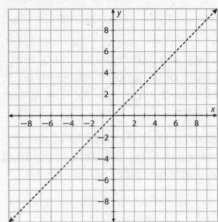

$f^{-1}(x) =$ _____

13. $f(x) = x^3 - 2$

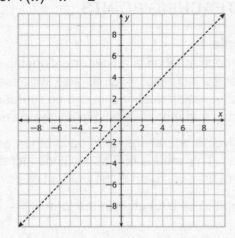

$f^{-1}(x) =$ _____

14. Explain the Error in finding the inverse function. Then find the correct solution.

$$y = \frac{1}{64}x^3$$

$$x = \frac{1}{64}y^3$$

$$64x = y^3$$

$$\sqrt[3]{64x} = \sqrt[3]{y^3}$$

$$8\sqrt[3]{x} = y$$

$$f^{-1}(x) = 8\sqrt[3]{x}$$

SKILL 16 INVERSE FUNCTIONS

Inverse Variation

KEY TEACHING POINTS

Example 1

Say: Direct variation is a linear relationship where the variables are in a constant ratio, and as x-values increase, y-values also increase. The constant ratio of variation is denoted as k. A direct variation relationship can be represented by a function in the form $y = kx$. The graph of a direct variation relationship always passes through the origin.

Say: Inverse operations undo each other, and inverse variation does the opposite of direct variation. This means that as x-values increase, y-values decrease. The constant of variation for an inverse variation is the product of x and y. An inverse variation relationship can be represented by a function in the form $y = \dfrac{k}{x}$.

Ask: If y varies inversely as x, and $y = 9$ when $x = 7$, how can you find the constant of variation? **[Substitute the values into the general form of an inverse variation.]**

Say: Remember, the constant of variation for inverse variation is the product of x and y.

Ask: In the equation $y = \dfrac{63}{x}$, is the constant of variation the product of the x- and y-values from the problem? **[Yes, (9)(7) = 63.]**

Ask: In the equation $y = \dfrac{63}{x}$, what is the value for y when x is 3? **[21]** What is the product of 3 and 21? **[63]**

Check

Ask: What is the product of 4 and 13? **[52]**

Ask: How do you find the equation for the inverse variation when you know a value for x and y? **[Substitute the known values into the inverse variation equation.]**

Show the following work:

$$y = \frac{k}{x}$$

$$4 = \frac{k}{13}$$

$$4(13) = 13\left(\frac{k}{13}\right)$$

$$52 = k$$

$$y = \frac{52}{x}$$

Ask: When y varies inversely as x, and $y = 10$ when $x = 7.5$, what is the constant of variation? **[75]** So then, if y varies inversely as x, and $y = 10$ when $x = 7.5$, what is the equation for the inverse variation? $\left[y = \dfrac{75}{x} \right]$

COMMON MISCONCEPTION

Ask: What is the Error in this problem?

Suppose y varies inversely as x, and $y = 9$ when $x = 12$. Then the equation $y = \frac{3}{4}x$ represents the inverse variation.

Reason incorrect: The constant of variation was found for direct variation, not inverse variation.

Solution:
$$y = \frac{k}{x}$$
$$9 = \frac{k}{12}$$
$$9(12) = 12\left(\frac{k}{12}\right)$$
$$108 = k$$
$$y = \frac{108}{x}$$

Ask: How could this error be avoided? **[Substitute the original values into the equation and see if it is true.]**

Remember, in an inverse variation, the constant of variation is the product of the variables, and the equation has the constant as a numerator.

KEY TEACHING POINTS

Example 2
Say: Remember, in inverse variation, as the x-value increases, the y-value decreases. In the real world, inverse variation occurs regularly. For example, as you move faster, it takes less time to cover a given distance, and as you drive farther, the amount of gas left in your tank decreases.

Ask: In an inverse variation, how can you find the constant of variation? **[Use the equation and substitute in the values, or multiply x times y.]**

Say: If the time varies inversely with the number of workers, and it takes 5 workers 48 hours, what is the constant of variation? $\left[(5)(48) = 240, \, k = 240\right]$

Ask: To build a fence in 20 working hours, 12 workers are needed. What is 12 times 20? **[240]**

Check
Ask: What does "the time varies inversely with the number of workers" mean? **[As the time increases, the number of workers decreases, and as the number of workers increases, the time decreases.]**

Ask: If it takes 15 workers 2.5 hours, what is the constant of variation? **[37.5]**

KEY TEACHING POINTS

Example 3

Say: Inverse variation functions never cross the origin.

Ask: When you substitute 0 into the inverse variation equation for *x*, what is the *y*-value? **[Undefined.]** Why? **[The result is a fraction with 0 in the denominator.]**

Say: Graphs of inverse variation functions include coordinates only in two quadrants and do not cross either axis.

Ask: Why will there never be a value where $y = 0$? **[Possible response: In order for *y* to be 0, the constant of variation would need to be 0. If the constant of variation is 0, then for every value of *x*, *y* is 0.]**

Check

Ask: What is the first step to graph the inverse function $y = \dfrac{-10}{x}$? **[Make a table of values.]**

Say: Because inverse variation equations are not linear, make sure you include values that are both negative and positive.

Complete a table of values as a class.

x	−10	−5	−2	−1	0	1	2	5	10
y	1	2	5	10	undef.	−10	−5	−2	−1

Ask: Why might these values have been chosen to graph? **[The *x*-values are all factors of 10, so they make division easy.]**

Ask: In what quadrants will the points lie? **[Quadrants II and IV]** Why not in Quadrants I and III? **[The constant of variation is negative, so the *x* and *y* terms always have opposite signs.]**

Look at the graph of $y = \dfrac{-10}{x}$ as a class.

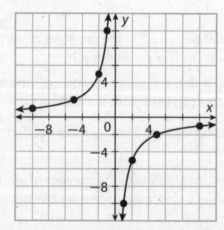

Say: Notice the points with negative and positive *x*-values reflect across the line $y = x$. When the constant of variation *k* is a positive value, the negative and positive *x*-values reflect across the line $y = -x$.

KEY TEACHING POINTS

Example 4

Ask: Look at the table in Part A. Do the *y*-values increase or decrease as *x* increases? **[Increase.]** How can you check if the table shows direct variation? **[See if the values have a constant ratio $\frac{y}{x}$.]**

Ask: How can you check if the table for Part B shows inverse variation? **[Multiply the *x*- and *y*-values and see if the product is constant.]**

Check

Ask: Look at the tables in Problems 10 and 11. How will the *x*- and *y*-values relate if these are direct variation relationships? **[If one increases, the other increases.]** If they are inverse variation relationships? **[If one increases, the other decreases.]**

ALTERNATE STRATEGY

Strategy: Compare the change.

1. You can recognize direct and inverse relationships in a table or graph by understanding how the values change.
2. **Say:** In a direct variation, when you multiply *x* by a constant, the value for *y* is multiplied by the same constant.
3. Look at the table from Part A. Compare the change from $x = 5$ to where $x = 10$. The value for *x* doubles. In a direct variation relationship, the value for *y* changes by the same factor.

x	2	5	9	10
y	−18	−45	−81	−90

4. **Ask:** Is $(2)(-45) = -90$? **[Yes.]** The relationship shows direct variation.
5. **Say:** In an inverse variation, when you multiply *x* by a constant, the value for *y* is multiplied by the reciprocal of that constant. For example, when *x* doubles, *y* halves.
6. Look at the table from Part B. Compare the change from $x = 4$ to where $x = 8$. The value for *x* doubles. In an inverse variation relationship, the value for *y* changes by the reciprocal factor, so it should change by a factor of $\frac{1}{2}$.

x	−2	1	4	8
y	−16	32	8	4

7. **Ask:** Is $\left(\frac{1}{2}\right)(8) = 4$? **[Yes.]** The relationship shows inverse variation.

ADDITIONAL ONLINE INTERVENTION RESOURCES

Use the following for students who have not mastered the concepts in Skill 17.

- Math on the Spot videos
- Personal Math Trainer with customized intervention
- Building Block worksheets (Skill 44: Graph Linear Functions)

SKILL 17 Inverse Variation

Example 1

An inverse variation is a relationship that can be represented by a function of the form $y = \dfrac{k}{x}$, or $xy = k$, where $k \neq 0$. The constant of variation for an inverse variation is k, or the product of the two nonzero variables x and y.

Suppose y varies inversely as x, and $y = 9$ when $x = 7$. Find the constant of variation. Then write an equation for the inverse variation.

$y = \dfrac{k}{x}$	Use the general form of an inverse variation.
$9 = \dfrac{k}{7}$	Substitute 7 for x and 9 for y.
$7(9) = 7\left(\dfrac{k}{7}\right)$	Multiply each side by 7.
$63 = k$	Simplify.
$y = \dfrac{63}{x}$	Write an equation. Substitute 63 for k.

The constant of variation k is 63. The equation $y = \dfrac{63}{x}$ represents the inverse variation.

Vocabulary

Inverse variation

Constant of variation (for inverse variation)

Direct variation

Check

Suppose y varies inversely as x. Write an equation for the inverse variation.

1. $y = 4$ when $x = 13$

2. $y = 6$ when $x = 6.5$

3. $y = 8.5$ when $x = 6$

4. $y = 10$ when $x = 7.5$

5. Explain the Error. Then find the correct solution.

Suppose y varies inversely as x, and $y = 9$ when $x = 12$. Then the equation $y = \dfrac{3}{4}x$ represents the inverse variation.

_____

Example 2

Many real-world problems can be modeled and solved with an inverse variation equation.

The time t that it takes a group of workers w to build a fence around a large pasture varies inversely as the number of workers. Suppose 5 workers can build a fence in 48 working hours. How many workers would be needed to build a fence in 20 working hours?

Step 1 Find the constant of variation k.

$$t = \frac{k}{w}$$ Use the general form of an inverse variation.

$$48 = \frac{k}{5}$$ Substitute 5 for w and 48 for t.

$$5(48) = 5\left(\frac{k}{5}\right)$$ Multiply each side by 5.

$$240 = k$$ Simplify.

Step 2 Find the number of workers needed.

$$t = \frac{240}{w}$$ Write an equation. Substitute 240 for k.

$$20 = \frac{240}{w}$$ Substitute 20 for t.

$$w(20) = w\left(\frac{240}{w}\right)$$ Multiply each side by w.

$$20w = 240$$ Simplify.

$$w = 12$$ Divide each side by 20.

To build a fence in 20 working hours, 12 workers are needed.

Check

Solve.

6. The time t that it takes a group of workers w to clean a stadium after an event varies inversely as the number of workers. Suppose 15 workers can clean the stadium in 2.5 hours. How many workers would be needed to clean the stadium in 0.5 hour?

   _____

7. The time t that a train travels varies inversely as the rate r at which the train travels. Suppose it takes the train 2 hours to travel a certain distance when it is traveling at a constant rate of 90 miles per hour. How long would it take the train to travel the same distance if it were traveling at a constant rate of 60 miles per hour?

   _____

Example 3

The graph of an inverse variation is a function that has two unconnected sections. You can graph an inverse variation function $y = \dfrac{k}{x}$, or $xy = k$, by making a table of values and plotting points.

Graph $y = \dfrac{24}{x}$.

Step 1 Make a table of values. Choose both negative and positive values for x.

x	−12	−6	−3	−1	0	1	3	6	12
y	−2	−4	−8	−24	undef.	24	8	4	2

Step 2 Plot the points in the table. Connect the points in Quadrant I with a smooth curve. Then connect the points in Quadrant III with a smooth curve.

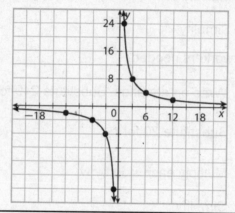

Check

Graph each inverse variation function.

8. $y = \dfrac{18}{x}$

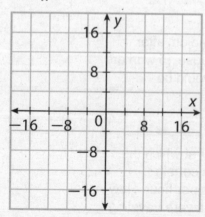

9. $y = \dfrac{-10}{x}$

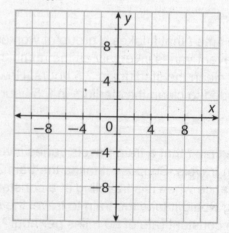

Example 4

You can use the following information to help you decide whether a situation represents a direct variation or an inverse variation:

- In a direct variation, the *ratio* of the variables x and y is constant.

- In an inverse variation, the *product* of x and y is constant.

A. Determine whether y varies directly or inversely as x.

x	2	5	9	10
y	−18	−45	−81	−90

It appears that y varies directly as x. Find the ratio $\frac{y}{x}$ for each ordered pair.

$$\frac{-18}{2} = -9 \qquad \frac{-45}{5} = -9 \qquad \frac{-81}{9} = -9 \qquad \frac{-90}{10} = -9$$

The ratio $\frac{y}{x}$ is the same for each ordered pair in the table, so y varies directly as x.

B. Determine whether y varies directly or inversely as x.

x	−2	1	4	8
y	−16	32	8	4

It appears that y varies inversely as x. Find the product xy for each ordered pair.

$$-2(-16) = 32 \qquad 1(32) = 32 \qquad 4(8) = 32 \qquad 8(4) = 32$$

The product xy is the same for each ordered pair in the table, so y varies inversely as x.

Check

Determine whether y varies directly or inversely as x.

10.

x	−5	−3	1	9
y	9	15	−45	−5

11.

x	−4	−2	3	5
y	−28	−14	21	35

_____ _____

SKILL 17 INVERSE VARIATION

Linear Functions

KEY TEACHING POINTS

Example 1

Say: Linear means line. The graph of a linear equation on the coordinate plane is a straight line.

Ask: How can you tell on a graph if an equation is a function? **[The vertical line test says that if you draw a vertical line anywhere on the graph it can only cross the graph of the equation one time.]**

Say: This means that the graph of a vertical line is a line, but it is not a function.

Say: So, the graph of a line does not always represent a function, as is seen in Graph (a), and the graph of a function is not always a line, as is seen in Graph (d).

Check

Say: The graph for Problem 1 shows a horizontal line.

Ask: Are horizontal lines on a coordinate graph linear functions? **[Yes.]**

Say: The graph for Problem 4 shows a vertical line.

Ask: Are vertical lines on a coordinate graph linear functions? **[No.]**

Say: Functions can have only one output, or y-value, for each input, or x-value. A vertical line on a coordinate graph shows an infinite number of y-values for one x-value.

Ask: In the graph for Problem 1, if $x = 3$, what is the value of y? **[–1]** Is this the only possible value for y? **[Yes.]** Item 1 is a function. In the graph for Problem 4, if $x = 3$, what is the value of y? **[All real numbers. There is no single value that is the answer.]** Item 4 is not a function.

Example 2

Say: All linear functions can be written using linear equations. When a function is written as a linear equation, you know it is a linear function.

Say: One form of the equation of a linear function is slope-intercept form. The linear equation $y = mx + b$ is called the slope-intercept form of a line because it tells the slope m and the y-intercept b directly in the equation. The y-intercept is the point where $x = 0$ and $y = b$.

Say: A second form of the equation of a linear function is standard form. The standard form of a linear equation is $Ax + By = C$, where A, B, and C are real numbers and A and B are not both 0.

Ask: Why can't A and B both be 0? **[If they are, then C is also 0. There is nothing to graph.]**

Ask: In either form of the equation of a linear function, what are the exponents of x and y? **[1]**

Say: If either variable has an exponent that is not 1, the equation does not represent a linear function.

Ask: Why does the equation $y = 5x^2 - 11$ not represent a linear function? **[The variable x has an exponent that is not 1.]**

Say: Look at the equation $xy - 7 = 14$. When the variables x and y are multiplied, the equation cannot be written in either slope-intercept or standard form. This is not a linear function.

Check

Say: Look at the equation $y = \dfrac{1}{x} + 6$. Try to write the equation in standard form. Let's start by subtracting 6 from both sides to get that fraction by itself. Then we can try to get x out of the denominator.

Show the following work:

$$y - 6 = \frac{1}{x} + 6 - 6$$

$$y - 6 = \frac{1}{x}$$

$$(y - 6)x = \left(\frac{1}{x}\right)x$$

$$xy - 6x = 1$$

Ask: Can the equation be written in standard form? **[No.]** This is not a linear equation.

Say: Look at the equation $-\dfrac{1}{4}x + 9 = y$.

Ask: What happens if you write the equation with the y on the left side and the expression on the right? **[It is written in slope-intercept form.]** What is the slope? $\left[-\dfrac{1}{4}\right]$ Lines that have a negative slope move down from left to right. Lines can have negative or positive slopes; they are still linear.

ALTERNATE STRATEGY

Strategy: Use a table.

1. **Say:** You can use a table of values to help decide if an equation represents a linear function.

2. For the equation $-\dfrac{1}{4}x + 9 = y$, create a table of values using integers from -2 to 2.

Demonstrate how to make a table of values using the equation. Substitute each x-value from the table into the equation to find the corresponding y-value.

x	-2	-1	0	1	2
y	$9\frac{1}{2}$	$9\frac{1}{4}$	9	$8\frac{3}{4}$	$8\frac{1}{2}$

3. In a linear relationship, for each unit that x changes, the value for y changes by a corresponding value. In the table, each x value increases by 1. From $x = -2$ to $x = -1$, the change in y is $9\frac{1}{4} - 9\frac{1}{2} = -\frac{1}{4}$ unit. From $x = -1$ to $x = 0$, the change in y is $9 - 9\frac{1}{4} = -\frac{1}{4}$. This shows that the slope of the graph between intervals is the same. This is true for any two consecutive points. In a linear function, the slope of the graph is always the same. This is a linear function.

4. For the equation $y = \frac{1}{x} + 6$, create a table of values using integers from 1 to 5. Substitute each x-value from the table into the equation to find the corresponding y-value.

x	1	2	3	4	5
y	7	$6\frac{1}{2}$	$6\frac{1}{3}$	$6\frac{1}{4}$	$6\frac{1}{5}$

5. In a linear relationship, for each unit that x changes, the value for y changes by a corresponding value. In the table, each x value increases by 1. From $x = 1$ to $x = 2$, the change in y is $6\frac{1}{2} - 7 = -\frac{1}{2}$ unit. From $x = 2$ to $x = 3$, the change in y is $6\frac{1}{3} - 6\frac{1}{2} = -\frac{1}{6}$. This shows that the slope of the graph changes. In a linear function, the slope of the graph is always the same. This is not a linear function.

KEY TEACHING POINTS

Example 3

Say: When you are given information about a linear function, such as the slope and y-intercept, you can write the equation of the linear function.

Ask: What is the slope-intercept form of a linear equation? [$y = mx + b$]

Ask: What does it mean when the y-intercept of a linear function is -5? [It means the line crosses the y-axis at -5.]

Check

Ask: If the y-intercept is -12 and the slope is 11, what value gets substituted in for m? [11] For b? [-12]

Say: The slope is 3 and the point $\left(0, -\frac{1}{4}\right)$ is on the graph.

Ask: Where on the graph is point $\left(0, -\frac{1}{4}\right)$? [On the y-axis.] What is the value for b? $\left[-\frac{1}{4}\right]$

COMMON MISCONCEPTION

Ask: What is the Error in this problem?

Susan is asked to write an equation representing a linear function with a y-intercept of $-\dfrac{5}{3}$ and a slope of 16. She writes $y = -\dfrac{5}{3}x + 16$.

Reason incorrect: The slope and y-intercept are reversed.

Solution: $y = 16x - \dfrac{5}{3}$

Say: Be sure to substitute the slope and y-intercept into the right parts of the slope-intercept form. In the equation $y = mx + b$, m is the slope and b is the y-intercept. Remember, slope comes before intercept in both the name and the equation.

KEY TEACHING POINTS

Example 4
Say: Finding the equation for a linear function can be done with just two points on the line or the slope and just one point on the line.

Ask: What is slope? **[It is the ratio of the change in *y* to the change in *x*.]** What does the slope tell you? **[The steepness and direction of a line.]**

Say: The sign of the slope tells you the direction, and the value tells you the steepness. A line with a slope of –2 moves down from left to right because it is negative. The value 2 tells you that the line moves down 2 units for every unit moved to the right.

Ask: What is the slope formula? $\left[m = \dfrac{y_2 - y_1}{x_2 - x_1} \right]$

Check
Say: You are given the fact that these are linear functions.

Ask: In Problem 14, how do you know what values to use to find the slope? **[It doesn't matter which values you choose, as long as they are corresponding *x* and *y* values.]**

Say: Is the slope in Problem 14 positive or negative? **[Positive.]** Can you tell without using the slope formula? **[Yes.]** How? **[As the *x*-values increase, the *y*-values also increase.]**

Ask: In Problem 15, the *x*-values are not in numeric order. Does this matter? **[No.]** Why not? **[When you use the slope formula, as long as the values for *x* and *y* correspond, it doesn't matter what order the points are in.]**

KEY TEACHING POINTS

Example 5

Say: Using the graph of a linear function, you can write an equation that represents the graph.

Ask: What values do you need to find from the graph? **[The slope and *y*-intercept.]**

Say: The *y*-intercept is the value for *y* where the graph crosses the *y*-axis.

Ask: How can you find the slope? **[Using two points on the line, you can use the slope formula.]**

Ask: Why might you want to choose the *x*- and *y*-intercepts? **[It is easy to work with zeros in the slope formula.]**

Say: Once you know the slope and *y*-intercept, use the slope-intercept form of the equation and substitute in the values.

Check

Ask: In the graph for Problem 16, is the slope positive or negative? **[Negative.]** What is the *y*-intercept? **[2]**

Say: Be careful when writing the equation. Remember, the slope is negative, but the *y*-intercept is positive.

COMMON MISCONCEPTION

Ask: What is the Error in this problem?

Write the equation for the linear function whose graph is shown.

$$y = \frac{2}{5}x - 3$$

Reason incorrect: The slope is the reciprocal of the correct slope.

Solution: $m = \dfrac{y_2 - y_1}{x_2 - x_1} = \dfrac{2-(-3)}{2-0} = \dfrac{5}{2}$

$$y = \frac{5}{2}x - 3$$

Say: Be sure to find the change in *y* over the change in *x*. Flipping the values gives you a slope that is the reciprocal of the correct slope.

KEY TEACHING POINTS

Example 6

Say: Contextual problems or real-world problems often include a rate. In a linear relationship, the rate, or rate of change, corresponds to the slope of the graph of the function.

Say: When you are told the temperature increases by 2 °F every hour, you know the slope is positive 2 because it is increasing at a rate of 2 degrees for 1 hour.

Say: You can decide which variable is x and which is y by asking yourself which is dependent and which is independent. In this problem, the change in temperature depends on the change in time, so the dependent variable y is the temperature. It may also help to say the rate out loud. "Degrees per hour." In a rate, the y-value, or dependent variable is always first.

Ask: What is the difference between a proportional relationship and a nonproportional relationship? **[A proportional relationship always crosses the coordinate graph at the origin, so for $x = 0$, $y = 0$.]**

Check

Ask: Say the rate out loud. **[gallons per hour]**

Ask: How can you tell the rate of change from the equation? **[The rate of change is the slope.]** Is the rate positive or negative? **[Negative.]** What does this mean in terms of the problem? **[The amount of gas in her truck is going down as she drives.]**

Ask: What is the y-intercept in terms of the problem? **[The amount of gas in her truck when she started.]**

Say: The graph of a linear function is a line, and it extends in both directions forever. In problems with context, this does not always make sense.

Ask: Why can the graph of the function for Problem 18 not extend forever and still make sense? **[Possible answer: Juanita will eventually run out of gas unless she puts more in the tank. Once the y-value reaches 0, there is no more gas and she has to stop driving.]**

ADDITIONAL ONLINE INTERVENTION RESOURCES

 Use the following for students who have not mastered the concepts in Skill 18.

- Math on the Spot videos

- Personal Math Trainer with customized intervention

- Building Block worksheets (Skill 1: Absolute Value; Skill 22: Connect Words and Algebra; Skill 23: Connect Words and Equations; Skill 27: Evaluate Expressions; Skill 41: Generate Ordered Pairs; Skill 42: Graph Equations; Skill 90: Solve for a Variable)

SKILL 18 — Linear Functions

Example 1

You can use graphs to identify linear functions. The graph of a linear function forms a line that is not vertical.

Tell whether each graph represents a linear function. Explain.

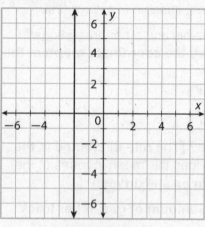

Graph (a)

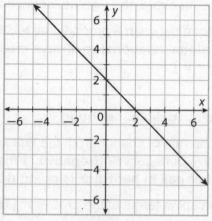

Graph (b)

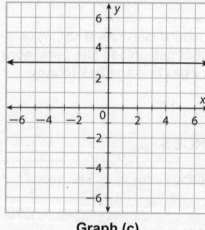

Graph (c)

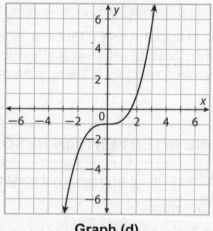

Graph (d)

- Graph (a) is a line, but it does not represent a linear function because it is vertical.

- Graph (b) represents a linear function because it is a graph of a non-vertical line.

- Graph (c) represents a linear function because it is a graph of a non-vertical line.

- Graph (d) does not represent a linear function because the graph is not a line.

Vocabulary

Linear functions
Standard form
Slope-intercept form
Rate of change
Proportional
Nonproportional

Check

Tell whether each graph represents a linear function. Explain.

1.
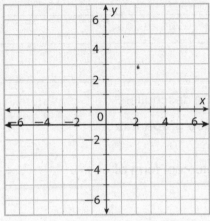

_____

_____

2.
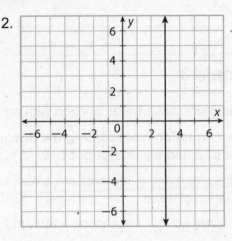

_____

_____

Example 2

You can also use equations to identify linear functions. The equation of a linear function can be written in standard form: $Ax + By = C$, where A, B, and C are real numbers and A and B are not both 0, or in slope-intercept form: $y = mx + b$, where m is the slope of the line, and b is the y-intercept.

Tell whether each equation represents a linear function. Explain.

(a) $-4x + y = -3$ (b) $y = 5x^2 - 11$ (c) $xy - 7 = 14$ (d) $y = 9x - 2$

- Equation (a) represents a linear function because it is in the standard form of a linear equation where $A = -4$, $B = 1$, and $C = -3$.

- Equation (b) does not represent a linear function because the exponent on x is not 1.

- Equation (c) does not represent a linear function because x and y are multiplied.

- Equation (d) represents a linear function because it is in the y-intercept form of a linear equation where $m = 9$ and $b = -2$.

Check

Tell whether each equation represents a linear function. Explain.

3. $y = \dfrac{1}{x} + 6$

4. $-\dfrac{1}{4}x + 9 = y$

_____

5. $8x - 5y = -1$ 6. $y^2 = 2x + 1$

_____   _____

Example 3

You can represent a linear function with an equation given a description.

Write an equation representing the linear function whose graph has a slope of 2 and a y-intercept of –5.

Since the slope and y-intercept are given, use the slope-intercept form of the equation of a line.

$y = mx + b$ Use slope-intercept form.

$y = 2x + (-5)$ Substitute 2 for m and –5 for b.

$y = 2x - 5$ Simplify.

An equation for the function is $y = 2x - 5$.

Check

Write an equation representing the linear function described.

7. The slope is 13 and the y-intercept is 4.

_____

8. The slope is $-\dfrac{7}{2}$ and the y-intercept is 17.

_____

9. The y-intercept is –12 and the slope is 11.

_____

10. The slope is 3 and the point $\left(0, -\dfrac{1}{4}\right)$ is on the graph.

_____

11. Explain the Error. Find the correct solution.

   Susan is asked to write an equation representing a linear function with a y-intercept of $-\dfrac{5}{3}$ and a slope of 16. She writes $y = -\dfrac{5}{3}x + 16$.

_____

Name _____ Date _____ Class_____

Example 4

You can represent a linear function with an equation given a set of points that satisfy the equation.

The table shows several points from the graph of a linear function. Write an equation for the function.

x	−1	3	5
y	6	−2	−6

Step 1: Calculate the slope using any two points. Choose $(−1, 6)$ and $(3, −2)$.

$\text{slope} = \dfrac{y_2 - y_1}{x_2 - x_1}$ — Use the slope formula.

$m = \dfrac{-2 - 6}{3 - (-1)}$ — Substitute values.

$= \dfrac{-8}{4}$ — Simplify the numerator and denominator.

$= -2$ — Simplify.

Step 2: Find the value of b using the fact that $m = -2$ and a point on the line is $(−1, 6)$.

$y = -2x + b$ — Write the function with the known value of m.

$6 = -2(-1) + b$ — Substitute −1 for x and 6 for y.

$6 = 2 + b$ — Simplify the right side of the equation.

$4 = b$ — Solve for b.

An equation for the function is $y = -2x + 4$.

Check

Write an equation representing the linear function that includes the points given in the table.

12.

x	−1	0	1	2
y	5	6	7	8

_____

13.

x	−4	−1	2	3
y	33	6	−21	−30

_____

14.

x	−4	−2	6	10
y	−12	−11	−7	−5

_____

15.

x	−2	3	5	2
y	9	6.5	5.5	7

_____

Example 5

You can represent a linear function with an equation given a graph.

Write an equation for the linear function whose graph is shown.

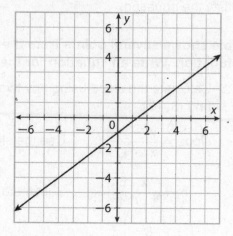

Use the slope-intercept form of a line, $y = mx + b$. Identify the y-intercept, b, shown on the graph. Then choose one other point to solve for m. Use the point $(4, 2)$.

$y = mx + (-1)$	Use slope-intercept form with $b = -1$.
$2 = m(4) + (-1)$	Substitute 4 for x and 2 for y.
$2 = 4m - 1$	Simplify the right side of the equation.
$3 = 4m$	Add 1 to both sides.
$\dfrac{3}{4} = m$	Divide by 4 to solve for m.

An equation for the function is $y = \dfrac{3}{4}x - 1$.

Check

Write an equation for the linear function whose graph is shown.

16.

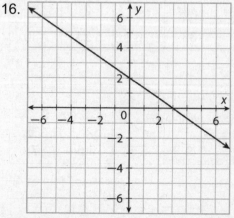

17.

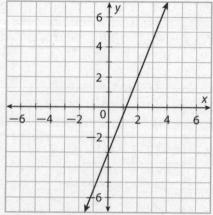

Example 6

You can describe a linear relationship from an equation. To determine the rate of change, use the slope. To determine whether the linear relationship is proportional, use the y-intercept. If $b = 0$, then the relationship between x and y is proportional. If $b \neq 0$, then it is nonproportional.

The temperature at dawn was 10°F. It increased by 2°F every hour. The temperature can be described by the equation $y = 2x + 10$.

a. What do the variables x and y represent in this situation?

The variable x represents time in hours. The variable y represents the temperature at time x.

b. What is the rate of change? Interpret the rate of change in terms of the problem situation.

The rate of change is the slope $m = 2$. For each hour, x, that goes by, the temperature, y, rises by 2°F.

c. Is the relationship between x and y proportional or nonproportional? Explain in terms of the problem situation.

The relationship between time, x, and temperature, y, is nonproportional because $b = 10 \neq 0$.

Check

Solve.

18. Juanita started a road trip with 16 gallons of gas in her truck. For every hour she drives, she uses 3.5 gallons of gas. The amount of gas in her truck can be modeled by the equation $y = -3.5x + 16$.

a. What do the variables x and y represent in this situation?

_____

b. What is the rate of change? Interpret the rate of change in terms of the problem situation.

_____

c. Is the relationship between x and y proportional or nonproportional? Explain in terms of the problem situation.

_____

SKILL 18 LINEAR FUNCTIONS

Linear Inequalities in Two Variables

KEY TEACHING POINTS

Example 1

Say: Linear equations are equations whose solutions can be shown on a coordinate plane as a line. Linear inequalities in two variables are graphed using a boundary line on a coordinate plane.

Say: The solution to a linear equation in two variables is a set of values, not just one value. The solution to a linear inequality in two variables is also a set of values.

Say: Linear inequalities can be written in standard form by solving the inequality for y. This form of the inequality is the same as the slope-intercept form of a linear equation and gives the boundary line of a graph of the solution set.

Ask: When solving an inequality, when do you need to reverse the direction of the inequality sign? **[When you multiply or divide by a negative value.]**

Say: When the inequality is greater than or less than, use a dashed line. The values that are on the line are not part of the solution set. When the inequality is less than or equal to or greater than or equal to, use a solid line. The values that are on the line are part of the solution set.

Ask: Once your boundary line is drawn, how do you decide which part of the graph to shade? **[If the y-value is greater than the expression, shade up. If the y-value is less than the expression, shade down.]**

Check

Say: Look at the inequality $20x \leq -24 - 8y$.

Ask: Will the boundary line be solid or dashed? **[Solid.]** What is the first step in finding the boundary line? **[Solve the inequality for y.]**

Say: To solve for y, get y alone on one side of the inequality.

Show the following work.

Let students know that there are other ways to solve the same problem. If you need to multiply or divide by a negative value, remember to reverse the signs.

$$20x \leq -24 - 8y$$
$$20x + 8y \leq -24$$
$$8y \leq -20x - 24$$
$$y \leq -\frac{3}{2}x - 3$$

Ask: What is the slope of the boundary line? $\left[-\dfrac{3}{2}\right]$ Where is the y-intercept? **[–3]**

Graph the boundary line as a class. Before shading the solution set, ask students how they determine which area to shade.

Say: The boundary line divides the plane into two regions. If you have any doubt over which region to shade, choose a test point. The origin is an easy point to test. Plug the values for the origin into the inequality.

Show the following work.

$$y \le -\frac{3}{2}x - 3$$

$$0 \le -\frac{3}{2}(0) - 3$$

$$0 \le -3$$

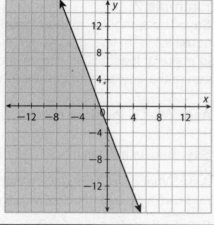

Ask: Is 0 less than or equal to negative 3? **[No.]** The region that contains the origin is not part of the solution set. Shade the other region.

COMMON MISCONCEPTION

Ask: What is the Error?

Farrah was asked to solve the inequality $18x - 27y \le 27$ for y and graph the solution set.

Her solution was $y \le \frac{2}{3}x - 1$, along with the graph shown. Where did she go wrong?

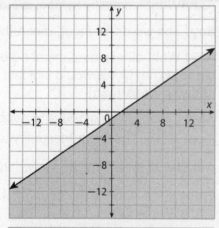

Reason incorrect: She divided by -27 and did not reverse the inequality symbol.

Solution: $18x - 27y \le 27$

$$-27y \le -18x + 27$$

$$y \ge \frac{2}{3}x - 1$$

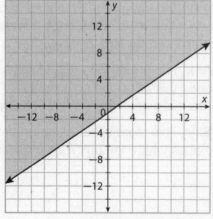

All of the values are the same, but the inequality sign is reversed. This results in the wrong region being shaded.

KEY TEACHING POINTS

Example 2

Say: The symbol $\geq$ means "greater than or equal to." Another way to say "greater than or equal to" is "at least." If you put the words into a context, they can be clearer. Jasmine wants to make at least $50 in commission. The lowest amount she wants to make is $50, and she can make any amount greater than that, so the amount is greater than or equal to $50.

Ask: What is the slope of the boundary line? $\left[-\dfrac{2}{5}\right]$ Where is the *y*-intercept? **[(0, 5)]**

Say: Because the symbol is $\geq$, the area above the boundary line is the solution set.

Ask: What does a negative *y*-value indicate? **[A negative number of shirts.]** What does a negative *x*-value indicate? **[A negative number of ties.]** Is this possible? **[No.]**

Say: The context of a question often adds limits to the solution set. In this case, the possible values are only positive, so they can only lie in the first quadrant.

Check

Ask: What inequality symbol is indicated by the words "at most"? **[Less than or equal to]**

Say: The words "at most" mean the value $15 is included, and any value less than $15.

Ask: What other words might be used to indicate less than or equal to? **[Possible answer: Up to]** What words would indicate that $15 is not included in the solution set? **[Possible answer: Less than]**

Say: If mangos *x* cost $2 and avocados *y* cost $1.50, the total $2x + 1.5y$ can be, at most, is 15. The linear inequality to start can be written as $2x + 1.5y \leq 15$.

Ask: What is the first step to writing this in standard form? **[Subtract 2*x* and divide by 1.5.]** What is the slope of the boundary line? $\left[-\dfrac{3}{5}\right]$ Is the boundary line solid or dashed? **[Solid.]**

Ask: Did you notice that in each of these combination problems, the slope of the boundary line is negative? How does this make sense in context? **[As there is more of one item, there can be less of the other.]**

Ask: It is unlikely that Omar will be allowed to buy half a mango or half an avocado. How does this affect the solution set? **[The values can only include whole number solutions.]** Are there any other limits? **[There are no negative values.]**

Say: This means that although the entire area is shaded, the actual solutions are only the places where the unit lines cross in the first quadrant.

ALTERNATE STRATEGY

Strategy: Use a graphing calculator.

1. **Say:** Linear inequalities can be graphed on a graphing calculator, much like a linear equation.

2. Explain that a calculator is a tool. In order to use this tool, you need to be able to translate from a word problem to the inequality, and in many cases, write the inequality in standard form.

3. Read the problem: Sheila sells custom jewelry. She makes $7.50 profit for each bracelet she sells and $12.50 for each necklace. She wants to earn at least $100. Find the number of bracelets, x, and necklaces, y, needed to make at least $100. The equation is $7.5x + 12.5y \geq 100$, or in standard form, $y \geq -\dfrac{3}{5}x + 8$.

4. To graph the inequality, enter $-\dfrac{3}{5}x + 8$ into Y_1.

   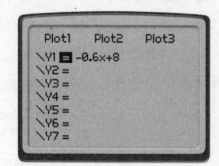

   The inequality can be entered using the decimal -0.6 instead of showing the slope as a fraction.
   Arrow over to the far left side of Y_1. Hit enter until the correct inequality symbol is shown. In some calculators, only greater than or less than are options. Remember, the only difference is that the boundary line is solid instead of dashed.

5. Press graph to see the graph.

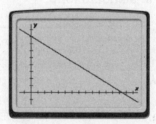

ADDITIONAL ONLINE INTERVENTION RESOURCES

 Use the following for students who have not mastered the concepts in Skill 19.

- Math on the Spot videos

- Personal Math Trainer with customized intervention

- Building Block worksheets (Skill 94: Solve One-Step Inequalities)

SKILL 19 — Linear Inequalities in Two Variables

Example 1

Vocabulary
Linear inequality in two variables
Solution of an inequality
Boundary line

A linear inequality in two variables results when the = sign is replaced with $<$, $>$, $\leq$, or $\geq$. For example, $5x + 3 \leq 30y$ is a linear inequality with the two variables x and y.

A solution of an inequality is an ordered pair (x, y) that makes the inequality true.

Solve the inequality $2x - 5y > -10$ for y. Then graph the solution set.

Step 1: First solve the inequality for y.

$$2x - 5y > -10$$

$$-5y > -10 - 2x \qquad \text{Subtract } 2x \text{ from both sides.}$$

$$y < \frac{-10 - 2x}{-5} \qquad \text{Divide both sides by } -5 \text{ and switch the inequality.}$$

$$y < 2 + \frac{2}{5}x \qquad \text{Simplify.}$$

$$y < \frac{2}{5}x + 2 \qquad \text{Write in standard form.}$$

Step 2: Graph the boundary line.

The inequality uses the symbol $<$, so the line will be *dashed*.

Step 3: Shade the appropriate part of the graph.

The inequality $y < \frac{2}{5}x + 2$

uses the symbol $<$, so shade *below* the boundary line.

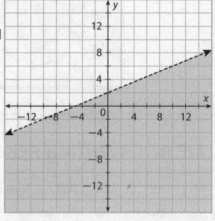

Check

Solve the inequality for *y*. Then graph the solution set.

1. $4y - 3x < 16$

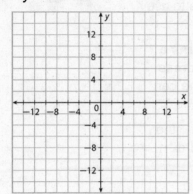

2. $-30 > 3x - 6y$

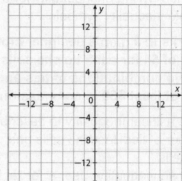

3. $20x \le -24 - 8y$

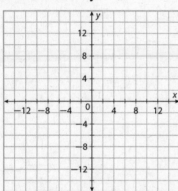

4. $21y - 42 \ge -7x$

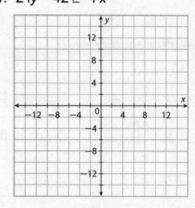

5. Explain the Error. Find the correct solution.

Farrah was asked to solve the inequality $18x - 27y \le 27$ for *y* and

graph the solution set. Her solution was $y \le \dfrac{2}{3}x - 1$, along with the

graph shown. Where did she go wrong?

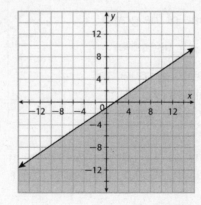

_____

_____

Example 2

Many real-world problems can be solved using linear inequalities in two variables. When writing an inequality for a situation, make sure to use the appropriate inequality symbol.

Jasmine works in a men's designer clothing store. She earns a commission of $4 for each tie she sells, and $10 for each dress shirt. Find two combinations of ties and shirts that Jasmine can sell to make at least $50 in commission.

Step 1: Write a linear inequality to describe the situation. Let x = the number of ties Jasmine sells and y = the number of shirts she sells.
Write an inequality. Use $\geq$ for "at least."

Commission on ties	plus	commission on shirts	is at least	$50.
$4x$	$+$	$10y$	$\geq$	50

Step 2: Solve the inequality for y.

$4x + 10y \geq 50$

$10y \geq 50 - 4x$ Subtract $4x$ from both sides.

$y \geq \dfrac{50 - 4x}{10}$ Divide both sides by 10.

$y \geq 5 - \dfrac{2}{5}x$ Simplify.

$y \geq -\dfrac{2}{5}x + 5$ Write in standard form.

Step 2: Graph the boundary line.

The inequality uses the symbol $\geq$, so the line will be *solid*.

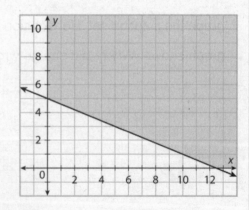

Step 3: Shade the appropriate part of the graph.

The inequality $y \geq -\dfrac{2}{5}x + 5$ uses the symbol $\geq$, so shade *above* the boundary line. Since the number of ties and shirts cannot be negative, shade the solutions in Quadrant 1 only.

Step 4: Since the line is solid, any point on or above the line in Quadrant 1 will be a solution, such as the points (0, 5) and (6, 4).

Two different combinations Jasmine could sell to make at least $50 are 0 ties and 5 shirts and 6 ties and 4 shirts.

Name _____ Date _____ Class _____

Check

Solve.

6. Omar can spend at most $15 on mangoes and avocados at the farmers' market. Mangoes cost $2.00 each, and avocados cost $1.50 each.

    a. Write a linear inequality that describes the number of mangoes, *x*, and avocados, *y*, that Omar can buy. Solve for *y*.

    b. Graph the solution set.

    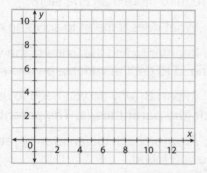

    _____

    c. Identify two combinations that Omar can afford.

    _____

7. Sheila sells custom jewelry. She makes $7.50 profit for each bracelet she sells and $12.50 for each necklace. She wants to earn at least $100.

    a. Write a linear inequality that describes the number of bracelets, *x*, and necklaces, *y*, that Sheila could sell to make at least $100. Solve for *y*.

    b. Graph the solution set.

    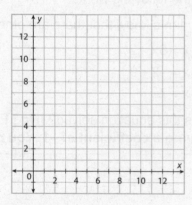

    _____

    c. Identify two combinations that Sheila could sell to make her goal.

    _____

SKILL 19 LINEAR INEQUALITIES IN TWO VARIABLES

Multi-Step Equations

KEY TEACHING POINTS

Example 1
Say: The same properties that are used to solve a one-step equation are used in equations that require more than one step.

Ask: What does it mean to solve an equation? **[Find the value of the variable.]**

Say: In order to find the value of the variable, you need to isolate the variable. This means you need to get the variable on one side of the equation by itself.

Ask: In part B, why do you need to use the Distributive Property first? **[Because $2x - 3$ is inside the parentheses. The parentheses need to be removed.]**

Say: Always check the answer by returning to the original equation and substituting in the value you found.

Ask: Why should you use the original equation and not one of the steps in between? **[If you made an error, you do not know which step the error is in, and you may check an incorrect equation.]**

Check
Say: Look at the equation $-9 + 7x = 8x - 2$.

Ask: What do you need to do first? **[Get the variables collected on one side.]**

Say: Let's get the variables on the left side.

Show the following work.

Let students know that there are other ways to solve the same problem.

$$-9 + 7x = 8x - 2$$
$$7x - 8x = -2 + 9$$
$$-x = 7$$

Ask: Is this equation solved? **[No.]** Explain. **[The variable is negative, which is the same as having a coefficient of –1. You can divide each side by –1 to get the variable alone.]**

COMMON MISCONCEPTION

Ask: What is the Error?

David solved an equation in the following way. Where did he go wrong?

$$-8(-8x - 6) = -6x - 22$$
$$64x - 48 = -6x - 22$$
$$70x - 48 = -22$$
$$70x = 26$$
$$x = \frac{26}{70}$$
$$x = \frac{13}{35}$$

Reason incorrect: When David used the Distributive Property, he didn't carry the negative sign to the second term.

Solution:
$$-8(-8x - 6) = -6x - 22$$
$$64x + 48 = -6x - 22$$
$$70x + 48 = -22$$
$$70x = -70$$
$$x = -1$$

Ask: What could David have done to avoid this error? **[Possible response: He could have checked his answer.]**

ALTERNATE STRATEGY

Strategy: Use algebra tiles.

1. Review the use of algebra tiles. A zero pair is a set of matching positive and negative tiles on the same side of the equation.

2. **Say:** Set up the equation $6n + 3 = 7 + 2n$ using algebra tiles.

3. Remember that you must always do the same action on each side of the equation to keep it balanced. Add two negative variable tiles to each side of the equation. Remove the zero pairs.

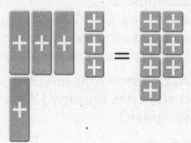

4. Add three negative unit tiles to each side to eliminate the constant on the right. Remove the zero pairs.

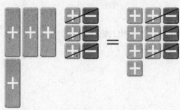

5. The tiles can be arranged in an equal number of rows, 4, on each side of the equation. When the tiles are arranged in this way, division can be used and the full set of tiles has the same value as the tiles in one row. The remaining tiles show that $x = 1$.

6. Check the result by substituting the answer into the original equation.

$$6n + 3 = 7 + 2n$$
$$6(1) + 3 = 7 + 2(1)$$
$$6 + 3 = 7 + 2$$
$$9 = 9$$

KEY TEACHING POINTS

Example 2
Say: Some equations have no solutions, while others have infinitely many solutions. An equation with no solutions is never true. An equation with infinitely many solutions is always true. Equations that are always true are called identities.

Ask: Compare the results in parts A and B. What is the first step in each solution? **[Use the Distributive Property.]** What is true of both solutions? **[They only contain numbers, no variables.]**

Check
Ask: After the equation is set up, what is the next step to solving the equation
$32 - 5x = 7 - 5(x - 5)$? **[Remove the parentheses using the Distributive Property.]**
Show the following work:
$$32 - 5x = 7 - 5(x - 5)$$
$$32 - 5x = 7 - 5x + 25$$

Ask: What is the next step? **[Combine like terms.]**
Continue the solution with the next step:
$32 - 5x = 32 - 5x$
Ask: When you add *5x* to each side of the equation, what is left? **[32 = 32]** Is this true? **[Yes.]** What is the equation that is always true called? **[An identity.]**

Example 3
Say: Situations in the real world often involve more than one step to find a solution.

Ask: How does writing a verbal model help solve the problem? **[Possible response: It helps you know what operations belong where in the equation.]**

Ask: How do you know what the variable should stand for? **[The variable should represent the unknown value that you are trying to find.]** What value are you trying to find? **[The number of hours it would take to make the two costs the same.]**

Check
Ask: What value are you trying to find? **[The number of months it would take for the cost of the two gyms to be the same.]**

Say: The verbal model for the situation might be:

Monthly rate for Shear Fitness = membership fee + monthly rate for Performance Plus

Ask: Using this verbal model, and the variable *m*, what equation is the starting point? **[$38.75m = 110 + 25m$]**

Ask: Solving for *m*, the result is $m = 8$. What does this mean in the context of the problem? **[At 8 months, the gyms will cost the same amount.]** So, if Sarah plans to use the gym for at least a full year, which gym will cost her less? Explain. **[Performance Plus because after 8 months, the monthly fee at Performance Plus is lower.]**

ADDITIONAL ONLINE INTERVENTION RESOURCES

 Use the following for students who have not mastered the concepts in Skill 20.

- Math on the Spot videos
- Personal Math Trainer with customized intervention
- Building Block worksheets (Skill 91: Solve Multi-Step Equations)

SKILL 20 — Multi-Step Equations

<table>
<tr><td>

Example 1

You can use the properties of equality, along with the Distributive Property to solve multi-step equations. When the variable appears on both sides of the equation, first collect the variable terms so that they are all on one side.

Solve each equation.

A. $4n - 5 = 2n + 1$

$4n - 5 = 2n + 1$	Set up the equation.
$2n - 5 = 1$	Use the Subtraction Property of Equality to subtract $2n$ from both sides.
$2n = 6$	Use the Addition Property of Equality to add 5 to both sides.
$n = 3$	Use the Division Property of Equality to divide both sides by 2.

Check: Substitute 3 for n in the original equation:

$$4(3) - 5 = 2(3) + 1$$
$$12 - 5 = 6 + 1$$
$$7 = 7 \checkmark$$

B. $-5(2x - 3) = 17 - 5x$

$-5(2x - 3) = 17 - 5x$	Set up the equation.
$-10x + 15 = 17 - 5x$	Use the Distributive Property to distribute -5.
$15 = 17 + 5x$	Use the Addition Property of Equality to add $10x$ to both sides.
$-2 = 5x$	Use the Subtraction Property of Equality to subtract 17 from both sides.
$-\dfrac{2}{5} = x$	Use the Division Property of Equality to divide both sides by 5.

Check: Substitute $-\dfrac{2}{5}$ for x in the original equation:

$$-5\left(2\left(-\frac{2}{5}\right) - 3\right) = 17 - 5\left(-\frac{2}{5}\right)$$
$$-5\left(-\frac{4}{5} - 3\right) = 17 + 2$$
$$4 + 15 = 19$$
$$19 = 19 \checkmark$$

</td><td>

Vocabulary

Properties of equality

Distributive Property

Multi-step equations

Variable

Identity

</td></tr>
</table>

Check

Solve each equation.

1. $6n + 3 = 7 + 2n$

   _____

2. $-9 + 7x = 8x - 2$

   _____

3. $-3(1 + 6y) = 14 - y$

   _____

4. $-2(1 - 7n) = 5n + 34$

   _____

5. $2p - 10 = 5(p - 7) - 8p$

   _____

6. $3x - 4(-5 - 2x) = 5(2x + 6)$

   _____

7. $5(-8y - 2) - 5(1 - 5y) = -4y - 8y$

   _____

8. $-(1 - 3a) - 5 = 7a - (5 + 5a) - 3$

   _____

9. Explain the Error. Find the correct solution.

   David solved an equation in the following way. Where did he go wrong?

   $$-8(-8x - 6) = -6x - 22$$
   $$64x - 48 = -6x - 22$$
   $$70x - 48 = -22$$
   $$70x = 26$$
   $$x = \frac{26}{70}$$
   $$x = \frac{13}{35}$$

   _____

Example 2

An identity is an equation that is always true. The solutions of an identity are all real numbers. Some equations are always false. Such equations have no solutions.

Solve each equation.

A. $6 - 2y + 4 = 8y - 10(y - 1)$

$6 - 2y + 4 = 8y - 10(y - 1)$	Set up the equation.
$6 - 2y + 4 = 8y - 10y + 10$	Distribute -10.
$10 - 2y = -2y + 10$	Combine like terms.
$10 = 10 \checkmark$	Add $2y$ to both sides.

The equation is an identity. The solution is all real numbers.

B. $4(4 - a) + 2 = 6a + 12 - 10a$

$4(4 - a) + 2 = 6a + 12 - 10a$	Set up the equation.
$16 - 4a + 2 = 6a + 12 - 10a$	Distribute 4.
$14 - 4a = 12 - 4a$	Combine like terms.
$14 = 12 \otimes$	Add $4a$ to both sides.

The equation is always false. There are no solutions.

Check
Solve each equation.

10. $-6(3 - k) = 3(2k - 2)$

11. $n + 8 = 3 + n + 3 + 2$

12. $32 - 5x = 7 - 5(x - 5)$

13. $12(2y + 11) = 12(2y + 12)$

Example 3

You can write and solve an equation to model a real-world situation.

As a mechanic, Shaheed has two options for daily pay at the auto repair shop. With Option A he makes a flat rate of $65.50 plus $8.25 per hour. With Option B he makes $21.35 per hour. How many hours would he need to work using Option B to make as much as he would if he had chosen Option A?

Step 1: Write a verbal model for the situation.
flat rate for Option A + hourly rate for Option A = hourly rate for Option B

Step 2: Let x be the number of hours he works.
$$65.5 + 8.25x = 21.35x$$

Step 3: Solve the equation.

$65.5 + 8.25x = 21.35x$ Set up the equation.

$65.5 = 13.1x$ Subtract $8.25x$ from both sides.

$x = 5$ Divide both sides by 13.1.

Shaheed would need to work 5 hours to earn as much with Option B as he would with Option A.

Check

Write and solve an equation that models the situation.

14. Sarah wants to join a gym. At Shear Fitness she would pay $38.75 per month. At Performance Plus she would pay a one-time membership fee of $110 and then $25 per month. How many months would she have to be a member of Performance Plus to pay as much as she would if she joined Shear Fitness?

_____

SKILL 20 MULTI-STEP EQUATIONS

Multiply and Divide Rational Numbers

KEY TEACHING POINTS

Example 1

Say: A number line can help you understand how to multiply rational numbers. Always begin at 0. Each move should be the rational distance, in this example, each move is –0.75 unit. Since this is a negative number, each move is to the left. The integer value, 2, tells you how many times to move. You will move 0.75 unit left, 2 times.

Ask: Multiplying and dividing integers with signs has rules. What is the rule for multiplying integers with different signs? **[The product of two factors with different signs is negative.]**

Say: Multiplying and dividing two signed rational numbers follows the same rules as multiplying and dividing integers. When the factors have the same sign, the product is positive. When the factors have different signs, the product is negative.

Check

Say: Problem 1 asks that you multiply 3(–0.5).

Ask: How can you say 0.5 in a different way? **[Half.]** Because it is negative 0.5, which direction should you move on the number line? **[Left.]** How many times should you move? **[3]** If you move from 0 to the left, will the result be positive or negative? **[Negative.]**

Say: When you multiply using the rules for signed numbers, the two factors have opposite signs, so the answer is negative. Multiply the rational numbers as if they don't have any signs.

Ask: What is (3)(0.5)? **[1.5]** So what is (3)(–0.5)? **[–1.5]** Make sure this is the same as the answer you found on the number line.

Say: Some rational numbers work well using a number line. For example, when the integer value is small and the rational number is one, that is easy to put on a number line. When the rational number is 0.5, it is easy to divide the number line in half. When the rational number is 1.2, the number line can be divided into tenths.

Ask: What units might you use to multiply using a number line for $12\left(-\dfrac{5}{6}\right)$? **[Sixths.]** If you use sixths, you move 5 tick marks each for 12 moves. What is $12\left(-\dfrac{5}{6}\right)$? **[–10]**

Ask: Rational numbers in real-world problems can be positive or negative. In problem 6, if you answer incorrectly, you lose 4.5 points. Is this a positive or negative value? **[Negative.]**

ALTERNATE STRATEGY

Strategy: Use fraction area models.

1. You can use the rules for multiplying rational numbers and fraction models to multiply rational numbers.

2. **Say:** The expression $6\left(-\dfrac{5}{7}\right)$ tells you to find 6 groups of $-\dfrac{5}{7}$. Ignore the negative symbols for the moment. Multiplication can be shown using an area model, because area is length times width. Draw a model that shows 6 units as the length and $\dfrac{5}{7}$, or 5 out of 7 parts of a whole, as the width.

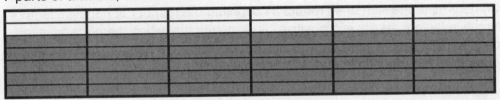

3. Now move the sections of fractions that are shaded from the right end to fill up the gaps starting at the top left.

4. There are 4 full units and $\dfrac{2}{7}$ of a unit, so you're left with $4\dfrac{2}{7}$. Because the signs of the rational factors were different, the sign of the product is negative.

$$6\left(-\dfrac{5}{7}\right) = -4\dfrac{2}{7}$$

KEY TEACHING POINTS

Example 2

Say: A number line can help you visualize this multiplication. Multiplying two positive numbers moves right on the number line. Multiplying when one of the numbers is negative reverses the direction and moves the total left.

Ask: In step 1, how many units should you move each time? **[1.5]**

Ask: If one negative reverses the direction of movement, what will two negatives do? **[Reverse the direction again.]** So in what direction will multiplying two negatives move on the number line? **[Right.]**

Say: Multiplying two negative values moves right on the number line, the same direction as multiplying two positives. This follows the rules for multiplying signed numbers. Two negative factors result in a positive product.

Check

Ask: How can you tell, without estimating, that $-5\left(-\dfrac{7}{8}\right)$ has a larger product than $-8\left(\dfrac{2}{7}\right)$?

[Look at the signs of the numbers.] Two negative factors have a positive product. A negative times a positive has a negative product. A positive number is always greater than a negative number.

Example 3

Ask: How does the multiplication change if you group the two negative factors? **[The two negative factors produce a positive product. Then you multiply two positive factors.]**

Say: You can determine the sign of a product by counting the number of negative factors. Every two negative factors results in a positive. This means that when there are an even number of negative factors, the product is positive. When there are an odd number of negative factors, the produce is negative.

Check

Ask: How many negative factors are in $\left(-\dfrac{4}{9}\right)\left(\dfrac{11}{12}\right)\left(-\dfrac{7}{8}\right)$? **[Two.]** Is the product negative or positive? **[Positive.]**

Say: When you are multiplying fractions, it is often helpful to simplify first.
Show the following work:

$\left(-\dfrac{\overset{1}{\cancel{4}}}{9}\right)\left(\dfrac{11}{12}\right)\left(-\dfrac{7}{\underset{2}{\cancel{8}}}\right)$ Simplify before multiplication.

$\left(\left(-\dfrac{1}{9}\right)\left(-\dfrac{7}{2}\right)\right)\left(\dfrac{11}{12}\right)$ Rearrange the factors with negative factors together.

$\left(\dfrac{7}{18}\right)\left(\dfrac{11}{12}\right)$ Multiply.

$\left(\dfrac{77}{216}\right)$ Multiply again.

Example 4

Say: The rules for signed numbers are the same for division as they are for multiplication.

Display rules:

- Multiply or divide like signs: positive product or quotient.

- Multiply or divide unlike signs: negative product or quotient.

Ask: How can you check your answer? **[Multiply. $-7(8.5) = -59.5$]**

Check

Ask: Problem 16 divides a negative by a negative. Is the quotient positive or negative? **[Positive.]**

KEY TEACHING POINTS

Example 5

Say: Complex fractions are simplified by rewriting the fraction as division. Divide the numerator by the denominator.

Ask: How are fractions divided? **[By multiplying by the reciprocal.]**

Say: Remember the rules for signed numbers. Dividing a negative by a positive results in a negative quotient. $-24 \div 4 = -6$

Check

Ask: How is $\dfrac{-\dfrac{1}{2}}{-\dfrac{1}{3}}$ written using multiplication? $\left[\left(-\dfrac{1}{2}\right)\left(-\dfrac{3}{1}\right)\right]$

COMMON MISCONCEPTION

Ask: What is the Error?

$$\frac{-\dfrac{2}{5}}{\dfrac{3}{10}} = -\frac{2}{5} \cdot \frac{3}{10} = \frac{-6}{50} = -\frac{3}{25}$$

Reason incorrect: The numerator was multiplied by the denominator instead of being divided by the denominator. The correct solution is $-\dfrac{20}{15}$, or $-\dfrac{4}{3}$.

Solution:

$$\frac{-\dfrac{2}{5}}{\dfrac{3}{10}} = -\frac{2}{5} \div \frac{3}{10} = -\frac{2}{5} \cdot \frac{10}{3} = \frac{-20}{15} = -\frac{4}{3} = -1\frac{1}{3}$$

ADDITIONAL ONLINE INTERVENTION RESOURCES

 Use the following for students who have not mastered the concepts in Skill 21.

- Math on the Spot videos
- Personal Math Trainer with customized intervention
- Building Block worksheets (Skill 60: Multiply and Divide Fractions; Skill 61: Multiply and Divide Integers)

SKILL 21 — Multiply and Divide Rational Numbers

Example 1

The product of two rational numbers with different signs is negative. You can use a number line to model the multiplication of two rational numbers with different signs.

Multiply 2(−0.75).

Step 1 Use a number line to find the product.

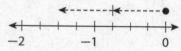

Start at 0. Move 0.75 unit to the left two times.

The result is −1.5.

So 2(−0.75) = −1.5.

Step 2 Use the rules for multiplying rational numbers to check your answer.

2(−0.75) = −1.5   A positive times a negative is a negative.

Check

Use a number line to find each product.

1. 3(−0.5) = _____

2. 4(−1.2) = _____

Multiply.

3. $6\left(-\dfrac{5}{7}\right)$

4. $12\left(-\dfrac{5}{6}\right)$

5. −3.4(4)

_____   _____   _____

6. In a trivia game, you lose points for each incorrect answer. You answer the first 5 questions incorrectly. Each question is worth 4.5 points. What is your score after answering the first 5 questions?

_____

Example 2

The product of two rational numbers with the same sign is positive. You can use a number line to model the multiplication of two rational numbers with the same sign.

Multiply −3(−1.5).

Step 1 First find the product +3(−1.5).

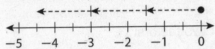

Start at 0. Move 1.5 units to the left three times.

The result is −4.5.

So +3(−1.5) = −4.5.

Step 2 Find the product −3(−1.5).

From Step 1, you know +3(−1.5) = −4.5.

So −3 groups of −1.5 must equal the *opposite* of −4.5.

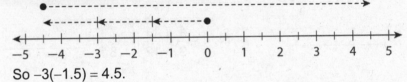

So −3(−1.5) = 4.5.

Step 3 Use the rules for multiplying rational numbers to check your answer.

−3(−1.5) = 4.5   A negative times a negative is a positive.

Check

Use a number line to find each product.

7. −2(−2.25) = _____   8. −4(−1.4) = _____

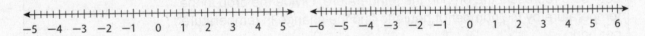

Multiply.

9. $-5\left(-\dfrac{3}{4}\right)$ 10. $-10\left(-\dfrac{2}{3}\right)$ 11. −0.75(−6)

_____   _____   _____

12. Without multiplying, tell which product is greater: $-5\left(-\dfrac{7}{8}\right)$ or $-8\left(\dfrac{2}{7}\right)$.

Explain. _____

Example 3

You can also multiply more than two rational numbers.

Multiply $\left(\dfrac{2}{3}\right)\left(-\dfrac{3}{5}\right)\left(-\dfrac{5}{8}\right)$.

$\left(\dfrac{2}{3}\right)\left(-\dfrac{3}{5}\right)\left(-\dfrac{5}{8}\right) = \left(\dfrac{2}{3} \cdot \left(-\dfrac{3}{5}\right)\right)\left(-\dfrac{5}{8}\right)$ Group the first two factors together.

$= \left(\dfrac{-6}{15}\right)\left(-\dfrac{5}{8}\right)$ Multiply the first two factors.

$= \left(-\dfrac{2}{5}\right)\left(-\dfrac{5}{8}\right)$ Simplify the product of the first two factors.

$= \dfrac{10}{40}$, or $\dfrac{1}{4}$ Multiply the remaining two factors. Simplify the product.

Check
Multiply.

13. $\left(\dfrac{1}{2}\right)\left(-\dfrac{3}{5}\right)\left(-\dfrac{7}{10}\right) =$ _____

14. $\left(-\dfrac{4}{9}\right)\left(\dfrac{11}{12}\right)\left(-\dfrac{7}{8}\right) =$ _____

Example 4

You divide two rational numbers in the same way you divide two integers.

The temperature drops 59.5 degrees in 8.5 hours. The temperature drops the same amount per hour. What is the change in the temperature each hour?

Let −59.5 represent the drop in the temperature. Divide the drop in the temperature by the number of hours to find the change in temperature per hour.

$\dfrac{-59.5}{8.5} = -7$ The quotient of a negative and a positive is negative.

Check
Find each quotient.

15. $\dfrac{4.2}{-7}$

16. $\dfrac{-1.21}{-1.1}$

17. $-\dfrac{7.2}{0.9}$

_____   _____   _____

Example 5

A complex fraction is a fraction that has a fraction in its numerator, in its denominator, or in both. You simplify a complex fraction by dividing its numerator by its denominator.

$$\frac{\frac{a}{b}}{\frac{c}{d}} = \frac{a}{b} \div \frac{c}{d}, \text{ where } b \neq 0, \ c \neq 0, \text{ and } d \neq 0.$$

Simplify $\dfrac{\frac{3}{4}}{-\frac{1}{8}}$.

$$\frac{\frac{3}{4}}{-\frac{1}{8}} = \frac{3}{4} \div \left(-\frac{1}{8}\right) \qquad \text{Write the complex fraction as a quotient.}$$

$$= \frac{3}{4} \cdot \left(-\frac{8}{1}\right) \qquad \text{To divide by a fraction, multiply by the reciprocal.}$$

$$= \frac{-24}{4} \qquad \text{Multiply.}$$

$$= -6 \qquad \text{Simplify.}$$

Check

Simplify.

18. $\dfrac{\frac{2}{3}}{-\frac{1}{6}}$

19. $\dfrac{-\frac{3}{7}}{\frac{5}{14}}$

20. $\dfrac{-\frac{1}{2}}{-\frac{1}{3}}$

21. Explain the Error. Then find the correct solution.

$$\frac{-\frac{2}{5}}{\frac{3}{10}} = -\frac{2}{5} \cdot \frac{3}{10} = \frac{-6}{50} = -\frac{3}{25}$$

SKILL 21 MULTIPLY AND DIVIDE RATIONAL NUMBERS

Multiply Polynomials

KEY TEACHING POINTS

Example 1

Say: The Distributive Property lets you multiply a sum of values by multiplying each addend separately, then adding. The Distributive Property can be applied to polynomial expressions.

Ask: In the expression $3(2x^2 + 7x - 5)$, how many terms are in the polynomial? **[3]** So you must distribute the factor 3 to each term 3 times.

Ask: The Distributive Property is used to distribute a factor over a sum. Why does this apply to a pair of binomials? **[A binomial is a sum of two terms, so the Distributive Property can be used.]**

Say: Multiplying two binomials is often organized using what is called the FOIL method. The acronym FOIL has four letters for First, Outer, Inner, and Last. There are four terms that result using this method.

Ask: What is the final step to solving part C? **[Combine like terms.]** Always try to write the solution in simplified form. Look over the solution and combine any like terms.

Check

Say: In problem 3 the expression $4b^2(2b^3 - 5b^2 + 9b + 2)$ multiplies a monomial by a trinomial.

Ask: After distributing, how many terms should be in the expression? **[3]**

ALTERNATE STRATEGY

Strategy: Use an organized method.

1. **Say:** The FOIL method is not the only way to multiply binomials. You can use any organized method to multiply, just make sure you don't miss any factors or addends.

2. Write the binomials on sticky notes in two different colors. Write the terms "$2m$" and "$+ 5$" on yellow notes and the terms "$+m$" and "-8" on blue notes. For each row and set of distribution, make a new set of sticky notes. Explain that because there are two terms in a binomial, the Distributive Property is applied in two steps.

3. In the first step, distribute the entire first binomial $(2m + 5)$ to each of the terms in the second binomial $(m - 8)$. Then distribute each of the terms, m and -8, over from $(m(2m + 5))$. The finished set should look like this:

2m	+5		m	−8

2m	+5	m		2m	+5	−8

2m	m		+5	m	2m	−8		+5	−8

4. Each set of notes in the final row are factors. Multiply the factors and combine like terms.

$2m^2 + 5m - 10m - 40$

$2m^2 - 5m - 40$

KEY TEACHING POINTS

Example 2

Say: Some special binomial products form patterns in their products. The square of a binomial always produces a trinomial made up of the square of the first term, double the product of the two terms, and the square of the third term.

Ask: What is the result when you multiply the sum and difference of the same two terms? **[The product is the square of the first term minus the square of the second term.]**

Check

Ask: What shortcut can you use to simplify problem 4? **[The Square of a Binomial Rule.]** What shortcut can you use to simplify problem 6? **[The Product of a Sum and a Difference Rule.]**

COMMON MISCONCEPTION

Ask: What is the Error?

$$(d-9)^2 = d^2 - (d)(9) + 9^2 = d^2 - 9d + 81$$

Reason incorrect: The square of a binomial rule was used incorrectly.

Solution: When you square a binomial, the center term in the resulting trinomial is double the product of the first and second terms. The center term should be doubled.

$$(d-9)^2 = d^2 - (d)(9) - (d)(9) + 9^2$$
$$= d^2 - 18d + 81$$

Say: When you are unsure about the rules for squaring binomials, you can write out the square as two binomial factors and use FOIL.

Ask: How would the product be different if the binomial was a sum instead of a difference? **[The center term would use addition instead of subtraction.]**

ADDITIONAL ONLINE INTERVENTION RESOURCES

Use the following for students who have not mastered the concepts in Skill 22.

- Math on the Spot videos

- Personal Math Trainer with customized intervention

- Building Block worksheets (Skill 24: Distributive Property; Skill 62: Multiply Binomials; Skill 64: Multiply Monomials and Polynomials)

SKILL 22 **Multiply Polynomials**

Example 1

<table>
<tr><td>

You can use the Distributive Property to multiply a monomial by a polynomial.

A. Simplify $3(2x^2 + 7x - 5)$.

$$3(2x^2 + 7x - 5) = 3(2x^2) + 3(7x) + 3(-5) \quad \text{Distribute the 3.}$$
$$= 6x^2 + 21x - 15 \qquad\qquad \text{Multiply.}$$

B. Simplify $5x(3x^2 - 8x + 5)$.

$$5x(3x^2 - 8x + 5) = 5x(3x^2) + 5x(-8x) + 5x(5) \quad \text{Distribute the } 5x.$$
$$= 15x^{1+2} - 40x^{1+1} + 25x^1 \qquad \text{Multiply coefficients. Add exponents.}$$
$$= 15x^3 - 40x^2 + 25x \qquad\qquad \text{Simplify.}$$

To multiply two binomials, you can use the Distributive Property or the FOIL method. To use the FOIL method, find the sum of the products of the First terms, the Outer terms, the Inner terms, and the Last terms of the binomials.

C. Simplify $(x + 2)(x + 7)$.

$$\qquad\qquad\qquad \text{First} \quad \text{Outer} \quad \text{Inner} \quad \text{Last}$$
$$(x + 2)(x + 7) = (x)(x) + (x)(7) + (2)(x) + (2)(7) \quad \text{FOIL}$$
$$= x^2 + 7x + 2x + 14 \qquad \text{Multiply.}$$
$$= x^2 + 9x + 14 \qquad\qquad\qquad \text{Combine like terms.}$$

D. Simplify $(4x^2 + 7)(x - 1)$.

$$\qquad\qquad\qquad \text{First} \qquad \text{Outer} \qquad \text{Inner} \quad \text{Last}$$
$$(4x^2 + 7)(x - 1) = (4x^2)(x) + (4x^2)(-1) + (7)(x) + (7)(-1) \quad \text{FOIL}$$
$$= 4x^3 + (-4x^2) + 7x + (-7) \qquad \text{Multiply.}$$
$$= 4x^3 - 4x^2 + 7x - 7 \qquad\qquad\qquad \text{Simplify.}$$

</td><td>

Vocabulary

Distributive Property

Monomial

Polynomial

Binomial

FOIL

Square of a binomial

Product of a Sum and Difference

</td></tr>
</table>

Check

Simplify each product.

1. $6(3x^2 - 5x + 2)$

2. $(p^2 + 10)(3p^2 - 3)$

3. $4b^2(2b^3 - 5b^2 + 9b + 2)$

_____   _____   _____

Example 2

You can use the Distributive Property several times to multiply two
polynomials with more than two terms.

A. Simplify $(x+3)(x^2+8x+15)$.

$(x+3)(x^2+8x+15) = x(x^2+8x+15)+3(x^2+8x+15)$ Distribute x and 3.

$= x(x^2)+x(8x)+x(15)+3(x^2)+3(8x)+3(15)$ Distribute again.

$= x^3+8x^2+15x+3x^2+24x+45$ Simplify.

$= x^3+11x^2+39x+45$ Combine like terms.

To simplify the square of a binomial or the product of a sum and difference,
you can use the FOIL method. Or you can use the following shortcuts.

Square of a Binomial: **Product of a Sum and Difference:**

$(a+b)^2 = a^2+2ab+b^2$ $(a+b)(a-b) = a^2-b^2$

$(a-b)^2 = a^2-2ab+b^2$

B. Simplify $(x-8)^2$.

$(x-8)^2 = x^2-2(x)(8)+8^2$ Use the Square of a Binomial Rule.

$= x^2-16x+64$ Simplify.

C. Simplify $(t+7)(t-7)$.

$(t+7)(t-7) = t^2-7^2$ Use the Product of a Sum and Difference Rule.

$= t^2-49$ Simplify.

Check
Simplify each product.

4. $(5y+9)^2$ 5. $(b+12)(b-12)$ 6. $(6n^2+1)(6n^2-1)$

_____   _____   _____

7. Explain the Error. Then find the correct solution.

$(d-9)^2 = d^2-(d)(9)+9^2 = d^2-9d+81$

_____

8. Use the FOIL method to show that $(a+b)^2 = a^2+2ab+b^2$. _____

SKILL 22 MULTIPLY POLYNOMIALS

One-Step Equations

KEY TEACHING POINTS

Example 1

Say: Solving an equation is done by isolating the variable.

Ask: What does isolate the variable mean? **[Get the variable on one side of the equation by itself.]**

Say: The properties of equality tell you that you can perform an operation on both sides of the equal side and the equation remains true.

Ask: What operation is in the equation $7.8 + t = -10$? **[Addition.]** What operation is performed on both sides? **[Subtraction.]**

Say: To isolate the variable t, the decimal 7.8 needs to be removed from that side of the equation. Because addition and subtraction are inverse operations, you can use subtraction to "undo" the addition.

Check

Ask: What operation is used in $-28 = -0.875h$? **[Multiplication.]** What operation is the inverse of multiplication? **[Division.]**

Say: When you divided each side of the equation by -0.875, will the quotient be positive, or negative? **[Positive.]** A negative divided by a negative has a positive quotient.

Example 2

Ask: What operation is used to find the difference between the amount of flour Fay needs and the amount of flour Fay has? **[Subtraction.]** What operation is the inverse of subtraction? **[Addition.]**

Ask: When you know the cost of one, what operation is used to find the cost of many? **[Multiplication.]** What operation is the inverse of multiplication? **[Division.]**

ALTERNATE STRATEGY

Strategy: Draw a diagram.

1. **Say:** Sometimes a diagram can help you set up the problem.

2. In January, the Sullivan family spent a total of $600 on food. This was $\frac{3}{20}$ of the family's monthly income. This problem tells you that the family spent a fraction of its income on food. Draw a model to show the fraction.

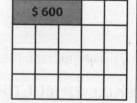

3. The model makes it clear that $\frac{3}{20}$ of the family's income is $600.

   The word *of* means multiplication. Multiply the income by the fraction.

4. Write the equation. $\dfrac{3}{20}m = 600$

5. The inverse of multiplication is division.

   To divide by a fraction, multiply by the reciprocal.

   The monthly income is $4000.

$$\dfrac{3}{20}m = 600$$

$$\left(\dfrac{20}{3}\right)\dfrac{3}{20}m = \left(\dfrac{20}{3}\right)600$$

$$m = 4000$$

COMMON MISCONCEPTION

Ask: What is the Error?

You have already read 104 pages of a book. You are two-thirds of the way through the book. How many pages are in the book?

$\dfrac{2}{3}p = 104$; $3\left(\dfrac{2}{3}p\right) = 3(104)$; $p = 312$ So the book has 312 pages.

Reason incorrect: The left side is incorrectly multiplied.

Solution: To isolate the variable p, you can multiply by the reciprocal of $\dfrac{2}{3}$.

$$\dfrac{2}{3}p = 104$$

$$\left(\dfrac{3}{2}\right)\left(\dfrac{2}{3}p\right) = \left(\dfrac{3}{2}\right)(104)$$

$$p = 156$$

So the book has 158 pages·

Say: The fraction is multiplied by the variable p. The inverse property of multiplication is division, so you must divide by $\dfrac{2}{3}$. Dividing by $\dfrac{2}{3}$ is the same as multiplying by the reciprocal, $\dfrac{3}{2}$.

ADDITIONAL ONLINE INTERVENTION RESOURCES

Use the following for students who have not mastered the concepts in Skill 23.

- Math on the Spot videos

- Personal Math Trainer with customized intervention

- Building Block worksheets (Skill 1: Absolute Value; Skill 89: Solve Equations with Fractions; Skill 90: Solve for a Variable)

SKILL 23 One-Step Equations

Example 1

	Vocabulary
	Properties of equality
	Inverse operations
	Isolate

To solve an equation, use the properties of equality and inverse operations to isolate the variable.

A. Solve $7.8 + t = -10$.

$$
\begin{aligned}
7.8 + t &= -10 \\
\underline{-7.8 \qquad\quad -7.8} & \\
t &= -17.8
\end{aligned}
$$
Subtract 7.8 from each side.

B. Solve $x - \dfrac{3}{4} = 12$.

$$
\begin{aligned}
x - \frac{3}{4} &= 12 \\
\underline{+\frac{3}{4} \qquad +\frac{3}{4}} & \\
x &= 12\frac{3}{4}
\end{aligned}
$$
Add $\dfrac{3}{4}$ to each side.

C. Solve $20 = -0.25p$.

$$
\begin{aligned}
20 &= -0.25p \\
\frac{20}{-0.25} &= \frac{-0.25p}{-0.25} \\
-80 &= p
\end{aligned}
$$
Divide each side by -0.25.

D. Solve $-\dfrac{m}{4.5} = 8.5$.

$$
\begin{aligned}
-\frac{m}{4.5} &= 8.5 \\
-\frac{m}{4.5}(-4.5) &= 8.5(-4.5) \\
m &= -38.25
\end{aligned}
$$
Multiply each side by -4.5.

Check

Solve each equation.

1. $w + 5.9 = -12.5$

2. $-\dfrac{3}{5} + n = 9$

3. $25 = -0.4c$

4. $-\dfrac{x}{5.2} = 10$

5. $d - \dfrac{4}{5} = \dfrac{7}{10}$

6. $-28 = -0.875h$

Example 2

You can solve some real-world problems by writing and solving a one-step equation.

A. Fay is baking a large batch of muffins. She has $5\frac{2}{3}$ cups of flour. She needs $12\frac{1}{3}$ cups of flour. Find how much more flour Fay needs.

$$5\frac{2}{3} + f = 12\frac{1}{3}$$ Write an equation. Let f represent how much more flour Fay needs.

$$\underline{-5\frac{2}{3} \qquad -5\frac{2}{3}}$$ Subtract $5\frac{2}{3}$ from each side.

$$f = \ 6\frac{2}{3}$$

Fay needs $6\frac{2}{3}$ more cups of flour.

B. Ari buys several T-shirts. He spends a total of $34.50. Each shirt costs $5.75. How many shirts does Ari buy?

$34.50 = 5.75t$ Write an equation. Let t represent the number of shirts Ari buys.

$$\frac{34.50}{5.75} = \frac{5.75t}{5.75}$$ Divide each side by 5.75.

$$6 = t$$

Ari buys 6 T-shirts.

Check

7. In January, the Sullivan family spent a total of $600 on food. This was $\frac{3}{20}$ of the family's monthly income. Write and solve an equation to find the family's monthly income for January.

_____

8. Explain the Error. Then find the correct solution.

You have already read 104 pages of a book. You are two-thirds of the way through the book. How many pages are in the book?

$\frac{2}{3}p = 104;\ 3\left(\frac{2}{3}p\right) = 3(104);\ p = 312$. So the book has 312 pages.

_____

SKILL 23 ONE-STEP EQUATIONS

One-Step Inequalities

KEY TEACHING POINTS

Example 1

Say: Solving an inequality involves getting the variable on one side of the inequality by itself. Just as in solving equations, you can add and subtract the same quantity to each side of an inequality and the inequality will still be true. Addition and subtraction have no effect on the inequality symbol.

Ask: After setting up the inequality, what is the first step in solving $x - 7 < -12$? **[Add 7 to both sides.]**

Ask: When graphing the solution, when are open and closed circles used? **[An open circle means the value is not included, a closed circle means the value is included.]** Should the circle be open or closed? **[Open.]** Why? **[The solution is $x < -5$. The value –5 is not part of the solution set.]**

Say: Look at the graph of the solution set, $x < -5$. The solution set means that any value for x that is less than –5 will make the inequality true. Compare the values that are included in the solution set to the original inequality.

Ask: Is the number –6 part of the solution set? **[Yes.]** If the variable x is replaced by the value 6 in the original inequality, is the inequality true? **[Yes.]**

Show the following work:

$$x - 7 < -12$$
$$(-6) - 7 < -12 \qquad \text{Substitute 6 for the variable.}$$
$$-13 < -12 \qquad \text{True.}$$

Ask: In part D, after the inequality is set up, what is the next step? **[Divide both sides of the inequality by –4.]**

Say: You can multiply and divide by the same quantity on each side of an inequality. When you multiply or divide by a negative number, the inequality sign is reversed.

Check

Say: Look at the inequality $11 \le 5 + m$.

Ask: What do you need to do first? **[Isolate the variable.]** What operation is used to isolate the variable? **[Subtraction.]**

Show the following work:

$$11 \le 5 + m$$
$$11 - 5 \le 5 - 5 + m$$
$$6 < m$$

Say: The variable in this inequality is on the right side of the equation. It is common for the variable to be written on the left side. In this case, saying "m is greater than 6" makes more sense than saying "6 is less than m." When you switch the variable and expression to opposite sides, make sure the correct end of the inequality symbol points toward the variable. In the inequality $6 < m$, the open end points toward the variable m. When the variable and expression switch sides, keep the open end pointing toward the variable, $m > 6$.

Ask: In the inequality $-47y \leq -1739$, what operation is used to solve the inequality? **[Division.]** Does the inequality sign reverse? **[Yes.]**

Show the following work:

$$-47y \leq -1739$$

$$\frac{-47y}{-47} \geq \frac{-1739}{-47}$$

$$y \geq 37$$

Ask: What value needs to be included on your number line? **[37 and the values around it.]**

Sketch a number line as a class.

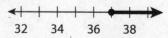

Ask: At the value 37 should the circle be open or closed? Why? **[Closed, because the value 37 is part of the solution set.]**

COMMON MISCONCEPTION

Ask: What is the Error?

Ellen was asked to solve $x - 1 < 3$ and graph the solution. Her answer is below. Where did Ellen go wrong?

$$x - 1 < 3$$
$$-1(x) > -1(3)$$
$$x > -3$$

Reason incorrect: Ellen multiplied by -1 instead of adding 1 to each side.

Solution:
$$x - 1 < 3$$
$$x - 1 + 1 < 3 + 1$$
$$x < 4$$

Ask: How could Ellen have caught her mistake? **[By checking her operations, or substituting values from the shaded part of the graph into the inequality.]**

Ask: If Ellen substituted 0 into the inequality, would she have found her own error? Explain. **[No. 0 is part of the solution set of the correct and incorrect answer.]** What values could she use to check? **[A number that is not close to the boundary, such as 100, or −100.]**

ALTERNATE STRATEGY

Strategy: Use algebra tiles.

1. Review the use of algebra tiles. Longer tiles are variable tiles and have a value of one unit of the variable. Shorter tiles have a value of 1. Red tiles show a negative value. When using algebra tiles, a zero pair is a set of a matching positive and negative tile on the same side of the equation. The positive and negative joined together have a value of zero, so they can be removed.

2. **Say:** Solving inequalities using algebra tiles is very similar to solving equations.

   Put tiles for the left side of the inequality on the left, and for the right side on the right.

   $$11 \le 5 + m$$

   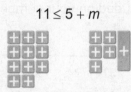

3. The goal is to isolate the variable. Remember that you must always do the same action on each side of the inequality to keep it true. Add five negative unit tiles to each side to eliminate the constant on the right. Remove the zero pairs.

   $$11 \le 5 + m$$

   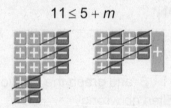

4. The remaining tiles show that $6 \le m$. You can switch the sides of the variable and number tiles, just be sure the open end of the inequality symbol follows the variable tile.

   $$6 \le m \qquad\qquad m \ge 6$$

   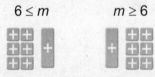

5. Graph the inequality using the form with the variable on the left. The boundary point is 6. Since the solution set includes 6, use a solid circle. When the inequality is written with the variable on the left, the inequality symbol points toward the direction that needs to be shaded. The symbol $\ge$ points right, so shade to the right of 6. This shows all of the values that are 6 or greater.

   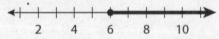

KEY TEACHING POINTS

Example 2

Say: Real world problems can be set up as inequalities using key words. The inequality in Example 2 uses the key phrase "no more than." "No more than" has the same meaning as "less than or equal to."

Ask: How can you check the answer for Example 2? **[Test eight payments to see if he can cover them with what is in his account, then test nine payments to see if it will be too much.]**

Say: If eight payments are taken from his account, $8 \times \$115 = \$920$ will be taken out, so there will be nothing left for the ninth payment. This is correct.

Check

Ask: In problem 11, what key words are used to tell you the inequality symbol needed? **[No colder than.]** What symbol does "no colder than" indicate? **[Greater than or equal to, $\geq$]**

Ask: If t represents the time in hours, what expression should be used on the left side of the inequality symbol? **[$-3t$]**

Say: The temperature is dropping by $3°$ each hour, so the coefficient is negative 3. The change in temperature should be added to the original temperature. Because the original temperature is $0°C$, the left side of the inequality is just $-3t$.

Show the following work:

$$-3t \geq -45$$
$$t \leq 15$$

Don't forget to switch the inequality symbol when you divide by a negative value.

Say: Check the result using the original problem. If the temperature drops $3°C$ each hour for 15 hours, it has dropped a total of $45°C$. Since the temperature started at $0°C$, the new temperature is $-45°C$.

Say: This is the coldest the cooler should get, so she can change the temperature for less than or equal to 15 hours. This is correct.

ADDITIONAL ONLINE INTERVENTION RESOURCES

Use the following for students who have not mastered the concepts in Skill 24.

- Math on the Spot videos

- Personal Math Trainer with customized intervention

- Building Block worksheets (Skill 1: Absolute Value; Skill 47: Graph Points on a Number Line; Skill 94: Solve One-Step Inequalities)

SKILL 24 — One-Step Inequalities

	Vocabulary
	Inequality

Example 1

You use the same process to solve an inequality that you do to solve an equation. The only difference is that you must reverse the inequality symbol when you multiply or divide by a negative number.

Solve each inequality and graph its solution.

A. $x - 7 < -12$

$x - 7 < -12$	Set up the inequality.
$x - 7 + 7 < -12 + 7$	Add 7 to both sides.
$x < -5$	Simplify.

Graph the solution.

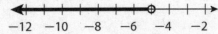

$$-12 \quad -10 \quad -8 \quad -6 \quad -4 \quad -2$$

B. $b + 8 > -4$

$b + 8 > -4$	Set up the inequality.
$b + 8 - 8 > -4 - 8$	Subtract 8 from both sides.
$b > -12$	Simplify.

Graph the solution.

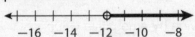

$$-16 \quad -14 \quad -12 \quad -10 \quad -8$$

C. $\dfrac{n}{3} \geq -6$

$\dfrac{n}{3} \geq -6$	Set up the inequality.
$3\left(\dfrac{n}{3}\right) \geq 3(-6)$	Multiply both sides by 3.
$n \geq -18$	Simplify.

Graph the solution.

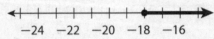

$$-24 \quad -22 \quad -20 \quad -18 \quad -16$$

D. $-4y \geq -4$

$-4y \geq -4$	Set up the inequality.
$\dfrac{-4y}{-4} \leq \dfrac{-4}{-4}$	Divide both sides by −4. Reverse the inequality symbol.
$y \leq 1$	Simplify.

Graph the solution.

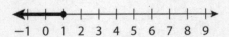

$$-1 \quad 0 \quad 1 \quad 2 \quad 3 \quad 4 \quad 5 \quad 6 \quad 7 \quad 8 \quad 9$$

Name _____ Date _____ Class_____

Check

Solve each inequality and graph its solution.

1. $-7 + p \geq -8$

2. $11 \leq 5 + m$

_____

3. $\dfrac{x}{5} \leq 2$

4. $-6p < -42$

_____

5. $x - 17 > -16$

6. $\dfrac{a}{5} \leq -\dfrac{3}{5}$

_____

7. $-47y \leq -1739$

8. $-166 < b - 83$

_____

9. Explain the Error. Find the correct solution.

Ellen was asked to solve $x - 1 < 3$ and graph the solution. Her answer is below. Where did Ellen go wrong?

$$x - 1 < 3$$
$$-1(x) > -1(3)$$
$$x > -3$$

_____

Example 2

Many real world problems can be solved using inequalities. When writing an inequality for a situation, make sure to use the appropriate inequality symbol.

Stephan has an account that he uses to pay his cell phone bill. Every month $115 is automatically withdrawn to pay his bill. He has enough savings to withdraw no more than $920. How many full monthly payments can Stephan make before needing to deposit more money in his account?

Step 1: Set up an equation that models the situation. Let t represent the number of monthly payments he can make.

monthly bill	times	number of payments	can be no more than	total in account
115	•	t	≤	920

Step 2: Solve the inequality.

$115t \leq 920$ Set up the inequality.

$\dfrac{115t}{115} \leq \dfrac{920}{115}$ Divide both sides by 115.

$x \leq 8$ Simplify.

Stephan can make no more than 8 monthly payments before needing to make a deposit.

Check

Solve.

10. Yolanda wants to spend no more than $150 to buy jeans and a coat for winter. She finds a pair of jeans that cost $65. What's the greatest amount she can spend on a coat?

   a. Write an inequality that models this situation. Let c represent the amount she can spend on a coat.

   _____

   b. Solve the inequality. How much can Yolanda spend on a coat?

   _____

   c. Suppose Yolanda decides to buy a pair of jeans on sale for $45 instead. How much would she have to spend on a coat in this situation?

   _____

11. For an experiment, a biologist needs to make sure that the temperature of a cooler with a starting temperature of 0°C gets no colder than –45°C. She changes the cooler's temperature at a steady rate of –3°C per hour. For how many hours can she continue to change the temperature?

   a. Write an inequality that models this situation. Let *t* represent the time in hours.

   _____

   b. Solve the inequality. How long can the biologist change the temperature of the cooler?

   _____

   c. Suppose the biologist decided to change the cooler's temperature at a rate of –5°C per hour. How long could the biologist change the temperature of the cooler in this situation?

   _____

12. A small airplane has a full flight of 25 passengers. The plane can carry up to 1700 pounds of luggage. What is the maximum weight of luggage each passenger can check onto the flight?

   a. Write an inequality that models this situation. Let *w* represent the maximum weight each passenger can check onto the flight.

   _____

   b. Solve the inequality. What is the maximum weight of luggage each passenger can check onto the flight?

   _____

SKILL 24 ONE-STEP INEQUALITIES

KEY TEACHING POINTS

Example 1

Say: Translations are a congruency transformation. This means when a figure is transformed, the image is congruent to the preimage. Translations move a figure left, right, up or down, without turning or flipping it, so a translation preserves its orientation.

Ask: To translate a figure 3 units to the left and 4 units up, how does each vertex need to be translated? **[3 units to the left and 4 units up.]**

Say: This is a triangle, so you need to translate three vertices. After the vertices are each translated, connect them to form the image. The original figure is called a preimage. The translated figure is called an image.

Ask: If you only saw the bottom graph, could you tell which figure was the preimage and which was the image? **[Yes.]** How? **[The translated image has vertices that are marked with a prime symbol.]**

Say: When a figure is transformed, the transformed vertices keep the same letter, but a prime symbol is used to show it is an image. A prime symbol looks like a single quotation mark, but the prime symbol is straight and does not curl.

Ask: What are the coordinates of vertex L? **[(4, 1)]** What are the coordinates of vertex L'? **[(1, 5)]** How does the x-coordinate change? **[It is 3 less.]** How does the y-coordinate change? **[It is 4 greater.]**

Check

Say: Look at Problem 1.
Do the translation as a class. Move each vertex 5 units left and 3 units down.
Have a student label the vertices.

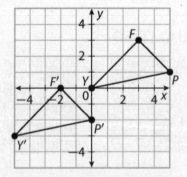

Ask: How are the line segments FP and $F'P'$ related? **[They are parallel.]**

Say: The image of a translation has sides that are parallel, have the same length, and have the same slope as the corresponding sides of the preimage.

Ask: You can check that you have translated each vertex correctly by seeing if the preimage and image have the same size, shape, and orientation.

ALTERNATE STRATEGY

Strategy: Use physical models.

1. Use a coordinate grid and paper cutouts to model translations.

2. Have students use two pieces of grid paper. The first is their coordinate grid and the second will be used to cut figures in the correct shape and size. It may be helpful to use colored grid paper for the shapes as a visual reinforcement.

3. Mark off the vertices, connect the points, and cut out the shape from Problem 2.

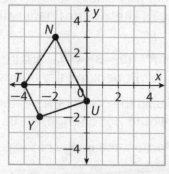

4. Use the shape to move the image 5 units right, then 2 units down. Follow one vertex without turning the shape in any way.

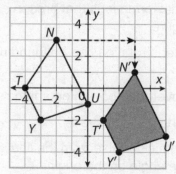

KEY TEACHING POINTS

Example 2

Say: Reflections are transformations that create a mirror image of the preimage across a line of reflection. Each vertex is the same distance from the line of reflection, but on the opposite side.

Ask: How is the image the same as the preimage? **[They are the same size and shape, but not always the same orientation.]** How might a preimage be reflected and have the same orientation? **[Possible answer: If there was more than one reflection performed.]**

Say: In a translation, each vertex moves the same distance and the same direction. In a reflection, the vertices move the same direction, but each may move a different distance.

Ask: In example 2, the figure is reflected over the *y*-axis. How far is point *E* from the *y*-axis? **[2 units]** How far is the image of point *E* from the *y*-axis? **[2 units]**

Ask: What are the coordinates of point *E*? **[(2, 1)]** What are the coordinates of point *E′*? **[(–2, 1)]**

Say: The *y*-coordinates stayed the same, because the figure did not move up or down. The *x*-coordinates became the opposite, because they moved to the point the same distance from the axis, but on the opposite side.

Ask: When a point is reflected across the *x*-axis, which coordinate changes? **[The y-coordinate.]**

Check

Ask: In problem 5, what axis is the figure reflected across? **[The x-axis.]** What coordinate will stay the same and what will change? **[The x-coordinate will stay the same and the y-coordinate will change.]**

Ask: What are the coordinates of point *X*? **[(3, –3)]** What are the coordinates of point *X′*? **[(3, 3)]** How did the *y*-coordinate change? **[It became the opposite.]**

Ask: If Point *R* began at (1, 0), what would the coordinates of the image be if it were reflected across the *x*-axis? **[The coordinates would not change: (1, 0).]**

Say: When a point is on the line of reflection, the image of the point is in the same place as the preimage.

Example 3

Say: Rotations are congruency transformations that preserve the size and shape, but not necessarily the orientation, of a figure.

Say: The vertices of the image after a rotation can be found using lines drawn to the center of rotation.

Demonstrate the following on an overhead or with geometric software.

Draw a line from Point *S* to the vertex.

Use a protractor to draw a 90° angle clockwise from the line you just drew with the vertex of the angle on the origin.

Using a compass, measure the distance from the origin to Point *S*. Draw Point *S′* the same distance from the vertex but on the second line. This is the image of the rotated point.

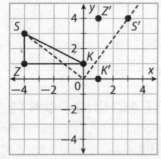

Say: In Example 3, the figure is rotated clockwise around the origin. This means the figure rotates in the same direction that the hands on a clock move, to the right. If a figure is rotated counterclockwise, it rotates in the opposite direction as the hands on a clock, to the left.

Ask: What are the coordinates of point *S*? **[(–4, 3)]** What are the coordinates of point *S′*? **[(3, 4)]**

Check

Ask: In problem 7, you are not told what direction to rotate the figure. Why? **[A 180° rotation results in the same image if you rotate clockwise or counterclockwise. A full rotation is a full circle of 360°, so a 180° rotation is halfway, either direction.]**

Ask: How do the coordinates in the preimage and image relate in a 180° rotation? **[Each coordinate becomes the opposite.]**

Say: Each counterclockwise rotation can be written as a clockwise rotation. A 90° clockwise rotation has the same result as a 270° counterclockwise rotation.

Ask: What clockwise rotation has the same result as a counterclockwise rotation of 90°? **[270° clockwise.]**

COMMON MISCONCEPTION

Ask: What is the Error?
A point with coordinates (1, –3) is rotated 270° clockwise about the origin. What are the coordinates of its image? Answer: (–3, –1)

Reason incorrect: The point was rotated counterclockwise instead of clockwise.

Solution: A clockwise rotation moves the point to the right around the axis. The *y*-coordinate will change to the opposite, and the coordinates will change position. The correct coordinates are (3, 1).

Ask: How could this mistake have been avoided? **[Think about what direction the hands on a clock move. Remember that there are 360° in a circle, so 270° should take the image $\frac{3}{4}$ of the way around a circle.]**

ADDITIONAL ONLINE INTERVENTION RESOURCES

Use the following for students who have not mastered the concepts in Skill 25.

- Math on the Spot videos

- Personal Math Trainer with customized intervention

- Building Block worksheets (Skill 41: Generate Ordered Pairs; Skill 103: Transformations)

Properties of Translations, Reflections, and Rotations

SKILL 25

Example 1

Vocabulary
Translations
Vertices
Reflections
Rotations

Translations preserve the size, shape, and orientation of a figure. To translate a figure in the coordinate plane, translate each of its vertices. Then connect the vertices to form the image.

The figure shows triangle CLU. Graph the image of the triangle after a translation of 3 units to the left and 4 units up.

Step 1: Translate point C.

Count left 3 units and up 4 units and plot point C'.

Step 2: Translate point L.

Count left 3 units and up 4 units and plot point L'.

Step 3: Translate point U.

Count left 3 units and up 4 units and plot point U'.

Step 4: Connect C', L', and U' to form triangle C'L'U'.

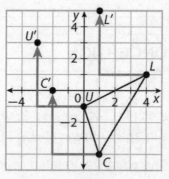
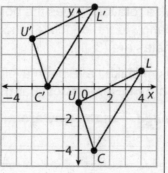

Each vertex is moved 3 units left and 4 units up.

Check
Draw the image of the figure after each translation.

1. 5 units left and 3 units down

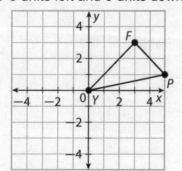

2. 5 units right and 2 units down

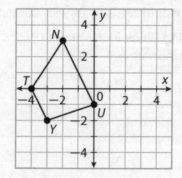

3. 1 unit right and 5 units up

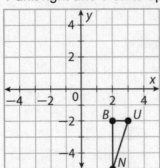

4. 2 units left and 1 unit down

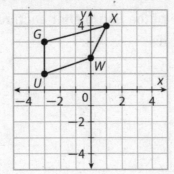

Example 2

Reflections preserve size and shape, but not orientation. To reflect a figure across a line of reflection, reflect each of its vertices. Then connect the vertices to form the image. Remember that each point and its image are the same distance from the line of reflection.

The figure shows triangle EIY. Graph the image of the triangle after a reflection across the y-axis.

Step 1: Reflect point E.

Point E is 2 units to the right of the y-axis. Count 2 units to the left of the y-axis and plot point E'.

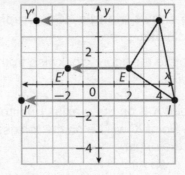

Step 2: Reflect point I.

Point I is 5 units to the right of the y-axis.

Count 5 units to the left of the y-axis and plot point I'.

Step 3: Reflect point Y.

Point Y is 4 units to the right of the y-axis. Count 4 units to the left of the y-axis and plot point Y'.

Step 4: Connect E', I', and Y' to form triangle E' I' Y'.

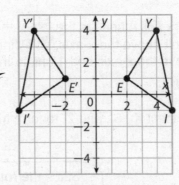

Each vertex of the image is the same distance from the y-axis as the corresponding vertex in the original figure.

Check

Draw the image of the figure after each reflection.

5. across the x-axis

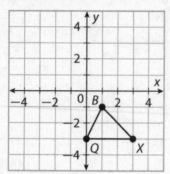

6. across the y-axis

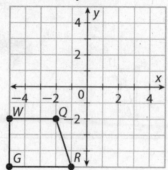

EXAMPLE 3

Rotations preserve size and shape, but change orientation. To rotate a figure in the coordinate plane, rotate each of its vertices. Then connect the vertices to form the image.

The figure shows triangle KSZ. Graph the image of triangle KSZ after a rotation of 90° clockwise.

Step 1: Rotate the figure clockwise from the y-axis to the x-axis.

Point K is on the y-axis, 1 unit above the origin, so Point K′ will be on the x-axis, 1 unit to the right of the origin.

Point S is 4 units to the left of the y-axis and 3 units above the x-axis, so Point S′ will be 4 units above the x-axis and 3 units to the right of the y-axis.

Point Z is 4 units to the left of the y-axis and 1 unit above the x-axis, so Point Z′ will be 4 units above the x-axis and 1 unit to the right of the y-axis.

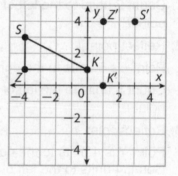

Step 2: Connect K′, S′, and Z′ to form triangle K′ S′ Z′.

Since the rotation is clockwise, the figure is turned *right* about the origin by the angle of rotation.

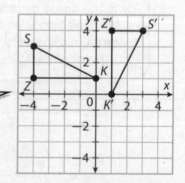

Check

Draw the image of the figure after each rotation.

7. 180° about the origin

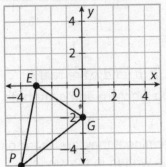

8. 90° clockwise about the origin

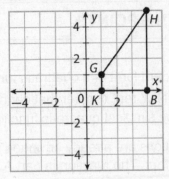

9. 90° counterclockwise about the origin

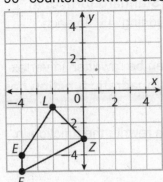

10. 270° counterclockwise about the origin

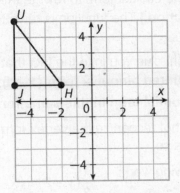

11. A point with coordinates (3, −2) is rotated 90° clockwise about the origin. What are the coordinates of its image?

_____

12. A point with coordinates (5, −2) is rotated 270° counterclockwise about the origin. What are the coordinates of its image?

_____

13. Explain the Error. Find the correct solution.

A point with coordinates (1, −3) is rotated 270° clockwise about the origin. What are the coordinates of its image? Answer: (−3, −1)

_____

SKILL 25 PROPERTIES OF TRANSLATIONS, REFLECTIONS, AND ROTATIONS

KEY TEACHING POINTS

Example 1

Say: In the standard form of a quadratic function, $y = ax^2 + bx + c$, a, b, and c are real numbers. The ONLY real number that cannot be 0 is a. The function where b and c are both 0 and a is 1 is the simplest quadratic function, $y = x^2$.

Say: Some functions are already arranged so that it is easy to determine if they are linear or quadratic, or neither. The function in part A has no exponents and is written in the slope-intercept form of a linear equation.

Ask: What is the easiest form to rewrite the function for part B in? **[Standard form of a quadratic function.]** The function is rewritten in standard form by adding $4x^2$ to each side.

Ask: What might clue you in to the fact that the function in part C can be rewritten in vertex form? **[The squared binomial term $(x-1)^2$. The vertex form of a quadratic function has a squared binomial term in this same form.]**

Say: You may not recognize the vertex form of a quadratic. You can rewrite the function in standard form also.

Show the following work:

$$\frac{1}{3}(y-2) = (x-1)^2$$

$$\frac{1}{3}(y-2) = x^2 - 2x + 1 \qquad \text{Evaluate the exponents.}$$

$$(y-2) = 3x^2 - 6x + 3 \qquad \text{Multiply by 3.}$$

$$y = 3x^2 - 6x + 5 \qquad \text{Subtract 2.}$$

Check

Ask: What is the highest exponent in a quadratic function? **[2]**

Say: In simplified form, if a function has an exponent greater than 2, it is not quadratic. All quadratic functions have a variable with an exponent 2. This means functions with no exponents are not quadratic.

Ask: How can you rewrite $-3.1(x + 2.6)^2 = y$ so that y is on the left? **[Just switch sides. $y = -3.1(x + 2.6)^2$]**

Say: When the sides of the equation are switched, you can see that the function is written in vertex form.

Ask: What form is the easiest to rewrite $7x^2 = y - 12 + 4x$ as? **[Standard form.]**

Ask: What about the function would lead you to believe it is a quadratic function? **[Possible answer: The squared binomial $(x + 5)^2$.]**

ALTERNATE STRATEGY

Strategy: Use a table of values.

1. In a linear function, there is a constant change, or rate of change, that is the slope. In a table of values, as the value for *x* increases by one unit, the value for *y* increases by a constant unit.

   Show an example table for the linear equation $y = 2x + 1$:

   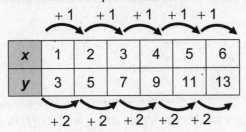

2. A quadratic function does not show a constant rate of change, but its change has a constant change of rate.

3. Consider the function $y = 11x^2 - 3x$. Check to see if it has a constant rate of change. If it does not, check to see if the rate of change has a constant rate of change.

   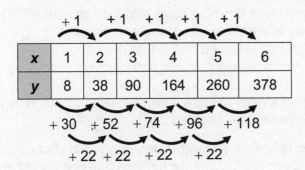

4. The rate of change has a constant rate of change: it increases by 22. This is a quadratic function.

KEY TEACHING POINTS

Example 2

Say: The graph of a linear function is always a line. The graph of a quadratic function is always a parabola. The vertex of a parabola y-coordinate at the minimum or maximum point, where the parabola changes direction. This point can be seen on the graph of a parabola.

Ask: In part A, is the vertex a minimum, or a maximum? **[A maximum.]** The y-coordinate at the maximum is 3, and there is no minimum.

Say: When the equation for a parabola is written in vertex form, $y = a(x - h)^2 + k$, the vertex is (h, k). The value of a determines if the parabola opens up or down.

Ask: In the equation $y = 3(x + 1)^2 - 4$, what is the value of a? **[3]** Because a is greater than 0, the parabola opens upward, so the parabola has a minimum. What are h and k? **[h is –1 and k is –4.]** The values of h and k tell you the vertex is at point (–1, –4).

Check

Ask: In problem 7, how do you know this is a quadratic function? **[The graph is a parabola.]** Does the parabola have a maximum, or minimum? Explain. **[The parabola has a minimum because the graph opens up.]** What is the minimum? **[–1]**

Ask: In the equation does the parabola open up or down? **[Down.]** How do you know? **[The value for a is less than 0.]** Does the parabola have a maximum, or a minimum? **[Maximum.]** What are h and k? **[4 and 11]** What is the vertex? **[(4, 11)]**

Example 3

Say: The zero of a function is the x-value that makes the function have a value of 0. When the value of a function is $y = 0$, the graph of a function crosses the x-intercept.

Ask: Describe a quadratic function that has no zeros. **[Possible answer: A parabola that opens down, with a vertex less than 0.]** Describe a quadratic function that has one zero. **[Possible answer: A parabola with a vertex on the x-axis.]**

Say: A graph is only as accurate as the person or program that makes the graph. When you determine the zeros of a function from a graph, you should always text the values in the equation of the function.

Ask: Why was there no value to test in part C? **[The graph of the function never crosses the x-axis.]**

Check

Ask: How many zeros does the quadratic function $y = -\frac{2}{3}(x - 1)^2 - \frac{1}{3}$ have? **[0]** How can you tell? **[The graph never crosses the x-axis.]**

Ask: How many zeros does the quadratic function $y = \frac{1}{2}x^2 - 2x + 2$ have? **[1]** How can you tell? **[The graph has a vertex on the x-axis.]** What does the zero appear to be? **[2]**

Say: Let's check the value by substituting it into the function. If it is correct, the function will have a value of 0 when $x = 2$.

KEY TEACHING POINTS

Example 4

Say: The graph of a parabola is symmetric. If the graph of a parabola is folded on a vertical line that passes through the vertex, the sides of the parabola will line up exactly. This line is called the axis of symmetry.

Say: Determining the axis of symmetry is done in the same way as determining the vertex. Since the axis of symmetry is a vertical line, it is given in an equation in the form $x = h$. The value for h is found in the vertex form of the equation of a quadratic function.

Ask: How can you determine the axis of symmetry from a graph? **[Find the vertex. The x-value of the vertex will tell you the axis of symmetry.]**

Check

Ask: In the equation $y = (x - 10)^2 + 15$, what are the values for a, h, and k? **[a = 1, h = 10, k = 15]** What does the value for a tell you? **[That the parabola opens up.]**

COMMON MISCONCEPTION

Ask: What is the Error?

Find the axis of symmetry for the quadratic function $y = 2(x + 5)^2 - 11$.

The axis of symmetry is $x = 5$.

Reason incorrect: The vertex form was misinterpreted and the negative missed.

Solution: The quadratic function is written in vertex form, $y = a(x - h)^2 + k$, where the value of $x = h$ is the axis of symmetry. For the sign inside the parentheses to be +, the axis of symmetry must be $x = -5$.

Ask: How could this mistake have been avoided? **[Substitute the value for h into the vertex form of the equation.]**

ADDITIONAL ONLINE INTERVENTION RESOURCES

 Use the following for students who have not mastered the concepts in Skill 26.

- Math on the Spot videos
- Personal Math Trainer with customized intervention
- Building Block worksheets (Skill 102: Symmetry)

SKILL 26

Quadratic Functions

Example 1

If a function is quadratic, it can be represented by an equation of the form $y = x^2 + bx + c$, where a, b, and c are real numbers and $a \neq 0$. This is called the standard form of a quadratic equation. The equation $y = a(x - h)^2 + k$ is called the vertex form of a quadratic function, where a, h, and k are real numbers and $a \neq 0$.

Determine whether the function represented by each equation is quadratic. Explain.

A. $y = -5x + 20$

   Compare $y = -5x + 20$ to $y = x^2 + bx + c$. This is not a quadratic function because $a = 0$.

B. $y - 4x^2 = 6$

   Rewrite the function in the form $y = x^2 + bx + c$.

   $y - 4x^2 = 6$

   $y = 4x^2 + 6$ Add $4x^2$ to both sides; $a = 4$, $b = 0$, and $c = 6$.

   This is a quadratic function in standard form where a, b, and c are real numbers and $a \neq 0$.

C. $\frac{1}{3}(y - 2) = (x - 1)^2$

   Rewrite the function in the form $y = a(x - h)^2 + k$.

   $\frac{1}{3}(y - 2) = (x - 1)^2$

   $y - 2 = 3(x - 1)^2$ Multiply both sides by 3.

   $y = 3(x - 1)^2 + 2$ Add 2 to both sides; $a = 3$, $h = 1$, and $k = 2$.

   This is a quadratic function in vertex form where a, h, and k are real numbers and $a \neq 0$.

Vocabulary

Quadratic

Standard form

Vertex form

Maximum

Minimum

Vertex

Parabola

Zeros

Axis of symmetry

Check

Determine whether the function represented by each equation is quadratic. Explain.

1. $y = 11x^2 - 3x$

2. $y - x = 7x + 2$

3. $-3.1(x + 2.6)^2 = y$

4. $7x^2 = y - 12 + 4x$

5. $y = x^3 + 2x - 9$

6. $12(x + 5)^2 = 4(y + 8)$

Example 2

You can identify the maximum or minimum of a quadratic function by a graph or an equation. On a graph, the y-coordinate of the vertex of a parabola is the maximum or minimum value of the equation represented by the parabola. Similarly, in the vertex form of a quadratic equation, $y = a(x - h)^2 + k$, the y-coordinate of the vertex (h, k) is the maximum or minimum value. If $a > 0$, then k is a maximum. If $a < 0$, then k is a minimum.

Determine the maximum or minimum value of each quadratic function from its graph or its equation. Explain.

A.
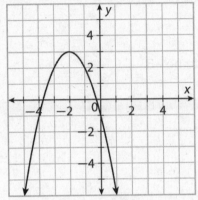

The parabola opens downward, so 3 is the maximum value.

B.
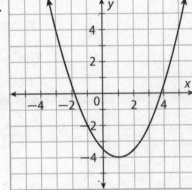

The parabola opens upward, so −4 is the minimum value.

C. $y = 3(x + 1)^2 - 4$

The vertex (h, k) is $(-1, -4)$. Because $a > 0$, the parabola opens upward. The minimum value of the function is −4.

D. $y = -5(x - 3)^2 + 6$

The vertex (h, k) is $(3, 6)$. Because $a < 0$, the parabola opens downward. The maximum value of the function is 6.

Check

Determine the maximum or minimum value of each quadratic function from its graph or its equation. Explain.

7.
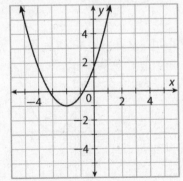

8. $y = -\frac{1}{3}(x - 4)^2 + 11$

_____   _____

Example 3

The zeros of a function are the *x*-intercepts of the graph of the function. A quadratic function may have one, two, or no zeros.

Find the zeros of each quadratic function from its graph.

A. $y = x^2 + 2x - 3$

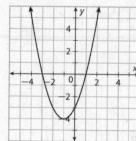

The zeros appear to be –3 and 1.

Check:

$y = x^2 + 2x - 3$ $y = x^2 + 2x - 3$

$= (-3)^2 + 2(-3) - 3$ $= (1)^2 + 2(1) - 3$

$= 9 - 6 - 3 = 0$ ✓ $= 1 + 2 - 3 = 0$ ✓

B. $y = -2(x + 3)^2$

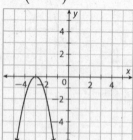

The only zero appears to be –3.

Check:

$y = -2(x + 3)^2$

$= -2((-3) + 3)^2$

$= -2(0)^2 = 0$ ✓

C. $y = 0.5(x - 2)^2 + 1$

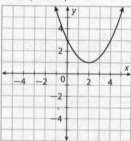

The graph does not cross the *x*-axis, so this function has no zeros.

Check

Find the zeros of each quadratic function from its graph.

9. $y = -\dfrac{2}{3}(x - 1)^2 - \dfrac{1}{3}$

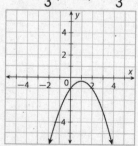

10. $y = x^2 - 4x$

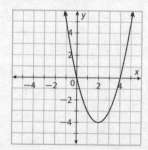

11. $y = \dfrac{1}{2}x^2 - 2x + 2$

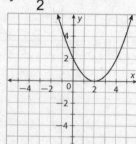

_____   _____   _____

Example 4

On a graph of a quadratic function, the axis of symmetry is a vertical line that passes through the x-coordinate of the vertex of the parabola. Similarly, in the vertex form of a quadratic equation, the x-coordinate of the vertex (h, k) tells you the axis of symmetry is $x = h$.

Determine the axis of symmetry of each parabola from its graph or its equation.

A.
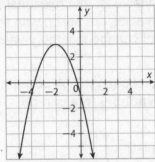

B. $y = -\dfrac{1}{3}(x - 1)^2 + 5$

The vertex is $(-2, 3)$. The x-coordinate of the vertex is -2, so the axis of symmetry is $x = -2$.

The vertex (h, k) is $(1, 5)$. The x-coordinate of the vertex is 1, so the axis of symmetry is $x = 1$.

Check

Determine the axis of symmetry of each parabola from its graph or its equation.

12.
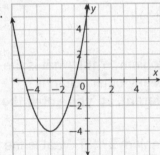

13.
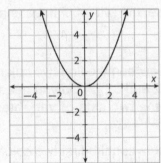

14. $y = (x - 10)^2 + 15$

_____   _____   _____

15. Explain the Error. Find the correct solution.

Find the axis of symmetry for the quadratic function $y = 2(x + 5)^2 - 11$.

The axis of symmetry is $x = 5$.

_____

SKILL 26 QUADRATIC FUNCTIONS

Rate of Change and Slope

KEY TEACHING POINTS

Example 1

Say: The dependent variable depends on what the independent variable is. In a relationship between x and y, x is typically the independent variable. Tables of values are set up with the x-values at the top, or on the left. Be careful when finding the rate of change that the y-value is the first term of the ratio.

Ask: What is the difference between a constant and a variable rate of change? [**A constant rate of change is the same, no matter what values you use. A variable rate can be different if you check different values.**]

Ask: What is the rate of change from one column in part A to the next? $\left[\dfrac{1}{2}\right]$

Say: In a constant function, the rate of change doesn't change. What happens when you choose columns that are not next to each other? Look at the values in the first and last columns of part A.

Show the following work:

$$\frac{9-3}{10-(-2)} = \frac{6}{12} = \frac{1}{2}$$

No matter what two values you use, the rate of change is always $\dfrac{1}{2}$.

Check

Ask: What is the rate of change between the first two columns in problem 1? [**8**] What is the rate of change between columns 2 and 3? [**2**] Do you need to check any other columns? Explain. [**No, the rates between the two sets of variables are different, so you know the rate of change is variable.**]

Ask: What is the rate of change between the first two columns in problem 2? [**3**] What is the rate of change between columns 2 and 3? [**3**] Do you need to check any other columns? Explain. [**Yes, the rate might be the same between some of the columns, but not all of them. You have to check all of the columns.**]

Example 2

Ask: The rate of change for the graph in part A has a constant rate of change. What does the graph look like? [**A straight line.**]

Ask: The rate of change for the graph in part B has a variable rate of change. What does the graph look like? [**It is a curve.**] Variable rates of change can be a curve, or a set of line segments with different slopes.

Say: Rates of change can be positive or negative. With a positive rate of change, as the independent variable increases, so does the dependent variable. With a negative rate of change, as the independent variable increases, the dependent variable decreases.

Say: In a graph, the graph moves up from left to right for a positive rate of change and down from left to right for a negative rate of change.

Check

Ask: What does the graph of the function for area in terms of side length look like? **[A curve that goes up.]** Is the rate of change constant or variable? **[Variable.]**

Ask: Without calculation, does the graph in problem 5 have a constant or variable rate of change? **[Constant.]** How can you tell? **[The graph is a straight line.]** Does the graph have a positive or negative rate of change? **[Negative.]**

Say: When the graph is a straight line moving down from left to right, the function has a constant negative rate of change. Let's look at the rates between 0 tickets and 5 tickets and between 0 tickets and 15 tickets.

Show the following work:

From 0 to 5: $\dfrac{50-75}{5-0} = \dfrac{-25}{5} = -5$

From 0 to 15: $\dfrac{0-75}{15-0} = \dfrac{-75}{15} = -5$

Say: Between any two points on the line, the rate of change is always the same, so it is constant.

Ask: Why might you want to use points that are on an axis, such as the ones for the purchase of 0 or 15 tickets, in your calculations? **[Possible response: When the points are on an axis, one of the coordinates is 0. This makes calculations easy.]**

Say: The rate of change for problem 5 is the ratio of the balance on a gift card to the number of tickets purchased. When more tickets are purchased, the balance is lower. The rate of change is moving down, or is negative.

Example 3

Say: The slope of a line tells you how a line moves up and down from left to right, or the steepness of the line.

Ask: What does the word "rise" mean? **[Possible answer: The change up and down.]** What does the word "run" mean? **[Possible answer: The change left to right.]**

Ask: In the graph of the line in part A, the rise is 6 and the run is –8. Why is the rise positive and the run negative? **[You can move up for a positive rise and left for a negative run to get from one point on a line to another point on the line.]**

Say: You can choose any two points on the line, and you can start at either point.

Ask: How do the rise and run change if you start on the left and move to the right? **[The run becomes positive and the rise becomes negative.]** Does this change the slope? **[No.]**

Say: The slope formula does the same thing as using the measure of rise over run. The difference between y-values is the rise and the difference between x-values is the run. When you use a graph to find the rise and run, you count the number of units between the points. The slope formula uses subtraction to find the number of units between the points.

Check

Ask: Does it matter which point you use for (x_1, y_1) and which is (x_2, y_2)? **[No, they just need to correspond.]**

Say: Let's check the points $(-5, -4)$ and $(0, -1)$ in both orders.

Show the following work:

$$\frac{y_2 - y_1}{x_2 - x_1} = \frac{-4 - (-1)}{-5 - 0} = \frac{-3}{-5} = \frac{3}{5} \qquad \frac{y_2 - y_1}{x_2 - x_1} = \frac{-1 - (-4)}{0 - (-5)} = \frac{3}{5}$$

The points you choose for the first and second point do not matter.

ALTERNATE STRATEGY

Strategy: Use a memory trick.

1. **Say:** You can remember the difference between slopes and how they relate to lines using a simple memory trick.

2. Draw the graphic on the right for the students. Explain each of the four types of slope.

3. A positive slope moves up, like the left eyebrow. The "+" sign open eye reminds you the slope is positive.

4. A negative slope moves down, like the right eyebrow. The "−" sign closed eye reminds you the slope is negative.

5. The nose is a vertical line. The "U" forming the bottom of the nose reminds you that a vertical line has an undefined slope.

6. The mouth is a horizontal line. The zeros at each end of the mouth remind you that a horizontal line has a slope of 0.

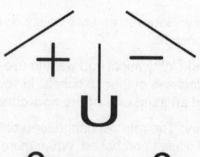

COMMON MISCONCEPTION

Ask: What is the Error?

In problem 7, Kinsey found that the slope of the line is $\frac{y_2 - y_1}{x_2 - x_1} = \frac{3 - (-5)}{-3 - 1} = \frac{8}{-4} = -2$.

Reason incorrect: The coordinates for point 1 and point 2 do not correspond.

Solution: $m = \frac{y_2 - y_1}{x_2 - x_1} = \frac{3 - (-5)}{1 - (-3)} = \frac{8}{4} = 2$

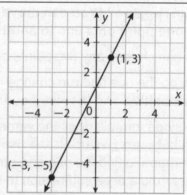

Ask: How could Kinsey have recognized her answer was not correct? **[The line moves up, not down, so the slope is positive, not negative.]**

KEY TEACHING POINTS

Example 4

Say: The slope of a line tells you how the line moves from left to right. A line with a greater slope is steeper. A line with a 0 slope has no steepness. It is flat or horizontal.

Say: The slope of a vertical line is undefined. Using the slope formula, the denominator has a result of 0. When a fraction has a 0 denominator, it is undefined.

Ask: When the slope of the line is steeper, what does that mean in terms of Mia's walk? **[She is covering more distance in the same amount of time, so she is moving faster.]**

Say: The graph represents distance from Mia's home. This means as the *y*-value on the graph is greater, Mia is farther from her home.

Ask: How would the graph look different if the *y*-axis represented the distance Mia walked? **[Segments 1, 2, and 3 would stay the same. The line would continue to move up in segments 4 and 5.]** Why? **[Possible answer: When Mia starts heading back toward home she is still walking more, so her total distance walked is still becoming greater.]**

Check

Ask: How can you tell which segment has the fastest rate? **[The line has the steepest slope.]**

Ask: How can you tell which segment has the slowest rate? **[The line has the flattest slope.]**

COMMON MISCONCEPTION

Ask: What is the Error?

Jamal says that Mia walks faster during Segment 2 than during Segment 5 because Segment 2 has a positive slope and Segment 5 has a negative slope.

Reason incorrect: The graph is showing distance from home, not total distance traveled.

Solution: Segment 5 is the steepest line in the graph, even though the steepness, or slope is negative. The segment with the steepest line is the segment during which Mia walked the fastest.

Say: The slope of the line represents Mia's speed. Distance is always a positive value, therefore speed is also always a positive value. The sign of the slope represents the direction Mia is walking in relation to her home.

ADDITIONAL ONLINE INTERVENTION RESOURCES

Use the following for students who have not mastered the concepts in Skill 27.

- Math on the Spot videos

- Personal Math Trainer with customized intervention

- Building Block worksheets (Skill 41: Generate Ordered Pairs; Skill 43: Graph Functions; Skill 44: Graph Linear Functions)

SKILL 27   Rate of Change and Slope

Vocabulary

Rate of change

Slope of a line

Example 1

A rate of change describes the relationship between two changing quantities. You can use the following formula to find rate of change:

$$\text{Rate of change} = \frac{\text{change in dependent variable}}{\text{change in independent variable}}$$

A. Tell whether the rate(s) of change is constant or variable.

x	−2	0	4	10
y	3	4	6	9

Find the rate of change from one column of the table to the next.

$$\frac{4-3}{0-(-2)} = \frac{1}{2} \qquad \frac{6-4}{4-0} = \frac{2}{4} = \frac{1}{2} \qquad \frac{9-6}{10-4} = \frac{3}{6} = \frac{1}{2}$$

The rate of change is constant and equals $\frac{1}{2}$.

B. Tell whether the rate(s) of change is constant or variable.

x	−4	−2	2	4
y	6	3	3	6

Find the rate of change from one column of the table to the next.

$$\frac{3-6}{-2-(-4)} = \frac{-3}{2} \qquad \frac{3-3}{2-(-2)} = \frac{0}{4} = 0 \qquad \frac{6-3}{4-2} = \frac{3}{2}$$

The rates of change are not the same, so they are variable.

Check

Tell whether the rate(s) of change is constant or variable.

1.

x	−2	0	1	3
y	−16	0	2	54

2.

x	−3	0	10	15
y	−14	−5	25	40

_____   _____

3. Kyle uses an app that keeps track of the total distance he runs throughout the month. Tell whether Kyle's rate of change in total distance over time is constant or variable.

Day of Month	5	13	18	31
Total Distance (mi)	22.5	58.5	81	139.5

_____

Example 2

You can also find rate of change from a graph.

A. Use the graph. Tell whether the rate(s) of change is constant or variable.

Find the rate of change from one ordered pair to the next.

$$\frac{32-16}{4-2}=\frac{16}{2}=8$$

$$\frac{48-32}{6-4}=\frac{16}{2}=8$$

$$\frac{64-48}{8-6}=\frac{16}{2}=8$$

The rate of change is constant and is equal to 8.

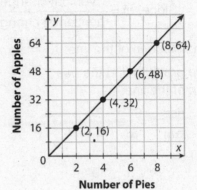

B. Use the graph. Tell whether the rate(s) of change is constant or variable.

Find the rate of change from one ordered pair to the next.

$$\frac{20-15}{2-1}=\frac{5}{1}=5$$

$$\frac{15-20}{3-2}=\frac{-5}{1}=-5$$

$$\frac{0-15}{4-3}=\frac{-15}{1}=-15$$

The rates of change are not the same, so they are variable.

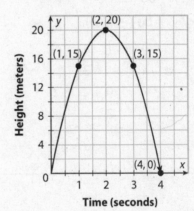

Check

Tell whether the rate(s) of change is constant or variable.

4.

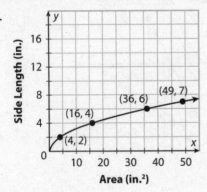

5.

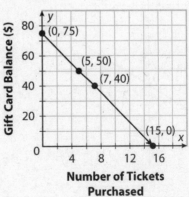

Example 3

When two quantities have a linear relationship, the rate of change is constant. The constant rate of change is called the slope of the line. You can use the following equivalent formulas to find the slope of a line:

$$\text{Slope, } m = \frac{\text{vertical change}}{\text{horizontal change}} = \frac{\text{rise}}{\text{run}} = \frac{y_2 - y_1}{x_2 - x_1}$$

A. Find the slope m of the line.

Use the graph to find the *rise* and *run* of the line.

$$\text{slope} = \frac{\text{rise}}{\text{run}} = \frac{6}{-8} = -\frac{3}{4}$$

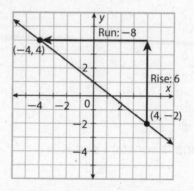

B. Find the slope m of the line.

Let (x_1, y_1) be $(2, 4)$.

Let (x_2, y_2) be $(-1, -5)$.

$$\text{slope} = \frac{y_2 - y_1}{x_2 - x_1} = \frac{-5 - 4}{-1 - 2}$$
$$= \frac{-9}{-3}$$
$$= 3$$

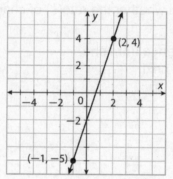

Check

Find the slope of each line.

6.

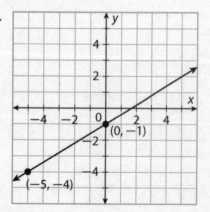

7.

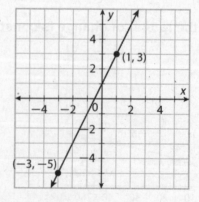

_____   _____

Example 4

You can use rate of change and slope to analyze a graph.

Mia goes for a walk. The graph shows her distance from home over time. Describe how Mia's time and distance from home are related at each section of the graph.

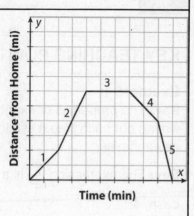

Segment 1 shows a line with a positive slope. This means that Mia's distance from home is increasing at a constant rate over time.

Segment 2 shows a steeper line with a positive slope. This means that Mia's distance from home is increasing at an even faster constant rate over time.

Segment 3 shows a line with a slope of 0. This means that Mia's distance from home is not changing during this period of time.

Segment 4 shows a line with a negative slope. This means that Mia's distance from home is decreasing at a constant rate over time.

Segment 5 shows a steeper line with a negative slope. This means that Mia's distance from home is decreasing at an even faster constant rate over time.

Check

Use the graph above to answer the following questions.

8. During which segment(s) does Mia walk at her fastest rate? _____

9. During which segment(s) does Mia walk at her slowest rate? _____

10. Which segment represents a period of time during which Mia may have stopped to take a break? _____

11. Explain the Error. Then find the correct solution. _____

   Jamal says that Mia walks faster during Segment 2 than during Segment 5 because Segment 2 has a positive slope and Segment 5 has a negative slope.

SKILL 27 RATE OF CHANGE AND SLOPE

Rational and Radical Exponents

KEY TEACHING POINTS

Example 1

Say: The properties of exponents allow you to simplify expressions with exponents without writing out each step. Let's look at the Quotient of Powers and Power of a Power properties as examples.

Say: The expression $\dfrac{4^5}{4^3}$ is a division of exponential expressions that each have the same base, 4.

Ask: What are exponents? **[Numbers that tell you how many times the base is a factor.]**

How can you rewrite $\dfrac{4^5}{4^3}$ without exponents? $\left[\dfrac{4 \cdot 4 \cdot 4 \cdot 4 \cdot 4}{4 \cdot 4 \cdot 4}\right]$

Say: You can reduce this fraction by canceling out factors.

Show the following work:

$$\frac{\cancel{4} \cdot \cancel{4} \cdot \cancel{4} \cdot 4 \cdot 4}{\cancel{4} \cdot \cancel{4} \cdot \cancel{4}} = \frac{4 \cdot 4}{1} = 4^2$$

Say: The Power of a Power property lets you multiply the exponents when a power is raised to a power.

Say: The expression $\left(2^3\right)^4$ can be written as $\left(2^3\right)\left(2^3\right)\left(2^3\right)\left(2^3\right)$. At this point, you could use the Product of Powers and add the exponents. $3 + 3 + 3 + 3 = 12$. Or you could continue to write the exponent as multiplication. Let's separate each $\left(2^3\right)$ into its factors.

$$\left[(2)(2)(2)\right]\left[(2)(2)(2)\right]\left[(2)(2)(2)\right]\left[(2)(2)(2)\right]$$

This can be written as one exponential expression. The base 2 is multiplied 12 times, so the expression is 2^{12}.

Check

Say: A negative exponent can be rewritten as the reciprocal with a positive exponent. The expression 3^{-4} written with a positive exponent is $\dfrac{1}{3^4}$.

Ask: How can you write $(-1)^{-3}$ with a positive exponent? **[$(-1)^3$]** The negative exponent moves to the numerator. -1 to any odd power is -1.

Say: Many times expressions can be simplified in more than one way. The Power of a Product property says that you can rewrite $(-5 \cdot 9)^2$ as $(-5)^2(9)^2$ which simplifies to $(25)(81) = 2025$. This expression can also be simplified by multiplying the values inside the parentheses first. $(-5 \cdot 9)^2 = (-45)^2 = 2025$

KEY TEACHING POINTS

Example 2

Say: A radical is the inverse of an exponent. Radicals and exponents do the opposite of each other. This means that $\sqrt{5^2} = 5$ because the radical and square undo each other.

Ask: What is the radicand in the expression $\sqrt[3]{8}$? **[8]**

Check

Say: The index of a radical expression tells how many times the value under the symbol is a factor.

Ask: What number, when multiplied by itself, is equal to 144? **[12]** So the value of $\sqrt{144}$ is 12.

Ask: What number, when multiplied by itself three times, is equal to 27? **[3]** So the value of $\sqrt[3]{27}$ is 3.

Ask: What non-negative number, when multiplied by itself four times, is equal to 81? **[3]** So the value of $\sqrt[4]{81}$ is 3. Is there a negative value that when multiplied by itself four times, is equal to 81? **[Yes, –3.]**

ALTERNATE STRATEGY

Strategy: Use algebra tiles.

1. **Say:** Algebra tiles can be used as an area model to find square roots.

2. To simplify the expression $\sqrt{16}$, you must find the number that, when multiplied by itself, results in 16.

3. Begin with 16 unit tiles. Set the tiles up so that they form a square. The area of a square is found by multiplying a side length by itself.

4. The square is a side length of 4 units. There are a total of 16 units. Therefore, $(4)(4) = 16$ and $\sqrt{16} = 4$.

KEY TEACHING POINTS

Example 3

Say: Fractional exponents have the same effect as a radical sign. The Power of a Power Property can be used to illustrate this. You've just seen that radicals and roots are opposite, so you know that $\sqrt{9} = \sqrt{3^2} = 3$ and the Power of a Power Property says that $\left(3^2\right)^{\frac{1}{2}} = 3^{(2)\left(\frac{1}{2}\right)} = 3^1 = 3$.

Say: Because both $\sqrt{3^2}$ and $\left(3^2\right)^{\frac{1}{2}}$ equal 3, they also equal each other. $\sqrt{3^2} = \left(3^2\right)^{\frac{1}{2}}$.

This means that the radical sign has the same effect as the exponent $\frac{1}{2}$.

Check

Ask: How can $(-1)^{\frac{1}{3}}$ be written as a radical? [$\sqrt[3]{-1}$]

Say: $1000^{\frac{1}{3}} - 144^{\frac{1}{2}}$ have different bases.

Complete the following work.

$\sqrt[3]{1000} - \sqrt{144}$	Rewrite each term using a radical symbol first.
$10 - 12$	Evaluate each term.
-2	Simplify.

Example 4

Say: The properties of exponents apply to fractional exponents in the same way as they do integer exponents.

Say: You can use the Power of a Power Property to break exponents into factors and rewrite them using the radical symbol.

Ask: What property of exponents is used in method 2? **[Product of Powers Property]**

Say: The product of powers says that when you multiply exponential expressions with the same base, you can add the exponents and keep the base. This means that you can also break the exponent into factors whose exponents have a sum of the original expression.

Check

Say: Both methods have the same result. Let's look at a problem with the difference of two fractional exponential expressions.

Say: $343^{\frac{2}{3}} - 243^{\frac{3}{5}}$ have different bases.

Complete the following work.

$343^{\frac{1}{3} \cdot 2} - 243^{\frac{1}{5} \cdot 3}$	Rewrite each term as a product.
$\left(343^{\frac{1}{3}}\right)^2 - \left(243^{\frac{1}{5}}\right)^3$	Use the Power of a Power property on each term.
$\left(\sqrt[3]{343}\right)^2 - \left(\sqrt[5]{243}\right)^3$	Rewrite each fractional exponent as a radical.
$\left(\sqrt[3]{7^3}\right)^2 - \left(\sqrt[5]{3^5}\right)^3$	Rewrite each radicand as a power.
$(7)^2 - (3)^3$	Simplify.
$49 - 27 = 22$	Simplify.

COMMON MISCONCEPTION

Ask: What is the Error?

$$16^{\frac{3}{4}} = 16^{\frac{1}{4} \cdot 3} = \left(16^{\frac{1}{4}}\right)^3 = \left(\sqrt[4]{16}\right)^3 = \left(\sqrt[4]{4^4}\right)^3 = (4)^3 = 64$$

Reason incorrect: 16 written as a power of 4 is 2^4, not 4^4.

Solution:

$$16^{\frac{3}{4}} = 16^{\frac{1}{4} \cdot 3} = \left(16^{\frac{1}{4}}\right)^3 = \left(\sqrt[4]{16}\right)^3 = \left(\sqrt[4]{2^4}\right)^3 = (2)^3 = 8$$

Say: Watch the index carefully. Not every radical is a square root.

KEY TEACHING POINTS

Example 5
Say: Finding unknown lengths in two- and three-dimensional figures often involves radicals or rational exponents.

Say: When you know the length of a side of a square, how can you find the area? **[Multiply it by itself, or square it.]**

Ask: When you know the area of a square, how can you find the side length? **[Find the square root.]** How can you write a square root using an exponent? **[Use a fractional exponent.]**

Ask: When you know the volume of a cube, how can you find the side length? **[Find the cube root.]** How can you write a cube root using an exponent? **[Use a fractional exponent.]**

Check
Say: The formula for the area of a circle is $A = \pi r^2$. When the formula is rewritten as the radius in terms of the Area, it is $r = \left(\dfrac{A}{\pi}\right)^{\frac{1}{2}}$.

Ask: How can you rewrite $r = \left(\dfrac{A}{\pi}\right)^{\frac{1}{2}}$ using a radical symbol? $\left[r = \sqrt{\dfrac{A}{\pi}} \right]$

ADDITIONAL ONLINE INTERVENTION RESOURCES

 Use the following for students who have not mastered the concepts in Skill 28.

- Math on the Spot videos
- Personal Math Trainer with customized intervention
- Building Block worksheets (Skill 29: Evaluate Powers; Skill 75: Properties of Exponents; Skill 100: Squares and Square Roots)

Rational and Radical Exponents

Example 1

Remember the following properties of exponents. You can use these properties to simplify expressions containing exponents.

Properties of Exponents		
Property		**Example**
Zero Exponent	$a^0 = 1$	$8^0 = 1$
Negative Exponent	$a^{-n} = \dfrac{1}{a^n}, \ a \neq 0$	$6^{-2} = \dfrac{1}{6^2} = \dfrac{1}{36}$
Product of Powers	$a^m \cdot a^n = a^{m+n}$	$3^2 \cdot 3^4 = 3^{2+4} = 3^6$
Quotient of Powers	$\dfrac{a^m}{a^n} = a^{m-n}, \ a \neq 0$	$\dfrac{4^5}{4^3} = 4^{5-3} = 4^2$
Power of a Product	$(a \cdot b)^n = a^n b^n$	$(2 \cdot 3)^4 = 2^4 \cdot 3^4$
Power of a Quotient	$\left(\dfrac{a}{b}\right)^n = \dfrac{a^n}{b^n}, \ b \neq 0$	$\left(\dfrac{3}{5}\right)^4 = \dfrac{3^4}{5^4}$
Power of a Power	$\left(a^m\right)^n = a^{mn}$	$\left(2^3\right)^4 = 2^{3 \cdot 4} = 2^{12}$

Vocabulary
Radical symbol
Square root
Cube root
Radicand
Radical expression
Rational exponents

Check
Simplify each expression.

1. 15^0 _____

2. 7.536^0 _____

3. $\left(\dfrac{3}{4}\right)^0$ _____

4. 2^{-2} _____

5. 3^{-4} _____

6. $(-1)^{-3}$ _____

7. $5^2 \cdot 5^4$ _____

8. $2^4 \cdot 2^{-3} \cdot 2^2$ _____

9. $(-6)^6 \cdot (-6)^{-3}$ _____

10. $\dfrac{9^{11}}{9^7}$ _____

11. $\dfrac{8^{10}}{8^{-4}}$ _____

12. $\dfrac{7^3 \cdot 7^6}{7 \cdot 7^2}$ _____

13. $(10 \cdot 3)^5$ _____

14. $(-5 \cdot 9)^2$ _____

15. $(-3 \cdot 8)^{-4}$ _____

16. $\left(\dfrac{3}{7}\right)^2$ _____

17. $\left(\dfrac{5}{12}\right)^3$ _____

18. $\left(\dfrac{-5}{8}\right)^4$ _____

19. $\left(12^2\right)^3$ _____

20. $\left(2^{-2}\right)^{-3}$ _____

21. $\left(13^2\right)^{-1}$ _____

Example 2

The radical symbol $\sqrt{}$ indicates a nonnegative square root. The symbol $\sqrt[3]{}$ indicates a cube root. In general, the symbol $\sqrt[n]{}$ indicates an nth root.

$\sqrt{25} = 5$ because $5 \cdot 5 = 25$. $\qquad$ $\sqrt[3]{8} = 2$ because $2 \cdot 2 \cdot 2 = 8$.

The expression under the radical symbol is the radicand. An expression that contains radicals is a radical expression.

Check

Simplify each expression.

22. $\sqrt{16}$ _____

23. $\sqrt{144}$ _____

24. $\sqrt[3]{27}$ _____

25. $\sqrt[3]{-125}$ _____

26. $\sqrt[4]{16}$ _____

27. $\sqrt[4]{81}$ _____

Example 3

An exponent can be expressed as a fraction. Fractional exponents are called rational exponents.

The equations $3 \cdot 3 = 9$ and $9^{\frac{1}{2}} = 3$ are equivalent. The equation $9^{\frac{1}{2}} = 3$ indicates that 3 is the positive number that, when used as a factor twice, equals 9.

In general, a number raised to the power of $\frac{1}{n}$ is equal to the nth root of that number: $a^{\frac{1}{n}} = \sqrt[n]{a}$, where $a \geq 0$ and n is an integer greater than 1. You can simplify powers that have a rational exponent.

Simplify $64^{\frac{1}{3}}$.

$64^{\frac{1}{3}} = \sqrt[3]{64}$ $\qquad$ Use the definition of $a^{\frac{1}{n}}$.

$\phantom{64^{\frac{1}{3}}} = \sqrt[3]{4^3}$ $\qquad$ Rewrite the radicand as a cube.

$\phantom{64^{\frac{1}{3}}} = 4$ $\qquad$ Simplify.

Check

Simplify each expression.

28. $(-1)^{\frac{1}{3}}$ _____

29. $121^{\frac{1}{2}}$ _____

30. $256^{\frac{1}{4}}$ _____

31. $0^{\frac{1}{5}}$ _____

32. $10{,}000^{\frac{1}{4}} + 1^{\frac{1}{5}}$ _____

33. $1000^{\frac{1}{3}} - 144^{\frac{1}{2}}$ _____

Example 4

You can use the properties of exponents to simplify expressions that contain rational exponents.

Simplify $81^{\frac{3}{4}}$.

Method 1

$81^{\frac{3}{4}} = 81^{\frac{1}{4} \cdot 3}$ Write the exponent as a product.

$= \left(81^{\frac{1}{4}}\right)^3$ Power of a Power Property

$= \left(\sqrt[4]{81}\right)^3$ Definition of $a^{\frac{1}{n}}$

$= \left(\sqrt[4]{3^4}\right)^3$ Rewrite the radicand as a power of 4.

$= (3)^3$ Simplify.

$= 27$ Simplify.

Method 2

$81^{\frac{3}{4}} = 81^{\frac{1}{4}} \cdot 81^{\frac{1}{4}} \cdot 81^{\frac{1}{4}}$ Rewrite the expression.

$= \sqrt[4]{81} \cdot \sqrt[4]{81} \cdot \sqrt[4]{81}$ Definition of $a^{\frac{1}{n}}$

$= \sqrt[4]{3^4} \cdot \sqrt[4]{3^4} \cdot \sqrt[4]{3^4}$ Rewrite each radicand as a power of 4.

$= 3 \cdot 3 \cdot 3$ Simplify.

$= 27$ Simplify.

Check

Simplify each expression.

34. $256^{\frac{3}{4}}$ _____

35. $64^{\frac{2}{3}}$ _____

36. $243^{\frac{4}{5}}$ _____

37. $625^{\frac{3}{4}}$ _____

38. $1000^{\frac{2}{3}} + 1^{\frac{3}{4}}$ _____

39. $343^{\frac{2}{3}} - 243^{\frac{3}{5}}$ _____

40. Explain the Error. Then find the correct solution.

$16^{\frac{3}{4}} = 16^{\frac{1}{4} \cdot 3}$

$= \left(16^{\frac{1}{4}}\right)^3$

$= \left(\sqrt[4]{16}\right)^3$

$= \left(\sqrt[4]{4^4}\right)^3$

$= (4)^3$

$= 64$

Example 5

You can solve real-world problems that involve radicals and rational exponents.

A. The relationship between the side length, *s*, of a square and its area, *A*, is $s = A^{\frac{1}{2}}$. What is the side length of a square that has an area of 169 square units?

$s = A^{\frac{1}{2}}$ Write the formula.

$= 169^{\frac{1}{2}}$ Substitute 169 for *A*.

$= \sqrt{13^2}$ Rewrite the radicand as a square.

$s = 13$ Simplify.

The side length of the square is 13 units.

B. The relationship between the side length, *s*, of a cube and its volume, *V*, is $s = V^{\frac{1}{3}}$. What is the side length of a cube that has a volume of 729 cubic units?

$s = V^{\frac{1}{3}}$ Write the formula.

$= 729^{\frac{1}{3}}$ Substitute 729 for *V*.

$= \sqrt[3]{9^3}$ Rewrite the radicand as a cube.

$s = 9$ Simplify.

The side length of the cube is 9 units.

Check

Solve.

41. Use the formula from Part A above. What is the side length of a square that has an area of 81 square units?

_____

42. The relationship between the radius, *r*, of a circle and its area, *A*, is $r = \left(\dfrac{A}{\pi}\right)^{\frac{1}{2}}$. What is the radius of a circle that has an area of 36π square units? _____

SKILL 28 RATIONAL AND RADICAL EXPONENTS

Rational Number Operations

KEY TEACHING POINTS

Example 1

Say: Signed rational numbers follow the same rules for operations as integers.

Remind students of the rules for addition and subtraction of signed numbers.

- When two signed numbers have the same sign, add their absolute values. The answer is the sum with the common sign.

- When two rational numbers have opposite signs, subtract their absolute values. The answer is the difference with the sign of the number with the greater absolute value.

Ask: In part A, what operation is used? **[Addition.]** Explain how you know. **[The recipe has two types of liquid. The question asks for the total, so you need to add.]**

Ask: Can you add the rational numbers without rewriting the mixed number as an improper fraction? **[Yes.]**

Show the following work:

$$1\frac{1}{3} + \frac{1}{4} = 1\frac{1 \cdot 4}{3 \cdot 4} + \frac{1 \cdot 3}{4 \cdot 3}$$ Rewrite the fraction part with the LCD.

$$= 1\frac{4}{12} + \frac{3}{12}$$ Simplify.

$$= 1\frac{7}{12}$$ Keep the whole number part, add the numerators.

Ask: In part B, what operation is used? **[Addition.]** Explain how you know. **[Jeremy has a bank balance, and he adds more money. This is addition.]**

Say: Sometimes thinking about what happens in the problem can help you tell if the answer makes sense. Jeremy starts with a negative balance in his account. Then he adds some money. He adds more money than his negative balance.

Ask: Should the new balance be negative, or positive? **[Positive.]**

Check

Ask: What operation is used in problem 1? **[Addition.]** Explain how you know. **[Amy walked a distance, then ran another distance. The problem asks for the total distance. This is addition.]**

Ask: The scuba diver in problem 2 is 73.6 feet below the surface. Is this a positive or negative value? **[Negative.]** The diver rises 24.7 feet. Is this a positive or negative addition? **[Positive.]** What rule for adding signed numbers should be used? **[Find the difference of the absolute values. The answer takes the sign of the addend with the greater absolute value.]**

Ask: How can you tell the sign of the answer in problem 2 without doing the computations? **[The diver starts below the surface, at a negative value. The diver rises, but not as far as they were from the surface. Because the diver does not make it back to the surface, the diver's depth is represented by a negative number.]**

KEY TEACHING POINTS

Example 2

Ask: In part A, what operation is used? **[Subtraction.]** Explain how you know. **[You are decreasing the temperature, this is subtraction.]**

Ask: How can this same problem be thought of as addition? **[You could think of decreasing the temperature as adding a negative temperature.]**

Ask: Both of the numbers are negative. What is the sum of two negative values? **[A negative value.]** Does a negative answer make sense in the problem? Explain. **[Yes, the temperature was below freezing and got colder, so it is still below freezing.]**

Say: Read the problem in part B carefully. What are you trying to find? **[The change in water level.]** You are being asked about the difference in the water level. Difference is subtraction.

Check

Say: Problem 4 is about a stake that is in the ground. A portion of the stake is above ground, and a portion is below ground. You can think of the stake as a vertical number line. One end of the stake is at $15\frac{5}{8}$ and the other is at $-6\frac{3}{4}$.

Ask: What are you trying to find? **[The length of the stake.]** How can you find the length of the stake? **[You can either subtract the negative length below the ground, or add the positive length below the ground.]**

Ask: What is the least common denominator of $15\frac{5}{8}$ and $-6\frac{3}{4}$? **[8]**

Complete the following together.

$$15\frac{5}{8} - \left(-6\frac{3}{4}\right) = 15\frac{5}{8} + 6\frac{3}{4} \quad \text{Rewrite subtraction as addition.}$$

$$= 15\frac{5}{8} + 6\frac{6}{8} \quad \text{Rewrite the fractions using the LCD.}$$

$$= 21\frac{11}{8} \quad \text{Add the whole numbers and add the fractions.}$$

$$= 22\frac{3}{8} \quad \text{Rewrite the improper fraction as part of the whole number.}$$

Ask: Does a positive answer make sense? **[Yes, the answer is a length, and length is always positive.]**

ALTERNATE STRATEGY

Strategy: Draw a sketch.

1. **Say:** A sketch can help you determine what is happening in the problem and what operation is needed to find the solution.

2. The temperature inside a refrigerator is −1.9°C.
   You adjust the setting of the refrigerator, and the temperature decreases by 3.9°C.

3. Let's think of the problem as a thermometer. The temperature started below 0, at 1.9°C. Make a simple sketch. It does not have to be detailed, it can be as simple as a line, like a vertical number line.

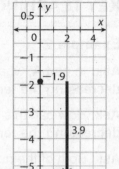

4. The temperature decreases by 3.9°C. Show this in your sketch by an arrow down, for decreasing.

5. From the sketch, you can tell that you should either subtract 3.9, or add a negative 3.9. You can also tell the answer is going to be a negative value because it is still below 0°C.

KEY TEACHING POINTS

Example 3
Ask: What are the rules for multiplying signed numbers? **[When the signs are the same, the product is positive. When the signs are different, the product is negative.]**

Ask: In part A, Laura is using her debit card to pay the same amount every day for 5 days. What operation is used? **[Multiplication.]** Is a debit a positive or negative value? **[Negative.]** Is the number of days positive or negative? **[Positive.]** What sign will the product be? **[Negative.]**

Say: In part B, the contractor is installing fence in sections that are all the same length. This is multiplication.

Check
Ask: Patrick is rappelling down. Is this positive or negative? **[Negative.]** He stops 8 times. Is this positive or negative? **[Positive.]** Is the overall change in altitude positive or negative? **[Negative.]**

COMMON MISCONCEPTION

Ask: What is the Error?

Tim has a large bag of birdseed. Each day during the summer, he scoops $2\frac{2}{3}$ cups of birdseed out of the bag and pours it into the feeder. After 30 days, what is the overall change in the amount of birdseed in the bag?

$30\left(2\frac{2}{3}\right) = 30\left(\frac{8}{3}\right) = \frac{240}{3} = 80$. So the overall change in the amount of birdseed is 80 cups.

Reason incorrect: Tim is removing birdseed from the bag, so the daily change in the bag is negative, not positive.

Solution: $30\left(-2\frac{2}{3}\right) = 30\left(-\frac{8}{3}\right) = -\frac{240}{3} = -80$

KEY TEACHING POINTS

Example 4

Say: Rational number division follows the same rules as multiplication. If the numbers have the same sign, the quotient is positive. If the numbers have different signs, the quotient is negative.

Ask: In part A, what are you trying to find? **[The change in the account balance each month.]**

Say: You are given the change for many months, and you need to find the change for one month. This is a division problem.

Ask: Is Sarah's total change in her account balance positive or negative? **[Negative.]** Is the change per month positive or negative? **[Negative.]**

Ask: What word in part B tells you this is a division problem? **[Divide.]** Sean starts with a 4-pound bag of nuts and bolts. He divides them into $\frac{2}{5}$-pound bags. Are there more or less than 4 bags? **[More.]** Explain. **[When a number is divided by a value between 0 and 1, the quotient is greater than the original number.]**

Check

Ask: Is the overall change in the volume of the water positive or negative? **[Negative.]**

Ask: What rational number represents the seagull's flight? **[−24.5]** How long did the descent take? **[3.5 seconds]** What expression represents the seagull's change in altitude per minute?

$$\left[\frac{-24.5}{3.5}\right]$$

ADDITIONAL ONLINE INTERVENTION RESOURCES

 Use the following for students who have not mastered the concepts in Skill 29.

- Math on the Spot videos

- Personal Math Trainer with customized intervention

- Building Block worksheets (Skill 4: Add and Subtract Integers; Skill 61: Multiply and Divide Integers)

Rational Number Operations

Example 1

To add rational numbers with the *same* sign, use the rules for adding integers. The sum has the same sign as the sign of the two numbers.

A. **A cornbread recipe calls for $1\frac{1}{3}$ cups of milk and $\frac{1}{4}$ cup of vegetable oil. How many cups of liquid does the recipe call for?**

Find $1\frac{1}{3} + \frac{1}{4}$.

$1\frac{1}{3} + \frac{1}{4} = \frac{4}{3} + \frac{1}{4}$ Write the mixed number as an improper fraction.

$= \frac{4 \cdot 4}{3 \cdot 4} + \frac{1 \cdot 3}{4 \cdot 3}$ Rewrite the fractions with the LCD.

$= \frac{16}{12} + \frac{3}{12}$ Simplify.

$= \frac{19}{12}$, or $1\frac{7}{12}$ Add the numerators. Write as a mixed number.

The recipe calls for $1\frac{7}{12}$ cups of liquid.

To add rational numbers with *different* signs, find the difference of their absolute values. The sum has the sign of the number with the greater absolute value.

B. **Jeremy's checking account balance is –$25.73. He makes a deposit of $45. What is his new account balance?**

Find $-25.73 + 45$.

$|-25.73| = 25.73$ and $|45| = 45$ Find the absolute value of each number.

$\begin{array}{r} 45 \\ -25.73 \\ \hline \end{array} \longrightarrow \begin{array}{r} 45.00 \\ -25.73 \\ \hline 19.27 \end{array}$ Subtract the lesser absolute value from the greater.

$-25.73 + 45 = 19.27$ The sum has the same sign as 45.

Jeremy's new account balance is $19.27.

Check

1. Amy walks $\frac{3}{4}$ mile. Then she runs $3\frac{2}{3}$ miles. Altogether, how far does

    Amy travel? _____

2. A scuba diver is 73.6 feet below the surface of the ocean. She rises

   24.7 feet. How far is the diver from the surface of the ocean? _____

Example 2

To subtract a rational number, add its opposite.

A. The temperature inside a freezer is –23.8°C. You adjust the setting of the freezer, and the temperature decreases by 6.2°C. What is the final temperature inside the freezer?

Find $-23.8 - 6.2$.

$$-23.8 - 6.2 = -23.8 + (-6.2)$$ To subtract 6.2, add its opposite.

$$= -30$$ Use the rules for adding rational numbers with the same sign: the sum of two negative numbers is negative.

The final temperature inside the freezer is –30°C.

B. The level of a lake is $\frac{1}{2}$ foot below full pool. The dam is opened so that water can be released. The level of the lake falls to $4\frac{3}{4}$ feet below full pool. What is the overall change in the level of the lake?

Find $-\frac{1}{2} - \left(-4\frac{3}{4}\right)$.

$$-\frac{1}{2} - \left(-4\frac{3}{4}\right) = -\frac{1}{2} + 4\frac{3}{4}$$ To subtract $-4\frac{3}{4}$, add its opposite.

$$= -\frac{1}{2} + \frac{19}{4}$$ Rewrite the mixed number as an improper fraction.

$$= -\frac{2}{4} + \frac{19}{4}$$ Rewrite the fractions using the LCD.

$$= \frac{17}{4}, \text{ or } 4\frac{1}{4}$$ Add the numerators. Write the answer as a mixed number.

The overall change in the level of the lake is $4\frac{1}{4}$ feet.

Check

3. The temperature inside a refrigerator is –1.6°C. You adjust the setting of the refrigerator, and the temperature decreases by 3.9°C. What is

   the final temperature inside the refrigerator? _____

4. A stake inserted in the ground rises $15\frac{5}{8}$ in. above ground level and

   extends $6\frac{3}{4}$ in. below ground level. How long is the stake? _____

Example 3

To multiply rational numbers, use the rules for multiplying integers. If the two factors have the same sign, the product is positive. If the two factors have different signs, the product is negative.

A. Laura uses her debit card each day to buy lunch. She buys a total of 5 lunches throughout the week, and each lunch costs $5.75. What is the overall change in the balance of her account?

Find $5(-5.75)$.

$5(-5.75) = -28.75$

The factors have different signs, so the product is negative.

The overall change in the balance of Laura's account is $-\$28.75$.

B. A contractor installs a fence around a playground. He uses a total of 35 sections of fencing. Each section is $8\frac{1}{4}$ feet long. What is the total length of the fence?

Find $35\left(8\frac{1}{4}\right)$.

$35\left(8\frac{1}{4}\right) = \frac{35}{1}\left(\frac{33}{4}\right)$ Write the mixed number as an improper fraction.

$= \frac{1155}{4}$ Multiply numerators. Then multiply denominators.

$= 288\frac{3}{4}$ Write the product as a mixed number.

The total length of the fence is $288\frac{3}{4}$ feet.

Check

5. Patrick rappelled down the side of a mountain. He stopped every 12.5 feet to rest. He stopped a total of 8 times. What was Patrick's

   overall change in altitude? _____

6. Explain the Error. Then find the correct solution.

   Tim has a large bag of birdseed. Each day during the summer, he

   scoops $2\frac{2}{3}$ cups of birdseed out of the bag and pours it into the

   feeder. After 30 days, what is the overall change in the amount of birdseed in the bag?

   $30\left(2\frac{2}{3}\right) = 30\left(\frac{8}{3}\right) = \frac{240}{3} = 80.$ So the overall change in the amount of

   birdseed is 80 cups. _____

Example 4

To divide rational numbers, use the rules for dividing integers. If the dividend and divisor have the same sign, the quotient is positive. If the dividend and divisor have different signs, the quotient is negative.

A. Over 12 months, Sarah used her debit card to pay a total of $580.20 to a grocery delivery service. She paid the same amount each month. What was the change in Sarah's account balance each month to pay for the service?

Find $\dfrac{-580.20}{12}$.

$\dfrac{-580.20}{12} = -48.35$ The dividend and divisor have different signs, so the quotient is negative.

The change in Sarah's account balance each month is –$48.35.

B. Sean wants to divide a 4-pound package of nuts and bolts into small bags. Each bag will hold $\dfrac{2}{5}$ pound of nuts and bolts. How many bags can Sean fill?

Find $4 \div \dfrac{2}{5}$.

$4 \div \dfrac{2}{5} = \dfrac{4}{1} \div \dfrac{2}{5}$ Write the dividend as a fraction.

$= \dfrac{4}{1} \cdot \dfrac{5}{2}$ To divide by the fraction, multiply by its reciprocal.

$= \dfrac{20}{2}$, or 10   Multiply numerators. Multiply denominators. Simplify.

Sean can fill 10 bags.

Check

Simplify each expression.

7. A swimming pool has a leak in its liner. The pool loses a total of $53\dfrac{3}{4}$ gallons of water in 5 days. On average, what is the change in the volume of the water in the pool each day?_____

8. A seagull descended 24.5 feet in 3.5 seconds. What was the seagull's average change in altitude per second? _____

SKILL 29 RATIONAL NUMBER OPERATIONS

Real Numbers

KEY TEACHING POINTS

Example 1

Say: Rational numbers can be written as ratios of integers, or fractions. All rational numbers can also be written as a decimal that either ends or has a repeating pattern in its digits.

Ask: Is 0.75 a rational number? **[Yes.]** How can you tell? **[It can be written as the ratio of 3 to 4 or $\frac{3}{4}$, or it is a terminating decimal.]**

Say: What is the difference between a terminating decimal and a repeating decimal? **[A terminating decimal ends and a repeating decimal keeps going forever in a pattern.]**

Ask: How do you convert a rational number that is written as a fraction into a decimal? **[Divide the numerator by the denominator.]**

Check

Say: You can tell quickly if some fractions are the equivalent of terminating decimals. The fraction $\frac{3}{25}$ has a 25 in the denominator. Denominators that are factors of powers of 10 will always result in a terminating decimal. The denominator 25 is a factor of 100. $\frac{3}{25}$ can be written as $\frac{3 \cdot 4}{25 \cdot 4} = \frac{12}{100} = 0.12$.

Ask: Is the decimal form of $\frac{19}{33}$ a terminating or repeating decimal? **[Repeating, $0.\overline{57}$.]**

Say: In some cases, only one digit repeats, while in others a pattern of digits repeats. Make sure that you include the fraction bar over the entire set of digits that repeats.

Example 2

Say: You can write any terminating or repeating decimal as a fraction. Terminating decimals can be written over a power of 10 and then simplified.

Ask: What is the purpose in multiplying the decimal $0.\overline{3}$ by 10? **[To remove the repeating part.]** Does this work when the repeating digit was not in the tenths place? Explain. **[Yes. The result after subtraction just has more decimal places.]**

Check

Ask: The decimal 0.825 is a terminating decimal. How do you decide what power of ten is in the denominator? **[There are 3 decimal places, so put in over the power of ten with 3 zeros, 1000.]**

Ask: In the decimal $0.\overline{37}$ there are 2 repeating digits. When you set $x = 0.\overline{37}$, what should you multiply by in the next step? **[100]**

KEY TEACHING POINTS

Example 3

Say: Irrational numbers cannot be written in fraction form. The decimal expansion of an irrational number is a decimal that never ends and never repeats.

Ask: Is a decimal with a pattern in the digits rational or irrational? **[It could be either.]** Decimals with repeating patterns are rational numbers, but not all patterns are repeating. For example, 0.123456789101112131415… does not ever repeat, but it does have a pattern.

Ask: What does the radical sign mean? **[To take the square root of a number.]** What is a square root? **[A square root is the number that when multiplied by itself will result in the number under the radical sign.]**

Ask: Are all numbers that are written as radicals also irrational? Explain. **[No. Rational numbers can be written as radicals before they are simplified, for example $\sqrt{49} = 7$, which is a rational number.]**

Check

Ask: Between what two perfect squares does 6 fall? **[4 and 9]** So, between what two whole numbers does $\sqrt{6}$ fall? **[2 and 3]** Does it fall closer to 2 or 3? **[2]** Using your calculator, what is the value of $\sqrt{6}$ to three decimal places? **[2.449]** Does this match your estimate? **[Yes.]**

Ask: Between what two perfect squares does 133 fall? **[121 and 144]** So, between what two whole numbers does $\sqrt{133}$ fall? **[11 and 12]** Does it fall closer to 11 or 12? **[Possible answer: 12, but it is close to right in the middle.]** Using your calculator, what is the value of $\sqrt{6}$ to three decimal places? **[11.533]** Does this match your estimate? **[Yes.]**

Example 4

Ask: Why is there always a real number between two real numbers? Explain. **[There is always a smaller division between values. If you look at two consecutive numbers to the thousandths place, like 0.332 and 0.333, there is an infinite set of values between that are to the ten-thousandths, hundred-thousandths, millionths place and so on.]**

Say: Let's approximate the value of $\sqrt{34}$ without using a calculator.

Ask: Between what two perfect squares does 34 fall? **[5 and 6]** 34 is close to 36, so $\sqrt{34}$ is closer to 6 than 5.

Say: To get a closer approximation, test some decimals in tenths.

Ask: What is 5.7^2? **[32.49]** What is 5.8^2? **[33.64]** What is 5.7^2? **[34.81]**

Say: 34 is closest to 33.64, so $\sqrt{34}$ is closest to 5.8.

Ask: How does the number line help you order numbers? **[When you plot them on the number line they are in order from least to greatest.]**

Check

Ask: How can you approximate the value of $2.\overline{41}$? **[Possible answer: Use a calculator.]** To the nearest ten, what is the approximate value of $\sqrt{2}$? **[1.4]** Is this enough of an approximation to order the numbers? **[No.]** Explain. **[$\sqrt{2}+1$ is too close to $2.\overline{41}$. $\sqrt{2}+1$ needs to be carried out to the ten-thousandths place, approximately 2.4142, to see that it is greater than $2.\overline{41}$.]**

COMMON MISCONCEPTION

Ask: What is the Error?

A teacher asked his students to write the numbers $\dfrac{116}{11}$, $\sqrt{116}$, and $10.\overline{45}$ in order from greatest to least.

Kevin wrote $10.\overline{45}$, $\dfrac{116}{11}$, $\sqrt{116}$. Where did he go wrong?

Reason incorrect: He wrote the set in order of least to greatest instead of greatest to least. Since $\dfrac{116}{11}=10.\overline{54}$ and $\sqrt{116}\approx10.8$, the correct solution is $\sqrt{116}$, $\dfrac{116}{11}$, $10.\overline{45}$.

Solution: Approximate the irrational values and convert the fractions to decimals.

$\dfrac{116}{11}=10.\overline{54}$.

$\sqrt{116}$ falls between 10 and 11 because $10^2=100$, and $11^2=121$. $10.7^2=114.49$ and $10.8^2=116.64$, so $\sqrt{116}\approx10.8$.

The number with the greatest value is $\sqrt{116}$, so it should be first.

In order from least to greatest, the numbers are, $\sqrt{116}$, $\dfrac{116}{11}$, $10.\overline{45}$.

Say: Always read the problem carefully. Some items will ask for least to greatest, and some for greatest to least.

KEY TEACHING POINTS

Example 5

Say: Numbers in real world situations are not always nice. Irrational numbers, and rational numbers that are repeating decimals occur frequently. Understanding the value of these numbers is important.

Ask: What formulas are needed to solve this problem? **[Area of a square and area of a circle.]** Does either formula include an irrational number? **[Yes, π is irrational.]** The formula for a circle is often memorized using the radius, $A_c=\pi(r)^2$. How can you find the radius of the circle? **[Divide the diameter in half.]**

ALTERNATE STRATEGY

Strategy: Use a number line.

1. **Say:** Number lines can be used to order real numbers in real-world or mathematical situations.

2. This problem provides real numbers in a table. You can add a row to the table for the approximate values. Use a calculator, or calculate the irrational number by hand to the nearest hundredth.

   Four classmates measured the width of their classroom using different methods. Their results are given in the table.

Distance Across the Classroom (ft)			
Angela	**Dean**	**Katie**	**Manny**
$12.\overline{6}$	$\sqrt{155}$	12.63	4π
$12.\overline{6}$	12.45	12.63	12.57

3. Graph the approximate location of each real number on a number line. Include to the nearest tenth on the number line.

   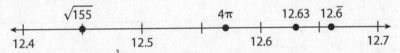

4. The question asks that you order the values from greatest to least. Greater numbers are on the right of a number line. Begin at the right and list the numbers from right to left.

   $$12.\overline{6},\ 12.63,\ 4\pi,\ \sqrt{155}$$

ADDITIONAL ONLINE INTERVENTION RESOURCES

Use the following for students who have not mastered the concepts in Skill 30.

- Math on the Spot videos

- Personal Math Trainer with customized intervention

- Building Block worksheets (Skill 18: Classify Real Numbers; Skill 20: Compare and Order Real Numbers; Skill 76: Reading and Writing Exponents; Skill 100 Squares and Square Roots; Skill 109: Write a Mixed Number as an Improper Fraction)

SKILL 30 — Real Numbers

Example 1

A rational number is any number that can be written in the form $\dfrac{a}{b}$, where a and b are integers and b is not 0. Every rational number can be written as a terminating decimal or a repeating decimal.

Write each fraction as a decimal.

A. $\dfrac{3}{4}$

$$\begin{array}{r} 0.75 \\ 4\overline{)3.00} \\ -28 \\ \hline 20 \\ -20 \\ \hline 0 \end{array}$$

Divide the numerator by the denominator.

Divide until the remainder is zero.

$\dfrac{3}{4} = 0.75$

B. $\dfrac{1}{6}$

$$\begin{array}{r} 0.166 \\ 6\overline{)1.000} \\ -6 \\ \hline 40 \\ -36 \\ \hline 40 \\ -36 \\ \hline 4 \end{array}$$

Divide until the digits in the quotient begin to repeat.

Write the decimal with a bar over the repeating digit(s).

$\dfrac{1}{6} = 0.1\overline{6}$

Check

Write each fraction as a decimal.

1. $\dfrac{3}{25}$

2. $\dfrac{19}{33}$

3. $\dfrac{7}{5}$

_____   _____   _____

Example 2

Write each decimal as a fraction in simplest form.

A. 0.125

$$0.125$$
$$= \dfrac{125}{1000}$$
$$= \dfrac{125 \div 125}{1000 \div 125}$$
$$= \dfrac{1}{8}$$

Write 0.125 as a fraction.

Divide the numerator and denominator by the GCF.

Simplify.

B. $0.\overline{3}$

$$x = 0.\overline{3}$$
$$(10)x = 0.\overline{3}(10)$$
$$10x = 3.\overline{3}$$
$$\underline{-x \quad -0.\overline{3}}$$
$$9x = 3$$
$$x = \dfrac{1}{3}$$

There is one repeating digit, so multiply both sides by $10^1 = 10$.

Because $x = 0.\overline{3}$, subtract x from one side and $0.\overline{3}$ from the other.

Simplify.

Check

Write each decimal as a fraction in simplest form.

4. 0.825

5. $0.8\overline{3}$

6. $0.\overline{37}$

_____

_____

Example 3

An irrational number is a number that is not rational. That is, it cannot be written in the form $\frac{a}{b}$, where a and b are integers and b is not 0. Unlike rational numbers, the decimal expansion of irrational numbers never terminate or repeat.

Estimate the value of $\sqrt{2}$ using the specified method.

A. Estimate the value of $\sqrt{2}$ without using a calculator. Use square roots of perfect squares to write the result as an inequality.

Step 1: Find two consecutive perfect squares that 2 is between. $\boxed{1} < 2 < \boxed{4}$

Step 2: Take the square root of each number. $\sqrt{\boxed{1}} < \sqrt{2} < \sqrt{\boxed{4}}$

Step 3: Simplify the square roots of the perfect squares. $1 < \sqrt{2} < 2$

B. Estimate the value of $\sqrt{2}$ to three decimal places using a calculator.

Step 1: Press the $\boxed{\sqrt{x}}$ button on your calculator.

Step 2: Press [2], then [ )], then ENTER.

Step 3: Round to three decimal places: $\sqrt{2} \approx 1.414$.

Check

Estimate without using a calculator. Use square roots of perfect squares to write the result as an inequality.

7. $\sqrt{6}$

8. $\sqrt{13}$

9. $\sqrt{133}$

_____

_____

_____

Estimate to three decimal places using a calculator.

10. $\sqrt{6}$

11. $\sqrt{13}$

12. $\sqrt{133}$

_____

_____

_____

Example 4

Between any two real numbers is another real number. To compare and order a set of real numbers, first approximate the irrational numbers as decimals. Then list the set of numbers from least to greatest.

Order $\sqrt{34}$, $5\frac{1}{2}$, and $\pi + 2$ from least to greatest.

Step 1: Approximate the irrational numbers.

Use a calculator to approximate $\sqrt{34}$ to one decimal place.
$\sqrt{34} \approx 5.8$

You already know that an approximate value of π is 3.14. So, an approximate value of $\pi + 2$ is 5.14.

Step 2: Order the numbers from least to greatest.

Since $5.14 < 5.5 < 5.8$, the ordered set is $\pi + 2$, $5\frac{1}{2}$, $\sqrt{34}$.

Note that you can also see order by plotting $\pi + 2$, $5\frac{1}{2}$, and $\sqrt{34}$ on a number line.

Check
Order the numbers from least to greatest.

13. $\sqrt{2} + 1$, $2.\overline{41}$, $\dfrac{12}{5}$

14. $\sqrt{83}$, $\dfrac{29}{3}$, 3π

15. $-\pi$, $-\sqrt{5}$, $-4\frac{1}{2}$

_____   _____   _____

16. **Explain the Error.** Find the correct solution.

A teacher asked his students to write the numbers $\dfrac{116}{11}$, $\sqrt{116}$, and $10.\overline{45}$ in order from greatest to least.

Kevin wrote $10.\overline{45}$, $\dfrac{116}{11}$, $\sqrt{116}$. Where did he go wrong?

_____

Example 5

Knowing how to estimate and order real numbers is useful for solving real world problems.

Kathy is considering two different shapes for the design of a courtyard fountain. One is a square with a side length of 4 feet. The other is a circle with a diameter of 5 feet. Which shape will give Kathy's fountain the greatest area?

Step 1: Find the areas for each shape.

Area of the square: $A_s = s^2 = 4^2 = 16 \text{ ft}^2$

Area of the circle: $A_c = \pi \left(\dfrac{d}{2}\right)^2 = \pi (2.5)^2 \approx 19.6 \text{ ft}^2$

Step 2: Compare the areas.

Since $16 < 19.6$, the circle will give Kathy's fountain the greatest area.

Check

Solve.

17. Four classmates measured the width of their classroom using different methods. Their results are given in the table.

Distance Across the Classroom (ft)			
Angela	**Dean**	**Katie**	**Manny**
$12.\overline{6}$	$\sqrt{155}$	12.63	4π

a. Use a calculator to estimate the irrational numbers to 2 decimal places.

_____

b. Order the lengths from greatest to least.

_____

SKILL 30 REAL NUMBERS

Slope and Slope-Intercept Form

KEY TEACHING POINTS

Example 1

Say: The solution to a linear equation in two variables forms a line when it is graphed on the coordinate plane. Any equation that can be written in the form $Ax + By = C$, where A, B, and C are real numbers and A and B are not both 0 is a linear equation.

Ask: Why can A and B both not be 0? **[If both are 0, the equation only says that 0 is equal to a constant, and so, C must be 0 also.]**

Ask: What linear equations are not functions? **[The ones that form vertical lines.]**

Say: If the value for B is 0, the solution set is a vertical line, so it is not a function.

Ask: What type of line is formed when A is 0? **[A horizontal line.]** Is this a function? **[Yes.]**

Say: The graph of $6x - 2y = 0$ is a line that passes through the origin. Lines that pass through the origin model proportional relationships.

Check

Ask: What is the first step in graphing the equation? **[Set up a table of values.]** What are good numbers to choose for the x-values? **[Possible response: Whole numbers, some positive and some negative.]**

Ask: What makes $-2x = y + 1$ a function? **[The graph forms a straight line that is not vertical.]**

Example 2

Ask: Which variable do you replace with 0 to find the x-intercept? **[y]** Why does replacing the variable y with 0 tell you the x-intercept? **[Where $y = 0$, the line is on the x-axis, so it is an x-intercept.]**

Ask: Are the intercepts enough information to graph the line? Explain. **[Yes. You only need to know two points to graph a line.]** Are there any intercepts where the x- and y-value are the same? **[Yes, at the origin.]**

Say: When the graph of a line passes through the origin, the x- and y-intercepts are the same point. You need to know at least one other point to graph a line.

Check

Ask: How do you determine the intercepts from a graph? **[Find the points on the graph where the line crosses the axes.]**

Ask: How do you determine the intercepts from an equation? **[Substitute 0 into the equation for x to find the y-intercept. Substitute 0 into the equation for y to find the x-intercept.]**

Say: To find the intercepts for the equation $-2x + \frac{1}{2}y = 2$, substitute 0 for x to find the y-intercept. Substitute 0 for y to find the x-intercept.

Show the following work:

x-intercept $\quad -2x + \dfrac{1}{2}y = 2$

$$-2x + \dfrac{1}{2}(0) = 2$$

$$-2x = 2$$

$$x = -1$$

y-intercept $\quad -2x + \dfrac{1}{2}y = 2$

$$-2(0) + \dfrac{1}{2}y = 2$$

$$\dfrac{1}{2}y = 2$$

$$y = 4$$

Ask: What are the coordinates of the intercepts? **[(−1, 0) and (0, 4).]**

COMMON MISCONCEPTION

Ask: What is the Error?

Graph $\dfrac{1}{2}(2x + 3y) = 3$ using the intercepts.

Reason incorrect: The intercepts are reversed.

Solution: Find the intercepts by substituting 0 into the equation for x then for y.

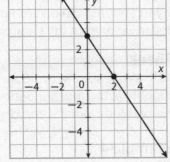

x-intercept $\quad \dfrac{1}{2}(2x + 3y) = 3$

$$\dfrac{1}{2}(2x + 3(0)) = 3$$

$$\dfrac{1}{2}(2x) = 3$$

$$x = 3$$

y-intercept $\quad \dfrac{1}{2}(2x + 3y) = 3$

$$\dfrac{1}{2}(2(0) + 3y) = 3$$

$$\dfrac{1}{2}(3y) = 3$$

$$\dfrac{3}{2}y = 3$$

$$\left(\dfrac{2}{3}\right)\dfrac{3}{2}y = \left(\dfrac{2}{3}\right)3$$

$$y = 2$$

The points for the intercepts are (3, 0) and (0, 2).

Plot the intercepts, then draw the line that passes through them.

Say: Remember, the x-intercept is the point where the line crosses the x-axis. The y-intercept is the point where the line crosses the y-axis.

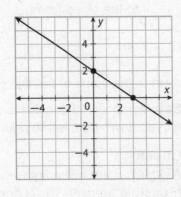

KEY TEACHING POINTS

Example 3

Say: Functions can be used to represent real world situations. Functions are often used as a way to show change over time. Situations that show a constant rate of change are represented by linear functions.

Say: The value of *y* depends on the value of *x*. The rate of change is the ratio of the dependent variable to the independent variable. If you say a rate aloud it may help you recognize which variable is which. Think, do you typically say "dollars per year" or "years per dollar" when you talk about a savings account? What would each phrase mean?

Ask: In Janice's savings account, which is the independent variable: time or money? **[Time.]** The dependent variable belongs in the denominator. What operation is used to find the change of time? **[Subtraction.]**

Say: It is important to make sure that you are doing the subtraction in corresponding order. If you subtract the earlier time from the later time, make sure you also subtract the early dollar value from the later dollar value.

Check

Ask: What are the two quantities in problem 9? **[Volume in gallons and distance.]** Which quantity is the independent variable? **[Miles.]** One of the quantities is not specifically given in the problem. What is the distance when Gavin has 11 gallons of fuel? **[0 miles.]**

Example 4

Say: When a linear relationship is graphed, the slope of the line is the same as the constant rate of change.

Ask: Can you use the opposite points for point 1 and 2 and still get the same slope? **[Yes.]**

Say: You can use any points on the line as point 1 or 2, as long as you keep the coordinates for *x* and *y* in the same order. Let's try this with the points in the opposite places.

Show the following work:

Let (x_1, y_1) be (4, 1).

Let (x_2, y_2) be (0, –2).

Substitute the coordinates into the slope formula.

$$\text{slope} = \frac{y_2 - y_1}{x_2 - x_1} = \frac{-2 - (1)}{0 - 4} = \frac{-3}{-4} = \frac{3}{4}$$

Ask: Is the slope of the line positive or negative? **[Positive.]**

Say: A line with a positive slope moves up from left to right. A line with a negative slope moves down from left to right.

Check

Ask: What are two points you can choose on the graph of problem 11 to find the slope? **[Possible answer: (3, 2) and (–3, 0)]** Does choosing points on the axis make sense? Why? **[Yes, the coordinates that are zero make the calculations easy.]** What are the coordinates of the intercepts? **[(0, 1) and (–3, 0)]**

Say: Let's find the slope using the intercepts.

Show the following work:

Let (x_1, y_1) be $(0, 1)$.

Let (x_2, y_2) be $(-3, 0)$.

Substitute the coordinates into the slope formula.

$$\text{slope} = \frac{y_2 - y_1}{x_2 - x_1} = \frac{0 - 1}{-3 - 0} = \frac{-1}{-3} = \frac{1}{3}$$

ALTERNATE STRATEGY

Strategy: Count units.

1. **Say:** The slope formula tells you the slope of a line. You can also count units on the graph of the line to find the rise over the run.

2. Find the slope of the line.
   Choose any two points on the line.
   Make sure the points are directly on grid lines.

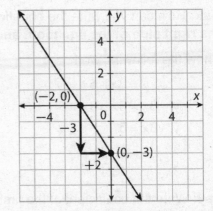

3. Count the number of units vertically between the points. If you start at $(-2, 0)$, you must move 3 units down, so the rise is -3.

4. Count the number of units horizontally between the points. You must move 2 units right, so the run is 2.

$$\text{Slope} = \frac{\text{rise}}{\text{run}} = \frac{-3}{2} = -\frac{3}{2}$$

5. You can begin at either point and the result is the same.

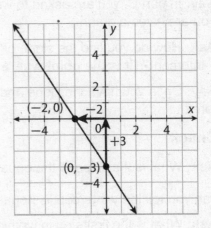

6. Count the number of units vertically. If you start at $(0, -3)$, you must move 3 units up, so the rise is 3.

7. Count the number of units horizontally. You must move 2 units left, so the run is -2.

$$\text{Slope} = \frac{\text{rise}}{\text{run}} = \frac{3}{-2} = -\frac{3}{2}$$

KEY TEACHING POINTS

Example 5

Say: The standard form of a line, $Ax + By = C$, where A, B, and C are real numbers and A and B are not both 0, and the slope-intercept form, $y = mx + b$, can both be used to describe the same line.

Say: The form of the equation used depends on the purpose. An equation in standard form may work well in a word problem, while the slope-intercept form is more useful when you are looking for the slope or y-intercept.

Ask: How do you rewrite an equation from standard form to slope-intercept form? **[Isolate the variable y on the left side of the equation.]**

Say: When you are given the slope and y-intercept of a line, all you need to do is substitute the values into the slope-intercept form. Be careful to watch the signs of the slope and y-intercept.

Ask: How can you write the equation from part B in standard form? **[Isolate the constant on the right side of the equation, and make the term with x the first term.]**

Show the following work:

$$y = 3x + 5$$
$$y - 3x = 3x - 3x + 5 \qquad \text{Subtract } 3x \text{ from each side.}$$
$$y - 3x = 5$$
$$-3x + y = 5 \qquad \text{Use the Commutative Property.}$$
$$3x - y = -5 \qquad \text{Multiply both sides by } -1.$$

Say: Write the coefficient of the first term as a positive value by multiplying by -1.

Say: In part C, you are asked to write the equation of a line in slope-intercept form when you are given a graph.

Ask: How do you find the slope of a line? **[The slope formula.]** How do you find the y-intercept? **[It is the point where the graph crosses the y-axis.]**

Say: Once you have the slope and y-intercept, substitute the values into the slope-intercept form.

Check

Ask: What is the slope of the equation $y = 2x - \dfrac{1}{2}$? **[2]** What is the y-intercept? $\left[-\dfrac{1}{2}\right]$ How can you tell the y-intercept is negative? **[The operation is subtraction.]**

Ask: What is the first step in writing $5x - 8y = 56$ in slope-intercept form? **[Isolate the variable y on the left side of the equation.]**

Complete the following with the class:

$$5x - 8y = 56$$

$$5x - 5x - 8y = 56 - 5x$$ Subtract 5x from each side.

$$-8y = -5x + 56$$ Use the Commutative Property to write the x term as the first term on the right.

$$\frac{-8y}{-8} = \frac{-5x}{-8} + \frac{56}{-8}$$ Divide each side by -8.

$$y = \frac{5}{8}x - 7$$

The slope is $\frac{5}{8}$ and the y-intercept is -7.

Say: In problem 18 you are given a graph and asked to write an equation for the line.

Ask: What do you need to find first? **[The slope and y-intercept.]** How do you find the slope? **[Choose two points on the line and use the slope formula.]**

Complete the following as a class.

Choose two points and plot them on the graph.

Let (x_1, y_1) be $(-3, 0)$.

Let (x_2, y_2) be $(3, 2)$.

Substitute the coordinates into the slope formula.

$$\text{slope} = \frac{y_2 - y_1}{x_2 - x_1} = \frac{2 - 0}{3 - (-3)} = \frac{2}{6} = \frac{1}{3}$$

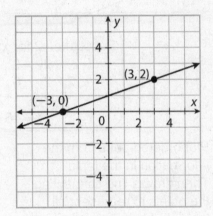

Find the y-intercept from the graph.

The y-intercept is 1.

Write the equation by substituting the values you just found into slope-intercept form.

$$y = mx + b$$

$$y = \frac{1}{3}x + 1$$

ADDITIONAL ONLINE INTERVENTION RESOURCES

 Use the following for students who have not mastered the concepts in Skill 31.

- Math on the Spot videos

- Personal Math Trainer with customized intervention

- Building Block worksheets (Skill 41: Generate Ordered Pairs; Skill 43: Graph Functions; Skill 44: Graph Linear Functions)

Slope and Slope-Intercept Form

SKILL 31

Example 1

A linear function is a function whose graph forms a line that is not vertical. A linear function can be represented by a linear equation. The standard form for the equation of a linear function is $Ax + By = C$, where A, B, and C are real numbers and A and B are not both 0.

Graph the equation $6x - 2y = 0$ and tell whether or not it is a function.

Step 1: Use the equation $6x - 2y = 0$ to make a table of values. Find the y value for each value of x.

x	−2	−1	0	1	2
y	−6	−3	0	3	6

Substitute −2 for x:
$$6(-2) - 2y = 0$$
$$-12 - 2y = 0$$
$$-2y = -12$$
$$y = -6$$

Step 2: Plot ordered pairs from the information in the table. Then draw a line connecting the points to represent all the possible solutions.

$6x - 2y = 0$ represents a linear function because its graph is a non-vertical line.

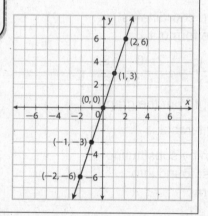

Vocabulary

Intercept

Linear equation

Linear function

Rate of change

Slope

Slope formula

Slope-intercept form

Standard form

x-intercept

y-intercept

Check

Graph the equation and explain why it is or is not a function.

1. $-2x = y + 1$

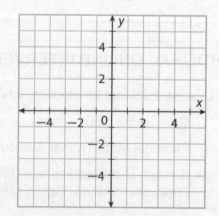

_____

Example 2

An intercept is where a graph crosses one of the axes.

A y-intercept is the y-coordinate of the point where the graph intercepts the y-axis. The x-coordinate of this point is always 0.

An x-intercept is the x-coordinate of the point where the graph intercepts the x-axis. The y-coordinate of this point is always 0.

A. Determine the x- and y-intercepts.

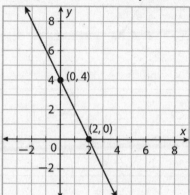

The graph crosses the x-axis at (2, 0).

The x-intercept is 2.

The graph crosses the y-axis at (0, 4).

The y-intercept is 4.

B. Graph $-3x + 4y = 12$ using the intercepts.

Step 1: Find the intercepts.

Replace y with 0 to find the x-intercept. Replace x with 0 to find the y-intercept.

$$-3x + 4(0) = 12$$
$$-3x = 12$$
$$x = -4$$

$$-3(0) + 4y = 12$$
$$4y = 12$$
$$y = 3$$

The x-intercept is –4.

The y-intercept is 3.

Step 2: Graph the line.

Plot the intercepts.

Draw the line that passes through both intercepts.

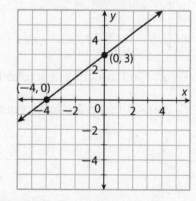

Check

Determine the *x*- and *y*-intercepts.

2.

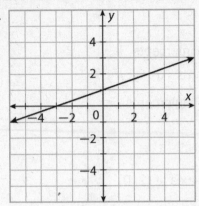

_____

3.

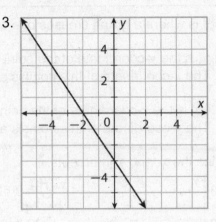

_____

4. $10x = -\dfrac{1}{2}y + 5$

_____

5. $y = 3x$

_____

Graph each line using the intercepts.

6. $\dfrac{1}{2}x = 2 - y$

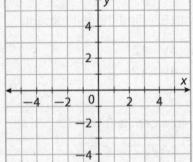

7. $-2x + \dfrac{1}{2}y = 2$

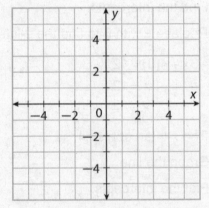

8. Explain the Error. Find the correct solution.

Graph $\dfrac{1}{2}(2x + 3y) = 3$ using the intercepts.

_____

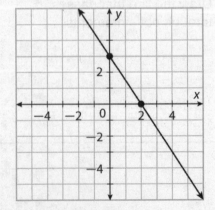

Example 3

The rate of change in a function is the ratio of the change in the dependent variable, *y*, to the change in the independent variable, *x*.

$$\text{rate of change} = \frac{\text{change in } y}{\text{change in } x}$$

When Janice was 10 years old, she had $250 in her savings account. By the time she turned 16, she had a balance of $1000. Find the rate of change for her savings account.

$$\text{rate of change} = \frac{\text{change in } y}{\text{change in } x} = \frac{1000 - 250}{16 - 10} = \frac{750}{6} = 125$$

The rate of change was $125 per year.

Find each rate of change.

9. Gavin's fuel tank had 11 gallons of fuel. He drove 135 miles, and had 5 gallons of fuel left.

10. In 2000, Myrna was 44 inches tall. In 2014, she was 62 inches tall.

Example 4

When two quantities have a linear relationship, the rate of change is constant. The constant rate of change is called the slope of the line. You can use the slope formula to find the slope of a line:

$$\text{Slope, } m = \frac{\text{vertical change}}{\text{horizontal change}} = \frac{\text{rise}}{\text{run}} = \frac{y_2 - y_1}{x_2 - x_1}$$

Find the slope *m* of the line.

Choose any two points on the line.

Let (x_1, y_1) be (0, –2).

Let (x_2, y_2) be (4, 1).

Substitute the coordinates into the slope formula.

$$\text{slope} = \frac{y_2 - y_1}{x_2 - x_1} = \frac{1 - (-2)}{4 - 0} = \frac{3}{4}$$

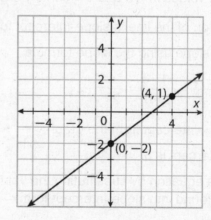

Check

Find the slope of each line.

11. _____

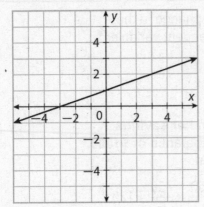

12. _____

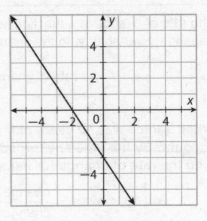

Example 5

The slope-intercept form of a linear equation, $y = mx + b$, uses the slope, m, and y-intercept b, to describe a line.

A. Find the slope and y-intercept of $-3x + 8y = 16$.

Rewrite the equation in slope-intercept form, $y = mx + b$, by isolating the variable y.

$$-3x + 8y = 16 \qquad \text{Add } 3x \text{ to each side.}$$

$$8y = 3x + 16 \qquad \text{Divide each side by 8.}$$

$$y = \frac{3}{8}x + 2$$

The slope is $\frac{3}{8}$ and the y-intercept is 2.

B. Write an equation for the line that has a slope of 3 and y-intercept of 5.

Substitute the values $m = 3$ and $b = 5$ into $y = mx + b$. $\qquad y = 3x + 5$

C. Write the equation of the line in slope-intercept form.

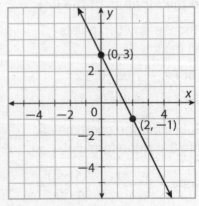

Step 1: Find the slope using the slope formula.

$$m = \frac{y_2 - y_1}{x_2 - x_1} = \frac{-1 - 3}{2 - 0} = \frac{-4}{2} = -2$$

Step 2: Find the y-intercept from the graph.

The y-intercept is 3.

Step 3: Write the equation by substituting the values you just found into slope-intercept form.

$$y = mx + b$$

$$y = -2x + 3$$

Check
Find the slope and *y*-intercept.

13. $y = 2x - \dfrac{1}{2}$

14. $5x - 8y = 56$

15. $3x + 2y = 8$

_____   _____   _____

Write the equation for each line.

16. Slope: -2

    y-intercept: -5

17. Slope: $\dfrac{3}{8}$

    y-intercept: 5

_____   _____

18.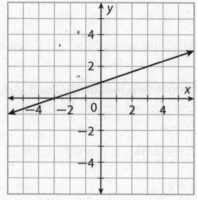

19.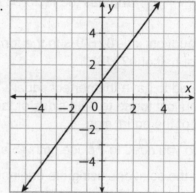

_____   _____

20. Tina started with $50 in her savings account. Each year she adds another $150. If *x* represents time in years, and *y* represents the balance in her account, what equation, in slope-intercept form, models her account over time?

_____

SKILL 31 SLOPE AND SLOPE-INTERCEPT FORM

Solving Quadratic Equations by Completing the Square

KEY TEACHING POINTS

Example 1

Say: Quadratic equations that cannot be solved using square roots or by factoring can be solved by completing the square to form a perfect square trinomial. A perfect square trinomial has a perfect square as the first and last term, and the term in the center is twice the product of the square roots of the first and last term. You can form a perfect square trinomial from the expression $x^2 + bx + c$ by replacing c with $\left(\dfrac{b}{2}\right)^2$. The new expression is in the form $x^2 + bx + \left(\dfrac{b}{2}\right)^2$ and has the factored form $\left(x + \dfrac{b}{2}\right)^2$.

Ask: The equation $x^2 - 8x = 9$ is in the form $x^2 - bx = -c$. What is the value of b? **[8]** What is the square of half of b? **[16]**

Say: You need to have the perfect square trinomial on one side of the equation by itself. Add the value you just found to both sides of the equation to form the perfect square trinomial on the left side of the equal sign.

Ask: Why do you need to include both +5 and –5? **[Both numbers when squared equal 25.]**

Say: Check the solutions using the original equation.

Show the following work :

$$x^2 - 8x = 9 \qquad\qquad x^2 - 8x = 9$$
$$(9)^2 - 8(9) = 9 \qquad\qquad (-1)^2 - 8(-1) = 9$$
$$81 - 72 = 9 \qquad\qquad 1 + 8 = 9$$
$$9 = 9 \qquad\qquad 9 = 9$$

Check

Ask: For the equation $x^2 + 11x - 17 = -5$, what is the first step to completing the square? **[Get the constants on the right side of the equation by adding 17 to each side.]** Once the constant is on the right, what is the value of b? **[11]** So, what value needs to be added to each side? **[30.25]**

Ask: What is the formula for the area of a rectangle? **[Area equals length times width.]** If you say w = width, what is the length in terms of w? **[w + 2]** Write the equation for Area A in terms of w. **[$A = (w)(w + 2)$ or $w^2 + 2w$]**

Say: Substitute the area from the problem into the equation to solve for w.

Show the following work:

$w^2 + 2w = 224$	
$w^2 + 2w + 1 = 225$	Complete the square.
$(w + 1)^2 = (15)^2$	Rewrite using perfect squares.
$w + 1 = 15$	Take the square root
$w = 14$	Subtract 1.
$l = w + 2 = 16$	Solve for length.

ALTERNATE STRATEGY

Strategy: Use algebra tiles.

1. **Say:** Algebra tiles can help you determine what constant you need to add in order to complete the square.

2. The equation $x^2 - 4x = 12$ has the expression $x^2 - 4x$ on the left. To determine what constant needs to be added to complete the square, set up the expression using algebra tiles. Set the tiles up with the squared tile in the upper left, and the same number of variable tiles along the top and side.

3. Add unit tiles to fill in the bottom right corner to complete a square. How many unit tiles did you use? **[4]** This is the number you need to add to both sides of the equation $x^2 - 4x = 12$ to complete the square.

   There are 4 unit tiles, so add 4 to each side.

   Show the work:

   $$x^2 - 4x + 4 = 16$$
   $$(x-2)^2 = (\pm 4)^2$$
   $$x - 2 = \pm 4$$
   $$x - 2 = 4 \qquad x - 2 = -4$$
   $$x = 6 \qquad x = -2$$

KEY TEACHING POINTS

Example 2
Say: You can use completing the square to solve quadratic equations when the coefficient of the squared variable is a perfect square.

Ask: Is the coefficient of the squared variable in the equation $25x^2 + 40x = 20$ a perfect square? **[Yes.]** What are the values of a and b? **[a = 25, b = 40]**

Check
Say: The solutions to quadratic equations are not always integer values. Let's look at the equation in problem 9.

Ask: What is the first step to solving the equation $9x^2 + 18x - 47 = 8$? **[Move the constants to the left side of the equal sign.]** Is the value for a a perfect square? **[Yes, $9 = 3^2$.]**

Work through the following as a class: $9x^2 + 18x - 47 = 8$ $\quad \dfrac{b^2}{4a} = \dfrac{324}{36} = 9$

$$9x^2 + 18x = 55$$

$$9x^2 + 18x + 9 = 64$$

$$(3x + 3)^2 = (\pm 8)^2$$

$$3x + 3 = \pm 8$$

$$3x + 3 = 8 \qquad 3x + 3 = -8$$

$$3x = 5 \qquad\qquad 3x = -11$$

$$x = \dfrac{5}{3} \qquad\qquad x = \dfrac{-11}{3}$$

Ask: What does the question ask in problem 10b? **[The amount of time the projectile will be in the air.]** Is a negative value possible? **[No.]** In some contexts, you can eliminate any negative values because they don't make sense.

Example 3

Say: Some quadratic equations can be solved by completing the square even when the leading coefficient is not a perfect square. Remember, as long as you do the same thing on both sides of an equation, the equation remains true. This means you can multiply or divide both sides of the equation to form a perfect square in the leading coefficient.

Ask: The leading coefficient 8 is not a perfect square. What factors or multiples of 8 are perfect squares? **[Possible answers: 4, 16 or 64]** Why might you choose to multiply both sides by $\dfrac{1}{2}$ instead of 2? **[Possible answers: Since all of the coefficients and constants are even, dividing by 2 still has integer results. Smaller numbers can be easier to work with.]**

Ask: Why is the solution left with a radical in the numerator? **[$3\sqrt{3}$ is an irrational number, it can't be written as a fraction of two integers, or as a decimal and be completely accurate. The solution would be approximate, not exact.]**

Check

Ask: In the equation $5x^2 - 10x - 47 = -3$, what is the first step in a solution? **[Get the constants on the right.]** What is the leading coefficient? **[5]** What factors or multiples of 5 are perfect squares? **[25]** What value must you add to both sides of the equation to complete the square? **[25]**

Say: Some equations look messy.

Show the following work :
$$5x^2 - 10x - 47 = -3$$

$$5x^2 - 10x = 44$$

$$25x^2 - 50x = 220 \quad \dfrac{b^2}{4a} = \dfrac{2500}{100} = 25$$

$$25x^2 - 50x + 25 = 245$$

$$(5x - 5)^2 = (\pm 7\sqrt{5})^2$$

$$5x - 5 = \pm 7\sqrt{5}$$

$$5x = 5 \pm 7\sqrt{5}$$

$$x = \dfrac{5 \pm 7\sqrt{5}}{5}$$

COMMON MISCONCEPTION

Ask: What is the Error?

Solve $-5x^2 + 16x + 15 = -9x^2$ by completing the square.

$$-5x^2 + 16x + 15 = -9x^2$$

$$4x^2 + 16x = -15$$

$$4x^2 + 16x + \left(\frac{16}{2}\right)^2 = -15 + \left(\frac{16}{2}\right)^2$$

$$4x^2 + 16x + 64 = 49$$

$$(2x + 8)^2 = 49$$

$$2x + 8 = \pm 7$$

So, $x = -\dfrac{1}{2}$ or $x = -\dfrac{15}{2}$.

Reason incorrect: The formula for completing the square when $a = 1$ was used incorrectly. In this case, $a \neq 1$, so the term that should have been added to complete the square is $\dfrac{b^2}{4a} = 16$.

Solution:

$$-5x^2 + 16x + 15 = -9x^2$$

$$4x^2 + 16x = -15$$

$$4x^2 + 16x + 16 = 1$$

$$(2x + 4)^2 = 1$$

$$2x + 4 = \pm\sqrt{1}$$

So, $x = -\dfrac{3}{2}$ or $x = -\dfrac{5}{2}$.

Say: Always check your solution by substituting it into the original equation. By checking this solution, the incorrect answers would have been spotted.

ADDITIONAL ONLINE INTERVENTION RESOURCES

Use the following for students who have not mastered the concepts in Skill 32.

- Math on the Spot videos
- Personal Math Trainer with customized intervention
- Building Block worksheets (Skill 21: Complete the Square; Skill 97: Solve Quadratic Equations)

SKILL 32

Solving Quadratic Equations by Completing the Square

Example 1

To complete the square for the expression $x^2 + bx + c$, replace c with $\left(\dfrac{b}{2}\right)^2$. The perfect-square trinomial is $x^2 + bx + \left(\dfrac{b}{2}\right)^2$, and it factors as $\left(x + \dfrac{b}{2}\right)^2$.

Vocabulary

Complete the square

Perfect-square trinomial

Perfect square

Solve $x^2 - 8x = 9$.

$$x^2 - 8x = 9$$

$$\left(\dfrac{8}{2}\right)^2 = 4^2 = 16 \qquad \text{Find } \left(\dfrac{b}{2}\right)^2.$$

$$x^2 - 8x + 16 = 9 + 16 \qquad \text{Complete the square.}$$

$$(x - 4)^2 = 25 \qquad \text{Factor and simplify.}$$

$$x - 4 = \pm 5 \qquad \text{Take the square root of both sides.}$$

$$x - 4 = 5 \text{ or } x - 4 = -5 \qquad \text{Write and solve two equations.}$$

$$x = 9 \text{ or } x = -1$$

Check

Solve each equation by completing the square.

1. $x^2 - 4x = 12$

2. $x^2 + 18x - 40 = 0$

3. $x^2 + 11x - 17 = -5$

4. $x^2 - 9x + 11 = -6$

Solve.

5. The length of a rectangle is 2 meters longer than the width. The area of the rectangle is 224 square meters.

   a. Set up an equation for the area of the rectangle.

   b. Find the length and the width.

Example 2

To complete the square for the expression $ax^2 + bx + c$, where a is a perfect square and $a \neq 1$, replace c with $\dfrac{b^2}{4a}$. Then factor the perfect-square trinomial $ax^2 + bx + \dfrac{b^2}{4a}$.

Solve $25x^2 + 40x = 20$.

$$25x^2 + 40x = 20$$

$$\dfrac{40^2}{4(25)} = \dfrac{1600}{100} = 16 \qquad \text{Find } \dfrac{b^2}{4a}.$$

$$25x^2 + 40x + 16 = 20 + 16 \qquad \text{Complete the square.}$$

$$(5x + 4)^2 = 36 \qquad \text{Factor and simplify.}$$

$$5x + 4 = \pm 6 \qquad \text{Take the square root of both sides.}$$

$$5x + 4 = 6 \text{ or } 5x + 4 = -6 \qquad \text{Write and solve two equations.}$$

$$x = \dfrac{2}{5} \text{ or } x = -2$$

Check

Solve each equation by completing the square.

6. $25x^2 - 15x = 10$

_____

7. $4x^2 + 16x = -12$

_____

8. $36x^2 + 9x + 36 = 63$

_____

9. $9x^2 + 18x - 47 = 8$

_____

Solve.

10. The height in feet, h, of a projectile launched from the top of a 108-foot cliff, with an initial velocity of 40 feet per second can be modeled using the equation $h = -16t^2 + 40t + 108$, where t is the time in seconds.

   a. Solve the equation for t by completing the square.

   _____

   b. Determine how long the projectile will be in the air. Round to the nearest hundredth.

   _____

Example 3

When the left side of an equation is in the form $ax^2 + bx + c$, such that the leading coefficient a is not a perfect square, you can transform the equation by multiplying both sides by a value such that a becomes a perfect square. Once a is a perfect square, proceed by adding $\dfrac{b^2}{4a}$ to both sides to begin solving.

Solve $8x^2 + 16x = 46$.

Step 1: Since the coefficient of x^2 is 8, which is not a perfect square, multiply both sides by a value so that the coefficient will be a perfect square, such as $\dfrac{1}{2}$.

$$\frac{1}{2}\left(8x^2 + 16x\right) = \frac{1}{2}(46)$$
$$4x^2 + 8x = 23$$

Step 2: Add $\dfrac{b^2}{4a}$ to both sides. In this case, $\dfrac{b^2}{4a} = \dfrac{8^2}{4(4)} = \dfrac{64}{16} = 4$.

$$4x^2 + 8x + 4 = 23 + 4 = 27$$

Step 3: Factor the left side of the equation as a perfect-square trinomial.

$$(2x + 2)^2 = 27$$

Step 4: Apply the definition of a square root. Write two equations, and solve each equation to find the two solutions:

$$2x + 2 = \pm\sqrt{27}$$ Take the square root of both sides.

$2x + 2 = \sqrt{27}$ or $2x + 2 = -\sqrt{27}$ Rewrite as two equations.

$2x = -2 + \sqrt{27}$ or $2x = -2 - \sqrt{27}$ Solve for x.

$x = \dfrac{-2 + \sqrt{27}}{2}$ or $x = \dfrac{-2 - \sqrt{27}}{2}$

$x = \dfrac{-2 + 3\sqrt{3}}{2}$ or $x = \dfrac{-2 - 3\sqrt{3}}{2}$ Simplify.

Check

Solve each equation by completing the square.

11. $3x^2 + 12x - 15 = 0$

12. $10x^2 - 20x - 30 = 0$

_____   _____

13. $6x^2 + 12x - 81 = -9$

_____

14. $5x^2 - 10x - 47 = -3$

_____

15. $4x^2 - 7x - 92 = 0$

_____

16. $8x^2 - 18x = 95$

_____

17. $3x^2 - 25 = 10x$

_____

18. $x^2 - 2x - 1 = -9x^2 - 4x + 7$

_____

19. Explain the Error. Find the correct solution.

Solve $-5x^2 + 16x + 15 = -9x^2$ by completing the square.

$$-5x^2 + 16x + 15 = -9x^2$$
$$4x^2 + 16x = -15$$
$$4x^2 + 16x + \left(\frac{16}{2}\right)^2 = -15 + \left(\frac{16}{2}\right)^2$$
$$4x^2 + 16x + 64 = 49$$
$$(2x + 8)^2 = 49$$
$$2x + 8 = \pm 7$$

So, $x = -\frac{1}{2}$ or $x = -\frac{15}{2}$.

_____

_____

_____

SKILL 32 SOLVING QUADRATIC EQUATIONS BY COMPLETING THE SQUARE

Solving Quadratic Equations by Factoring

KEY TEACHING POINTS

Example 1

Say: A quadratic equation in the form $ax^2 + bx + c = 0$, where $a \neq 0$, can be solved using the related quadratic function that replaces 0 with y.

Say: The graph of a quadratic function is a parabola. The parabola may open up or down. The solution to the related quadratic equation is the set of points where the graph crosses the x-axis.

Ask: What is the coordinate value of y at the x-axis? **[0]**

Say: The points where a quadratic function crosses the x-axis are called its zeroes.

Say: A quadratic equation may have 0, 1, or 2 solutions.

Ask: What does the graph of the related quadratic function with no solution look like? **[The parabola's vertex is above the x-axis and opens up or is below the y-axis and opens down.]**

Ask: What does the graph of the related quadratic function with one solution look like? **[The vertex lies exactly on the axis.]**

Check

Ask: What is the related function of $x^2 - x - 2 = 0$? **[$y = x^2 - x - 2$]**

Ask: What values might you choose as x for a table of values to graph the function $y = x^2 - x - 2$? **[Possible answer: Integer values between –2 and 2.]**

Create the following table of values as a class. Remind students to substitute their chosen values for x into the equation and solve for y.

x	$x^2 - x - 2$	y
–2	$(-2)^2 - (-2) - 2$	4
–1	$(-1)^2 - (-1) - 2$	0
0	$0^2 - 0 - 2$	–2
1	$1^2 - 1 - 2$	–2
2	$2^2 - 2 - 2$	0

Say: The graph of the parabola opens up. Choosing the integers between –2 and 2 does not give you the minimum value that is the vertex.

Ask: To find the zeros of the function, do you need to know the vertex? **[No.]**

Say: Even when you can estimate the vertex of the graph, you can still find the exact answers to the equation because the points of intersection are integer values.

Ask: Can you solve the equation without graphing the function? Explain. **[Yes. The values where $y = 0$ are the solutions, and there are two values for x in the table where $y = 0$.]**

KEY TEACHING POINTS

Example 2

Say: In the equation $(x + 1)(x - 2) = 0$ the two factors are $(x + 1)$ and $(x - 2)$. You can set each factor equal to zero in two equations, $(x + 1) = 0$ and $(x - 2) = 0$.

Ask: In the related function, what do the solutions -1 and 2 represent? **[The points where the parabola crosses the x-axis.]**

Say: When factoring a quadratic expression with the form $x^2 + bx + c$, the sign of c tells you the sign in the factors. When c is positive, the factors of c both have the same sign. When c is negative, one factor is negative and one is positive.

Let's find the factors of the expression $x^2 + 11x + 28$.

$(\quad)(\quad)$	Use ( ) to set up a product of two binomials.
$(x \quad)(x \quad)$	Write the factors of the first term, x^2.
$(x + \quad)(x + \quad)$	Since c is positive, the factors will have the same signs. Since the middle term, $11x$, is positive, the signs are both positive.
$(x + 4)(x + 7)$	The factors of 28 are $1 \cdot 28$, $2 \cdot 14$, or $4 \cdot 7$. The pair that has a sum of 11 is 4 and 7.

The factored form of $x^2 + 11x + 28 = 0$ is $(x + 4)(x + 7) = 0$.

Check

Ask: What is the standard form of the equation $x^2 + 2x = 99$? **[$x^2 + 2x - 99 = 0$]**

Ask: What is the factored form of $x^2 + 2x - 99 = 0$? **[$(x + 11)(x - 9) = 0$]**

Ask: What is the next step to solve $x^2 + 2x = 99$? **[Set each factor equal to zero and solve each equation for x.]**

ALTERNATE STRATEGY

Strategy: Use algebra tiles.

1. **Say:** You can use algebra tiles to find the factors of quadratic expressions.
2. Model the quadratic expression $x^2 + 9x + 18$ using algebra tiles.

3. Arrange the tiles so that the x^2 tile is in the upper left and the unit tiles are in the bottom right corner of a rectangle. Fill in the missing area with x tiles. The tiles must form a perfect rectangle with no gaps and no extra tiles.

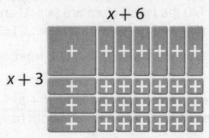

$x + 6$

$x + 3$

4. The area of a rectangle is the product of the length and width. The rectangle forms an area model for the two binomials that equal the quadratic expression when they are multiplied. The dimensions of the rectangle are the binomial factors.

5. The length of the rectangle is $x + 6$ and the width is $x + 3$. Multiply the two binomials to be sure they are the factors of $x^2 + 9x + 18$.

6. Show the work:
$$(x + 6)(x + 3) = x^2 + 6x + 3x + 18$$
$$= x^2 + 9x + 18$$

COMMON MISCONCEPTION

Ask: What is the Error?

$$x^2 + 6x = 16$$
$$x(x + 6) = 16$$

$$x = 16 \text{ or } x + 6 = 16$$
$$x = 10$$

Reason incorrect: The Zero Product Property is only true when the product is zero.

Solution: Write the equation in standard form first.

$$x^2 + 6x = 16$$
$$x^2 + 6x - 16 = 0$$
$$(x + 8)(x - 2) = 0$$
$$(x + 8) = 0 \quad \text{or} \quad (x - 2) = 0$$
$$x = -8 \qquad\qquad x = 2$$

Ask: How can you check your solutions? **[Substitute each solution into the original equation.]**

KEY TEACHING POINTS

Example 3

Say: Quadratic equations that are in the form $ax^2 + bx + c = 0$, when a does not equal 1, can also be solved using factoring. The key is to choose factors for both a and c so that the sum of the outer and inner products is equal to bx.

Say: The equation $2x^2 + 7x + 3 = 0$ has $a = 2$ and $c = 3$. The factors of 2 are 1 and 2. The factors of 3 are 1 and 3. To have a sum of the outer and inner products that is $7x$, the 2 and 3 must both be in the outer terms.

Ask: What is the first step in solving $3x^2 + 9x = 2x + 6$? **[Write the equation in standard form.]**

Check

Say: In Problem 16 you are given the volume of a rectangular prism. You are also given the dimensions of the prism.

Ask: What is the formula for the volume of a rectangular prism? **[$V = lwh$]**

Say: Substituting the dimensions into the volume formula, the equation to solve is $3(x + 9)(x + 7) = 105$.

Example 4

Say: Remember, in a perfect square trinomial, the first and last terms are perfect squares. The middle term is twice the product of the square roots of the first and last term.

Ask: How many solutions are there when the quadratic equation is a perfect square trinomial? **[1]** Explain. **[The factors in a perfect square are both the same.]**

Ask: How are the solutions in a quadratic equation that is the difference of two squares related? **[They are opposites.]**

Check

Ask: What is the greatest common factor in the expression $5x^2 - 20x + 20$? **[5]** After 5 is factored out, what type of expression is left? **[A perfect square trinomial.]**

Ask: What is the greatest common factor in the expression $9x^2 - 9 = 0$? **[9]** After 9 is factored out, what type of expression is left? **[A difference of two squares.]** If 9 is not factored out, what type of expression is $9x^2 - 9 = 0$? **[A difference of two squares.]** Is it necessary to factor out 9 to get the correct answer? Explain. **[No, the answers are the same, $x = 1$.]**

ADDITIONAL ONLINE INTERVENTION RESOURCES

Use the following for students who have not mastered the concepts in Skill 33.

- Math on the Spot videos

- Personal Math Trainer with customized intervention

- Building Block worksheets (Skill 34: Factor Trinomials; Skill 97: Solve Quadratic Equations; Skill 100: Squares and Square Roots)

SKILL 33

Solving Quadratic Equations by Factoring

Example 1

Remember that a quadratic equation is an equation that can be written in the form $ax^2 + bx + c = 0$, where $a \neq 0$.

You can solve a quadratic equation by graphing the related quadratic function $y = ax^2 + bx + c$. The x-intercepts of the function are the solutions of the equation.

Solve $x^2 + 2x - 8 = 0$ by graphing.

Make a table of values for the related quadratic function $y = x^2 + 2x - 8$.

x	y
−5	7
−4	0
0	−8
2	0
3	7

Plot the points and connect with a U-shaped curve.

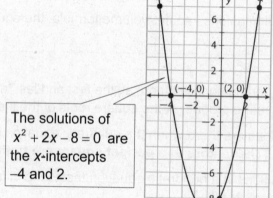

The solutions of $x^2 + 2x - 8 = 0$ are the x-intercepts −4 and 2.

The solutions are −4 and 2.

Vocabulary

Quadratic equation

Quadratic function

x-intercept

Zero Product Property

Difference of Two Squares

Perfect-Square Trinomial

Check

Solve the quadratic equation by graphing.

1. $x^2 - x - 2 = 0$

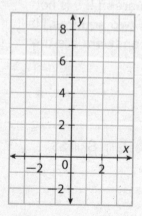

2. $x^2 - 3x - 10 = 0$

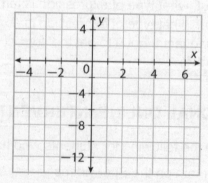

Example 2

You can solve some quadratic equations by using the Zero Product Property.

Zero Product Property For all real numbers a and b, if $ab = 0$, then $a = 0$ or $b = 0$.

A. Solve $(x+1)(x-2)=0$.

$$(x+1)(x-2)=0$$

$x+1=0$ or $x-2=0$ Use the Zero Product Property.
       $x=-1$ $x=2$ Solve each equation for x.

The solutions are -1 and 2.

In some cases, you have to factor the quadratic expression before you can use the Zero Product Property to solve the quadratic equation.

B. Solve $x^2 + 11x = -28$.

$$x^2 + 11x = -28$$

$x^2 + 11x + 28 = 0$ Write the equation in standard form.

$(x+4)(x+7)=0$ Factor. Find the factors of 28 that have a sum of 11.

$x+4=0$ or $x+7=0$ Use the Zero Product Property.
      $x=-4$ $x=-7$ Solve for x.

The solutions are -4 and -7.

Check

Solve the quadratic equation.

3. $(x-3)(x+9)=0$

4. $0=(x+5)(x-8)$

5. $(x+12)(x+12)=0$

6. $x^2 + 9x + 18 = 0$

7. $x^2 - 3x - 70 = 0$

8. $x^2 + 2x = 99$

9. Explain the Error. Then find the correct solution.

$$x^2 + 6x = 16$$
$$x(x+6) = 16$$

$x = 16$ or $x + 6 = 16$
            $x = 10$

Example 3

You can also solve quadratic equations of the form $ax^2 + bx + c = 0$ by factoring and using the Zero Product Property. First write the equation in standard form, factor the quadratic expression, and then solve.

A. Solve $2x^2 + 7x + 3 = 0$.

$$2x^2 + 7x + 3 = 0$$

$$(2x + 1)(x + 3) = 0 \qquad \text{Factor.}$$

$$2x + 1 = 0 \quad \text{or} \quad x + 3 = 0 \qquad \text{Use the Zero Product Property.}$$

$$2x = -1 \qquad\qquad x = -3$$

$$x = -\frac{1}{2} \qquad\qquad \text{Solve for } x.$$

The solutions are $-\dfrac{1}{2}$ and -3.

B. Solve $3x^2 + 9x = 2x + 6$.

$$3x^2 + 9x = 2x + 6$$

$$3x^2 + 9x - 2x - 6 = 0 \qquad \text{Subtract } 2x \text{ and 6 from each side.}$$

$$3x^2 + 7x - 6 = 0 \qquad \text{Combine like terms.}$$

$$(3x - 2)(x + 3) = 0 \qquad \text{Factor.}$$

$$3x - 2 = 0 \quad \text{or} \quad x + 3 = 0$$

$$3x = 2 \qquad\qquad x = -3 \qquad \text{Use the Zero Product Property.}$$

$$x = \frac{2}{3} \qquad\qquad\qquad \text{Solve for } x.$$

The solutions are $\dfrac{2}{3}$ and -3.

Check

Solve the quadratic equation.

10. $2x^2 - 5x - 12 = 0$

11. $3x^2 - 14x - 5 = 0$

12. $4x^2 - 19x - 30 = 0$

_____

_____

_____

13. $4x^2 + 7x = 3x - 1$

14. $12x^2 + 16x = -5$

15. $10x^2 + 9 = 21x$

_____

_____

_____

16. A rectangular prism has a volume of 105 cm^3. Its dimensions are 3 cm, $(x + 9)$ cm, and $(x + 7)$ cm. What is the value of x?

_____

Example 4

You can sometimes solve a quadratic equation by using one of the factoring patterns listed below.

Difference of Two Squares $\quad a^2 - b^2 = (a+b)(a-b)$

Perfect-Square Trinomial $\quad a^2 + 2ab + b^2 = (a+b)(a+b) = (a+b)^2$

$\qquad\qquad\qquad\qquad\qquad a^2 - 2ab + b^2 = (a-b)(a-b) = (a-b)^2$

A. Solve $3x^2 - 12x + 12 = 0$.

$3x^2 - 12x + 12 = 0$

$3(x^2 - 4x + 4) = 0$ Factor out the GCF, 3.

$3(x - 2)(x - 2) = 0$ Factor the perfect-square trinomial.

$x - 2 = 0$ Use the Zero Product Property

$x = 2$ to solve for x.

B. Solve $5x^2 - 45 = 0$.

$5x^2 - 45 = 0$

$5(x^2 - 9) = 0$ Factor out the GCF, 5.

$5(x + 3)(x - 3) = 0$ Factor the difference of two squares.

$x = -3 \text{ or } x = 3$ Use the Zero Product Property

     to solve for x.

C. Solve $4x^2 + 48x + 144 = 0$.

$4x^2 + 48x + 144 = 0$

$4(x^2 + 12x + 36) = 0$ Factor out the GCF, 4.

$4(x + 6)(x + 6) = 0$ Factor the perfect-square trinomial.

$x + 6 = 0$ Use the Zero Product Property

$x = -6$ to solve for x.

Check

Solve the quadratic equation.

17. $4x^2 + 40x + 100 = 0$ 18. $2x^2 + 28x + 98 = 0$ 19. $2x^2 - 72 = 0$

_____   _____   _____

20. $9x^2 - 9 = 0$ 21. $5x^2 - 20x + 20 = 0$ 22. $3x^2 - 24x + 48 = 0$

_____   _____   _____

SKILL 33 SOLVING QUADRATIC EQUATIONS BY FACTORING

Solving Systems of Linear Inequalities

KEY TEACHING POINTS

Example 1

Say: The solution set of a system of linear inequalities is graphed on a coordinate plane. The solution set is the set of all ordered pairs that make all the inequalities true.

Say: A boundary line is graphed for each inequality. The boundary line is the graph of the related linear equation.

Say: When the line is included in the solution set, it is drawn as a solid line. When the line is not a part of the solution set, it is drawn as a dashed line.

Ask: What inequality symbols include the line in the solution set? **[The symbols for less than or equal to and greater than or equal to, $\leq$ and $\geq$.]**

Ask: What inequality symbols do not include the boundary line in the solution set? **[The symbols for less than and greater than, $<$ and $>$.]**

Say: The linear system $\begin{cases} 4x - 2y \leq 4 \\ x + 3y > -6 \end{cases}$ includes the symbols $\leq$ and $>$. One boundary line is solid, the other is dashed. Step 1 graphs the inequality $4x - 2y \leq 4$.

Ask: How do you find the x- and y-intercepts? **[To find the x-intercept, substitute 0 into the equation for y. To find the y-intercept, substitute 0 into the equation for x.]**

Complete the following work as a class:

$$4x - 2y = 4 \qquad\qquad 4x - 2y = 4$$
$$4(0) - 2y = 4 \qquad\qquad 4x - 2(0) = 4$$
$$0 - 2y = 4 \qquad\qquad 4x - 0 = 4$$
$$y = -2 \qquad\qquad x = 1$$

Use the intercepts to graph the solid line.

Ask: How can you tell if (0, 0) is a solution to the inequality? **[Substitute the coordinates into the original inequality. If the inequality is true, the point is part of the solution set.]**

Complete the following work as a class:

$$4x - 2y \leq 4$$
$$4(0) - 2(0) \leq 4$$
$$0 - 0 \leq 4 \qquad$$ Because the inequality is true, shade the side of the line that includes (0, 0).
$$0 \leq 4$$

Ask: Why might you choose the origin as your test point? **[Possible response: Because both coordinates are zero, they are easy numbers to put into the inequalities.]**

Say: The solution to the system includes all of the points that are shaded by the graph of each inequality. The points where grid lines meet are only part of the solution set; all of the points inside the gridded boxes are also included.

Ask: The point $(-3, -1)$ is on the dashed boundary line of $x + 3y > -6$ and is in the shaded region for $4x - 2y \leq 4$. Is it part of the solution set for the system? Explain. **[No. Even though it satisfies one of the inequalities, it does not satisfy both, so it is not part of the solution set.]**

Check

Ask: Let's look at the system $\begin{cases} 3x - 2y < 0 \\ y \leq 2 \end{cases}$. What are the x- and y-intercepts for the boundary line of $3x - 2y < 0$? **[The line passes through the origin, so the intercepts are both at the origin.]** How can you graph the boundary line without knowing the intercepts? **[Possible answer: Write the related equation in slope-intercept form. Use the slope to move from the origin for a second point.]**

Complete the following work as a class.

$3x - 2y < 0$

$\quad -2y < -3x \qquad$ Subtract $3x$ from each side.

$\quad y > \dfrac{3}{2}x \qquad$ Divide each side by -2.

$\qquad\qquad\qquad$ Remember to reverse the inequality symbol.

Ask: What is the slope of the boundary line? $\left[\dfrac{3}{2}\right]$ If the boundary line passes through the origin and has a slope of $\dfrac{3}{2}$, what point can be used as a second point? **[Possible answer: (2, 3)]**

Ask: Is the boundary line solid or dashed? **[Dashed.]**

The other inequality in the system is $y \leq 2$. How can you graph the boundary line for $y \leq 2$? **[This is already in slope-intercept form. There is no slope, so the boundary line is a horizontal line passing through $y = 2$.]**

ALTERNATE STRATEGY

Strategy: Use the inequality symbol.

1. **Say:** When the boundary line of an inequality is written in slope-intercept form, the inequality symbol can sometimes tell you which part of the graph is shaded. Let's look at the system $\begin{cases} x + y \leq 4 \\ x - 2y > -2 \end{cases}$.

2. Write each inequality in slope-intercept form.

$\quad x + y \leq 4 \qquad\qquad x - 2y > -2$

$\qquad y \leq -x + 4 \qquad\qquad -2y > -x - 2$

$\qquad\qquad\qquad\qquad\qquad\qquad y < \dfrac{1}{2}x + 2$

---

3. Graph the boundary line for $x + y \leq 4$ using the slope and y-intercept from the slope-intercept form, $y \leq -x + 4$.

Look at the inequality symbol in the slope-intercept form.

  • When the inequality is $<$ or $\leq$, shade below the line.

  • When the inequality is $>$ or $\geq$, shade above the line.

The symbol is $\leq$, so shade below the boundary line.

4. Graph the boundary line for $x - 2y > -2$ using the slope-intercept form, $y < \dfrac{1}{2}x + 2$.

In slope-intercept form, the inequality symbol is $<$, so shade below the boundary line.

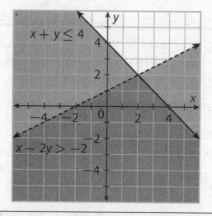

COMMON MISCONCEPTION

Ask: What is the Error?

$$\begin{cases} 2x - 3y < -6 \\ 2x + 5y \geq 10 \end{cases}$$

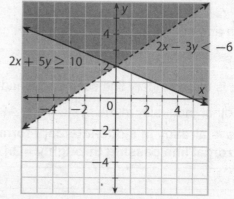

Reason incorrect: Each inequality was shaded on the wrong side of the boundary line.

Solution: After graphing each boundary line, check the origin by substituting zeros into the original inequality.

$2x - 3y < -6$
$2(0) - 3(0) < -6$
$\qquad 0 < -6 \qquad$ False

$2x + 5y \geq 10$
$2(0) + 5(0) \geq 10$
$\qquad 0 \geq 10 \qquad$ False

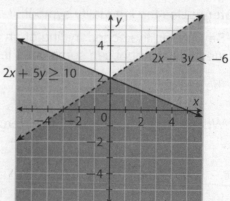

KEY TEACHING POINTS

Example 2

Say: When the boundary lines of the inequalities in a system have the same slope, the lines are parallel. As a result, the solution set will either be between the two boundary lines, be the same as one of the inequalities, or there will be no solution.

Ask: When the boundary lines in a system of two inequalities intersect, the coordinate plane is divided into four regions. When the boundary lines are parallel, how many regions are in the coordinate plane? **[Three.]**

Say: Let's look at the system $\begin{cases} 2x + y \geq -1 \\ 2x + y > 6 \end{cases}$. The graph shows that the solution set is the same solution set as $2x + y > 6$.

Ask: How would the solution set change if the inequality symbol for $2x + y \geq -1$ was reversed? **[The shading for that inequality would be on the other side of the boundary line. There would be no solution set.]**

Ask: How would the solution set change if both inequality symbols were reversed? **[The shading for both inequalities would move to the other side of the boundary lines. The solution set would be the same as the one for $2x + y \leq -1$.]**

Ask: How could you change the inequality symbols so that the solution set lies between the boundary lines and on the boundary line given by $2x + y \geq -1$? **[The shading for the inequality $2x + y > 6$ would need to be on the other side of the boundary line, so change the inequality to $2x + y < 6$.]**

Check

Ask: Does the solution set for $\begin{cases} 3x - 4y > -4 \\ 3x - 4y < 16 \end{cases}$ include any boundary lines? Explain. **[No. Both lines are dashed so neither line is included in the solution set.]**

ADDITIONAL ONLINE INTERVENTION RESOURCES

Use the following for students who have not mastered the concepts in Skill 34.

- Math on the Spot videos
- Personal Math Trainer with customized intervention
- Building Block worksheets (Skill 44: Graph Linear Equations)

SKILL 34

Solving Systems of Linear Inequalities

Example 1

A system of linear inequalities is made up of two or more linear inequalities in the same two variables. The solutions of a system of linear inequalities are all the ordered pairs that make all the inequalities in the system true.

Solve the system by graphing. 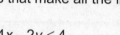 $\begin{cases} 4x - 2y \le 4 \\ x + 3y > -6 \end{cases}$

Step 1 Graph $4x - 2y \le 4$.

The equation of the boundary line is $4x - 2y = 4$.

The x-intercept is 1. The y-intercept is –2.

The inequality symbol is $\le$, so use a solid line.

Shade above the boundary line because (0, 0) is a solution of the inequality.

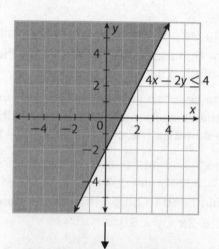

Step 2 Graph $x + 3y > -6$.

The equation of the boundary line is $x + 3y = -6$.

The x-intercept is –6. The y-intercept is –2.

The inequality symbol is >, so use a dashed line.

Shade above the boundary line because (0, 0) is a solution of the inequality.

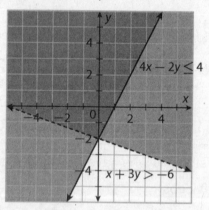

Step 3 Identify the solutions.

The solutions are the points in the region where the graphs of the individual inequalities overlap.

Step 4 Check your answer.

(0, 0) is in the solutions region. Make sure (0, 0) satisfies each inequality in the system:

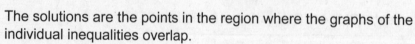

$4x - 2y \le 4$	$x + 3y > -6$
$4(0) - 2(0) \le 4?$	$0 + 3(0) > -6?$
$0 \le 4$	$0 > -6$

Vocabulary

System of linear inequalities

Solutions of a system of linear inequalities

Check
Solve the system of inequalities by graphing.

1. $\begin{cases} x + y \le 4 \\ x - 2y > -2 \end{cases}$

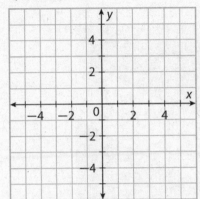

2. $\begin{cases} 3x - 4y < 12 \\ x + 2y \le 4 \end{cases}$

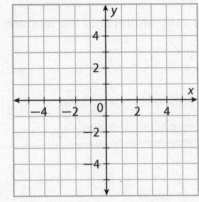

3. $\begin{cases} 3x - 2y < 0 \\ y \le 2 \end{cases}$

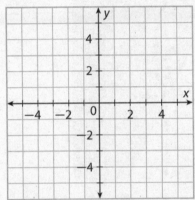

4. $\begin{cases} x - 2y < -1 \\ 3x - y \le -3 \end{cases}$

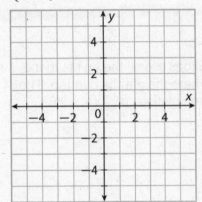

5. Explain the Error. Then graph the correct solution.

$\begin{cases} 2x - 3y < -6 \\ 2x + 5y \ge 10 \end{cases}$

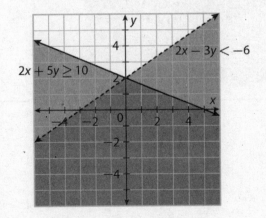

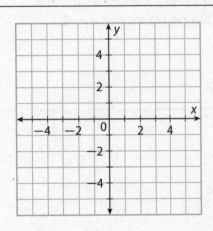

Example 2

The graphs of the linear inequalities in a system may have boundary lines that are parallel.

A. Describe the solutions of the system.

$$\begin{cases} x - 2y \le -2 \\ x - 2y > 6 \end{cases}$$

The two regions do not overlap.

The system has no solution.

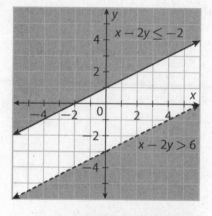

B. Describe the solutions of the system.

$$\begin{cases} 2x + y \ge -1 \\ 2x + y > 6 \end{cases}$$

The solutions are all the points in the region where the graphs overlap. They are all the solutions of $2x + y > 6$.

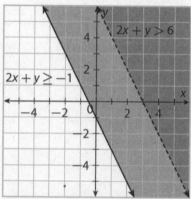

C. Describe the solutions of the system.

$$\begin{cases} y < 3 \\ y \ge -2 \end{cases}$$

The solutions are all the points in the regions between the boundary lines and on the boundary line $y = -2$.

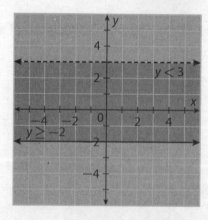

Check

Describe the solutions of each system of inequalities.

6. $\begin{cases} x + 4y \geq 4 \\ x + 4y \leq -12 \end{cases}$

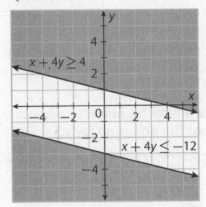

7. $\begin{cases} x - y \leq -2 \\ x - y < 3 \end{cases}$

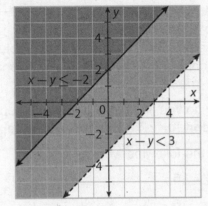

8. $\begin{cases} 3x - 4y > -4 \\ 3x - 4y < 16 \end{cases}$

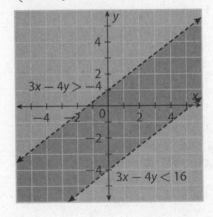

9. $\begin{cases} y \geq 0 \\ y \geq 2 \end{cases}$

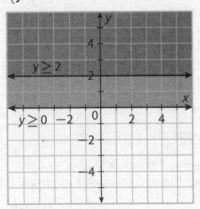

10. Suppose you have a system of two linear inequalities in which the boundary lines intersect. Is it possible that the system has no solution? Explain your reasoning.

_____

SKILL 34 SOLVING SYSTEMS OF LINEAR INEQUALITIES

Systems of Two Linear Equations

KEY TEACHING POINTS

Example 1
Say: Some problems ask you to find a solution that is true for more than one linear equation. The solution to a system of linear equations is the set of values that makes all of the equations true.

Ask: How do you find the *x*- and *y*-intercepts? **[To find the *x*-intercept, substitute 0 into the equation for *y*. To find the *y*-intercept, substitute 0 into the equation for *x*.]**

Complete the following work as a class:

For $x + 4y = 16$

$$x + 4y = 16$$
$$(0) + 4y = 16$$
$$4y = 16$$
$$y = 4$$

$$x + 4y = 16$$
$$x + 4(0) = 16$$
$$x = 16$$

The intercepts are $y = 4$ and $x = 16$.

For $3x - 2y = 6$

$$3(0) - 2y = 6$$
$$-2y = 6$$
$$y = -3$$

$$3x - 2(0) = 6$$
$$3x = 6$$
$$x = 2$$

The intercepts are $y = -3$ and $x = 2$.

Say: Graphing the solution to a system of linear equations can help you locate the intersection, but you still need to check the point.

Check

Say: Let's look at the linear system $\begin{cases} 3x + 2y = -6 \\ 6x + 4y = -12 \end{cases}$.

Ask: How can you tell both equations are linear? **[They are both written in the standard form of a linear equation.]**

Say: Let's find the intercepts and graph this system.

Complete the following work as a class:

Find the intercepts for $3x + 2y = -6$.

$$3x + 2y = -6$$
$$3(0) + 2y = -6$$
$$2y = -6$$
$$y = -3$$

$$3x + 2y = -6$$
$$3x + 2(0) = -6$$
$$3x = -6$$
$$x = -2$$

The intercepts are $y = -3$ and $x = -2$.

Graph the equation using the intercepts.

Say: Now let's graph $6x + 4y = -12$.

Find the intercepts.

$6x + 4y = -12$ $6x + 4y = -12$
$6(0) + 4y = -12$ $6x + 4(0) = -12$
$\quad\ \ 4y = -12$ $\quad\ \ 6x = -12$
$\qquad y = -3$ $\qquad x = -2$

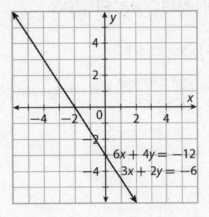

The intercepts are $y = -3$ and $x = -2$.

The intercepts are the same, so the line is the same.

ALTERNATE STRATEGY

Strategy: Use slope-intercept form.

1. **Say:** In some cases you can't use the x- and y-intercept to graph a line. In those cases, you can use the slope-intercept form.

    Look at the linear system $\begin{cases} x - 2y = 0 \\ x - 2y = -6 \end{cases}$. The equation $x - 2y = 0$ passes through the

    origin. Both the x- and y-intercepts are the same point.

2. Write the equations in slope-intercept form.

    $x - 2y = 0$ $x - 2y = -6$
    $\ \ -2y = -x$ $\ \ -2y = -x - 6$
    $\qquad y = \dfrac{1}{2}x$ $\qquad y = \dfrac{1}{2}x + 3$

3. Graph the equations using the slope-intercept form.

    $y = \dfrac{1}{2}x$ has a y-intercept of 0 and a slope of $\dfrac{1}{2}$.

    Mark a point at the origin. Move up
    one unit and right two units to mark a second
    point. Connect the points to graph the line.

    $y = \dfrac{1}{2}x + 3$ has a y-intercept of 3 and a slope

    of $\dfrac{1}{2}$. Mark a point at $y = 3$. Move up one unit

    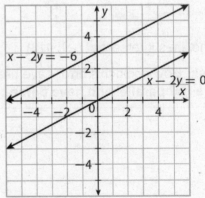

    and right two units to mark a second point.
    Connect the points to graph the line.

4. Because the slopes of the lines are the same, there is no solution.

COMMON MISCONCEPTION

Ask: What is the Error?

The system $\begin{cases} 4x - 3y = 3 \\ x - y = 4 \end{cases}$ has no solution because the lines do not intersect.

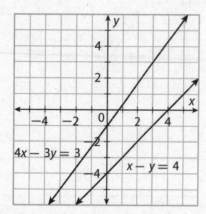

Reason incorrect: The given window for the graph is too small.

Solution: Create a graph with a greater window to find the intersection.

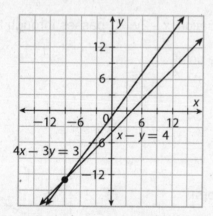

The lines intersect at (−9, −13).

Ask: How could this error have been avoided? **[Possible response: By noticing the lines are not parallel and have different slopes.]**

KEY TEACHING POINTS

Example 2

Say: The substitution method of solving a linear system solves one of the equations for one of the variables and then replaces that variable in the second equation.

Say: The equation $x + y = 12$ has no coefficients. This equation can be solved for either variable by simply subtracting the other variable from both sides. In the equation $5x - y = 0$, the variable y has no coefficients. It can be solved for y by adding y to each side.

Ask: In Step 1, which equation is solved? **[5x − y = 0]** Which variable is solved for? **[y]**

Ask: In Step 2, which equation is y replaced by in the expression found in Step 1? **[x + y = 12]**

Say: Be careful to substitute your answer for Step 1 into the other equation. Because we have removed the variable y from the equations, solving the new equation gives us the value for x in the solution.

Say: Once you know the value for x, you can use either equation to find the value for y.

Ask: Does it matter which equation you use or which variable you solve for in the first step? **[No.]**

Say: Let's try solving for x first in the equation $x + y = 12$ and see if we get the same results.

Complete the following as a class:

$x + y = 12$
$\quad x = -y + 12 \qquad$ Solve for x.

Substitute the expression $(-y + 12)$ into the other equation for x.

$\quad\quad 5x - y = 0$
$5(-y + 12) - y = 0 \qquad$ Replace the variable x.
$\quad -5y + 60 - y = 0 \qquad$ Use the Distributive Property.
$\quad\quad -6y + 60 = 0 \qquad$ Combine like terms.
$\quad\quad\quad -6y = -60 \qquad$ Subtract 60 from each side.
$\quad\quad\quad\quad y = 10 \qquad$ Divide each side by -6.

The y-value is the same as the one we found using the other variable and equation.

Check

Say: Let's look at the linear system $\begin{cases} 2x - y = -1 \\ 6x - 3y = 2 \end{cases}$.

Ask: What variable and equation look like they might be easiest to solve for? **[Possible answer: Solve for y in 2x − y = −1.]**

Complete the following work as a class:

$2x - y = -1 \qquad$ Solve for y.
$\quad -y = -1 - 2x$
$\quad\quad y = 2x + 1$

$$6x - 3y = 2$$
$$6x - 3(2x + 1) = 2 \qquad \text{Replace } y \text{ with the equivalent expression.}$$
$$6x - 6x - 3 = 2 \qquad \text{Use the Distributive Property.}$$
$$-3 = 2 \qquad \text{Combine like terms.}$$

Say: This is impossible. When the two sides of the equation are constants that are not equal, the system has no solutions.

Say: Let's look at the linear system $\begin{cases} x + 5y = 8 \\ 3x + 15y = 24 \end{cases}$.

Ask: What variable and equation look like they might be easiest to solve for? **[Possible answer: Solve for x in x + 5y = 8.]**

Complete the following work as a class:

$$x + 5y = 8 \qquad \text{Solve for } x.$$
$$x = -5y + 8$$

$$3x + 15y = 24$$
$$3(-5y + 8) + 15y = 24 \qquad \text{Replace } x \text{ with the equivalent expression.}$$
$$-15y + 24 + 15y = 24 \qquad \text{Use the Distributive Property.}$$
$$24 = 24 \qquad \text{Combine like terms.}$$

Say: This is always true. When both sides of the equation are equal constants, the two equations in the system are graphed by the same line. There are infinite solutions.

Example 3

Say: In the system $\begin{cases} 6x + 3y = -12 \\ x - 3y = -9 \end{cases}$, the two equations have opposite coefficients for y.

Combining the two equations into one eliminates the variable y and leaves an equation that can be solved for x.

Say: This system made it easy to eliminate a variable. In some systems you will need to use multiplication to find equivalent equations.

Say: In the system $\begin{cases} 4x + 10y = -60 \\ x - 5y = 15 \end{cases}$, the second equation is multiplied by 2 to eliminate y.

Because 5 is a factor of 10, we only need to change one of the equations.

Ask: How could you eliminate x instead? **[Multiply the second equation by –4.]**

Say: There are often many different ways to solve a system, but each method, if done correctly, will have the same result.

Ask: In Part D, the variable *x* is eliminated by creating the coefficients 6 and −6. What are other possible ways to use elimination? **[Possible answer: Eliminate *y* by creating the coefficients 10 and −10.]**

Check

Say: Let's look at the linear system $\begin{cases} 3x + 2y = 16 \\ 4x + 5y = 5 \end{cases}$.

Ask: What variable can be eliminated using what coefficients? **[Possible answer: Eliminate *y* by creating the coefficients 10 and −10.]** How would you create those coefficients? **[Multiply the first equation by 5 and the second equation by −2.]**

Ask: Is there another way to eliminate a variable? **[Yes. Possible answer: Eliminate *x* by multiplying the first equation by 4 and the second equation by −3.]**

Ask: In the system $\begin{cases} x - 2y = -2 \\ 2x - 4y = 12 \end{cases}$, what variable can be eliminated, and using what coefficients? **[Possible answer: Eliminate *x* by multiplying the first equation by −2.]**

Show the following work.

$$\begin{cases} x - 2y = -2 \\ 2x - 4y = 12 \end{cases} \longrightarrow \begin{array}{r} -2x + 4y = 4 \\ +\ \ 2x - 4y = 12 \\ \hline 0x + 0y = 16 \\ 0 = 16 \end{array}$$

Say: When eliminating a variable results in an equation that is not true, the system has no solutions. When the result is an identity, the system has infinite solutions.

Say: Problem 21 solves a problem about purchases using a system of equations. In the problem, you are given the total number of shirts and pants combined that were purchased, the cost of each item, and the total price.

Say: Since Sasha bought shirts and pants, the variables used are *s* and *p*.

Ask: How was the first equation in the system derived? **[The number of shirts added to the number of pants equals the total number of items.]**

Ask: How was the second equation in the system derived? **[The cost of a shirt times the number of shirts added to the cost of a pair of pants multiplied by the number of pants equals the total amount that was spent.]**

ADDITIONAL ONLINE INTERVENTION RESOURCES

Use the following for students who have not mastered the concepts in Skill 35.

- Math on the Spot videos
- Personal Math Trainer with customized intervention
- Building Block worksheets (Skill 44: Graph Linear Equations; Skill 91: Solve Multi-Step Equations)

Systems of Two Linear Equations

Example 1

A system of linear equations, or a linear system, is made up of two or more linear equations in the same two variables. A solution of a system of linear equations is the ordered pair that makes all the equations in the system true.

You can solve a linear system by graphing.

- If the lines in a system intersect at one point, the system has exactly one solution.

- If the lines in a system are parallel, the system has no solution.

- If the lines in a system are the same line, then the system has infinitely many solutions.

Solve the linear system by graphing. $\begin{cases} x + 4y = 16 \\ 3x - 2y = 6 \end{cases}$

Step 1 Find the x- and y-intercepts for the graphs of both equations. Then graph both equations in the same coordinate plane.

$x + 4y = 16$: x-intercept: 16; y-intercept: 4

$3x - 2y = 6$: x-intercept: 2; y-intercept: −3

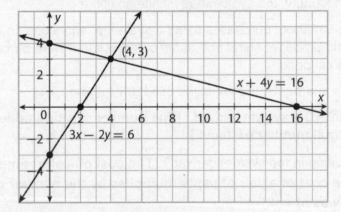

Step 2 Find the point of intersection.

The lines appear to intersect at (4, 3).

Step 3 Check to see if (4, 3) makes each equation true.

$x + 4y = 16$	$3x - 2y = 6$
$4 + 4(3) = 16$?	$3(4) - 2(3) = 6$?
$4 + 12 = 16$?	$12 - 6 = 6$?
$16 = 16$	$6 = 6$

The solution of the system is (4, 3).

Vocabulary

System of linear equations

Linear system

Solutions of a system of linear equations

Substitution method

Elimination method

Check
Solve the linear system by graphing.

1. $\begin{cases} x + y = 6 \\ x - 3y = -6 \end{cases}$ _____

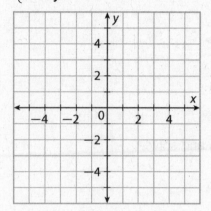

2. $\begin{cases} 3x - 4y = 12 \\ x + 4y = 4 \end{cases}$ _____

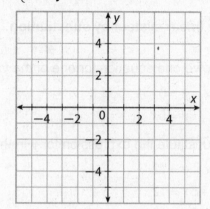

3. $\begin{cases} 3x + 2y = -6 \\ 6x + 4y = -12 \end{cases}$ _____

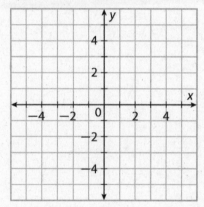

4. $\begin{cases} x - 2y = 0 \\ x - 2y = -6 \end{cases}$ _____

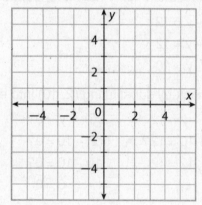

5. Explain the Error. Then graph the correct solution.

The system $\begin{cases} 4x - 3y = 3 \\ x - y = 4 \end{cases}$ has no solution because the lines do not intersect.

_____

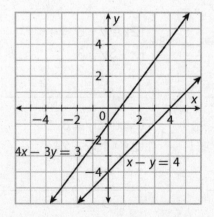

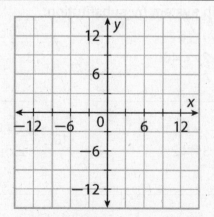

Example 2

You can also solve a linear system using the substitution method.

Solve the linear system by substitution. $\begin{cases} x + y = 12 \\ 5x - y = 0 \end{cases}$

Step 1 Solve one equation for one of the variables.

$$5x - y = 0$$
$$y = 5x$$

Step 2 Substitute the expression for y in the other equation and solve.

$$x + y = 12$$
$$x + 5x = 12$$
$$6x = 12$$
$$x = 2$$

Step 3 Substitute 2 for x into either equation, and solve for y.

$$x + y = 12$$
$$2 + y = 12$$
$$y = 10$$

Step 4 Check by substituting (2, 10) into each equation.

$x + y = 12$	$5x - y = 0$
$2 + 10 = 12?$	$5(2) - 10 = 0?$
$12 = 12$	$10 - 10 = 0?$
	$0 = 0$

The solution is (2, 10).

When solving a linear system, if you get an identity, such as $4 = 4$, then the system has infinitely many solutions. If you get a false statement, such as $-2 = 9$, then the system has no solution.

Check

Solve each system by substitution.

6. $\begin{cases} x - y = -6 \\ 2x + 2y = 40 \end{cases}$

7. $\begin{cases} x - y = -7 \\ 3x + 4y = 14 \end{cases}$

8. $\begin{cases} 2x + y = 6 \\ x - 3y = 3 \end{cases}$

_____ _____ _____

9. $\begin{cases} 2x - y = -1 \\ 6x - 3y = 2 \end{cases}$

10. $\begin{cases} 4x - 2y = 2 \\ 2x + y = 6 \end{cases}$

11. $\begin{cases} x + 5y = 8 \\ 3x + 15y = 24 \end{cases}$

_____ _____ _____

Example 3

You can also use the elimination method to solve a linear system.

A. Solve the linear system by elimination. $\begin{cases} 6x + 3y = -12 \\ x - 3y = -9 \end{cases}$

Step 1 Eliminate one variable. Since $3y$ and $-3y$ are opposites, *add* the equations to eliminate y.

$$6x + 3y = -12$$
$$\underline{+ \quad x - 3y = \ -9}$$
$$7x + 0 = -21 \qquad \text{Add equations to eliminate } y.$$
$$7x = -21 \qquad \text{Solve for } x.$$
$$x = -3$$

Step 2 Substitute -3 for x in either equation to solve for y.

$$x - 3y = -9$$
$$-3 - 3y = -9$$
$$-3y = -6$$
$$y = 2$$

The solution is $(-3, 2)$.

When both equations of a linear system have the same term, you can subtract the equations to eliminate the variable.

B. Solve the linear system by elimination. $\begin{cases} 3x + 2y = -2 \\ 3x - 6y = 30 \end{cases}$

Step 1 Eliminate one variable. Since $3x$ is a term of both equations, *subtract* the equations to eliminate x.

$$3x + 2y = -2$$
$$\underline{- \ (3x - 6y = 30)}$$
$$0x + 8y = -32 \qquad \text{Subtract equations to eliminate } x.$$
$$8y = -32 \qquad \text{Solve for } y.$$
$$y = -4$$

Step 2 Substitute -4 for y in either equation to solve for x.

$$3x + 2y = -2$$
$$3x + 2(-4) = -2$$
$$3x - 8 = -2$$
$$3x = 6$$
$$x = 2$$

The solution is $(2, -4)$.

For some linear systems, you may have to first multiply one equation by a constant before you can eliminate one of the variables.

C. Solve the linear system by elimination. $\begin{cases} 4x + 10y = -60 \\ x - 5y = 15 \end{cases}$

Step 1 Multiply the second equation by 2 so you can eliminate y. Then add the resulting equations.

$$4x + 10y = -60$$
$$2(x - 5y = 15) \longrightarrow$$

$$\begin{aligned} 4x + 10y &= -60 \\ + \ 2x - 10y &= \ 30 \\ \hline 6x + 0y &= -30 \\ 6x &= -30 \\ x &= -5 \end{aligned}$$

Add equations to eliminate y.

Solve for x.

Step 2 Substitute -5 for x in either equation to solve for y.

$$x - 5y = 15$$
$$-5 - 5y = 15$$
$$-5y = 20$$
$$y = -4$$

The solution is $(-5, -4)$.

Sometimes you may have to multiply both equations in a linear system by a constant before you can eliminate a variable.

D. Solve the linear system by elimination. $\begin{cases} 2x + 5y = 26 \\ 3x + 2y = 17 \end{cases}$

Step 1 Multiply the first equation by 3 and the second equation by -2 so you can eliminate x. Then add the resulting equations.

$$3(2x + 5y = 26)$$
$$-2(3x + 2y = 17) \longrightarrow$$

$$\begin{aligned} 6x + 15y &= 78 \\ + \ -6x - 4y &= -34 \\ \hline 0x + 11y &= 44 \\ y &= 4 \end{aligned}$$

Add equations to eliminate x.

Solve for y.

Step 2 Substitute 4 for y in either equation to solve for x.

$$3x + 2y = 17$$
$$3x + 2(4) = 17$$
$$3x + 8 = 17$$
$$3x = 9$$
$$x = 3$$

The solution is $(3, 4)$.

Check

Solve each system by elimination.

12. $\begin{cases} 3x - 2y = 0 \\ 4x + 2y = 21 \end{cases}$

13. $\begin{cases} 3x + 3y = -9 \\ -3x + 4y = -5 \end{cases}$

14. $\begin{cases} 5x - y = 0 \\ -3x - y = -32 \end{cases}$

15. $\begin{cases} 5x + 6y = 39 \\ 5x + 3y = 27 \end{cases}$

16. $\begin{cases} x + 2y = 4 \\ 3x - 4y = 12 \end{cases}$

17. $\begin{cases} 3x - y = -3 \\ x - 2y = -1 \end{cases}$

18. $\begin{cases} 3x + 2y = 16 \\ 4x + 5y = 5 \end{cases}$

19. $\begin{cases} 3x - 3y = -12 \\ 5x + 4y = -83 \end{cases}$

20. $\begin{cases} x - 2y = -2 \\ 2x - 4y = 12 \end{cases}$

21. Sasha has to purchase shirts and pants to wear to her after-school job. Altogether, she buys 20 items of clothing. A shirt costs $7. A pair of pants costs $10. She spends a total of $155. Solve the system below to find how many shirts and pairs of pants Sasha purchased.

$\begin{cases} s + p = 20 \\ 7s + 10p = 155 \end{cases}$

SKILL 35 SYSTEMS OF TWO LINEAR EQUATIONS

The Quadratic Formula

KEY TEACHING POINTS

Example 1

Say: The quadratic formula can be used to solve any quadratic equation. In order to know the correct values to put into the formula, you must first write the equation in standard form.

Ask: What is the standard form of a quadratic equation? **[$ax^2 + bx + c = 0$, where $a \neq 0$]**

Ask: What do the subtraction signs in the equation $2x^2 - x - 15 = 0$ tell you about the values for b and c? **[They are negative.]**

Say: When you substitute the values for a, b, and c into the quadratic formula, putting the values inside parentheses helps keep the correct sign for each value.

Ask: What is a radicand? **[The value under the radical symbol.]** What is the radicand in $x = \dfrac{1 \pm \sqrt{121}}{4}$? **[121]**

Say: Because 121 is a perfect square, you can evaluate the square root as 11.

Ask: Why do you need to write two equations? **[The symbol $\pm$ in the numerator means there are two different solutions.]** Why is the symbol $\pm$ included as part of the solution? **[There are two possible solutions to a square root, either a positive value or a negative value.]**

Check

Ask: What is the first step to solving $-4x^2 - 4x + 4 = 3$? **[Write the equation in standard form.]** What is the equation in standard form? **[$-4x^2 - 4x + 1 = 0$]**

Ask: Are there any common factors in $-4x^2 - 4x + 1 = 0$? **[No.]**

Ask: Is $-4x^2 - 4x + 1 = 0$ a perfect square or the difference of two squares? **[No.]**

Ask: Is $-4x^2 - 4x + 1 = 0$ a perfect square trinomial? **[No.]**

Ask: Does the equation $-4x^2 - 4x + 1 = 0$ work well to complete the square? Why or why not? **[It will work, but you will need to factor out a –1 first, and the numbers are not going to be integer values.]**

Ask: What are the values for a, b, and c? **[$a = -4$, $b = -4$, $c = 1$]**

Say: Let's put those values into the quadratic formula.

Complete the following as a class.

$$x = \frac{-b \pm \sqrt{b^2 - 4ac}}{2a}$$

$$x = \frac{-(-4) \pm \sqrt{(-4)^2 - 4(-4)(1)}}{2(-4)}$$

Remember to use parentheses around the values you substitute into the formula.

$$x = \frac{4 \pm \sqrt{32}}{-8}$$

Simplify the radicand and the denominator.

Keep track of the signs carefully.

$$x = \frac{4 \pm 4\sqrt{2}}{-8}$$

Evaluate the square root. Because 32 is not a perfect square, keep the radical symbol in your solution for an exact answer.

$$x = \frac{1 \pm \sqrt{2}}{-2}$$

Reduce the fraction.

Because there is a radical in the answer, it does not need to be broken down further. It is common to write the negative symbol either in the numerator or in front of the fraction, so the solutions are $x = \frac{-1 \pm \sqrt{2}}{2}$.

Say: Quadratic equations are commonly used to model the flight of a projectile, as in Problem 9. The flight path at any given time is represented by the equation. At what height, the value for h, will the ball no longer be in the air? **[When h is 0.]** When h is 0, the value for t is the number of seconds from when the ball hits the bat (the initial time) to when it hits the ground.

Ask: Why does the baseball problem only have one solution? **[The ball was hit at $t = 0$, so the negative solution is not during the ball's post-hit trajectory.]**

COMMON MISCONCEPTION

Ask: What is the Error?

Solve $-3x^2 = -4 + 3x$ using the quadratic formula.

Solution:

$$-3x^2 - 3x + 4 = 0$$

$$x = \frac{-(3) \pm \sqrt{(3)^2 - 4(-3)(4)}}{2(-3)}$$

$$x = \frac{-3 \pm \sqrt{57}}{-6}$$

$$x = \frac{3 \pm \sqrt{57}}{6}$$

Reason incorrect: The sign for $b = 3$ was picked up as a positive value instead of a negative value.

Solution: Substitute the values for a, b, and c into the quadratic formula.

$$-3x^2 - 3x + 4 = 0$$

$$a = -3, \ b = -3, \ c = 4$$

$$x = \frac{-(-3) \pm \sqrt{(-3)^2 - 4(-3)(4)}}{2(-3)}$$

$$x = \frac{3 \pm \sqrt{57}}{-6}$$

$$x = \frac{-3 \pm \sqrt{57}}{6}$$

Say: It is very easy to pick up the wrong sign for the variable b, particularly in the first term in the numerator.

KEY TEACHING POINTS

Example 2

Say: The part of the quadratic formula that is under the radical sign is the discriminant and can be used to determine the number of real solutions. Real solutions are points where the graph of the related quadratic function crosses the x-axis.

Say: Let's look at just what this means.

- If the discriminant is greater than 0, $b^2 - 4ac > 0$, there are two real solutions, so the graph crosses the x-axis at two points.

- If the discriminant is exactly 0, $b^2 - 4ac = 0$, there is exactly one real solution. The graph touches the x-axis at exactly one point. This means the parabola has its vertex on the x-axis.

- If the discriminant is less than 0, $b^2 - 4ac < 0$, there are no real solutions. This means the graph never crosses the x-axis.

Ask: How many real solutions does the equation $4x^2 + 4x + 1 = 0$ have? **[One.]** How can this be used? **[Possible response: To check your answer.]**

Say: Let's find the solution and see if this is accurate. Use the quadratic formula.

Complete the following as a class.

Substitute the values for a, b, and c into the quadratic formula.

$$4x^2 + 4x + 1 = 0$$

$$a = 4, \quad b = 4, \quad c = 1$$

$$x = \frac{-(4) \pm \sqrt{(4)^2 - 4(4)(1)}}{2(1)}$$

$$x = \frac{-4 \pm \sqrt{0}}{2}$$

$$x = -2$$

There is only one solution. Since the value for a is positive, the graph is a parabola that opens up, with its vertex at $x = -2$.

ALTERNATE STRATEGY

Strategy: Sketch a graph.

Say: A quick sketch can help you understand word problems.

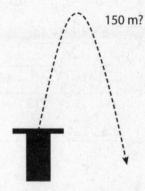

150 m?

1. A model rocket is launched with an initial velocity of 50 meters per second from a launch pad 2 meters tall. The equation for the rocket's height h at time t seconds can be modeled by the equation $h = -4.9t^2 + 50t + 2$.

2. What might the path of the rocket look like over time? Make a sketch. It does not have to be perfect, just good enough that you understand it.

3. The question asks how the discriminant can be used to determine whether the rocket will reach a height of 150 meters. Use the sketch to show the question.

4. If the discriminant has no solutions, it means the rocket never reaches that height.

ADDITIONAL ONLINE INTERVENTION RESOURCES

Use the following for students who have not mastered the concepts in Skill 36.

- Math on the Spot videos
- Personal Math Trainer with customized intervention
- Building Block worksheets (Skill 100: Squares and Square Roots)

SKILL 36

The Quadratic Formula

Example 1

Vocabulary
Quadratic formula
Standard form
Real solutions
Discriminant

The quadratic formula, $x = \dfrac{-b \pm \sqrt{b^2 - 4ac}}{2a}$, can be used to solve any

quadratic equation written in standard form, $ax^2 + bx + c = 0$, where $a \neq 0$. To use the formula, check that the equation is in standard form. If not, rewrite it in standard form. Then substitute the values of a, b, and c into the formula.

Solve $2x^2 - x = 15$ using the quadratic formula.

$2x^2 - x - 15 = 0$	Write in standard form.
$a = 2$, $b = -1$, $c = -15$	Identify a, b and c.
$x = \dfrac{-b \pm \sqrt{b^2 - 4ac}}{2a}$	Use the quadratic formula.
$x = \dfrac{-(-1) \pm \sqrt{(-1)^2 - 4(2)(-15)}}{2(2)}$	Substitute the identified values into the quadratic formula.
$x = \dfrac{1 \pm \sqrt{121}}{4}$	Simplify the radicand and the denominator.
$x = \dfrac{1 \pm 11}{4}$	Evaluate the square root.
$x = \dfrac{1 + 11}{4}$ or $x = \dfrac{1 - 11}{4}$	Write as two equations.
$x = 3$ or $x = -\dfrac{5}{2}$	Simplify both equations.

The solutions are 3 and $-\dfrac{5}{2}$.

Check

Solve each equation using the quadratic formula.

1. $2x^2 - x - 6 = 0$

2. $x^2 + 4x - 8 = 0$

3. $x^2 - 2x - 6 = -4$

4. $2x^2 + 5x - 2 = 5$

5. $-4x^2 - 4x + 4 = 3$

6. $-2x^2 - x + 5 = 2$

_____

_____

7. $4x^2 + 6 = 7 - 3x$

8. $-5x^2 + 11 = -5$

_____

_____

Solve.

9. A baseball is hit by a bat 4 feet above the ground and has an initial velocity of 72 feet per second. The height of the baseball t seconds after being hit can be modeled by the equation $h = -16t^2 + 72t + 4$.

   a. How can the quadratic formula be used to determine how long the ball stays in the air?

   _____

   _____

   b. How long does the ball stay in the air? Round your answer to the nearest tenth.

   _____

10. Explain the Error. Find the correct solution.

    Solve $-3x^2 = -4 + 3x$ using the quadratic formula.

    Solution:

    $$-3x^2 - 3x + 4 = 0$$

    $$x = \frac{-(3) \pm \sqrt{(3)^2 - 4(-3)(4)}}{2(-3)}$$

    $$x = \frac{-3 \pm \sqrt{57}}{-6}$$

    $$x = \frac{3 \pm \sqrt{57}}{6}$$

    _____

    _____

    _____

    _____

Example 2

A quadratic equation can have two, one, or no real solutions. By evaluating the part of the quadratic formula under the radical sign, $b^2 - 4ac$, called the discriminant, you can determine the number of real solutions.

- If $b^2 - 4ac > 0$, the equation has two real solutions.

- If $b^2 - 4ac = 0$, the equation has one real solution.

- If $b^2 - 4ac < 0$, the equation has no real solutions.

Find the discriminant. Then state the number of real solutions of each quadratic equation using the discriminant.

A. $3x^2 + 2x - 1 = 0$

$a = 3,\ b = 2,\ c = -1$	Identify a, b, and c.
$b^2 - 4ac$	Use the discriminant.
$(2)^2 - 4(3)(-1)$	Substitute the identified values into the discriminant.
$4 + 12 = 16$	Simplify.

Since $b^2 - 4ac > 0$, the equation has two real solutions.

B. $4x^2 + 4x + 1 = 0$

$a = 4,\ b = 4,\ c = 1$	Identify a, b, and c.
$b^2 - 4ac$	Use the discriminant.
$(4)^2 - 4(4)(1)$	Substitute the identified values into the discriminant.
$16 - 16 = 0$	Simplify.

Since $b^2 - 4ac = 0$, the equation has one real solution.

C. $-2x^2 - 3 = 0$

$a = -2,\ b = 0,\ c = -3$	Identify a, b, and c.
$b^2 - 4ac$	Use the discriminant.
$(0)^2 - 4(-2)(-3)$	Substitute the identified values into the discriminant.
$0 - 24 = -24$	Simplify.

Since $b^2 - 4ac < 0$, the equation has no real solutions.

Check

Find the discriminant. Then state the number of real solutions of each quadratic equation using the discriminant.

11. $x^2 + 2x + 1 = 0$

12. $-x^2 - x - 5 = 0$

13. $8x^2 + 2x + 5 = 6$

14. $8x^2 - 8x + 8 = 3$

_____

_____

15. $-2x^2 - 2 = 4x$

16. $4x^2 + 5x = 0$

_____

_____

17. $5x^2 - 6x = -2 - 5x^2$

18. $3x^2 + x - 3 = 7$

_____

_____

Solve.

19. A model rocket is launched with an initial velocity of 50 meters per second from a launch pad 2 meters tall. The equation for the rocket's height h at time t seconds can be modeled by the equation $h = -4.9t^2 + 50t + 2$.

   a. How can the discriminant be used to determine whether the rocket will reach a height of 150 meters?

   _____

   _____

   b. Calculate the discriminant for a height of 150 meters. Will the rocket reach that height? Explain.

   _____

   _____

   _____

   _____

   _____

   _____

SKILL 36 THE QUADRATIC FORMULA

Transforming Cubic Functions

Example 1

Say: The parent cubic function, $f(x) = x^3$, is the most basic cubic function. On a graph, the parent cubic function looks similar to a parabola that has been twisted at the origin so that the section in negative x-values goes down instead of up.

Say: The general form of a cubic function is $f(x) = a(x-h)^3 + k$. Each of the variables a, h, and k transforms the parent cubic function in its own way. The variables h and k translate the function. The variable h translates it left and right, and the variable k translates it up and down. The variable a vertically stretches and compresses as well as reflects the function.

Ask: How does a value of 3 for a transform a cubic function? **[It vertically stretches the function by a factor of 3.]** How does a value of –1 for a transform a cubic function? **[It reflects the function about the x-axis.]** Then, how does a value of –3 for a transform a cubic function? **[It combines both by stretching the function and reflecting it.]**

Say: Stretches and compressions can get confusing. Remember, the y-value changes by the factor. For a stretch of 3, the values for y are 3 times what they are in the parent function.

Check

Ask: In $g(x) = -\dfrac{1}{2}(x+2)^3 - 1$, what is the value of a? $\left[-\dfrac{1}{2}\right]$ How does $a = -\dfrac{1}{2}$ transform the parent function? **[It compresses by a factor of $-\dfrac{1}{2}$ and reflects about the x-axis.]**

Ask: In the same function, what is the value of h? **[–2]** The operation is addition, so the value of h is negative. How does $h = -2$ transform the parent function? **[It translates the function two units to the left.]**

Ask: What is the value of k? **[–1]** How does $k = -1$ transform the parent function? **[It translates the function one unit down.]**

ALTERNATE STRATEGY

Strategy: Use a graphing calculator.

1. **Say:** A graphing calculator will show you the transformed function and is a tool you can use to understand how different values transform functions.

2. Enter the parent function x^3 into Y_1.

3. Enter the transformed function $(x-4)^3$ into Y_2.

4. Press "graph" to see the functions graphed on the same screen.

5. Compare the two graphs to determine how a positive value of 4 as the variable h transforms the function. You can see on the graph that a positive value translates the graph 4 units to the right.

6. In order to understand the transformations, try changing the values of a, h, and k and watch what transformations are produced for each.

COMMON MISCONCEPTION

Ask: What is the Error?

The graph of $f(x) = x^3$ is vertically compressed by a factor of $\dfrac{1}{3}$ and translated 2 units to the right and 6 units down. Write the equation for the new function.

Solution: $g(x) = \dfrac{1}{3}(x+2)^3 - 6$

Reason incorrect: The horizontal shift in the solution translates to the left.

Solution: The value given for the horizontal shift to the right is incorrect. Using the general form, $f(x) = a(x-h)^3 + k$, the correct equation for the transformation is $g(x) = \dfrac{1}{3}(x-2)^3 - 6$.

ADDITIONAL ONLINE INTERVENTION RESOURCES

 Use the following for students who have not mastered the concepts in Skill 37.

- Math on the Spot videos

- Personal Math Trainer with customized intervention

- Building Block worksheets (Skill 41: Generate Ordered Pairs; Skill 43: Graph Functions; Skill 76: Reading and Writing Exponents)

SKILL 37

Transforming Cubic Functions

Example 1

<table>
<tr><td>

$f(x) = x^3$ is the parent function from which other cubic functions are formed. You can transform the parent cubic function by changing the values of a, h, and k in the general form of cubic functions.

$$f(x) = a(x - h)^3 + k$$

</td><td>

Vocabulary

Cubic function
Transform
Translate
Stretch
Compress
Reflect

</td></tr>
</table>

The value of h will translate $f(x) = x^3$ horizontally left or right.

- If $h > 0$, the graph of $f(x) = x^3$ is translated h units to the right.
- If $h < 0$, the graph of $f(x) = x^3$ is translated $|h|$ units to the left.

The value of k will translate $f(x) = x^3$ vertically up or down.

- If $k > 0$, the graph of $f(x) = x^3$ is translated k units up.
- If $k < 0$, the graph of $f(x) = x^3$ is translated $|k|$ units down.

The value of a will vertically stretch or compress $f(x) = x^3$ and may also reflect $f(x) = x^3$ across the x-axis.

- If $|a| > 1$, the graph of $f(x) = x^3$ is stretched by a factor of $|a|$.
- If $|a| < 1$, the graph of $f(x) = x^3$ is compressed by a factor of $|a|$.
- If $a < 0$, the graph of $f(x) = x^3$ is reflected across the x-axis.

Describe the transformation $g(x)$ on the graph of $f(x) = x^3$. Then graph $f(x)$ and $g(x)$ on the same coordinate plane.

A. $g(x) = (x - 3)^3 + 2$

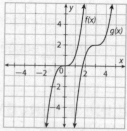

   $g(x)$ translates $f(x)$ horizontally 3 units to the right and vertically 2 units up.

B. $g(x) = -3(x + 1)^3 - 2$

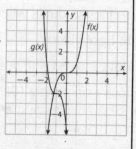

   $g(x)$ vertically stretches $f(x)$ by a factor of 3, reflects it across the x-axis, and translates it horizontally 1 unit to the left and vertically 2 units down.

Check

Describe the transformation $g(x)$ on the graph of $f(x) = x^3$.

Then graph $g(x)$ alongside $f(x)$.

1. $g(x) = x^3 + 1$

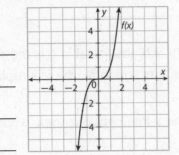

_____

_____

_____

2. $g(x) = (x - 4)^3$

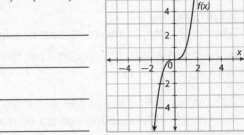

_____

_____

_____

3. $g(x) = 2(x - 3)^3 - 2$

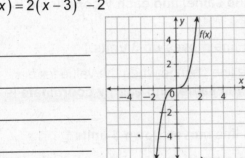

_____

_____

_____

_____

4. $g(x) = -\dfrac{1}{2}(x + 2)^3 - 1$

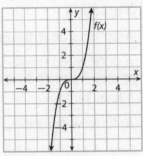

_____

_____

_____

Solve.

5. The graph of the function $f(x) = x^3$ is reflected across the x-axis and translated 12 units to the left. Write the equation for the new function.

_____

6. Explain the Error. Find the correct solution.

   The graph of $f(x) = x^3$ is vertically compressed by a factor of $\dfrac{1}{3}$ and translated 2 units to the right and 6 units down. Write the equation for the new function.

   Solution: $g(x) = \dfrac{1}{3}(x + 2)^3 - 6$

_____

SKILL 37 TRANSFORMING CUBIC FUNCTIONS

Transforming Linear Functions

KEY TEACHING POINTS

Example 1

Say: In the slope-intercept form of a line, $y = mx + b$, the variable b is the y-intercept, which is the point where the line crosses the y-axis. In function form, the y is replaced by $f(x)$, $f(x) = mx + b$.

Ask: When a line keeps the same slope, but the y-intercept changes, what is the effect on the graph? **[The line moves up or down.]**

Ask: How do the coordinates of each point on the line change when the value for b is changed from 0 to 3? **[The x-coordinates stay the same, and each y-coordinate is 3 greater.]**

Ask: How does the graph of the line move? **[The line moves up 3 units.]**

Ask: How do the coordinates of each point on the line change when the value for b is changed from 0 to –5? **[The x-coordinates stay the same, and each y-coordinate is 5 less.]**

Ask: How does the graph of the line move? **[The line moves down 5 units.]**

Say: A positive value for b moves the line up, and a negative value for b moves the line down.

Ask: How can you write the equation for a line that begins with the parent function $f(x) = x$, and moves the line down 3 units? **[$f(x) = x - 3$]**

Ask: How can you write the equation for a line that begins with the parent function $f(x) = x$, and moves the line up 5 units? **[$f(x) = x + 5$]**

Check

Ask: In the function $f(x) = x + 1$, what is the value of b? **[1]** How is the graph of $f(x) = x + 1$ related to the graph of $f(x) = x$? **[The graph of $f(x) = x + 1$ is the graph of $f(x) = x$ translated up 1 unit.]**

Ask: In the function $f(x) = x - 2$, what is the value of b? **[–2]** How is the graph of $f(x) = x - 2$ related to the graph of $f(x) = x$? **[The graph of $f(x) = x - 2$ is the graph of $f(x) = x$ translated down 2 units.]**

Say: The function $f(x) = x + 4.5$ has a slope of 1 and a y-intercept of 4.5.

Ask: What is the slope of $f(x) = x$? **[1]** What is the y-intercept? **[0]** How is this different than the function $f(x) = x + 4.5$? **[The y-intercept is different.]**

Ask: Describe the graph of $f(x) = x$? **[A line through the origin with a slope of 1.]**

Say: Let's graph the function $f(x) = x$.

Complete the following as a class.

Draw a point at the y-intercept, which is the origin.

Since the slope is 1, move up 1 unit and right one unit. Draw a point at (1, 1).

Draw the line that passes through both the origin and the point you drew.

Ask: Describe the graph of $f(x) = x - \dfrac{7}{2}$. **[A line through $\left(0, -\dfrac{7}{2}\right)$ with a slope of 1.]**

Say: Let's graph the function $f(x) = x - \dfrac{7}{2}$.

Complete the following as a class.

Draw a point at the *y*-intercept, which is $\left(0, -\dfrac{7}{2}\right)$.

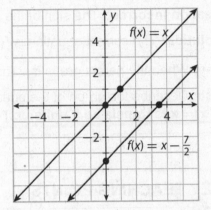

Since the slope is 1, you can move the same distance both up and to the right.

Ask: If you move up $\dfrac{7}{2}$ units, and right $\dfrac{7}{2}$ units, what are the coordinates? $\left[\left(\dfrac{7}{2}, 0\right)\right]$

Draw the line that passes through both the *y*-intercept and the point you drew.

In all eight lines that you graphed, what was the slope? **[1]**

ALTERNATE STRATEGY

Strategy: Make a table of values.

1. **Say:** You can see how the graphs are different by comparing the *y*-values on a table of values. Let's look at the function $f(x) = x - 2$.

2. Set up a table of values with three columns. One for *x*, one for the parent function $f(x) = x$ and one for the translated function $f(x) = x - 2$.

3. Choose values for *x* that work well in both functions. Any integer values will work well for these functions.

4. Fill in the values for *f(x)* by substituting *x* into the expression.

5. Compare the values for *f(x)* in the parent function and the translated function. The translated function always has a value for *f(x)* that is 2 less than the parent function. This means each point on the translated line is 2 units lower than its corresponding point on the line of the parent function.

x	$f(x) = x$	$f(x) = x - 2$
-2	-2	-4
0	0	-2
2	2	0
4	4	2
6	6	4

COMMON MISCONCEPTION

Ask: What is the Error?

Your friend was asked to write the equation of the line that is the graph of $f(x) = x$ translated 4 units down. Your friend wrote the equation $f(x) = x + 4$.

Reason incorrect: The sign of the y-intercept that your friend used is incorrect.

Solution: The correct equation is $f(x) = x - 4$.

Say: When the parent graph is translated down, the value for b is negative.

Ask: Describe the graph of the equation your friend wrote. **[The graph of $f(x) = x$ is translated 4 units up.]**

KEY TEACHING POINTS

Example 2

Say: In the slope-intercept form of a linear function, $f(x) = mx + b$, the variable m is slope, which tells both the direction and steepness of the line.

Say: The greater the absolute value of m, the steeper the line.

Ask: What is the value for m in a line that has no slope, or is horizontal? **[0]**

Ask: Which of the following lines has the steeper slope: $f(x) = 2x$ or $f(x) = \frac{1}{4}x$? **[$f(x) = 2x$]**

Explain. **[2 has a greater absolute value than $\frac{1}{4}$, so the slope is steeper.]**

Say: The slope of parent function $f(x) = x$ changes by a factor of m. This means that for each x-coordinate, the y-coordinate will be m times what it is on the parent graph.

Ask: What is the y-value when $x = 2$ for the parent function $f(x) = x$? **[2]** What is the y-value when $x = 2$ for the function $f(x) = 2x$? **[4]**

Say: Notice that the y-value for the transformed function is 2 times the y-value for the parent function.

Ask: What is the y-value when $x = 4$ for the parent function $f(x) = x$? **[4]** What is the y-value when $x = 4$ for the function $f(x) = \frac{1}{4}x$? **[1]**

Say: Notice that the y-value for the transformed function is $\frac{1}{4}$ of the y-value for the parent function.

Say: In part C, the sign of the slope is negative. Since there is no coefficient, the slope of the parent function is 1 and the coefficient, or m, is -1 for the transformed function.

Ask: How does a factor of -1 change a value? **[It reverses the sign.]**

Ask: What is the y-value when $x = 2$ for the parent function $f(x) = x$? **[2]** What is the y-value when $x = 2$ for the function $f(x) = -x$? **[–2]**

Review the following:

- When the value for m is greater than 1, the line becomes steeper by a factor of m.
- When the value for m is less than 1, the line becomes less steep by a factor of m.
- When the value for m is positive, the line moves up from left to right.
- When the value for m is negative, the line moves down from left to right.

Check

Ask: How is the steepness of the graph of $f(x) = -5x$ related to the steepness of the graph of $f(x) = x$? **[The graph of $f(x) = -5x$ is five times steeper than the graph of $f(x) = x$.]**

Ask: How is the direction of the graph of $f(x) = -5x$ related to the direction of the graph of $f(x) = x$? **[The graph of $f(x) = -5x$ moves down from left to right instead of up.]**

Say: Let's graph the functions $f(x) = x$ and $f(x) = -5x$.

Complete the following as a class.

We've already graphed $f(x) = x$, so lets graph $f(x) = -5x$.

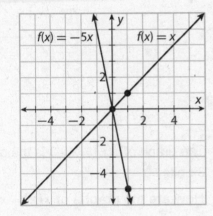

Draw a point at the y-intercept, which is the origin.

Since the slope is –5, move 5 units down and 1 unit right. Draw a point.

Draw the line that passes through both the y-intercept and the point you drew.

Ask: What is the y-value when $x = 1$ for the parent function $f(x) = x$? **[1]** What is the y-value when $x = 1$ for the function $f(x) = -5x$? **[–5]**

ADDITIONAL ONLINE INTERVENTION RESOURCES

 Use the following for students who have not mastered the concepts in Skill 38.

- Math on the Spot videos
- Personal Math Trainer with customized intervention
- Building Block worksheets (Skill 103: Transformations)

SKILL 38 Transforming Linear Functions

Example 1

You can transform, or change, the graph of the linear function $f(x) = mx + b$ by changing the value of m or b. The value of b translates, or slides, the graph of $f(x) = mx + b$ up or down.

A. How are the graphs of $f(x) = x$ and $f(x) = x + 3$ related?

Find the slope and y-intercept for the graphs of both functions. Then graph both functions in the same coordinate plane.

$f(x) = x$: y-intercept: 0; slope: 1 $f(x) = x + 3$: y-intercept: 3; slope: 1

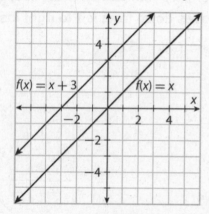

The graph of $f(x) = x + 3$ is the graph of $f(x) = x$ translated up 3 units.

B. How are the graphs of $f(x) = x$ and $f(x) = x - 5$ related?

Find the slope and y-intercept for the graphs of both functions. Then graph both functions in the same coordinate plane.

$f(x) = x$: y-intercept: 0; slope: 1 $f(x) = x - 5$: y-intercept: −5; slope: 1

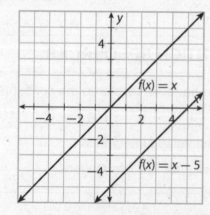

The graph of $f(x) = x - 5$ is the graph of $f(x) = x$ translated down 5 units.

Original content Copyright © by Houghton Mifflin Harcourt. Additions and changes to the original content are the responsibility of the instructor.

Vocabulary

Transform

Linear function

Translate

Slope

y-intercept

Check
Describe how the graph of each function is related to the graph of $f(x) = x$. Then graph both functions in the same coordinate plane.

1. $f(x) = x + 1$ _____

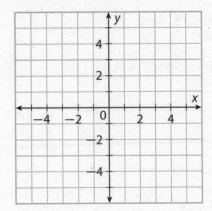

2. $f(x) = x - 2$ _____

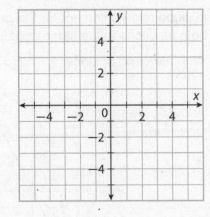

3. $f(x) = x + 4.5$ _____

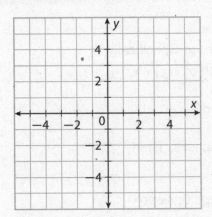

4. $f(x) = x - \dfrac{7}{2}$ _____

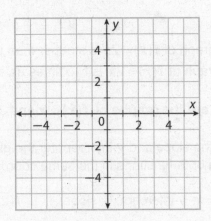

5. Refer to your answers for Questions 1–4 above. How are the graphs of the functions similar? How are they different?

_____

6. In general, what values of b translate the graph of $f(x) = x$ up? What values of b translate the graph of $f(x) = x$ down?

_____

7. Explain the Error. Then find the correct equation.

Your friend was asked to write the equation of the line that is the graph of $f(x) = x$ translated 4 units down. Your friend wrote the equation $f(x) = x + 4$.

_____

Example 2

The value of m affects the steepness of the graph of $f(x) = mx + b$.

A. How are the graphs of $f(x) = x$ and $f(x) = 2x$ related?

Find the slope and y-intercept for the graphs of both functions. Then graph both functions in the same coordinate plane.

$f(x) = x$: y-intercept: 0; slope: 1 $f(x) = 2x$: y-intercept: 0; slope: 2

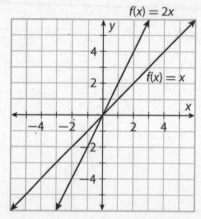

The graph of $f(x) = 2x$ is steeper than the graph of $f(x) = x$. Specifically, the graph of $f(x) = 2x$ is two times as steep as the graph of $f(x) = x$.

B. How are the graphs of $f(x) = x$ and $f(x) = \dfrac{1}{4}x$ related?

Find the slope and y-intercept for the graphs of both functions. Then graph both functions in the same coordinate plane.

$f(x) = x$: y-intercept: 0; slope: 1 $f(x) = \dfrac{1}{4}x$: y-intercept: 0; slope: $\dfrac{1}{4}$

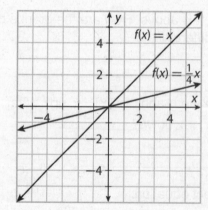

The graph of $f(x) = \dfrac{1}{4}x$ is less steep than the graph of $f(x) = x$. Specifically,

the graph of $f(x) = \dfrac{1}{4}x$ is one-quarter times as steep as the graph of $f(x) = x$.

C. How are the graphs of $f(x) = x$ and $f(x) = -x$ related?

Find the slope and *y*-intercept for the graphs of both functions. Then graph both functions in the same coordinate plane.

$f(x) = x$: *y*-intercept: 0; slope: 1

$f(x) = -x$: *y*-intercept: 0; slope: –1

The graphs of $f(x) = x$ and $f(x) = -x$ have the same steepness. The graph of $f(x) = -x$ is the reflection of the graph of $f(x) = x$ across the *y*-axis.

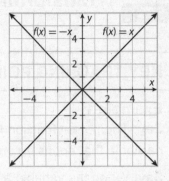

Check

Describe how the graph of each function is related to the graph of $f(x) = x$. Then graph both functions in the same coordinate plane.

8. $f(x) = 4x$ _____

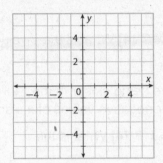

9. $f(x) = \dfrac{2}{3}x$ _____

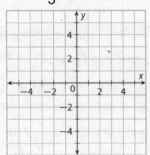

10. $f(x) = -5x$ _____

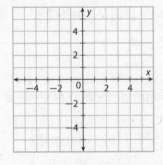

11. $f(x) = -\dfrac{3}{4}x$ _____

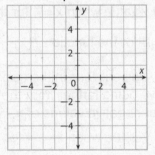

SKILL 38 TRANSFORMING LINEAR FUNCTIONS

Transforming Quadratic Functions

KEY TEACHING POINTS

Example 1

Say: The parent function for a quadratic function is $f(x) = x^2$. The graph of $f(x) = x^2$ is a parabola that opens up and crosses the points (1, 1) and (−1, 1).

Say: When the variable a is introduced as a coefficient, $g(x) = ax^2$, the graph of $f(x) = x^2$ is transformed. The value of a determines which direction the parabola opens and how wide the parabola is. Example 1 considers positive values for a.

Say: Values for a that have a greater absolute value than 1 result in a parabola that is narrower than the graph of $f(x) = x^2$. A greater value means the value for x^2 is multiplied by a greater factor. This results in a greater y-value for the same x-value as the parent function $f(x) = x^2$.

Ask: What is the y-value when $x = 2$ for the parent function $f(x) = x^2$? **[4]** What is the y-value when $x = 2$ for the function $f(x) = 2x^2$? **[8]**

Say: The y-value is greater by a factor of 2. This results in the curve being closer to the y-axis, which makes a narrower parabola. Let's see if this is true for negative values of x also.

Ask: What is the y-value when $x = -2$ for the parent function $f(x) = x^2$? **[4]** What is the y-value when $x = -2$ for the function $f(x) = 2x^2$? **[8]**

Say: The points on either side of the parabola are greater by a factor of 2 when $a = 2$.

Ask: What is the y-value when $x = 4$ for the parent function $f(x) = x^2$? **[16]** What is the y-value when $x = 4$ for the function $f(x) = \frac{3}{4}x^2$? **[12]**

Say: Notice the y-value is less in the transformed function than in the parent function. This results in the curve being farther from the y-axis, which makes a wider parabola. Let's see if this is also true for negative values of x.

Ask: What is the y-value when $x = -4$ for the parent function $f(x) = x^2$? **[16]** What is the y-value when $x = -4$ for the function $f(x) = \frac{3}{4}x^2$? **[8]**

Say: The points on either side of the parabola are less by a factor of $\frac{3}{4}$ when $a = \frac{3}{4}$.

Ask: Are any of the values for y the same in the parent function and the transformed function? **[Yes, the vertex is at the origin in each case.]**

Check

Say: Look at the values on the *y*-axis of the graphs for Problems 1 through 4.

Ask: Why don't they increase by one unit each? **[Possible response: A quadratic function increases very quickly, so the *y*-axis needs to include greater numbers.]**

Say: In each graph, the parent function has already been graphed for you.

Ask: How can you tell by looking at the function whether the transformed function will be narrower or wider than the parent function? **[If the value of *a* is greater than 1, it will be narrower. If the value of *a* is greater than 1, it will be wider.]**

Ask: Describe the graph of $f(x) = 4x^2$ as it relates to the parent function. **[The graph of $f(x) = 4x^2$ is narrower than the parent function.]** How are the *y*-values of the two functions related? **[The corresponding *y*-values for the transformed function are each 4 times greater than the ones from the parent function.]**

Say: Let's graph the function $g(x) = 4x^2$.

Graph the following as a class.

Ask: What are good values to choose for *x*? **[Possible response: Integers that are close to the origin.]**

Make a table of values.   Graph the function.

x	$g(x) = 4x^2$
−3	27
−2	16
−1	4
0	0
1	4
2	16
3	27

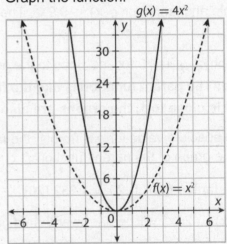

The graph of $g(x)$ is narrower than the graph of $f(x) = x^2$.

Example 2

Say: The graph of the parent function for a quadratic function $f(x) = x^2$ is a parabola that opens up, has its vertex on the origin, and crosses the points (1, 1) and (−1, 1).

Say: In the quadratic function $g(x) = ax^2$ the graph of $f(x) = x^2$ is transformed. When *a* is a negative value, the parabola opens down.

Say: The absolute value of a determines the width of the parabola. Parabolas that open down follow the same rules as those that open up.

Review the following:

- $|a| > 1$, the graph of the function $g(x) = ax^2$ is narrower than the graph of $f(x) = x^2$

- $|a| < 1$, the graph of the function $g(x) = ax^2$ is wider than the graph of $f(x) = x^2$

- $a > 0$, the graph of the function $g(x) = ax^2$ opens up

- $a < 0$, the graph of the function $g(x) = ax^2$ opens down

Ask: How are the graphs of $f(x) = x^2$ and $f(x) = -x^2$ related? **[$f(x) = -x^2$ is a reflection of $f(x) = x^2$ across the x-axis.]**

Say: A factor of –1 reflects the parent function across the x-axis.

Say: Just as with positive values for a, the corresponding y-values are changed by a factor from the parent function. For example, in the function $g(x) = -3x^2$, each y-value is –3 times the value of the corresponding y-value in the parent function $f(x) = x^2$.

Say: Look at the table and graph for $g(x) = -0.9x^2$. The dotted line represents the function $g(x) = 0.9x^2$.

Ask: Why is the graph of $g(x) = 0.9x^2$ so close to the graph of the parent function $f(x) = x^2$? **[Possible response: The parent function is like the function $g(x) = ax^2$ with a value for a of 1. Because 0.9 is close to 1, the graphs are also close.]**

Say: The farther the absolute value for a is from 1, the farther the graph of the function $g(x) = ax^2$ is from the graph of the parent function $f(x) = x^2$.

Ask: Which value is farther from 1: 20 or 1.25? **[20]**

Say: A graph for $g(x) = -20x^2$ will be narrower than a graph for $h(x) = -1.25x^2$.

Ask: Which graph will be wider: $g(x) = -0.4x^2$ or $h(x) = -0.25x^2$? Explain. **[The graph for $h(x)$ will be wider than the graph of $g(x)$ because the absolute value of 0.25 is farther from 1 than the absolute value of 0.4.]**

Check

Say: Let's graph the function $g(x) = -\dfrac{3}{5}x^2$.

Ask: What are good values to choose for x? **[Possible response: Integers that are close to the origin.]**

Ask: What can you tell about the function before you start graphing? **[Possible responses: It will open down. It is wider than the parent function.]**

Ask: Where will the vertex be on the graph of $g(x) = -\dfrac{3}{5}x^2$? **[at the origin]**

Make a table of values.

x	$g(x) = -\dfrac{3}{5}x^2$
-3	$-5\dfrac{2}{5}$
-2	$-2\dfrac{2}{5}$
-1	$-\dfrac{3}{5}$
0	0
1	$-\dfrac{3}{5}$
2	$-2\dfrac{2}{5}$
3	$-5\dfrac{2}{5}$

Graph the function.

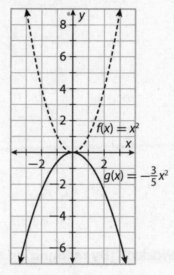

Say: The graph of $g(x)$ is wider than the graph of $f(x) = x^2$, and opens down.
Notice the graphs share a vertex on the origin.

COMMON MISCONCEPTION

Ask: What is the Error?

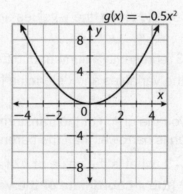

Reason incorrect: The graph of $g(x) = -0.5x^2$ should open down.

Solution: Make a table of values.

x	$g(x) = -0.5x^2$
-3	-4.5
-2	-2
-1	-0.5
0	0
1	-0.5
2	-2
3	-4.5

Graph the function.

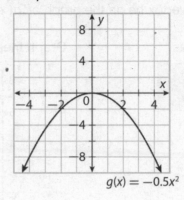

$g(x) = -0.5x^2$

Ask: How can this error be avoided? **[By recognizing a negative value for _a_ results in the parabola opening down.]**

KEY TEACHING POINTS

Example 3

Say: The vertex form of a quadratic function, $g(x) = a(x - h)^2 + k$, includes a value for _a_ that tells you the direction and width of the graph, but it also includes values for _h_ and _k_ that give you a vertex for the parabola, (h, k).

Ask: In the quadratic function $g(x) = -2(x + 1)^2 - 3$, what is the value of _a_? **[-2]**

Ask: What does the value $a = -2$ tell you about the graph? **[The graph will open down, and will be narrower than the graph of $f(x) = x^2$.]**

Ask: Will each _y_-value of the transformed function be greater or less than the corresponding _y_-value in the parent function by a factor of _a_? **[No]**

Say: Because the vertex is no longer on the origin, the _y_-values are not direct products of _a_ and the value for _x_.

Say: The function $g(x) = -2(x + 1)^2 - 3$ represents a number of different transformations of the parent function. Let's look at each of the variables and determine how it affects the parent function.

Say: The value for _a_ is -2. This tells you the graph of the transformed function has been reflected over the _x_-axis, and the graph is narrower than the parent graph.

Ask: In the function $g(x) = -2(x + 1)^2 - 3$, what is the value of _h_? **[-1]** What does the value of _h_ tell you in the graph of the function? **[the _x_-coordinate of the vertex]** How is this different than the graph of the parent function? **[The parent function has its vertex at the origin, so the new _x_-coordinate for the vertex is 1 unit left of the _x_-coordinate of the parent function's vertex.]**

Say: The value for h translates the function left or right. Since h is -1, the graph translates 1 unit left.

Ask: In the function $g(x) = -2(x+1)^2 - 3$, what is the value of k? **[–3]** What does the value of k tell you in the graph of the function? **[the *y*-coordinate of the vertex]** How is this different than the graph of the parent function? **[The parent function has its vertex at the origin, so the new *y*-coordinate for the vertex is 3 units down from the *y*-coordinate of the parent function's vertex.]**

Say: The value for k translates the function up or down. Since k is -3, the graph translates 3 units down.

Check

Ask: Without graphing, what do you know about the graph of the function $g(x) = \frac{1}{2}(x-1)^2 - 3$? **[The graph opens up because *a* is positive, and the graph is wider than the graph of the parent function. The vertex of the parabola is at (1, –3).]**

ALTERNATE STRATEGY

Strategy: Use a graphing calculator.

1. **Say:** A graphing calculator will show you the transformed function and is a tool you can use to understand how different values transform functions.

2. Enter the parent function x^2 into Y_1.

3. Enter the transformed function $-1(x+2)^2 - 5$ into Y_2.

4. Press graph to see the functions graphed on the same screen.

5. Compare the two graphs to determine how the parent graph has been transformed. You can see that the graph is the same shape as the parent function, it but has been reflected over the *x*-axis and has been translated to a new vertex of $(-2, -5)$.

6. In order to understand the transformations, try changing the values of a, h, and k and watch what transformations are produced for each.

ADDITIONAL ONLINE INTERVENTION RESOURCES

Use the following for students who have not mastered the concepts in Skill 39.

- Math on the Spot videos
- Personal Math Trainer with customized intervention
- Building Block worksheets (Skill 43: Graph Functions; Skill 103: Transformations)

SKILL 39 — Transforming Quadratic Functions

Example 1

Consider the graph of the quadratic function $g(x) = ax^2$. When $a > 0$, the graph of $g(x)$ opens upward.

If $|a| > 1$, the graph of $g(x) = ax^2$ is narrower than the graph of $f(x) = x^2$.

A. Graph $g(x) = 2x^2$.

Make a table of values.

x	$g(x) = 2x^2$
−3	18
−2	8
−1	2
0	0
1	2
2	8
3	18

Graph the function.

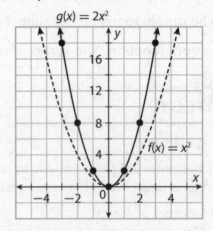

The graph of $g(x)$ is narrower than the graph of $f(x) = x^2$.

If $0 < |a| < 1$, the graph of $g(x) = ax^2$ is wider than the graph of $f(x) = x^2$.

B. Graph $g(x) = \dfrac{3}{4}x^2$.

Make a table of values.

x	$g(x) = \dfrac{3}{4}x^2$
−6	27
−4	12
−2	3
0	0
2	3
4	12
6	27

Graph the function.

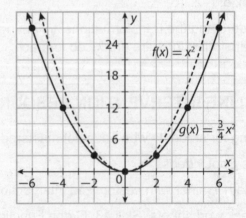

The graph of $g(x)$ is wider than the graph of $f(x) = x^2$.

Vocabulary

Vertex form (of a quadratic function)

Vertex (of the graph of a quadratic function)

Check

Graph each quadratic function.

1. $g(x) = 4x^2$

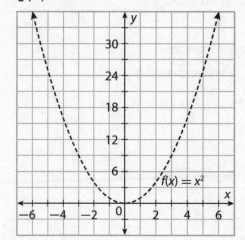

2. $g(x) = 3.5x^2$

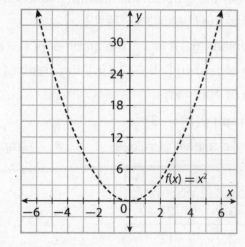

3. $g(x) = \dfrac{2}{3}x^2$

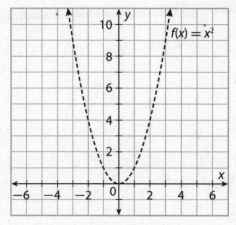

4. $g(x) = 0.8x^2$

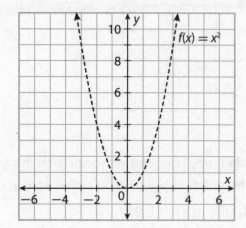

5. Without graphing, write the following quadratic functions in the correct column of the table below.

   $g(x) = 5x^2 \quad g(x) = \dfrac{3}{5}x^2 \quad g(x) = 7.25x^2 \quad g(x) = 0.85x^2$

Narrower Than $f(x) = x^2$	Wider Than $f(x) = x^2$

Example 2

Consider the graph of the quadratic function $g(x) = ax^2$. When $a < 0$, the graph of $g(x)$ opens downward.

Remember that if $|a| > 1$, the graph of $g(x) = ax^2$ is narrower than the graph of $f(x) = x^2$. If $0 < |a| < 1$, the graph of $g(x) = ax^2$ is wider than the graph of $f(x) = x^2$.

A. Graph $g(x) = -3x^2$.

Make a table of values.

x	$g(x) = -3x^2$
−3	−27
−2	−12
−1	−3
0	0
1	−3
2	−12
3	−27

Graph the function.

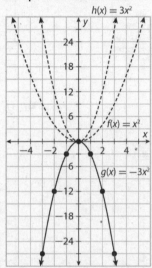

The graph of $g(x)$ is narrower than the graph of $f(x) = x^2$.

The graph of $g(x)$ is a reflection across the x-axis of $h(x) = 3x^2$.

B. Graph $g(x) = -0.9x^2$.

Make a table of values.

x	$g(x) = -0.9x^2$
−3	−8.1
−2	−3.6
−1	−0.9
0	0
1	−0.9
2	−3.6
3	−8.1

Graph the function.

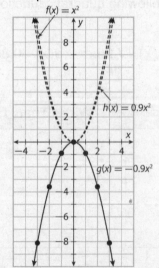

The graph of $g(x)$ is wider than the graph of $f(x) = x^2$.

The graph of $g(x)$ is a reflection across the x-axis of $h(x) = 0.9x^2$.

Check

Graph each quadratic function.

6. $g(x) = -2x^2$

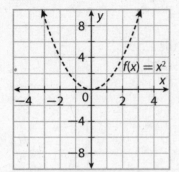

7. $g(x) = -4.25x^2$

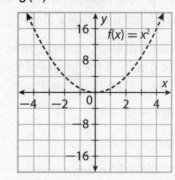

8. $g(x) = -\dfrac{3}{5}x^2$

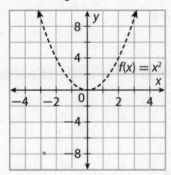

9. $g(x) = -0.7x^2$

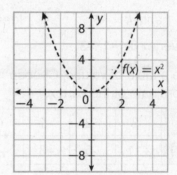

10. Explain the Error. Then graph the correct solution.

$g(x) = -0.5x^2$

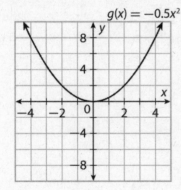

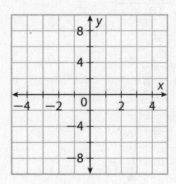

_____

_____

_____

Example 3

You can also write a quadratic function in vertex form, $g(x) = a(x - h)^2 + k$, where (h, k) represents the vertex of the graph of the function.

If the graph of the quadratic function opens upward, the vertex is the *lowest* point of the graph. If the graph of the function opens downward, the vertex is the *highest* point of the graph.

Graph $g(x) = -2(x + 1)^2 - 3.$

Step 1 Identify the vertex.

$$g(x) = -2(x + 1)^2 - 3$$

$$g(x) = -2(x - (-1))^2 + (-3)$$ Write the function in vertex form.

$h = -1$ and $k = -3$ Identify the values of h and k.

The vertex is $(-1, -3)$.

Step 2 Make a table of values. Choose x-values on either side of the x-coordinate of the vertex, -1.

x	-3	-2	-1	0	1
$g(x)$	-11	-5	-3	-5	-11

Step 3 Plot the points. Draw a smooth curve through them.

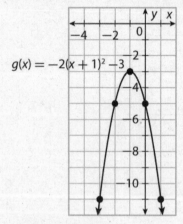

Things to Note:

- Because $a = -2 < 0$, the graph opens *downward*.

- Because $|a| = 2 > 1$, the graph is *narrower* than the graph of $f(x) = x^2$.

- Because the graph opens downward, the vertex $(-1, -3)$ is the *highest* point of the graph.

Check

Identify the vertex of each quadratic function. Then graph the function.

11. $g(x) = 2(x-3)^2 + 2$

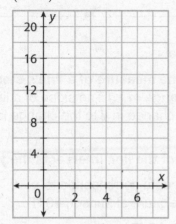

12. $g(x) = -1(x+2)^2 - 5$

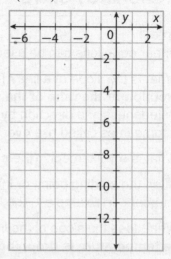

13. $g(x) = \dfrac{1}{2}(x-1)^2 - 3$

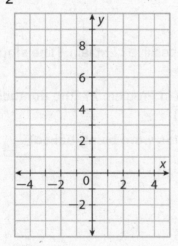

14. $g(x) = -0.25(x+1)^2 + 4$

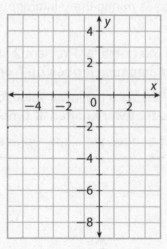

SKILL 39 TRANSFORMING QUADRATIC FUNCTIONS

Writing Linear Equations

KEY TEACHING POINTS

Example 1

Say: Linear equations can be used to model real-world data.

Ask: What is the slope of a line? **[Possible response: The measure of a line's steepness and direction or the ratio of the change in *y* to the change in *x*.]** The slope of a line tells you its steepness and direction by finding the ratio of the change in *y* to the change in *x*. This is also sometimes called rise over run.

Ask: What is a *y*-intercept? **[the point where the graph of the line intersects the *y*-axis]**

Say: Often the starting point, or initial value, of real-world data corresponds to $x = 0$. This is the *y*-intercept. In Example 1, the initial value is the temperature at sunset, 80 °F.

Ask: What does the slope of the line tell you in this example? **[Possible response: how fast the temperature is dropping]**

Ask: Is the slope negative or positive? Why? **[The slope is negative. A negative slope moves down from left to right.]**

Say: Remember, when writing an equation in slope-intercept form, $y = mx + b$, the value for the slope is *m* and the *y*-intercept is *b*.

Check

Ask: In the graph for Problem 2, is the slope negative or positive? Explain. **[The slope is positive because it goes up from left to right.]**

Ask: What does the initial value, or *y*-intercept, represent in Problem 2? **[the number of muffins that were baked at time 0, or at the start time]**

Ask: What does the slope represent? **[the rate the muffins were being baked]**

KEY TEACHING POINTS

Example 2

Ask: How can you decide which variable is dependent and which is independent? **[Since the number of pages you read depends on how many days you read, the number of days is the independent variable *x*.]**

Say: In this problem, the initial value is the number of pages that were read when you started keeping track. So, on day 0, how many pages had you already read? **[75]**

Ask: What does the slope represent? **[The rate the pages are read.]** How many pages are read each day? **[23]**

Check

Say: In Problem 4, the equation models the boiling point of water at different altitudes.

Ask: What are the independent and dependent variables? **[The temperature depends on the altitude, so the altitude is independent, or *x*. The temperature is dependent, so it is the *y*-value.]**

Say: In ordered pairs, the information is listed as (altitude, temperature).

Ask: What are the two ordered pairs you are given? **[(2000, 206), (10,000, 194)]**

Ask: Without calculating, is the slope negative or positive? Explain. **[The slope is negative because as the altitude gets higher, the boiling point is lower.]**

Say: Use the slope formula to find the slope.

Complete the following as a class.

$$m = \frac{y_2 - y_1}{x_2 - x_1} = \frac{194 - 206}{10,000 - 2000} = \frac{-12}{8000} = \frac{-3}{2000}$$

Say: Be careful to use the *y*-values in the numerator and *x*-values in the denominator. Make sure you put the values in the same order.

Say: Use the slope and values from one of the points to find the *y*-intercept.

Complete the following as a class.

$$y = mx + b$$
$$206 = \frac{-3}{2000}(2000) + b$$
$$206 = -3 + b$$
$$209 = b$$

Say: You know the values for the slope and *y*-intercept. Substitute them into the equation.

$$y = \frac{-3}{2000}x + 209$$

ALTERNATE STRATEGY

Strategy: Make a table.

1. **Say:** Sometimes it helps to make a table to understand the problem.

2. Look at Example 2. You can make a table that shows the number of days and the number of pages. Since you have read up to 6 days, you can include columns for days 0 to 6, even if you don't fill them in. Fill in the values that you know.

Number of days	0	1	2	3	4	5	6
Number of pages read			121				213

3. To write an equation in slope-intercept form, you need to know the initial value, or number of pages on day 0, as well as the rate of change per day.

4. You know the number of pages you read by day 2 and by day 6. To get from day 2 to day 6, there are 4 days. Find the number of pages you read between day 2 and 6 using subtraction. $213 - 121 = 92$

5. Find the rate of change using division. If you read 92 pages in 4 days, then you read $92 \div 4 = 23$ pages each day.

6. Find the initial value, the number of pages on day 0. $121 - 23 = 98$ pages on day 1. $98 - 23 = 75$ pages on day 0.

7. You know the initial value for the y-intercept is 75, and the rate of change, or slope, is 23. Use these values to write the equation.
$y = 23x + 75$

KEY TEACHING POINTS

Example 3
Say: When information is given to you in a table, the y-intercept is the value where the independent variable x is equal to 0.

Ask: What is the y-intercept? **[35]**

Ask: How can you find the slope in a table where the x-values increase by 1? **[Subtract any y-value from the next consecutive y-value.]**

Ask: How does the graph help you find the equation of the line? **[Possible response: The graph makes it clear that the slope is positive and the y-intercept is at y = 35.]**

Check
Ask: In Problem 6, if you want to graph this line, what values could you use on the axis? **[Possible answer: Units of 1 on the x-axis, and units of 5 or 10 on the y-axis.]**

Ask: What is the slope? **[6]** What is the y-intercept? **[72]**

Ask: What do the slope and y-intercept represent? **[The slope is the rate that grades improve with studying and the y-intercept is the grade that was achieved with no study time.]**

KEY TEACHING POINTS

Example 4

Ask: How can you find the slope from a table where the x-values increase by a value other than 1? **[Use the slope formula.]**

Ask: What are two ways you can find the y-intercept? **[Possible answers: Subtract from the distance at 5 hours or substitute values in the slope-intercept form that you know.]**

Say: Once you know the values for m and b, substitute them into the slope-intercept form of the equation.

COMMON MISCONCEPTION

Ask: What is the Error?

Number of Days, x	7	14	21	28	35
Height of Bamboo (in.), y	180	348	516	684	852

Your friend says that after 10 days, the height of the bamboo will be 240 inches.

Reason incorrect: The y-intercept was not included in the calculations.

Solution: The equation of the line that models the data is $y = 24x + 12$.

Substitute in the number of days, 10, as the value for x.

$y = 24(10) + 12$
$y = 240 + 12$
$y = 252$

Ask: How can this error be avoided? **[Check the equation is true by substituting the values for x, 10, and y, 240.]**

ADDITIONAL ONLINE INTERVENTION RESOURCES

Use the following for students who have not mastered the concepts in Skill 40.

- Math on the Spot videos

- Personal Math Trainer with customized intervention

- Building Block worksheets (Skill 52: Inverse Operations; Skill 111: Write Fractions as Decimals)

SKILL 40

Writing Linear Equations

Example 1

	Vocabulary
	Slope-intercept form (of a linear equation)
	Slope
	y-intercept

You can write a linear equation in slope-intercept form to model the data given in a graph.

A weather app records the outdoor temperature at sunset and then at each hour throughout the night. The results are shown in the graph. Write an equation in slope-intercept form to represent the temperature y in degrees Fahrenheit, x hours since sunset.

Step 1   Find the slope of the line that passes through the points.

Use (0, 80) and (8, 48).

$$m = \frac{y_2 - y_1}{x_2 - x_1}$$

$$= \frac{80 - 48}{0 - 8}$$

$$m = \frac{32}{-8}, \text{ or } -4$$

Outdoor Temperature Since Sunset

[graph: Temperature (°F) on y-axis from 0 to 80, Number of Hours Since Sunset on x-axis from 0 to 8, showing points descending from (0,80) to (8,48)]

Step 2   Use the graph to find the y-intercept of the line.

$b = 80$

Step 3   Write the equation in slope-intercept form.

$y = -4x + 80$ Substitute –4 for m and 80 for b.

Check

Write a linear equation that models the data in each graph.

1.   **Amount Owed on Loan**

[graph: Amount Owed ($), y on y-axis, Number of Payments Made, x on x-axis, point labeled (1, 105)]

2.   **Number of Muffins Baked**

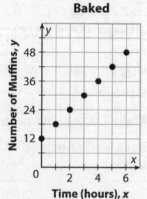

[graph: Number of Muffins, y on y-axis from 0 to 48, Time (hours), x on x-axis from 0 to 6]

Example 2

You can also write a linear equation in slope-intercept form to model the information given in a verbal description.

The number of pages you have read in a book over time can be modeled with a linear equation. After 2 days, you have read 121 pages. After 6 days, you have read 213 pages. Write an equation in slope-intercept form that models the number of pages you have read.

Step 1 Identify the independent and dependent variables.

The number of pages you have read depends on the number of days you read. So, the independent variable is the number of days. The dependent variable is the number of pages you have read.

Step 2 Write the given information as ordered pairs.

After 2 days, you have read 121 pages: (2, 121).

After 6 days, you have read 213 pages: (6, 213).

Step 3 Find the slope of the line that passes through the 2 points.

$$m = \frac{y_2 - y_1}{x_2 - x_1} = \frac{213 - 121}{6 - 2} = \frac{92}{4}, \text{ or } 23$$

Step 4 Find the y-intercept.

$y = mx + b$ Use slope-intercept form.

$121 = 23(2) + b$ Substitute 23 for m, 2 for x, and 121 for y.

$121 = 46 + b$ Simplify.

$b = 75$ Solve for b.

Step 5 Write the equation.

$y = 23x + 75$ Substitute 23 for m and 75 for b.

Check

3. The amount you spend for frozen yogurt can be modeled with a linear equation. A cup of yogurt with 1 topping costs $3.35. A cup of yogurt with 3 toppings costs $4.85. Write an equation in slope-intercept form that models the cost y, in dollars, of a cup of yogurt with x toppings.

_____

4. The relationship between altitude and the temperature at which water boils can be modeled with a linear equation. At an altitude of 2000 feet, water boils at a temperature of 209 °F. At an altitude of 10,000 feet, water boils at a temperature of 182 °F. Write an equation in slope-intercept form that models the temperature y at which water boils, in degrees Fahrenheit, at an altitude of x feet.

_____

Example 3

You can write a linear equation to model the information given in a table.

The data in the table have a linear relationship. Write an equation in slope-intercept form that models the data.

Number of Movies Rented, x	0	1	2	3	4
Amount of Cable Bill ($), y	35	41	47	53	59

Step 1 Graph the ordered pairs. Draw a dotted line through the points.

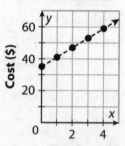

Cost of Monthly Cable Bill

Step 2 Find the slope of the line.

$$m = \frac{y_2 - y_1}{x_2 - x_1}$$

$$= \frac{41 - 35}{1 - 0}$$

$$= \frac{6}{1}, \text{ or } 6$$

Step 3 Use the table or graph to find the y-intercept.

$b = 35$

Step 4 Write an equation.

$y = mx + b$

$y = 6x + 35$ Substitute 6 for m and 35 for b.

Check

The data in each table have a linear relationship. Write an equation that models the data.

5.

Temperature (°C), x	0	5	10	15	20
Temperature (°F), y	32	41	50	59	68

_____

6.

Time Spent Studying (hr), x	0	1	2	3	4
Grade, y	72	78	84	90	96

_____

Example 4

You can write a linear equation to model the information given in a table without graphing the data.

The data in the table have a linear relationship. Write an equation in slope-intercept form that models the data.

Time (hr), x	5	10	15	20	25
Distance (mi), y	285	510	735	960	1185

Step 1 Find the slope of the line that passes through the points.

$$m = \frac{y_2 - y_1}{x_2 - x_1} = \frac{510 - 285}{10 - 5} = \frac{225}{5} = 45$$

Step 2 Find the y-intercept of the line.

$y = mx + b$ Use slope-intercept form.

$285 = 45(5) + b$ Substitute 45 for m, 5 for x, and 285 for y.

$285 = 225 + b$ Simplify.

$b = 60$ Solve for b.

Step 3 Write an equation.

$y = mx + b$ Use slope-intercept form.

$y = 45x + 60$ Substitute 45 for m and 60 for b.

Check

Use the data in the table to answer Questions 7 and 8.

Number of Days, x	7	14	21	28	35
Height of Bamboo (in.), y	180	348	516	684	852

7. Write an equation that models the data. _____

8. Explain the Error. Then find the correct solution.

Your friend says that after 10 days, the height of the bamboo will be 240 inches.

_____

SKILL 40 WRITING LINEAR EQUATIONS

KEY TEACHING POINTS

Example 1

Say: Box plots are a visual way to show how data is spread around the median, or center value.

Ask: How many values are in the data set for Example 1? **[12]** There are 12 months, so there are 12 values.

Say: The median is the center value. Because there are an even number of values, the median is the value that falls halfway between the sixth and seventh value.

Ask: What is the median? **[13]**

Say: Quartiles divide data into four sections with the same number of values in each, so 25% of the values are in each section. Once you know the median, find the center value of the data that falls below the median. This is the first quartile. The center value of the data above the median is the third quartile. The median is the second quartile.

Ask: There are six values below the median and six values above the median. How do you find the first and third quartile and what are they? **[The quartiles are the values that divide the upper and lower sections evenly. The first quartile is halfway between 11 and 12, so it is 11.5. The third quartile is halfway between 15 and 16, so it is 15.5.]**

Say: A box plot graphs the quartiles using a box and line segments. A point shows the minimum and maximum, and a rectangular box covers the range between the first and third quartile. A line shows the division created by the median.

ALTERNATE STRATEGY

Strategy: Make a physical model.

1. Give each of 17 students an index card with the values from problem 2 written on them. Have the students stand in order from least to greatest with duplicate values stacking behind each other.

2. Have students determine which person is the center, being careful to include the "stacked" students. This person is the median. Mark him or her with a flag or colored yardstick.

3. Have students determine which person is the first and third quartile. Emphasize that there should be the same number of students between the endpoints and each quartile.

4. Students who are the first and third quartiles should each hold the end of a roll of paper (wrapping paper, paper towels, etc.) The median student should hold his or her flag or yardstick so it is visible in front of the paper.

5. The minimum and first quartile students should each hold one end of a string or narrow paper, as should the third and maximum students, creating a physical model of a box plot.

KEY TEACHING POINTS

Example 2

Say: Graphing two box plots on the same number line makes it easier to compare data. Minimums, maximums, medians, and other quartile values can be compared easily by looking at the box plots.

Say: Comparing the medians of two data sets compares the center value. Comparing the interquartile range compares the middle 50% of the data values.

Ask: How is the interquartile range represented in a box plot? **[It is the box part.]** What does the value on the left side of the box represent? **[The first quartile.]** What does the value on the right side of the box represent? **[The third quartile.]**

Ask: The lower section of the box for 2000 is shorter than the lower section of the box for 2010. What does this mean? **[Possible response: There was a larger concentration of cities with similar populations in the smaller box.]** A longer box means there is a greater range; a shorter box means there is a smaller range.

Ask: Could you conclude that every metropolitan area surveyed has grown by looking at the box plot? Explain. **[Possible response: No. Individual data can't be compared on the box plot. Some of the areas many have remained the same, or even declined; however, the description from the problem that tells you the data is from the fastest growing areas in the United States leads you to believe they have all grown.]**

COMMON MISCONCEPTION

Ask: What is the Error?

Overall, Boston's average high monthly temperatures are greater than Atlanta's because the box plot for Boston is longer than the box plot for Atlanta.

Reason incorrect: The length of the box plot indicates the *range* of the average high monthly temperatures—actual temperature values.

Solution: Overall, Atlanta's average high monthly temperatures are greater because its minimum, maximum, and quartile temperatures are each greater than Boston's minimum, maximum, and quartile temperatures, respectively.

ADDITIONAL ONLINE INTERVENTION RESOURCES

Use the following for students who have not mastered the concepts in Skill 41.

- Math on the Spot videos

- Personal Math Trainer with customized intervention

- Building Block worksheets (Skill 6: Analyze Data; Skill 115: Find Range; Skill 116: Find Median and Mode)

SKILL 41

Box Plots

Example 1

A box plot is a graph that uses a number line to show how the values in a data set are distributed. A box plot is made up of a "box" and two "whiskers":

- The left whisker connects the minimum value to the first quartile, (Q_1).

- The box connects the first quartile to the third quartile. It has a vertical line through the second quartile (Q_2), or median.

- The right whisker connects the third quartile(Q_3) to the maximum value.

The table shows the average number of clear days per month in Flagstaff, Arizona. Use the data to make a box plot.

Month	J	F	M	A	M	J	J	A	S	O	N	D
Avg. No. of Clear Days	12	11	12	12	15	18	9	10	16	17	15	14

Step 1 Order the data values from least to greatest. Identify the minimum, maximum, and quartiles.

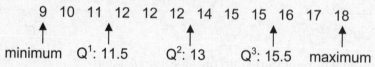

9 10 11 12 12 12 14 15 15 16 17 18

minimum Q^1: 11.5 Q^2: 13 Q^3: 15.5   maximum

Step 2 Draw the box plot.

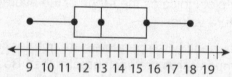

9 10 11 12 13 14 15 16 17 18 19

Vocabulary
Box plot
First quartile
Second quartile
Median
Third quartile

Check

Make a box plot for each set of data.

1. Price for the Same Pair of Sneakers at Different Stores

   $52 $60 $55 $42 $51 $35
   $50 $50 $60 $41 $49 $35

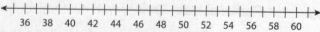

   36 38 40 42 44 46 48 50 52 54 56 58 60

2. Number of Points Scored in Each Game During One Football Season

   23 13 23 30
   13 30 27 27
   55 20 34 34
   27 20 41 34 16

   10   15   20   25   30   35   40   45   50   55   60

Name _____ Date _____ Class_____

Example 2

You can put two box plots on the same number line.

The box plots show the populations, in thousands of people, of the 10 fastest-growing metropolitan areas in the United States in 2000 and in 2010. Use the box plots to compare the data sets.

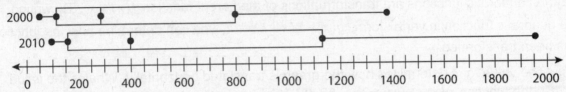

Step 1   Use the medians to compare the data sets.
The median population in 2000 was about 300,000. The median population in 2010 was about 400,000. So the median population in 2010 was about 100,000 greater than in 2000.

Step 2   Use the interquartile ranges to compare the data sets.
The "box" for 2010 is longer than the "box" for 2000. So the data set for 2010 has the greater interquartile range. This means that the middle 50% of the populations in 2010 varied more widely than the middle 50% of the populations in 2000.

Step 3   Use the maximum values to compare the data sets.
The maximum population in 2000 was about 1,400,000. The maximum population in 2010 was about 1,950,000. The maximum population in 2010 was about 550,000 greater than in 2000.

Check

The box plots show the average high monthly temperatures (in °F) for two cities. Use the box plots to answer the questions that follow.

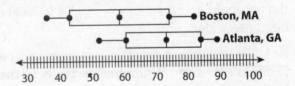

3. Which city has the greater median average high monthly temperature? Explain your reasoning.

4. Explain the Error. Then find the correct solution.
   Overall, Boston's average high monthly temperatures are greater than Atlanta's because the box plot for Boston is longer than the box plot for Atlanta.

SKILL 41 BOX PLOTS

Combining Transformations of Quadratic Functions

KEY TEACHING POINTS

Example 1

Say: All quadratic functions are transformations of the parent function $f(x) = x^2$. By writing the quadratic function in vertex form, $g(x) = a(x-h)^2 + k$, you can determine how the function has been transformed.

Ask: The value for h determines how the graph is translated horizontally. What is the value for h in the function $g(x) = -2(x-3)^2 + 8$? **[3]** This means the graph is translated 3 units to the right.

Ask: When the graph is translated 3 units to the right from the parent function $f(x) = x^2$, what is the x-coordinate of the new vertex? **[3]** The value for h is the x-coordinate of the vertex.

Ask: The value for k determines how the graph is translated vertically. What is the value for k in the function $g(x) = -2(x-3)^2 + 8$? **[8]** This means the graph is translated 8 units up.

Ask: When the graph is translated 8 units up from the parent function $f(x) = x^2$, what is the y-coordinate of the new vertex? **[8]** The value for k is the y-coordinate of the vertex.

Say: The vertex is (3, 8). The value for a tells you the scale factor for the transformation. Because a is negative, the parabola opens down.

Ask: Does a scale factor of -2 indicate a vertical stretch, or a compression? **[A vertical stretch.]**

Say: The scale factor changes the shape of the parabola. In a vertical stretch, the graph of the parabola becomes narrower. In a vertical compression, the shape of the parabola becomes wider.

Ask: To transform a function, why might you want to perform the stretch or compression first? **[Possible answer: When the vertex is at the origin, the factors are easy to work with. You can just multiply the y-value from the parent function by the scale factor to find the transformed y-value.]**

Check

Say: To graph a transformation that is given as an equation, begin with a table of values for the transformed function $g(x)$. Let's look at Problem 4.

Ask: What is the vertex for the function $g(x) = -0.4(x+4)^2 + 1$? **[(-4, 1)]**

Say: The vertex gives you a starting point for your table of values. Use x-values that are on either side of the x-coordinate of the vertex.

Complete the following table of values as a class. Work through each point by substituting each x-value into the transformed function. Then plot the points and draw the parabola.

x	$-0.4(x + 4)^2 + 1$	$g(x)$
–6	$-0.4((-6) + 4)^2 + 1 = -0.4(-2)^2 + 1$	–0.6
–5	$-0.4((-5) + 4)^2 + 1 = -0.4(-1)^2 + 1$	0.6
–4	$-0.4((-4) + 4)^2 + 1 = -0.4(0)^2 + 1$	1
–3	$-0.4((-3) + 4)^2 + 1 = -0.4(1)^2 + 1$	0.6
–2	$-0.4((-2) + 4)^2 + 1 = -0.4(2)^2 + 1$	–0.6

Ask: What is the value of a? **[–0.4]** What does this tell you about the transformed function? **[It is a vertical compression with a scale factor of 0.4, and is a reflection over the x-axis.]**

Ask: What do the h and k values tell you about the transformed function? **[It is a vertical shift of 1 unit up and a horizontal shift of 4 units left.]**

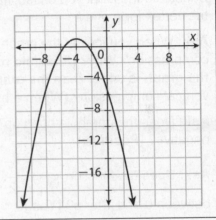

COMMON MISCONCEPTION

Ask: What is the Error?

To transform the graph of $f(x) = x^2$ to the graph of $g(x) = -4(x + 3)^2 - 5$, first reflect across the x-axis, stretch vertically by a factor of 4, and then translate 3 units to the right and 5 units down.

Reason incorrect: The value for h is negative, so the function is translated left instead of right.

Solution:

To transform the graph of $f(x) = x^2$ to the graph of $g(x) = -4(x + 3)^2 - 5$, reflect across the x-axis, stretch vertically by a factor of 4, and then translate 3 units to the left and 5 units down.

Say: The value for h can be easily reversed if you aren't careful. The vertex form, $g(x) = a(x - h)^2 + k$, subtracts h, so a negative value for h shows as addition in the equation.

Example 2

Say: The vertex is the point on the graph that is the maximum or minimum, or the place where the *y*-value is least or greatest. It is also the point on a parabola where the graph changes direction.

Ask: On the graph for Example 2, what is the *x*-value at the lowest point? **[–2]** What is the *y*-value at the lowest point? **[–4]** The vertex is at (–2, –4).

Say: Once you know the vertex, you can choose any point on the graph to find the value for *a*. Choose a point on the graph where the parabola crosses the intersection of two grid lines. Substitute the point you chose into the function using your point as the *x*- and *y*-values and the vertex for *h* and *k*.

Ask: When you look at the graph of the function, does it appear to be a vertical stretch or compression? Why? **[Possible response: It looks like a vertical compression because the graph is wider than the graph of the parent function.]** What values of *a* result in a vertical compression? **[When *a* has an absolute value between 0 and 1.]**

Ask: Does the parabola open up or down? **[Up.]** Should the value for *a* be positive or negative? **[Positive.]**

Ask: Does the function $g(x) = \frac{1}{2}(x+2)^2 - 4$ have a positive value with an absolute value between 0 and 1 for *a*? **[Yes.]**

Check

Say: For Problem 7, the graph of this parabola opens down, so the vertex is a maximum.

Ask: What is the *x*-value at the highest point on the graph? **[8]** What is the *y*-value at the highest point? **[80]** The vertex is at (8, 80). A point on the graph is given to you; what is that point? **[(24, 48)]**

Say: Substitute the point you know into the function for the *x*- and *y*-values and the vertex for *h* and *k*.

Complete the following work as a class.

$g(x) = a(x-8)^2 + (80)$ Write the function in vertex form with the vertex coordinates.

$48 = a(24-8)^2 + (80)$ Substitute in the known values for *x* and *y*.

$48 = a(16)^2 + (80)$

$48 = 256a + 80$

$-32 = 256a$ Solve for *a*.

$-\frac{1}{8} = a$

Say: What is the function for Problem 7? $[\, g(x) = -\frac{1}{8}(x-8)^2 + 80 \,]$

KEY TEACHING POINTS

Example 3
Say: A function can be transformed from another function that is not the parent function. In Example 3, the two functions have the same value for *a* and *h*. The values for *k* are different.

Ask: What does the variable *k* tell you in the function $g(x) = a(x-h)^2 + k$?

[The *y*-coordinate of the vertex.] What is the difference between the two graphs?
[One is 20 units up from the other.]

Check
Ask: In Problem 8, the equation $h(t) = -16t^2 + c$ is used to describe the height of balls dropped from 80 feet and 120 feet. What is the difference in the two functions? **[The value for *c*, which is the *y*-coordinate of the vertex.]** What transformation will map the function for the 80-foot height onto the function for the 120-foot height? **[A vertical translation 40 units up.]**

Ask: How does translating the function 40 units up affect the time it takes for the ball to reach the ground? **[It takes 0.5 second longer to reach the ground.]**

ALTERNATE STRATEGY

Strategy: Use algebra.

1. Let's look at Example 3. Using the function $h(t) = -16t^2 + c$ and substituting in the heights 16 and 36, you have the functions $h(t) = -16t^2 + 16$ and $h(t) = -16t^2 + 36$.

2. The graphing calculator tells you that for the function $h(t) = -16t^2 + 16$, the *x*-intercept, or time when the object reaches the ground, is 1 second after it is dropped, and from 36 feet up, the time when the object hits the ground is at 1.5 seconds. For each function, substitute the values in letting $y = 0$.

$$h_1(t) \overset{?}{=} -16t^2 + 16 \qquad\qquad h_2(t) \overset{?}{=} -16t^2 + 36$$

$$0 \overset{?}{=} -16(1)^2 + 16 \qquad\qquad 0 \overset{?}{=} -16(1.5)^2 + 36$$

$$0 \overset{?}{=} -16(1) + 16 \qquad\qquad 0 \overset{?}{=} -16(2.25) + 36$$

$$0 \overset{?}{=} -16 + 16 \qquad\qquad 0 \overset{?}{=} -36 + 36$$

$$0 = 0 \qquad\qquad\qquad 0 = 0$$

The results check algebraically.

ADDITIONAL ONLINE INTERVENTION RESOURCES

Use the following for students who have not mastered the concepts in Skill 42.

- Math on the Spot videos

- Personal Math Trainer with customized intervention

- Building Block worksheets (Skill 40: Function Tables; Skill 45: Graph Ordered Pairs; Skill 102: Symmetry; Skill 103: Transformations)

SKILL 42

Combining Transformations of Quadratic Functions

Example 1

Vocabulary

Quadratic
function

Parent
function

Vertex form

Vertex

Translation

Stretch

Compression

Reflection

Zeros

Any quadratic function can be expressed as a combination of transformations of the quadratic parent function $f(x) = x^2$ by the vertex form $g(x) = a(x - h)^2 + k$. The values of a, h, and k determine how to transform the graph of $f(x)$. (h, k) is the vertex of $g(x)$ and expresses the translation of h units horizontally and k units vertically. $|a|$ gives the scale factor of the vertical stretch or compression. If $a < 0$, then there is a reflection across the x-axis.

A. Graph $g(x) = -2(x - 3)^2 + 8$.

Identify the vertex: $h = 3$ and $k = 8$, so the vertex is $(3, 8)$. Plot the vertex.

Make a table of values for the function.

Plot the points and draw a parabola.

x	$g(x)$
1	0
2	6
3	8
4	6
5	0

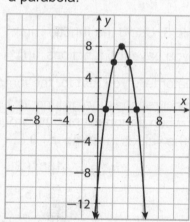

The parabola is a transformation of the graph of $f(x) = x^2$.

B. List the transformations needed to obtain the graph of
$g(x) = -2(x - 3)^2 + 8$ **from the graph of** $f(x) = x^2$.

Reflect across the x-axis.

Vertically stretch by a factor of 2.

Translate 3 units to the right.

Translate 8 units up.

Check

Graph each quadratic function and then list the transformations needed to obtain the graph of the function from the graph of $f(x) = x^2$.

1. $g(x) = 2(x-5)^2 + 3$

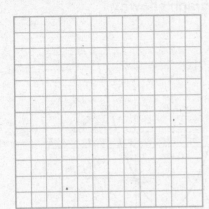

_____

_____

2. $g(x) = \dfrac{1}{2}(x+3)^2 - 1$

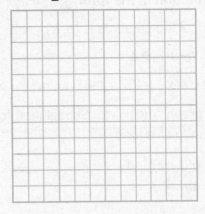

_____

_____

3. $g(x) = -3(x-3)^2 + 4$

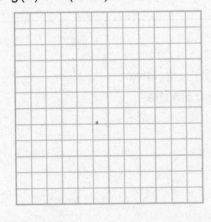

_____

_____

4. $g(x) = -0.4(x+4)^2 + 1$

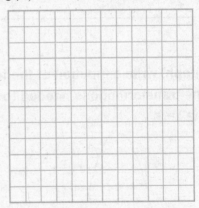

_____

_____

5. Explain the Error. Then describe the correct transformation.

To transform the graph of $f(x) = x^2$ to the graph of $g(x) = -4(x+3)^2 - 5$, first reflect across the y-axis, stretch vertically by a factor of 4, and then translate 3 units to the right and 5 units down.

_____

_____

_____

Example 2

By understanding transformations, you can determine the quadratic function, in vertex form, from its graph.

Write a function of the form $g(x) = a(x - h)^2 + k$ for the graph shown.

The vertex of the parabola is $(h, k) = (-2, -4)$.

Substitute for h and k.

$$g(x) = a(x - (-2))^2 + (-4), \text{ or } g(x) = a(x + 2)^2 - 4$$

From the graph, $g(0) = -2$. Substitute 0 for x and -2 for $g(x)$ and solve for a.

$$-2 = a(0 + 2)^2 - 4$$
$$-2 = 4a - 4$$
$$\frac{1}{2} = a$$

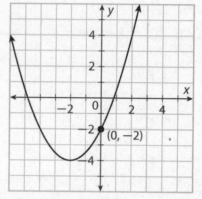

Substitute for a.

$$g(x) = \frac{1}{2}(x + 2)^2 - 4$$

Check

For each graph, write a function of the form $g(x) = a(x - h)^2 + k$. Then describe the transformations needed to obtain the graph from the graph of $f(x) = x^2$.

6.

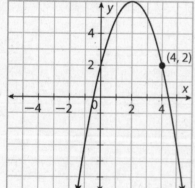

_____

_____

_____

7.

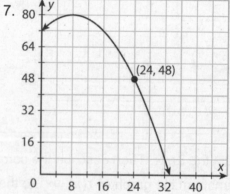

_____

_____

_____

Example 3

Use the quadratic function of the form $h(t) = -16t^2 + c$ to approximately describe the height $h(t)$ in feet above the ground of an object dropped after t seconds from a height of c feet.

A. Two identical objects are dropped from heights of 16 feet and 36 feet. Write the height function for each and compare their graphs.

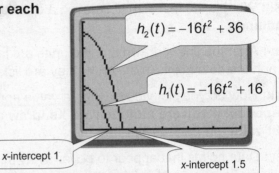

$h_1(t) = -16t^2 + 16 \leftarrow$ Dropped from 16 feet.

$h_2(t) = -16t^2 + 36 \leftarrow$ Dropped from 36 feet.

Using a graphing calculator, the graph of h_2 is the vertical translation of the graph of h_1 by 20 feet up.

B. Use the graph to tell how long it takes each object to reach the ground.

The *x*-intercept of each graph tells how long it takes for the object to reach the ground. Use your graphing calculator to find the zeros.

The first object reaches the ground in 1 second.

The second object reaches the ground in 1.5 seconds.

Check

8. One ball is dropped from a height of 80 feet. Another ball is dropped from a height of 120 feet.

   a. Write the height function for each ball. Then use a graphing calculator to compare their graphs.

   _____

   _____

   _____

   b. Use the graphs to tell when each ball reaches the ground. Round to the nearest tenth.

   _____

   _____

SKILL 42 COMBINING TRANSFORMATIONS OF QUADRATIC FUNCTIONS

Data Distributions and Outliers

KEY TEACHING POINTS

Example 1

Ask: What is the first step in creating a dot plot? [**Possible response: Choose the scale and units.**]

Say: After the line is drawn and the units are labeled, there is no need to order the data. Graph the data points in the order they are listed.

Ask: How do you plot values when a value appears more than once in a data set? [**Possible response: If you are plotting with Xs, draw an X directly above the X that is already at that value on the number line.**]

Say: Data points that appear to be far away from the rest of the points are sometimes outliers. To be an outlier, a point must be at least one and a half times the interquartile range away from the middle half of the data.

Ask: What points are the endpoints of the interquartile range? [**Quartile 1 and 3**] Quartile 1 and 3 separate the middle half of the data.

Ask: If a point looks far away from the median, does that make it an outlier? Explain. [**Possible responses: No, looking far away is not enough. You must check to make sure the point meets the requirements in distance from the interquartile.**]

Check

Ask: What is the minimum data value in the set of the number of gold medals? [**1**] What is the maximum data value? [**13**] It is not necessary to label every unit on the dot plot, but since there are so many odd numbers included in the set, be sure there is a tick mark for each unit.

Graph the data set on a dot plot as a class in the order given in the problem.

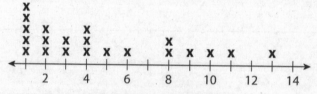

Number of Gold Medals

Ask: How do you find the quartiles and interquartile range? [**Order the values and find the quartiles and then find the difference between quartile 1 and quartile 3.**]

Say: Let's find the quartiles and interquartile range for the data when the country that won 18 gold medals in Problem 3 is included.

Order the data first.

1, 1, 1, 1, 1, 2, 2, 2, 3, 3, 4, 4, 4, 5, 6, 8, 8, 9, 10, 11, 13, 18

Say: The middle value, or median, is between two of the 4s. The median is 4. Quartile 1 is 2 and Quartile 3 is 8. The interquartile range is $8 - 2 = 6$.

Ask: For a value to be an outlier that lies in the upper part of the data, what is the lowest possible value? Explain. **[The inequality $x > Q_3 + 1.5(IQR)$ can be solved to find the lowest value for an outlier. $x > 8 + 1.5(6)$; $x > 17$, so an outlier must be greater than 17.]**

Say: 18 is greater than 17, so the new value is an outlier.

COMMON MISCONCEPTION

Ask: What is the Error?

Maria says that 13 is an outlier in the data set because $13 < 8 + 1.5(6.5)$.

Reason incorrect: The inequality sign is the wrong direction.

Solution: First arrange the values in numeric order and find the quartiles and interquartile range.

$$\boxed{1, 1, 1, 1, 1, 2, 2, 2, 3, 3,}\ 4, \boxed{4, 4, 5, 6, 8, 8, 9, 10, 11, 13}$$

The first quartile (Q_1) is $\dfrac{1+2}{2} = 1.5$. The third quartile (Q_3) is $\dfrac{8+8}{2} = 8$.

So, the IQR is $8 - 1.5 = 6.5$.

To determine if 13 is an outlier, use the inequality $x > Q_3 + 1.5(IQR)$, or

$$13 > 8 + 1.5(6.5) = 17.75.$$

13 is not an outlier because the inequality is not true.

ALTERNATE STRATEGY

Strategy: Draw a diagram.

1. You can use the dot plot to determine if there are any outliers.
2. Let's look at Example 1, Part B.
3. When you draw the dot plot, the values in the data set are placed in order on the number line.
4. There are 16 values. The median falls between the eighth and ninth value on the dot plot, 78 and 79, so the median is 78.5.
5. There are eight values on each side of the median. Quartile 1 is between the 4th and 5th value, 74 and 75, so it is 74.5. Quartile 3 is between the 12th and 13th values, 81 and 81, so it is 81. Draw a dotted line to represent the quartile marks.

6. The interquartile range is 81 − 74.5 = 6.5. Outliers must be one and a half times the interquartile range, or (6.5)(1.5) = 9.75 values away from the middle half of the data, marked by the quartiles.

7. The upper limit is 81 + 9.75 = 90.75. This is not even on the graph, so you know there are no outliers that fall above the data.

8. The lower limit is 74.5 − 9.75 = 64.75. Mark this point on the graph using a solid line. Any data points that fall outside the solid line are outliers. Since the data point 63 is below the solid line at 64.75, it is an outlier.

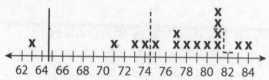

Height, in Inches, of Players on a Professional Basketball Team

KEY TEACHING POINTS

Example 2

Say: Data that are symmetric have values that are evenly distributed on each side of the mean, in roughly the same shape. If you were to fold the dot plot vertically along the mean, the sides would correspond to each other.

Ask: How are the mean and median related in a data distribution that is symmetric? Explain. **[The mean and median will be very close to each other and at the center of the data distribution. This is because the values are equally distributed on each side of the center.]**

Say: Data distributions of real-world data often have values that are heavier on one side or the other. For example, if everyone in a class put in extra time studying, it is likely that the test scores will be heavier in the upper part of the data.

Say: A skewed distribution has one side with a hump, where the data values appear more often, and what looks like a tail on the other side, where there are few data values. The terms skewed to the left and skewed to the right are easy to get confused.

Ask: How can you remember which is which? **[Possible response: The tail in a data distribution is on the side that it is skewed toward. So, if the tail is on the left side, the data are skewed to the left.]**

Say: Compare the two dot plots in Exercise 2.

Ask: Without calculating, what could you say about the median and mean for the data for Class 1? **[The median and mean are likely to be very close to each other.]** What could you say about the median and mean for the data for Class 2? **[The median is likely to be greater than the mean. Since the data are skewed to the left, there are more data points in the higher scores, which will move the median into the higher scores. Even one or two low values have a greater effect on the mean than on the median.]**

Say: Let's do the calculations for the mean and median for Class 2. Find the mean by adding all of the data values and dividing by the total number of values. There are 30 scores recorded in all.

Show the following work.

$$\frac{2(70) + 3(75) + 3(80) + 4(85) + 5(90) + 7(95) + 6(100)}{30} = \frac{2660}{30} = 88.\overline{6}$$

The mean is a little less than 89.

The median is found by finding the middle data value. If there are 30 students, the median score is the score between the 15th and 16th student when they are placed in order. Use the dot plot and count up 15 dots. The median is between two of the scores of 90. In this data set, even though the data are skewed, the median and mean are close together.

Check

Ask: In Class 3, what is the low value? **[70]** What is the high value? **[100]** What unit is a good choice for the dot plot? Explain. **[Possible response: 5, the data values increase in increments of 5, so it is a good choice]**

Ask: When the data are plotted, are more of the values on the left or the right? **[Left]** When more values are on the left end, which end has a tail? **[The right end.]** If the tail of the data is on the right, how do you describe the distribution? **[Skewed to the right]**

Ask: If the data is skewed to the right, are more values on the left or the right of the mean? **[There are more data values on the left of the mean when the data distribution is skewed to the right.]** How does this affect the relationship between the mean and the median? **[The median might be on the left of the mean instead of the same or very close.]**

ADDITIONAL ONLINE INTERVENTION RESOURCES

 Use the following for students who have not mastered the concepts in Skill 43.

- Math on the Spot videos
- Personal Math Trainer with customized intervention
- Building Block worksheets (Skill 115: Find Range; Skill 116: Find Median and Mode; Skill: 117 Find Mean)

SKILL 43 Data Distributions and Outliers

Example 1

A dot plot, or line plot, is a graph that uses a number line and X's, dots, or other symbols to represent frequency.

A. **The heights, in inches, of the players on a professional basketball team are listed below. Make a dot plot of the data.**

  81, 77, 80, 75, 77, 74, 83, 81, 81, 78, 84, 71, 73, 81, 79

The minimum height is 71 inches and the maximum height is 84 inches, so a number line from 70 to 84 seems reasonable. Place an X above the appropriate number on the number line for each time the value appears in the data set.

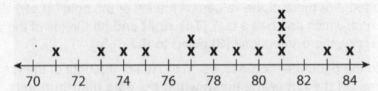

**Height, in Inches, of Players on a
Professional Basketball Team**

An outlier is a value in a data set that is either much greater than or much less than most of the other values in the data set. You can use the first quartile or the third quartile, along with the interquartile range (IQR), to determine if a value is an outlier.

A data value x is an outlier if $x < Q_1 - 1.5(\text{IQR})$ or if $x > Q_3 + 1.5(\text{IQR})$.

B. **Suppose the list of heights in Part A is expanded to include a player that is 63 inches tall. Is the height of 63 inches an outlier in the new data set?**

  63, 81, 77, 80, 75, 77, 74, 83, 81, 81, 78, 84, 71, 73, 81, 79

Step 1: Make a dot plot for the revised data set.

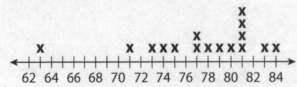

**Height, in Inches, of Players on a
Professional Basketball Team**

Vocabulary
Dot plot
Line plot
Outlier
First quartile
Third quartile
Interquartile range (IQR)
Symmetric
Skewed to the left
Skewed to the right

Step 2: Find the first quartile (Q_1), the third quartile (Q_3), and the IQR.

$Q_1 = 74.5$

$Q_3 = 81$

$IQR = 81 - 74.5$, or 6.5

Step 3: Determine if 63 is an outlier.

Because 63 is *less than* all the other values in the data set, determine if $63 < Q_1 - 1.5(IQR)$.

$63 < Q_1 - 1.5(IQR)$

$63 < 74.5 - 1.5(6.5)$

$63 < 74.5 - 9.75$

$63 < 64.75$

So, 63 is an outlier.

Check

The numbers of gold medals won by different countries during the Winter Olympics are listed below. Use the data to answer Questions 1–3.

13, 9, 11, 10, 8, 8, 4, 4, 2, 6, 3, 3, 2, 2, 1, 5, 4, 1, 1, 1, 1

1. Make a dot plot of the data.

2. Explain the Error. Then find the correct solution.

   Maria says that 13 is an outlier in the data set because $13 < 8 + 1.5(6.5)$.

   _____

3. Suppose a different country won 18 gold medals during the same Winter Olympics. Is 18 an outlier in the revised data set? Explain your reasoning.

   _____

Example 2

You can describe a set of data as symmetric, skewed to the left, or skewed to the right, depending on the overall shape of the distribution in a dot plot.

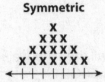

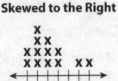

The table lists the test scores of the students in two different math classes on the same test. Make a dot plot and determine the type of distribution for each class. Explain what each distribution means in terms of the problem situation.

Score	70	75	80	85	90	95	100
Class 1	3	4	5	5	4	3	1
Class 2	2	3	3	4	5	7	6

Make a dot plot for Class 1.

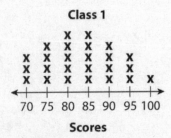

The data for Class 1 show a distribution that is almost symmetric. This means that the test scores are approximately evenly distributed about the mean test score.

Make a dot plot for Class 2.

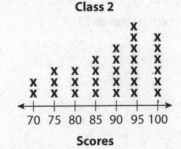

The data for Class 2 show a distribution that is skewed to the left. This means that more than half of the test scores are greater than the mean test score.

Check

The table lists the test scores of the students in a third math class.
Use the data to answer Questions 4–6.

Score	70	75	80	85	90	95	100
Class 3	6	7	6	5	3	2	1

4. Make a dot plot for Class 3.

5. Describe the distribution of the dot plot as skewed to the left, skewed
   to the right, or symmetric.

   _____

6. Explain what the distribution means in terms of the problem situation.

   _____

SKILL 43 DATA DISTRIBUTIONS AND OUTLIERS

Distance and Midpoint Formulas

KEY TEACHING POINTS

Example 1

Start by pointing out a common distance in the classroom. For example, ask students to estimate the halfway point between their own desk and the door, their desk and the trashcan, etc.

Ask: How many steps does it take to get from your desk to the classroom door? **[Answers will vary: Sample answer: 12 steps]**

Ask: How many steps does it take to get halfway from your desk to the classroom door? **[Answers will vary: Sample answer: 6 steps]**

Say: Notice that the halfway point means that the distance is divided equally in two.

Direct students' attention to Example 1. Point out the segment on the grid and ask students to approximate the halfway distance on the segment and plot a point. This will be their guess.

Say: Now let's learn how to find the midpoint exactly.

Ask: Look at just the x-axis. Where does the segment start on the left? **[at the −6]**

Ask: At which x-value does the segment stop on the right? **[at the 2]**

Remind students that the average of two numbers is found by adding the numbers and dividing by 2.

Ask: What is the average of −6 and 2? Explain how you got your answer. **[−2; I added −6 and 2 to get −4. Then I divided −4 by 2 to get −2.]**

Repeat for the y-coordinates to show that the average of the y-coordinates is 2.5. Be sure to point out that the midpoint is not necessarily an integer.

Check
Problems 1–2

Encourage students to write the ordered pairs at each endpoint on the graph. For example, problem 1 is from (1, 3) to (3, −3). Allow students to draw vertical and horizontal lines if desired to help them see the distance between the x-values and the distance between the y-values.

Problem 5

Students may be confused when averaging the x-values and see that 2 + −2 = 0. Point out that the segment is 2 units to the left of 0 and 2 units to the right of 0 so the average is 0.

Ask: What is 0 divided by any number (other than 0)? **[0]**

Example 2

Connect students' prior knowledge by having them create right triangles using the segment as the hypotenuse. It may be necessary to review the parts of a right triangle.

Work through Example 2 with students. Have them practice tracing the dashed line to create the right triangle. Point out that the legs of the right triangle will always be vertical and horizontal lines.

Ask: The legs of the right triangle in the example were drawn above the segment. Will the triangle be the same if we draw the legs below the segment? **[Yes.]**

Encourage students to draw another triangle below the segment in the example to verify that it does not matter where the triangle is drawn. Some students may remember this method for finding slope. If time permits, allow students to explore the difference in using the right triangles this way. Help students recall that slope is determined by dividing the vertical distance by the horizontal distance.

Ask: What does 4^2 mean? **[It means 4 × 4 or 16.]**

Ask: What does 6^2 mean? **[It means 6 × 6 or 36.]**

Take a few minutes to review square roots with students. List common square roots on the board and a draw number line to help students estimate. Next, have students estimate where $\sqrt{52}$ will be located on the number line.

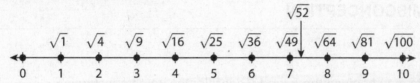

Check
Problems 6–7
Remind students to start at the endpoint, then trace only on the horizontal or vertical line to get to the other endpoint.

Ask: Does the length of the segment depend on whether the segment is sloping up or down? Why or why not? **[No, because direction does not matter when finding distance.]**

Example 3
The Distance Formula can be difficult to memorize, so help students see the connection to the Pythagorean Theorem.

Ask: How might you describe the Distance Formula in words? **[Sample answer: Take the difference of the *x*-values and the difference of the *y*-values, square both, and then add them together and take the square root.]**

Direct students, attention to the Sample in Example 3. Point out that keeping track of labeling each coordinate pair can help when using the formula.

Refer to the number line to help students estimate $\sqrt{117}$.

Check
Problem 10
Use this problem to encourage students to think about the distance before applying the formula.

Ask: What are the *x*-coordinates? **[8 and 8]**

Ask: What do you know about the line segment if the *x*-coordinates are the same? **[This is a vertical line.]**

Ask: Can you think of a simpler way to calculate the length of a vertical line? What is it? **[Yes, find the difference of the *y*-coordinates.]**

Ask: Would the Distance Formula still give the correct solution? Explain. **[Yes. If the *x*-coordinates are the same, the difference of *x*-values will be 0 and $0^2 = 0$.]**

ALTERNATE STRATEGY

Strategy: Visual Representation of Midpoint

1. If students have difficulty with understanding midpoint of a segment, allow them to trace the segment on a piece of patty paper or other tracing paper.

2. Then, have them fold the paper so the endpoints are aligned. Direct them to place a point on the line segment at the crease.

3. Finally, have students lay the traced segment over the original segment to the midpoint found using the algebraic method.

4. Students can use this tracing method to help them estimate before finding the midpoint algebraically or after to check their answers.

COMMON MISCONCEPTION

Check
Problem 12
Error: Students may confuse the x- and y-coordinates when substituting into the Distance Formula.

Ask: What are the x-coordinates? **[3 and −5]**

Ask: What are the y-coordinates? **[−8 and 1]**

Encourage students to use colored pencils or other markings to remind themselves that the difference of the x-coordinates and the difference of the y-coordinates must be found.

Solution: Find the distance between (3, −8) and (−5, 1).

$$d = \sqrt{\left(3-(-5)\right)^2 + \left(-8-1\right)^2}$$
$$d = \sqrt{8^2 + (-9)^2}$$
$$d = \sqrt{64+81}$$
$$d = \sqrt{145}$$
$$d \approx 12.0$$

Error: Students often have difficulty simplifying the Distance Formula.

Encourage students to avoid algebraic mistakes by writing steps carefully. Most errors will occur when subtracting negatives as some students believe the exponent means they can ignore the negative sign. Point out that order of operations specifies they add/subtract in the parentheses before applying the exponent.

Problem 13
Students may make assumptions about lengths from graphs because of the orientation of the segment. Point out that precision is necessary and all segment lengths must be calculated before the triangle can be classified.

ADDITIONAL ONLINE INTERVENTION RESOURCES

 Use the following for students who have not mastered the concepts in Skill 44.

- Math on the Spot videos
- Personal Math Trainer with customized intervention
- Building Block worksheets (Skill 10 Area of Polygons; Skill 11 Area of Squares, Rectangles, Triangles; Skill 27 Evaluate Expressions; Skill 38 Find the Square of a Number; Skill 45 Graph Ordered Pairs (First Quadrant); Skill 69 Order of Operations; Skill 70 Ordered Pairs; Skill 98 Solve Two-Step Equations; Skill 100 Squares and Square Roots)

SKILL 44

Distance and Midpoint Formulas

Example 1

Vocabulary
Midpoint
Hypotenuse
Legs

A midpoint is a point that divides a segment into two congruent segments.

The midpoint of any segment is the "average" of the coordinates.

$$x = \frac{x_1 + x_2}{2} \qquad y = \frac{y_1 + y_2}{2}$$

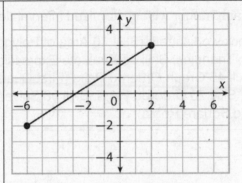

Endpoints: (−6, −2) and (2, 3)

$$x = \frac{x_1 + x_2}{2} = \frac{-6 + 2}{2} = \frac{-4}{2} = -2$$

$$y = \frac{y_1 + y_2}{2} = \frac{2 + 3}{2} = \frac{5}{2} = 2.5$$

The midpoint is (−2, 2.5).

Check

State the midpoint of each line segment.

1.

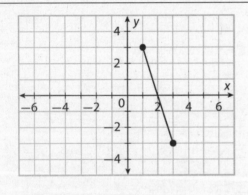

_____

2.

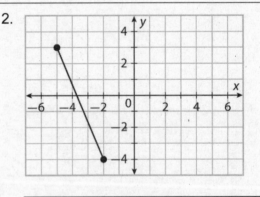

_____

3. Segment with endpoints at (−4, 10) and (−6, −2)   _____

4. Segment with endpoints at (−1, 15) and (3, 0)   _____

5. Segment with endpoints at (2, −3) and (−2, −5)   _____

Example 2

The length of any segment, in a right triangle, can be found using the Pythagorean theorem.

The Pythagorean theorem states: In any right triangle where *a* and *b* are legs and *c* is the hypotenuse, then $a^2 + b^2 = c^2$. The hypotenuse is the side opposite the right angle in a right triangle. The legs are the sides adjacent to the right angle.

Calculate the length of $\overline{JK}$.	Step 1 Draw a triangle so that $\overline{JK}$ is the hypotenuse.	Step 2 Use the Pythagorean theorem.
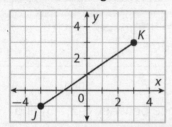	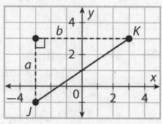 $a = 4$ and $b = 6$	$4^2 + 6^2 = c^2$ $16 + 36 = c^2$ $52 = c^2$ $\sqrt{52} = c$ $7.2 \approx c$

Check

Create a right triangle with the segment as the hypotenuse. Then calculate the length.

6.
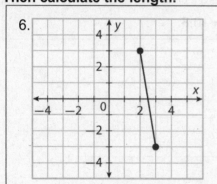

_____

_____

7.
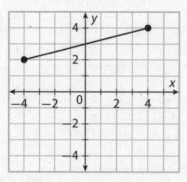

_____

_____

8.

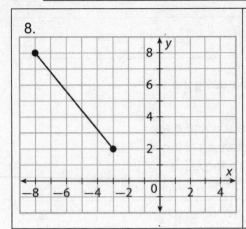

_____

_____

Example 3

The distance formula is based on the Pythagorean theorem.

$$c^2 = a^2 + b^2$$

$$c^2 = (x_2 - x_1)^2 + (y_2 - y_1)^2$$

$$c = \sqrt{(x_2 - x_1)^2 + (y_2 - y_1)^2}$$

The distance formula is:

$$d = \sqrt{(x_2 - x_1)^2 + (y_2 - y_1)^2}.$$

Sample

What is the distance between (−2, −5) and (7, 1)?

Let $(x_1, y_1) = (-2, -5)$ and $(x_2, y_2) = (7, 1)$

$$d = \sqrt{(7 - (-2))^2 + (1 - (-5))^2}$$

$$d = \sqrt{9^2 + 6^2}$$

$$d = \sqrt{81 + 36}$$

$$d = \sqrt{117}$$

$$d \approx 10.8$$

Check

Calculate the distance between each set of ordered pairs.

9. (13, −2) and (−5, 7)

_____

_____

10. (8, −6) and (8, 7)

_____

_____

11. (−11, 5) and (6, 0)

_____

_____

Name _____ Date _____ Class_____

12. Explain the Error. Find the solution.

Find the distance between (3, −8) _____
and (−5, 1).

_____

$d = \sqrt{(3-(-8))^2 + (-5-1)^2}$

$d = \sqrt{11^2 + (-6)^2}$ _____

$d = \sqrt{121+36}$

$d = \sqrt{157}$ _____

$d \approx 12.5$

13. Is △CDE a scalene, isosceles, or
    equilateral triangle?
    (Hint: First, find the measure of each side.)

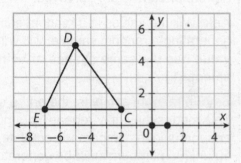

    A What is CD? _____

    B What is DE? _____

    C What is CE? _____

    D Classify △CDE by its sides. _____

14. A map is shown on a coordinate system as shown.
    What is the distance on the map between Springfield
    and Chester? Each unit is 1 cm.

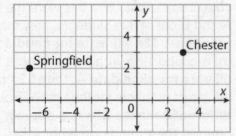

    _____

15. The map legend states that 1 cm = 5 miles. What is the
    real distance between cities?

    _____

SKILL 44 DISTANCE AND MIDPOINT FORMULAS

Generating Random Samples

KEY TEACHING POINTS

Example 1

Say: Instead of testing an entire population, you can use random samples to make predictions about the entire population.

Say: In Part A, the school newspaper is taking a survey of whom students intend to vote for. Since there are 900 students, each student is assigned a unique number. A graphing calculator is used to generate random numbers, and the students assigned those numbers are the ones who are surveyed.

Ask: Will the values in a random sample always be evenly distributed? **[No.]** When you are generating a random sample, will values repeat? Explain. **[Yes. In a random sample, each value has the same chance of being selected, even the ones that have already been selected.]**

Say: In random samples, the entire set of values has the same chance for each sampling. This means they may repeat. You must continue to generate random samples until you have enough unique numbers to complete the sample. In this case the staff wants 50 students, so 50 unique numbers must be generated.

Say: The generated numbers chose random students to survey, but the results need to be interpreted.

Ask: Of the 50 students surveyed, 18 said they will vote for candidate A, and 17 said they will vote for candidate B. If this were the exact ratio of students who actually vote for candidates A and B out of 900 students, how many will vote for candidates A and B? Explain. **[Possible response: 324 will vote for candidate A and 306 will vote for candidate B. You can set up a proportion with the numbers from the survey and the total population. If 18 out of 50 vote for candidate A, then 324 out of 900 vote for candidate A.]** Are these likely to be the exact numbers for the vote? Explain. **[The numbers will probably be close but slightly different because this is a survey, and until the actual vote takes place, students may change their minds on whom they will vote for.]**

Check

Ask: The computer company wants a sample of 80 out of 2000 chips. Do you think this is a large enough sample? **[Possible answer: Yes, a sample of this size, if it is truly random, is likely to produce a good representation of the chips.]**

Ask: What percent of the chips tested were defective? **[2.5%]** What inference can you make? **[Possible response: Most of the chips are not defective, or only a small percent of the chips are defective.]**

Ask: If the expected rate of defective chips is 1%, would this batch be likely to meet the tolerance rate? Explain. **[Possible response: No, if 2 of the randomly chosen 80 were defective, this is more than double the tolerance rate. It might be a good idea to test another set or a larger set of the chips.]**

COMMON MISCONCEPTION

Ask: What is the Error?

To generate a random sample of 20 out of 1000, enter **randInt(20, 1000)** into a graphing calculator and press ENTER 20 times.

Reason incorrect: This eliminates numbers 1 to 19, so only 980 of the numbers are actually possible.

Solution: To generate a random sample of 20 out of 1000, enter **randInt(1, 1000)** into a graphing calculator and press ENTER 20 times.

Say: Remember, it is important to know your calculator. There are a number of calculator functions that look similar to randInt, but they will not produce usable random numbers.

KEY TEACHING POINTS

Example 2

Say: In this simulation, it is assumed that the students are evenly divided on what candidate to vote for.

Ask: How many times do you expect each candidate to receive a vote? **[Possible answer: About 10 times each since they are evenly divided and there are 3 candidates and 30 samples.]**

Ask: The candidates did not receive 10 votes each in the simulation in Example 2. Why not? **[Possible response: Because this is random, the votes are not evenly distributed, and a simulation could possibly end up having all of the votes for one candidate.]**

Say: You can use multiple simulations to see how much difference or variance there is between samples. If all of your samples have similar results, you can make a good prediction from the data.

Check

Ask: When you ran your own simulation, were the results more of what you expected? Explain. **[Possible response: Yes, I expected the votes to be evenly split. My results were closer to even, but not exact.]**

Ask: When you combined the data with the rest of the class, were the results closer to what you expected? Why do you think this is true? **[Possible response: Yes, when the results were combined and the average taken, the votes were very close to evenly split. Using a combination and average gives a more accurate result.]**

Ask: What is another way you can get a more accurate result? **[Possible response: Taking a larger survey could give a more accurate result.]**

ALTERNATE STRATEGY

Strategy: Perform an experiment.

1. **Say:** Experiments that produce results similar to those in Example 2 can be performed without using technology.

2. There are three possible candidates and 900 students voting. One way you can produce a random sample is to use a different colored marble to represent each candidate.

3. In Example 2 it was assumed that the students were evenly divided among candidate choices. To simulate this, you could use 300 marbles of 3 different colors. For example, let 300 red marbles represent the students who choose candidate A, 300 white marbles represent students who choose candidate B, and 300 black marbles represent students who choose candidate C.

4. Place all of the marbles in a bag or box. Without looking, pick out one of the marbles. Use a chart or tally marks to record the color of the marble.

5. Replace the marble and repeat the procedure until you have enough data.

6. **Ask:** Why must you replace the marble before you draw the next marble? **[Possible response: For each draw to have the same chance, all of the marbles must be present for each draw.]**

7. An experiment such as this yields the same type of results as the random number generator in Example 2. The sample size and number of times the experiment is performed affects the accuracy of predictions made using the data.

8. **Ask:** How might the experiment be affected if each color marble had a different weight? **[Possible response: The heavier marbles might go to the bottom, so the lighter marbles might have a better chance of being chosen.]**

KEY TEACHING POINTS

Example 3
Say: In this simulation, a teacher rolls two number cubes.

Ask: How many possible numbers are there on each number cube? **[6]** With six sides on each number cube, how many possible combinations can be made? **[36]**

Ask: Why might it be a good idea to have two different colored number cubes? **[Possible response: If the number cubes are the same color, you might use the column when the row should be used. For example, if a 1 and a 6 are rolled, how can you distinguish it from a 6 and a 1?]**

Say: The number cubes were rolled and 6 random values chosen.

Ask: How can you find the average of those 6 heights? **[Find the total of the heights, and then divide it by 6.]**

Say: The average height of the sample is called the sample mean. The sample mean is lower than the population mean, or average height of the entire population.

Ask: What could you do to generate a more accurate sample? **[Possible response: Use a larger sample size, or generate more samples and take the average.]**

Say: This sample was taken by generating numbers by rolling number cubes. Could you have generated random numbers by dropping a pencil onto the table? **[Possible response: No, a pencil would cover a set of numbers, which would make them not random.]**

Check

Ask: How can you select a random sample from the table without using technology? **[Possible response: Number the table cells and draw numbers from a hat or bag.]**

Ask: How do you find the average number of pounds of fruit a tree produces from the sample? **[Add the number of pounds produced by each tree in the sample, and then divide by 10.]**

Ask: How do you find the projected number of pounds produced by all of the trees? **[Possible response: There are 64 trees in all, so multiply the average expected for one tree by 64.]**

Ask: How did the average for 16 trees compare to the average for 10 trees? **[Possible response: The average number of pounds was slightly lower/higher.]**

Say: Let's find the average number of pounds for the entire 64-tree population. If all of the weights are added together, the sum is 7958 pounds.

Ask: How does this compare to the projected number of pounds from problem 9? **[The actual total is larger.]** What is the average number of pounds produced by each tree? **[124.34]** How much of a difference is there between your answer for problem 8 and the population average? **[Almost 5 pounds]** How do these answers compare to the ones you found using your own 10-tree sample? What about your own 16-tree sample? **[Answers will vary depending on student samples.]**

Ask: If you were to find 20 samples of 10 trees each, what would you expect from the results? **[Possible response: It is likely that the average of the 20 samples would be closer to the population average than a single sample average.]**

ADDITIONAL ONLINE INTERVENTION RESOURCES

Use the following for students who have not mastered the concepts in Skill 45.

- Math on the Spot videos

- Personal Math Trainer with customized intervention

- Building Block worksheets (Skill 96: Solve Proportions Using Cross Products; Skill 115: Find Range; Skill 117: Find Mean)

SKILL 45 — Generating Random Samples

Vocabulary
Random sample

Example 1

You can use technology or tables as a means to generate random samples.

A. In a school, 900 students are voting for 1 of 3 candidates for student body president. In order to see who is the leading candidate, the school newspaper decides to select a random sample of 50 students to survey whom they intend to vote for. How can the paper use technology to help select the random sample?

The newspaper staff members first assign a unique number from 1 to 900 to each student. They then follow these steps on a graphing calculator.

- Press the MATH button, scroll right to select **PRB**, and then select **5: randInt**.

- Enter the least possible value, a comma, and then the greatest possible value.

- Press ENTER until there are enough unique numbers for the random sample.

Here, the staff members use **randInt(1, 900)** and press ENTER at least 50 times until they have 50 unique numbers.

The screen shot shows three of their results, so students who were assigned 366, 661, and 40 are surveyed by the paper.

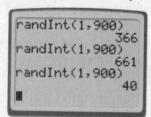

```
randInt(1,900)
                366
randInt(1,900)
                661
randInt(1,900)
                 40
■
```

B. Of the 50 students surveyed, 18 say they will vote for candidate A, 17 say they will vote for candidate B, and 23 say they will vote for candidate C. How might the paper rank the candidates from the results?

The paper might conclude that candidate C is the leading candidate and has the support of about $\frac{23}{50} = 46\%$ of the students at the school.

The results of the survey are too close to determine between candidate A and candidate B.

Check

A company produces 2000 memory chips in a batch and wants to take a random sample for testing.

1. Describe how you could use a graphing calculator to help select 80 chips as a random sample for testing.

   _____

   _____

2. Of the 80 chips tested, 2 were found to be defective. What might you infer from this result?

   _____

   _____

3. Explain the Error. Then describe the correct procedure.

   To generate a random sample of 20 out of 1000, enter **randInt (20, 1000)** into a graphing calculator and press ENTER 20 times.

   _____

   _____

Example 2

You can also simulate random samples using a calculator to see the value of a sample size.

Suppose in Example 1 that the school is evenly divided among the candidates. How could the paper run 10 simulations to see how much statistical measures vary for different samples of size 30?

The paper can use **randInt(1, 900)** to generate 30 unique numbers. Staff members assign numbers 1 to 300 for candidate A, 301 to 600 for candidate B, and 601 to 900 for candidate B.

They then run the simulation a total of 10 times to see how much variation they get. In one simulation they run, they get the following 30 numbers.

306, 896, 181, 719, 857, 199, 333, 8, 842, 98, 6, 495, 771, 880, 251, 248, 110, 48, 651, 12, 380, 277, 875, 26, 755, 557, 185, 887, 653, 272

With this simulation, candidate A receives 14 votes, candidate B receives 5 votes, and candidate C receives 11 votes. Thus, one simulation of a random sample size of 30 could be misleading.

Check

4. For Example 2, run your own simulation. What do your results show?

_____

5. Compare your results with your class. Compile the results of at least 20 simulations and take the average result for each candidate. Based on your results, who do you think is likely to win?

_____

_____

6. Besides running more simulations, what else could you do to get a more accurate simulation?

_____

Example 3

A table can also be used to generate a random sample.

A. **The table shows the heights of 36 students in a math class. To randomly select 6 students, the teacher rolls two number cubes. One cube represents the row, and the other cube represents the column. The heights selected are bolded in the table. What is the average height of the students in the sample?**

62	68	60	59	64	66
61	66	64	70	**66**	67
65	63	63	60	63	**65**
68	62	**59**	63	67	58
69	65	67	64	63	64
61	**63**	65	66	65	64

The average height of the sample is $\dfrac{66 + 65 + 59 + 69 + 61 + 63}{6} \approx 63.8$ inches.

B. **How does the sample compare to the actual average height?**

The average of all 36 heights is about 64 inches. The average of the sample was slightly lower than the actual average.

Check

**An orange grower has 64 trees of the same maturity and age. The
production in pounds of each tree from the most recent season is
shown in the 8-by-8 table. The orange grower selects a random sample
of 10 trees. His results are the bolded numbers.**

118	100	147	**105**	100	127	143	149
114	114	106	102	136	**100**	121	115
149	101	142	**131**	110	150	136	115
112	148	**147**	**102**	105	135	150	132
115	104	150	110	120	105	**112**	143
119	130	130	103	100	100	135	135
144	118	105	**122**	150	135	**127**	**132**
147	134	140	128	**117**	111	131	144

7. Describe a way you can select the numbers in the table randomly
without using technology.

_____

_____

8. What is the average number of pounds produced in the orange grower's
randomly selected sample?

_____

9. What is the projected number of pounds produced for all of the trees?

_____

10. Randomly select a sample of 10 trees. How does the average number of
pounds of your sample compare with the orange grower's sample?

_____

11. Randomly select a sample of 16 trees. How does the average number of this
sample compare to the other samples? Which sample do you think you
should use to estimate the production for all the trees?

_____

_____

SKILL 45 GENERATING RANDOM SAMPLES

Histograms

KEY TEACHING POINTS

Example 1

Say: A histogram is a specific type of bar graph.

Ask: What are the characteristics of a histogram? **[Possible responses: Bars represent intervals, not individual values. The bars touch but don't overlap.]**

Say: In a histogram, each bar represents the same interval; for example, the bars in the histogram in Example 1 represent 10 values each.

Ask: What factors go into choosing the intervals? **[Possible responses: the range of values or the number of bars you would like to include]**

Ask: What does the word *frequency* mean? **[Possible response: the number of times something occurs]**

Say: A frequency table records the number of times a value within each interval occurs. It is important to be sure you have included every item of data in your frequency table.

Ask: How could you check your table for accuracy? **[Possible response: Find the sum of the frequencies in the table, and count the number of values in the list. The two totals should be the same.]**

Say: Notice that in the histogram each bar is the same width. This makes sense since each bar represents the same interval. The height of the bar is used to show the number of data values that fall within the interval.

Ask: Can you tell by looking at a histogram the number of times an individual value occurs? Explain. **[Possible response: No. A histogram only shows the frequency of any value in the interval, not individual values.]**

Check

Ask: How many values are in the data for Problem 1? **[20]** What are the minimum and maximum prices in the data? **[The minimum is $5; the maximum is $561.]** How many dollars are included in each interval? **[100]**

Say: Count the number of phones in each price interval and record them in the frequency table. Let's complete the table together.

Complete the table as a class. Ask for the frequency of phones that occur in each interval.

Ask: What is the frequency for 0–99? **[3]**

Ask: What is the frequency for 300–399? **[4]**

Say: Sometimes there will be a gap where an interval has no data values. Be sure to include an area for the bar for this interval anyway, or the histogram could be misleading.

Price ($)	Frequency
0–99	3
100–199	3
200–299	4
300–399	4
400–499	4
500–599	2

Ask: What is the sum of the numbers in the frequency column? **[20]**

ALTERNATE STRATEGY

Strategy: Make a tally chart.

1. **Say:** Sometimes it is easy to lose count of the number of values that belong in each interval. Larger data sets make this even more likely. A tally chart can help you keep track of the data.

2. The data from Problem 2 have a minimum value of 410 and a maximum value of 836. The intervals have already been chosen. In a separate table or a separate column do a tally count from the data set.

3. Beginning with the first value in the set, 836, make one tally mark in the row for 800–899. When you make the tally mark, cross the value out of the list. To keep the list of data intact, it is best to make a copy of the entire list first.

4. When all of the data has been tallied, write the number that corresponds to the tally marks in the frequency column.

~~836~~ ~~506~~ ~~706~~ ~~505~~ ~~462~~ ~~460~~
~~500~~ ~~464~~ ~~451~~ ~~453~~ ~~590~~ ~~468~~
~~586~~ ~~614~~ ~~668~~ ~~501~~ ~~449~~ ~~425~~
~~406~~ ~~444~~ ~~446~~ ~~410~~ ~~420~~ ~~425~~

Depth (m)	Frequency	Tally Count
400–499	14	~~卌~~ ~~卌~~ IIII
500–599	6	~~卌~~ I
600–699	2	II
700–799	1	I
800–899	1	I

5. There are 24 data values, and the total from the frequency columns is also 24. Even if you've used tally marks and crossed out the data, it is still a good idea to total the values in the frequency column and compare that number to the number of data values in the data set.

6. Draw the histogram using the data from the frequency table. There are 5 intervals, so draw 5 bars. The graph title, labels, and units have already been given, so all you need to do is draw the correct bars.

KEY TEACHING POINTS

Example 2

Say: Although individual data values are not available once data have been transferred into a histogram, you can still use the histogram to estimate statistical data for the set.

Ask: What is a mean and how do you find the mean? **[Possible response: The mean is the average. The mean is found by adding all of the data values and then dividing by the number of values.]**

Say: Because the actual data values are not available in a histogram, an estimate is used. The total value for each bar is estimated as a group using the midpoint of the interval.

Ask: How can you find the midpoint of an interval? Give an example. **[Add the first and last values in the interval, and then divide by 2. As an example, for the interval from 2000 to 2499, the sum is 2499 + 2000 = 4499. Divided by 2, this is 2249.5, so 2249.5 is the midpoint.]**

Ask: The mean is estimated at 2022.2 square feet. Does this make sense when you look at the histogram? Explain. **[Possible response: Yes, because it is a little lower than the center of the histogram and there appear to be more values that are on the lower end of the histogram.]**

Say: The median is the center value in a data set. A histogram allows you to know the total number of items in a data set, so you can determine in which interval the median falls.

Ask: You can locate where the median falls in relation to the intervals and the other data values. What factors may cause your estimate to not be accurate? **[Possible response: The values may be heavier in one part of the interval than in another.]** When estimating the median, this method uses the assumption that the data values within each interval are evenly spaced. When they are heavily skewed to one side or the other, it can cause the estimate to be less accurate.

Check

Ask: What is the first step in finding the mean length of the movies? **[Possible response: Find the center value for each interval and multiply it by the number of values in that interval.]**

COMMON MISCONCEPTION

Ask: What is the Error?

The median is the 11th value.

Use the histogram to find which interval contains the 11th value. There is 1 value in the first interval, 3 values in the second interval, 6 values in the third interval, and 10 values in the fourth interval, for a total of 20 values. So the 11th value must be in the 4th interval, 150–169.

The median is the 1st value in this interval. The interval has 20 values. To estimate how far into the interval the median is located, find $\frac{1}{20} = 0.05$, or 5%, of the interval width, 20. Then add the result to the interval's least value, 150.

Median: 0.05(20) + 150 = 151 minutes

Reason incorrect: The number of values in the interval is 10 instead of 20.

Solution: The median is the 1st value in this interval. The interval has 10 values. To estimate how far into the interval the median is located, find $\frac{1}{10} = 0.1$, or 10%, of the interval width, 20. Then add the result to the interval's least value, 150.
Median = 0.1(20) + 150 = 152 min

ADDITIONAL ONLINE INTERVENTION RESOURCES

Use the following for students who have not mastered the concepts in Skill 46.

- Math on the Spot videos
- Personal Math Trainer with customized intervention
- Building Block worksheets (Skill 90: Read a Table; Skill 118: Read Bar Graphs)

SKILL 46 Histograms

Example 1

Vocabulary
Histogram
Frequency
Frequency table
Mean
Median

A histogram is a bar graph that displays the frequency of data values that are divided into equal intervals.

• Each interval has one bar.

• The height of a bar shows the frequency, or number, of data values within the interval.

• The bars have equal width.

• The bars touch but do not overlap.

The data below represent the fuel efficiency, in miles per gallon (MPG), of various cars on the road. Make a histogram for this data.

37 37 37 50 50 43 35 42 23 23

31 28 24 16 16 14 14 14 25 25

Step 1 Make a frequency table.

The minimum value is 14.
The maximum value is 50.
Use intervals of 10.

In the first column of the table, list the intervals.

Count and record the number of data values in each interval.

MPG	Frequency
11–20	5
21–30	6
31–40	5
41–50	4

Step 2 Draw the histogram.

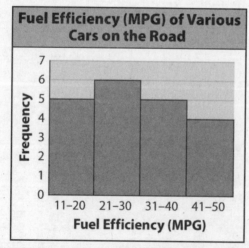

Fuel Efficiency (MPG) of Various Cars on the Road

Check

Make a frequency table and histogram for each set of data.

1. Prices for Smartphones:

$429	$5	$129	$504	$39
$44	$149	$237	$221	$299
$149	$354	$380	$491	$399
$454	$250	$561	$419	$307

Price ($)	Frequency
0–99	
100–199	
200–299	
300–399	
400–499	
500–599	

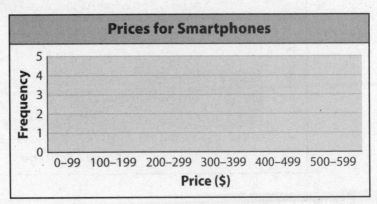

2. Depths of Lakes (meters)

836	506	706	505	462	460
500	464	451	453	590	468
586	614	668	501	449	425
406	444	446	410	420	425

Depth (m)	Frequency
400–499	
500–599	
600–699	
700–799	
800–899	

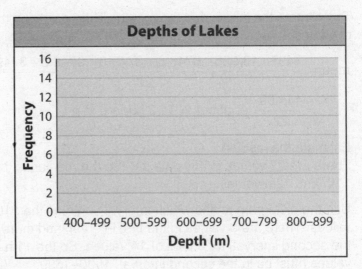

Example 2

You can use a histogram to estimate several statistics of a data set.

Use the histogram below to estimate the mean and median square footage of homes for sale in a certain neighborhood.

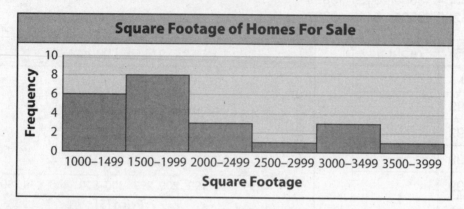

A. Estimate the mean.
Find the midpoint of each interval. Then multiply the midpoint by the frequency.

1st interval: 1249.5(6) = 7497   2nd interval: 1749.5(8) = 13,996

3rd interval: 2249.5(3) = 6748.5   4th interval: 2749.5(1) = 2749.5

5th interval: 3249.5(3) = 9748.5   6th interval: 3749.5(1) = 3749.5

To estimate the mean, add the results. Then divide by the total number of values.

$$\text{mean: } \frac{7497 + 13,996 + 6748.5 + 2749.5 + 9748.5 + 3749.5}{22}$$

$$= \frac{44,489}{22}, \text{ or about 2022.2 square feet}$$

B. Estimate the median.
There are 22 values in this data set. So the median is the average of the 11th and 12th values.

Use the histogram to find which interval contains the 11th and 12th values. There are 6 values in the first interval, and there are 8 values in the second interval, for a total of 14 values. So the 11th and 12th values must be in the second interval, 1500–1599.

The median is the average of the 5th and 6th values in this interval. This interval has 8 values. To estimate how far into the interval the median is located, find $\frac{5.5}{8} \approx 0.69$, or 69%, of the interval width, 500. Then add the result to the interval's least value, 1500.

Median: 0.69(500) + 1500 ≈ 1845 square feet

Name _____ Date _____ Class_____

Check
Use the histogram to answer the questions that follow.

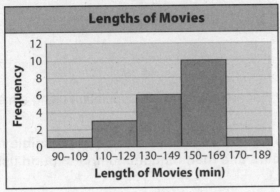

3. How many movies were between 130 and 149 minutes long?

_____

4. How many movies were longer than 129 minutes?

_____

5. How many movies are included in the histogram?

_____

6. Estimate the mean length of the movies included in the histogram.

7. Explain the Error. Then find the correct solution.

The median is the 11th value.

Use the histogram to find which interval contains the 11th value. There is 1 value in the first interval, 3 values in the second interval, 6 values in the third interval, and 10 values in the fourth interval, for a total of 20 values. So the 11th value must be in the fourth interval, 150–169.

The median is the 1st value in this interval. The interval has 20 values. To estimate how far into the interval the median is located, find

$\frac{1}{20} = 0.05$, or 5%, of the interval width, 20. Then add the result to the

interval's least value, 150.

Median: $0.05(20) + 150 = 151$ minutes

SKILL 46 HISTOGRAMS

SKILL 47 — Making Inferences from a Random Sample

KEY TEACHING POINTS

Example 1

Say: Random samples are samples that are taken from a population using a method that is unbiased.

Ask: What method could be used to choose quiz scores randomly? **[Possible response: Students could be assigned numbers and then random numbers found using a random number generator on a calculator.]**

Say: The first step in making a dot plot or box plot is knowing the least and greatest values in the data set. These are necessary to draw the starting number line.

Ask: What are the least and greatest values in the data set? **[72 and 100.]** Why was the number line for this dot plot drawn using multiples of 4? **[Possible response: All of the values are multiples of 4, so it is possible that each question was worth 4 points.]**

Ask: How do you plot values when a value appears more than once in a data set? **[Possible response: If you are plotting with Xs, draw an X directly above the X that is already at that value on the number line.]**

Ask: There are no scores in the sample that are less than 72. Can you infer that there are no quiz scores in the entire set of quizzes that are below 72? **[Possible response: No, the data are from a sample, so you could infer that it is not likely there are scores below 72, but you can't say for certain there are no scores below 72.]**

Say: A box plot uses the median and quartiles to graph data. The median is the value that is in the exact center when the data values are put in order.

Ask: The lower section of the box is longer than the upper section of the box. What does this mean? **[Possible response: There was a larger concentration of scores in the upper range.]** A longer box means there is a greater range; a shorter box means there is a smaller range.

Ask: What percent of the sample data falls between the first and third quartile? **[50%]**

Check

Ask: What is the minimum data value in the sample of people living in a student's household? **[2]** What is the maximum data value? **[8]**

Ask: There are 14 values in the sample. That means there is no value that is directly in the middle. How do you find the median and what is the median? **[The median is the mean of the two center values. The seventh value is 3 and the eighth value is 4, so the median is halfway between 3 and 4, which is 3.5.]**

Graph the data in a box plot as a class.

Ask: Since the interquartile covers the middle half of the data, between what two values does 50% of the population lie? **[3 and 4]** This is an exact answer for the sample. Is it an exact answer for the population? Explain. **[No. However this is a good estimate.]**

ALTERNATE STRATEGY

Strategy: Make a physical model.

1. Give each of 11 students an index card with the values from Example 1 Part B written on them. Have the students stand in order from least to greatest with duplicate values stacking behind each other.

2. Have students determine which person is the center, being careful to include the "stacked" students. This person is the median. Mark them with a flag or colored yardstick.

3. Have students determine which person is the first and third quartile. Emphasize that there should be the same number of students between the endpoints and each quartile.

4. Students who are the first and third quartiles should each hold the end of a roll of paper (wrapping paper, paper towels, etc.) The median student should hold his or her flag or yardstick so it is visible in front of the paper.

5. The minimum and first quartile students should each hold one end of a string or narrow paper to represent the lower whisker, as should the third and maximum students. The wider paper, narrower paper or string, and flags create a physical model of a box plot.

KEY TEACHING POINTS

Example 2

Say: Proportional reasoning finds two ratios that have the same value. Because you have a random sample, the resulting value for the population is a prediction, not an exact value.

Ask: What value is the question asking you to find? **[Possible response: the number of students in Washington High School who intend to continue their education]**

Ask: How many students were surveyed? **[50]** How many of the sample intended to continue their education? **[30]** So, 30 out of 50, or $\frac{3}{5}$, intend to continue their education in some form after high school.

Say: One way to solve the problem is to set up a proportion with the sample data on one side and the population data on the other.

Ask: Is there a different proportion you can set up? **[Possible response: Yes. You can compare the ratios of total number sampled to total population and the sample that plans to continue education to the population that plans to continue education.]**

Set up and solve the proportion as a class.

$$\frac{\text{plan to continue education in sample}}{\text{plan to continue education in population}} = \frac{\text{size of sample}}{\text{size of population}}$$

$\frac{30}{x} = \frac{50}{1280}$ Substitute in the known values.

$\frac{30}{x} = \frac{5}{128}$ Reduce the ratio.

$(5)(x) = (30)(128)$ Cross multiply.

$5x = 3840$

$x = 768$ Divide.

The result is the same. There are a number of different ways the proportion can be set up to start the problem and still be correct.

Check

Ask: What is the question asking you to find in Problem 10? **[the number of discs that are likely to be cracked or warped]** What ratio of the sampled discs were cracked or warped? $\left[\textbf{4 out of 200, or } \frac{1}{50} \right]$

COMMON MISCONCEPTION

Ask: What is the Error?

Sharon wrote the proportion $\dfrac{7}{x} = \dfrac{200}{7{,}200}$ and found that 2,520 of the discs

from the day's production are likely to not have replicated correctly.

Reason incorrect: incorrect computation with multiples of ten

Solution: Sharon wrote a correct proportion.

$\dfrac{7}{x} = \dfrac{200}{7{,}200}$ Reduce the ratio on the right by dividing each term by 200.

$\dfrac{7}{x} = \dfrac{1}{36}$

$x = (7)(36)$
$x = 252$ Cross multiply.

There are likely to be around 252 discs that have not replicated correctly.

ADDITIONAL ONLINE INTERVENTION RESOURCES

Use the following for students who have not mastered the concepts in Skill 47.

- Math on the Spot videos

- Personal Math Trainer with customized intervention

- Building Block worksheets (Skill 6 Analyze Data; Skill 20: Compare and Order Real Numbers; Skill 39: Fractions, Decimals, and Percents)

Making Inferences from a Random Sample

Example 1

A random sample can be organized into a dot plot or box plot to make inferences about a population.

The mathematics quiz scores of a random sample of students are shown below.

> **92, 96, 72, 80, 76, 92, 92, 100, 84, 96, 84**

A.   Use a dot plot to analyze the data and draw conclusions.

Find the least and greatest values in the data set.

Draw a number line from 72 to 100. Place a dot or X above each number for each time it appears in the data set.

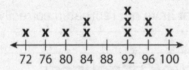

Quiz Scores

From the dot plot you can draw conclusions about the data that can be inferred about the population.

Most students scored between an 84 and a 96 on the quiz.

More than half of the students scored at least an 84 on the quiz.

B.   Use a box plot to analyze the data and draw conclusions.

Step 1:   Order the values from least to greatest. Find the least value, greatest value, and median.

Step 2:   Find the first and third quartile by finding the median for the lower half and the median for the upper half.

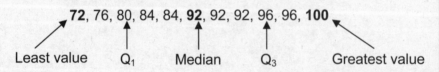

Vocabulary
Box plot
Dot plot
Inference
Proportional reasoning

Step 3: Draw the box plot using the values you found in Step 2.

- Draw a number line and plot each of the values.

- Draw a box from quartile 1 to quartile 3.

- Draw a vertical line through the box at the median.

- Connect the least and greatest values with a line segment to the box.

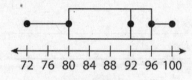

Quiz Scores

From the box plot, you can draw conclusions about the data that can be inferred about the population.

50% of the students scored between an 80 and a 96.

Almost every student passed the quiz.

A good estimate for the most likely score is 92.

Check
The number of people living in a household for a random sample of students is listed below. Use the data to answer Questions 1–9.

2, 3, 3, 5, 2, 8, 4, 4, 3, 2, 4, 6, 4, 3

1. Make a dot plot of the data.

Use the dot plot to complete the following statements.

2. Most students have _____ two people living in their households.

3. Most students have fewer than _____ people living in their households.

4. Most students have between _____ and _____ people living in their households.

5. Make a box plot of the data.

Use the box plot to complete the following statements.

6. 50% of the population have between _____ and _____
   living in their households.

7. A good estimate for the most likely number of people in a household is

   _____.

8. Almost every student has at least _____ people living in his or
   her household.

9. Are there any other conclusions you can draw based on the sample?

   _____

Example 2

Proportional reasoning is used to make inferences or predictions based
on a random sample.

**Washington High School has a population of 1280 students. A
random sample of 50 students found that 30 planned to continue
their education in some form after high school. How many students
from Washington High School are likely to intend to continue their
education?**

Step 1: Set up a proportion.

$$\frac{\text{plan to continue education in sample}}{\text{size of sample}} = \frac{\text{plan to continue education in population}}{\text{size of population}}$$

Step 2: Substitute values into the proportion.

$$\frac{30}{50} = \frac{x}{1280}$$

Substitute in the known values.
Use x to represent the number of
students in the population who
intend to continue their education.

$$\frac{3}{5} = \frac{x}{1280}$$

Reduce the ratio.

$$1280 \cdot \frac{3}{5} = \frac{x}{1280} \cdot 1280$$

Multiply both sides by 1280.

$$768 = x$$

Simplify.

Based on the sample, you can predict that 768 students in Washington
High School intend to continue their education after high school.

Check

**A replicator of compact discs produces 7,200 discs each day.
A quality control specialist took a random sample of 200 discs from
one day's production and found that 4 discs were cracked or warped
during replication and 7 discs did not replicate correctly and would
not play. Use the data to answer Questions 10 and 11.**

10. How many discs from the day's production are likely to be cracked or
warped?

    _____

11. Explain the Error. Then find the correct solution.

    Sharon wrote the proportion $\dfrac{7}{x} = \dfrac{200}{7,200}$ and found that 2,520 of the

    discs from the day's production are likely to not have replicated
    correctly.

    _____

SKILL 47 MAKING INFERENCES FROM A RANDOM SAMPLE

Making Predictions with Probability

KEY TEACHING POINTS

Example 1
Make sure students understand how to solve proportions.

Say: When you make a prediction based on a sample, you make an assumption that the ratio of the preferences in the sample will be the same as the ratio of the preferences of a larger group.

Ask: How can you write a ratio for the number of students who ride the bus using the survey results? **[Compare the number of students who ride the bus to the total number of students in the survey.]**

Ask: How many of the students surveyed ride a bus to school? **[22]**

Ask: How can you find the total number of students surveyed? **[Add the number of responses in the table.]** How many students were surveyed? **[40]**

Ask: What ratio of the students surveyed ride a bus? **[22 out of 40, or $\frac{22}{40}$, or $\frac{11}{20}$]**

Say: Remember that a proportion states that two ratios are equivalent. If you want to find an equivalent ratio for a larger group, you can solve a proportion.

Ask: How can you represent the ratio for the number of students who ride a bus in the entire school? $\left[\frac{n}{300}\right]$

Work through the steps to solve the proportion. Have students check their answers by showing that the ratios are equivalent since $\frac{11}{20} = 0.55$ and $\frac{165}{300} = 0.55$.

Ask: Do you know for certain that 165 students in the school ride the bus? **[No; it is only a prediction.]**

Check
Make sure students can set up proportions correctly.

Problem 1
Ask: What proportion can you write to represent the problem? $\left[\frac{3}{8} = \frac{n}{1200}\right]$

Problem 3
Ask: How many students were surveyed? **[80]**

Ask: What is the ratio of students who want to learn German to the total number of students surveyed? $\left[\frac{12}{80}\right]$

KEY TEACHING POINTS

Example 2

Make sure students can convert between fractions, decimals, and percents.

Say: Probability is a ratio. It compares the number of favorable outcomes to the number of possible outcomes.

Ask: What is the favorable outcome? **[blocking a shot]**

Ask: What are the possible outcomes? **[blocking a shot and not blocking a shot]**

Ask: What are you trying to predict? **[the number of shots that were scored]**

Say: If a team scores a point that means that the shot was not blocked.

Ask: Do you want to find the number of shots that were blocked or the number of shots that were not blocked? **[not blocked]**

Say: You are given the probability that a goalie will block a shot. If the goalie blocks 12 out of 15 attempts, then the goalie does not block 3 out of 15 attempts. So, the probability of not blocking a shot is $\frac{3}{15} = \frac{1}{5}$ or 20%.

Check
Problem 4

Ask: What is the ratio of 25% coupons to the total number of coupons? **[5 out of 75 or 1 out of 15]**

Problem 5

Ask: What is $\frac{3}{5}$ written as a decimal and a percent? **[0.6; 60%]** Point out that the answer is not an integer so it is given as an approximation.

Problem 6

Students can approach the problem in two ways. They can determine the probability of not winning a prize and then make a prediction, or they can make a prediction for the people who will win a prize and subtract that number from 120 to find the number of people who will not win a prize.

Ask: What are the possible outcomes of spinning the wheel? **[winning a prize and not winning a prize]**

Ask: What is the probability of winning a prize? $\left[\frac{1}{15}\right]$

Ask: What is the probability of not winning a prize? $\left[\frac{14}{15}\right]$

ALTERNATE STRATEGY

Strategy: Use a different approach.

Example 2

Show students that you can also solve the problem by using the given probability to find the number of blocked shots. Then subtract the number of blocked shots from the total number of attempts to find the number of scores.

Say: There were 25 attempts to score a goal. The probability of blocking a shot is $\frac{4}{5}$. Use this probability to find the number of shots blocked.

$$\frac{4}{5} \cdot 25 = 20$$

Ask: If 20 out of 25 shots were blocked, how many shots were not blocked? Explain.
[5 shots; 25 − 20 = 5]

KEY TEACHING POINTS

Example 3

Say: The probability of rolling a 4 is $\frac{1}{6}$ since 1 out of the 6 numbers on the cube is a 4. This means that you expect to roll a 4 one time out of every six rolls. To find how many times you expect to roll a 4 out of 100 tosses, use a proportion.

Ask: In the proportion, why is the denominator 100 in the second ratio? **[The number cube is rolled 100 times.]**

Ask: Is it possible to roll a number cube 100 times, and land on 4 more than 17 times or less than 17 times? **[Yes; 17 is only a prediction.]**

Check
Problem 10

Ask: How many different kinds of fruit are in the dried fruit mix? **[6]**

Ask: What is the probability of randomly choosing a raisin? $\left[\frac{1}{6}\right]$

Problem 12

Ask: How many cards were purchased altogether as shown in the table? **[60]**

Ask: What is the ratio of birthday cards purchased to the total number of cards? $\left[\frac{30}{60} \text{ or } \frac{1}{2}\right]$

Ask: What is the ratio of thank you cards purchased to the total number of cards? $\left[\frac{12}{60} \text{ or } \frac{1}{5}\right]$

COMMON MISCONCEPTIONS

Problem 6
The question asks for the number of people who will NOT win a prize. Students may have misread the question or forgotten to find the complement. Remind students to read problem statements carefully and look for key words.

Problem 11
The question asks for the number of monkeys left in the box. The solution given, 16 monkeys, is the result of finding the number of monkeys that have been given out so far, instead of finding the number of monkeys left in the box. Students do not need to recognize that 16 is the number of monkeys given away, but they should know that the correct equation is $\frac{1}{4} \cdot 36 = 9$.

Ask: How many stuffed animals have been given away? **[64]**

Ask: How many stuffed animals are left in the box? **[36]**

Ask: What is the probability of randomly choosing a monkey? **[1 out of 4 or $\frac{1}{4}$]**

Ask: Is it reasonable to predict that 16 out of 36 stuffed animals left in the box are monkeys? **[No; only about $\frac{1}{4}$ of the stuffed animals should be monkeys.]**

Error: There were 16 monkeys that were given away, not left in the box. There are 36 stuffed animals left in the box. The probability of randomly choosing a monkey is $\frac{1}{4}$ and $\frac{1}{4} \cdot 36 \neq 16$.

Solution: The number of monkeys left in the box should be $\frac{1}{4} \cdot 36 = 9$ monkeys.

ADDITIONAL ONLINE INTERVENTION RESOURCES

 Use the following for students who have not mastered the concepts in Skill 48.

- Math on the Spot videos
- Personal Math Trainer with customized intervention
- Building Block worksheets (Skill 6: Analyze Data; Skill 95: Solve Proportions)

Making Predictions with Probability

Example 1

Vocabulary
Survey
Sample
Probability
Outcome

Surveys are used to collect information about a group.
Sometimes the group is too large to survey every individual.
A sample can be used to predict the actions of a larger group.

Suppose you randomly surveyed a group of students in your
school about the transportation they use to get to school.
The table shows the results of a survey.

Transportation to School	
Bus	22
Walk	6
Bicycle	5
Car	7

If there are 300 students at the school, predict how
many students ride a bus to school.

Write a ratio for the number of students who ride a
bus to the total number of students surveyed.

Students who ride bus: 22

Total number of students surveyed: 22 + 6 + 5 + 7 = 40

Ratio: $\frac{22}{40}$ or $\frac{11}{20}$

The survey shows that 11 out of every 20 students
surveyed ride a bus to school. Set up a proportion to
find the number of n students out of 300 who ride a
bus.

$\frac{11}{20} = \frac{n}{300}$ Write a proportion.

$11 \cdot 300 = 20 \cdot n$ Find the cross products.

$3300 = 20n$ Multiply.

$165 = n$ Divide each side by 20.

So, the survey predicts that about 165 students in
the school ride the bus.

Check

1. The manager of a movie theater kept track of the number of tickets sold for each type of movie for one week. The manager found that 3 out of every 8 people bought tickets for action films. If the movie theater sold 1200 tickets during a weekend, predict how many people watched an action film.

_____

2. The results of a survey show that 42 out of 100 people take a vitamin every day. How many people would you expect to take a vitamin every day out of 2000 people?

_____

3. The table shows the results of a survey that asked incoming students what foreign language they were interested in learning. If 240 students signed up for a foreign language class, predict how many students chose German.

Language	Number of Students
French	24
Spanish	36
German	12
Latin	8

_____

Example 2

The probability of an event is a ratio that compares the number of favorable outcomes to the total number of possible outcomes. In soccer, a shot is an attempt to score a goal. When a goal is attempted, there are two possible outcomes: the shot is blocked or the shot is scored.

During soccer practice, a goalie blocks 12 out of 15 attempts to score a goal. Find the probability that the goalie will block a shot on the goal.

The number of favorable outcomes is 12 blocked shots and the total number of outcomes is 15 attempts. So, the probability that the goalie will block a shot is $\frac{12}{15}$ or $\frac{4}{5}$.

You can write probability as a fraction, a decimal, or a percent: $\frac{4}{5} = 0.8 = 80\%$.

Suppose that in a game there were 25 attempts to score a goal by the other team. Predict how many shots were scored.

If the goalie blocks 80% of the shots, then 20% of the shots are scored. Multiply the probability by the number of attempts.

$n = 0.2 \cdot 25$ $20\% = 0.20$

$n = 5$

A good prediction is that 5 shots were scored.

Check

4. A clothing store is giving coupons to its customers worth 10%, 15%, 20%, or 25% off every purchase. The company prints five 25% off coupons out of every 75 coupons. What is the probability that you will choose a 25% off coupon out of a box with 300 coupons?

_____

5. The probability that a basketball player makes a basket during a game is $\frac{3}{5}$.

   During a recent game, the player attempted 24 shots. Predict how many shots she made.

_____

6. In a carnival game, participants spin a wheel to win a prize. The probability of winning a prize is 1 out of every 15 spins. If 120 people play the game, predict how many people will not win a prize.

_____

Use the following information 7–8.
A toothbrush manufacturer determines that 3 out of 150 toothbrushes have a defect.

7. What is the probability that a randomly chosen toothbrush has a defect?

_____

8. Predict how many toothbrushes will have a defect out of a box of 1000 toothbrushes.

_____

Example 3

Some outcomes have an equal probability of occurring.

If you roll a number cube with numbers 1–6 on the faces, the probability of rolling each number is equally likely. Since there are 6 possible outcomes, the probability of rolling each number is $\frac{1}{6}$.

Predict how many times you will roll a 4 if you roll a number cube 100 times.

$\frac{1}{6} = \frac{n}{100}$	Write a proportion.
$1 \cdot 100 = 6 \cdot n$	Find the cross products.
$100 = 6n$	Multiply.
$16.7 \approx 6n$	Divide each side by 6.

You should expect to roll a 4 about 17 times.

Check

9. A spinner has 8 equal sections numbered 1–8.
How many times would you expect to land on
an even number out of 20 spins?   _____

10. A package of dried fruit mix contains apricots,
bananas, raisins, pineapple cubes, dates, and
cranberries in equal amounts. If you take a
random handful of 20 pieces, predict how
many apricots you will get.   _____

11. Explain the Error. Find the correct solution.

    A zoo is having a customer appreciation day and is giving away stuffed animals to every
    visitor. In the first hour, the zoo gives away 64 stuffed animals that are randomly chosen
    from a box with 100 stuffed animals.

    If the box contains an equal number of elephants, tigers, monkeys, and bears, there should
    be about 16 monkeys left in the box.

    _____

    _____

12. The table shows the number of cards that were purchased last week at a gift shop. The
    store manager is placing an order for 500 cards. How many more birthday cards should the
    manager order than thank you cards? Show your work.

Type of Card	Number of Cards
Birthday	30
Get Well	13
Thank You	12
Sympathy	5

_____

SKILL 48 MAKING PREDICTIONS WITH PROBABILITY

Measures of Center and Spread

KEY TEACHING POINTS

Example 1

Say: A measure of center is a way to describe an entire data set using only one value.

Ask: What is another word for *mean*? **[Average.]** How do you find the average of three numbers? **[Possible response: Add the numbers and then divide by three.]**

Say: The data for Isaiah's exercise time covers each day for a week. There is one value for each day, so there are a total of seven values. To find the mean, add the minutes for each day, then divide by 7.

Say: The median is the middle value of a set.

Ask: What must you do first to find the middle value? **[Order the values.]** Once the values are in order, how can you find the middle value? **[Possible response: You can count in from each side to find the number left in the center.]**

Ask: The mean and median for both sets of data in Exercise 1 are different values. The mean is the average and the median is the center value. In Part A, why might Isaiah choose to use the mean instead of the median value? **[Possible responses: to have a higher value to report so it looks like he is exercising more]**

Say: When the values in a data set are evenly spread, the mean and median are both good measures. When the values in the entire set are very similar, or clustered around a value, the mean and median are both good measures.

Ask: If all of the values in a set are clustered around a particular value, except one very low outlier, how is the mean affected? **[Possible response: The outlier causes the mean to be lower than what might be considered an accurate representation of the center.]** In this instance, the median may give a better description of the data set.

Say: When there is an odd number of values in a data set, the median is the value with the same number of values on each side when the values are placed in order. When there is an even number of values, there is no middle value. Find the two values at the center, and find the mean, or average, of those two middle values.

Ask: How can you find the center value in a large set of values? Give an example. **[Possible responses: If the set has an even number of values, you can divide the number of values in the set by 2 to find how many values are on each side of the median. For example, if there are 150 values in all, there should be 75 values on each side of the median, so the median is the average of values 75 and 76. If there is an odd number of values, such as 75, subtract 1 to get an even number, 74. Then divide by 2 to get 37. There are 37 values on each side of the median, and the median is value number 38.]**

Check

Ask: How many values are in the data set for Problem 1? **[10]** How do you find the mean of the data set? **[Add the values, then divide by 10.]** What is the sum of the values? **[131]** What is the mean? **[13.1]**

Say: Let's find the median together.

Ask: What is the first thing that must be done to find the median? **[Order the values.]**

Say: You can order the values by writing the values from least to greatest, and marking each item in the original data as you go to make sure you don't miss any.

Complete the following as a class.

4, 4, 5, 7, 8, 9, 16, 18, 21, 39

Say: There are 10 values, so the data set has an even number of values.

Ask: What are the two center values? **[8 and 9]** What is the mean of 8 and 9? **[8.5]** The median of the data set is 8.5.

Ask: How many values are in the data set for Problem 2? **[13]** Is the median one of the values in the data set? **[Yes, it is the center value.]**

Complete the following as a class.

6, 12, 14, 24, 35, 51, 57, 115, 143, 155, 162, 240, 320

Ask: How many values are on each side of the median? **[6]** If the values were numbers from 1 to 13, what value would be the median? **[Number 7]**

Say: In problem 2, the mean number of followers is 102.6 and the median number of followers is 57. These values are very different.

Ask: Are the data values clustered around a particular number? **[No.]** Are there any values that are much higher or much lower than the others? **[Yes, but there are both high and low values.]** Why are the mean and median so different? **[Possible response: The values have a large range between them, or cover a large area. The mean averages those values, but the median is one of the values.]**

Ask: The owner reports that his users have 103 followers. Is this measure an accurate representation? Why or why not? **[Possible response: Yes, the owner used the mean and there are both very low and very high values with about the same number of values less than and greater than 103.]**

COMMON MISCONCEPTION

Ask: What is the Error?

The monthly high temperature, in degrees Fahrenheit, each month for 12 months:

67, 71, 77, 85, 95, **104**, **106**, 105, 100, 89, 76, 66

The median monthly high temperature is $\frac{104+106}{2} = \frac{210}{2}$, or 105°F.

Reason incorrect: The data was not ordered first.

Solution: The median is the center value when the values are arranged in order.
First arrange the values in numeric order.

66, 67, 71, 76, 77, **85**, **89**, 95, 100, 104, 105, 106

The median monthly high temperature is $\frac{85+89}{2} = \frac{174}{2}$, or 87°F.

ALTERNATE STRATEGY

Strategy: Use visual learning.

1. **Say:** It is easy to confuse the measures of center. You can use memory tricks to help you remember how to calculate each measure. The two measures of center we are working with are mean and median.

2. Give seven students pieces of paper cut to lengths in centimeters that match the values from Example 1 Part A. Write the value on the paper.

3. **Say:** Median is the value that happens in the middle. The letter *d* can help you remember that median means middle.

4. Students should stand in order from shortest paper strip to longest paper strip. To find the median, have one student on each end move off to the side at a time. The student left in the middle is the median.

5. **Say:** Mean, or arithmetic mean, is the average. You can use a sentence to remember mean, such as *It just sounds mean to say a person is average* or *It's mean for teachers to make us work this hard to find the average.*

6. Have the students tape all of the papers together end to end. Ask what they can do to get a result in which each student has the same length. Fold and cut the combined length of paper into seven equal sections and then measure the length. This is the mean length.

KEY TEACHING POINTS

Example 2

Say: Measures of spread are used to tell how the data are spread out around the center.

Ask: What is the range of a data set and how do you find it? **[Possible response: The range is the difference between the greatest and least values in the data set. It is a value that tells you over how many values the data are spread.]**

Say: Quartiles are values that divide a data set into four equal parts. Quartiles can be found by first finding the median to divide the set into two equal parts and then dividing the lower half of the set into two equal parts and the upper half of the set into two equal parts.

Ask: What percent or fraction of the data values fall between the first quartile and the third quartile? Explain. **[50% or half of the data values fall between the first and third quartile. If each quartile has the same number of values and there are four quartiles, then two of them are between the first and third. Two out of four is half, or 50%.]**

Say: The interquartile range is the difference between the first and third quartile. This value tells you over how many values the middle half of the data is spread. In Example 2, the middle half of the data is spread over a range of 183 pages.

Check

Ask: Is the median part of the upper half, lower half, both halves, or neither when you find the first and third quartile? **[Possible response: The median is a value that is not included in either computation for quartiles.]**

KEY TEACHING POINTS

Example 3

Say: Standard deviation is a measure of how spread out the values in a data set are.

Say: Deviation is difference. You might say, *How far does your grade deviate from the typical grade?* and you would be asking what is the difference between your grade and the average grade. To find the standard deviation, you need to find the difference between each value and the mean.

Ask: What is the first value you need to find to calculate the standard deviation? **[the mean]**

Say: Some of the data values are less than the mean and some are greater than the mean. To account for this, square the differences, find the mean of the squares, and then take the square root.

Ask: Why is it helpful to use a table when finding the standard deviation? **[Possible response: If there are very many data values, they can get easily confused or some of them can be missed.]**

Check

Ask: In Question 6, there are five values. What is the mean of the values? **[52.8]** How do you find the deviation between a value and the mean? **[Subtract.]**

Say: After finding the deviation, or difference, between each value and the mean, square the deviations, and find the mean of the squared deviations.

Ask: How do you find the mean of the squared deviations? **[Add them and divide by the number of values.]** What is the mean of the squares of each difference? **[316.96]**

Say: The standard deviation is the square root of the mean of the squares of the differences.

Ask: What is the standard deviation? **[About 17.8]**

ADDITIONAL ONLINE INTERVENTION RESOURCES

Use the following for students who have not mastered the concepts in Skill 49.

- Math on the Spot videos
- Personal Math Trainer with customized intervention
- Building Block worksheets (Skill 115: Find Range; Skill 116: Find Median and Mode; Skill 117: Find Mean)

SKILL 49

Measures of Center and Spread

Example 1

Vocabulary
Mean
Median
Range
Interquartile range (IQR)
Quartile
First quartile (Q_1)
Third quartile (Q_3)
Standard deviation

The *mean* and *median* of a data set are two commonly used measures of center. A measure of center is a value that represents a center, or typical, value of a data set.

- The mean is the sum of the data values, divided by the total number of data values.
- The median is the middle value in a data set when the values are arranged in numerical order. If a data set contains an even number of values, the median is the mean of the two middle data values.

A. **The number of minutes that Isaiah exercises each day for a week is shown. Find the mean and median for the set of data.**

$$25, 40, 35, 50, 60, 20, 30$$

Mean: $\dfrac{25 + 40 + 35 + 50 + 60 + 20 + 30}{7} = \dfrac{260}{7}$ Find the sum. Divide by the number of values.

$$\approx 37.1 \quad \text{Simplify.}$$

Median: 20, 25, 30, **35**, 40, 50, 60   Order the values. Find the middle value.

Mean: about 37.1 minutes per day

Median: 35 minutes per day

B. **The number of pages that Eloise reads from a book each day for 8 days is shown. Find the mean and median for the set of data.**

$$25, 42, 14, 38, 8, 32, 47, 84$$

Mean: $\dfrac{25 + 42 + 14 + 38 + 8 + 32 + 47 + 84}{8} = \dfrac{290}{8}$ Find the sum. Divide by the number of values.

$$= 36.25 \quad \text{Simplify.}$$

Median: 8, 14, 25, **32**, **38**, 42, 47, 84   Order the values.

$$\dfrac{32 + 38}{2} = \dfrac{70}{2} = 35 \quad \text{Find the mean of the two middle values.}$$

Mean: 36.25 pages per day

Median: 35 pages per day

Check
Find the mean and median of each data set.

1. The number of miles 10 different people in the same office drive to work:

    5, 4, 18, 4, 8, 21, 9, 16, 7, 39

    _____

2. The number of followers 13 different people have on a social media website:

    14, 35, 143, 115, 240, 57, 320, 12, 6, 24, 155, 162, 51

    _____

3. Explain the Error. Then find the correct solution.

    The monthly high temperature, in degrees Fahrenheit, each month for 12 months:

    67, 71, 77, 85, 95, **104**, **106**, 105, 100, 89, 76, 66

    The median monthly high temperature is $\dfrac{104+106}{2} = \dfrac{210}{2}$, or 105°F.

    _____

Example 2

The *range* and *interquartile range* of a data set are two commonly used measures of spread. A measure of spread describes how spread out the values in a data set are.

- The range is the difference between the greatest and least values in a data set.

- The interquartile range (IQR) is the difference between the third and first quartiles in a data set. Quartiles divide a data set into four equal parts. The first quartile (Q_1) is the median of the lower half of a data set. The third quartile (Q_3) is the median of the upper half of a data set.

The number of pages in 11 textbooks is shown. Find the median, range, and IQR for the set of data.

$$946, 887, 763, 913, 730, 768, 746, 1040, 1165, 929, 787$$

Step 1: Order the values from least to greatest.

730, 746, 763, 768, 787, 887, 913, 929, 946, 1040, 1165

Step 2: Find the median, minimum, maximum, and range.

730, 746, 763, 768, 787, **887**, 913, 929, 946, 1040, **1165**

The median is 887 pages.

The minimum is 730, and the maximum is 1165. So the range is 1165 – 730, or 435 pages.

Step 3: Use the first and third quartiles to find the IQR.

730, 746, **763**, 768, 787, 887, 913, 929, **946**, 1040, 1165

The first quartile (Q_1) is 763. The third quartile (Q_3) is 946. So the IQR is 946 – 763, or 183 pages.

Check

Find the median, range, and IQR for each set of data.

4. The sizes of certain files, in kilobytes (KB), on a computer

   2400, 238, 3992, 227, 2177, 26, 23, 4423, 2100, 3487, 275

5. The prices per pound, in dollars, of different types of produce in a grocery store

   1.15, 3.85, 1.67, 0.96, 4.30, 1.45, 2.70, 1.19, 0.86, 1.12

Example 3

Standard deviation is a measure of spread that represents the average of the distances between the values of a data set and the mean.

standard deviation $= \sqrt{\dfrac{\left(x_1 - \overline{x}\right)^2 + \left(x_2 - \overline{x}\right)^2 + ... + \left(x_n - \overline{x}\right)^2}{n}}$, where $x_1, x_2, ..., x_n$ are

the data values, $\overline{x}$ is the mean of the data set, and n is the number of data values.

The average numbers of hours of daylight per season in a certain area are 9, 14.7, 15.5, and 9.7. Calculate the standard deviation.

Step 1: Find the mean.

mean: $\dfrac{9 + 14.7 + 15.5 + 9.7}{4} = \dfrac{48.9}{4} \approx 12.2$

Step 2: Complete the table to find the difference between each data value and the mean, $x - \overline{x}$, and the square of each difference, $(x - \overline{x})^2$.

Data Value, x	Deviation from Mean, $x - \overline{x}$	Squared Deviation, $(x - \overline{x})^2$
9	$9 - 12.2 = -3.2$	$(-3.2)^2 = 10.24$
14.7	$14.7 - 12.2 = 2.5$	$(2.5)^2 = 6.25$
15.5	$15.5 - 12.2 = 3.3$	$(3.3)^2 = 10.89$
9.7	$9.7 - 12.2 = -2.5$	$(-2.5)^2 = 6.25$

Step 3: Find the mean of the squares of each difference.

mean: $\dfrac{10.24 + 6.25 + 10.89 + 6.25}{4} = \dfrac{33.63}{4} \approx 8.4$

Step 4: To find the standard deviation, take the square root of the mean of the squares of each difference.

Standard deviation: $\sqrt{8.4} \approx 2.9$

The standard deviation is approximately 2.9.

Check

Find the standard deviation of each set of data.

6. 63, 63, 68, 51, 19

7. 72, 88, 7, 5, 44, 9

SKILL 49 MEASURES OF CENTER AND SPREAD

Normal Distributions

KEY TEACHING POINTS

Example 1

Say: When a normal distribution is plotted on a graph as a curve that represents a histogram, the curve creates a symmetric bell shape with a tail on each end.

Ask: What value is represented at the high point of the normal curve? **[the mean.]**

Say: In a normal distribution, the top of the curve is on a line of reflection. At the top of the point, exactly half of the values are on either side of the point, which makes it the median. This means that the mean and median are the same and are at the exact center of the curve. This also means that the mean is the center value of the distribution.

Ask: A normal distribution can be completely described using only two values. What are those values? **[the mean and standard deviation]**

Ask: Part A asks that a normal curve is sketched and the quiz scores at one, two, and three standard deviations be shown. How do you find the quiz score at one standard deviation? **[Possible responses: Since a standard deviation is 5, you add 5 to the mean to find the score that is one standard deviation above the mean. To find the score that is one standard deviation below the mean, subtract 5.]**

Say: When you have found the values and labeled the normal curve, you can use the data to find what percent of the values are in a given range. Because the normal curve percentages are always the same, it is important to know them. Remember the following:

- 68% of the values are between one standard deviation below and one standard deviation above the mean.
- 95% of the values are between two standard deviations below and two standard deviations above the mean.
- 99.7% of the values are between three standard deviations below and three standard deviations above the mean.
- 0.3% of the values are more than three standard deviations from the mean.

Ask: In Part B, you are asked to find the percent of scores that are between 72 and 92. How many standard deviations is 72 from the mean? **[2]** How many standard deviations is 92 from the mean? **[2]** What percent of the scores fall between 72 and 82? **[47.5%]** What percent of the scores fall between 82 and 92? **[47.5%]**

Check

Ask: In Question 1, what is the value at the high point, or center, of the normal curve? **[100]** The center is the mean, so the value at the center is 100.

Say: There are tick marks along the bottom axis of the graph that represent one standard deviation each. You know the mean, so label that mark first.

Complete the values on the curve as a class as you ask the following questions.

Ask: What is one standard deviation? **[15]** What value is one standard deviation below the mean? **[85]** What value is one standard deviation above the mean? **[115]**

Ask: What are two standard deviations? **[30]** What value is two standard deviations below the mean? **[70]** What value is two standard deviations above the mean? **[130]**

Ask: What are three standard deviations? **[45]** What value is three standard deviations below the mean? **[55]** What value is three standard deviations above the mean? **[145]**

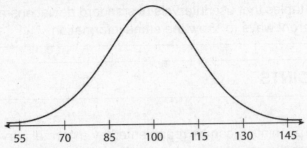

Say: The normal curve lets you see the percent of scores that are between given values.

Ask: What scores are one standard deviation above and below the mean? **[85 and 115]** What percent of the data falls within one standard deviation? **[68%]** Therefore, 68% of the scores are between 85 and 115.

Ask: What score is three standard deviations above the mean? **[145]** What percent of the data falls more than three standard deviations above the mean? **[0.15%]** Therefore, 0.15% of the scores are greater than 145.

ALTERNATE STRATEGY

Strategy: Make a table

1. **Say:** When you need to find the percent of values that fall between given scores, a relative frequency table can be helpful. A normal curve contains all of the information needed to set up a relative frequency table.

2. Use the information you are given in the problem to find the intervals for the table. Each row represents a set of values between standard deviations, from values that are more than 4 standard deviations below the mean to more than 4 standard deviations above the mean. In Problem 1, the mean is 100 and the standard deviation is 15.

3. Set up the following table as a class.

Deviation from Mean	Scores	Relative Frequency
$x < -3\sigma$	< 55	0.15%
$-3\sigma < x < -2\sigma$	55 – 70	2.35%
$-2\sigma < x < -1\sigma$	70 – 85	13.5%
$-1\sigma < x < \overline{X}$	85 – 100	34%
$\overline{X} < x < +1\sigma$	100 – 115	34%
$+1\sigma < x < +2\sigma$	115 – 130	13.5%
$+2\sigma < x < +3\sigma$	130 – 145	2.35%
$x > +3\sigma$	>145	0.15%

4. Use the table to find the percent of scores that fall between 85 and 115. From 85 to 100 is 34% and from 100 to 115 is 34%. 34% + 34% = 68%.

5. Relative frequency tables that use intervals of standard deviations and graphs of normal curves are two different ways to show the same information.

KEY TEACHING POINTS

Example 2

Say: When you know a population can be represented by a normal curve, you can use the area under the curve to make estimates and predictions about the population.

Ask: What percent of the area under the curve is greater than 70 inches? Explain. **[0.15%]** Knowing that 0.15% of the area under the curve includes women's heights greater than 70 inches tells you that the probability of a randomly chosen woman having a height greater than 70 inches is 0.15% or 0.0015.

Say: It is important to remember that real-world data is unlikely to form an exact bell curve. However, the percents in normally-distributed data are very close to correct, so a good accurate prediction can be made.

Check

Complete the values on the curve as a class as you ask the following questions.

Ask: What is the mean? **[175]** Label the center value on the normal curve 175.

Ask: What is one standard deviation? **[8]** What value is one standard deviation below the mean? **[167]** What value is one standard deviation above the mean? **[183]**

Ask: What are two standard deviations? **[16]** What value is two standard deviations below the mean? **[159]** What value is two standard deviations above the mean? **[191]**

Ask: What are three standard deviations? **[24]** What value is three standard deviations below the mean? **[151]** What value is three standard deviations above the mean? **[199]**

Ask: Where does a weight of 167 pounds fall on the normal curve? **[One standard deviation below the mean.]** How much of the area under the normal curve is above one standard deviation below the mean? **[84%]**

Say: Since 84% of the area includes mean with weight greater than 167 pounds, the probability of a randomly chosen man having a weight greater than 167 pounds is 0.84.

Ask: Where does a weight of 159 pounds fall on the normal curve? **[Two standard deviations below the mean.]** Where does a weight of 183 pounds fall on the normal curve? **[One standard deviation above the mean.]** What is the probability that a randomly chosen man has a weight between 159 pounds and 183 pounds? **[0.815]**

Say: When you are familiar with the normal curve and percents, you can calculate predictions quickly. In Problem 6, if you recognize that the data within two standard deviations represent 95% and the data between one standard deviation above and two standard deviations above represent 13.5%, you can subtract 95 − 13.5 = 81.5, so the probability is 0.815.

COMMON MISCONCEPTION

Ask: What is the Error?

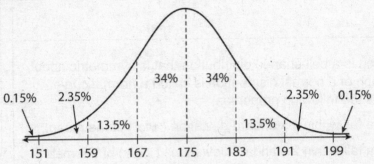

Jackson says that the probability that a randomly chosen man has a weight less than 183 pounds is 34%.

Reason incorrect: The 34% represents the values between the mean and one standard deviation in one direction, so it does not include the bottom half of the data.

Solution: The probability that a randomly chosen man has a weight less than 183 pounds is 0.15% + 2.35% + 13.5% + 34% + 34% = 84% or 50% + 34% = 84%.

ADDITIONAL ONLINE INTERVENTION RESOURCES

Use the following for students who have not mastered the concepts in Skill 50.

- Math on the Spot videos
- Personal Math Trainer with customized intervention
- Building Block worksheets (Skill 72: Percents and Decimals; Skill 117: Find Mean)

SKILL 50

Normal Distributions

Example 1

A normal distribution is a bell-shaped distribution that is symmetric about the mean. The graph of a normal distribution is called a *normal curve*. A normal curve has the following properties:

- 68% of the data fall within 1 standard deviation ($\pm 1\sigma$) of the mean.

- 95% of the data fall within 2 standard deviations ($\pm 2\sigma$) of the mean.

- 99.7% of the data fall within 3 standard deviations ($\pm 3\sigma$) of the mean.

The symmetry of a normal curve separates the area under the curve into eight parts. You can use these to determine what percent of the data are contained in each part.

Vocabulary

Normal
   distribution

Mean

Normal curve

Standard
   deviation

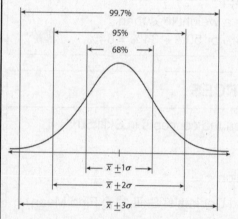

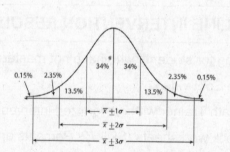

The scores of students on a science quiz are normally distributed with a mean of 82 and a standard deviation of 5.

A. Sketch a normal curve showing the quiz scores at one, two, and three standard deviations from the mean.

Because the scores are normally distributed, the mean, 82, is the "center" of the normal curve.

1 Standard Deviation From Mean: $82 - 5 = 77$ and $82 + 5 = 87$

2 Standard Deviations From Mean: $82 - 2(5) = 72$ and $82 + 2(5) = 92$

3 Standard Deviations From Mean: $82 - 3(5) = 67$ and $82 + 3(5) = 97$

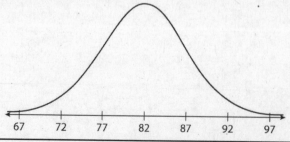

B. Find the percent of quiz scores that are between 72 and 92.

Method 1:

Use the properties of the normal curve to label the normal curve from Part A with the correct percents:

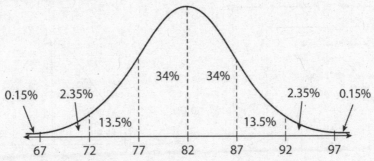

To find the percent of scores that are between 72 and 92, add the percents for 72–77, 77–82, 82–87, and 87–92:

13.5% + 34% + 34% + 13.5% = 95%

So, 95% of the quiz scores are between 72 and 92.

Method 2:

Find the distance between 72 and the mean: 82 − 72 = 10, which is twice the standard deviation of 5. So 72 is 2 standard deviations below the mean.

Find the distance between 92 and the mean: 92 − 82 = 10, which is twice the standard deviation of 5. So 92 is 2 standard deviations above the mean.

95% of the data in a normal distribution fall within 2 standard deviations of the mean, so 95% of the quiz scores are between 72 and 92.

Check

The scores of students on an IQ test are normally distributed with a mean of 100 and a standard deviation of 15. Use this information to answer Questions 1 and 2.

1. Sketch a normal curve showing IQ scores at one, two, and three standard deviations from the mean.

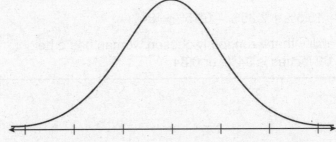

2. What percent of IQ test scores are between 85 and 115? Explain.

_____

_____

Example 2

You can use a normal curve to make predictions about a population that is represented by a normally-distributed sample of data.

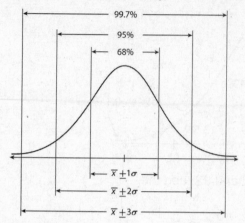 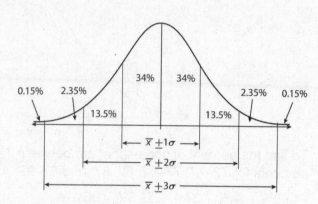

The heights of women in a survey are normally distributed with a mean of 64 inches and a standard deviation of 2 inches. What is the probability that a randomly chosen woman has a height greater than 62 inches?

Step 1: Sketch a normal curve showing the heights at one, two, and three standard deviations from the mean. Label the areas under the curve with the correct percents.

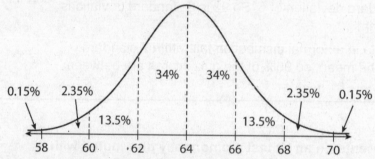

Step 2: Use the normal curve to find the probability.

Look at the parts of the curve that represent heights that are greater than 62 inches. Add the percents for 62–64, 64–66, 66–68, 68–70, and 70+.

34% + 34% + 13.5% + 2.35% + 0.15% = 84%

So, the probability that a randomly chosen woman has a height greater than 62 inches is 84%, or 0.84.

Check

The weights of men in a survey are normally distributed with a mean of 175 pounds and a standard deviation of 8 pounds. Use this information to answer Questions 3–7.

3. Sketch a normal curve showing the weights at one, two, and three standard deviations from the mean. Label the curve with the correct percents.

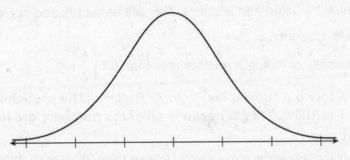

4. What is the probability that a randomly chosen man has a weight greater than 167 pounds? Explain your reasoning.

_____

5. What is the probability that a randomly chosen man has a weight less than 175 pounds? Explain your reasoning.

_____

6. What is the probability that a randomly chosen man has a weight between 159 pounds and 183 pounds? Explain your reasoning.

_____

7. Explain the Error. Then find the correct solution.

Jackson says that the probability that a randomly chosen man has a weight less than 183 pounds is 34%.

_____

SKILL 50 NORMAL DISTRIBUTIONS

Probability of Compound Events

KEY TEACHING POINTS

Example 1

Encourage students to build upon their prior knowledge by thinking of the probability of compound events as the sum of simple events. Be aware that students might ask questions in which mutual exclusivity must be taken into account. This will be addressed in Example 2.

Work through the example with students.

Ask: What would be the probability of rolling a number less than 6? $\left[\dfrac{5}{6}\right]$

Ask: What is the probability of rolling a number less than 7? Explain. **[The probability of rolling a number less than 7 is 100%. This is because all of the numbers are less than 7 and it is certain to happen.]**

Ask: How can you show this using the addition method? **[P(less than 7) = P(1) + P(2) + P(3) + P(4) + P(5) + P(6) = $\dfrac{1}{6} + \dfrac{1}{6} + \dfrac{1}{6} + \dfrac{1}{6} + \dfrac{1}{6} + \dfrac{1}{6} = \dfrac{6}{6} = 1$]**

Check
Problem 2

Explore with students by asking them to think about which compound event would have the highest probability. Guide students to see that the probability of selecting a green or red marble would result in a greater probability because there are a greater number of green and red marbles.

Example 2

The concept of mutual exclusivity can be a confusing one to students. Point out that the word mutual means that it is the same for both events. The word exclusive usually means that something is excluded. In this case, mutually exclusive is the idea that the events are excluded from each other.

With the students, read through the situation in the example. Spend time discussing the data given in the table. Ask several questions so that students focus on reading the correct information in the rows and columns.

Ask: How many boys are in choir? **[3]**

Ask: How many students are in choir? **[7]**

Ask: How many students are there in total? **[20]**

Continue as time permits so that students feel comfortable with the data.

Direct students' attention to the solution method.

Ask: How many students are girls? **[12]**

Ask: How many students are in choir? **[7]**

Ask: How many students are girls and in choir? **[4]**

Ask: What answer would you get if you forgot to subtract the girls in choir? What would that mean? **[I would get $\frac{19}{20}$ which means that if a student were randomly selected, it is almost certain the student would be a girl or in the choir.]**

Point out that students should check that their answers make sense each time.

Check
Problem 5
If students forget to subtract the number of patients with a fever and an earache, they will get an answer of 110%.

Ask: Can the probability of an event be 110%? Explain. **[No, if the probability of an event is 100%, it is certain to happen. So, a probability of 110% makes no sense.]**

Remind students that probability must be between 0% and 100% inclusive. Students can use this information to see if their answers make sense.

Example 3
Explain to students that often a difficult part of probability is finding the total number in the sample space. A tree diagram or list can help a student visualize the possible outcomes.

Because the tree diagram or list provides every possible outcome, the probability of this compound event can be determined by simply counting the appropriate events.

Check
Problem 10
Students are often confused about when to use the totals in a table.

Ask: What is the total number of students in the 10th grade? **[17]**

Ask: What is the total number of females? **[45]**

Ask: Are these events mutually exclusive? Explain. **[No, because a student can be female and in the 10th grade.]**

Ask: How many students are females and in the 10th grade? **[6]**

Say: Now, determine the probability by adding the individual probabilities and subtracting the number counted twice.

Problem 11
Continue questioning in the same manner as Problem 10 so that students understand how the calculation is different for events that are mutually exclusive.

Ask: What is the total number of students in the 11th grade? **[39]**

Ask: What is the total number of students in the 12th grade? **[21]**

Ask: Are these events mutually exclusive? Explain. **[Yes, because a student cannot be in the 11th and 12th grade at the same time.]**

Ask: How many students are in the 11th and 12th grade? **[0]**

Say: Notice you can still think about subtracting the number of students who are double counted. But because these events are mutually exclusive, the amount is 0.

ALTERNATE STRATEGY

Strategy: Manipulatives and Prediction

Use colored discs or other manipulatives and guide students through the following activity.

1. Place 10 yellow discs, 10 green discs, 1 blue disc, and 1 red disc in a box.

   Ask: How likely is it to get a yellow or green disc? **[very likely]**

2. Conduct several trials by randomly selecting a disc to verify the student's prediction. Then, continue asking and conducting trials to verify the predictions.

   Ask: How likely is it to get a yellow or red disc? **[likely]**

   Ask: How likely is it to get a red or blue disc? **[unlikely]**

3. Point out to students that a compound event using *or* means that there are more ways for the compound event to occur. Thus, it makes sense to add the probabilities together to yield a higher probability.

4. Continue by marking 5 yellow discs and 5 green discs with a large X.

   Ask: How likely is it to get a yellow disc or a disc with an X? **[likely]**

5. Point out that now there are some yellow discs with an X. So adding the yellow discs to the discs with an X would mean some of the discs are double counted. Encourage students to see that by subtracting the double counted items, the correct probability can be determined.

COMMON MISCONCEPTION

Problem 6

Ask: What are the even numbers? **[2, 4, 6, 8, 10]**

Ask: What are the numbers less than 6? **[1, 2, 3, 4, 5]**

Ask: What numbers are even and less than 6? **[2, 4]**

Error: Students may forget to consider whether the events are mutually exclusive. If events are mutually exclusive, they cannot happen at the same time. An even number and a number less than 6 are not mutually exclusive. Therefore, some of the numbers were double counted.

Show students a Venn diagram to help them visualize the double counted numbers.

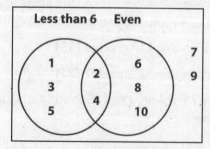

Solution: $P(\text{even or less than } 6) = \dfrac{5}{10} + \dfrac{5}{10} - \dfrac{2}{10} = \dfrac{8}{10} = 80\%$

ADDITIONAL ONLINE INTERVENTION RESOURCES

 Use the following for students who have not mastered the concepts in Skill 51.

- Math on the Spot videos

- Personal Math Trainer with customized intervention

- Building Block worksheets (Skill 37 Find the Percent of a Number; Skill 39 Fractions, Decimals, and Percents; Skill 65 Multiply with Fractions and Decimals; Skill 72 Percents and Decimals; Skill 82 Simplify Fractions; Skill 86 Simplify Ratios; Skill 95 Solve Proportions; Skill 112 Write Ratios)

SKILL 51

Probability of Compound Events

Example 1

A compound event is more than one outcome.

What is the probability of rolling a number less than 5?

Sample Space Method

P(rolling a number less than 5) = ?

Outcome of "less than 5": 4, 3, 2, 1

Sample Space: 1, 2, 3, 4, 5, 6

P(rolling a 4) = $\dfrac{4}{6}$

Addition Method

P(less than 5) = $P(1) + P(2) + P(3) + P(4)$

$\dfrac{1}{6} + \dfrac{1}{6} + \dfrac{1}{6} + \dfrac{1}{6} = \dfrac{4}{6}$

Vocabulary

Compound event

Mutually exclusive

Check

Determine the probability.

1. A drawer holds 8 black socks and 6 brown socks and 4 blue socks. What is the probability of randomly selecting a brown or black sock?

   _____

2. A box contains 12 chocolate chip cookies, 10 sugar cookies, and 5 oatmeal cookies. What is the probability of randomly selecting a sugar or oatmeal cookie?

   _____

3. A bag of marbles contains 8 green, 8 red, and 4 yellow. What is the probability of randomly selecting a green or yellow marble?

   _____

Example 2

Some events cannot happen at the same time. For example, a coin can't land heads and tails. Events that cannot happen at the same time are mutually exclusive.

Some events can happen at the same time. For example, a number can be both less than 4 and odd. These events are not mutually exclusive.

When compound events are not mutually exclusive, the probability of the event happening at the same time must be subtracted.

The table shows boys and girls in drama and choir. What is the probability of randomly selecting a student who is a girl or in choir?

	Girls	Boys	Total
Drama	8	5	13
Choir	4	3	7
Total	12	8	20

Addition Method

$P(\text{girl or choir}) = P(\text{girl}) + P(\text{choir}) - P(\text{girl and choir})$

$$\frac{12}{20} + \frac{7}{20} - \frac{4}{20} = \frac{15}{20}$$

Check

Calculate each probability.

4. A number cube is rolled. What is the probability of rolling a number that is less than 5 or odd?

_____

5. At a hospital, 70% of patients have a fever and 40% have an earache. 25% of patients have a fever and an earache. What is the probability that a patient randomly selected will have a fever or an earache?

_____

6. Explain the Error. Find the solution.

Question: The numbers 1–10 are in a box and will be drawn randomly. What is the probability of selecting an even number or a number less than 6?

_____

_____

Solution: The probability of selecting

_____

an even number is $\frac{5}{10}$. The probability

of selecting a number less than 6 is $\frac{5}{10}$.

Therefore, P(even or less than 6) =

$\frac{5}{10} + \frac{5}{10} = \frac{10}{10} = 1$.

Example 3

You can use a tree diagram or list to help organize and count events in a sample space. A family has 3 children. What is the probability the family has at least 2 girls?

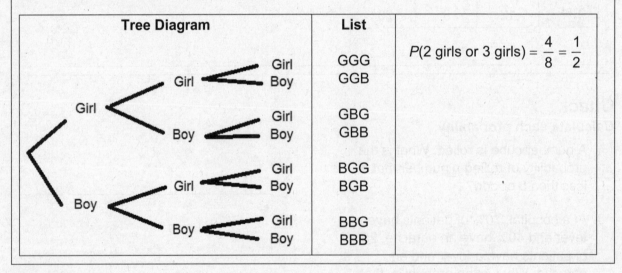

Tree Diagram	List	
	GGG	P(2 girls or 3 girls) = $\frac{4}{8} = \frac{1}{2}$
	GGB	
	GBG	
	GBB	
	BGG	
	BGB	
	BBG	
	BBB	

Check

Draw a tree diagram.

7. A coin is tossed and a number cube is rolled.

Use the tree diagram to calculate the probabilities.

8. What is the probability of tossing a head or a 3? _____

9. What is the probability of tossing a tails or an even number? _____

Use this information for 10–13.

A school is looking for a student representative to the city council. One hundred students applied. The data is shown. The representative will be chosen randomly.

	Female	Male	Total
9th	14	8	22
10th	6	11	17
11th	17	23	39
12th	8	13	21
Total	45	55	100

10. What is the probability the student representative is in 10th grade or female? _____

11. What is the probability the student representative is in 11th or 12th grade? _____

12. What is the probability the student representative is male or in 9th grade? _____

13. Which event or events described above are mutually exclusive? Explain.

_____

_____

SKILL 51 PROBABILITY OF COMPOUND EVENTS

Probability of Simple Events

KEY TEACHING POINTS

Example 1
Some students have a difficult time visualizing the sample space of experiments. Refer to the alternate strategy for ideas on how to use experimental probability to help students understand.

Start the class by flipping a coin in the air. Ask students to choose which side will come up. Repeat several times.

Say: When you called out heads or tails, you were predicting the event you thought would occur. So "heads" and "tails" are events.

Ask: How come you only called "heads" or "tails" when I flipped the coin? **[Because there are no other sides to the coin.]**

Say: The sample space is all the types of events that could occur. Because only heads and tails are possible, there are only two possible events in the sample space.

Direct students' attention to Example 1. Have students read through the vocabulary descriptions and examples.

Ask: How come no one would predict the number 27 when rolling a number cube? **[Because 27 is not a number on the cube.]**

Remind students that the sample space includes only those events that are possible.

Check
Problem 2
Allow students to experiment with two coins to determine the total sample space. Some students might argue that HT and TH are one single event. To help students understand these are two separate events, make a mark on one coin to distinguish it from another. You may also use a coin that is a different color or a different value to help explain. For example, students might see that a dime landing heads and a penny landing tails is different from a dime landing tails and a penny landing heads.

Problem 4
Although not addressed specifically, point out that the areas on the spinner are equal, which means each number has an equal chance of being selected.

Example 2
Direct students' attention to the Probability ratio and guide them through the samples. If students are confused by the probability notation, help them understand by writing P (rolling a 4) rather than $P(4)$. Continue until students understand the shortened meaning.

In sample 2, point out that students can list the sample space if preferred. However, the probability ratio only requires the number of events in the sample space.

Ask: How can you determine the sample space without listing all the marble colors? **[Just add 5 green marbles plus 7 blue marbles to get 12 marbles.]**

To help students understand the meaning of the fractional probability, encourage them to state the probability in the following way:

Sample 1

Say: A probability of $\frac{1}{6}$ means there is 1 way to get the number out of 6 possible numbers.

Sample 2

Say: A probability of $\frac{5}{12}$ means there are 5 ways to get the marble out of 12 possible marbles.

Check
Problem 6

Have the students write each letter in the word DEFINITION vertically to help them see the individual letters composing the word. If necessary, review that the vowels are A, E, I, O, U. All other letters are consonants.

Problem 7

Remind students that the apple pies are also included in the sample space. If desired, prompt students to think about the probability of selecting a different pie.

Example 3

Review the meaning of probability with students to help them understand that probability will always be between 0% and 100% inclusive.

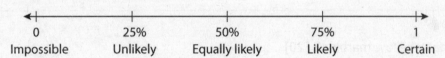

| 0 | 25% | 50% | 75% | 1 |
| Impossible | Unlikely | Equally likely | Likely | Certain |

Guide students through the probability calculation.

Ask: Which company's phone has a higher probability of being defective? **[Company A]**

Ask: Which company would you prefer to buy a phone from? Why? **[Company B; because I am less likely to get a defective phone]**

Say: One student said that Company B makes more defective phones because they had 6 defective phones in the sample and Company A only had 2.

Ask: What might you say to the student to explain the error? **[Possible answer: You have to compare how large the sample is to see which has the greater percent or probability.]**

Check
Problem 10

Remind students to count the number of possible events in the sample space to determine the denominator of the probability fraction.

ALTERNATE STRATEGY

Strategy: Experimental Probability

Have students conduct experiments using number cubes, coins, and cards to help them become comfortable with the vocabulary and its meaning.

1. Provide each student with a number cube or any manipulative that can be used to generate random numbers. Tell students they will conduct an experiment by rolling the manipulative and writing down the event that occurs. Continue to use the vocabulary with students and encourage them to use it while discussing.

2. Have students conduct their experiments 10–20 times, time permitting. Direct students to take a look at the results of their experiment. Answers to the following questions will depend on the number generator used.

   Ask: What numbers did you roll? **[Answers will vary. Sample answer: 2, 5, 6, 4, 1]**

   Say: These are called events.

   Ask: What numbers were possible to roll? **[Answers will vary. Sample answer: 1, 2, 3, 4, 5, 6]**

   Say: This is called the sample space.

3. Throughout the lesson, encourage students to create a hands-on method to understand what is happening in each experiment. For example, in Problem 6, have students write each letter of the word DEFINITION on an index card. Then have them mix the cards up, write the sample space and sort the vowels (E, I, O) from the consonants. Help students see that the repeated "I" counts as three events.

COMMON MISCONCEPTION

Problem 6

Ask: How many yellow marbles? **[20]**

Ask: How many red marbles? **[30]**

Ask: How many marbles are in the sample space? Explain. **[50; because 20 + 30 = 50]**

Error: Students may forget to include the desired event in the sample space. Encourage students to visualize the experiment to determine the actual number of items in the sample space.

Solution: $P(\text{yellow}) = \dfrac{20}{50} = \dfrac{2}{5}$

Problem 11

When the events involve numbers, students often confuse the number of the event with the number of times the event can happen. If students mistakenly believe that $P(5) = \dfrac{5}{6}$, restate the question and emphasize how many times.

Say: How many times will the 5 occur?

Problem 12

If students make an error, point out that they can check their answers by adding all the probabilities. If the sum is not equal to 1, then one or more of the probabilities is incorrect.

ADDITIONAL ONLINE INTERVENTION RESOURCES

Use the following for students who have not mastered the concepts in Skill 52.

- Math on the Spot videos

- Personal Math Trainer with customized intervention

- Building Block worksheets (Skill 6: Analyze Data; Skill 12: Certain, Impossible, Likely, Unlikely; Skill 39: Fractions, Decimals, Percents)

SKILL 52 **Probability of Simple Events**

Example 1

An <mark>experiment</mark> is anything from which an observer can obtain data.

      Experiment: Rolling a six-sided number cube

An <mark>event</mark> is the result of one experiment.

      Event: the number cube shows "4"

The <mark>sample space</mark> is the set of all possible events of an experiment.

      Sample space: 1, 2, 3, 4, 5, 6

Vocabulary
Event
Experiment
Probability of event
Sample Space

Check

List a possible event and the sample space for each experiment.

1. Flipping one coin

      Possible event: _____

      Sample space: _____

2. Flipping two coins

      Possible event: _____

      Sample space: _____

3. Answering a multiple choice question with choices A, B, C, D, E

      Possible event: _____

      Sample space: _____

4. Spinning a spinner shown

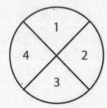

      Possible event: _____

      Sample space: _____

Example 2

The probability of an event is the likelihood that a certain thing or event will occur.
To calculate the probability of an event:

$$P(\text{event}) = \frac{\text{number of ways event can happen}}{\text{total number of events in the sample space}}$$

Sample 1	Sample 2
A number cube is rolled. What is the probability of rolling a 4?	A box has 5 green marbles and 7 blue marbles. What is the probability of selecting a marble at random and getting a green marble?
$P(4) = ?$	$P(\text{green}) = ?$

Step 1   Event: rolling a 4
          Sample Space:
          1, 2, 3, 4, 5, 6
	Step 1 Event: green
	          Sample Space: 5 green and 7 blue OR
	          G, G, G, G, G, B, B, B, B, B, B, B,

Step 2 $P(4) = \dfrac{1}{6}$	Step 2 $P(\text{green}) = \dfrac{5}{12}$

Check
Determine the probability of each event.

5. There are 15 boys and 20 girls in a class. What is the probability of selecting a student at random and selecting a boy?

6. The word DEFINITION has vowels and consonants. What is the probability of selecting a letter at random and selecting a vowel?

7. A bakery has 3 apple pies, 4 lemon pies, and 5 blueberry pies. What is the probability of selecting a pie at random and selecting apple?

8. Find the Error. Explain the solution.

   A bag has 20 yellow marbles and 30 red marbles. What is the probability that a marble selected at random will be yellow?

   $$P(\text{yellow}) = \frac{20}{30} = \frac{2}{3}$$

Example 3

Probability is often shown as a percentage so comparisons can be made. The higher the probability, the more likely the event is to occur.

Sample:

Two companies manufacture phones. Company A found 2 defective phones in a sample of 50. Company B found 6 defective phones in a sample of 250.

What is the probability of buying a phone at random from each company and getting a defective phone?

$$P(\text{defective phone}) = \frac{\text{number of defective phones}}{\text{total number of phones}}$$

Company A	Company B
$P(\text{defective phone}) = \dfrac{2}{50} = 0.04 = 4\%$	$P(\text{defective phone}) = \dfrac{6}{250} = 0.04 = 0.024 = 2.4\%$

Check

9. A manufacturer of car parts for air conditioners found 5 defective hoses out of 200. What is the probability that a hose selected at random will be defective?

   _____

10. A multiple choice test question has choices A, B, C, D. If a student guesses the answer randomly, what is the probability the student will guess correctly?

   _____

Determine the probability for each event. Write your answer as a fraction.

11. A six-sided number cube is rolled. What is the probability of rolling a 5?

   _____

12. A vase holds 9 roses, 5 tulips, 3 carnations, and 3 lilies. A flower is selected at random. Find each probability.

   $P(\text{rose})$ _____

   $P(\text{tulip})$ _____

   $P(\text{carnation})$ _____

   $P(\text{lily})$ _____

Use probability as percent for 13–15.

13. A software company finds that one of its programs is not working. It was reported that the program crashes 3 times out of 30 times being opened. What is P(crash)?

_____

_____

14. The company is trying to sell more of its programs. Instead of mentioning how many times it crashes, it would like to mention how many times the program is successful. What is P(not crashing)?

_____

_____

_____

15. How are P(crash) and P(not crash) related? What do you notice? Explain.

_____

_____

_____

16. A manufacturer of computer chips checks batches of chips. The manufacturer found that 5 items in a batch of 200 were defective. Find the probability of a defective chip.

_____

Find the probability of a chip that is not defective.

_____

SKILL 52 PROBABILITY OF SIMPLE EVENTS

The Pythagorean Theorem

KEY TEACHING POINTS

Ask: What are some properties of triangles? **[Answers may vary. Sample answer: the measures of the interior angles have a sum of 180°]**

Remind students that there are several types of triangles such as right triangles, isosceles triangles, and equilateral triangles. Explain that while some properties hold for all triangles, some are specific to one type of triangle.

Ask: What property defines a right triangle? **[The triangle has one interior angle of 90°]**

Ask: Which side is called the hypotenuse? **[The side opposite the right angle]**

On the board, draw a right triangle and label the hypotenuse and two legs as shown below. Explain that in the formula for the Pythagorean Theorem, the lengths of the legs are a and b and that the length of the hypotenuse is c.

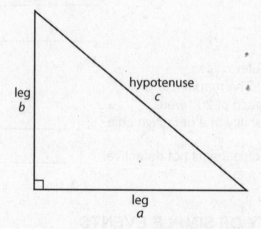

Write the Pythagorean Theorem on the board next to the right triangle so that students can see where the values come from.

Say: The Pythagorean Theorem is a property that applies only to right triangles so it can't be used to find side lengths for other types of triangles.

Explain to students that either leg can be thought of as the one with length a and the other as the one with length b. Encourage them to label which side they decide is a and which side they decide is b so that they will be consistent while working the problem. Reiterate that the lengths of the legs can't be interchanged with the length of the hypotenuse when working with the formula.

Example 1
Say: Let's let $a = 6$ and $b = 4$. Since x is the length of the hypotenuse, $c = x$.

Start with the Pythagorean Theorem and replace each value with the values from the problem.

Work through how to find the value of x and explain that only the positive square root is a solution since x represents a side length and side lengths are positive. It may be necessary to review how to simplify square roots.

Check
Problem 1
Students may assume every final answer must be simplified and therefore need verification that $\sqrt{13}$ is completely simplified. Remind them that 13 has factors of only 13 and 1 and that neither are perfect squares.

Problem 3
Once students have successfully worked this problem, point out that this triangle is both a right triangle and an isosceles triangle.

Ask: Is it possible for an equilateral triangle to also be a right triangle? **[No. The angles within an equilateral triangle all have a measure of 60°]**

Problem 5
Encourage students to sketch the right triangle formed by the height from the ground, horizontal extension of the loading platform, and the actual length of the loading platform.

Ask: Which of the three pieces of information represents the length of the hypotenuse? **[The length of the loading platform]**

Example 2
Say: Since the Pythagorean Theorem includes three variables, given the values of two of them, we can find the value of the third. We just saw this when we were given the lengths of each leg and then found the length of the hypotenuse. But, given the length of the hypotenuse and the length of one leg, it is also possible to find the length of the remaining leg.

Say: Since the leg lengths are 5 and x, let's let $a = 5$ and $b = x$. The length of the hypotenuse is 10, so $c = 10$.

Start with the basic form of the Pythagorean Theorem and then show students that by substituting in these values for a, b, and c you get the equation in the example.

Work through solving the equation step by step with the students.

Check
Problem 8
Students may have trouble squaring the length of the hypotenuse. To help them remember how to compute this value, remind them that exponents can be distributed across multiplication but not addition. Point out that since $3\sqrt{2} = 3 \times \sqrt{2}$, $\left(3\sqrt{2}\right)^2 = 3^2\left(\sqrt{2}\right)^2 = 9(2) = 18$. You may need to remind them that squaring $\sqrt{a}$ will always result in a.

Problem 9
Have students select whether a or b will represent the leg of length 5 and then use this to write an equation such as $3^2 + b^2 = 5^2$. For some, drawing the picture of the right triangle may assist them with understanding which values are missing. If this is done, be sure to check that the hypotenuse is correctly labeled with a length of 5 and that 5 was not used as a leg length.

Problem 10
Since each side length is the same, have the students give that side length a value such as x. When they then apply the Pythagorean Theorem, they will have the equation $2x^2 = 32$.

KEY TEACHING POINTS

Example 3

Remind students what it means for a statement to be a converse of another statement and explain that the Pythagorean Theorem is an "if and only if" statement.

Explain to students that this means the Pythagorean Theorem can be used to check if a triangle is a right triangle.

Ask: In a right triangle, which side has the longest measure? **[The hypotenuse]**

Say: Since the hypotenuse has the longest measure, we can check if three numbers could be sides of a right triangle by seeing if the square of the longest side is the sum of the squares of the two shorter sides.

Work through Example 3 step by step.

Check
Problem 15

In this problem, the given values do not represent lengths of the sides of a right triangle. Once students have verified this, ask them to find a length for the hypotenuse which could be used with leg lengths 5 and 12 to define the sides of a right triangle.

To do this correctly, they will need to calculate c when $5^2 + 12^2 = c^2$. The only correct answer is 13.

Problem 17

There are many correct answers to this question. If students have trouble finding one, encourage them to simply choose values for a and b and then find what value of c would be needed for the statement $a^2 + b^2 = c^2$ to hold.

ALTERNATE STRATEGY

Strategy: Verifying the Pythagorean Theorem

1. Have students create several different sized right triangles from poster board or other easy-to-measure material. Ideally the triangles will have whole number side lengths measured in either inches or centimeters.

2. For each triangle, have students measure the lengths of the legs and the hypotenuse using a ruler and record them in a table.

3. Ask students to verify that the Pythagorean Theorem holds for these triangles by finding the sum of the squared leg lengths and comparing that sum to the square of the length of the hypotenuse.

COMMON MISCONCEPTION

Problem 12

Commonly, students will simply take the two known values and use these as leg lengths in the formula for the Pythagorean Theorem. Here, the leg lengths should be x and 4, but the hypotenuse was instead treated as though it has length x.

In order to avoid this mistake, have students mark the side opposite the right angle with the letter c and label the other sides as a and b. If they do this, they can rewrite the formula needed to find x as:

$$x^2 + 4^2 = 5^2$$

The correct answer will be $x = 3$.

ADDITIONAL ONLINE INTERVENTION RESOURCES

Use the following for students who have not mastered the concepts in Skill 53.

- Math on the Spot videos
- Personal Math Trainer with customized intervention
- Building Block worksheets (Skill 38 Find the Square of a Number; Skill 46 Graph Ordered Pairs (First Quadrant); Skill 100 Squares and Square Roots)

SKILL 53 The Pythagorean Theorem

<table>
<tr><td>

Example 1

The Pythagorean Theorem describes a relationship between the lengths of the legs of a right triangle and the length of its hypotenuse.

If the legs have lengths a and b and the hypotenuse has length c, then $a^2 + b^2 = c^2$.

Find the value of x in the triangle below.

</td><td>

Vocabulary

Leg

Hypotenuse

</td></tr>
</table>

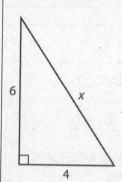

Calculate $a^2 + b^2$

$6^2 + 4^2 = x^2$

$36 + 16 = x^2$

$52 = x^2$

Find and simplify the positive square root.

$x = \sqrt{52} = \sqrt{4 \cdot 13} = 2\sqrt{13}$

Check

Find the value of x for each of the triangles below.

1.

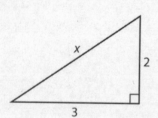

2.

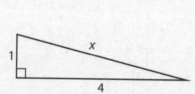

3.

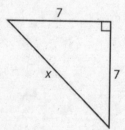

4. A right triangle has legs with lengths of 3 and 9 units. What is the length of the hypotenuse?

_____

5. As shown below, the loading platform extends out 6 feet from the back of a truck and is 3 feet above the ground at its highest point. To the nearest tenth of a foot, what is the length of the platform?

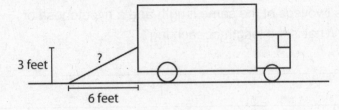

_____

_____

Example 2

The Pythagorean Theorem can be used to find the length of either leg in a right triangle.

Find the value of x in the triangle below.

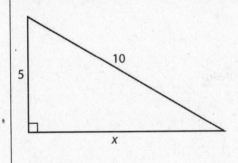

Write an equation using the Pythagorean Theorem.

$$5^2 + x^2 = 10^2$$
$$25 + x^2 = 100$$

Solve for x.

$$x^2 = 75$$
$$x = \sqrt{75} = \sqrt{3 \cdot 25} = 5\sqrt{3}$$

Check
Find the value of x in each of the triangles below.

6.

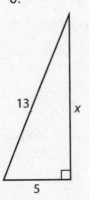

7.

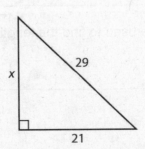

8.

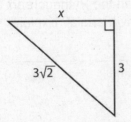

9. A right triangle has a leg with a length of 3 units and a hypotenuse with a length of 5 units. What is the length of the other leg?

_____

10. A right triangle has two legs of the same length and a hypotenuse of length $4\sqrt{2}$ units. What is the length of each leg?

_____

_____

11. As shown below, a 10 foot ladder is placed against a tree. If the bottom of the ladder is 6 feet from the bottom of the tree, then how many feet above the ground does the ladder touch the tree?

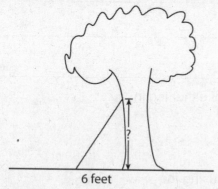

6 feet

_____

_____

_____

12. Explain the Error. Find the correct solution.

In the triangle below, the value of x is found using the Pythagorean Theorem as shown.

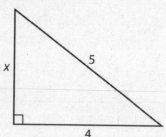

$$5^2 + 4^2 = x^2$$
$$25 + 16 = x^2$$
$$41 = x^2$$
$$\sqrt{41} = x$$

_____

_____

_____

13. Can the Pythagorean Theorem be used to find the length of a side of any triangle? Explain.

_____

_____

Example 3

The converse of the Pythagorean Theorem is also true.

If the square of one side of a triangle is equal to the sum of the squares of the other two sides, then the triangle is a right triangle.

Determine if a triangle with sides of length 10, 24, and 26 is a right triangle.

Let the longest side equal c and the other sides be a and b.

$c = 26$, $a = 10$, and $b = 24$ and then check if $a^2 + b^2 = c^2$

$c^2 = 26^2 = 676$

$a^2 + b^2 = 10^2 + 24^2 = 100 + 576 = 676$

Solution: Since $10^2 + 24^2 = 26^2$, the triangle with these side lengths is a right triangle.

Check

Determine if the given numbers could be the side lengths of a right triangle. If yes, explain why and if not, explain why not.

14. 9, 12, 15

_____

15. 5, 12, 14

_____

16. $8\sqrt{2}$, 8, 8

_____

17. Give an example of three numbers that could be side lengths of a right triangle. Justify your answer.

_____

SKILL 53 THE PYTHAGOREAN THEOREM

Scatter Plots and Association

KEY TEACHING POINTS

Example 1

Say: Scatter plots use a coordinate grid and are often limited to only the first quadrant where both the *x* and *y* values are positive. Real-world data is often limited to only positive values.

Say: Scatter plots are used to find an association or relationship in bivariate data. Bivariate data have two variables. In Example 1, the variables are the amount for the gasoline and the price paid for the gasoline.

Ask: Do you need to order the data before you plot it on the scatter plot? Explain. **[Possible response: No. The order in the table doesn't matter because when it is plotted on the grid, it shows in order by the number of gallons purchased.]**

Check

Ask: In Question 1, what two variables are being compared? **[the age of a car and its value.]**

Say: The values in the table don't match the grid lines on the coordinate grid. In problems where you are looking for a general association between two sets of data, the values on a hand-graphed grid do not need to be exact.

Plot the points on the graph as a class as you ask the following questions.

Ask: The first value in the table is 0 years and $12,000. Where does the point belong? **[Possible response: Since it is 0 years, it is going to be on the vertical axis. There is a grid line of $12,000, so put the point on the vertical axis at $12,000.]**

Ask: The second point is 3.5 years. Where is 3.5 years on the graph? **[Possible response: The axis is labeled every even year, but there are grid lines for each year. 3.5 years is halfway between the grid line for 3 years and the grid line for 4 years.]** The value at 3.5 years is $5200. Where is $5200? **[There are grid lines for every $500. The line for $5500 is between $5000 and $6000. The point belongs a little closer to $5000 than $5500.]**

Continue having students describe each point.

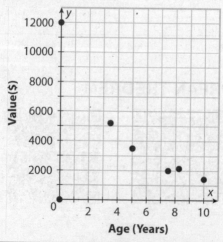

KEY TEACHING POINTS

Example 2

Say: In a positive association, as the value on the horizontal axis increases, so do the values on the vertical axis. The data points move up from left to right.

Ask: Can you think of a situation where data might show a positive association? **[Possible response: The number of hours a person works and the amount that person earns.]**

Say: You may have realized as you were trying to think of a situation that both sets of data must use some kind of numeric value. For example, plotting age to favorite color cannot be done on a scatter plot because color is not numeric.

Say: In a negative association, as the values on the horizontal axis increase, the values on the vertical axis decrease. The data points move down from left to right.

Ask: Can you think of a situation where data might show a negative association? **[Possible response: the distance a person drives and the amount of fuel left in the tank]**

Ask: What connection do associations and the slope of a line have? **[Possible response: An association is positive when both values are increasing. A slope is positive when both values are increasing. A line with a positive slope moves up from left to right. An association is negative when as one value increases, the other decreases. A slope is negative when one value decreases as the other increases. A line with a negative slope moves down from left to right.]**

Say: Sometimes a scatter plot will have points that do not appear to have any association at all. Data that are not related are said to have no association.

Ask: Can you think of a situation where data might show no association? **[Possible response: The height of a person and the distance that person drives to work.]**

Ask: In Question 3, the price of some item per pound and the year from when the cost was first tracked are compared. Do the data points appear to move up, down, or neither as you look from left to right? **[Neither.]** What does this tell you about the data? **[There is no association, they are unrelated.]** Is this a result you would expect when comparing price to time? **[Possible response: No, I would expect the price to go up as time went forward.]**

Say: In many cases, an association might be expected, but when data are studied, no real relationship is found. In other cases, where you might not expect to see an association when data are studied, an association is found.

Ask: In some cases, data may show a positive association for a portion of the data, and a negative association for another portion. Can you think of any situations where that might be the case? **[Possible responses: The amount of time spent playing sports and age. You might play more and more as you age from a young child to a teen or young adult but then play less as you get older.]**

COMMON MISCONCEPTION

Ask: What is the Error?

Emily says that the two sets of data represented in the scatter plot at the right have a positive association because all of the data values are positive.

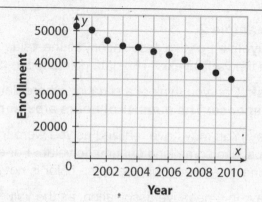

Reason incorrect: The association between two sets of data is unrelated to the actual data point values but is related to how the values are related to each other.

Solution: In this case, as the year increases, the enrollment decreases, so there is a negative association. And because the points lie basically along a line, the two sets of data exhibit linear association.

In both positive and negative associations, it is possible to have both positive and negative values. An example of this may be the temperature of an item and the amount of time it has been in a freezer. The longer the item is in the freezer, the colder it gets, and if the temperature is below zero, the item will have a negative temperature at some point.

KEY TEACHING POINTS

Example 3

Say: Clusters are groups of data points that appear to all be in a tight bunch. Outliers are points that are off by themselves away from any other points. In data that show an association, an outlier will be one point that is out of the trend of the rest of the points, while a cluster may be a set of points that are close together along a linear association.

Ask: There are two obvious clusters of points on the graph and one outlier. Do you see any associations in the data? **[Possible response: The data does appear to move up from left to right, so it could have a positive association. It also appears to be along a line, but there are gaps in the data.]**

Say: Sometimes data that are collected and recorded don't give enough information. The data for Example 3 represent the number of times a player is at bat compared to the number of hits. The gaps are where there are no players that have had that number of times up to bat when the data were recorded.

Ask: What is the outlier in this data? **[641 times at bat with 193 hits.]** Why might an outlier like this occur? **[Possible response: The player may be a known hitter, so is put up to bat more often.]**

Ask: What could a cluster of points indicate in this data? **[Possible response: That different players that have been up to bat the same number of times tend to have the same number of hits.]**

ALTERNATE STRATEGY

Strategy: Visualize clusters and outliers

1. **Say:** Clusters of data form a tight group around a point. It may help you to identify clusters and outliers if you mark them on your graph.

2. Let's look at the scatter plot of highest grossing films used in Questions 7 and 8.

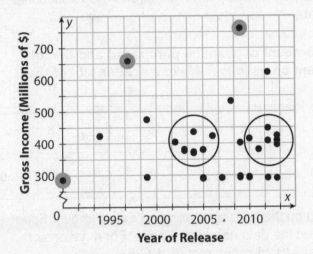

3. Draw a circle around any clusters of data you see. Anywhere a set of data points is closer together than the rest of the points appear to be is a cluster.

4. Mark with a highlight any points that appear to be outliers. Outliers are points that are noticeably far away from the rest of the data.

ADDITIONAL ONLINE INTERVENTION RESOURCES

 Use the following for students who have not mastered the concepts in Skill 54.

- Math on the Spot videos

- Personal Math Trainer with customized intervention

- Building Block worksheets (Skill 45 Graph Ordered Pairs; Skill 47: Graph Points on a Number Line; Skill 54: Locate Points on a Number Line; Skill 70: Ordered Pairs; Skill 114: Read a Table)

SKILL
54

Scatter Plots and Association

Example 1

A scatter plot is a graph with plotted points that shows the relationship between two sets of data.

The table shows the amount of gasoline purchased and the total amount of money spent on gasoline. Make a scatter plot of the data.

Gallons Purchased	5.3	4	8.7	10.5	18.1	20	11.8	15.2
Total Amount Spent ($)	22.70	13.25	24	37.75	61	62	44	51.50

Plot Gallons Purchased on the horizontal axis and Total Amount Spent on the vertical axis. Treat the data as ordered pairs. For 4 gallons of gasoline purchased and $13.25 spent, plot (4, 13.25).

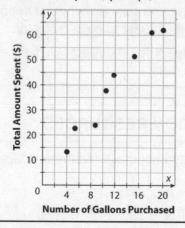

Check

1. The table shows the age of a car and the value of a car. Make a scatter plot of the data.

Age (Years)	Value ($)
0	12,000
3.5	5200
8.25	2150
10	1425
7.5	2000
5	3500

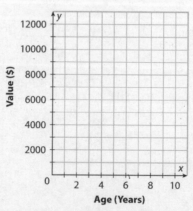

Vocabulary

Scatter plot
Association
Positive association
Negative association
No association
Linear association
Nonlinear association
Cluster
Outlier

Example 2

A scatter plot will show one of three types of association.

- Two sets of data have a positive association when both sets of data tend to increase.
- Two sets of data have a negative association when one set of data tends to decrease as the other set of data tends to increase.
- Two sets of data have no association when they are not related.

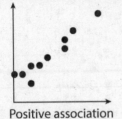
Positive association

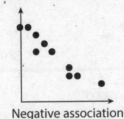
Negative association

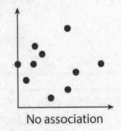
No association

If two sets of data show a positive or negative association and lie basically along a linear line, they exhibit linear association. If two sets of data show a positive or negative association but do not lie basically along a linear line, they exhibit nonlinear association.

The scatter plot shows the relationship between the amount of time spent exercising and the number of calories burned. Describe the association between the two sets of data.

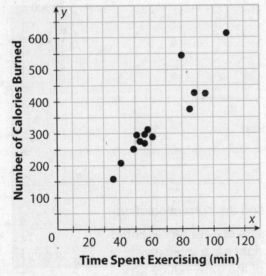

As the amount of time spent exercising increases, the number of calories burned also increases. So there is a positive association between the two sets of data. Because the data points do not lie basically along a line, the association is nonlinear.

Check

Describe the type of association each scatter plot shows. Give your answer in terms of the two sets of data shown in the scatter plot.

2.

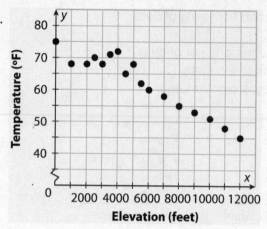

3.

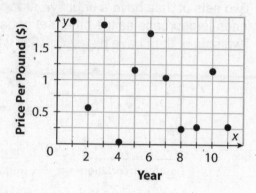

_____

_____

4.

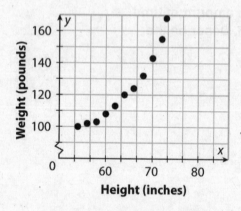

5.

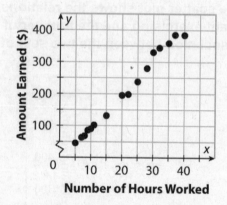

_____

_____

6. Explain the Error. Then find the correct solution.

Emily says that the two sets of data represented in the scatter plot at the right have a positive association because all of the data values are positive.

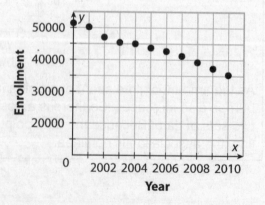

_____

Example 3

A scatter plot may have clusters or outliers. A cluster is a closely grouped set of data. An outlier is a data point that is very different from the other data points in the set.

The scatter plot shows the number of at-bats and number of hits for 17 different players on a professional baseball team. Describe any clusters you see in the scatter plot. Identify any outliers.

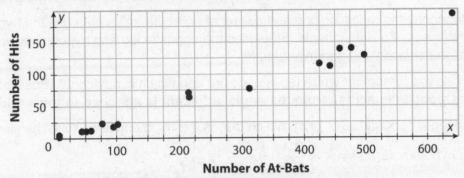

There is a large cluster in the 0–100 at-bats range. There is another cluster in the 400–500 at-bats range.

The point (641, 193) is an outlier because 641 at-bats is much greater than the other numbers of at-bats and 193 hits is much greater than the other numbers of hits.

Check

The scatter plot shows the year of release and the gross income of some of the highest-grossing films of all time. Use the scatter plot to answer Questions 7 and 8.

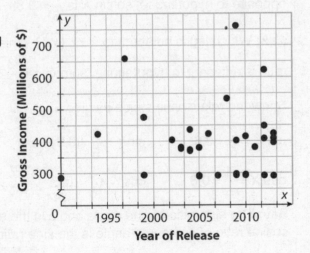

7. Describe any clusters you see in the scatter plot.

   _____

8. Identify two outliers you see in the scatter plot.

   _____

SKILL 54 SCATTER PLOTS AND ASSOCIATION

Sine and Cosine Ratios

KEY TEACHING POINTS

Example 1

Say: When the side lengths of right triangles are written as ratios, the ratios are constant for acute angles that have the same measure. This is because triangles with the same angle measures are similar, so their sides are in proportion. These ratios are called trigonometric ratios.

Say: The trigonometric ratios for sine and cosine of an acute angle both use the hypotenuse and one of the legs of a right triangle. Sine uses the opposite leg and hypotenuse while cosine uses the adjacent leg and hypotenuse.

Ask: How can you remember which leg is opposite and which is adjacent? **[Possible response: Opposite is across from the angle, adjacent is attached to the angle.]**

Ask: Which leg is opposite $\angle X$? **[$\overline{YZ}$]** Which side is the hypotenuse? **[$\overline{XY}$]** The sine ratio is opposite to hypotenuse, so sin X is $\dfrac{3}{5} = 0.6$.

Ask: Which leg is adjacent to $\angle X$? **[$\overline{XZ}$]** Which side is the hypotenuse? **[$\overline{XY}$]** The cosine ratio is adjacent to hypotenuse, so cos X is $\dfrac{4}{5} = 0.8$.

Say: The trigonometric ratios of the two acute angles in a right triangle will always be related. Let's look at the ratios for angle Y.

Ask: Which leg is opposite $\angle Y$? **[$\overline{XZ}$]** Which side is the hypotenuse? **[$\overline{XY}$]** The sine ratio is opposite to hypotenuse, so sin X is $\dfrac{4}{5} = 0.8$.

Ask: Which leg is adjacent to $\angle Y$? **[$\overline{YZ}$]** Which side is the hypotenuse? **[$\overline{XY}$]** The cosine ratio is adjacent to hypotenuse, so cos Y is $\dfrac{3}{5} = 0.6$.

Show the relationships side by side.

$$\sin X = \frac{3}{5} = 0.6 \qquad \sin Y = \frac{4}{5} = 0.8$$

$$\cos X = \frac{4}{5} = 0.8 \qquad \cos Y = \frac{3}{5} = 0.6$$

Say: The sine ratio of one acute angle is the same as the cosine ratio of the other. The cosine ratio of one acute angle is the sine ratio of the other. This is true for all right triangles.

Check

Set up the following ratios as a class. Complete the work while asking the following leading questions:

Ask: What is the hypotenuse? **[$\overline{EF}$]** What is the length of the hypotenuse? **[26]**

Ask: Which leg is opposite $\angle E$? **[$\overline{DF}$]** What is the length of $\overline{DF}$? **[10]** Which leg is adjacent to $\angle E$? **[$\overline{DE}$]** What is the length of $\overline{DE}$? **[24]**

Ask: Which leg is opposite $\angle F$? **[$\overline{DE}$]** What is the length of $\overline{DE}$? **[24]** Which leg is adjacent to $\angle F$? **[$\overline{DF}$]** What is the length of $\overline{DF}$? **[10]**

$$\sin E = \frac{10}{26} = \frac{5}{13} \qquad \sin F = \frac{24}{26} = \frac{12}{13}$$

$$\cos E = \frac{24}{26} = \frac{12}{13} \qquad \cos F = \frac{10}{26} = \frac{5}{13}$$

Example 2

Say: The question asks that you find the length of $\overline{KL}$. You know the measure of angle J and the length of the hypotenuse.

Ask: How is $\overline{KL}$ related to $\angle J$? **[It is opposite.]** What trigonometric ratio relates the side you know, the hypotenuse, and the side you don't know, the opposite side? **[The sine ratio.]**

Say: You can find the length of the opposite side by substituting in the values you know into the equation for the sine ratio. Be careful to always use the correct trigonometric ratio and side when setting up your equation.

Ask: Is $\overline{NP}$ the hypotenuse or a leg? **[Hypotenuse.]** How is the side you know, $\overline{MP}$, related to the angle you know, $\angle N$? **[It is opposite.]** What trigonometric ratio relates the side you know, the opposite, and the side you don't know, the hypotenuse? **[The sine ratio.]**

Say: When you don't know the denominator part of the ratio, it takes one more step to solve for the missing length. First multiply by the unknown side, then divide by the sine of the angle.

Check

Say: Problem 7 is a real world problem. It's recommended that a ladder be placed with the horizontal angle no greater than 75°. The length of the ladder affects how high a ladder will reach on a wall. In this problem, the length of the ladder, which is the hypotenuse, is the missing value. The angle and the distance from the house are enough information to find the length of the ladder.

Ask: What is the relationship between the known leg and the known angle? **[The leg is adjacent to the angle.]** Which trigonometric ratio should be used to find the hypotenuse length? **[The cosine ratio.]**

Complete the following work as a class:

$$\cos 73° = \frac{3}{x}$$

$x(\cos 73°) = 3$ Multiply each side by x.

$x \approx \dfrac{3}{\cos 73°}$ Divide each side by cos 73°.

$x \approx \dfrac{3}{0.2923717}$ Use a calculator to find cos 73°.

$x \approx 10.260910859$ Evaluate.

Therefore, the ladder is about 10 feet long.

COMMON MISCONCEPTION

Ask: What is the Error?

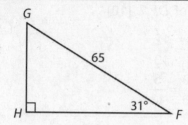

$$\sin 31° = \frac{FH}{65}$$

$$65(\sin 31°) = FH$$

$$33 \approx FH$$

Reason incorrect: The wrong ratio, sine, was used instead of cosine.

Solution:

$$\cos 31° = \frac{FH}{65}$$

$$65(\cos 31°) = FH$$

$$65(0.8571673) \approx FH$$

$$55.7 \approx FH$$

Say: Always check the ratio carefully. Make sure you've chosen the ratio that has the side you know and the side you are trying to find. Be sure you have the correct values in the correct locations.

ALTERNATE STRATEGY

Strategy: Use an acronym.

1. **Say:** To remember the trigonometric ratios, an acronym or a sentence can be helpful. The three most commonly used ratios are for sine, cosine, and tangent.

2. Let's look at the three common ratios.

   $$\sin x = \frac{\text{opposite}}{\text{hypotenuse}} \qquad \text{SOH}$$

   $$\cos x = \frac{\text{adjacent}}{\text{hypotenuse}} \qquad \text{CAH}$$

   $$\tan x = \frac{\text{opposite}}{\text{adjacent}} \qquad \text{TOA}$$

3. SOHCAHTOA, a nonsense word formed by the first letter of each ratio and side name, can be pronounced "SOCK-a-toe-ah" or "Sew-cah-toe-ah" or really any way that you want as long as you remember the letters.

4. Some sentences formed by the first letters are "Sister Olive Had Coats And Hats To Offer All" or "Silly Old Harry Chased A Horse Through Our Attic."

KEY TEACHING POINTS

Example 3

Say: Inverse trigonometric functions are used when you know side lengths, but want to know an angle. Scientific calculators can be used to find the inverse sine or cosine by pressing the inverse key before the trigonometric ratio key.

Say: Let's look at the sine ratio for angle B as an example. The inverse sine is the inverse of sine, so it undoes the sine. You can think of it as $\sin^{-1}(\sin B) = m\angle B$.

So, when you take the inverse sine on each side of the equation, you are left with

$$\sin B = \frac{96}{146}$$

$$\sin^{-1}(\sin B) = \sin^{-1}\left(\frac{96}{146}\right)$$

$$m\angle B = \sin^{-1}\left(\frac{96}{146}\right) \approx 41.1$$

The measure of $\angle B$ is approximately 41.1°. You found that $m\angle A \approx 48.9°$. $41.1 + 48.9 = 90$, so this makes sense.

Check

Ask: In Problem 9, you know the leg length adjacent to $\angle A$ and the length of the hypotenuse. You want to find the measure of angle A. Set up the cosine ratio, then take the inverse cosine of each side.
Complete the following work together:

$$\cos A = \frac{42}{58}$$

$$\cos^{-1}(\cos A) = \cos^{-1}\left(\frac{42}{58}\right) \qquad \text{Take the inverse cosine of each side.}$$

$$m\angle A = \cos^{-1}\left(\frac{42}{58}\right)$$

$$m\angle A = \cos^{-1}(0.7241379) \qquad \text{Divide.}$$

$$m\angle A \approx 43.6° \qquad \text{Simplify using your calculator.}$$

ADDITIONAL ONLINE INTERVENTION RESOURCES

Use the following for students who have not mastered the concepts in Skill 55.

- Math on the Spot videos

- Personal Math Trainer with customized intervention

- Building Block worksheets (Skill 79: Rounding and Estimation; Skill 90: Solve for a Variable; Skill 95: Solve Proportions; Skill 99: Special Right Triangles; Skill 104: Triangle Sum Theorem)

SKILL 55 **Sine and Cosine Ratios**

Example 1	**Vocabulary**

Consider the right triangle below with legs $\overline{AC}$ and $\overline{BC}$ and hypotenuse $\overline{AB}$. The leg that is adjacent to $\angle A$ is the leg that forms one side of $\angle A$. The leg that is opposite $\angle A$ is the leg that does not form a side of $\angle A$.

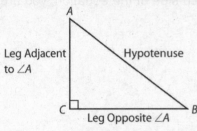

The sine of $\angle A$, written sin A, is $\dfrac{\text{length of leg opposite } \angle A}{\text{length of hypotenuse}}$, or $\dfrac{BC}{AB}$.

The cosine of $\angle A$, written cos A, is $\dfrac{\text{length of leg adjacent to } \angle A}{\text{length of hypotenuse}}$, or $\dfrac{AC}{AB}$.

Find the sine and cosine of $\angle X$.

$\sin X = \dfrac{\text{length of leg opposite } \angle X}{\text{length of hypotenuse}}$

$= \dfrac{YZ}{XY}$

$= \dfrac{3}{5}$, or 0.6

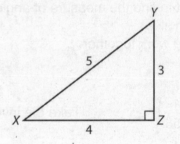

$\cos X = \dfrac{\text{length of leg adjacent to } \angle X}{\text{length of hypotenuse}}$

$= \dfrac{XZ}{XY}$

$= \dfrac{4}{5}$, or 0.8

Vocabulary

Legs (of a right triangle)

Hypotenuse

Adjacent (leg of a right triangle)

Opposite (leg of a right triangle)

Sine (of an acute angle of a right triangle)

Cosine (of an acute angle of a right triangle)

Inverse sine

Inverse cosine

Check

Find the sine and cosine of both acute angles in each right triangle.

1.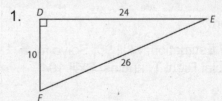

2.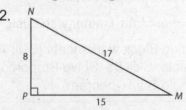

_____   _____

Example 2

You can use the sine ratio to find missing lengths in a right triangle, given the length of one side of the triangle and the measure of an acute angle.

A. What is the length of $\overline{KL}$? Round your answer to the nearest tenth.

You know the measure of $\angle J$.

You know the length of the *hypotenuse*.

You are looking for the length of the leg *opposite* $\angle J$.

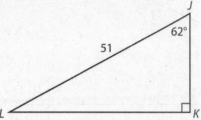

Use the sine ratio.

$$\sin J = \frac{\text{length of leg opposite } \angle J}{\text{length of hypotenuse}}$$ Use the definition of sine.

$$\sin J = \frac{KL}{JL}$$ Substitute the correct side lengths.

  Substitute 62° for m$\angle J$ and 51 for JL.

$$\sin 62° = \frac{KL}{51}$$ Cross multiply.

$$51(\sin 62°) = KL$$ Use a calculator to find sin 62°.

$$51(0.8829475929) \approx KL$$ Simplify. Round to the nearest tenth.

$$45.0 \approx KL$$

B. What is the length of $\overline{NP}$? Round your answer to the nearest tenth.

You know the measure of $\angle N$.

You know the length of the leg *opposite* $\angle N$.

You are looking for the length of the *hypotenuse*.

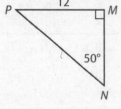

Use the sine ratio.

$$\sin N = \frac{\text{length of leg opposite } \angle N}{\text{length of hypotenuse}}$$ Use the definition of sine.

$$\sin N = \frac{MP}{NP}$$ Substitute the correct side lengths.

$$\sin 50° = \frac{12}{NP}$$ Substitute 50° for m$\angle N$ and 12 for MP.

$$NP(\sin 50°) = 12$$ Cross multiply.

$$NP = \frac{12}{\sin 50°}$$ Divide each side by sin 50°.

$$\approx \frac{12}{0.7660444431}$$ Use a calculator to find sin 50°.

$$NP \approx 15.7$$ Simplify. Round to the nearest tenth.

Similarly, you can also use the cosine ratio to find missing lengths in a right triangle.

Name _____ Date _____ Class_____

Check

For each right triangle, find the length of $\overline{ST}$. Round your answer to the nearest tenth.

3.

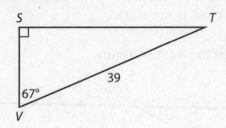

_____

4.

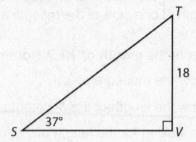

_____

5.

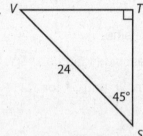

_____

6.

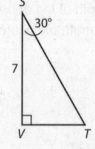

_____

7. Harry places the base of a ladder 3 feet away from his house, as shown at the right. The ladder forms an angle of 73° with the ground. To the nearest foot, how long is the ladder?

_____

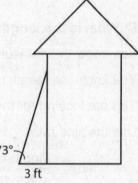

8. Explain the Error. Then find the correct solution.

$$\sin 31° = \frac{FH}{65}$$

$$65(\sin 31°) = FH$$

$$33 \approx FH$$

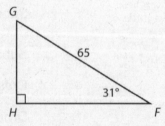

_____

_____

Example 3

You can use the inverse sine of ∠A, written $\sin^{-1} A$, or the inverse cosine of ∠A, written $\cos^{-1} A$, to find the measure of ∠A, given that ∠A is an acute angle of a right triangle. In general, the following are true:

- If $\sin A = x$, then $\sin^{-1} x = m\angle A$.

- If $\cos A = x$, then $\cos^{-1} x = m\angle A$.

What is m∠A? Round to the nearest tenth of a degree.

You know the length of the leg *adjacent* to ∠A.

You know the length of the hypotenuse.

Use the cosine ratio to write and solve an equation.

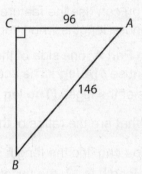

$\cos A = \dfrac{AC}{AB}$ Use the definition of cosine.

$\cos A = \dfrac{96}{146}$ Substitute 96 for AC and 146 for AB.

$\cos^{-1}\left(\dfrac{96}{146}\right) = m\angle A$ Use the definition of inverse cosine.

$48.9 \approx m\angle A$ Use a calculator to simplify.

Similarly, to find m∠B, you could use the inverse sine of ∠B.

Check

For each right triangle, find m∠A. Round your answer to the nearest tenth of a degree.

9.

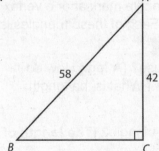

10.

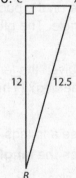

_____   _____

SKILL 55 SINE AND COSINE RATIOS

Special Right Triangles

KEY TEACHING POINTS

Example 1

Say: Right triangles with special features that make calculations or formulas easy are called special right triangles. An isosceles right triangle has angle measures in the ratio 1 : 1 : 2. The degree measurements of the angles are 45° – 45° – 90°. The two leg lengths are the same, and the hypotenuse is $\sqrt{2}$ times the length of a leg.

Say: You can use the features of a 45° – 45° – 90° triangle to find missing leg and hypotenuse lengths when you only know the length of one side.

Ask: In Part A, one side of the triangle is given. Is the given measure a leg or the hypotenuse? **[A leg.]** The acute angles each measure 45°. What does this tell you about the lengths of the legs? **[The leg lengths are the same.]** What is the length of $\overline{AC}$? **[12]**

Ask: What are the ratios of the side lengths in a 45° – 45° – 90° triangle? **[1 : 1 : $\sqrt{2}$]**

Say: You can find the length of the hypotenuse by multiplying a leg length by $\sqrt{2}$. So, since the leg length is 12, the hypotenuse length is $12\sqrt{2}$.

Say: In Part B, the length given is the hypotenuse. A 45° – 45° – 90° triangle is an isosceles triangle, so the legs are the same length. The hypotenuse length is $\sqrt{2}$ times the leg length, so you can divide the hypotenuse length by $\sqrt{2}$ to find the length of the legs.

Ask: What does it mean to rationalize the denominator? **[To rewrite a number so that there are no radicals in the denominator.]** How do you rationalize the denominator? **[Multiply the numerator and denominator by the same radical.]**

Check

Say: Look over each triangle on the page. Notice, each has a right angle mark at one vertex showing that it is a right triangle. The other angles are marked 45°. Each of these triangles is a right isosceles triangle.

Ask: In Problem 1, are you given the length of a leg or the hypotenuse? **[A leg.]** How do you find the length of the other leg? **[The legs are the same length.]** What is the length of the $\overline{XZ}$? **[8]**

Ask: How are the hypotenuse and legs related in an isosceles right triangle? **[The length of the hypotenuse is $\sqrt{2}$ times the length of a leg.]**

Complete the following as a class.

$$\text{hypotenuse} = \sqrt{2} \cdot \text{leg}$$

$XY = \sqrt{2} \cdot YZ$ Substitute the correct side lengths.

$XY = \sqrt{2} \cdot 8$ Substitute 8 for XY.

$XY = 8\sqrt{2}$ Simplify.

Ask: In Problem 3, are you given the length of a leg or the hypotenuse? **[A leg.]** How do you find the length of the hypotenuse? **[Multiply the length of the leg by $\sqrt{2}$.]**

Say: In this problem, the side length includes a radical.

Complete the following as a class.

$$\text{hypotenuse} = \sqrt{2} \cdot \text{leg}$$

$GJ = \sqrt{2} \cdot HJ$	Substitute the correct side lengths.
$GJ = \sqrt{2} \cdot 18\sqrt{2}$	Substitute $18\sqrt{2}$ for HJ.
$GJ = 18\sqrt{4}$	
$GJ = 18(2) = 36$	Simplify.

Say: In Problem 5, the hypotenuse length is given and includes a radical.

Ask: How do you find the length of a leg in a $45° - 45° - 90°$ triangle when you know the hypotenuse? **[Divide by $\sqrt{2}$.]** What is $3\sqrt{2}$ divided by $\sqrt{2}$? **[3]** The length of each leg is 3.

Ask: Look at Problem 7. What is the line drawn from non-adjacent vertices called? **[A diagonal.]** The diagonal of a square forms two $45°- 45° - 90°$ triangles. You are given the distance for each side. Do the sides of the square form the legs or hypotenuse of the triangles? **[The legs.]** How do you use the length of a side to find the length of the hypotenuse? **[Multiply by $\sqrt{2}$].**

ALTERNATE STRATEGY

Strategy: Use the distance formula.

1. **Say:** What if you don't remember the ratio of leg to hypotenuse? You can use the Pythagorean Theorem or the distance formula to find the length of the legs or hypotenuse.

2. Think of the right triangle as having its right angle at the origin and each leg on an axis.

   You know that because this is an isosceles triangle, each leg has the same length, so each leg is 8 units long.

3. The distance formula tells you that the distance that is the hypotenuse is the square root of the sum of the square of the change in run and the change in rise, or

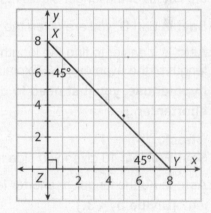

   $$d = \sqrt{(\text{run})^2 + (\text{rise})^2}.$$

   The rise and run are each 8. Substitute this into the distance formula.

   $$d = \sqrt{(8)^2 + (8)^2} = \sqrt{2(8)^2} = 8\sqrt{2}$$

4. At this point you may remember that the ratio of leg length to hypotenuse length is $1 : \sqrt{2}$. Remember, in any right triangle, you can use the distance formula to find the length of the hypotenuse. To find the length of a leg, you can substitute the length of the hypotenuse in for distance and use a variable to represent the length of a leg. Since the leg lengths are the same, use the same variable, and solve for that variable.

KEY TEACHING POINTS

Example 2

Say: A second special right triangle has angle measures in the ratio 1 : 2 : 3. The angle measures are 30°, 60°, and 90°. The side lengths are in the ratio $1 : \sqrt{3} : 2$. Remember, the hypotenuse is twice as long as the short leg.

Illustrate the relationship between an equilateral triangle and a 30° – 60° – 90° triangle by drawing a sketch and saying the following:

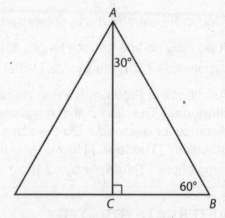

Say: One way you can remember where each side belongs in the ratio is to think of an equilateral triangle with an altitude drawn. The altitude divides the triangle exactly in half. The half triangle is a right triangle that retains one of the 60° angles, has one of the 60° angles split in half to form a 30° angle, and has a right angle at the base. One side of the equilateral triangle forms the hypotenuse of the 30° – 60° – 90° triangle, with the shorter leg being exactly half of one of the original sides.

Ask: In part A, one side of the triangle is given. Is it the shorter leg, the longer leg, or the hypotenuse? **[The shorter leg.]** How can you find the length of the hypotenuse in a 30° – 60° – 90° triangle when you know the length of the shorter leg? **[Double the length of the shorter leg.]** What is the length of the hypotenuse *AB*? **[20]**

Ask: How can you find the length of the longer leg in a 30° – 60° – 90° triangle when you know the length of the shorter leg? **[Multiply the length of the shorter leg by $\sqrt{3}$.]** What is the length of the longer side, *AC*? **[$10\sqrt{3}$]**

Say: In part B, you are given the length of the hypotenuse.

Ask: Is it easier to find the length of the longer leg or the shorter leg first when you know the length of the hypotenuse? Explain. **[The shorter leg. Since the shorter leg is half the hypotenuse, you just need to divide by 2. The longer leg is $\sqrt{3}$ times the length of the shorter leg.]**

Check

Say: Problem 10 gives you side length $KJ = 2$ and $m\angle J = 30°$.

Ask: Is *KJ* the longer or shorter leg? **[Longer.]** How can you find the length of the shorter leg? **[Divide by $\sqrt{3}$.]**

Say: Dividing by a radical can result in a fraction with a radical in the denominator. Remember to rationalize denominators that contain a radical.

Say: Once you have the shorter leg length, you can double it to find the length of the hypotenuse.

COMMON MISCONCEPTION

Ask: What is the Error?

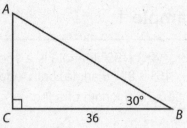

longer leg $= 3 \cdot$ shorter leg

$\quad BC = 3 \cdot AC$

$\quad 36 = 3 \cdot AC$

$\quad AC = \dfrac{36}{3}$

$\quad AC = 12$

hypotenuse $= 2 \cdot$ shorter leg

$\quad AB = 2 \cdot AC$

$\quad AB = 2 \cdot 12$

$\quad AB = 24$

Reason incorrect: The longer leg is $\sqrt{3}$ times the shorter leg, not 3 times the shorter leg.

Solution:

longer leg $= \sqrt{3} \cdot$ shorter leg

$\quad BC = \sqrt{3} \cdot AC$

$\quad 36 = \sqrt{3} \cdot AC$

$\quad AC = \dfrac{36}{\sqrt{3}}$

$\qquad = \dfrac{36}{\sqrt{3}} \cdot \dfrac{\sqrt{3}}{\sqrt{3}}$

$\qquad = \dfrac{36\sqrt{3}}{3}$

$\quad AC = 12\sqrt{3}$

hypotenuse $= 2 \cdot$ shorter leg

$\quad AB = 2 \cdot AC$

$\qquad = 2 \cdot 12\sqrt{3}$

$\quad AB = 24\sqrt{3}$

Ask: How could this error have been spotted? **[Possible response: In the incorrect answer, the leg was longer than the hypotenuse, but the hypotenuse is always the longest side.]**

ADDITIONAL ONLINE INTERVENTION RESOURCES

 Use the following for students who have not mastered the concepts in Skill 56.

- Math on the Spot videos

- Personal Math Trainer with customized intervention

- Building Block worksheets (Skill 50: Identify Similar Figures; Skill 91: Solving Multi-Step Equations; Skill 99: Special Right Triangles; Skill 100: Squares and Square Roots)

SKILL 56

Special Right Triangles

Vocabulary
45° − 45° − 90° triangle
Right triangle
Leg (of a right triangle)
Hypotenuse
30° − 60° − 90° triangle

Example 1

A 45° − 45° − 90° triangle is a special type of right triangle. In a 45° − 45° − 90° triangle, both legs are congruent, and the hypotenuse is $\sqrt{2}$ times the length of a leg.

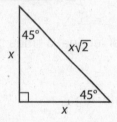

A.   Find the unknown side lengths in △ABC.
Find AC and AB.
The legs are congruent, so AC = BC = 12.
The hypotenuse is $\sqrt{2}$ times the length of a leg:
hypotenuse = $\sqrt{2}$ • leg

$AB = \sqrt{2} \cdot BC$ Substitute the correct side lengths.

$AB = \sqrt{2} \cdot 12$ Substitute 12 for BC.

$AB = 12\sqrt{2}$ Simplify.

B.   Find the unknown side lengths in △XYZ.
Find YZ and XZ.

The hypotenuse is $\sqrt{2}$ times the length of a leg:
hypotenuse = $\sqrt{2}$ • leg

$XY = \sqrt{2} \cdot YZ$ Substitute the correct side lengths.

$15 = \sqrt{2} \cdot YZ$ Substitute 15 for XY.

$\dfrac{15}{\sqrt{2}} = YZ$ Divide each side by $\sqrt{2}$.

$YZ = \dfrac{15}{\sqrt{2}} \cdot \dfrac{\sqrt{2}}{\sqrt{2}}$ Rationalize the denominator.

$YZ = \dfrac{15\sqrt{2}}{2}$ Simplify.

The legs are congruent, so $XZ = YZ = \dfrac{15\sqrt{2}}{2}$.

Name _____ Date _____ Class _____

Check

Find the unknown side lengths in each triangle. Write your answers in simplest radical form.

1.
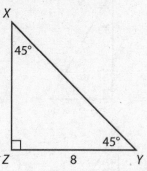
Triangle with vertex X (45°), right angle at Z, 45° at Y, side Z to Y labeled 8.

_____

2.
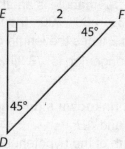
Triangle with right angle at E, side E to F labeled 2, 45° at F, 45° at D.

_____

3.
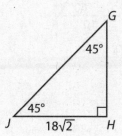
Triangle with G at top (45°), 45° at J, right angle at H, side J to H labeled $18\sqrt{2}$.

_____

4.
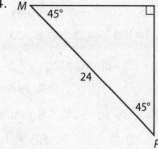
Triangle with M (45°), right angle at N, 45° at P, side M to P labeled 24.

_____

5.
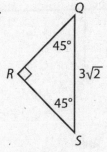
Triangle with Q at top (45°), right angle at R, 45° at S, side Q to S labeled $3\sqrt{2}$.

_____

6.
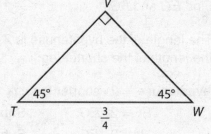
Triangle with right angle at V, 45° at T, 45° at W, side T to W labeled $\frac{3}{4}$.

_____

7. The infield of a baseball field is a square with 90-foot sides. What is the distance from first base to third base? Round your answer to the nearest tenth of a foot. Explain how you found your answer.

_____

Square diagram labeled "90 ft", "third base", "first base".

Example 2

A 30° – 60° – 90° triangle is another special type of right triangle. In a 30° – 60° – 90° triangle, the length of the hypotenuse is 2 times the length of the shorter leg. The length of the longer leg is $\sqrt{3}$ times the length of the shorter leg.

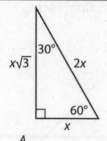

A. **Find the unknown side lengths in △ABC.**

Find AC and AB.

The length of the hypotenuse is 2 times the length of the shorter leg:

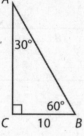

hypotenuse = 2 • shorter leg

$AB = 2 \cdot BC$ Substitute the correct side lengths.

$AB = 2 \cdot 10$ Substitute 10 for BC.

$AB = 20$ Simplify.

The length of the longer leg is $\sqrt{3}$ times the length of the shorter leg:

longer leg = $\sqrt{3}$ • shorter leg

$AC = \sqrt{3} \cdot BC$ Substitute the correct side lengths.

$AC = \sqrt{3} \cdot 10$ Substitute 10 for BC.

$AC = 10\sqrt{3}$ Simplify.

B. **Find the unknown side lengths in △EFG.**

Find EG and FG.

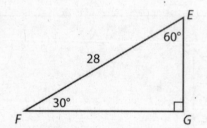

The length of the hypotenuse is 2 times the length of the shorter leg:

hypotenuse = 2 • shorter leg

$EF = 2 \cdot EG$ Substitute the correct side lengths.

$28 = 2 \cdot EG$ Substitute 28 for EF.

$EG = \dfrac{28}{2}$, or 14   Simplify.

The length of the longer leg is $\sqrt{3}$ times the length of the shorter leg:

longer leg = $\sqrt{3}$ • shorter leg

$FG = \sqrt{3} \cdot EG$ Substitute the correct side lengths.

$FG = \sqrt{3} \cdot 14$ Substitute 14 for EG.

$FG = 14\sqrt{3}$ Simplify.

Name _____ Date _____ Class _____

Check

Find the unknown side lengths in each triangle. Write your answers in simplest radical form.

8.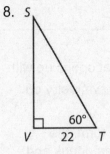

9.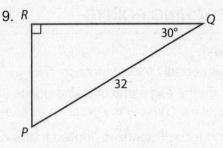

10.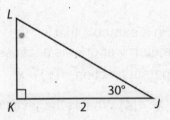

11.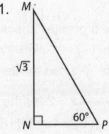

12. Explain the Error. Then find the correct solution.

longer leg $= 3 \cdot$ shorter leg

$$BC = 3 \cdot AC$$

$$36 = 3 \cdot AC$$

$$AC = \frac{36}{3}$$

$$AC = 12$$

hypotenuse $= 2 \cdot$ shorter leg

$$AB = 2 \cdot AC$$

$$AB = 2 \cdot 12$$

$$AB = 24$$

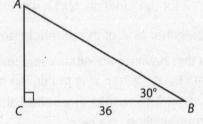

SKILL 56 SPECIAL RIGHT TRIANGLES

Stretching, Compressing, and Reflecting Quadratic Functions

KEY TEACHING POINTS

Example 1

Say: The quadratic parent function $f(x) = x^2$, when graphed, is a parabola that opens up with its vertex on the origin and crossing points $(1, 1)$ and $(-1, 1)$. It has an axis of symmetry on the y-axis, which means the graph is a reflection of itself across the y-axis.

Say: When a coefficient a is applied to the quadratic parent function in vertex form, the function is transformed. The value of a determines which direction the parabola opens and how wide the parabola is. Positive values of a produce a parabola that opens up, like the parent function.

Say: Values for a that have a greater absolute value than 1 result in a parabola that is narrower than the graph of $f(x) = x^2$. Greater values for a produce narrower graphs because the factor results in a greater y-value for the same x-value as the parent function, $f(x) = x^2$.

Ask: What is the y-value when $x = 2$ for the parent function $f(x) = x^2$? **[4]** What is the y-value when $x = 2$ for the function $g(x) = 4x^2$? **[16]**

Say: The y-value is greater by a factor of 4. This results in the curve being closer to the y-axis, which makes a narrower parabola. Let's see if this is true for negative values of x also.

Ask: What is the y-value when $x = -2$ for the parent function $f(x) = x^2$? **[4]** What is the y-value when $x = -2$ for the function $f(x) = 4x^2$? **[16]**

Say: The points on either side of the parabola are greater by a factor of 4 when $a = 4$.

Say: Values for a that have an absolute value less than 1 result in a parabola that is wider than the one for $f(x) = x^2$. When x^2 is multiplied by a factor less than 1, the product is smaller than the original value. This results in y-values that are less for the same x-values as the y-values for the parent function, $f(x) = x^2$.

Ask: What is the y-value when $x = 4$ for the parent function $f(x) = x^2$? **[16]** What is the y-value when $x = 4$ for the function $g(x) = \frac{1}{4}x^2$? **[4]**

Say: Notice the y-value is less in the transformed function than in the parent function. This results in the curve being farther from the y-axis, which makes a wider parabola. Let's see if this is true for negative values of x also.

Ask: What is the y-value when $x = -4$ for the parent function $f(x) = x^2$? **[16]** What is the y-value when $x = -4$ for the function $f(x) = \frac{1}{4}x^2$? **[4]**

Say: The points on either side of the parabola are less by a factor of $\frac{1}{4}$ when $a = \frac{1}{4}$.

Ask: Are any of the values for *y* the same in the parent and transformed function? **[Yes, the vertex is at the origin in each case.]**

Say: The value for *a* does not affect the vertex of the graph. The vertex of all quadratic functions in the form $g(x) = ax^2$ is at the origin.

Check

Ask: How can you tell without graphing whether the transformed function will be narrower or wider than the parent function? **[If the value of *a* is greater than 1, it will be narrower. If the value of *a* is greater than 1, it will be wider.]**

Ask: Describe the graph of $g(x) = 3x^2$ as it relates to the parent function. **[The graph of $f(x) = 3x^2$ is narrower than the parent function.]** How are the *y*-values of the two functions related? **[The corresponding *y*-values for the transformed function are each 3 times greater than the ones from the parent function.]**

Say: You are given a blank grid.

Ask: What is the vertex for each of the parabolas given by $g(x) = ax^2$? **[(0, 0)]** Do the graphs open up or down? **[Up.]** In your graphs, you should include positive values for *y*, and both positive and negative values for *x*.

Ask: Why might you choose to have different units on the *x*- and *y*-axis? **[Possible response: An exponential function increases very quickly, so the *y*-axis could include greater numbers than the *x*-axis.]**

Graph the following as a class.

Ask: What are good values to choose for *x*? **[Possible responses: Integers that are close to the origin.]**

In our graph, let's include the parent function for comparison.

Make a table of values.   Graph the function.

x	$g(x) = 3x^2$
–3	27
–2	12
–1	3
0	0
1	1
2	12
3	27

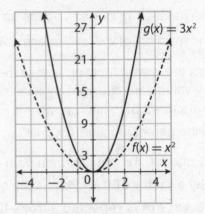

Say: Notice the transformed function is closer to the *y*-axis than the parent function. This is a vertical stretch. Imagine a rubber band fastened at the origin. As it is stretched, or pulled up the *y*-axis, the band becomes narrower and closer to the *y*-axis. If the band is pushed toward the origin, it becomes wider and farther from the *y*-axis.

COMMON MISCONCEPTION

Ask: What is the Error?

The graph of $g(x) = \frac{3}{2}x^2$ is vertically compressed to the x-axis and is wider than the graph of $f(x) = x^2$.

Reason incorrect: The value for a is greater than 1.

Solution:

The graph of $g(x) = \frac{3}{2}x^2$ is vertically stretched and is narrower than the graph of $f(x) = x^2$.

Say: Although $\frac{3}{2}$ is a fraction, it is an improper fraction, and has a value greater than one.

KEY TEACHING POINTS

Example 2

Say: In the quadratic function $g(x) = ax^2$, the graph of $f(x) = x^2$ is transformed. When a is a negative value, the parabola opens down, and the absolute value of a determines the width of the parabola.

Review the following:

- $|a| > 1$, the graph of the function $g(x) = ax^2$ is narrower than the graph of $f(x) = x^2$
- $|a| < 1$, the graph of the function $g(x) = ax^2$ is wider than the graph of $f(x) = x^2$
- $a > 0$, the graph of the function $g(x) = ax^2$ opens up
- $a < 0$, the graph of the function $g(x) = ax^2$ opens down

Say: A factor of –1 reflects the parent function across the x-axis. Just as with positive values for a, the corresponding y-values are changed by a factor from the parent function. For example, in the function $g(x) = -2.5x^2$, each y-value is –2.5 times the value of the corresponding y-value in the parent function $f(x) = x^2$.

Ask: How is the graph of $h(x) = 0.4x^2$ transformed from the parent function $f(x) = x^2$? **[It is vertically compressed by a factor of 0.4.]** How is the graph of $g(x) = -0.4x^2$ transformed from the graph of $h(x) = 0.4x^2$? **[It is reflected across the x-axis.]** Therefore, how is the graph of $g(x) = -0.4x^2$ transformed from the parent graph? **[It is vertically compressed by a factor of 0.4 and reflected across the x-axis.]**

Check

Ask: Is the graph of $g(x) = 2x^2$ or $h(x) = 3x^2$ closer to the graph of the parent function? **[The graph of $g(x) = 2x^2$ is closer to the graph of the parent function.]** The farther the value of a is from 1, the farther the graph is from the parent graph. This is also true of a values that are less than one. Is the graph of $g(x) = 0.4x^2$ or $h(x) = 0.8x^2$ closer to the graph of the parent function? **[h(x) is closer that g(x).]** 0.8 is closer to 1 than 0.4.

Ask: How can you order quadratic functions expressed as $g(x) = ax^2$ according to which is narrowest without graphing the functions? **[The absolute value of a tells you the width of the graph. The narrowest graphs have the greatest absolute values for a.]**

Ask: What is the value of a in the function $d(x) = -x^2$? **[−1]** Is the graph of $d(x)$ wider or narrower than the graph of the parent function $f(x) = x^2$? **[Neither, it is the same shape, but reflected across the x-axis.]**

Ask: Which of the functions in Problem 8 have graphs that are narrower than the parent function? **[c(x) and e(x).]** Which graph is the narrowest? Explain. **[e(x) had the narrowest graph because the value for a has the greatest absolute value.]**

ALTERNATE STRATEGY

Strategy: Use a graphing calculator.

1. **Say:** A graphing calculator will show you the transformed function, and it is a tool you can use to understand how different values transform functions.

2. Enter the parent function x^2 into Y_1.

3. Enter the transformed function $g(x) = -0.25x^2$ into Y_2.

4. Press graph to see the functions graphed on the same screen.

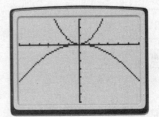

5. Compare the two graphs to determine how the parent graph has been transformed. You can see that the graph has been reflected over the x-axis and is wider than the parent graph.

6. In order to understand the transformations, try changing the values of a and watch the different transformations that take place.

ADDITIONAL ONLINE INTERVENTION RESOURCES

 Use the following for students who have not mastered the concepts in Skill 57.
  • Math on the Spot videos

  • Personal Math Trainer with customized intervention

  • Building Block worksheets (Skill 40: Function Tables; Skill 45: Graph Ordered Pairs; Skill 102: Symmetry)

SKILL 57 Stretching, Compressing, and Reflecting Quadratic Functions

Example 1

The graph of $g(x) = ax^2$ is a vertical stretch or vertical compression of the graph of the quadratic parent function $f(x) = x^2$.

When $a > 0$, the graph of $g(x)$ opens upward.

A. Graph $g(x) = 4x^2$.

When $|a| > 1$, the graph is vertically stretched away from the x-axis and narrower than the graph of $f(x)$.

Make a table of values.

x	g(x)
−2	16
−1	4
0	0
1	4
2	16

Plot the points and draw.

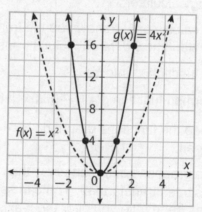

B. Graph $g(x) = \dfrac{1}{4}x^2$.

When $|a| < 1$, the graph is vertically compressed to the x-axis and wider than the graph of $f(x)$.

Make a table of values.

x	g(x)
−4	4
−2	1
0	0
2	1
4	4

Plot the points and draw.

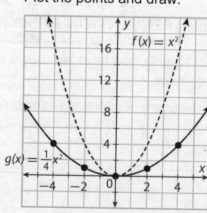

Vocabulary
Parent function
Vertical stretch
Vertical compression
Reflection

Check

Graph each quadratic function. Describe how the graph of $g(x)$ compares to the graph of $f(x) = x^2$.

1. $g(x) = 3x^2$

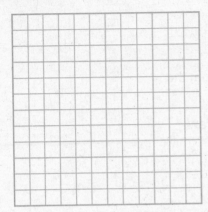

_____

_____

2. $g(x) = \dfrac{2}{3}x^2$

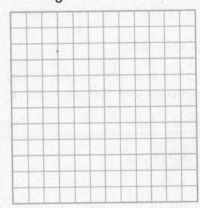

_____

_____

3. $g(x) = 0.75x^2$

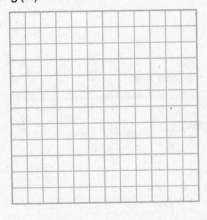

_____

_____

4. $g(x) = 1.5x^2$

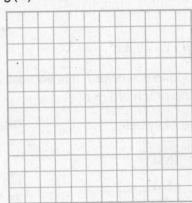

_____

_____

5. Explain the Error. Then write the correct description.

The graph of $g(x) = \dfrac{3}{2}x^2$ is vertically compressed to the x-axis and is

wider than the graph of $f(x) = x^2$.

_____

_____

Example 2

When $a < 0$, the graph of $g(x) = ax^2$ opens downward. The graph of $g(x)$ is a reflection of the parent function $f(x) = x^2$ across the x-axis, followed by a vertical stretch or compression.

A. Graph $g(x) = -2.5x^2$.

The graph opens downward. It is vertically stretched away from the x-axis and narrower than the graph of $f(x)$.

Make a table of values.

x	g(x)
−2	−10
−1	−2.5
0	0
1	−2.5
2	−10

Plot the points and draw.

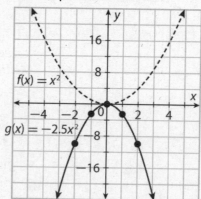

B. Graph $g(x) = -0.4x^2$.

The graph opens downward. It is vertically compressed to the x-axis and wider than the graph of $f(x)$.

Make a table of values.

x	g(x)
−4	−6.4
−2	−1.6
0	0
2	−1.6
4	−6.4

Plot the points and draw.

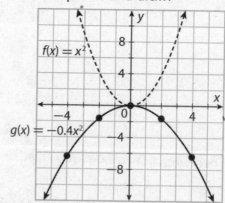

Check

Graph each quadratic function. Describe how the graph of $g(x)$ compares to the graph of $f(x) = x^2$.

6. $g(x) = -4x^2$

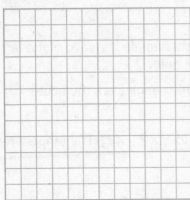

_____

_____

7. $g(x) = -0.25x^2$

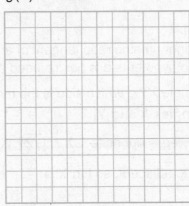

_____

_____

8. Order the functions from narrowest (most vertically stretched) to widest (most vertically compressed).

$a(x) = -\dfrac{5}{3}x^2$; $b(x) = 0.5x$; $c(x) = 2x^2$; $d(x) = -x^2$; $e(x) = -3x^2$

_____

9. The graph compares the heights in feet of two balls that are dropped as time passes in seconds.

a. If each graph represents a translation of a function of the form $g(x) = ax^2$, are the coefficients a positive or negative? Explain.

_____

_____

b. How do the coefficients of the two graphs compare? Explain.

_____

_____

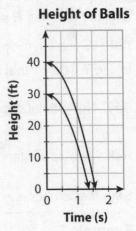

Height of Balls

SKILL 57 STRETCHING, COMPRESSING, AND REFLECTING QUADRATIC FUNCTIONS

Tangent Ratio

KEY TEACHING POINTS

Example 1

Say: The trigonometric ratio tangent of an acute angle of a right triangle is a ratio of the leg lengths. The hypotenuse is not included as part of the tangent ratio.

Ask: In triangle *XYZ*, which side is the hypotenuse? **[$\overline{XY}$]** Which angles are the acute angles? **[Angles *X* and *Y*]**

Ask: Which leg is opposite ∠*X*? **[$\overline{YZ}$]** Which leg is adjacent to ∠*X*? **[$\overline{XZ}$]** The tangent ratio is opposite to adjacent, so tan *X* is $\frac{3}{4}$.

Ask: Which leg is opposite ∠*Y*? **[$\overline{XZ}$]** Which leg is adjacent to ∠*Y*? **[$\overline{YZ}$]** The tangent ratio is opposite to adjacent, so tan *Y* is $\frac{4}{3}$.

Ask: What is the relationship between tan *X* and tan *Y*? **[They are reciprocals.]** Explain. **[The two angles use the same side lengths for tangent but in the opposite order.]**

Ask: Why would you not ask for tan *Z*? **[Angle *Z* is the right angle. The trigonometric ratios are only defined for the acute angles in a right triangle.]**

Check

Ask: In triangle *DEF*, which side is the hypotenuse? **[$\overline{EF}$]** Which angles are the acute angles? **[Angles *E* and *F*]**

Ask: Which leg is opposite ∠*E*? **[$\overline{DF}$]** What is the length of $\overline{DF}$? **[5]** Which leg is adjacent to ∠*E*? **[$\overline{DE}$]** What is the length of *DE*? **[12]**

Say: The ratio of opposite length to adjacent length is $\frac{5}{12}$.

Ask: What is the tangent ratio for ∠*F*? $\left[\dfrac{12}{5}\right]$

Say: Remember, the tangent ratios for the two acute angles are always reciprocals.

Example 2

Say: In a right triangle, for a given angle measure, the trigonometric ratios are constant. This means that for every 28° acute angle in a right triangle, the tangent ratio is approximately 0.5317094317. Since you know this is a constant, the ratio can be used to find an unknown side length.

Say: The question asks that you find the length of $\overline{JL}$. You can use a tangent ratio because you know one of the leg lengths and you know the measure of one of the acute angles, ∠*L*.

Ask: Which leg is opposite ∠*L*? **[$\overline{JK}$]** This is the unknown length we are looking for. Which leg is adjacent to ∠*L*? **[$\overline{KL}$]** What is the length of $\overline{KL}$? **[15]**

Ask: Does the length of $\overline{KL}$ belong in the first or second term of the ratio? **[Second.]** It is important that you make sure you place the known side length in the correct term of the ratio.

Check

Say: Problem 5 is a real-world problem. It's recommended that a ladder be placed with the horizontal angle no greater than 75°. This affects how high a ladder will reach on a wall. In this problem, we don't know the length of the ladder, which is the hypotenuse, but we do know the angle and the distance from the wall. This is enough to find how high the ladder will reach on the wall.

Ask: Using x as the value for the unknown side, what is the tangent equation that uses the 70° angle? $[\tan 70° = \dfrac{x}{4}]$

Complete the following work as a class:

$$\tan 70° = \frac{x}{4}$$

$4(\tan 70°) = x$ Multiply each side by 4.

$x \approx 4(2.747477)$ Use a calculator to find tan 70°.

$x \approx 10.9899$ Simplify.

Therefore, the ladder will reach about 11 feet up the side of the house.

Example 3

Say: When the opposite leg length is known and you want to know the adjacent leg length, an additional computation step is needed.

Say: Set up the tangent ratio. When the unknown is in the denominator, multiply both sides of the equation by the unknown, leg length NP, first. Then divide both sides of the equation by the tangent ratio, tan 71°. This isolates the unknown side length.

Check

Say: In problem 7, you want to find the length of $\overline{GH}$. You know that angle G measures 30°, $\overline{FH}$ measures 2 units, and $\overline{GH}$ is adjacent to angle G.

Ask: Using GH as the value for the unknown side, what is the tangent equation?

$[\tan 30° = \dfrac{2}{GH}]$

Complete the following work as a class:

$$\tan 30° = \frac{2}{GH}$$

$GH(\tan 30°) = 2$ Multiply each side by GH.

$GH = \dfrac{2}{\tan 30°}$ Divide each side by tan 30°.

$GH \approx \dfrac{2}{0.577350269°}$ Use a calculator to find tan 70°.

$GH \approx 3.5$ Simplify.

ALTERNATE STRATEGY

Strategy: Use the other acute angle.

1. **Say:** You've seen that the tangent ratios for the two acute angles are reciprocals. It may help for you to use the other acute angle when the unknown side length is in the denominator.

2. The sum of the interior angles of a triangle is always 180°. This means that if you know the measure of one of the acute angles in a right triangle, you also know the measure of the other. Since one of the angles is a right angle, the other two angles must have a sum of 90°.

   If the measure of angle G is 30°, the measure of angle F must then be 90° − 30° = 60°.

   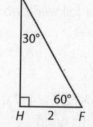

3. Now you can use the tangent ratio with angle F to find the opposite side length, $\overline{GH}$.

$$\tan 60° = \frac{GH}{2}$$

$2(\tan 60°) = GH$ Multiply each side by 2.

$GH \approx 2(1.732050875)$ Use a calculator to find tan 60°.

$GH \approx 3.5$ Simplify.

COMMON MISCONCEPTION

Ask: What is the error?

$$\tan 59° = \frac{GH}{33}$$

$33(\tan 59°) = GH$

$54.9 \approx GH$

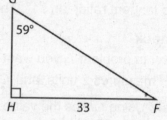

Reason incorrect: The opposite and adjacent sides are reversed.

Solution:

$$\tan 59° = \frac{33}{GH}$$

$GH(\tan 59°) = 33$

$$GH = \frac{33}{\tan 59°}$$

$GH \approx 19.8$

Say: Always check the ratio carefully to make sure you have the correct values in the correct locations.

KEY TEACHING POINTS

Example 4

Say: Inverse trigonometric functions are used when you know side lengths, but want to know an angle. Scientific calculators can be used to find the inverse tangent by pressing the inverse key before the tangent key.

Say: The inverse tangent is the inverse of tangent, so it undoes the tangent. You can think of it as $\tan^{-1}(\tan A) = m\angle A$.

So, when you take the inverse tangent on each side of the equation, you are left with

$$\tan A = \frac{48}{55}$$

$$\tan^{-1}(\tan A) = \tan^{-1}\left(\frac{48}{55}\right)$$

$$m\angle A = \tan^{-1}\left(\frac{48}{55}\right)$$

Check

Ask: In Problem 1, you know the leg lengths and want to find the measure of angle A. Set up the tangent ratio, then take the inverse tangent of each side.
Complete the following work together:

$$\tan A = \frac{21}{20}$$

$$\tan^{-1}(\tan A) = \tan^{-1}\left(\frac{21}{20}\right) \quad \text{Take the inverse tangent of each side.}$$

$$m\angle A = \tan^{-1}\left(\frac{21}{20}\right)$$

$$m\angle A = \tan^{-1}(1.05) \quad \text{Divide.}$$

$$m\angle A \approx 46.397° \quad \text{Simplify using your calculator.}$$

ADDITIONAL ONLINE INTERVENTION RESOURCES

Use the following for students who have not mastered the concepts in Skill 58.

- Math on the Spot videos

- Personal Math Trainer with customized intervention

- Building Block worksheets (Skill 79: Rounding and Estimation; Skill 90: Solve for a Variable; Skill 95: Solve Proportions; Skill 99: Special Right Triangles; Skill 104: Triangle Sum Theorem)

SKILL 58

Tangent Ratio

Example 1

Consider the right triangle below with legs $\overline{AC}$ and $\overline{BC}$ and hypotenuse $\overline{AB}$. The leg that is adjacent to $\angle A$ is the leg that forms one side of $\angle A$. The leg that is opposite $\angle A$ is the leg that does not form a side of $\angle A$.

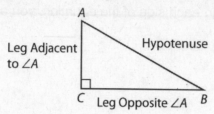

The tangent of an acute angle of a right triangle is the ratio of the length of the leg opposite the acute angle to the length of the leg adjacent to the acute angle. So in $\triangle ABC$ above, the tangent of $\angle A$, written tan A, is

$$\frac{\text{length of leg opposite } \angle A}{\text{length of leg adjacent to } \angle A}, \text{ or } \frac{BC}{AC}.$$

Find the tangent of $\angle X$ and the tangent of $\angle Y$.

$$\tan X = \frac{\text{length of leg opposite } \angle X}{\text{length of leg adjacent to } \angle X}$$

$$= \frac{YZ}{XZ}$$

$$= \frac{6}{8}, \text{ or } \frac{3}{4}$$

$$\tan Y = \frac{\text{length of leg opposite } \angle Y}{\text{length of leg adjacent to } \angle Y}$$

$$= \frac{XZ}{YZ}$$

$$= \frac{8}{6}, \text{ or } \frac{4}{3}$$

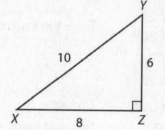

Vocabulary

Legs (of a right triangle)

Hypotenuse

Adjacent (leg of a right triangle)

Opposite (leg of a right triangle)

Tangent (of an acute angle of a right triangle)

Inverse tangent (of an acute angle of a right triangle)

Check

Find the tangent of both acute angles in each right triangle.

1.

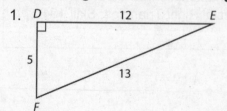

_____

2.

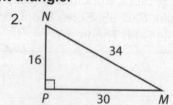

_____

Example 2

You can use the tangent ratio to find the length of the leg that is opposite an acute angle of a right triangle, given the length of the side adjacent to the angle and the measure of the angle.

What is the length of $\overline{JK}$? Round your answer to the nearest tenth.

You know the measure of $\angle L$.

You know the length of the leg *adjacent* to $\angle L$.

You are looking for the length of the leg *opposite* $\angle L$.

So use the tangent ratio to write and solve an equation.

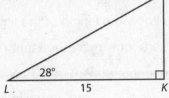

$\tan L = \dfrac{\text{leg opposite } \angle L}{\text{leg adjacent to } \angle L}$	Use the definition of tangent.
	Substitute the correct side lengths.
$\tan L = \dfrac{JK}{KL}$	Substitute 28° for $m\angle L$ and 15 for KL.
$\tan 28° = \dfrac{JK}{15}$	Cross multiply.
$15(\tan 28°) = JK$	Use a calculator to find $\tan 28°$.
$JK \approx 15(0.5317094317)$	Simplify. Round to the nearest tenth.
$JK \approx 8.0$	

Check

For each right triangle, find the length of $\overline{ST}$. Round your answer to the nearest tenth.

3.

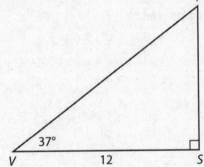

4.

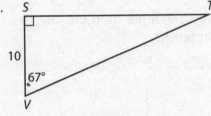

_____   _____

5. Jenna places the base of a ladder 4 feet away from her house, as shown at the right. The ladder forms an angle of 70° with the ground. To the nearest foot, how far up the side of the house does the ladder reach?

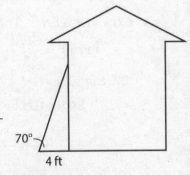

_____

Example 3

You can also use the tangent ratio to find the length of the leg that is adjacent to an acute angle of a right triangle, given the length of the side opposite the angle and the measure of the angle.

What is the length of $\overline{NP}$? Round your answer to the nearest tenth.

You know the measure of $\angle N$.

You know the length of the leg *opposite* $\angle N$.

You are looking for the length of the leg *adjacent to* $\angle N$.

So use the tangent ratio to write and solve an equation.

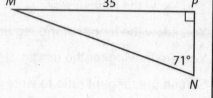

$\tan N = \dfrac{\text{leg opposite } \angle N}{\text{leg adjacent to } \angle N}$ Use the definition of tangent.

$\tan N = \dfrac{MP}{NP}$ Substitute the correct side lengths.

$\tan 71° = \dfrac{35}{NP}$ Substitute 71° for m$\angle N$ and 35 for MP.

$NP(\tan 71°) = 35$ Cross multiply.

$NP = \dfrac{35}{\tan 71°}$ Divide each side by tan 71°.

$NP \approx \dfrac{35}{2.904210878}$ Use a calculator to find tan 71°.

$NP \approx 12.1$ Simplify. Round to the nearest tenth.

Check

For each right triangle, find the length of $\overline{GH}$. Round your answer to the nearest tenth.

6.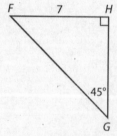

_____

7.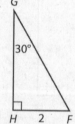

_____

8. Explain the Error. Then find the correct solution.

$\tan 59° = \dfrac{GH}{33}$

$33(\tan 59°) = GH$

$54.9 \approx GH$

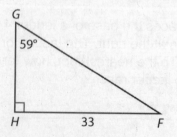

_____

Example 4

You can use the inverse tangent of $\angle A$.

In general, if $\tan A = x$, then $\tan^{-1} x = m\angle A$.

What is m$\angle A$? Round to the nearest tenth of a degree.

You know the length of the leg *opposite* $\angle A$.

You know the length of the leg *adjacent to* $\angle A$.

So use the tangent ratio to write and solve an equation.

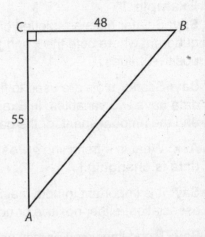

$$\tan A = \frac{\text{leg opposite } \angle A}{\text{leg adjacent } \angle A}$$

$\tan A = \dfrac{BC}{AC}$ Use the definition of tangent.

$\tan A = \dfrac{48}{55}$ Substitute 48 for BC and 55 for AC.

$\tan^{-1}\left(\dfrac{48}{55}\right) = m\angle A$ Use the definition of inverse tangent.

$41.1 \approx m\angle A$ Use a calculator to simplify.

Check

For each right triangle, find m$\angle A$. Round your answer to the nearest tenth of a degree.

9.

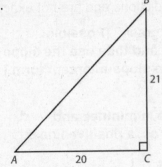

10.

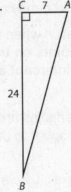

SKILL 58 TANGENT RATIO

Trend Lines and Predictions

KEY TEACHING POINTS

Example 1

Say: Scatter plots are plotted on a coordinate grid and are often limited to only the first quadrant where both the *x* and *y* values are positive. Real-world data is often limited to only positive values.

Say: Scatter plots are used to find an association or relationship in bivariate data. Bivariate data have two variables. In Example 1, the variables are the amount of gasoline purchased and the amount spent for the gasoline.

Ask: What is a trend line? **[Possible response: A line that shows approximately how the data is changing.]**

Say: It is important to note that not all data show a trend. Only data that have a clear linear association, either positive or negative, should be modeled using a trend line.

Say: Trend lines may or may not go through any of the data points. Approximately half of the data points should be on each side of the trend line.

Ask: Does the trend line drawn in Part A pass through any of the plotted points? **[Yes, 2 points.]** How many points are plotted on the grid? **[11]** There are about 6 points that are very close to the trend line. How many of the points that are not very close are above the trend line? **[3]** How many are below? **[2]**

Say: Trend lines are not used to find exact values. You should draw a trend line as accurately as possible, but keep in mind that trend lines are used to make predictions and are not exact.

Ask: How do you write an equation when you are given a line on a graph? **[Possible response: You can use two points on the line to find the slope and then use the slope and either point to find the *y*-intercept and write the equation in slope-intercept form.]**

Check

Ask: In Question 1, what two variables are being compared? **[Time in minutes and calories burned.]** Does there appear to be a linear association? **[Yes, a positive linear association.]**

Say: Scatter plots sometime have clusters of data and outliers. Outliers should be ignored, and as often as possible, trend lines should pass through the center of clusters.

Ask: Can you draw a trend line that passes through every point? **[Possible response: If the data are an exact rate it will be in a line, but in a scatter plot you should not try to hit every data point, or even any data point. Instead, try to keep the data points evenly spread out on each side of the trend line.]**

Draw a trend line on the graph as a class as you ask the following questions.

Ask: How many values are plotted on the graph for Question 1? **[14]** How should the data fall around the trend line? **[About 7 points on each side of the line.]**

Say: The trend lines drawn may not all be exactly the same, but they should be close.

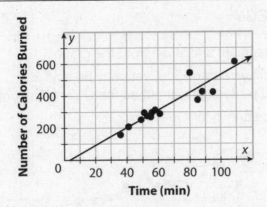

Ask: The first step in finding the equation of a trend line is choosing two points on the line. What are two points that appear to lie very close to the line? **[Possible response: (40, 200) and (95, 500)]**

Ask: How do you find the slope of the line? **[Use the slope formula.]**

Do the following work as a class

$$m = \frac{y_2 - y_1}{x_2 - x_1}$$ Use the slope formula.

$$= \frac{500 - 200}{95 - 40}$$ Substitute (40, 200) for (x_1, y_1) and (96, 500) for (x_2, y_2).

$$= \frac{300}{55}$$ Simplify.

$$m \approx 5.5$$ Round to the nearest tenth.

Ask: How do you find the y-intercept of the line? **[Use the slope and a point.]**
Do the following work as a class:

$$y = mx + b$$ Use slope-intercept form.

$$200 = 5.5(40) + b$$ Substitute 200 for y, 5.5 for m, and 40 for x.

$$200 = 220 + b$$ Simplify.

$$b = -20$$ Solve for b.

Say: You know the slope and y-intercept. Write the equation in slope-intercept form. The equation of the trend line is $y = 5.5x - 20$.

Ask: What are some reasons you might have a different equation? **[Possible response: The drawn trend lines might be slightly different, or you may have chosen different points that are close to the line.]**

ALTERNATE STRATEGY

Strategy: Estimate the *y*-intercept and slope from the graph.

1. **Say:** Once you have drawn a trend line, you may be able to estimate the slope and *y*-intercept without as many computations.

2. Let's look at a trend line drawn for Question 2.

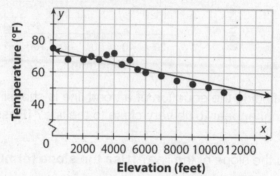

3. The *y*-intercept can be estimated by looking at where the trend line crosses the *y*-axis. The intercept appears to be just above 75, so a good estimate is 76.

4. Slope is the change in rise over the change in run. Estimate two points that are easy to work with. Let's say *x*-values of 0 and 10,000. From where $x = 0$ to where $x = 10,000$, the rise is about $76 - 51 = -25$, and the run is $10,000 - 0 = 10,000$, so the slope is approximately $\dfrac{-25}{10,000}$, or -0.0025.

5. Use the approximate slope and intercept to write the equation $y = -0.0025x + 76$.

KEY TEACHING POINTS

Example 2

Say: Trend lines can be used to estimate values that are between known values or to predict what values outside the range of known values might be. You can remember that interpolation is inside the known data by connecting the beginnings of the words—inter and inside. You can remember that extrapolation predicts values outside by connecting the beginnings of the words—extra and outside.

Ask: In Example 2, the trend line and the equation of the trend line are given to you. How can you estimate amounts of money that are earned for a given number of hours? **[Substitute the hours into the equation of the trend line.]**

Ask: Does it make sense in terms of the known data that a person who works 17 hours would earn about $165.50? Why? **[Possible response: A person who worked 20 hours earned a little less than $200. A person who worked 15 hours earned a little less than $150. The amount fits where it should be, between the two.]**

Ask: Part B is an extrapolation. How are the computations different to interpolate or extrapolate? Explain. **[Possible response: The calculations are done in the same way.**

You substitute in the value you want to estimate or predict the earnings for. The only difference is that there are points on either side, left or right, of the value you interpolate but only on one side of the value you extrapolate.]

Check

Ask: For what years would you need to interpolate to find the enrollment? **[Between year 0 and year 9.]**

Say: Question 3 begins with the word *estimate*. Estimation with trend lines is interpolation. Question 4 begins with the word *predict*. Prediction using trend lines is called extrapolation.

COMMON MISCONCEPTION

Ask: What is the Error?

Luis uses the equation of the trend line to predict the enrollment at the university in Year 35:

$$y = -1620x + 51,953$$
$$= -1620(35) + 51,953$$
$$= -56,700 + 51,953$$
$$y = -4747$$

Luis concludes that the enrollment in Year 35 will be about −4747.

Reason incorrect: Luis did the work correctly, but he came to the wrong conclusion.

Solution: In this case, although all of the calculations are correct, you must take into account restrictions on the data because of the context. In the context of the problem, Luis is looking for the enrollment in Year 35 and the equation of the trend line yielded a negative result. It is not possible for the university to have a negative number of students. The trend line cannot be used to predict an accurate enrollment as far into the future as Year 35.

ADDITIONAL ONLINE INTERVENTION RESOURCES

Use the following for students who have not mastered the concepts in Skill 59.

- Math on the Spot videos
- Personal Math Trainer with customized intervention
- Building Block worksheets (Skill 6: Analyze Data; Skill 43: Graph Equations; Skill 89: Solve Equations with Fractions; Skill 90: Solve for a Variable; Skill 91: Solve Multi-Step Equations)

Trend Lines and Predictions

SKILL 59

Example 1

When a scatter plot shows a linear association between two sets of data, you can use a *trend line* to model the association more clearly. A trend line passes through the points on a scatter plot and has about the same number of points above it and below it.

You can estimate the coordinates of two points on a trend line and use those coordinates to write an equation of the trend line.

The scatter plot shows the amount of gasoline purchased and the total amount of money spent.

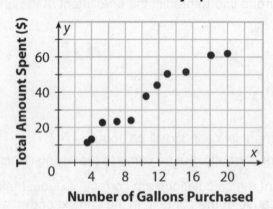

A. Draw a trend line.

Use a straightedge to draw a line through the points. There should be about the same number of points above the line as below it.

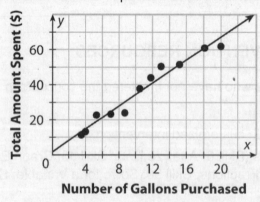

Vocabulary

Scatter plot
Linear association
Trend line
Interpolate
Extrapolate

B. **Write an equation of the trend line.**

Step 1: Estimate the coordinates of two points on the trend line.

The line comes close to passing through (7, 24) and (18, 60).

Step 2: Find the slope of the trend line.

$m = \dfrac{y_2 - y_1}{x_2 - x_1}$ Use the slope formula.

$= \dfrac{60 - 24}{18 - 7}$ Substitute $(7, 24)$ for (x_1, y_1) and $(18, 60)$ for (x_2, y_2).

$= \dfrac{36}{11}$ Simplify.

$m \approx 3.27$ Round to the nearest cent.

Step 3: Find the y-intercept of the trend line.

$y = mx + b$ Use the slope slope-intercept form

$60 = 3.27(18) + b$ Substitute 60 for y, 3.27 for m, and 18 for x.

$60 = 58.86 + b$ Simplify.

$b = 1.14$ Solve for b.

Step 4: Use your slope and y-intercept to write an equation.

$y = mx + b$ Use slope-intercept form

$y = 3.27x + 1.14$ Substitute 3.27 for m and 1.14 for b.

An equation of the trend line is $y = 3.27x + 1.14$.

Check

For each scatter plot, draw a trend line and write an equation of the trend line.

1.

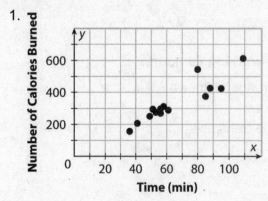

2.

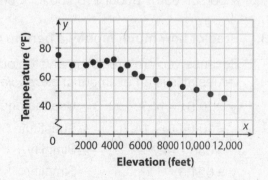

_____   _____

Example 2

You can use the equation of a trend line to *interpolate* or *extrapolate* data values.

- To interpolate is to estimate a value between two known data values.
- To extrapolate is to predict a value outside the range of known data values.

The scatter plot and trend line show the relationship between the number of hours worked and the amount of money earned.

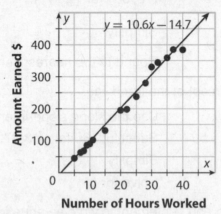

A. **Estimate how much money a person earns for working 17 hours.**

Because you are estimating a value *between* two known values, this is an example of *interpolation*.

$y = 10.6x - 14.7$	Use the equation of the trend line.
$= 10.6(17) - 14.7$	Substitute 17 for x.
$= 180.2 - 14.7$	Simplify.
$y = 165.5$	Simplify.

A person earns about $165.50 for working 17 hours.

B. **Predict how much money a person earns for working 60 hours.**

Because you are predicting a value *outside* the range of known values, this is an example of *extrapolation*.

$y = 10.6x - 14.7$	Use the equation of the trend line.
$= 10.6(60) - 14.7$	Substitute 60 for x.
$= 636 - 14.7$	Simplify.
$y = 621.3$	Simplify.

A person earns about $621.30 for working 60 hours.

Check

The scatter plot and trend line show the student enrollment over time at a large university. Use the scatter plot to answer Questions 3–5.

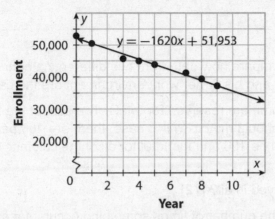

3. Estimate the enrollment at the university in Year 2. Is this an example of interpolation or extrapolation? Explain your reasoning.

_____

4. Predict the enrollment at the university in Year 16. Is this an example of interpolation or extrapolation? Explain your reasoning.

_____

5. Explain the Error. Then find the correct solution.

   Luis uses the equation of the trend line to predict the enrollment at the university in Year 35:

   $y = -1620x + 51,953$

   $ = -1620(35) + 51,953$

   $ = -56,700 + 51,953$

   $y = -4747$

   Luis concludes that the enrollment in Year 35 will be about –4747.

_____

SKILL 59 TREND LINES AND PREDICTIONS

KEY TEACHING POINTS

Example 1

Say: Two-way tables are used to compare how data from two different categories are related. In this example, the sex of a person and his or her work environment are the categories.

Say: The final row and the final column are reserved for totals. The sum of the totals of the rows and the totals of the columns should match. In this case, there are 150 people surveyed, so the total for all of the rows should be 150 and the total for all of the columns should be 150.

Ask: How many women were surveyed in all? **[72]**

Say: The word "frequency" means the number of times something occurs; for example, you might score over 10,000 points in a game 12 different times. The frequency of a score over 10,000 is 12. Relative frequency is the ratio of the frequency of an event, such as scoring over 10,000 points, to the number of total times it was possible. If the game was played 12 times, the relative frequency is 12 out of 12, or 100%. However, if the game was played 200 times, the relative frequency is 12 out of 200, or 6%.

Say: The relative frequency in a two-way table relates a subtotal, such as the number of women, to the entire number surveyed, 150. This means the relative frequency of a woman being surveyed for this study is 72 out of 150, or 48%.

Say: Relative frequencies can be used to determine if there is an association between two categories. Part A compares the total percentage of people who work inside their homes to the percent of women who work in the home. The percent of women is much higher than the total percent, so it is likely that there is an association between being a woman and working inside the home.

Ask: The conclusion in Part B is that there is no association between being a high school student and being left-handed. What two relative frequencies are compared to reach this conclusion? **[The relative frequency of being left-handed for the total set and the relative frequency of being left-handed for high school students]**

Check

Say: To determine if there are associations between categories, you must compare two relative frequencies.

Ask: To look for an association between living 1 mile or less from school and walking to school, which two relative frequencies should you compare? **[The relative frequency of walking to school for the entire data set and the relative frequency of walking to school for students who live 1 mile or less from school]**

Ask: What is the relative frequency of walking to school? **[0.45]** What is the relative frequency of walking to school if students live 1 mile or less from school? **[About 0.77]** Is there an association? **[Yes, students who live 1 mile or less from school are much more likely to walk.]**

ALTERNATE STRATEGY

Strategy: Make a Venn diagram.

1. **Say:** Sometimes a Venn diagram helps you to understand the data. A simple Venn diagram can be used to show the same information as a two-way frequency table.

2. Let's look at the data from part B. One hundred and twenty elementary and high school students were surveyed about whether they are left- or right-handed. To make a Venn diagram, begin with one of the categories. Let's begin with the level of the students.

3. A rectangle can be used to represent the entire set of students who were surveyed. Let a circle inside the rectangle represent the number of elementary students. Do NOT write any numbers in the diagram yet.

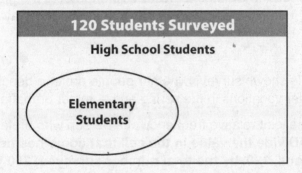

4. A second circle represents students who are left-handed. Any students outside this circle are right-handed. At this point, there are four regions in the Venn diagram, and each represents one of the four cells that are not "total" cells in the frequency table.

5. **Ask:** What category does the area where the circles overlap represent? **[Elementary students who are left-handed]** What category does the area outside of the circles represent? **[High school students who are right-handed]**

6. Complete the diagram by filling in the values.

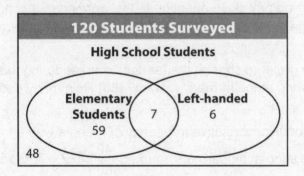

KEY TEACHING POINTS

Example 2

Say: A two-way relative frequency table does not give actual numbers in the table cells, but instead shows the relative frequency for each cell. The lower right cell is the total, so the relative frequency in that cell should always be 1, or 100%.

Ask: What do you divide the value in each cell of the table by to create a relative frequency table? **[The total number surveyed, or total number of the population, which is in the lower right cell.]**

Say: There are two types of relative frequencies shown in a relative-frequency table. Joint relative frequency relates the individual values that are not row or column totals to the grand total. Marginal relative frequency relates a row or column total to the grand total. Marginal relative frequencies are found in the final row and column of a two-way relative frequency table.

Check

Say: The frequency table shown surveys whether people prefer a beach or mountain vacation and if they prefer vacations in the spring and summer or the fall and winter.

Ask: How do you find the joint relative frequency of a person who prefers a beach vacation in the spring or summer? **[Divide the value in the cell that combines beach and spring/summer vacations, 120, by the total number surveyed, 250.]**

Ask: Are all of the values divided by the same number? Explain. **[Yes, relative frequency is found by dividing each cell value by the grand total.]**

Example 3

Say: One type of relative frequency uses an individual cell and a row or column total. Conditional relative frequency limits the possible options by using the phrase *given that*. In Part A, the phrase *given that the person shops at the farmers' market* limits the possible people surveyed to only those who shop at the farmers' market.

Say: It is important that you pay close attention to the wording of a conditional relative frequency. In the table given, there are eight different possible conditional relative frequencies.

Ask: How many people prefer to shop at the farmers' market during the week? **[42]** How many people prefer to shop at the farmers' market? **[60]** How many people prefer to shop during the week? **[105]**

Say: You can find the conditional relative frequency of people who shop during the week, given that they prefer to shop at the farmers' market, $\frac{42}{60} = 0.7 = 70\%$, or you can reverse the options and find the conditional relative frequency of people who shop for groceries at the farmers' market, given that they prefer to shop during the week, $\frac{42}{105} = 0.4 = 40\%$.

Ask: What does the conditional relative frequency of people who shop for groceries at the farmers' market, given that they prefer to shop during the week, tell you? **[Possible response: That of the 105 people who prefer to shop during the week, 40% shop at the farmers' market]**

COMMON MISCONCEPTION

Ask: What is the Error?

	During the Week	On the Weekend	TOTAL
Supermarket	63	77	140
Farmers' Market	42	18	60
TOTAL	105	95	200

The conditional relative frequency that a person shops at the farmers' market, given that the person shops during the week, is $\frac{42}{200} = 0.21 = 21\%$.

Reason incorrect: $\frac{42}{200}$ is the *joint relative frequency* of people who shop at the farmers' market during the week.

Solution: The conditional relative frequency that a person shops at the farmers' market, given that the person shops during the week, is found by dividing the number of people who shop at the farmers' market during the week, 42, by the number of people who shop during the week, 105. $\frac{42}{105} = 0.40 = 40\%$

Say: Remember:

- Relative frequency is the ratio of any subtotal to the grand total found in the lower right cell of the table.

- Joint relative frequency is a ratio of a value that is not a row or column total to the grand total.

- Marginal relative frequency is a ratio of a row or column total to the grand total.

- Conditional relative frequency is a ratio of a value that is not a row or column total to a row or column total.

ADDITIONAL ONLINE INTERVENTION RESOURCES

Use the following for students who have not mastered the concepts in Skill 60.

- Math on the Spot videos

- Personal Math Trainer with customized intervention

- Building Block worksheets (Skill 37: Find the Percent of a Number; Skill 39: Fractions, Decimals, and Percents; Skill 72: Percents and Decimals; Skill 82: Simplify Fractions; Skill 114: Read a Table)

Two-Way Tables

SKILL 60

Example 1

You can use a two-way table and relative frequency to decide whether there is an association between two variables or events. Relative frequency is the ratio of a subtotal value to the grand total.

A. 150 working adults were polled about whether they work outside or inside the home. Is there an association between being a woman and working inside the home?

	Work Outside the Home	Work Inside the Home	TOTAL
Men	65	13	78
Women	41	31	72
TOTAL	106	44	150

Step 1 Find the relative frequency of working inside the home.

$$\frac{\text{subtotal of working inside home}}{\text{total number of adults polled}} = \frac{44}{150} \approx 0.293 = 29.3\%$$

Step 2 Find the relative frequency of working inside the home among women.

$$\frac{\text{subtotal of women working inside home}}{\text{total number of women}} = \frac{31}{72} \approx 0.431 = 43.1\%$$

Step 3 Compare the relative frequencies.

The percent of adults who were polled who work inside the home is 29.3%. The percent of women who were polled who work inside the home is 43.1%, which is significantly greater than 29.3%. So there is an association between being a woman and working inside the home.

B. Data from 120 elementary and high school students were collected. Students were asked whether they were left-handed or right-handed. Is there an association between being a high school student and being left-handed? Explain.

	Left-Handed	Right-Handed	TOTAL
Elementary	7	59	66
High	6	48	54
TOTAL	13	107	120

Step 1 Find the relative frequency of being left-handed.

$$\frac{\text{subtotal of left-handed students}}{\text{total number of students polled}} = \frac{13}{120} \approx 0.108 = 10.8\%$$

Step 2 Find the relative frequency of being left-handed among high school students.

$$\frac{\text{high schoolers who are left-handed}}{\text{total number of high schoolers}} = \frac{6}{54} \approx 0.111 = 11.1\%$$

Step 3 Compare the relative frequencies.

The percent of students polled who are left-handed is 10.8%. The percent of high school students who were polled who are left-handed is 11.1%, which is **not** significantly greater than 10.8%. So, there is **no** association between being a high school student and being left-handed.

Check

1. The results of a survey at school are shown in the two-way table. Is there an association between living 1 mile or less from school and walking to school? Explain.

	School Bus	Walk	TOTAL
1 Mile or Less	6	20	26
More Than 1 Mile	49	25	74
TOTAL	55	45	100

_____

2. The results of a survey at a medical office are shown in the two-way table. Patients were asked how long they had to wait before seeing their caregivers. Is there an association between seeing a doctor and waiting more than 15 minutes? Explain.

	Wait 15 Min or Less	Wait More Than 15 Min	TOTAL
Saw a Doctor	12	64	76
Saw a Nurse Practitioner	13	71	84
TOTAL	25	135	160

_____

Example 2

You can use a two-way table to create a two-way relative frequency table. A two-way relative frequency table shows joint relative frequencies and marginal relative frequencies.

- A joint relative frequency is the ratio of a value that is **not** a Row Total or a Column Total to the Grand Total.

- A marginal relative frequency is the ratio of a Row Total or Column Total to the Grand Total.

Use the two-way table to create a two-way relative frequency table.

	Before School	After School	TOTAL
Work Out at Home	34	52	86
Work Out at a Gym	18	76	94
TOTAL	52	128	180

Divide each value in the two-way table by the grand total. Write each quotient as a decimal.

	Before School	After School	TOTAL
Work Out at Home	$\frac{34}{180} \approx 0.19$	$\frac{52}{180} \approx 0.29$	$\frac{86}{180} \approx 0.48$
Work Out at a Gym	$\frac{18}{180} = 0.10$	$\frac{76}{180} \approx 0.42$	$\frac{94}{180} \approx 0.52$
TOTAL	$\frac{52}{180} \approx 0.29$	$\frac{128}{180} \approx 0.71$	$\frac{180}{180} = 1.00$

Check

Use the two-way table to answer Questions 3–5.

	Spring/Summer	Fall/Winter	TOTAL
Beach	120	15	135
Mountains	55	60	115
TOTAL	175	75	250

3. Create a two-way relative frequency table for the data above.

4. What is the joint relative frequency of people surveyed who prefer to vacation at the beach in the spring or summer?

_____

5. What is the marginal relative frequency of people surveyed who prefer to vacation in the mountains?

_____

Example 3

You can also calculate conditional relative frequency from a two-way frequency table. A conditional relative frequency is the ratio of a value that is **not** a Row Total or Column Total to the frequency's Row Total or Column Total.

Use the two-way table to find each conditional relative frequency.

	During the Week	On the Weekend	TOTAL
Supermarket	63	77	140
Farmers' Market	42	18	60
TOTAL	105	95	200

A. **Find the conditional relative frequency that a person shops for groceries during the week, given that the person shops at the farmers' market.**

Divide the number of people who shop for groceries during the week at the farmers' market by the number of people who shop at the farmers' market.

$$\frac{42}{60} = 0.7 = 70\%$$

B. **Find the conditional relative frequency that a person shops at the supermarket, given that the person prefers to shop on the weekend.**

Divide the number of people who shop at the supermarket on the weekend by the number of people who shop on the weekend.

$$\frac{77}{95} \approx 0.81 = 81\%$$

Check

Use the two-way table above to answer Questions 6 and 7.

6. Find the conditional relative frequency that a person shops for groceries on the weekend, given that the person shops at the supermarket.

_____

7. Explain the Error. Then find the correct solution.
   The conditional relative frequency that a person shops at the farmers' market, given that the person shops during the week is $\frac{42}{200} = 0.21 = 21\%$.

_____

SKILL 60 TWO-WAY TABLES

Answer Key

Module Pre-Tests

Pre-Test Module 1

1. (−8, −9), (−3, 1), (0, 7)
2. (−2, −12), (3, −2), (6, 4)
3. (3, −9), (8, 1), (11, 7)
4. (−2, −7), (3, 3), (6, 9)
5. $y = -x - 2$
6. $y = 4x + \dfrac{3}{2}$
7. $y = 5x - \dfrac{23}{2}$
8.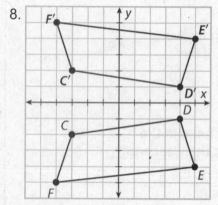
9. (6, −2)
10. A Constant B Constant C Variable D Variable
11. $\dfrac{3}{4}$

Pre-Test Module 2

1. $y = 2.5x - 3$
2. A No B Yes C No D Yes
3. a. 3; b. −3
4.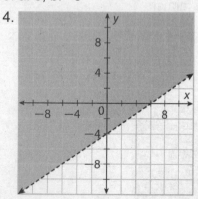

5. A Divide by −2.1. B Add 3.4. C Multiply by −5. D Subtract 9.3.
6. $k \le -4$

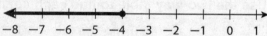

7. $w < 11$

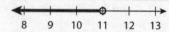

8. $p < -6$

Pre-Test Module 3

1. A No B Yes C No D Yes
2. a. $-16t < -240$

   b. $t > 15$; Yes, the balloon will take greater than 15 minutes, so it is possible to reach the ground in less than 20 minutes.
3. A Negative B Positive C Positive D Positive
4. 2.375
5. $2\dfrac{2}{3}$
6. $x = -4, 8$
7. $x = -12, -4$
8. length: 32 meters; width: 18 meters
9. 6
10. −2 and 1

Pre-Test Module 4

1. $\left(7, \dfrac{5}{2}\right)$, $\left(3, \dfrac{1}{2}\right)$, (−2, 0)
2. slope: −6; y-intercept 25
3. $k = -2$
4. $c = 25$
5. $c = \dfrac{49}{4}$
6. $c = \dfrac{9}{49}$
7. $x = -7, 8$

8. $x = -2, 12$

9. $x = -8, 6$

10. $x = 7, 12$

11.
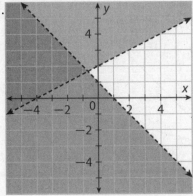

12. $x = 21, y = 7$

13. A No B Yes C Yes D No

14. $g(x) = 0.45x^2$

Pre-Test Module 5

1. $5x^4, 6x^3, 3x^2, 1$

2. A True B False C False D True

3. $-16a^5 + 13a^3 - 5a^2 + 4a + 14$

4. A Yes B No C No D Yes

5. maximum; -6

6. $x = -1$

7. $x = -2$, $x = 3$

8. A Yes B No C Yes D Yes

9.
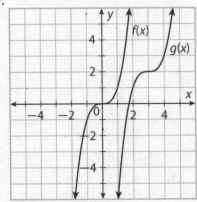

Pre-Test Module 6

1. $-8c^6 + 14c^3 - 25c^2 + 12$

2. $5x^3 + 3x^2 + 26x - 10$

3. A No B No C No D Yes

4. $4x^3$

5. A Yes B No C Yes D No

6. A False B True C True D True

7. $(9x^2 + y)(9x^2 - y)$

8. $(x - 8)(x + 7)$

9. $(x + 11)(x - 3)$

10. $(x + 7)(x - 2)$

11. $20x^2 + 45x - 30$

12. $81n^4 + 90n + 25$

13. Find the sum of the products of the first terms, outer terms, inner terms, and last terms of the binomials.

14. $42x^3 + 72x^2 + 54x$ units

Pre-Test Module 7

1. $-2\frac{1}{4}$

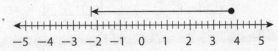

2. -5

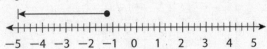

3. $3\frac{1}{4}$

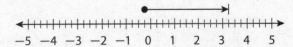

4. -2.25

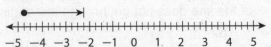

5. A Yes B Yes C No D Yes

6. A True B False C False D True

7. $x = -2$

8. $3.\overline{28}, \dfrac{143}{37}, \sqrt{5} + 2$

9. $\sqrt{45}, 7.\overline{14}, 3\pi - 2$

10. 4.359

11. -2.646

12. $3\frac{8}{9}$

Pre-Test Module 8

1. A No B Yes C No D Yes
2. A True B False C True D False
3. slope $= -2$; y-intercept $= -3$
4. A True B True C False D False
5. A Direct B Inverse C Inverse D Direct
6. $y = \dfrac{24}{x}$

Pre-Test Module 9

1. A Yes B No C No D Yes
2. $y = 6x$; $y = 66$
3. a.

x	-1	0	1	2
y	-5	-2	1	4

b.
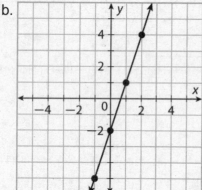

c. It is not proportional because the graph of the line does not go through the origin.
4. $y = 5x$
5. $y = 22x$, where x represents the time he spends reading and y represents the total number of pages he reads.
6. $y = 6x$
7. 24
8. $y = \dfrac{39}{x}$

Pre-Test Module 10

1. $\dfrac{1}{256}$
2. A False B True C True D False
3. 729
4. 100,000
5. A Yes B No C No D Yes

6. -512
7. $f^{-1}(x) = -6x + 2$
8. A No B Yes C No D Yes
9. $f^{-1}(x) = \dfrac{3}{4}\sqrt{x}$

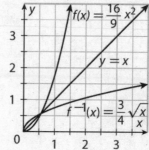

10. $y = \dfrac{1}{2}\sqrt[4]{x}$

Pre-Test Module 11

1. $\dfrac{1}{216}$
2. A True B True C False D False
3. $\dfrac{1}{4096}$
4. 39
5. $\sqrt[3]{63}$
6. A True B True C True D False
7. 1000
8. $f^{-1}(x) = -8x + 2$
9. A Yes B No C No D Yes
10. $f^{-1}(x) = \dfrac{3}{2}\sqrt{x}$

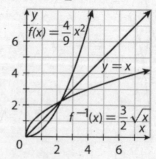

11. $y = \dfrac{1}{2}\sqrt[5]{x}$

Pre-Test Module 12

1. 29
2. A No B Yes C Yes D No

3. $3x^4y^3 - x^3$

4. A Yes B No C No D Yes

5. $-\dfrac{2}{3}$

6. a. $a_n = \dfrac{1}{18} \cdot 6^{n-1}$

   b. $a_8 = 15,5882$

7. $c = 0$

8. $x = -2$

9. a. $40 + 0.1x = 30 + 0.15x$

   b. $x = 200$ min

Pre-Test Module 13

1. -120

2.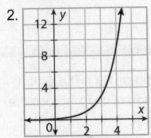

3. A True B False C False D True

4. 19,408

5. $-\dfrac{3}{2}$

6. $f(n) = 2(-3)^{n-1}$

7. A Yes B No C Yes D No

8. a. $a_n = 768 \cdot \left(\dfrac{1}{2}\right)^{n-1}$

   b. $a_8 = 6$

9. A No B Yes C Yes D No

10. $2.\overline{09}$

11. $\dfrac{5}{9}$

12. $8.\overline{42},\ 3\pi - 1,\ \sqrt{72}$

Pre-Test Module 14

1. $x = \dfrac{5}{16}$

2. $x = \dfrac{3}{2}$

3. $x = -\dfrac{1}{3}$

4. $\dfrac{1}{36}$

5. 1

6. $y = 4x$

7. x-intercept: 15; y-intercept: 3

8. A Yes B No C No D Yes

9. $y = 6x - 7$

10. $g(x) = x - 13$

11. The graphs of $g(x) = 3x$ and $h(x) = -3x$ are both 3 times as steep as the graph of $f(x) = x$. The graph of $h(x) = -3x$ is the reflection of $g(x) = 3x$ across the y-axis.

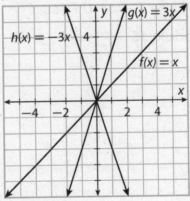

12. $y = 20x + 50$

Pre-Test Module 15

1. $\dfrac{1}{64}$

2. A True B False C True D False

3. $\dfrac{1}{3}$

4. 14

5. $\sqrt[4]{54}$

6. A True B False C True D False

7. 10,000

8. a.

x	-1	0	1	3
y	-1	$-\dfrac{1}{2}$	0	1

b.

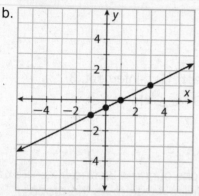

c. It is not proportional because the graph of the line does not go through the origin.

9. A True B False C True D False

Pre-Test Module 16

1. $x = \dfrac{1}{6}$

2. $x = 2$

3. $x = -\dfrac{3}{2}$

4. $\dfrac{1}{729}$

5. A False B True C False D True

6. $\dfrac{1}{125}$

7. 117

8. $2\sqrt[3]{9}$

9. A True B False C False D True

10. 10,000,000

11. $c = 0$

12. $x = \dfrac{-4}{5}$

13. no solution

14. a. $40 + 0.4x = 30 + 0.5x$

    b. 100 miles

Pre-Test Module 17

1. (2, 1)

2. $\sqrt{106}$

3. Yes, because
$9^2 + 40^2 = 81 + 1600 = 1681 = 81^2$.

4. ≈ 72.2 miles

5. A False B True C True D False

6. ≈ 8.5 ft

7. 10

8. A True B False C True D False

9. 3

10. $\angle R$

Pre-Test Module 18

1. $g(x) = x - 13$

2. The graphs of $g(x)$ and $h(x)$ are both $\dfrac{1}{2}$ as steep as the graph of $f(x)$. The graph of $g(x)$ is the reflection of $h(x)$ across the y-axis.

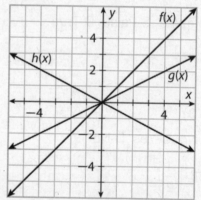

3. A False B True C False D True

4. $a(x) = -\dfrac{5}{3}x^2$, $d(x) = 1.6x^2$, $c(x) = \dfrac{2}{3}x^2$,
$b(x) = -0.6x^2$

5. A Yes B No C No D Yes

6. Reflect across the x-axis. Compress vertically by a factor of 4. Translate 40 units to the left and 20 units down.

7. Stretch vertically by a factor of $\dfrac{5}{3}$.

Translate 23 units to the right and 35 units up.

Pre-Test Module 19

1. $\frac{3}{7} \approx 0.429$

2. $\frac{9}{14} \approx 0.643$

3. $\frac{5}{21} \approx 0.238$

4. No; the two events can occur at the same time. There are freshmen who preferred 2nd period study hall.

5. HH, TT, HT, TH

6. $\frac{2}{5}$

7. $\frac{7}{10}$

8. $\frac{3}{10}$

9. 20%

10. 80%

11. Sample answer: a number less than 3 is rolled.

Pre-Test Module 20

1. 340 m^2

2. 85 in^2

3. 1056 cm^2

4. 0.55

5. 87.5%

6. 12.5%

7. No; the events can occur at the same time because there are full-time employees working at location A.

8. 0.2

Pre-Test Module 21

1. 1, 2, 3, 4, 5

2. $\frac{3}{5}$

3. $\frac{3}{5}$

4. 8 times

5. 12 times

6. 100 employees

7. 16%

8. 80%

9. 60 employees

10. 6%

11. 144 light bulbs

12. 3.75%

13. Yes; because the percent probability of a defective light bulb was lower after the adjustment, the company's improvement worked.

Pre-Test Module 22

1.
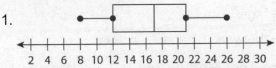

2.
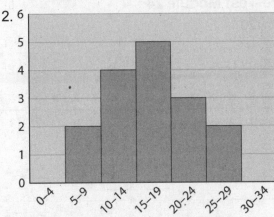

3. A True B False C True D False

4. A Yes B No C No D Yes

5.

	Like	Do Not Like	TOTAL
Boys	90	30	120
Girls	78	52	130
TOTAL	168	82	250

Pre-Test Module 23

1.
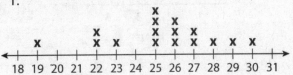

2. A False B True C True D False

3. skewed left

4. 11

5. 25.3125

6. 2.7

7.

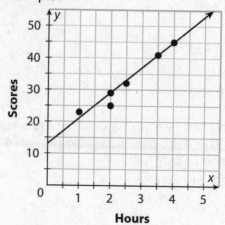

8. 16%

9. 34%

10. 97.5%

11. 2.5%

12. 50%

13. between 62 and 72 inches

Pre-Test Module 24

1. 420

2.

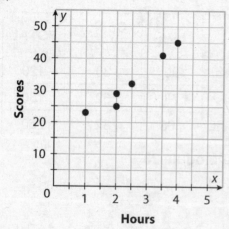

3.

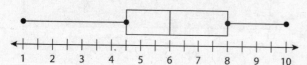

4. A False B True C False D False

5.

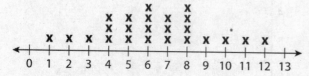

6. positive correlation

7. Sample:

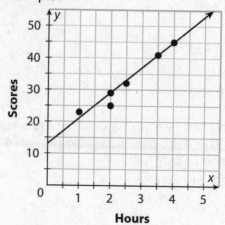

8. Possible answer: $y = 8x + 13$

9. Possible answer: 37

10. interpolation

Answer Key

Skills Post-Tests

Post-Test Skill 1

1. $3\dfrac{3}{4}$

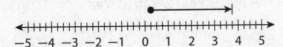

2. -4.5

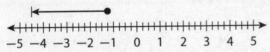

3. $1\dfrac{3}{4}$

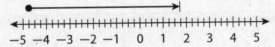

4. A No B Yes C Yes D No

5. 4.1

6. A False B True C False D True

7. 13

8. $-\dfrac{3}{4}$

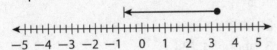

9. -4.25

10. 2

11. $1\dfrac{3}{4}$

12. A True B True C True D True

13. 6.18 m

14. -24.33

Post-Test Skill 2

1. $9k^3,\ -18k^2,\ 12k,\ -6$

2. not like terms

3. Associative Property of Addition

4. D

5. $4m^3 + m^2 + 4$

6. $-7n^3 + 3$

7. A False B False C True D True

8. $19b^5 + 19b^3 - 11b^2 + 4b - 11$

9. $3c^4 + 30c^2 + 13c + 24$

10. $16v^2 - 425v + 4800$

11. $-10f^3 + 4f^2 - 8f + 18$

12. C

13. $5c^4 - 15c^2 - 4c$

Post-Test Skill 3

1. 29

2. 15

3. 31

4. A No B Yes C No D Yes

5. $8x$

6. $10p^2 - 6$

7. $4x^3y^2 - 3x^2$

8. $-6x^2 + \dfrac{8}{3}x$

9. $10a^3b - 5ab - 2$

10. A True B False C False D True

11. $7y + 5$

12. $\dfrac{2m + 3}{6 - m}$

13. $7t^3(t - 12)$

14. A Yes B No C No D No

Post-Test Skill 4

1. $(1, 5), (4, -1),$ and $(8, -9)$

2. $(-4, 3), (-1, -3),$ and $(3, -11)$

3. $(-7, 5), (-4, -1),$ and $(0, -9)$

4. $(-4, 12), (-1, 6),$ and $(3, -2)$

5. A Yes B No C Yes D No

6. A False B True C True D False

7. A No B Yes C No D Yes

8. (4, –3), (2, –1), and (–3, 4)

9.

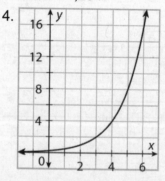

10. (–3, –6), (0, 3), and (2, 9)

Post-Test Skill 5

1. $3a^4$, $-7a^3$, $5a^2$, -3

2. Like terms

3. A True B True C False D False

4. –13

5. D

6. 6

7. A False B True C True D False

8. 1

9. $-15m^5 - 17m^3 + 4m^2 + 9m + 16$

10. A

11. Binomial

12. A False B True C True D False

13. C

14. D

Post-Test Skill 6

1. A No B Yes C No D Yes

2. This equation represents a direct variation because it can be written in the form $y = kx$. The constant of variation is 3.

3. This equation does not represent a direct variation because it cannot be written in the form $y = kx$.

4. This is a direct variation because it can be written as $y = kx$, where $k = 7$.

5. This is not a direct variation because it cannot be written as $y = kx$.

6. A True B True C False D True

7. $y = 6x$; when $x = 11$, $y = 66$

8. $y = -0.5x$; when $x = -2$, $y = 1$

9. $y = 5x$; when $x = 2$, $y = 10$; it would take 10 sec to hear thunder from lightning that strikes 2 mi away.

10. $y = 3.75x$; when $x = 24$, $y = 90$; it would cost $90 for 24 tickets.

Post-Test Skill 7

1. A No B Yes C Yes D Yes

2. $x = \dfrac{1}{5}$

3. $x = -\dfrac{2}{3}$

4. $x = \dfrac{1}{2}$

5. $x = -\dfrac{5}{2}$

6. $x = -\dfrac{2}{7}$

7. A True B True C False D False

8. $700 + 35x = 800 + 25x$

9. after 10 months

Post-Test Skill 8

1. B

2. –108

3. about 11,234

4.

5. A True B True C True D False

6. B

7. A True B True C False D False

8. about 28,496

9. about $6201.13

Post-Test Skill 9

1. $\dfrac{1}{7^3} = \dfrac{1}{343}$

2. A True B False C True D True

3. Keep the base and add the exponents.

4. $10^6 = 1,000,000$

5. C

6. $(-3)^4 (2)^4 = 81(16) = 1296$

7. A False B True C False D True

8. $4^{-6} = \dfrac{1}{4^6} = \dfrac{1}{4096}$

9. Possible answer: Use multiplication: $4 \cdot 4 \cdot 4 \cdot 4 \cdot 4 = 1024$.

10. A

11. $\sqrt[3]{512}$

12. A True B True C True D False

13. D

14. 84

Post-Test Skill 10

1. $4m^2$

2. A False B True C True D False

3. Answers will vary. Sample: $5x^3$, $10x^3$, $15x^3$

4. $2x^2$

5. $7b^2(b^4 - 4)$ or $7b^2(b^2 + 2)(b^2 - 2)$

6. A

7. No. The GCF of the terms of the polynomial is $10x^3$, not $5x$. So $10x^3$ should have been factored out of each term. The correct factorization is $10x^3(x - 2)$.

8. $2x + 3$

9. A Yes B No C No D Yes

10. A

11. $8x^5$

12. $(2x^2 - 7)(9x^3 + 1)$

Post-Test Skill 11

1. perfect-square trinomial

2. A False B True C False D True

3. $(h + 8)^2$

4. Look at the middle term of the trinomial. If it is positive, use the form $(a + b)^2$. If it is negative, use the form $(a - b)^2$.

5. $(6x - 7)^2$

6. D

7. No. Because the middle term of the trinomial is negative, its factored form should be in the form $(a - b)^2$. The correct factored form is $(4m - 7)^2$.

8. $(10s + 7)$

9. Both terms are perfect squares and one term is subtracted from the other term.

10. A No B Yes C Yes D No

11. C

12. $(4y^2 + z)(4y^2 - z)$

13. The values of a and b are incorrect. $4d^6 - 81f^4$ is a difference of two squares, with $a = 2d^3$ and $b = 9f^2$. The correct factored form is $(2d^3 + 9f^2)(2d^3 - 9f^2)$.

Post-Test Skill 12

1. A True B False C True D True

2. $(x - 4)(x - 9)$

3. $(x + 6)(x - 7)$

4. $(x + 3)(x + 11)$

5. $(x - 10)(x + 13)$

6. a. length: $x + 2$ ft; width: $x + 3$ ft

   b. length: $x + 7$ ft; width: $x + 4$ ft

7. A No B Yes C Yes D No

8. $(2x - 5)(x + 2)$

9. $(5x + 3)(x - 5)$

10. $(2x + 3)(5x + 3)$

11. $(11x - 6)(2x - 1)$

12. $(9x - 5)(3x + 7)$

13. $3x + 1$ ft

Post-Test Skill 13

1. A No B Yes C No D Yes

2. $r = 6$

3. $r = 4$

4. $r = \dfrac{1}{3}$

5. $a_1 = 4$, $a_n = 3 \cdot a_{n-1}$

6. $a_1 = 625$, $a_n = \dfrac{1}{5} \cdot a_{n-1}$

7. $a_1 = -2$, $a_n = 6 \cdot a_{n-1}$

8. $a_n = 3 \cdot 5^{n-1}$

9. $a_n = -2.5 \cdot 2^{n-1}$

10. $a_n = 5 \cdot \left(\dfrac{1}{4}\right)^{n-1}$

11. A No B No C Yes D Yes

12. a. $a_n = 3 \cdot 5^{n-1}$

   b. $a_8 = 234,375$

Post-Test Skill 14

1. A No B Yes C Yes D Yes

2. a.

x	−1	0	2	3
y	−5	−3	1	3

b.

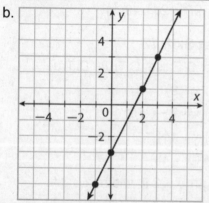

c. It is not proportional because the graph of the line does not go through the origin.

3. A True B False C False D True

4. slope: $-\dfrac{1}{2}$; y-intercept: (0, 1)

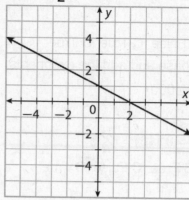

5. $b \neq 0$

Post-Test Skill 15

1. $y = 3x$

2. $y = 18x$, where y represents the number of muffins and x represents time in hours

3. A Yes B No C Yes D No

4. $y = 8x$

5. A True B True C False D True

6. slope $= -\dfrac{1}{2}$, y-intercept $= 4$

7. D

Post-Test Skill 16

1.

x	5	6	9	14
$f^{-1}(x)$	0	1	2	3

2. $f^{-1}(x) = -4x - 2$

3. A Yes B No C Yes D No

4. $s(V) = \sqrt[3]{V}$; 4 units

5.

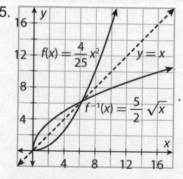

$$f^{-1}(x) = \dfrac{5}{2}\sqrt{x}$$

6. A True B True C False D False

7. D

Post-Test Skill 17

1. 36

2. $y = \dfrac{36}{x}$

3. A Inverse B Direct C Direct D Inverse

4. $y = \dfrac{22}{x}$

5. A True B False C False D True

6.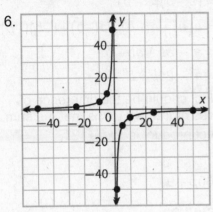

7. C

Post-Test Skill 18

1. No; The line is vertical, so it does not represent a linear function.

2. A No B Yes C Yes D No

3. $y = 5x - \dfrac{1}{2}$

4. $y = \dfrac{4}{5}x - \dfrac{2}{3}$

5. $y = -\dfrac{1}{2}x + 7$

6. $y = \dfrac{2}{3}x + 1$

7. a. The variable x represents time in minutes. The variable y represents the amount of yogurt the machine has produced at time x.

b. The rate of change is the slope, $m = \dfrac{4}{3}$.

For each minute, x, that goes by, the amount of yogurt produced increases by $\dfrac{4}{3}$ cups.

c. The relationship between time, x, and the amount of yogurt, y, is proportional because $b = 0$.

Post-Test Skill 19

1. A No B Yes C No D Yes

2. $y > \dfrac{3}{4}x + 6$;

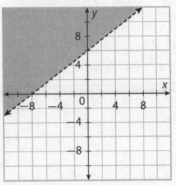

3. $y < \dfrac{10}{11}x + 9$;

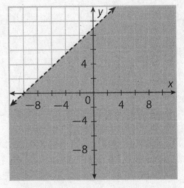

4. $y \le -\dfrac{5}{2}x - 6$;

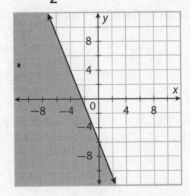

5. a. $3.75x + 2.5y \le 20$; $y \le -\dfrac{3}{2}x + 8$

b.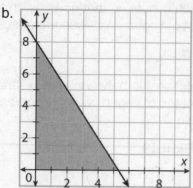

c. Possible answer: Two different combinations are: 0 movies and 8 books and 2 movies and 2 books.

Post-Test Skill 20

1. A No B Yes C Yes D No
2. $n = 0$
3. $p = -1$
4. no solution
5. $y = 5$
6. $x = -1$
7. A False B True C False D True
8. a. $21 + 0.25x = 0.6x$
   b. $x = 60$ mi

Post-Test Skill 21

1. -11.2
2. -42 degrees
3. A Negative B Negative C Positive D Positive
4. -4.8

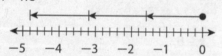

5. A False B True C True D False
6. $\dfrac{21}{360} = \dfrac{7}{120}$
7. A
8. $-\dfrac{55}{56}$

Post-Test Skill 22

1. $12x^2 + 32x + 16$
2. $\left(10x^3 + 55x^2 + 25x\right)$ square units
3. D
4. Find the sum of the products of the first terms, outer terms, inner terms, and last terms of the binomials.
5. A False B False C True D True
6. $49n^4 + 126n^2 + 81$
7. $(a-b)^2 = (a-b)(a-b)$
   $= a(a) + a(-b) + a(-b) + (-b)(-b)$
   $= a^2 - ab - ab + b^2$
   $= a^2 - 2ab + b^2$
8. The product should be the difference of the squares of the two terms, not the sum. The correct product is $9x^2 - 121$.
9. C
10. $100p^2 - 60p + 9$

Post-Test Skill 23

1. subtraction
2. $1\dfrac{7}{10}$, or $\dfrac{17}{10}$
3. D
4. Yes, both equations have a solution of 24.
5. A: Subtract 5.4. B: Add 0.89. C: Divide by -1.5. D: Multiply by -2.
6. $165.75
7. 1250 students
8. 144 minutes
9. B
10. 12 pies

Post-Test Skill 24

1. A No B No C Yes D Yes
2. $s \le 14$

3. $x \ge 1$

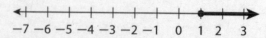

4. $t < -4$

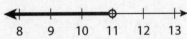

5. $y < 11$

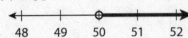

6. $b \le -3$

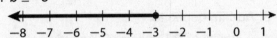

7. $r > 50$

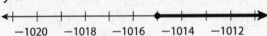

8. $p \ge 7$

9. $x < -6$

10. $y \ge -1015$

11. A No B Yes C No D Yes

12. a. $-13t < -195$

   b. $t > 15$; No, the submarine will not reach the shipwreck in less than 12 seconds.

Post-Test Skill 25

1. A Yes B No C Yes D No

2.

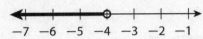

3.

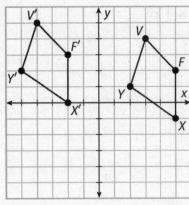

4. $(-1, 3)$

5.

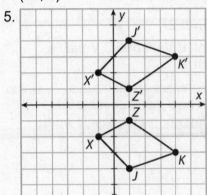

6.

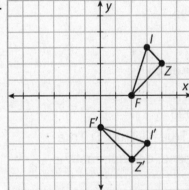

7.

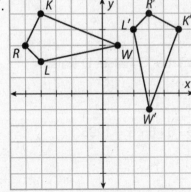

8. $(0, -2)$

Post-Test Skill 26

1. A Yes B No C No D Yes
2. max: 5
3. min: −8
4. −3 and 4
5. no zeros
6. $x = 7$
7. $x = -1$
8. $x = -6.5$
9. A No B Yes C No D Yes

Post-Test Skill 27

1. A Constant B Variable C Variable
   D Constant
2. Yes, it is constant and it equals −5, which represents how many points each incorrect answer on the test is worth.
3. $\dfrac{4}{5}$
4. A
5. A Yes B Yes C Yes D No
6. $\dfrac{3}{2}$

Post-Test Skill 28

1. $\dfrac{1}{8^4}$, or $\dfrac{1}{4096}$
2. A True B True C True D True
3. Keep the base, and subtract the exponents.
4. 11^7
5. A
6. −8000
7. A False B True C False D False
8. $\dfrac{1}{5^{12}}$
9. Because $6 \cdot 6 \cdot 6 \cdot 6 = 1296$
10. A
11. $\sqrt[5]{32}$
12. A True B True C True D False
13. B

14. 14
15. 11 units

Post-Test Skill 29

1. $2\dfrac{5}{12}$ cups
2. C
3. Add its opposite.
4. A Positive B Positive C Negative
   D Positive
5. −2.7°C
6. −45 cups
7. −$13.65
8. A Positive B Negative C Negative
   D Negative
9. 18 bags

Post-Test Skill 30

1. A No B Yes C Yes D Yes
2. 0.375
3. $1.\overline{72}$
4. $22.8\overline{3}$
5. $\dfrac{8}{9}$
6. $3\dfrac{7}{8}$ or $\dfrac{31}{8}$
7. A Yes B No C Yes D No
8. A False B True C True D False
9. 3.464
10. −2.828
11. $2.\overline{73}$, $\dfrac{137}{50}$, $\sqrt{3} + 2$
12. $\sqrt{27}$, $5.\overline{28}$, $2\pi - 1$
13. a. square: 56.25 ft^2; circle: 50.27 ft^2

    b. The square garden has the greatest area.

Post-Test Skill 31

1. A Yes B No C No D Yes
2. x-intercept: 15
   y-intercept: 3
3. x-intercept: −1
   y-intercept: −2

4.

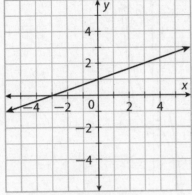

5. 2 peaches per minute

6. A No B Yes C Yes D No

7. a. $m = -1$

   b. $b = -2$

   c. $y = -x - 2$

Post-Test Skill 32

1. A Yes B No C Yes D No

2. $c = 4$

3. $c = \dfrac{9}{4}$

4. $c = \dfrac{25}{121}$

5. $x = 3, 5$

6. $x = -13, 3$

7. $x = -5, 10$

8. length: 22 cm; width: 11 cm

9. A True B False C False D True

10. $x = -7, 3$

11. $x = -\dfrac{10}{3}, \dfrac{4}{3}$

12. $x = -1, 3$

13. about 1.7 sec

Post-Test Skill 33

1. −1 and 3

2. A True B False C False D True

3. C

4. −5 and 4

5. Factor the quadratic expression into $(x - 9)(x + 4)$. Then set each factor equal to 0 and solve for x.

6. C

7. 11

8. 9

9. C

10. −11 and 11

Post-Test Skill 34

1. B

2. A True B False C False D False

3.

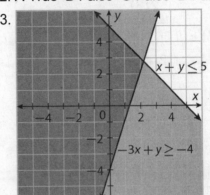

4. A True B True C True D False

5.

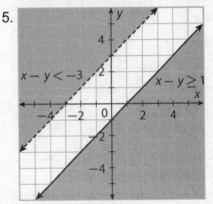

Post-Test Skill 35

1. no solution

2. (1, 4)

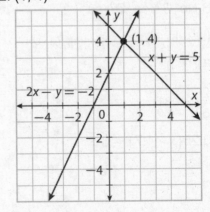

3. A True B True C False D False

4. (28, 7)

5. (4, −5)

6. A

Post-Test Skill 36

1. A Yes B Yes C No D No

2. $x = \dfrac{-(-5) \pm \sqrt{(-5)^2 - 4(3)(-13)}}{2(3)}$

3. $x = \dfrac{-(7) \pm \sqrt{(7)^2 - 4(4)(-30)}}{2(4)}$

4. $x = \dfrac{-(0) \pm \sqrt{(0)^2 - 4(-1)(7)}}{2(-1)}$

5. $x = 3, -4$

6. $x = \pm \dfrac{\sqrt{15}}{3}$

7. $x = \dfrac{3 \pm \sqrt{41}}{4}$

8. $x = 3 \pm \sqrt{11}$

9. A Yes B No C Yes D Yes

10. 0; one real solution

11. −92; no real solutions

12. 256; two real solutions

13. a. about 3.2 seconds

   b. −508; since the discriminant is negative, there are no real solutions. The baseball will not reach a height of 50 feet.

Post-Test Skill 37

1. A Yes B No C Yes D Yes

2. $g(x) = (x + 4)^3$

3. $g(x) = 4x^3 - 9$

4. $g(x) = \dfrac{2}{5}(x - 3)^3$

5. $g(x) = 0.25(x - 4.7)^3 - 3.1$

6.

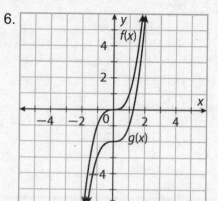

7.

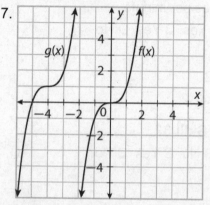

8. A Yes B No C Yes D No

Post-Test Skill 38

1. B

2. The graph of $f(x) = x + 4$ is the graph of $f(x) = x$ shifted 4 units up.

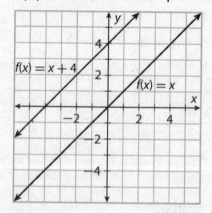

3. $f(x) = x + 10$

4. The graph of $f(x) = x - 12$ is the graph of $f(x) = x$ shifted 12 units down.

5. A True B False C False D True

6. The graphs of $f(x) = 2x$ and $f(x) = -2x$ are both 2 times as steep as the graph of $f(x) = x$. The graph of $f(x) = -2x$ is the reflection of $f(x) = 2x$ across the y-axis.

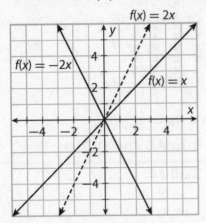

Post-Test Skill 39

1. B

2. The graph of $h(x) = 4x^2$ and $g(x) = -4x^2$ are both narrower than the graph of $f(x) = x^2$. The graph of $g(x) = -4x^2$ is a reflection across the x-axis of $h(x) = 4x^2$.

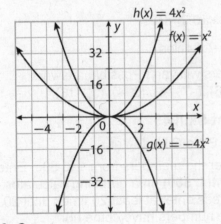

3. C

4. downward

5. A False B True C True D False

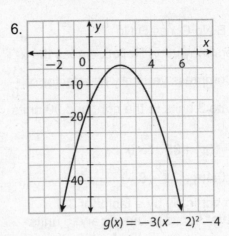

$g(x) = -3(x-2)^2 - 4$

Post-Test Skill 40

1. A False B True C True D True

2. $y = 2.5x$

3. $y = 95x + 110$

4. B

5. $y = 35x + 1000$

Post-Test Skill 41

1. A True B True C False D False E True

2.

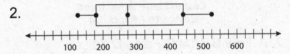

3. $400

4. $260

5. A True B False C True

6. A True B False C True D True

7. 5.5 − 3, or about 2.5 in.

8. Seattle. This means that the middle 50% of Seattle's average monthly precipitation amounts vary more widely than those of Nashville.

Post-Test Skill 42

1.

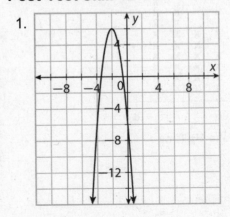

2. A Yes B No C Yes D No

3. Answers may vary. Reflect across the x-axis. Compress vertically by a factor of $\frac{1}{8}$. Translate 3 units to the right and 90 units up.

4. $h(t) = -16t^2 + 35$, $t > 0$

5. $g(x) = 0.4(x - 2)^2 - 8$

6. Stretch vertically by a factor of 3.5. Translate 3 units to the left and 5 units down.

7. A False B False C True D True

Post-Test Skill 43

1.
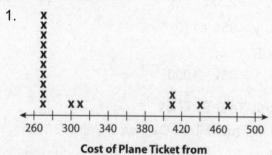
Cost of Plane Ticket from Boston to Atlanta, ($)

2. A True B True C False D False

3. Yes. In the revised data set, $Q_1 = 270$, $Q_3 = 310$, so the IQR $= 90$. To determine if 125 is an outlier, use the inequality $x < Q_1 - 1.5(\text{IQR})$:
$125 < 270 - 1.5(40)$; $125 < 210$, which is true. So \$125 is an outlier.

4. skewed to the right

5. Most of the prices are around \$270.

6.
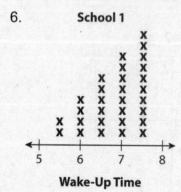
School 1
Wake-Up Time

7.
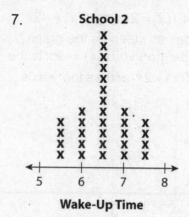
School 2
Wake-Up Time

8. A False B True C True D True

Post-Test Skill 44

1. $(-3, 5)$

2. $(-2, 1.5)$

3. $(-4.5, -4)$

4. $(6, 0)$

5. $(-2, 8)$

6. $(8, -0.5)$

7. $(-3, -6)$

8. $(-1.5, -4.5)$

9. $\sqrt{104} \approx 10.2$ miles

10. $\sqrt{50} \approx 7.1$ miles

11. Answers will vary. Possible answers: $(13, -6)$, $(-7, -6)$, $(3, 4)$, $(3, -16)$

Post-Test Skill 45

1. A Yes B No C No D Yes

2. Number the members from 1 to 500. Enter **randInt(1, 500)** on a graphing calculator and press enter at least 20 times until 20 unique numbers have come up.

3. Sample answer: Generate a random sample by using **randInt(1, 500)** on a graphing calculator. Press enter at least 40 times to generate 40 unique numbers. Let numbers 1 to 10 represent defective phones.

4. Sample answer: Roll two six-sided numbers cubes. One represents the row number and the other represents the column number. Roll until ten numbers from the table are selected.

5. 13.9 years

6. The actual average age is about 14.3. The average age of the sample is a good comparison to the actual average age.

Post-Test Skill 46

1. A True B False C False D True

2.

Distance Traveled (mi)	Frequency
0–249	5
250–499	3
500–749	2
750–999	0
1000–1249	3
1250–1499	1

3.
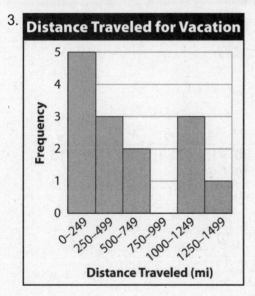

4. 3

5. 6

6. 14

7. about 514

8. about 525

Post-Test Skill 47

1. A False B True C False D False E True

2.
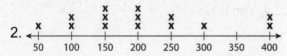

3. 100; 250

4. less than

5. more than

6.
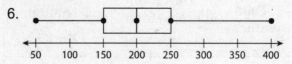

7. A True B False C True

8. 120

9. 1,365

Post-Test Skill 48

1. choosing a "Lose a Turn" card

2. choosing a "Lose a Turn" card and not choosing a "Lose a Turn" card

3. 6 times

4. 260 cards

5. 24 phones

6. 2040 people

7. 18 times

8. 100 people

9. $\frac{3}{10}$

10. 288 people

11. 2 foul shots

12. 20 green mints, 50 pink mints, 80 yellow mints

Post-Test Skill 49

1. A True B True C False D False

2. $63.78

3. $75

4. median. Sample explanation: $11, $16, and $30 are so much less than the costs of the other watches, and this affects the mean, but not the median.

5. minimum: 77; maximum: 98

6. 21

7. Q_1: 82; Q_3: 88

8. 6

9. 297.75 lb

10.

Data Value, x	Deviation From Mean, $x - \overline{x}$	Squared Deviation, $(x - \overline{x})^2$
300	2.25	5.0625
296	−1.75	3.0625
295	−2.75	7.5625
300	2.25	5.0625

11. 2.2776

Post-Test Skill 50

1. A True B True C False D True

2.

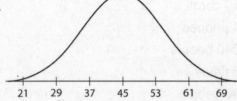

3. 95%. $61 - 45 = 45 - 29 = 16$, which is twice the standard deviation of 8. So 61 is two standard deviations above the mean, and 29 is two standard deviations below the mean. In a normal distribution 95% of the data fall within 2 standard deviations of the mean.

4.

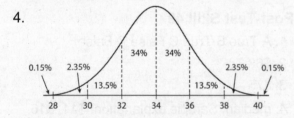

5. 81.5%. Add the percents for 30–32, 32–34, and 34–36: $13.5\% + 34\% + 34\% = 81.5\%$.

6. A True B False C True

Post-Test Skill 51

1. $\dfrac{2}{8} = \dfrac{1}{4}$

2. $\dfrac{5}{8}$

3. $\dfrac{11}{26}$

4. Yes, it is not possible to get one prize that is both medium and large.

5. $\dfrac{29}{37}$

6. 70%

7. 68%

8. 63%

9. 31–50 year olds or over 50

10. A No B Yes C No

Post-Test Skill 52

1. 15, 16, 17, 18, 19, 20

2. $\dfrac{3}{6} = \dfrac{1}{2}$

3. $\dfrac{2}{6} = \dfrac{1}{3}$

4. $\dfrac{2}{11}$

5. $\dfrac{4}{11}$

6. A $\dfrac{2}{30} = \dfrac{1}{15}$ B $\dfrac{8}{30} = \dfrac{4}{15}$ C $\dfrac{4}{30} = \dfrac{2}{15}$ D $\dfrac{16}{30} = \dfrac{8}{15}$

7. $\dfrac{3}{30} = \dfrac{1}{10}$

8. $\dfrac{6}{30} = \dfrac{1}{5}$

9. $\dfrac{8}{100} = 0.08 = 8\%$

10. $\dfrac{3}{60} = \dfrac{1}{20} = 0.05 = 5\%$

11. Because the percent probability of getting a leaky pen was lower after the machine adjustment was made, the company's improvement worked.

12. A Yes B No

Post-Test Skill 53

1. $3\sqrt{10}$

2. 4

3. No; The triangle is not a right triangle and the Pythagorean Theorem only applies to right triangles.

4. No; $16^2 + 30^2 \neq 31^2$

5. 72.2 miles

6. Sample answer: 3, $\sqrt{13}$

7. $\sqrt{3}$

Post-Test Skill 54

1.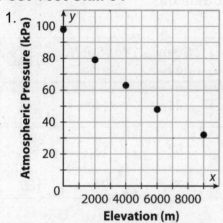

2. A False B True C True D False

3. As the number of years since investing increases, the account balance also increases, so there is a positive association. Because the data points do not lie basically along a straight line, the association is nonlinear.

4. Answers may vary. Sample: There is a cluster in the years of about 1850–1870 with ages from 60 to 75. There is a larger cluster in the years of about 1900–1950 with ages from about 53 to 90.

5. Answers may vary. Any two of the following data points: (1906, 11), (1912, 35), (1914, 37), (1938, 0), (1953, 0).

Post-Test Skill 55

1. A True B True C False D True

2. $\dfrac{12}{13}$

3. $\dfrac{12}{13}$

4. They are equal.

5. 8

6. approximately 35 ft

7. $\angle B$

8. 37°

Post-Test Skill 56

1. A False B False C True D True

2. The length of the hypotenuse is $\sqrt{2}$ times the length of a leg.

3. 24

4. $24\sqrt{2}$

5. A True B True C False D True

6. 8 mm

7. 18

8. $18\sqrt{3}$

Post-Test Skill 57

1. A Yes B No C No D Yes

2.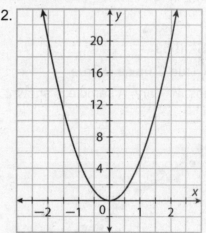

3. The graph of $g(x)$ is stretched away from the x-axis and is narrower than the graph of $f(x) = x^2$.

4. $c(x) = \dfrac{4}{3}x^2$, $b(x) = -1.25x^2$, $d(x) = 0.7x^2$,

$a(x) = -\dfrac{3}{5}x^2$

5.

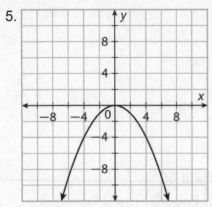

6. The graph of $g(x)$ is reflected across the x-axis. It is compressed to the x-axis and is wider than the graph of $f(x) = x^2$.

7. A True B False C True D False

Post-Test Skill 58

1. A False B True C False D False

2. 3

3. $\angle X$

4. They are reciprocals.

5. 5.0

6. about 238.2 in.

7. 42°

Post-Test Skill 59

1. A True B True C False D True

2. Trend lines will vary. A sample is shown.

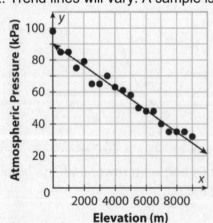

3. Equations will vary.
   Sample: $y = -0.0069x + 90$

4. about 175.36 lb

5. extrapolation because you are predicting a value outside the range of known data values

6. about 146.92 lb

7. interpolation because you are estimating a value between two known data values

8. No, because a person who is 100 inches tall would be 8 ft 4 in. tall, which is an unreasonable height for a person. So this trend line cannot be used to accurately predict the height or weight of someone who is beyond about 7 feet tall (84 inches).

Post-Test Skill 60

1.

	Seen Movie	Not Seen Movie	TOTAL
Read Book	21	14	35
Not Read Book	52	13	65
TOTAL	73	27	100

2. A True B False C False D True

3. $\frac{73}{100} = 0.73 = 73\%$

4. $\frac{21}{35} = 0.6 = 60\%$

5. Yes, there is an association. Students who have read the book are less likely to have seen the movie than the general population. The relative frequencies (from Questions 3 and 4) show that students who have read the book are less likely to have seen the movie than the general population of students polled in the survey.

6. $\frac{60}{96} = 0.625 = 62.5\%$

7. $\frac{26}{62} \approx 0.419 = 41.9\%$

8.

	Runs	Does Not Run	TOTAL
Male	0.30	0.18	0.48
Female	0.39	0.13	0.52
TOTAL	0.69	0.31	1.00

9. $\frac{78}{200} = 0.39 = 39\%$

10. $\frac{62}{200} = 0.31 = 31\%$

Answer Key

Reteach

Reteach 1-1

1. $(-\infty, -2]$

2. $(0, 3]$

3. $+\infty; +\infty$

4. $-\infty; -\infty$

Reteach 1-2

1. $(-\infty, +\infty)$

   0

   $(0, +\infty)$

   $(-\infty, 0)$

   $0; 0$

2. $(-\infty, +\infty)$

   $(-\infty, +\infty)$

Reteach 1-3

1. Graph shifts left 1 unit

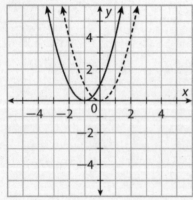

2. Graph shifts down 2 units

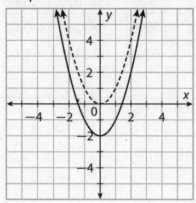

3. Graph shifts down 4 units

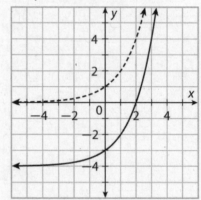

4. Graph shifts right 1 unit

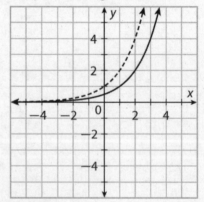

Reteach 1-4

1. $f^{-1}(x) = \dfrac{x - 5}{2}$

2. $f^{-1}(x) = -\dfrac{x - 8}{3}$

3.

Inverse Function	
x	**y**
5	1
2	2
−1	3

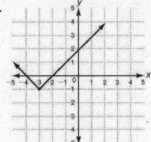

Reteach 2-1

1.

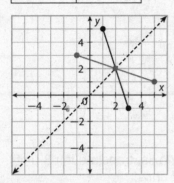

$(1, 2)$; all x; $y \geq 2$

2.

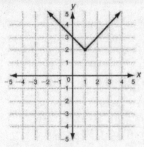

$(-3, -1)$; all x; $y \geq -1$

3.

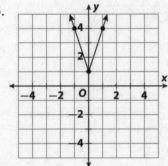

$(0, 1)$; all x; $y \geq 1$

Reteach 2-2

1. $x = -6$ or $x = 10$

2. $x = -15$ or $x = 1$

3. $x = 0$ or $x = 10$

4. $x = -3$ or $x = 3$

Reteach 2-3

1. $x > -4$ AND $x < 4$

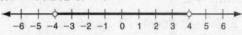

2. $x \geq -3$ AND $x \leq 5$

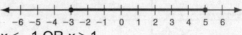

3. $x \leq -1$ OR $x \geq 1$

4. $x < -5$ OR $x > 1$

Reteach 3-1

1. $2i\sqrt{11}$

2. $\dfrac{i}{3}\sqrt{5}$

3. $\pm 2\sqrt{5}$

4. $\pm 4i\sqrt{3}$

Reteach 3-2

1. $-8 + 7i$

2. $-11 - 37i$

3. $16 + 4i$

4. $-68 + 128i$

5. $52 + 58i$

6. $-7 + 3i$

Reteach 3-3

1. $-\dfrac{3 \pm 3\sqrt{5}}{2}$

2. $\dfrac{7 \pm i\sqrt{71}}{6}$

3. $\dfrac{5 \pm \sqrt{57}}{4}$

4. $\dfrac{-2 \pm i}{5}$

Reteach 4-1

1. $r = \sqrt{5^2 + 12^2} = \sqrt{169} = 13;$
$(x-3)^2 + (y+7)^2 = 169$

2. $r = \sqrt{(10-4)^2 + (13-5)^2} = \sqrt{6^2 + 8^2}$
$= \sqrt{100} = 10; \ (x-4)^2 + (y-5)^2 = 100$

Reteach 4-2

1. $(2, 3);$ $-1;$ down; $(2, 2);$ $y = 4;$ $x = 2;$

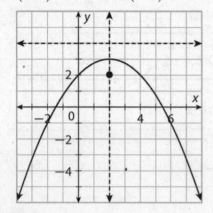

Reteach 4-3

1. $(2, -1), (5, 2)$

2. $(-2, -2)$

3. no solution

Reteach 4-4

1. $(3, 0, -5)$

2. $(1, -1, 2)$

Reteach 5-1

1. Vertical stretch by 3, reflection over *x*-axis, translate right 4, translate up 1;
$(-1, -1) \rightarrow (3, 4)$
$(0, 0) \rightarrow (4, 1)$
$(1, 1) \rightarrow (5, -2)$

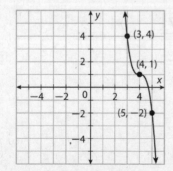

2. Vertical compression by $\frac{1}{2}$, translate right 2 units, translate down 4 units;
$(-1, -1) \rightarrow (0, -8)$
$(0, 0) \rightarrow (2, -4)$
$(1, 1) \rightarrow (4, 0)$

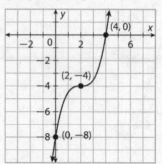

3. Reflect over *x*-axis, translate left 3 units, translate up 2 units;
$(-1, -1) \rightarrow (-4, 3)$
$(0, 0) \rightarrow (-3, 2)$
$(1, 1) \rightarrow (-2, 1)$

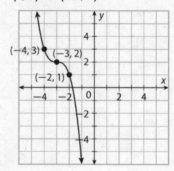

Reteach 5-2

1.

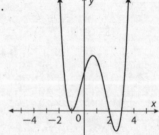

2.

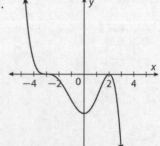

3.

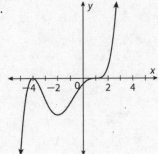

4.

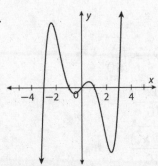

Reteach 6-1

1. $6x^4 + 10x^3 - x^2 + 3x - 11$
2. $4x^3 + 6x^2 - x - 13$
3. $4a^4 - 2a^3 - 9a^2 - 2a + 14$
4. $-3y + 7$
5. $-6x^4 - 4x^3 + 6x^2 - 2x - 9$
6. $3x^4 - x^3 + 4x^2 - 5x - 8$
7. $2c^4 - 5c^3 + c^2 + 7c - 17$
8. $3r^3 + 2r^2 + r$

Reteach 6-2

1. $-2x^3 - 15x^2 + 14x + 48$
2. $2x^3 - 13x^2 + 23x - 12$
3. $2x^3 - x^2 - 23x + 24$
4. $-12x^3 - x^2 + 38x - 5$

Reteach 6-3

1. $1 \cdot 8x^3 + 3 \cdot 4x^2y + 3 \cdot 2xy^2 + 1 \cdot y^3$;

   $8x^3 + 12x^2y + 6xy^2 + y^3$

2. ${}_4C_0x^4(3y)^0 + {}_4C_1x^3(3y)^1 + {}_4C_2x^2(3y)^2 +$
   ${}_4C_3x^1(3y)^3 + {}_4C_4x^0(3y)^4$;

   $1 \cdot x^4 + 4 \cdot (3x^3y) + 6 \cdot (9x^2y^2) + 4 \cdot$

   $(27xy^3) + 1 \cdot (81y^4)$;

   $x^4 + 12x^3y + 54x^2y^2 + 108xy^3 + 81y^4$

Reteach 6-4

1. $(3x + 1)(9x^2 - 3x + 1)$
2. $\left(m + \dfrac{1}{2}\right)\left(m^2 - \dfrac{1}{2}m + \dfrac{1}{4}\right)$
3. $(p + 6)(p^2 - 6p + 36)$
4. $(2x - 1)(4x^2 + 2x + 1)$
5. $(b - 10)(b^2 + 100b + 100)$
6. $(5t - 7)(25t^2 + 35t + 49)$

Reteach 6-5

1. Quotient: $3x^2 + 2x + 5$; Remainder: -6
2. Quotient: $-2x^2 + 2x + 6$; Remainder: 15
3. Quotient: $5x^2 - 14x + 49$; Remainder: -188
4. Quotient: $-2x^3 - 2x^2 - x + 11$; Remainder: 12

Reteach 7-1

1. Zeros: -4, $\dfrac{1}{2}$, and 3;

   $f(x) = (x + 4)(x - 3)(2x - 1)$

2. Zeros: -1, 2, and 10;

   $f(x) = (x + 1)(x - 2)(x - 10)$

3. Zeros: 0, -4, -1, and 6;

   $f(x) = x(x + 4)(x + 1)(x - 6)$

4. Zeros: -5, 1, and 2;

   $f(x) = (x + 5)(x - 1)(x - 2)$

Reteach 7-2

1. $1 + i$
2. $-1 - 3i$
3. $2i$
4. $x^4 - 5x^3 + 2x^2 + 22x - 20$
5. $x^4 - 2x^3 - 11x^2 - 8x - 60$

Reteach 8-1

1. $x = 5$; $y = -3$
2. $x = -3$; $y = -1$
3. $x = 4$; $y = 6$
4. $x = 0$; $y = 7$
5. $y = \dfrac{3}{x + 1} - 4$

6. $y = \dfrac{-1}{x-2} + 1$

Reteach 8-2

1. $x = 6$, $x = -2$; no holes; $(-6, 0)$; $\left(0, -\dfrac{1}{2}\right)$

2. $x = 2$; $x = -4$; $(-3, 0)$; $\left(0, -\dfrac{3}{2}\right)$

3. $x = 4$; no holes; $(1, 0)$, $(-1, 0)$; $\left(0, \dfrac{1}{4}\right)$

4. no vertical asymptotes; no holes; $(-2, 0)$; $(0, 1)$

Reteach 9-1

1. $\dfrac{x^2 + 6x - 13}{(x+2)(x-5)}$; $x \neq -2$, $x \neq 5$

2. $\dfrac{x^2 + 9x - 14}{x(x-2)}$; $x \neq 0$, $x \neq 2$

3. $\dfrac{12x - 14}{(x-3)(x-1)}$; $x \neq 1$, $x \neq 3$

4. $\dfrac{3x^2 - 15x - 4}{(x-5)(x+6)}$; $x \neq -6$, $x \neq 5$

5. $\dfrac{x^2 - 7x + 5}{(x+3)(x-3)}$; $x \neq -3$, $x \neq 3$

6. $\dfrac{7x + 13}{(x+3)(x+1)(x-2)}$; $x \neq -3$, $x \neq -1$, $x \neq 2$

Reteach 9-2

1. $\dfrac{(x-7)(x-5)}{x-4}$; $x \neq -4$, $x \neq -2$, $x \neq 4$

2. $\dfrac{x + 8}{(x-3)(x-1)}$; $x \neq 0$, $x \neq 1$, $x \neq 2$, $x \neq 3$

3. $\dfrac{(x-9)}{2(2x-1)(x+5)}$; $x \neq -5$, $x \neq 0$,

   $x \neq \dfrac{1}{2}$, $x \neq 5$

4. $\dfrac{(x-9)}{(x+4)(x-1)}$; $x \neq -4$, $x \neq -2$,

   $x \neq 4$, $x \neq 1$

5. $(x+1)(x-5)$; $x \neq -5$, $x \neq -1$

6. $\dfrac{(x-1)(2x+1)}{6}$; $x \neq 0$, $x \neq \dfrac{1}{2}$

Reteach 9-3

1. $x = 5$

2. $x = 3$, $x = -\dfrac{4}{3}$

3. $x = 1$, $x = -\dfrac{3}{2}$

4. $x = 0$, $x = 7$

Reteach 10-1

1. $\{x \mid x \geq 0\}$; $f^{-1}(x) = \sqrt{\dfrac{x}{10}}$;

   $f^{-1}(f(x)) = \sqrt{\dfrac{(10x^2)}{10}}$

   $= \sqrt{\dfrac{(\cancel{10}x^2)}{\cancel{10}}}$

   $= \sqrt{x^2}$

   $= x$

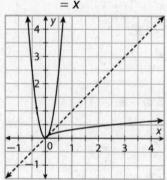

2. $\{x \mid x \geq 0\}$; $f^{-1}(x) = \sqrt{7x}$;

   $f^{-1}(f(x)) = \sqrt{7\left(\dfrac{x^2}{7}\right)}$

   $= \sqrt{\cancel{7}\left(\dfrac{x^2}{\cancel{7}}\right)}$

   $= \sqrt{x^2}$

   $= x$

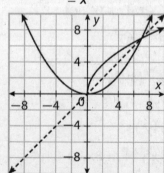

3. $\{x \mid x \geq -6\}$; $f^{-1}(x) = \sqrt{x+6}$;

$$f^{-1}(f(x)) = \sqrt{(x^2 - 6) + 6}$$
$$= \sqrt{x^2}$$
$$= x$$

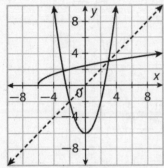

4. $\{x \mid x \geq 2\}$; $f^{-1}(x) = \sqrt{x-2}$;

$$f^{-1}(f(x)) = \sqrt{(x^2 + 2) - 2}$$
$$= \sqrt{x^2}$$
$$= x$$

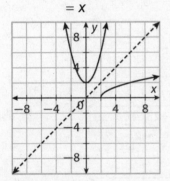

Reteach 10-2

1. Reflect across x-axis; horizontal shift right 5 units; vertical shift up 3 units

2. Horizontal shrink by $\dfrac{1}{2}$; horizontal shift left 4 units; vertical shift up 1 unit

3. Reflect across y-axis; horizontal stretch by 3; vertical shift down 6 units

4. Vertical compression by 0.4; horizontal shift left 8 units; vertical shift down 10 units

Reteach 10-3

1. $f(x) = 3\sqrt[3]{x+2} + 2$

2. $f(x) = \sqrt[3]{\dfrac{1}{2}(x+3)} - 2$

3. $f(x) = -2\sqrt[3]{x-1} - 2$

Reteach 11-1

1. 125

2. 9

3. −7776

4. 48.5

5. 3

6. 49

7. $\dfrac{1}{8}$

8. −32

Reteach 11-2

1. $243a^{\frac{5}{3}}$

2. $4b^{\frac{4}{5}}$

3. $9x^{\frac{1}{2}}$

4. $\dfrac{1}{x^6}$

5. $\dfrac{5}{y}$

6. $z^{\frac{1}{5}}$

Reteach 11-3

1. $x = 19$

2. $x = 1$

3. $x = 3$ ($x = -3$ is extraneous)

4. $x = 10$

5. $x = 1$ ($x = -4$ is extraneous)

6. $x = \dfrac{9}{5}$

Reteach 12-1

1. No

2. Yes; $d = -2$; $f(n) = 14 + (-2)(n - 1)$

3. No

4. $f(1) = -5$, $f(n) = f(n - 1) + 5$, for $n \geq 2$; $f(n) = -5 + 5(n - 1)$

5. $f(1) = 7$, $f(n) = f(n - 1) + (-3)$, for $n \geq 2$; $f(n) = 7 + (-3)(n - 1)$

6. $f(1) = 4$, $f(n) = f(n - 1) + 3$, for $n \geq 2$; $f(n) = 4 + 3(n - 1)$

7. 6, 9, 12

8. $16, 15\frac{1}{2}, 15$

9. 20, 10, 0

Reteach 12-2

1. $f(n) = 0.5 \cdot (3)^n$;

$f(n) = 3 \cdot f(n-1), n \geq 1, f(0) = 0.5$

2. $f(n) = 6 \cdot \left(\frac{1}{2}\right)^n$;

$f(n) = \frac{1}{2} \cdot f(n-1), n \geq 1, f(0) = 6$

3. $f(n) = \frac{1}{4} \cdot (4)^n$;

$f(n) = 4 \cdot f(n-1), n \geq 1, f(0) = \frac{1}{4}$

4. $f(n) = 162 \cdot \left(\frac{1}{9}\right)^n$;

$f(n) = \left(\frac{1}{9}\right) \cdot f(n-1), n \geq 1, f(0) = 162$

Reteach 12-3

1. 410

2. 4092

Reteach 13-1

1. Domain $\{x | -\infty < x < \infty\}$;

Range $\{y | y > 1\}$;

Reference points (1, 4) and (2, 13);

Asymptote $y = 1$;

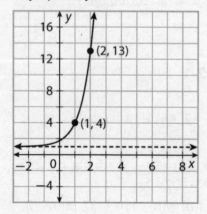

2. Domain $\{x | -\infty < x < \infty\}$;

Range $\{y | y > -2\}$;

Reference points $(3, -3.5)$ and $(4, -3)$;

Asymptote $y = -4$;

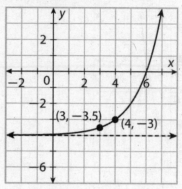

3. Domain $\{x | -\infty < x < \infty\}$;

Range $\{y | y > -5\}$;

Reference points $(-5, -4)$ and $(-4, 5)$;

Asymptote $y = -5$;

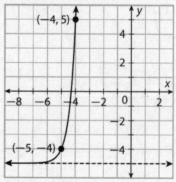

4. Domain $\{x | -\infty < x < \infty\}$;

Range $\{y | y > -5\}$;

Reference points (1, 3) and (2, 13);

Asymptote $y = -2$;

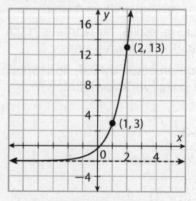

Reteach 13-2

1. $f(x) = \left(\dfrac{1}{2}\right)^x$; $b = \dfrac{1}{2}$; $y = -2$; $(3, 2)$, $(2, 6)$

2. $f(x) = \left(\dfrac{1}{10}\right)^x$; $b = \dfrac{1}{10}$; $y = 1$; $(-2, 8)$, $(-3, 71)$

3. $f(x) = 0.3^x$; $b = 0.3$; $y = -3$; $(-3, 3)$, $(-4, 17)$

4. $f(x) = \left(\dfrac{1}{4}\right)^x$; $b = \dfrac{1}{4}$; $y = -5$; $(6, -6)$, $(5, -9)$

5. $f(x) = \left(\dfrac{2}{3}\right)^x$; $b = \dfrac{2}{3}$; $y = 9$; $(0, 10)$, $(-1, 10.5)$

6. $f(x) = \left(\dfrac{3}{10}\right)^x$; $b = \dfrac{3}{10}$; $y = 7$; $(4, 5)$, $\left(3, \dfrac{1}{3}\right)$

Reteach 13-3

1. $g(x) = -2e^{x+1} - 3$

2. $g(x) = 3e^{x-9} + 4$

3. $g(x) = 0.5e^{x-2} - 0.1$

4. $g(x) = -e^{x+3} + 2$

Reteach 13-4

1. About 18.8 years
2. About 11.6 years

Reteach 14-1

1. $y = 1.2 \cdot 1.3^x$

2. $y = 56 \cdot 0.9^x$

3. $y = -20 \cdot 1.1^x$

4. $y = 3.0 \cdot 2.1^x$

5. $y = 100 \cdot 0.8^x$

6. $y = -5 \cdot 0.5^x$

Reteach 14-2

1. $f(x) = 0.598 \cdot 2.402^x$

2. $f(x) = 2.156x + 13.642$

3. $f(x) = 0.526x^2 - 7.803x + 81.341$

4. $f(x) = 203.67 \cdot 0.95^x$

Reteach 15-1

1. $\log_2 64 = 6$

2. $\log_4 \dfrac{1}{16} = -2$

3. $\log_{\frac{1}{3}} \dfrac{1}{27} = 3$

4. $7^2 = 49$

5. $2^{-4} = \dfrac{1}{16}$

6. $8^x = 48$

7. 4

8. $\dfrac{1}{3}$

9. -2

Reteach 15-2

1. $x = -2$; $(-1, -1)$, $(0, 4)$;

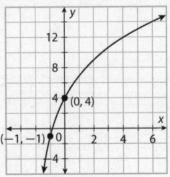

2. $x = -5$; $(-4, 2)$, $(5, 1)$;

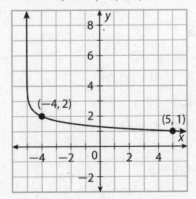

3. $x = 5$; $(5, -2)$, $(10, 1)$;

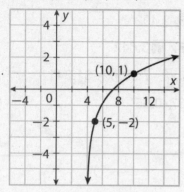

4. $x = -9$; $(-8, 3)$, $(-1, 1)$;

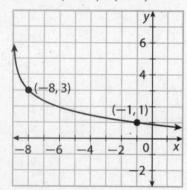

Reteach 16-1

1. $\log_2 16 = 4$

2. $\log xy = 2\log_8 24$

3. $\log_{\frac{1}{5}} \dfrac{1}{5} = 1$

4. $\log_8 576$

5. $\log_7 a$

6. $\log 10 = 1$

7. $x\log_6 6 = x$

8. $5\log_a a = 5$

9. $2\log x$

Reteach 16-2

1. $x = -2.5$; $4^{-(-2.5)} = 32$

2. $x \approx 1.024$; $3^{4(1.024)} \approx 90.01$

3. $\log 5^{x-3} = \log 600$

   $(x - 3)\log 5 = \log 600$

   $x \approx 6.975$

   $5^{6.975-3} \approx 600.352$

Reteach 17-1

1. $\dfrac{8\pi}{9}$ radians

2. $144°$

3. about 3.8 cm

4. about 11 inches

5. about 6.3 m

6. about 243.5 mm

Reteach 17-2

1. $\dfrac{\sqrt{3}}{2}$

2. $-\dfrac{1}{2}$

3. $-\dfrac{\sqrt{3}}{2}$

4. $-\dfrac{\sqrt{2}}{2}$

Reteach 17-3

1. $\sin\theta \approx 0.370$

2. $\cos\theta \approx -0.836$

3. $\sin\theta \approx -0.915$

4. $\cos\theta \approx 0.985$

Reteach 18-1

1. $y = 2\sin 4x$

2. $y = -\sin\dfrac{1}{2}x$

Reteach 18-2

1. $y = 2\tan\left(\dfrac{\pi}{4}x\right)$

2. $y = -\tan\left(\dfrac{1}{2}x\right)$

Reteach 18-3

1. possible solution:

$$f(x) = 0.5\sin\left[\dfrac{1}{2}\left(x + \dfrac{\pi}{2}\right)\right] - 1$$

2. possible solution:

$$f(x) = 4\sin\left[\dfrac{\pi}{2}(x - 1)\right] + 2$$

Reteach 18-4

1. $f(x) = 0.4\sin\left[1.7(x - 0.9)\right] + 2.1$

2. $f(x) = 24.9\sin\left[0.5(x - 4.8)\right] + 53.7$

Reteach 19-1

1.

Description of Subset	Set Notation	Number of Elements in Subset	Number of Elements in Universal Set
Multiples of 3	$A = \{3, 9, 15\}$	$n(A) = 3$	$n(U) = 7$
Multiples of 5	$B = \{5, 15\}$	$n(B) = 2$	$n(U) = 7$

2. $\dfrac{3}{7}$

3. $\dfrac{2}{7}$

4.

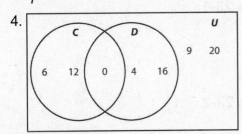

Reteach 19-2

1. a–d.
 | 8 | 7 | 6 | 5 |

   e. $8 \cdot 7 \cdot 6 \cdot 5 = 1680$

2. a. 120

   b. $\dfrac{1}{14}$

Reteach 19-3

1. permutation

2. combination

3. a. 990

   b. 6

   c. $\dfrac{990}{6} = 165$

4. a. $\dfrac{60}{6} = 10$

   b. $\dfrac{2}{33}$

Reteach 19-4

1. overlapping

2. mutually exclusive

3. mutually exclusive

4. overlapping

5. $\dfrac{1}{2}$

6. $\dfrac{2}{3}$

7. $\dfrac{4}{13}$

Reteach 20-1

1. a. 55

   b. 35

   c. about 64%

2. a. 45

   b. 25

   c. about 56%

Reteach 20-2

1. a. $\dfrac{2}{3}$

   b. $\dfrac{2}{3}$

   c. yes

2. a. $\dfrac{2}{3}$

   b. $\dfrac{4}{5}$

   c. $\dfrac{8}{15}$

   d. yes

3. $\dfrac{1}{5}$

Reteach 20-3

1. independent
2. dependent
3. a. $\dfrac{4}{52}$ or $\dfrac{1}{13}$

   b. $\dfrac{3}{51}$ or $\dfrac{1}{17}$

   c. $\dfrac{1}{221}$

Reteach 21-1

1. Possible answer: Assign numbers 1 through 5 to each of the friends/movies. Use randInt(1, 5) on the graphing calculator to choose a movie.

2. Possible answer: Assign numbers to each player for each dollar amount of candy sold. Those with more sales will have more numbers. Use randInt(1, total amount of money raised) on the graphing calculator to choose a player to win the prize.

3. Possible answer: Assign numbers to each student for each point earned throughout the week. Those with more points will have more numbers. Use randInt(1, total number of points) on the graphing calculator to choose a student to win the prize.

Reteach 21-2

1. 53%
2. 2.8%

Reteach 22-1

1. 151 tickets
2. 4.4 tickets
3. $\dfrac{11}{60} \approx 18\%$ of the audience were other community members, so the drama department did reach the goal.

Reteach 22-2

1. $\bar{x} \approx 84.9$; $s \approx 2.67$
   median $= 84.2$; IQR $= 5.2$
2. $\bar{x} \approx 0.55$; $s \approx 0.092$
   median $= 0.55$; IQR $= 0.2$

Reteach 23-1

1. 80%
2. 50%
3. 100%

Reteach 23-2

1. 68%
2. 97.5%
3. 95%
4. 99.7%

Reteach 23-3

1. 119 cm to 125 cm
2. 16%
3. 118.2 mL to 121.8 mL
4. 0.15%

Reteach 24-1

1. 0.28 to 0.44
2. 0.73 to 0.81
3. 0.0050 to 0.017

Reteach 24-2

1. Survey
2. Experiment
3. Observational Study
4. Survey
5. Observational Study

Reteach 24-3

1. The difference in mean crop yield between the old and new fertilizer is about 0.
2. 4 bushels/acre
3. 0.05
4. The result is significant. The null hypothesis is rejected. The new fertilizer does have an effect on crop yield.

Answer Key

Skills

Skill 1

1. $4\frac{3}{4}$

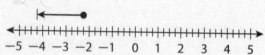

2. −3.75

3. $-4\frac{1}{4}$

4. $1\frac{3}{4}$

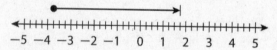

5. −2.5

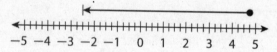

6. $\frac{3}{4}$ cups

7. −12

8. $2\frac{3}{4}$

9. $-\frac{2}{3}$

10. −21.4

11. $-35\frac{1}{4}$

12. $-1\frac{1}{2}$

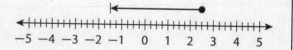

13. −2

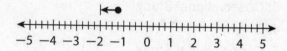

14. $-2\frac{1}{4}$

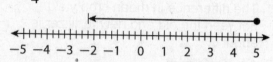

15. The starting point is at −0.75 instead of −1.25. $-1.25 - 2.5 = -3.75$.

16. −0.75

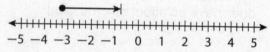

17. $3\frac{3}{4}$

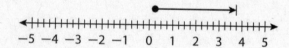

18. 15.24 cm

19. −11.1

20. $3\frac{3}{4}$

21. $-10\frac{1}{4}$

22. −5.35

23. 2.69 was grouped with the positive numbers instead of negative numbers when adding the opposite. The correct answer is −0.65.

Skill 2

1. Not like terms
2. Like terms
3. Like terms
4. Not like terms
5. Associative Property of Addition
6. Commutative Property of Addition
7. Commutative Property of Addition
8. Associative Property of Addition

9. $3x + 3$

10. $16y^2 - 2$

11. $15wz^2 - 2wz^3$

12. 0

13. $15a^3 + 12a^5 + 6$

14. $2x^2 - 12x - 32$

15. $-10b^4 - 10b - 10$

16. $16y^3 - y^2 + 2$

17. $10j^3 + 19j + 9$

18. $19k^5 + 6k^2 - 20$

19. $9m + 5$

20. $20n^3 + 16n^2 + 12n + 26$

21. $-18n^2 + 158n + 2275$

22. $9x^5 - 5x^2 + 5x$

23. $11y^2 + 9y - 11$

24. $25w^3 + 5w$

25. $7z^4 - 12z^3 + 12z^2$

26. In the polynomial being subtracted, only the first term, $11m^2$, was changed to its opposite; -4 should have been changed to $+4$. The correct answer is $-4m^2 + 9$.

Skill 3

1. 29

2. -28

3. 85

4. 4

5. 0

6. 13

7. $-11x$

8. $\dfrac{23}{6}s$

9. $-2x^2 + 2x - 4$

10. $3.5p^2 + 1.8$

11. $-\dfrac{3}{2}m^2n - \dfrac{11}{3}n^2$

12. $-13.5r^5s^2 + 6.8r^3s^2$

13. $18r - 44$

14. $x^2 + 3x - 11$

15. $-23s^2 + 10s - 2$

16. $\dfrac{11}{3}x^2 - \dfrac{17}{3}x - 8$

17. $8a^3b - a^2b$

18. $x^3y^2 - 2x^2$

19. $x + 8$

20. $12 - y$

21. $3(t - 4)$

22. $\dfrac{m - n}{m + n}$

23. $\dfrac{y^2 + 5}{7}$

24. $(t + 8)(s^3 - 2)$

25. like terms were not correctly combined: all coefficients and exponents were added. The correct answer is $a^5b^3 + a^2b$.

Skill 4

1. Points on transformation: $(-4, 2)$, $(-2, 0)$, and $(2, -4)$.

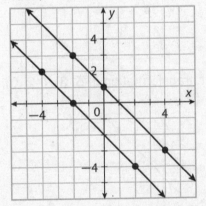

2. Points on transformation: $(-5, -1)$, $(-3, 1)$, and $(1, 5)$.

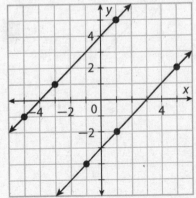

3. Points on transformation: (−2, 1), (2, −1), and (4, −2).

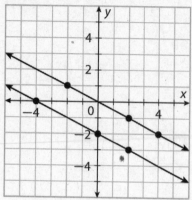

4. Points on transformation: (−5, −2), (−4, 0), and (−1, 6).

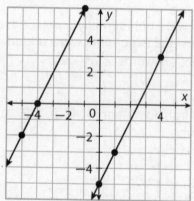

5. Points on transformation: (−5, 3), (−2, 0), and (3, −5).

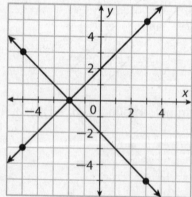

6. Points on transformation: (1, −4), (−1, 2), and (−2, 5).

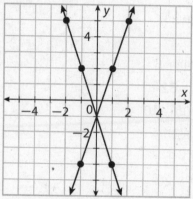

7. Error: the points were reflected across the y-axis instead of the x-axis; Corrected points on transformation: (−3, 5), (−1, 3), and (3, −1);

Corrected graph:

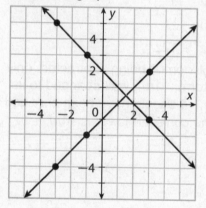

8. Points on transformation: (−4, 20), (−1, −10), and (1, −30).

9. Points on transformation: (−8, 4), (−2, −2), and (2, −6).

10. Points on transformation: (−3, −1), $\left(0, \dfrac{1}{2}\right)$, and (3, 2).

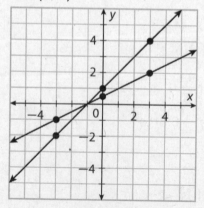

11. Points on transformation: $(-1, -2)$, $(0, 1)$ and $(1, 4)$.

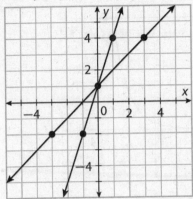

12. The incorrect points include a reflection about the x-axis. The correct points on the transformation are: $(-2, -6)$, $(2, -2)$, $(6, 2)$.

Skill 5

1. Not like terms
2. Like terms
3. Not like terms
4. Like terms
5. 8
6. 3
7. 9
8. 0
9. $2x^5 + x^4 + 20x^3$; 2
10. $17x^2 - 17x + 16$; 17
11. $-2x^4 - x - 5$; -2
12. $2y^4 + 7y^3 - 4y^2 + 3$; 2
13. Trinomial
14. Monomial
15. Binomial
16. Polynomial
17. Answers will vary. Possible answer: $x^4 + 2x^3 + x$
18. The polynomial was incorrectly classified as a binomial because its degree is 2. However, the polynomial should be classified as a trinomial because it has 3 terms.

Skill 6

1. This equation represents a direct variation because it can be written in the form $y = kx$. The constant of variation is $-\dfrac{1}{3}$.
2. This equation does not represent a direct variation because it cannot be written in the form $y = kx$.
3. This equation represents a direct variation because it can be written in the form $y = kx$. The constant of variation is $\dfrac{3}{4}$.
4. This equation does not represent a direct variation because it cannot be written in the form $y = kx$.
5. This is a direct variation because it can be written as $y = kx$, where $k = 3$.
6. This is not a direct variation because it cannot be written as $y = kx$.
7. This is a direct variation because it can be written as $y = kx$, where $k = 5$.
8. This is a direct variation because it can be written as $y = kx$, where $k = \dfrac{1}{3}$.
9. This is not a direct variation because it cannot be written as $y = kx$.
10. This is a direct variation because it can be written as $y = kx$, where $k = 1.5$.
11. $y = 2x$; When $x = 10$, $y = 20$.
12. $y = -8x$; When $x = 5$, $y = -40$.
13. $y = -\dfrac{1}{6}x$; When $x = 24$, $y = -4$.
14. $y = \dfrac{3}{5}x$; When $x = -15$, $y = -9$.
15. $y = 21.5x$; When $x = 8$, $y = 172$: it would cost \$172 to buy 8 tickets.
16. $y = 3.5x$; When $x = 10$, $y = 35$: the delivery service could deliver 35 packages in 10 hours.
17. $y = 7x$; When $x = 7$, $y = 49$: a 7-year-old dog is considered 49 years old in human years.

18. When solving for k, the x- and y-values were incorrectly switched:

$y = kx$

$15 = k(6)$ Incorrect.

$k = 2.5$

The correct way to solve for k is:

$y = kx$

$6 = k(15)$

$k = 0.4$

So, the equation is $y = 0.4x$. When $x = 35$, $y = 0.4(35) = 14$.

Skill 7

1. $x = 3$

2. $x = 2$

3. $x = \dfrac{11}{15}$

4. $x = 2$

5. You need to apply the Power to a Power Property on the right side of the equation between steps 2 and 3 of the solution. The correct solution is:

$15^{-x} = 225^{2x+1}$

$15^{-x} = \left(15^2\right)^{2x+1}$

$-x = 4x + 2$

$-5x = 2$

$x = -\dfrac{2}{5}$

6. $x \approx 2.32$

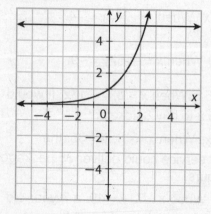

7. $x \approx 2.77$

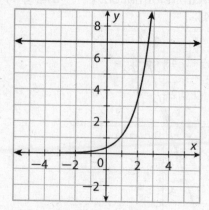

8. $x \approx 18.39$

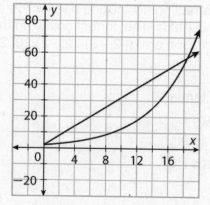

9. $x \approx 15.08$

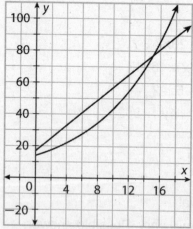

10. $x \approx 32.92$, so Company B will have more employees than Company A after 33 months.

11. $x \approx 9.35$, so North town will have more residents than Middleburg after 10 years.

12. At 3 years, Job B offers a higher monthly salary. At 4 years, Job A offers a higher monthly salary.

Skill 8

1. 54

2. 128

3. −50,000

4. 427.15

5. About 638 deer

6. $y = 3(3)^x$

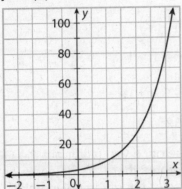

7. $y = \frac{1}{2}(4)^x$

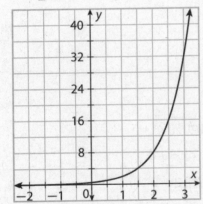

8. $y = 6\left(\frac{1}{3}\right)^x$

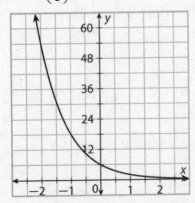

9. $y = 220,000(1.02)^t$; The value of the home in 15 years will be about $296,091.03.

10. The growth factor should be 1.04, instead of 1.4, because the growth rate is 4%, or 0.04. The correct function is $y = 8500(1.04)^t$. The cost of tuition in 8 years will be about $11,632.84 per year.

11. $y = 128(1 - 0.5)^t$; One team will remain in the tournament at the end of 7 rounds.

12. $y = 18,000(1 - 0.08)^t$; The value of the car in 10 years will be about $7818.99.

Skill 9

1. 1

2. 1

3. 1

4. $\frac{1}{3^5} = \frac{1}{243}$

5. $\frac{1}{6^4} = \frac{1}{1296}$

6. $\frac{1}{(-8)^3} = -\frac{1}{512}$

7. $4^8 = 65,536$

8. $5^7 = 78,125$

9. $(-3)^5 = -243$

10. $12^4 = 20,736$

11. $10^8 = 100,000,000$

12. $6^2 = 36$

13. $8^3 \cdot 5^3 = 512 \cdot 125 = 64,000$

14. $(-4)^2(10)^2 = 16(100) = 1600$

15. $(-2)^{-3}(7)^{-3} = \frac{1}{(-2)^3} \cdot \frac{1}{7^3} =$ $-\frac{1}{8}\left(\frac{1}{343}\right) = -\frac{1}{2744}$

16. $\frac{9^2}{5^2} = \frac{81}{25}$

17. $\frac{4^3}{11^3} = \frac{64}{1331}$

18. $\frac{(-3)^4}{10^4} = \frac{81}{10,000}$

19. $11^8 = 214,358,881$

20. $3^{15} = 14,348,907$

21. $12^{-2} = \dfrac{1}{12^2} = \dfrac{1}{144}$

22. Because a power is raised to a power, the exponents should be multiplied, not added: $\left(7^4\right)^5 = 7^{4(5)} = 7^{20}$.

23. Possible answers: $\left(5^1\right)^{12}$, $\left(5^2\right)^6$, $\left(5^3\right)^4$.

24. 9

25. 13

26. 2

27. –1

28. 10

29. 4

30. 2

31. 11

32. 3

33. 0

34. 4

35. 0

36. 8

37. 9

38. 16

39. 27

40. 26

41. 19

Skill 10

1. $12y^5$

2. m^3

3. $-4b^2$

4. 1

5. $4x^2\left(x^3 + 6\right)$

6. $6x\left(x^2 - 7\right)$

7. $9y^2\left(y^3 + 3y - 2\right)$

8. $-11z^2\left(z^4 + 2z - 11\right)$

9. $\left(x + 6\right)\left(7 - 9x\right)$

10. $\left(m^3 + 2\right)\left(-m + 1\right)$

11. $(y + 1)(3y - 5)$

12. Not factorable

13. When the GCF was factored out of the polynomial, the other factor was written incorrectly. The correct factorization is $(w - 3)(4w - 5)$.

14. $\left(x^2 + 5\right)\left(3x^3 + 2\right)$

15. $(x + 7)\left(2x^2 + 1\right)$

16. $\left(4x^5 - 3\right)\left(2x^2 + 1\right)$

17. $\left(x^4 - 3\right)\left(-5x^2 + 2\right)$

18. No, because once you factor out the GCF from each group, there are no common factors to factor out of the polynomial.

Skill 11

1. $(d + 5)^2$

2. $(f - 9)^2$

3. $(4x + 3)^2$

4. $(5g - 2)^2$

5. $(m + 12)(m - 12)$

6. $(2y + 11)(2y - 11)$

7. $\left(3m^3 - 9n\right)\left(3m^3 + 9n\right)$

8. $(5x + 8y)(5x - 8y)$

9. In $4c^2 - 36$, $a = 2c$, not $4c$. So $4c^2 - 36 = (2c + 6)(2c - 6)$.

Skill 12

1. $(x + 4)(x + 1)$

2. $(x - 3)(x + 6)$

3. $(x + 2)(x - 7)$

4. $(x - 5)(x - 11)$

5. $(x + 12)\ m$

6. $(2x + 1)(x + 3)$

7. $(3x - 2)(x + 4)$

8. $(3x - 1)(2x - 5)$

9. $(5x + 1)(3x - 7)$

10. The factors are correct, but the signs are reversed. The correct answer is $(7x - 2)(x + 6)$.

Skill 13

1. $r = 2$

2. $r = \dfrac{1}{2}$

3. $r = 3$

4. $r = \dfrac{1}{3}$

5. recursive: $a_1 = 4$, $a_n = 4 \cdot a_{n-1}$; explicit: $a_n = 4 \cdot 4^{n-1}$

6. recursive: $a_1 = -1$, $a_n = 3 \cdot a_{n-1}$; explicit: $a_n = -3^{n-1}$

7. recursive: $a_1 = 0.25$, $a_n = 4 \cdot a_{n-1}$; explicit: $a_n = 0.25 \cdot 4^{n-1}$

8. recursive: $a_1 = 5$, $a_n = \dfrac{2}{3} \cdot a_{n-1}$; explicit: $a_n = 5 \cdot \left(\dfrac{2}{3}\right)^{n-1}$

9. a. $r = \dfrac{1}{2}$

   b. $a_1 = 48$, $a_n = \dfrac{1}{2} \cdot a_{n-1}$

   c. $a_n = 48 \cdot \left(\dfrac{1}{2}\right)^{n-1}$

10. The common ratio was found for terms moving right to left instead of left to right. The common ratio should be $\dfrac{1}{3}$, not 3.

    The correct rules are: Recursive: $a_1 = 108$, $a_n = \dfrac{1}{3} \cdot a_{n-1}$; Explicit: $a_n = 108 \cdot \left(\dfrac{1}{3}\right)^{n-1}$

11. $a_n = 3 \cdot 2^{n-1}$

12. $a_n = -3 \cdot 2^{n-1}$

13. $a_n = 125 \cdot \left(\dfrac{1}{5}\right)^{n-1}$

14. $a_n = -4 \cdot 5^{n-1}$

15. a. $a_n = 25 \cdot 20^{n-1}$

    b. 80,000,000

    c. Level 8: 32,000,000,000

Skill 14

1.

x	−4	−2	0	2	4
y	−4	−3	−2	−1	0

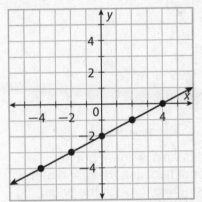

The relationship is linear but not proportional because the graph of the line does not go through the origin.

2.

x	−3	−1	2	3	5
y	4.5	2.5	−0.5	−1.5	−3.5

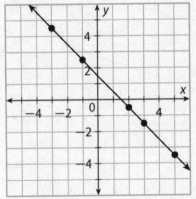

The relationship is linear but not proportional because the graph of the line does not go through the origin.

3. a.

Time (hrs)	0	1	2	3	4
Total Earnings ($)	50	65	80	95	110

b.

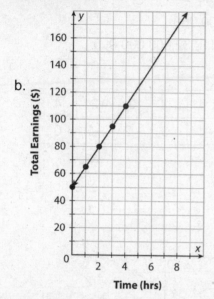

c. The relationship is linear but not proportional because the graph of the line does not go through the origin.

4. slope: $-\dfrac{1}{4}$; y-intercept: (0, 9)

5. slope: −52; y-intercept: (0, 19)

6.

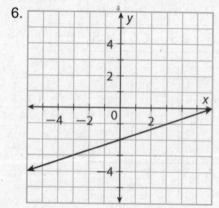

7.

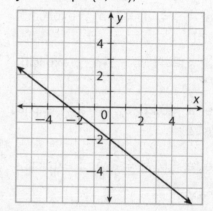

8. The slope and y-intercept were switched. The correct solution is slope: $-\dfrac{3}{4}$; y-intercept: (0, −2);

Skill 15

1. $\dfrac{20}{4}=5$, $\dfrac{40}{8}=5$, $\dfrac{50}{10}=5$, $\dfrac{60}{12}=5$, $y=5x$

2. $\dfrac{4.5}{3}=1.5$, $\dfrac{9}{6}=1.5$, $\dfrac{13.5}{9}=1.5$, $\dfrac{18}{12}=1.5$, $y=1.5x$

3. Jonah did not find $\dfrac{y}{x}$ for each ordered pair. If he had, he would have noticed that the ratio is not the same for each ordered pair: $\dfrac{5}{2}\neq\dfrac{7}{3}$. Therefore, the relationship between x and y is not proportional.

4. $y=9x$, where x is time and y is earnings.

5. $y=4x$, where x is side length and y is perimeter.

6. slope $=\dfrac{1}{3}$, y-intercept $=2$

7. slope $=-2$, y-intercept $=-1$

8. $\dfrac{76-49}{6-3}=\dfrac{27}{3}=9,\quad \dfrac{103-76}{9-6}=\dfrac{27}{3}=9,$

$\dfrac{130-103}{12-9}=\dfrac{27}{3}=9;$ rate of change $=9,$

initial value $=22$

9. $\dfrac{36-60}{3-1}=\dfrac{-24}{2}=-12,$

$\dfrac{12-36}{5-3}=\dfrac{-24}{2}=-12,\quad \dfrac{0-12}{6-5}=\dfrac{-12}{1}=-12;$

rate of change $=-12,$ initial value $=72$

Skill 16

1.

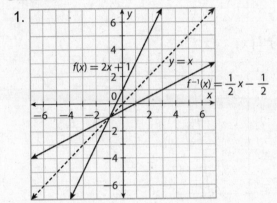

$$f^{-1}(x)=\dfrac{1}{2}x-\dfrac{1}{2}$$

2.

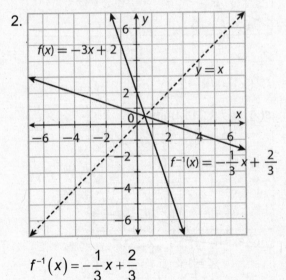

$$f^{-1}(x)=-\dfrac{1}{3}x+\dfrac{2}{3}$$

3.

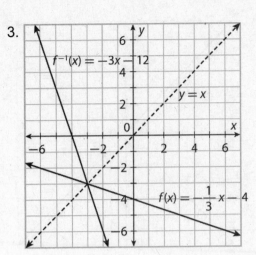

$$f^{-1}(x)=-3x-12$$

4.

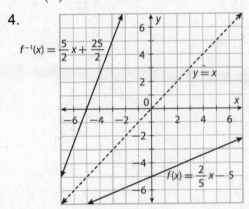

$$f^{-1}(x)=\dfrac{5}{2}x+\dfrac{25}{2}$$

5.

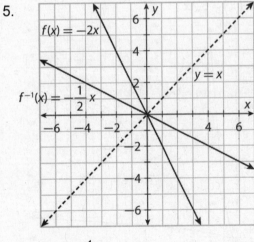

$$f^{-1}(x)=-\dfrac{1}{2}x$$

6.

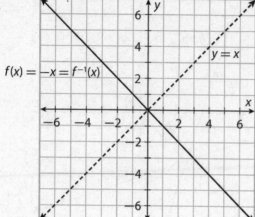

$$f(x) = -x = f^{-1}(x)$$

$y = x$

$$f^{-1}(x) = -x$$

7.

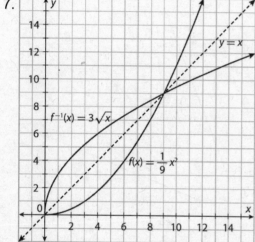

$y = x$

$$f^{-1}(x) = 3\sqrt{x}$$

$$f(x) = \frac{1}{9}x^2$$

$$f^{-1}(x) = 3\sqrt{x}$$

8.

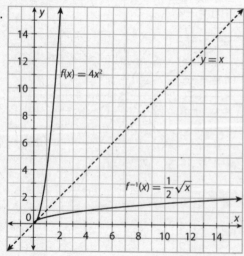

$y = x$

$$f(x) = 4x^2$$

$$f^{-1}(x) = \frac{1}{2}\sqrt{x}$$

$$f^{-1}(x) = \frac{1}{2}\sqrt{x}$$

9.

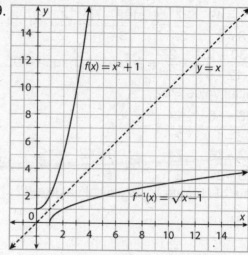

$$f(x) = x^2 + 1$$

$y = x$

$$f^{-1}(x) = \sqrt{x-1}$$

$$f^{-1}(x) = \sqrt{x-1}$$

10.

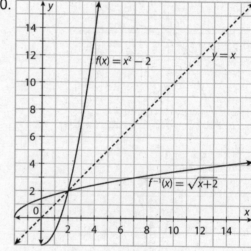

$$f(x) = x^2 - 2$$

$y = x$

$$f^{-1}(x) = \sqrt{x+2}$$

$$f^{-1}(x) = \sqrt{x+2}$$

11. $s(A) = \sqrt{A}$; 11 units

12.

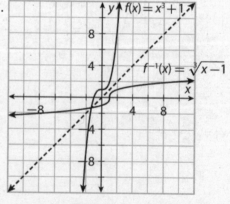

$$f(x) = x^3 + 1$$

$$f^{-1}(x) = \sqrt[3]{x-1}$$

$$f^{-1}(x) = \sqrt[3]{x-1}$$

13.

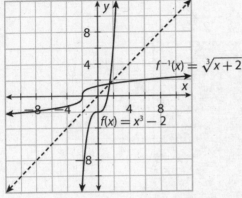

$f^{-1}(x) = \sqrt[3]{x+2}$

$f^{-1}(x) = \sqrt[3]{x+2}$

14. The square root of 64 is given, instead of the cube root of 64. The actual inverse function is $f^{-1}(x) = 4\sqrt[3]{x}$.

Skill 17

1. $y = \dfrac{52}{x}$

2. $y = \dfrac{39}{x}$

3. $y = \dfrac{51}{x}$

4. $y = \dfrac{75}{x}$

5. The constant of variation was found for a direct variation, not for an inverse variation. The inverse variation equation should be $y = \dfrac{108}{x}$.

6. 75 workers

7. 3 hours

8.

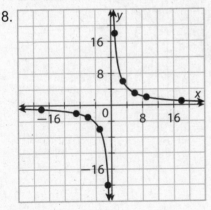

9.

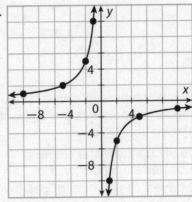

10. inversely

11. directly

Skill 18

1. Yes; It is a graph of a non-vertical line.

2. No; The line is vertical, so it does not represent a linear function.

3. No; It is not a linear function because x is in the denominator.

4. Yes; It is a linear function in slope-intercept form with $m = -\dfrac{1}{4}$ and $b = 9$.

5. Yes; It is a linear function in standard form with $A = 8$, $B = -5$, and $C = -1$.

6. No; It is not a linear function because the exponent on y is not 1.

7. $y = 13x + 4$

8. $y = -\dfrac{7}{2}x + 17$

9. $y = 11x - 12$

10. $y = 3x - \dfrac{1}{4}$

11. Susan switched the slope and y-intercept in the equation. The correct equation is $y = 16x - \dfrac{5}{3}$.

12. $y = x + 6$

13. $y = -9x - 3$

14. $y = \dfrac{1}{2}x - 10$

15. $y = -0.5x + 8$

16. $y = -\dfrac{2}{3}x + 2$

17. $y = \dfrac{5}{2}x - 3$

18. a. The variable x represents time in hours. The variable y represents the amount of gas in the truck at time x.

   b. The rate of change is the slope, $m = -3.5$. For each hour, x, that Juanita drives, the amount of gas in her tank goes down by 3.5 gallons.

   c. The relationship between time, x, and the amount of gas, y, is nonproportional because $b = 16 \neq 0$.

Skill 19

1. $y < \dfrac{3}{4}x + 4$;

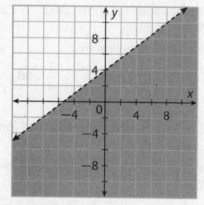

2. $y > \dfrac{1}{2}x + 5$;

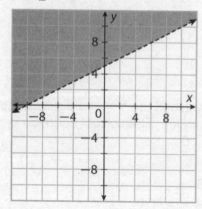

3. $y \leq -\dfrac{5}{2}x - 3$;

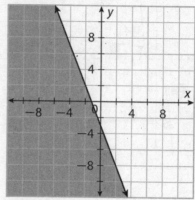

4. $y \geq -\dfrac{1}{3}x + 2$;

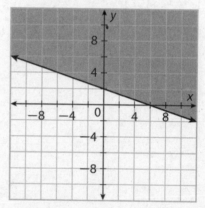

5. She forgot to switch the inequality when dividing by -27; The correct solution is $y \geq \dfrac{2}{3}x - 1$;

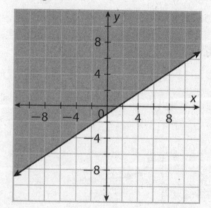

6. a. $2x + 1.5y \le 15$; $y \le -\dfrac{4}{3}x + 10$

b.
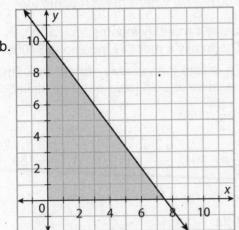

c. Possible answer: Two different combinations are: 0 mangoes and 10 avocados and 2 mangoes and 2 avocados.

7. a. $7.5x + 12.5y \ge 100$; $y \ge -\dfrac{3}{5}x + 8$

b.
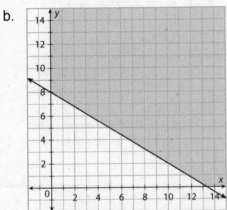

c. Possible answer: Two different combinations are: 0 bracelets and 8 necklaces and 10 bracelets and 4 necklaces.

Skill 20

1. $n = 1$
2. $x = -7$
3. $y = -1$
4. $n = 4$
5. $p = -5$
6. $x = 10$
7. $y = -5$
8. $a = -2$

9. In the second step, he did not distribute -8 correctly: the left side of the equation should be $64x + 48$. The correct solution is $x = -1$.
10. no solution
11. all real numbers
12. all real numbers
13. no solution
14. $110 + 25m = 38.75m$; $m = 8$ months

Skill 21

1. -1.5
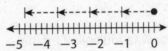

2. -4.8

3. $-\dfrac{30}{7}$

4. -10

5. -13.6

6. -22.5

7. 4.5

8. 5.6

9. $\dfrac{15}{4}$

10. $\dfrac{20}{3}$

11. 4.5

12. 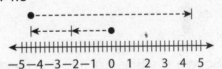 $-5\left(-\dfrac{7}{8}\right)$ is greater. The product $-5\left(-\dfrac{7}{8}\right)$ is positive because a negative times a negative is a positive. The product $-8\left(\dfrac{2}{7}\right)$ is negative because a negative times a positive is negative. A positive value is always greater than a negative value.

13. $\dfrac{21}{100}$

14. $\dfrac{308}{864}$, or $\dfrac{77}{216}$

15. -0.6

16. 1.1

17. -8

18. -4

19. $-\dfrac{42}{35}$, or $-\dfrac{6}{5}$

20. $\dfrac{3}{2}$

21. The numerator was multiplied by the denominator instead of being divided by the denominator. The correct solution is $-\dfrac{20}{15}$, or $-\dfrac{4}{3}$.

Skill 22

1. $18x^2 - 30x + 12$

2. $3p^4 + 27p^2 - 30$

3. $8b^5 - 20b^4 + 36b^3 + 8b^2$

4. $25y^2 + 90y + 81$

5. $b^2 - 144$

6. $36n^4 - 1$

7. The Square of a Binomial rule was used incorrectly: the middle term is incorrect. The correct simplification is $d^2 - 18d + 81$.

8. $(a+b)^2 = (a+b)(a+b)$
$= a(a) + a(b) + b(a) + b(b)$
$= a^2 + ab + ab + b^2$
$= a^2 + 2ab + b^2$

Skill 23

1. -18.4

2. $9\dfrac{3}{5}$

3. -62.5

4. -52

5. $\dfrac{3}{2}$

6. 32

7. $600 = \dfrac{2}{3}m$, where m represents the family's monthly income; $m = 4000$. The family's monthly income is $4000.

8. To isolate the variable, each side of the equation should have been multiplied by $\dfrac{3}{2}$, not 3.

$\dfrac{2}{3}p = 104;\ \dfrac{3}{2}\left(\dfrac{2}{3}p\right) = \dfrac{3}{2}(104);\ p = 156$

So the book has 156 pages.

Skill 24

1. $p \geq -1$

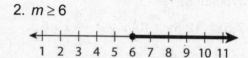

2. $m \geq 6$

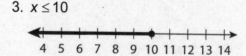

3. $x \leq 10$

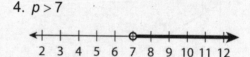

4. $p > 7$

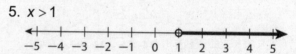

5. $x > 1$

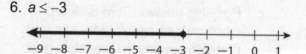

6. $a \leq -3$

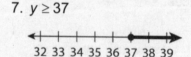

7. $y \geq 37$

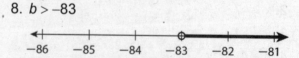

8. $b > -83$

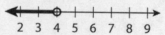

9. Ellen solved by multiplying both sides by -1 rather than adding 1 to both sides. The correct solution is $x < 4$;

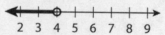

10. a. $65 + c \leq 150$

b. $c \leq 85$; She can spend up to $85 on a coat.

c. She could spend up to $105 on a coat.

11. a. $-3t \geq -45$

b. $t \leq 15$; She can change the temperature for 15 or fewer hours.

c. She could change the temperature for 9 or fewer hours.

12. a. $25w \leq 1700$

b. $w \leq 68$; Each passenger can check up to 68 pounds of luggage.

Skill 25

1.
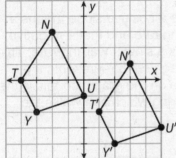

2.
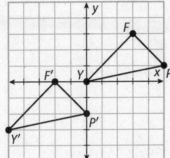

3.
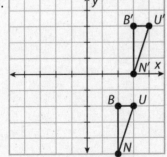

4.
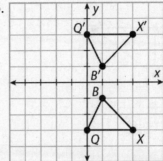

5.
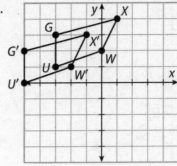

6.
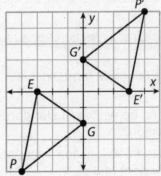

7.
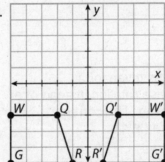

8.
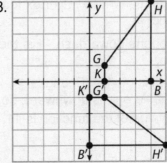

9.

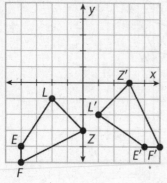

10.

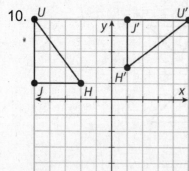

11. (−2, −3)

12. (−2, −5)

13. The answer was given for a counterclockwise rotation instead of a clockwise rotation. The correct coordinates are (3, 1).

Skill 26

1. This function is in standard form, so it is quadratic.

2. This is not a quadratic function because $a = 0$.

3. This function is in vertex form, so it is quadratic.

4. This function can be written in standard form, so it is quadratic.

5. This is not a quadratic function because there is an exponent of 3 on x.

6. This function can be written in vertex form, so it is quadratic.

7. The parabola opens upward, so −1 is the minimum value.

8. The vertex (h, k) is (4, 11). Because $a < 0$, the parabola opens downward, so the maximum value of the function is 11.

9. no zeros

10. 0 and 4

11. 2

12. $x = -3$

13. $x = 0$

14. $x = 10$

15. Since the vertex form of an equation is $y = a(x - h)^2 + k$, the x-value of the vertex would be −5, not 5, for the quadratic function $y = 2(x + 5)^2 - 11$. The correct solution is $x = -5$.

Skill 27

1. variable

2. constant: 3

3. constant: 4.5

4. variable

5. constant: −5

6. $\dfrac{3}{5}$

7. 2

8. Segment 5

9. Segments 1 and 4

10. Segment 3

11. Jamal thinks a positive slope means a faster walking rate and that a negative slope means a slower walking rate. This is incorrect. Segment 5 represents the steepest line on the graph, so this is the segment during which Mia walks the fastest.

Skill 28

1. 1

2. 1

3. 1

4. $\dfrac{1}{4}$

5. $\dfrac{1}{81}$

6. −1

7. 5^6, or 15,625

8. 2^3, or 8

9. $(-6)^3$, or −216

10. 9^4, or 6561

11. 8^{14}

12. 7^6, or 117,649

13. 30^5, or 24,300,000

14. 2025

15. $\dfrac{1}{(-24)^4}$, or $\dfrac{1}{331,776}$

16. $\dfrac{9}{49}$

17. $\dfrac{125}{1728}$

18. $\dfrac{625}{4096}$

19. 12^6, or 2,985,984

20. 64

21. $\dfrac{1}{169}$

22. 4

23. 12

24. 3

25. −5

26. 2

27. 3

28. −1

29. 11

30. 4

31. 0

32. 11

33. −2

34. 64

35. 16

36. 81

37. 125

38. 101

39. 22

40. 16 written as a power of 4 is 2^4, not 4^4. The correct solution is 8.

41. 9 units

42. 6 units

Skill 29

1. $4\dfrac{5}{12}$ mi

2. 48.9 feet below the surface, which can be represented with the rational number −48.9

3. −5.5°C

4. $22\dfrac{3}{8}$ in.

5. −100 ft

6. The change in the amount of birdseed in the bag per day should have been represented with the rational number $-2\dfrac{2}{3}$. The overall change is actually −80 cups.

7. $-10\dfrac{3}{4}$ gal

8. −7 ft/second

Skill 30

1. 0.12

2. $0.\overline{57}$

3. 1.4

4. $\dfrac{33}{40}$

5. $\dfrac{5}{6}$

6. $\dfrac{37}{99}$

7. $2 < \sqrt{6} < 3$

8. $3 < \sqrt{30} < 4$

9. $11 < \sqrt{133} < 12$

10. $\sqrt{6} \approx 2.449$

11. $\sqrt{13} \approx 3.606$

12. $\sqrt{133} \approx 11.533$

13. $\dfrac{12}{5}$, $2.\overline{41}$, $\sqrt{2}+1$

14. $\sqrt{83}$, 3π, $\dfrac{29}{3}$

15. $-4\dfrac{1}{2}$, π, $-\sqrt{5}$

16. He wrote the set in order of least to greatest instead of greatest to least.

Since $\frac{116}{11} = 10.\overline{54}$ and $\sqrt{116} \approx 10.8$,

the correct solution is $\sqrt{116}$, $\frac{116}{11}$, $10.\overline{45}$.

17. a. $\sqrt{155} \approx 12.45$; $4\pi \approx 12.57$

b. $12.\overline{6}$, 12.63, 4π, $\sqrt{155}$

Skill 31

1.

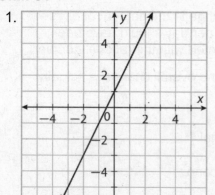

Yes, it is a linear function because the graph is a non-vertical line.

2. x-intercept: −3
   y-intercept: 1

3. x-intercept: −2
   y-intercept: −3

4. x-intercept: $\frac{1}{2}$
   y-intercept: 10

5. x-intercept: 0
   y-intercept: 0

6.

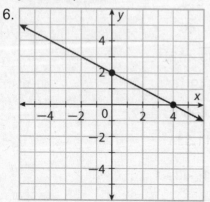

7.

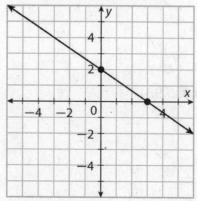

8. The intercepts are reversed.

9. The rate of change is −22.5 miles per gallon.

10. The rate of change is 4.5 inches per year.

11. $\frac{1}{3}$

12. $-1\frac{1}{2}$

13. Slope: 2; y-intercept: $-\frac{1}{2}$

14. Slope: $\frac{5}{8}$; y-intercept: −7

15. Slope: $-\frac{3}{2}$; y-intercept: 4

16. $y = -2x - 5$

17. $y = \frac{3}{8}x + 5$

18. $y = \frac{1}{3}x + 1$

19. $y = \frac{4}{3}x + 1$

20. $y = 150x + 50$

Skill 32

1. $x = -2, 6$

2. $x = -20, 2$

3. $x = -12, 1$

4. $x = \dfrac{9 \pm \sqrt{13}}{2}$

5. a. $x^2 + 2x = 224$

   b. length: 16 m; width 14 m

6. $x = -\dfrac{2}{5}, 1$

7. $x = -3, -1$

8. $x = -1, \dfrac{3}{4}$

9. $x = -\dfrac{11}{3}, \dfrac{5}{3}$

10. a. $t = \dfrac{1}{4}\left(5 \pm \sqrt{133}\right)$

    b. $t \approx 4.13$ sec (reject negative answer)

11. $x = -5, 1$

12. $x = -1, 3$

13. $x = -1 \pm \sqrt{13}$

14. $x = \dfrac{5 \pm 7\sqrt{5}}{5}$

15. $x = -4, \dfrac{23}{4}$

16. $x = -\dfrac{5}{2}, \dfrac{19}{4}$

17. $x = -\dfrac{5}{3}, 5$

18. $x = -1, \dfrac{4}{5}$

19. The formula for completing the square when $a = 1$ was used incorrectly. Notice the error between the 3rd and 4th steps: $(2x + 8)^2 \neq 4x^2 + 16x + 64$

    In this case, $a \neq 1$, so the term that should have been added to complete the square is $\dfrac{b^2}{4a} = 16$. The correct solution is:

$$-5x^2 + 16x + 15 = -9x^2$$
$$4x^2 + 16x = -15$$
$$4x^2 + 16x + 16 = 1$$
$$(2x + 4)^2 = 1$$
$$2x + 4 = \pm\sqrt{1}$$

So, $x = -\dfrac{3}{2}$ or $x = -\dfrac{5}{2}$.

Skill 33

1. -1 and 2

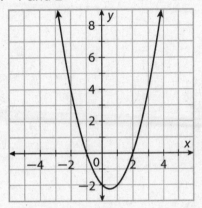

2. -2 and 5

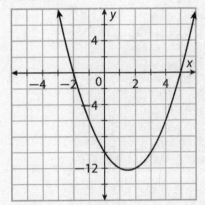

3. -9 and 3

4. -5 and 8

5. -12

6. -6 and -3

7. -7 and 10

8. -11 and 9

9. The Zero Product Property was used even though the equation is set equal to 16 instead of 0. The correct solutions are -8 and 2.

10. $-\dfrac{3}{2}$ and 4

11. $-\frac{1}{3}$ and 5

12. $-\frac{5}{4}$ and 6

13. $-\frac{1}{2}$

14. $-\frac{5}{6}$ and $-\frac{1}{2}$

15. $\frac{3}{5}$ and $\frac{3}{2}$

16. –2

17. –5

18. –7

19. –6 and 6

20. –1 and 1

21. 2

22. 4

Skill 34

1.
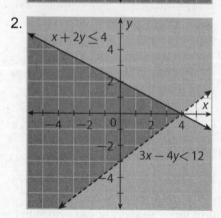

2.

3.
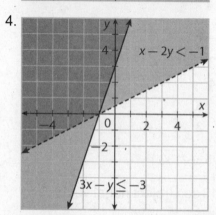

4.

5. The shading for both inequalities is incorrect.

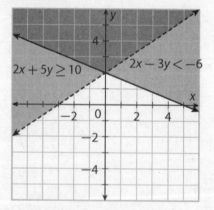

6. no solution

7. all points in the region where the graphs overlap, i.e., all the solutions of $x - y \le -2$

8. all points in the region between the boundary lines

9. all points in the region where the graphs overlap, i.e., all the solutions of $y \ge 2$

10. No. Given a system of two linear inequalities in which the boundary lines intersect, there will always be 4 regions formed by the intersection. One of those regions will contain solutions of the system. One or both of the boundary lines may also contain solutions of the system.

Skill 35

1. (3, 3)

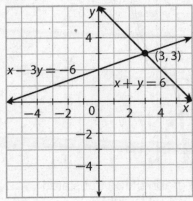

2. (4, 0)

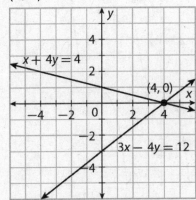

3. infinitely many solutions

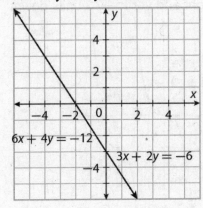

4. no solution

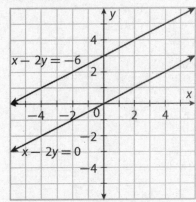

5. The given window for the graph is too small. The lines intersect at (−9, −13).

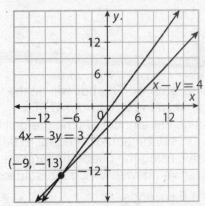

6. (7, 13)

7. (−2, 5)

8. (3, 0)

9. no solution

10. $\left(\dfrac{7}{4}, \dfrac{5}{2}\right)$

11. infinitely many solutions

12. $\left(3, \dfrac{9}{2}\right)$

13. (−1, −2)

14. (4, 20)

15. (3, 4)

16. (4, 0)

17. (−1, 0)

18. (10, −7)

19. (−11, −7)

20. no solution

21. 15 shirts and 5 pairs of pants

Skill 36

1. $x = 2, -\dfrac{3}{2}$

2. $x = -2 \pm 2\sqrt{3}$

3. $x = 1 \pm \sqrt{3}$

4. $x = 1, -\dfrac{7}{2}$

5. $x = \dfrac{-1 \pm \sqrt{2}}{2}$

6. $x = -\dfrac{3}{2}, 1$

7. $x = \dfrac{1}{4}, -1$

8. $x = \pm \dfrac{4\sqrt{5}}{5}$

9. a. Possible answer: The ball will hit the ground when the height, $h = 0$. To determine the amount of time the ball is in the air, set the equation equal to 0 and solve using the quadratic formula. The positive answer will be the solution.

   b. about 4.6 seconds

10. The solution uses $b = 3$ instead of $b = -3$ in the quadratic formula. The correct solution is $x = \dfrac{-3 \pm \sqrt{57}}{6}$.

11. 0; one real solution

12. −19; no real solutions

13. 36; two real solutions

14. −96; no real solutions

15. 0; one real solution

16. 25; two real solutions

17. −44; no real solutions

18. 121; two real solutions

19. a. Let $h = 150$ in the equation and find the discriminant. If the discriminant is positive, then there are real solutions; the rocket can reach a height of 150 meters. If the discriminant is negative, then there are no real solutions; the rocket cannot reach a height of 150 meters.

   b. −400.8; since the discriminant is negative, there are no real solutions. The rocket will not reach a height of 150 meters.

Skill 37

1. $g(x)$ is the graph of $f(x)$ translated vertically 1 unit up.

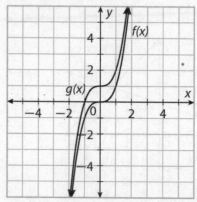

2. $g(x)$ is the graph of $f(x)$ translated horizontally 4 units right.

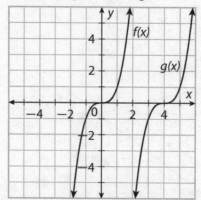

3. $g(x)$ is the graph of $f(x)$ vertically stretched by a factor of 2 and translated horizontally 3 units right and vertically 2 units down.

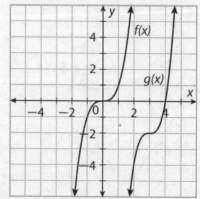

4. $g(x)$ is the graph of $f(x)$ vertically compressed by a factor of $\dfrac{1}{2}$, reflected across the x-axis, and translated horizontally 2 units left and vertically 1 unit down.

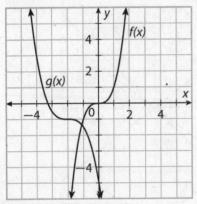

5. $g(x) = -(x+12)^3$

6. The value given for the horizontal shift to the right is incorrect. Using the general form, $a(x+h)^3 + k$, the correct equation for the transformation is

$$g(x) = \dfrac{1}{3}(x-2)^3 - 6.$$

Skill 38

1. The graph of $f(x) = x+1$ is the graph of $f(x)$ translated up 1 unit.

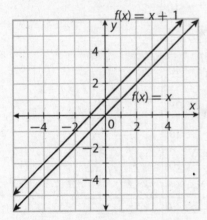

2. The graph of $f(x) = x-2$ is the graph of $f(x)$ translated down 2 units.

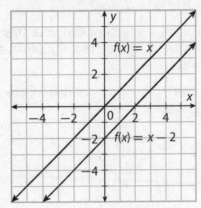

3. The graph of $f(x) = x + 4.5$ is the graph of $f(x)$ translated up 4.5 units.

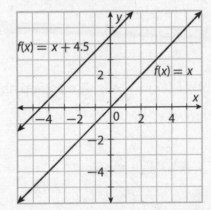

4. The graph of $f(x) = x - \dfrac{7}{2}$ is the graph of $f(x)$ translated down $\dfrac{7}{2}$ units.

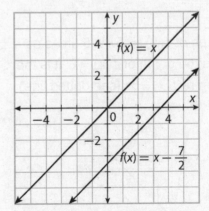

5. All the lines have the same slope, 1, but different y-intercepts.

6. Positive values of b translate the graph of $f(x) = x$ up. Negative values of b translate the graph of $f(x) = x$ down.

7. The sign of the y-intercept that your friend used is incorrect. The correct equation is $f(x) = x - 4$.

8. The graph of $f(x) = 4x$ is 4 times as steep as the graph of $f(x)$.

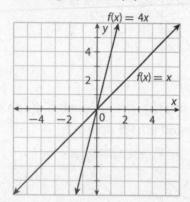

9. The graph of $f(x) = \dfrac{2}{3}x$ is $\dfrac{2}{3}$ as steep as the graph of $f(x) = x$.

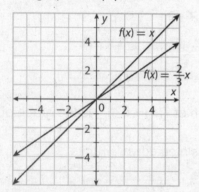

10. The graph of $f(x) = -5x$ is 5 times as steep as the graph of $f(x) = x$. It is the reflection of $f(x) = 5x$ (see dotted line) across the y-axis.

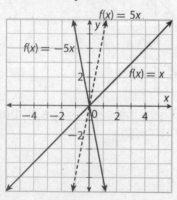

11. The graph of $f(x) = -\dfrac{3}{4}x$ is $\dfrac{3}{4}$ as steep as the graph of $f(x) = x$. It is the reflection of $f(x) = \dfrac{3}{4}x$ (see dotted line) across the y-axis.

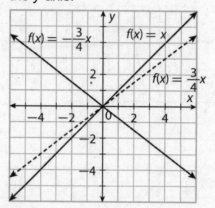

Skill 39

1.

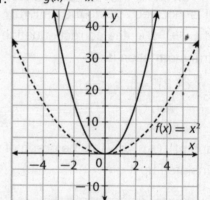

2.

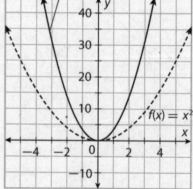

3.

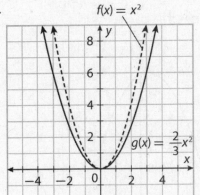

$f(x) = x^2$

$g(x) = \frac{2}{3}x^2$

4.

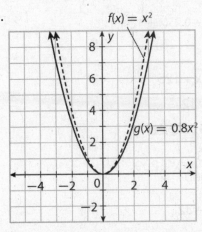

$f(x) = x^2$

$g(x) = 0.8x^2$

5. Narrower Than $f(x) = x^2$: $g(x) = 5x^2$, $g(x) = 7.25x^2$; Wider Than $f(x) = x^2$: $g(x) = \frac{3}{5}x^2$, $g(x) = 0.85x^2$

6.

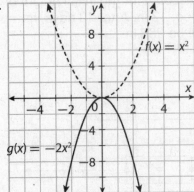

$f(x) = x^2$

$g(x) = -2x^2$

7.

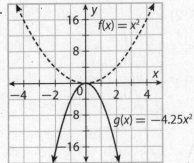

$f(x) = x^2$

$g(x) = -4.25x^2$

8.

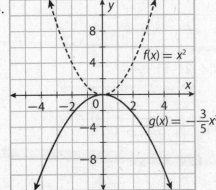

$f(x) = x^2$

$g(x) = -\frac{3}{5}x^2$

9.

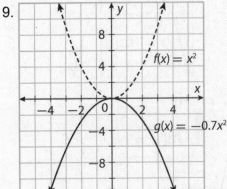

$f(x) = x^2$

$g(x) = -0.7x^2$

10.

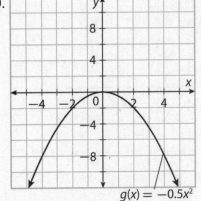

$g(x) = -0.5x^2$

The graph is the correct width, but it opens up. It has a negative coefficient on x^2, so it should open down.

11. vertex: (3, 2)

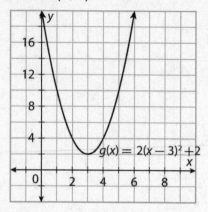

$g(x) = 2(x-3)^2 + 2$

12. vertex: (−2, −5)

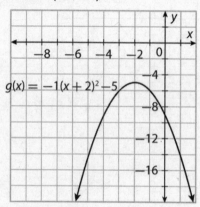

$g(x) = -1(x+2)^2 - 5$

13. vertex: (1, −3)

$g(x) = \frac{1}{2}(x-1)^2 - 3$

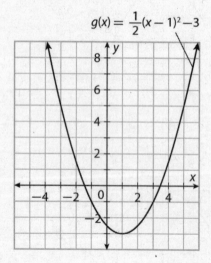

14. vertex: (−1, 4)

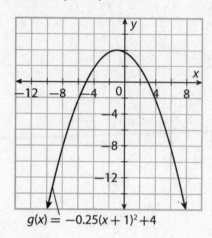

$g(x) = -0.25(x+1)^2 + 4$

Skill 40

1. $y = -20x + 125$

2. $y = 6x + 12$

3. $y = 0.75x + 2.60$

4. $y = -\dfrac{3}{2000}x + 209$

5. $y = \dfrac{9}{5}x + 32$

6. $y = 6x + 72$

7. $y = 24x + 12$

8. Your friend multiplied 10 days by the slope, or growth rate, 24 in. per day, but forgot to account for the initial height of the bamboo, 12 in. After 10 days, its height will be 252 in.

Skill 41

1.

2.

3. Atlanta's median average high monthly temperature is about 73° F. Boston's median average high monthly temperature is about 58° F. So Atlanta's median average high monthly temperature is greater.

4. The length of the box plot indicates the *range* of the average high monthly temperatures—not how low or high the average high monthly temperatures are. Overall, Atlanta's average high monthly temperatures are greater because its minimum, maximum, and quartile temperatures are each greater than Boston's minimum, maximum, and quartile temperatures, respectively.

Skill 42

1.

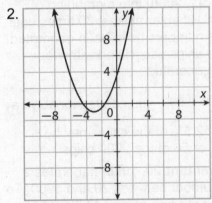

Vertically stretch by a factor of 2. Translate 5 units to the right and 3 units up.

2.

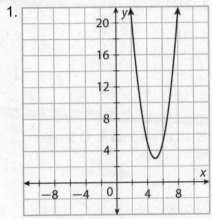

Vertically compress by a factor of $\frac{1}{2}$.
Translate 3 units to the left and 1 unit down.

3.

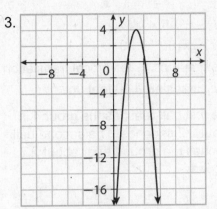

Reflect across the x-axis. Vertically stretch by a factor of 3. Translate 3 units to the right and 4 units up.

4.

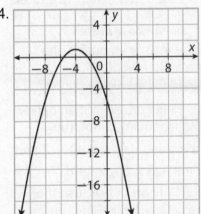

Reflect across the x-axis. Vertically compress by a factor of 0.4. Translate 4 units to the left and 1 unit up.

5. There are two errors. The graph is reflected across the y-axis and translated 3 units to the left. The correct answer is the following:

To transform the graph of $f(x) = x^2$ to the graph of $g(x) = -4(x + 3)^2 - 5$, first reflect across the x-axis, stretch vertically by a factor of 4, and then translate 3 units to the left and 5 units down.

6. $g(x) = -(x - 2)^2 + 6$

Reflect across the x-axis. Translate 2 units to the right and 6 units up.

7. $g(x) = -\frac{1}{8}(x - 8)^2 + 80$

Reflect across the x-axis. Vertically compress by a factor of $\frac{1}{8}$. Translate 8 units to the right and 80 units up.

8. a. $h_1(t) = -16t^2 + 80$;
   $h_2(t) = -16t^2 + 120$
   The graph of h_2 is vertical translation of h_1, translated 40 feet up.

   b. The first ball reaches the ground in about 2.2 seconds. The second ball reaches the ground after about 2.7 seconds.

Skill 43

1.

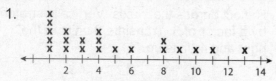

Number of Gold Medals

2. To determine if 13 is an outlier, the inequality $x > Q_3 + 1.5(IQR)$, or $13 > 8 + 1.5(6.5) = 17.75$, should have been used. 13 is actually not an outlier because the inequality is not true.

3. Yes. In the revised data set, $Q_1 = 2$ and $Q_3 = 8$, so the IQR $= 8 - 2$, or 6. To determine if 18 is an outlier, use the inequality $x > Q_3 + 1.5(IQR)$: $18 > 8 + 1.5(6)$; $18 > 17$, which is true. So 18 is an outlier.

4.

Class 3

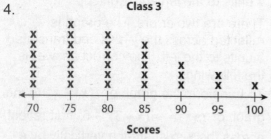

Scores

5. Skewed to the right

6. More than half of the test scores are less than the mean test score.

Skill 44

1. (2, 0)

2. (–3.5, –0.5)

3. (–5, 4)

4. (1, 7.5)

5. (0, –4)

6. $\sqrt{37} \approx 6.1$

7. $\sqrt{68} \approx 8.2$

8. $\sqrt{61} \approx 7.8$

9. $\sqrt{405} \approx 20.1$

10. 13

11. $\sqrt{314} \approx 17.7$

12. The student found the difference of the x- and y-values instead of just the x-values and then just the y-values.
$$d = \sqrt{(3 - (-5))^2 + (-8 - 1)^2}$$
$$d = \sqrt{8^2 + (-9)^2}$$
$$d = \sqrt{64 + 81}$$
$$d = \sqrt{145}$$
$$d \approx 12.0$$

13. A 5 units B $\sqrt{20} \approx 4.5$ units C 5 units D isosceles

14. $\sqrt{101} \approx 10.0$

15. $(10)(5) = 50$ miles

Skill 45

1. Number the chips from 1 to 2000. Then enter **rand(1, 2000)** into a graphing calculator. Hit enter at least 80 times until 80 unique numbers have been generated. Select the chips associated with the numbers generated.

2. Since $\frac{2}{80} = 2.5\%$, you can reasonably say that about 2.5% of the chips may be defective, or 50 of the 2000 chips.

3. Entering **randInt(20, 1000)** generates a random number between 20 and 1000. To generate a random sample of 20 out of 1000, enter **randInt(1, 1000)** into a graphing calculator and press ENTER at least 20 times until there are 20 unique numbers.

4. Check students' answers.

5. Check students' answers. Results should be close to even among the three candidates.

6. Sample answer: Increasing the sample size should result in a more accurate simulation.

7. Sample answer: Write 8 numbers to draw out of a bag. Draw one number for the row and then put it back in the bag. Then draw another number for the column. Repeat at least 10 times until there are ten unique answers.

8. 119.5 pounds

9. 7648 pounds

10. Check students' answers.

11. Check students' answers. Sample: Use the sample with 16 trees since it has a greater sample size.

Skill 46

1.

Price ($)	Frequency
0–99	3
100–199	3
200–299	4
300–399	4
400–499	4
500–599	2

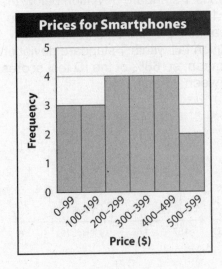

2.

Depth (m)	Frequency
400–499	14
500–599	6
600–699	2
700–799	1
800-899	1

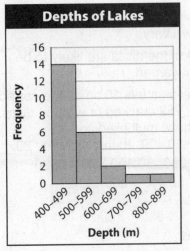

3. 6

4. 17

5. 21

6. about 146.2 min

7. The first two paragraphs are correct. In the 3rd paragraph, the number of values in the interval should be 10 instead of 20:

The median is the 1st value in this interval. The interval has 10 values. To estimate how far into the interval the median is located, find $\frac{1}{10} = 0.1$, or 10%, of the interval width, 20. Then add the result to the interval's least value, 150: Median = 0.1(20) + 150 = 152 min.

Skill 47

1.

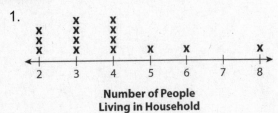

Number of People Living in Household

2. greater than

3. five

4. 2; 4

5.

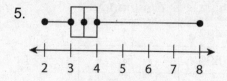

Number of People Living in Household

6. 3; 4

7. 3 or 4

8. 2

9. Answers will vary.

10. About 144 of the discs are likely to be cracked or warped.

11. Sharon's estimate is 10 times the correct prediction, 252 cracked or warped discs. She may have multiplied correctly, $7 \times 7200 = 50,400,$ then divided by 20 instead of 200, $50,400 \div 20 = 2520$ instead of $50,400 \div 200 = 252$.

Skill 48

1. 450 people

2. 840 people

3. 36 students

4. $\dfrac{1}{15}$

5. about 14 shots

6. 112 people

7. $\dfrac{1}{50}$ or 2%

8. 20 toothbrushes

9. 10 times

10. about 3 apricots

11. There were predicted to be 16 monkeys that were given away, so there should be about 9 monkeys left in the box.

12. 150 more birthday cards; $\dfrac{30}{60}$ or 50% of the cards should be birthday cards and $\dfrac{12}{60}$ or 20% of the cards should be thank you cards. $0.5(500) - 0.2(500) = 250 - 100$ or 150 cards

Skill 49

1. mean: about 13.1 mi; median: 8.5 mi

2. mean: about 103 followers; median: 57 followers

3. The values were not arranged in numerical order before finding the average of the two middle terms. The actual median is 87°F.

4. median: 2100 KB; range: 4400 KB; IQR: 3260 KB

5. median: $1.32; range: $3.44; IQR: $1.58

6. 17.8

7. 33.1

Skill 50

1.

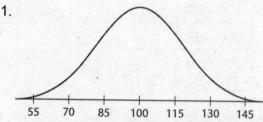

2. 68%. 85 is 1 standard deviation below the mean. 115 is 1 standard deviation above the mean. 68% of the data in a normal distribution fall within 1 standard deviation of the mean, so 68% of the IQ test scores are between 85 and 115.

3.

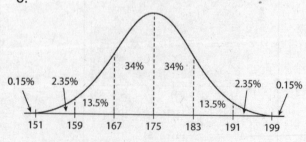

4. 84%. Add the percents for 167–175, 175–183, 183–191, 191–199, and 199+: 34% + 34% + 13.5% + 2.35% + 0.15% = 84%.

5. 50%. Add the percents for 151 or less, 151–159, 159–167, and 167–175: 0.15% + 2.35% + 13.5% + 34% = 50%.

6. 81.5%. Add the percents for 159–167, 167–175, and 175–183: 13.5% + 34% + 34% = 81.5%.

7. The given probability, 34%, actually represents the probability that a randomly chosen man has a weight less than 183 pounds but greater than 175 pounds. The probability that a randomly chosen man has a weight less than 183 pounds is 0.15% + 2.35% + 13.5% + 34% + 34%, or 84%.

Skill 51

1. $\dfrac{14}{18} = \dfrac{7}{9}$

2. $\dfrac{15}{27} = \dfrac{5}{9}$

3. $\dfrac{12}{20} = \dfrac{3}{5}$

4. $\dfrac{5}{6}$

5. 85%

6. The student did not subtract the probability of a number being even and less than 6. The solution is, $P(\text{even or less than 6}) = \dfrac{5}{10} + \dfrac{5}{10} - \dfrac{2}{10} = \dfrac{8}{10} = \dfrac{4}{5}$.

7.

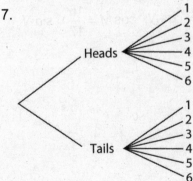

8. $\dfrac{7}{12}$

9. $\dfrac{9}{12} = \dfrac{3}{4}$

10. $\dfrac{56}{100} = 56\%$

11. $\dfrac{60}{100} = 60\%$

12. $\dfrac{69}{100} = 69\%$

13. The mutually exclusive event is the probability of the student being from 11th or 12th grade because a student cannot be in both grades at the same time.

Skill 52

1. Possible event: H; Sample Space: H, T

2. Possible event: HH; Sample Space: HH, HT, TH, TT

3. Possible event: C; Sample Space: A, B, C, D, E

4. Possible event: 2; Sample Space: 1, 2, 3, 4

5. $\dfrac{15}{35} = \dfrac{3}{7}$

6. $\dfrac{5}{10} = \dfrac{1}{2}$

7. $\dfrac{3}{12} = \dfrac{1}{4}$

8. The student forgot to include all the events in the sample space. $P(\text{yellow}) = \dfrac{20}{50} = \dfrac{2}{5}$

9. $\dfrac{5}{200} = \dfrac{1}{40} = 0.025 = 2.5\%$

10. $\dfrac{1}{4} = 0.25 = 25\%$

11. $\dfrac{1}{6}$

12. $P(\text{rose}) = \dfrac{9}{20}; P(\text{tulip}) = \dfrac{5}{20};$ $P(\text{carnation}) = \dfrac{3}{20}; P(\text{lily}) = \dfrac{3}{20}$

13. $P(\text{crash}) = \dfrac{3}{30} = \dfrac{1}{10} = 0.1 = 10\%$

14. $P(\text{not crashing}) = \dfrac{27}{30} = \dfrac{9}{10} = 0.9 = 90\%$

15. They both add to 1 because the software will either crash or not crash.

16. $P(\text{defective}) = \dfrac{5}{200} = 2.5\%$;

$P(\text{not defective}) = \dfrac{195}{200} = 97.5\%$

Skill 53

1. $\sqrt{13}$

2. $\sqrt{17}$

3. $7\sqrt{2}$

4. $3\sqrt{10}$

5. 6.7 feet

6. 12

7. 20

8. 3

9. 4 units

10. 4 units

11. 8 feet

12. Error: Treating 5 as a leg length instead of the hypotenuse. Correct solution is $x = 3$.

13. No; The Pythagorean Theorem only applies to right triangles.

14. Yes; $9^2 + 12^2 = 15^2$.

15. No; $5^2 + 12^2 \neq 14^2$.

16. Yes; $8^2 + 8^2 = \left(8\sqrt{2}\right)^2$.

17. Sample answer: 3, 4, 5. The justification should show that the Pythagorean Theorem holds for the given 3 numbers; in this case $3^2 + 4^2 = 5^2$.

Skill 54

1.

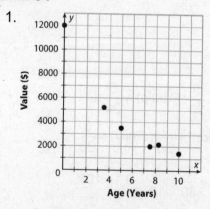

2. As the elevation increases, the temperature decreases, so there is a negative association. Because the points lie basically along a linear line, they exhibit linear association.

3. There is no association between the year and the price per pound.

4. As the height increases, the weight also increases, so there is a positive association. Because the points do not basically lie along a linear line, they exhibit nonlinear association.

5. As the number of hours worked increases, the amount earned also increases, so there is a positive association. Because the points lie basically along a linear line, they exhibit linear association.

6. The values of the individual data points do not determine if the two sets of data have a positive association. In this case, as the year increases, the enrollment decreases, so there is a negative association. And because the points lie basically along a linear line, the two sets of data exhibit linear association.

7. Answers may vary. Sample: There is a cluster in the 2002–2006 range and another cluster in the 2009–2013 range.

8. Answers may vary. Sample: (1990, 286), which is much less than all the other data values, and (2009, 761), which is much greater than all the other data values.

Skill 55

1. $\sin E = \dfrac{5}{13} = \cos F$; $\cos E = \dfrac{12}{13} = \sin F$

2. $\sin M = \dfrac{8}{17} = \cos N$; $\cos M = \dfrac{15}{17} = \sin N$

3. 35.9

4. 29.9

5. 17.0

6. 8.1

7. about 10 ft

8. To find *FH*, cosine should be used instead of sine:

$$\cos 31° = \frac{FH}{65}$$

$$65(\cos 31°) = FH$$

$$FH \approx 55.7$$

9. $43.6°$

10. $73.7°$

Skill 56

1. $XZ = 8$; $XY = 8\sqrt{2}$

2. $DE = 2$; $DF = 2\sqrt{2}$

3. $GH = 18\sqrt{2}$; $GJ = 36$

4. $MN = NP = 12\sqrt{2}$

5. $QR = RS = 3$

6. $TV = VW = \dfrac{3\sqrt{2}}{8}$

7. About 127.3 ft. The segment connecting first and third bases divides the square into two $45° - 45° - 90°$ triangles with 90-ft legs. The segment connecting first and third bases is the hypotenuse of the triangle:

$$\text{hypotenuse} = \sqrt{2} \cdot \text{leg}$$

$$= \sqrt{2} \cdot 90$$

$$= 90\sqrt{2}$$

$$\approx 127.3$$

8. $ST = 44$; $SV = 22\sqrt{3}$

9. $PR = 16$; $QR = 16\sqrt{3}$

10. $KL = \dfrac{2\sqrt{3}}{3}$; $JL = \dfrac{4\sqrt{3}}{3}$

11. $NP = 1$; $MP = 2$

12. In a $30° - 60° - 90°$ triangle, the longer leg is $\sqrt{3}$ times the length of the shorter leg—not 3 times the length of the shorter leg.

$$\text{longer leg} = \sqrt{3} \cdot \text{shorter leg}$$

$$BC = \sqrt{3} \cdot AC$$

$$36 = \sqrt{3} \cdot AC$$

$$AC = \frac{36}{\sqrt{3}}$$

$$= \frac{36}{\sqrt{3}} \cdot \frac{\sqrt{3}}{\sqrt{3}}$$

$$= \frac{36\sqrt{3}}{3}$$

$$AC = 12\sqrt{3}$$

Use the correct length of $\overline{AC}$ to find the correct length of $\overline{AB}$:

$$\text{hypotenuse} = 2 \cdot \text{shorter leg}$$

$$AB = 2 \cdot AC$$

$$= 2 \cdot 12\sqrt{3}$$

$$AB = 24\sqrt{3}$$

Skill 57

1.

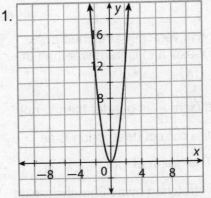

The graph is vertically stretched away from the *x*-axis and is narrower than the graph of $f(x)$.

2.

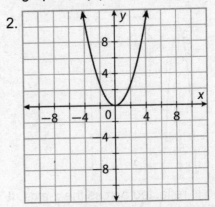

The graph is vertically compressed to the *x*-axis and is wider than the graph of $f(x)$.

3.

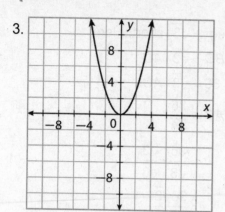

The graph is vertically compressed to the x-axis and is wider than the graph of $f(x)$.

4.

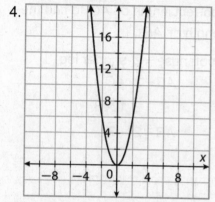

The graph is vertically stretched away from the x-axis and is narrower than the graph of $f(x)$.

5. The coefficient $\frac{3}{2}$ is greater than 1, not less, so the correct description is as follows: The graph of $g(x) = \frac{3}{2}x^2$ is vertically stretched away from the x-axis and is narrower that than the graph of $f(x) = x^2$.

6.

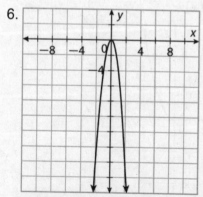

The graph is reflected across the x-axis. It is vertically stretched away from the x-axis and is narrower than the graph of $f(x)$.

7.

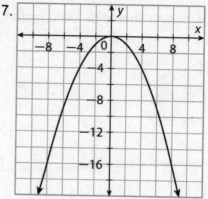

The graph is reflected across the x-axis. It is vertically compressed to the x-axis and is wider than the graph of $f(x)$.

8. $e(x) = -3x^2$, $c(x) = 2x^2$, $a(x) = -\frac{5}{3}x^2$,

$d(x) = -x^2$, $b(x) = 0.5x$

9. a. They are negative, because the graphs open downward.

b. The coefficients are the same because the graphs have the same shape.

Skill 58

1. $\tan E = \frac{5}{12}$; $\tan F = \frac{12}{5}$

2. $\tan M = \frac{16}{30}$, or $\frac{8}{15}$; $\tan N = \frac{30}{16}$, or $\frac{15}{8}$

3. $ST \approx 9.0$

4. $ST \approx 23.6$

5. about 11 ft

6. $GH = 7$

7. $GH \approx 3.5$

8. In the first step, the side adjacent to $\angle G$ is incorrectly given in the numerator and the side opposite $\angle G$ is incorrectly given in the denominator. The correct solution is

$$\tan 59° = \frac{33}{GH}$$

$$GH(\tan 59°) = 33$$

$$GH = \frac{33}{\tan 59°}$$

$$GH \approx 19.8$$

9. 46.4°

10. 73.7°

Skill 59

1. Trend lines and equations will vary.
   Sample: $y = 5.5x - 18.5$

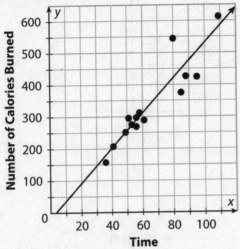

2. Trend lines and equations will vary.
   Sample: $y = -0.002x + 74$

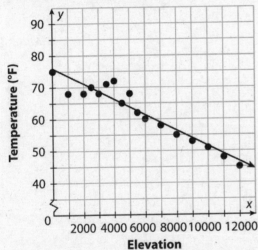

3. about 48,713; interpolation because you are estimating a value between two known values

4. about 26,033; extrapolation because you are predicting a value outside the range of known values

5. Luis' work is correct, but his answer does not make sense in the context of the situation: student enrollment cannot be a negative value. For that reason, this trend line cannot be used to accurately predict the enrollment in Year 35.

Skill 60

1. Yes. The relative frequency of walking to school is $\dfrac{45}{100} = 0.45 = 45\%$. The relative frequency of living 1 mile or less from school and walking to school is $\dfrac{20}{26} \approx 0.769 = 76.9\%$, which is significantly greater than 45%. So there is an association between living 1 mile or less from school and walking to school.

2. No. The relative frequency of waiting more than 15 minutes is $\dfrac{135}{160} \approx 0.844 = 84.4\%$. The relative frequency of seeing a doctor and waiting more than 15 minutes is $\dfrac{64}{76} \approx 0.842 = 84.2\%$, which is virtually the same as 84.4%. So there is no association between seeing a doctor and waiting more than 15 minutes.

3.

	Spring/Summer	Fall/Winter	TOTAL
Beach	$\dfrac{120}{250} = 0.48$	$\dfrac{15}{250} = 0.06$	$\dfrac{135}{250} = 0.54$
Mountains	$\dfrac{55}{250} = 0.22$	$\dfrac{60}{250} = 0.24$	$\dfrac{115}{250} = 0.46$
TOTAL	$\dfrac{175}{250} = 0.70$	$\dfrac{75}{250} = 0.30$	$\dfrac{250}{250} = 1.00$

4. 0.48, or 48%

5. 0.46, or 46%

6. $\dfrac{77}{140} = 0.55 = 55\%$

7. $\dfrac{42}{200}$ is the *joint relative frequency* of people who shop at the farmers' market during the week. The conditional relative frequency that a person shops at the farmers' market, given that the person shops during the week, is $\dfrac{42}{105} = 0.40 = 40\%$.